Fodor's

I0834764

POLAND

First Edition

**Where to Stay and Eat
for All Budgets**

**Must-See Sights
and Local Secrets**

Ratings You Can Trust

Fodor's Travel Publications   New York, Toronto, London, Sydney, Auckland
www.fodors.com

FODOR'S POLAND

Editor: Douglas Stallings

Editorial Contributors: Dorota Wąsik, Marcin Jasionowicz, Dorota Leśniak–Rychlak, Marta Ślusarczyk–Snoch, Sylwia Trzaska
Editorial Production: Evangelos Vasilakis
Maps: David Lindroth, *cartographer;* Rebecca Baer and Bob Blake, *map editors*
Design: Fabrizio La Rocca, *creative director;* Guido Caroti, *art director;* Moon Sun Kim, *cover designer;* Melanie Marin, *senior picture editor*
Production/Manufacturing: Colleen Ziemba
Cover Photo (Piwna Street in Warsaw's Old Town): Walter Bibikow/age fotostock

SPECIAL SALES

This book is available at special discounts for bulk purchases for sales promotions or premiums. Special editions, including personalized covers, excerpts of existing books, and corporate imprints, can be created in large quantities for special needs. For more information, write to Special Markets/Premium Sales, 1745 Broadway, MD 6-2, New York, New York 10019, or e-mail specialmarkets@randomhouse.com.

AN IMPORTANT TIP & AN INVITATION

Although all prices, opening times, and other details in this book are based on information supplied to us at press time, changes occur all the time in the travel world, and Fodor's cannot accept responsibility for facts that become outdated or for inadvertent errors or omissions. So **always confirm information when it matters,** especially if you're making a detour to visit a specific place. Your experiences—positive and negative—matter to us. If we have missed or misstated something, **please write to us.** We follow up on all suggestions. Contact the Poland editor at editors@fodors. com or c/o Fodor's at 1745 Broadway, New York, NY 10019.

PRINTED IN THE UNITED STATES OF AMERICA

10 9 8 7 6 5 4 3 2 1

Be a Fodor's Correspondent

Your opinion matters. It matters to us. It matters to your fellow Fodor's travelers, too. And we'd like to hear it. In fact, we *need* to hear it.

When you share your experiences and opinions, you become an active member of the Fodor's community. That means we'll not only use your feedback to make our books better, but we'll publish your names and comments whenever possible. Throughout our guides, look for "Word of Mouth," excerpts of your unvarnished feedback.

Here's how you can help improve Fodor's for all of us.

Tell us when we're right. We rely on local writers to give you an insider's perspective. But our writers and staff editors—who are the best in the business—depend on you. Your positive feedback is a vote to renew our recommendations for the next edition.

Tell us when we're wrong. We're proud that we update most of our guides every year. But we're not perfect. Things change. Hotels cut services. Museums change hours. Charming cafés lose charm. If our writer didn't quite capture the essence of a place, tell us how you'd do it differently. If any of our descriptions are inaccurate or inadequate, we'll incorporate your changes in the next edition and will correct factual errors at fodors.com *immediately*.

Tell us what to include. You probably have had fantastic travel experiences that aren't yet in Fodor's. Why not share them with a community of like-minded travelers? Maybe you chanced upon a beach or bistro or B&B that you don't want to keep to yourself. Tell us why we should include it. And share your discoveries and experiences with everyone directly at fodors.com. Your input may lead us to add a new listing or highlight a place we cover with a "Highly Recommended" star or with our highest rating, "Fodor's Choice."

Give us your opinion instantly at our feedback center at www.fodors.com/feedback. You may also e-mail editors@fodors.com with the subject line "Poland Editor." Or send your nominations, comments, and complaints by mail to Poland Editor, Fodor's, 1745 Broadway, New York, NY 10019.

You and travelers like you are the heart of the Fodor's community. Make our community richer by sharing your experiences. Be a Fodor's correspondent.

Szczęśliwej podróży! (Or simply: Happy traveling!)

Tim Jarrell, Publisher

CONTENTS

UNDERSTANDING POLAND

CLOSEUPS

CONTENTS

MAPS

ABOUT THIS BOOK

Our Ratings

Sometimes you find terrific travel experiences and sometimes they just find you. But usually the burden is on you to select the right combination of experiences. That's where our ratings come in.

As travelers we've all discovered a place so wonderful that its worthiness is obvious. And sometimes that place is so unique that superlatives don't do it justice: you just have to be there to know. These sights, properties, and experiences get our highest rating, **Fodor's Choice**, indicated by orange stars throughout this book.

Black stars highlight sights and properties we deem **Highly Recommended**, places that our writers, editors, and readers praise again and again for consistency and excellence.

By default, there's another category: any place we include in this book is by definition worth your time, unless we say otherwise. And we will.

Disagree with any of our choices? Care to nominate a place or suggest that we rate one more highly? Visit our feedback center at www.fodors.com/feedback.

Budget Well

Hotel and restaurant price categories from ¢ to $$$$ are defined in the opening pages of each chapter. For attractions, we always give standard adult admission fees; reductions are usually available for children, students, and senior citizens. Want to pay with plastic? **AE, DC, MC, V** following restaurant and hotel listings indicate whether American Express, Diner's Club, MasterCard, and Visa are accepted.

Restaurants

Unless we state otherwise, restaurants are open for lunch and dinner daily. We mention dress only when there's a specific requirement and reservations only when they're essential or not accepted—it's always best to book ahead.

Hotels

Hotels have private bath, phone, TV, and air-conditioning and operate on the European Plan (aka EP, meaning without meals), unless we specify that they use the Continental Plan (CP, with a continental breakfast), Breakfast Plan (BP, with a full breakfast), or Modified American Plan (MAP, with breakfast and dinner). We always list fa-

cilities but not whether you'll be charged an extra fee to use them, so when pricing accommodations, find out what's included.

Many Listings

★	Fodor's Choice
★	Highly recommended
✉	Physical address
✛	Directions
⌖	Mailing address
☎	Telephone
🖷	Fax
⊕	On the Web
✍	E-mail
⌨	Admission fee
☯	Open/closed times
Ⓜ	Metro stations
▭	Credit cards

Hotels & Restaurants

🏨	Hotel
⌂	Number of rooms
◊	Facilities
⏣	Meal plans
✕	Restaurant
⌂	Reservations
🏛	Dress code
↘	Smoking
⌕	BYOB
✕🏨	Hotel with restaurant that warrants a visit

Outdoors

🏌	Golf
⛺	Camping

Other

☺	Family-friendly
☎	Contact information
⇨	See also
✉	Branch address
☞	Take note

Poland

Zatoka
Gdańska
Zalew Wiślany

RUSSIA
LITHUANIA
BELARUS
UKRAINE
SLOVAKIA

ńsk
Kaliningrad
Frombork
Górowo
Iławeckie
Bartoszyce
Węgorzewo
Suwałki
Elbląg
Pasłęk
Lidzbark Warm.
Giżycko
Ełk
Augustów
Malbork
Mrągowo
16
Sztum
Olsztyn
Kwidzyn
16
Ostróda
Szczytno
Szczuczyn
Grajewo
udziądz
Nowe Miasto
Lubawskie
Nidzica
52
Czarna
Białostocka
52
Mława
Łomża
61
Białystok
Ostrołęka
Ciechanów
60
Zambrów
Bielsk
Podlaski
10
Ostrów
Mazowiecki
19
w
Włocławek
Wkra R.
Wyszków
Siemiatycze
Płock
62
Bug R.
wice
Żelazowa Wola
Warsaw
E30
Sokołów
Podlaski
Siedlce
Brest
Kutno
Minsk
Mazowiecki
2
Łowicz
Żyrardów
Otwock
Biała
Podlaska
Zgierz
Grójec
Garwolin
Radzyń
Podl
Łódź
E67
Pilica R.
E77
Wisła R.
17
Kock
19
Włodawa
Zduńska
Wola
Tomaszów
Mazowiecki
Radom
44
Puławy
Wieprz R.
8
Piotrków
Trybunalski
Kazimierz
Dolny
Lublin
Bug R.
luń
E75
Radomsko
74
Skarżysko
Kamienna
Chełm
Krasnystaw
Kielce
Kraśnik
iniec
Ostrowiec
Świętokrzyski
Janów
Zamość
Częstochowa
Jędrzejów
Sandomierz
78
Stalowa
Wola
San R.
Tomaszów
Lubelski
Bytom
Sosnowiec
Miechów
Wisła R.
Mielec
Leżajsk
w
Jaworzno
9
Jarosław
wice
Kraków
Tarnów
E40
Rzeszów
Oświęcim
E40
Dębica
Przemyśl
E462
Myślenice
Krosno
Bielsko
Biała
Rabka
96
Nowy
Sącz
Gorlice
Sanok
Zakopane
Krynica

0   60 miles
0   90 km

WHAT'S WHERE

WARSAW & MAZOVIA	The charms of Poland's capital are not immediately obvious; you need to seek them out with some patience. Painstakingly rebuilt after World War II, Warsaw is a mix of (mostly reconstructed) historical architecture, "vintage" communist leftovers, and brand-new developments. To the southwest of Warsaw, the city of Łódź is sometimes called the "Polish Manchester." With its rich, prewar industrial heritage and vibrant contemporary arts scene, it is one of the trendiest and fastest developing cities in Poland. Between the two cities, you will find a rustic landscape dotted with small towns and villages quite in contrast to that metropolitan-cosmopolitan frenzy. Chopin's birthplace in the manor at Żelazowa Wola, Łowicz with its folk art traditions, and medieval Tum Basilica are definitely worth side trips or detours.
SILESIA	Silesia is perhaps the most distinctly Polish region of the country, and yet it is sometimes overlooked as a tourist destination. Lower Silesia and its capital Katowice are associated mostly with coal mining and heavy industry But Silesia is more than gray, coal-dusted cities. Częstochowa and its Shrine of Black Madonna speak to the country's fervent religious base. Wrocław, the capital of Upper Silesia, gives Kraków a run for its money as the "hottest" destination in Poland. Other destinations are more remote. South of Wrocław, the Sudeten Mountains abound with hiking and sightseeing opportunities, while south of Katowice, Pszczyna and Cieszyn are charming towns (and you shouldn't be discouraged by their almost unpronounceable names!).
WIELKOPOLSKA 	Wielkopolska ("Great Poland") is the oldest part of the Polish state, and it is here that the first Polish ruler, Mieszko, embraced Christianity in AD 966. Reminders of the dawn of Poland's early history can be found throughout Wielkopolska: the wonderful cathedral in Gniezno, Poland's first capital; the prehistoric settlement at Biskupin; as well as Poznań, the current capital of the region. And from the post-medieval era, you can see great palaces in both Kórnik and Rogalin. Farther north lies Toruń, the birthplace of Nicolas Copernicus and a UNESCO World Heritage Site. Orderly and picturesque, the infrastructure here is well-developed, and the rolling hills and fertile plains are perfectly suited for agriculture and the popular pursuits of horseback riding and golf.

THE BALTIC COAST & POMERANIA	Although Poland is not the first destination that springs to mind when you think about seaside holidays, 400 km (249 mi) of beautiful coastline along the Baltic guarantee a fair share of sandy beaches. Although warm temperatures are not always in the package, there are other distractions in the region along the Baltic coast, including historic cities (such as Gdańsk, part of the Tri-City), formidable castles (such as Malbork), and nature reserves (such as Wolin Island). Farther inland in Pomerania, you will find mushroom-laden forests and fish-filled lakes (for instance in Pojezierze Drawskie). These are perfect destinations for a long and lazy holiday, but not for a quick visit; if your time is limited, it is possibly better to focus on the Tri-City area.
MAZURY & EASTERN POLAND 	Eastern Poland is vast and varied, though on the whole it is probably the poorest and least developed region of the country. The disadvantage for the traveler is a more rudimentary tourism infrastructure with fewer modern hotels; the advantage is also significant: a much more authentic atmosphere. Two areas in particular are favorites of visitors, and for good reason. The Mazury Lake District (and also the Suwalskie Lake District further south) in the northeast are prime sailing and kayaking destinations. In the southeast, Lublin is the biggest city in eastern Poland, a pleasant destination in itself and a convenient jumping-off point for such marvels as Kazimierz Dolny, a picturesque town favored by generations of artists; Zamość, an "ideal" city built from nothing during the Renaissance; and Łańcut, with its dreamlike aristocratic palace and grounds.
KRAKÓW 	If you had to choose only one city in Poland to visit, it would have to be Kraków, the number one destination for both domestic and international tourists. Poland's capital for more than 500 years (and still considered its cultural and spiritual, if not administrative, center), Kraków was miraculously spared from destruction during World War II. And while Kraków is by no means undiscovered, mass tourism has not ruined its charm; rather, it has forced the city to improve its infrastructure, something good for both tourists and residents. To enjoy Kraków to the fullest, you should slow down and give yourself a few days, perhaps using it as a jumping-off point for further exploration, including Wieliczka, Auschwitz, and Zakopane (in Małopolska) and Częstochowa (in Lower Silesia).

MAŁOPOLSKA & THE TATRAS

Roughly translated, Małopolska is "little Poland," and in a way it is Poland in miniature. In addition to Kraków, its regional capital (which was also the capital of Poland for centuries), there are many other must-see tourist destinations in the area, both natural and cultural. Most are a mix of both. Highlights include the wondrous, medieval salt mines at Wieliczka; the sobering Auschwitz-Birkenau Memorial Museum; the Renaissance castle and rock formations in Ojców National Park; the rafting routes through Pieniny Gorge; and the spectacular Tatra Mountains with the fashionable resort of Zakopane, a popular skiing and hiking base. Though you can explore the region using Kraków as your base, you'll enjoy the trip more if you slow down and savor the offerings.

WHEN TO GO

°F GDAŃSK °C

°F KRAKÓW °C

°F WARSAW °C

°F ZAKOPANE °C

Late spring and early autumn are probably the nicest traveling seasons in Poland. It is neither too hot nor too cold, there is relatively little rain, and most destinations are less crowded than during the summer, when prices are also the highest.

Summer is travel season in Poland, especially for the more remote areas and those you visit for their natural beauty and outdoor activities. Many of the smaller lakeside and seaside resorts close down for the winter. Some activities and transit options, such as ferries and rafting trips, are also seasonal (usually operating from mid-April to mid-October).

Winter is ski season, when the mountain resorts are busiest—particularly on weekends. In winter, some hiking trails are closed, and only experienced mountaineers should try to ascend to the upper trails and mountaintops.

Cities are less seasonal, though most festivals are concentrated in the summer season. Recently, there have been visible efforts to spread the cultural offerings more evenly throughout the year.

Climate

The Polish climate is a mix between moderate continental and moderate maritime climates, making it a bit unpredictable. Spring begins cold and windy but usually ends up warm and sunny. Summer can be warm and even hot at times, with some short, heavy rainstorms. Autumn starts warm, but by November, the weather turns cold, damp, and foggy. There may be a few days of really fine weather in October during *babie lato,* the Polish Indian summer. Winter will almost certainly bring periods of snow; January and February are the coldest months. However, be prepared for short periods of extreme temperatures: over 30C (86F) in the summer, and below -15C (5F) in the winter.

The following are the average daily maximum and minimum temperatures for major cities in the region.

🛈 Forecasts **Weather Channel Connection** (☎ 900/932-8437 95¢ per minute ⊕ www.weather.com).

QUINTESSENTIAL POLAND

All Roads Lead to Rome

Religion infuses every aspect of Polish life, even though Polish Catholicism is neither monolithic nor orthodox. Nevertheless, religious traditions are observed even by many nonbelievers. Religious rites often take on aesthetically pleasing, colorful, and festive forms. Easter week and Corpus Christi are times of processions, and during the Christmas season you can see beautiful and imaginative nativity scenes in every church. On All Saints' Day, Poles visit the graves of their ancestors, and cemeteries all over the country are lighted with candles and chrysanthemums. A glimpse of a Sunday mass speaks volumes, and a trip to the shrine of Black Madonna in Częstochowa is an unforgettable experience and an insight into the Polish psyche. Another way to understand the Poles' religious experience is to follow the footsteps of John Paul II (today, you can do it in style, by boarding the modern Pope's Train connecting Kraków to Wadowice, Karol Wojtyła's birthplace).

Say It With Flowers

Tulips, daffodils, roses, irises, sunflowers, violets, forget-me-nots, daisies, lilies-of-the-valley, carnations, dahlias: the Poles love buying and giving all kinds of flowers. In addition to obvious celebrations, there are endless other opportunities to perform this quintessential ceremony. Even in the gray days of Communism, every lady received a carnation on March 8 (International Women's Day). Any excuse will do: an evening out, or a meal in. It is a very welcome gesture to bring flowers when you are invited to someone's home. You will see flowers (mostly chrysanthemums) adorning graves in cemeteries, and many flower petals are shed in the Corpus Christi processions. To buy your bouquet, head for any local market (*targ*) or to a florist (*kwiaciarnia*)—in Poland, even the smallest village is bound to have one. This is a genuine and inexpensive way to participate in one of the country's favorite rituals.

If you want to get a sense of contemporary Polish culture, and indulge in some of its pleasures, start by familiarizing yourself with the rituals of daily life. These are a few highlights—things you can take part in with relative ease.

Polish Comfort Food

The *bar mleczny* (literally: milk bar) is a typically Polish fast-food restaurant, invented in the People's Republic in the 1960s. These days it might look like a fossil that has miraculously survived from a long-past era. Milk bars serve delicious, simple food, mostly based on dairy products, eggs, and flour. Their most faithful patrons include chronically broke students, elderly people with their painfully insufficient pensions, and impoverished vagrants, but no one will be surprised to see a well-dressed businessman or a tourist among the customers. Prices are incredibly low, often calculated with a touching precision: for instance, 1 złoty 63 grosze for a soup. Interiors are often tacky and slightly battered, and the chipped crockery and aluminum cutlery will undoubtedly have seen better days. But they hold a certain nostalgic charm for many in Poland; for others, they are still vital institutions and a means of survival.

The Art of Drinking Vodka

For better and for worse, vodka is an integral part of Polish culture. Clear vodka is king, best consumed ice-cold, and traditionally accompanied with a bite of pickled cucumbers (*ogórki kiszone*), a ritual sometimes eliminated in today's more elegant establishments. At some point, you are likely to be offered a *flagowiec* (the flagship), which is a combination of thick, red pomegranate juice with pure white vodka poured slowly on top of it to create a liquid Polish flag. But vodka comes in many flavors as well. *Żubrówka* has the sharp tang of the grass from Białowieża virgin forest, on which the native bison feed. *Pieprzówka* has the spiciness of pepper, *orzechówka* the bitter aroma of unripe walnuts. If you imbibe too much of the national spirit, red *barszcz* (borscht) or white *żurek* (sour rye) soup should help.

IF YOU LIKE

Majestic Castles & Grand Palaces

Poland has its fair share of imposing castles and magnificent, aristocratic residences, exemplifying various architectural styles. Even two world wars and 50 years of Communism did not erase that heritage.

- **Wawel Castle, Kraków.** The royal seat for more than 500 years, Wawel is the spiritual center of Poland. Wandering through kings' and queens' private apartments evokes centuries past.

- **Malbork Castle, The Baltic Coast & Pomerania.** This medieval stronghold of the Teutonic Knights has a powerful and ominous presence. A tour through its dungeons and halls will send shivers down your spine.

- **Łańcut Palace, Mazury & Eastern Poland.** Originally built as a fortified castle, the grandiose garden residence we see today is the pet project of the "Blue Marchioness" Izabela Lubomirska, who had it revamped in the rococo style.

- **Rogalin Palace, Wielkopolska.** The magnificent park and palace were the ancestral home of the Raczyński family, and each generation added new memories and new treasures.

- **Zamek Królewski, Warsaw & Mazovia.** Warsaw's Royal Castle is impressive despite—or perhaps because—it is a meticulous 1970s-era reconstruction (it was reduced to ruins during World War II). Artworks amid the royal purple and gold include Canaletto's views of Warsaw, which were used to plan the city's reconstruction.

Rivers Deep & Mountains High

Poland has 23 national parks (8 of them UNESCO Biosphere Reserves) and countless protected areas, spanning an infinite variety of landscapes: from the Baltic shores, the lakes and rivers of northern Poland, and the fertile plains of the interior, to the rolling hills and high mountains in the south.

- **Hiking in the Tatras, Zakopane, Małopolska & the Tatras.** To make acquaintance with eagles and mountain goats and breathe pine-scented mountain air, you can do an easy hike to reach beautiful views or even climb Poland's highest peak, Rysy, for the sense of achievement.

- **Slow Rafting, the Dunajec Gorge, Małopolska & the Tatras.** As the *flisacy*—local highlander "gondoliers"—steer their rafts through the Dunajec River gorge, each turn opens a new fantastic view of the rocks and peaks of the Pieniny Mountains. This trip is particularly beautiful in the fall, when the leaves are turning.

- **Kayaking, Krutynia, Mazury & Eastern Poland.** Krutynia is justly considered one of the loveliest lowland kayaking trails in Poland. This mellow river meanders through the ancient forest of Puszcza Piska, as well as through numerous picturesque lakes, and the trip is not too strenuous even for beginners.

- **Woliński National Park, The Baltic Coast & Pomerania.** It's one of the smallest national parks in Poland but also one of the most splendid: with steep cliffs, ancient forests of beech and pine, lovely lakes, and numerous species of rare plants.

Café Culture

A café (*kawiarnia*) is part and parcel of everyday culture in any Polish city, as much as in Paris or Vienna. It is a place to socialize, hold a business meeting, have a romantic tryst, read a paper, or just linger. The *cukiernia* is a kind of a cafeteria that serves sweets.

- **Jama Michalikowa, Kraków.** This café is a dark green art nouveau oasis, filled with authentic artworks by late-19th-century customers, who often paid their bills in kind. (Today, you will have to pay for yours in cash).

- **Wedel, Warsaw, Warsaw & Mazovia.** Excellent hot chocolate in a charming and cozy, classic *pijalnia czekolady* (chocolaterie) will take you back to 19th-century Warsaw, where Mr. Wedel opened his little shop to the delight of generations of chocoholics to come.

- **Cocorico, Wielkopolska.** Something between a Viennese café and a Parisian bistro, this is a perfect place to laze away an afternoon or get tempted by that hot cherry sundae.

- **Blikle, Warsaw, Warsaw & Mazovia.** The oldest cake shop in Poland's capital has a black-and-white-tile café with chocolates, pies, biscuits, buns, and cakes. But Blikle's famous doughnuts.

- **Massolit, Kraków.** This is a double bonus: great coffee and apple pie in a relaxed and informal café-cum-bookshop with miles and miles of shelves laden with books in English.

Sleeping Like the Gods

An old Polish proverb goes: Gość w dom, Bóg w dom("A guest coming to visit is like God visiting your home"). Below are some of the best hostelries in Poland, including boutique hotels and plush accommodations in lovingly restored, converted historic buildings.

- **Gródek, Kraków.** A noble place with a lot of personality, this small hotel hides in a cozy cul-de-sac next to the Planty and is one of the best places to stay in Kraków, kept in perfect tune with the city's ancient and romantic spirit.

- **Le Regina, Warsaw, Warsaw & Mazovia.** Are we really in the center of a busy metropolis? Le Regina is an oasis of peace, with spacious, serene rooms, marvelous suites, a lovely patio, and a superb location at the top of Warsaw's Old Town.

- **Hotel Monopol, Katowice, Silesia.** Entering the Monopol is like entering into a different era, namely the 1930s, the hotel's golden age. This art deco beauty was resuscitated and then dressed in marble, exotic wood, luxurious fabrics, and Oriental carpets, and given a worthy reintroduction.

- **Dwór Oliwski, Gdańsk, The Baltic Coast & Pomerania.** Dwór Oliwski is a Zen experience: low, thatched buildings of a renovated manor are surrounded by a lovely park within vast woods. Large rooms are furnished with luxurious simplicity, and some ground-floor rooms come with French doors opening directly onto the garden.

IF YOU LIKE

The Sound of Music

Your travel to Poland is likely to be accompanied with music, played not just in concert halls but also in churches, regional restaurants, and in the streets. Throughout the year, but especially in summer, there are a multitude of music festivals: classical, rock, blues, jazz, folk . . . you name it.

- **Piano recitals at Żelazowa Wola, Warsaw & Mazovia.** In this modest and charming 19th-century manor house, the birthplace of Fryderyk Chopin, the piano seems to be playing mazurkas even when nobody is touching the keys. It has often been said that Chopin's music is in harmony with the Polish landscape, and it is easy to see that here.

- **The Pipe Organ, Oliwa Cathedral, Gdańsk, The Baltic Coast & Pomerania.** The magnificent, slender cathedral in Gdańsk's northwestern suburb houses one of the most impressive rococo organs you're ever likely to hear—or see. It has more than 6,000 pipes, and when a special mechanism is activated, wooden angels ring bells and a wooden star climbs up a wooden sky.

- **The Jewish Culture Festival, Kraków.** Usually in the fist week in July, synagogues and streets of Kraków's Kazimierz District fill with the sound of Klezmer duos and kantors singing. There are occasions for both serious meditations and joyous dances under the rainbow of music.

Folk Art

Poles cherish their indigenous art, and you can still find many living examples in the architecture of old wooden churches, in folk music, in painted eggs for Easter, and in the colorful patterns on regional costumes. Crafts and traditions are alive, especially in the foothills of the Tatras.

- **Sądecki Park Etnograficzny, Małopolska & the Tatras.** This excellent *skansen* (open-air museum) in Nowy Sącz presents the folk-art heritage and traditional rural architecture in natural surroundings.

- **Muzeum Nikifora, Krynica, Małopolska & the Tatras.** The "primitive," modest, and magical paintings of one of the most intriguing Polish artists, the painter Nikifor, are here.

- **Zalipie, Małopolska & the Tatras.** In Poland, this village is almost synonymous with folk tradition, embodied in colorful paintings of flowers adorning nearly everything from a church to a dog kennel, tablecloths, china cups, and wooden spoons.

- **Muzeum Stylu Zakopiańskiego im. Stanisława Witkiewicza, Zakopane, Małopolska & the Tatras.** This museum presents the "vernacular" style created in the late 19th century, based on Podhale's folk traditions. The building itself, the Willa Koliba embodies the Zakopane style.

- **Cepelia, Warsaw, Warsaw & Mazovia.** Any of the shops in the Cepelia chain (which are found in Warsaw and other major cities and run by a foundation aimed at protecting traditional Polish folk traditions) sells genuine folk art.

20th-Century History

Even though Poland's history is 1,000 years old and counting, the 20th century was particularly tempestuous. Some witnesses to the century's most dramatic events—particularly World War II—are still with us, but with every year there are fewer of them.

- **Nowa Huta, Kraków.** A trip to the steelworks and "model socialist town" built in the 1950s next to Kraków, is a fascinating experience. Nowa Huta is slowly rediscovered, and visitors marvel at its mind-boggling scale.

- **Memorial Museum of Auschwitz-Birkenau, Małopolska & the Tatras.** A visit to the former German extermination camp in occupied Poland is a painful and unforgettable history lesson. More than 1.5 million people—90% of them Jews from Poland and Europe—died in the Nazis' largest death-camp.

- **Gdańsk Shipyard, Gdańsk, The Baltic Coast & Pomerania.** The former Lenin Shipyards was the cradle of the Solidarity movement, which triggered democracy in Poland and throughout the former Soviet bloc. It is here that the Gdańsk Agreements were signed.

- **Warsaw Rising Museum, Warsaw, Warsaw & Mazovia.** This interactive museums tells the story of the 1944 uprising with life-size reconstructions, real-life objects, video footage, and audio recordings. It is a day-by-day account of the heroic struggle of the insurgents—most of them in their twenties—often told in their own words.

Great Churches

Since Mieszko I embraced Christianity in 966, the church has always been important in the Polish state, and one of the results has been a large outpouring of magnificent religious architecture, be it in the form of modest wooden chapels, austere Romanesque basilicas, exuberant baroque temples, or modern houses of prayer.

- **Kościół Mariacki, Kraków.** Although each and every one of Kraków's churches (there are well over 100) are temples of great beauty, artistic quality, and historical significance, the Kościół Mariacki stands out.

- **Dębno Church, Małopolska & the Tatras.** This tiny, 15th-century timber church in a village east of Nowy Targ, is probably the oldest surviving wooden building in the Podhale region. Its medieval wall paintings and wooden sculptures have landed it on the UNESCO World Heritage list.

- **Klasztor Paulinów, Częstochowa, Silesia.** In this chapel on the Jasna Góra (Hill of Light) you'll find Poland's holiest shrine, the Black Madonna, which welcomes 5 million pilgrims a year.

- **Tum Church, Warsaw & Mazovia.** This 12th-century collegiate church may be in the middle of nowhere, but it is one of the most magnificent in Poland, its portal framed by adoring angels.

- **Gniezno Cathedral, Wielkopolska.** This 10th-century cathedral was Poland's first bishopric. Its famous doors depict intricate bas-relief scenes from the life of Saint Adalbert.

GREAT ITINERARIES

THE VISTULA RUNS THROUGH IT

This itinerary follows the course of Poland's largest and most important river, the Vistula, which flows from the Beskidy Mountains, across the middle of the country, and empties into the Vistulan Lagoon and the Bay of Gdańsk in the Baltic Sea.

Days 1 & 2: Kraków

Wake up to the bugle call from the tower of the Church of Our Lady in the Rynek. Linger in the largest medieval square in Europe to sip coffee and buy some folk souvenirs in Sukiennice, or flowers from the stalls. Pay a visit to the Collegium Maius of the old university and Leonardo's Lady in the Muzeum Czartoryski. Have a quick tour of Nowa Huta, then listen to an opera or a music concert.

On Day 2, climb Wawel Hill to visit the royal digs and descend through the dragon's den to the river. In summer, sail on the Wisła River to Tyniec, a Benedictine monastery where monks chant their evensong and arrange ikebana. The latter may inspire you to check out the Manggha Japanese museum before you cross the river again and walk through the Pauline monastery garden. Visit the three main synagogues and then enjoy an evening of traditional Yiddish music and the famous nightlife scene of Kazimierz. ⇨ Chapters 6 & 7.

Day 3: Warsaw

The viewing platform high atop the Stalinist Palace of Culture & Science is a good spot to begin exploring Warsaw. Afterward, head for the museum of the 1944 Warsaw Rising, followed by a tour of the Royal Castle. Stroll around the cobblestone streets of the Old Town, then make your way through the Warsaw University campus toward the river to see the Warsaw University Library. Climb to the roof garden with a view of the Vistula. In the evening, check what's on at the National Theater or at Fabryka Trzciny, a contemporary arts center in the Praga District. ⇨ Chapter 1.

Day 4: Puławy to Kazimierz Dolny

Take a train from Warsaw to Puławy, where you can make a brief stop at the 18th-century romantic park and palace. Then take a boat to Kazimierz, founded by a medieval Polish king Kazimierz the Great, and nicknamed "Kazimierz Dolny" (Kazimierz the Lower) to distinguish it from the town upriver, now part of Kraków. In the 16th and 17th centuries, it was an important port; today it's known as a charming holiday town and an artists' colony. Wander around the square and pop in the Vistula Valley Museum and the Parish Church before you enjoy a double feast of food and music at U Fryzjera. ⇨ Chapter 5.

Day 5: Kazimierz Dolny

Take in two castles—or what is left of them. First, climb to the ruins of the 14th-century Kazimierz Castle, a watchtower to protect the Vistula trade route, then take the ferry to the Firlej Castle ruins across the river in Janowiec. In summer, there may be a concert at either castle. Back on the right bank of the Vistula, follow one of the walking trails into the Kazimierz Landscape Reserve, then relax in your hotel's spa. ⇨ Chapter 5.

Day 6: Toward Gdańsk

Travel onto Gdańsk via Puławy and Warsaw, arriving for a late lunch in the Old Town. Enjoy an afternoon in the oldest part

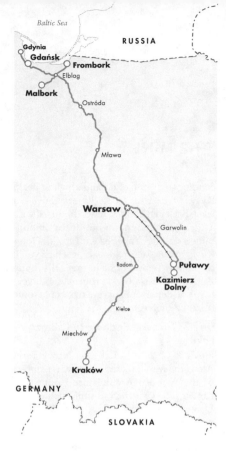

Look for Nicolas Copernicus's epitaph in the Frombork Cathedral; it is here that the great astronomer spent the last decades of his life. Return to the Tri-City for the night. ⇨ Chapter 4.

Day 8: The Tri-City

In the morning, visit the cradle of Solidarity, the Gdańsk Shipyard, and the "Roads to Freedom" exhibition. Have fish for lunch in Sopot, then head for Gdynia. In Gdynia's docklands, tour the ships *Dar Pomorza* and *Błyskawica*. In the afternoon, head for Oliwa to see the cathedral and hear the sound of its venerable organ, before retiring to Dwór Oliwski, a serene and luxurious hotel in a woodland park. ⇨ Chapter 4.

TIPS

❶ Convenient express trains connect Kraków, Warsaw, and Gdańsk. Local trains connect Warsaw to Puławy, and Gdańsk to Malbork; but other sections have to be done by bus or by car.

❷ You can get around locally mostly by foot or public transit, but in Warsaw, you might need to hop in a taxi.

❸ The boat from Puławy to Kazimierz Dolny (or vice versa) runs only in the summer.

❹ If you're driving, it will be more logical to begin your trip in Kraków, then travel to Puławy and Kazimierz Dolny before Warsaw; visit Malbork and Frombork on the way to Gdańsk.

---

of Gdańsk—where you shouldn't miss St. Mary's Church or the Neptune Fountain— and do some shopping. Check out the old Harbor Crane by the Motława River, one of the many threads through which the mighty Vistula trickles to the sea. Just before sunset, head for a pier in Gdynia-Orłowo or Sopot. Choose a quiet stroll on the beach and a dinner, or a much less quiet night touring Sopot's bars and clubs. ⇨ Chapter 4.

Day 7: Malbork & Frombork

Head southeast to see one of the greatest castles in Poland: Malbork, which was built by Teutonic Knights in the late 13th century. Continue northeast toward Frombork on the Vistulan Lagoon (you can stop in Kadyny Country Club for lunch).

GREAT ITINERARIES

UP THE MOUNTAIN, DOWN THE MINE

This itinerary is a series of ups and downs: it climbs down to medieval Salt Mines, and up to the peaks of the Tatra and Pieniny mountains, then carries you through the not-so-troubled waters of a mountain gorge. It stops at the birthplace of a dedicated mountaineer, the late Pope John Paul II, then descends to the hell of the former Auschwitz death camp. Finally, it crosses the industrialized landscape of Upper Silesia on the way to the Jasna Góra (Hill of Light) monastery, which enshrines the holy image of the Black Madonna.

Day 1: Wieliczka & Zakopane

Starting from Kraków, visit the Wieliczka Salt Mine in the morning (book your tickets in advance or plan to spend considerable time in line). Marvel at the salty underground lakes, chambers, and chapels where everything—down to the beads in crystal chandeliers—has been carved in salt. Go back to Kraków for lunch or, if you're driving, continue to Zakopane. On arrival in Zakopane, take the cable-car to Gubałówka to admire a panorama of the Tatras, but get back down in time to visit the wooden church and Cmentarz na Pęksowym Brzyzku at dusk. In the evening, listen to folk music at a regional restaurant and/or see a play at the Teatr im. Stanisława Ignacego Witkiewicz (Witkacy Theatre). ⇨ Chapter 7.

Day 2: A Hike in the Tatras

Choose a trail to follow within the Tatra National Park, depending on the kind of mountain walking you like and how fit you feel. Head into Dolina Kościeliska for an easy valley walk, or even hire a horse-drawn carriage to bring you into the heart of the valley. The fittest may want to try as-cending to the top of Poland's highest peak, Rysy, which rises to 8,199 feet above sea level. Back in the valley, reward yourself with a snack at a mountain hut or tea "mountaineers' style" (fortified with spirit). Don't forget to buy some regional souvenirs; you'll find many temptations in the stalls lining Zakopane's Krupówki promenade; and before you depart, make sure to sample some *oscypek* sheep cheese. ⇨ Chapter 4.

Day 3: Through Podhale to Czorsztyn Lake

Head to Czorsztyn Lake via Nowy Targ. Along the way, look for the brown signposts of the Wooden Architecture Route: you can stop to visit the old timber church in Dębno. Visit Niedzica Castle and Osada Turystyczna Czorsztyn village in Kluszkowce, both overlooking Czorsztyn Lake. Search for the Incas treasure at the castle, or at least get a panoramic view of the Spisz landscape from its upper terrace. Dine, lodge, and relax in Kluszkowce, an old village rescued from the man-made lake; the lovely, 19th-century villas offer top-notch accommodations. ⇨ Chapter 7.

Day 4: The Pieniny

Take a rafting trip through the Dunajec Gorge, a tourist attraction since the 19th century (the first organized tour group floated through the gorge in 1840). Sit back and enjoy the changing views as local highlanders steer their rafts like expert gondoliers. Disembark at Szczawnica, where you can take a hike or simply the chair-lift to Palenica mount and beyond. Retire in Szczawnica-Jaworki to enjoy an evening concert of jazz, blues, or folk in the excellent "Music Sheep-Fold" cultural center. ⇨ Chapter 7.

Day 5: A Long Journey to Auschwitz

Make your way northwest—either take a bus to Kraków, and then another bus or a train to Oświęcim, or drive up, but it's a long drive. If you have a car, you could stop at the Chabówka Railway Museum as well as Karol Wojtyła's birthplace in Wadowice. Spend the afternoon in Oświęcim, and visit the Auschwitz-Birkenau Memorial Museum in the former Nazi death camps. For supper and bed, drive to the 19th-century Hotel Noma Residence in Kobiór, but if you rely on public transportation, head straight for Katowice to the marvelous art deco Hotel Monopol. ⇨ Chapters 2 & 7.

Day 6: Through Upper Silesia to the Hill of Light

Spend a few hours in Katowice—perhaps visiting the Silesian Museum, with its collection of 19th- and 20th-century Polish art, and Giszowiec, a model coal miner's settlement constructed in the early 20th century. Continue north to Częstochowa, home to the 14th-century Pauline Monastery at Jasna Góra (meaning the Bright Mountain, or Hill of Light). It enshrines the famous wood-pane painting of a dark-skinned Madonna and child. The icon of the "Queen of Poland" is believed to be miraculous, and

it attracts thousands of pilgrims every year. Return to Katowice or Kraków for the night. ⇨ Chapter 2.

TIPS

❶ It would be useful to have a car for this itinerary, but most places can also be accessed by public transport, even if it takes a little longer.

❷ In the hilly southern Poland, the bus network is better developed than the railways, and buses tend to be faster than trains.

❸ Consider guided tours from Kraków for busy tourist destinations.

❹ If you don't have a car, take a bus from Zakopane to Czorsztyn via Nowy Targ and from Szczawnica to Kraków, and then it is easy enough to take a train, bus, or minibus to Auschwitz.

GREAT ITINERARIES

POLAND WASN'T BUILT IN A DAY

This itinerary is a trip through Polish history, including its first capital. It calls at stately homes of aristocratic families and explores important cities of Poland's west and center: Wrocław, Poznań, and Łódź.

Day 1: Wrocław

In Wrocław, the capital of the Lower Silesia, you'll cross dozens of bridges over the canals and tributaries of the Oder while you wander through the Market Square and around the Cathedral Island. Don't miss an important icon of 20th-century architecture, Max Berg's Centennial Hall, and the nearby Japanese Garden, which itself is nearly 100 years old. Try to include visits to the Museum of Architecture and the Racławice Panorama. If you're lucky, you'll be able to visit during a festival or listen to a concert. ➪ Chapter 2.

Day 2: The Cult of the Sun & the Churches of Peace

From Wrocław, head southwest toward the "Silesian Mount Olympus," Mount Ślęża in Sobótka, the holy place of ancient pagan tribes for whom the Sun was the ruling god. Afterward, visit the curious Churches of Peace—in Świdnica and Jawor—Protestant temples erected after the Peace of Westphalia of 1648, which ended the Thirty Years' War. These impressive structures, capable of holding thousands of people, were built with no nails, only with wood, straw, sand, and clay (they weren't meant to last), and their construction was finished in less than a year. Today they are UNESCO World Heritage Sites. Head back to Wrocław for the night. ➪ Chapter 2.

Day 3: Stately Homes of Greater Poland

Depart from Wrocław early and head toward Poznań and take in two stately homes on the way. Rogalin is a magnificent, part-baroque, part-classic palace where the Raczyński family gathered some real treasures of art and built an English-style landscape park. Kórnik is a neo-Gothic palace with Oriental traits, filled with cultured clutter of rare books and antiques, with the bonus of an old arboretum. At the end of the day, do some sightseeing in Poznań itself, including a stop at Old Town Square, where you can watch the billy goats fight on the Town Hall Clock and eat in one of the charming cafeterias. ➪ Chapter 3.

Day 4: From Poznań to Gniezno, Poland's First Capital

Leave Poznań and head toward Gniezno, Poland's first capital. Stopping at Ostrów Lednicki and the nearby Wielkopolski Park Etnograficzny on the shore of Lednickie Lake. Take a detour to the nearby open-air archaeological museum, which has a reconstruction of the prehistoric town of Biskupin, before continuing to Gniezno, which takes its name from the nesting site of a white eagle. Visit the cathedral with its magnificent 12th-century cast-bronze Doors of Gniezno before you set off for Toruń for the night. ➪ Chapter 3.

Day 5: Copernicus's Birthplace

In the morning, wander around the beautiful medieval city of Toruń, which is in the historic Kujawy region. Stop at the Nicolaus Copernicus Museum, and just absorb the atmosphere of this ancient town, which has some magnificent churches, Gothic burgher houses, and Renaissance and

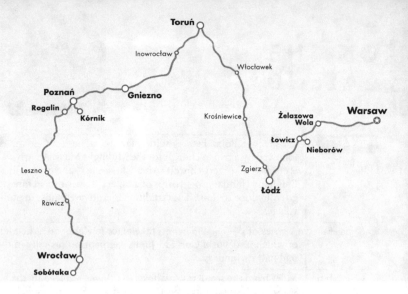

baroque mansions. Make sure to bite into one of the ginger cakes (*pierniki*) the town is famous for, or buy a packet to take home. In the early hours of the afternoon, head out to Łódź, stopping at Tum, a 12th-century Romanesque collegiate church, on your way. ⇨ Chapters 1 & 3.

Day 6: Łódź, the Promised Land

Welcome to the promised land of Łódź, a city that developed rapidly owing to the textile industry boom in the 19th century. Visit the industrialists' residences at Księży Młyn, the Modern Art Museum, and the Textile Museum. Promenade along the city's main street, Piotrkowska, either by foot or rickshaw. For shopping and events head to Manufaktura, a retail and cultural center, which occupies several converted factory buildings. Take in the city's vibrant nightlife scene, which includes some of Poland's best clubs. ⇨ Chapter 1.

Day 7: The Homes of Mazovia

From Łódź, head back toward Warsaw, stopping by the spectacular Radziwiłł family estate. Enter the impressive baroque palace at Nieborów, designed by Tilman van Gameren in the late 17th century, and its regular, symmetrical baroque park. Wander around the romantic park at Arkadia, the imaginary realm of happiness, landscaped

in the English style at the turn of the 19th century. Then head, via Łowicz, to Żelazowa Wola, a charming 19th-century manor house where Fryderyk Chopin was born. Try to capture a chord or a passage of music, and perhaps a glimpse of the composer's shadow. Warsaw will be your ultimate destination for the night. ⇨ Chapter 1.

TIPS

❶ Trains are probably the best means to cover the major distances of this itinerary. Take Intercity Express wherever possible.

❷ Driving a car will give you more flexibility, especially when you explore the surroundings of Wrocław, visit places around Poznań and Gniezno on the way to Toruń, and make stopovers in Mazovia.

❸ This itinerary can be combined with the second one; they can be bridged either via Łódź–Częstochowa or Katowice–Wrocław. On the evening of Day 7, you'll arrive in Warsaw, where you can pick up at Day 3 of the first itinerary.

ON THE CALENDAR

WINTER Dec.–Jan.	**Christmas** in Poland starts with a family supper on Christmas Eve, followed by a trip to church for the Midnight Mass. A nativity scene is displayed in every church. After Christmas—and especially on the Epiphany (January 6)–groups of carolers, sometimes in fancy dress, go from door to door. This tradition is cultivated most in mountain villages.
Jan.–Feb.	A series of **ski-jumping events** take place in Zakopane, the highlight of which is a World Cup Ski Jump competition (usually in the second half of January).
Feb.	Miles from the sea, Kraków hosts the **Shanties,** allegedly the biggest sea songs festival in the world, held since 1981 in late February.
SPRING Mar.–Apr.	On **Palm Sunday** (a week before Easter Sunday), colorful palms are brought to churches; a famous competition of giant palms takes place in Lipnica Murowana.
	Leading to **Easter,** "God's Graves" are displayed in churches on Good Friday. On Easter Saturday people bring food to church in little baskets, to be sprinkled with holy water as a blessing for a plentiful year. Easter Monday is *śmigus dyngus,* when it is the human's turn to be sprinkled with water.
	In several places in Poland during Easter Week, you can find **reenactments of the Passion.** The most famous ones take place in Kalwaria Zebrzydowska.
	Usually overlapping with Easter week, the **Ludwig van Beethoven Easter Festival** in Warsaw is one of the top classical music events of the year, with interesting programs and excellent performers.
May	The **Procession of Saint Stanislaus** commemorates martyrdom of Kraków's patron saint on May 8.
	The tradition of *Juvenalia*—the official fiesta of students—started in Kraków but spread to other Polish university towns.
	Łańcut Music Festival, held since 1961, fills the interiors of the splendid rococo palace.
	The **"No Frontiers" International Theatre Festival** enlivens the charming, sleepy border town of Cieszyn.
SUMMER June	Eight days before the religious holiday of Corpus Christi (a moveable feast), the colorful *Lajkonik* pageant parades through Kraków.
	Corpus Christi processions led by children—some in their white First Communion robes and some in regional costumes—can be seen all

	over the country. One of the most famous parades takes place in Łowicz.
	Poznań's **St. John's Fair** goes back to the 15th century; today, shopping for artisan goods can be combined with enjoyment of street theater and music concerts. It's usually held from June 10 to June 20.
	The shortest night of the year (the summer solstice)—the pagan festival of Noc Kupały for Ancient Slavs—is called **St. John's Night** in the Christian tradition. Of course, it's an excuse for celebrations. Popular fests are organized in different cities, the most famous of which is Kraków's *wianki,* when flowery wreaths are cast upon the waters of the Wisła River.
June–July	The **Zamość Theatrical Summer** descends on the very apt setting of this ideal Renaissance town.
July	The **Malta International Theatre Festival** in Poznań features theater, music, and other performance arts in an open-air setting.
	Usually in the first week of the month, the unique **Jewish Culture Festival** in Kraków's Kazimierz District has brilliant concerts, workshops, lectures, films, and exhibitions.
	The castle at Golub-Dobrzyń becomes a scene of **knights' tournaments**, organized by modern knightly fraternities since the mid-1970s, usually held in the second weekend of July.
	Both Warsaw and Gdynia hold their **Summer Jazz Days**, while Kraków's **Summer Jazz Festival** at Piwnica Pod Baranami continues throughout July and August.
	In the last ten days of the month, the **Era New Horizons Film Festival** in Wrocław is the best international film festival in Poland.
	During the **International Festival of Street Theater**, Kraków's Old Town is a stage for constant performances, morning until night. The late-night shows feature special lighting effects.
	Zakopane hosts the **Karol Szymanowski's Music Days**, with performances of works by the great Polish composer, who lived at the foot of the Tatras.
	Mrągowo on the Mazury lakes turns into a Polish Nashville during the **Piknik Country Music Festival**.

ON THE CALENDAR

July–Aug.	On summer weekends, the **International Festivals of Organ Music** in Kamień Pomorski and Gdańsk-Oliwa are a series of concerts that bring out the best of two wonderful and ancient instruments.
Aug.	For several weeks, Gdańsk hosts the traditional **Dominican Fair** with stalls laden with arts, crafts, antiques, and traditional food products, plus an arts program packed with concerts and shows.
	A regatta called the **Gdynia Sailing Days** is a World Cup event in Poland's biggest harbor.
	The **International Chopin Festival** in Duszniki-Zdrój has attracted generations of pianists, having run every year since 1946.
	The island of Wolin turns back the clock by some 1,000 years for the annual **Vikings' Festival,** where you may suddenly find yourself in the middle of an Icelandic saga.
	On the stages of the Tri-City, theatrical troupes from the world over take part in the **International Shakespearean Festival.**
	The **Jan Kiepura European Festival** in Krynica Zdrój features mostly "lighter classical" music, including operetta, in a fashionable mountain spa resort. It commemorates the famous Polish tenor Jan Kiepura (1902–66).
	In the second half of August, the **Music in Old Cracow** festival (since 1971) has classical music concerts in historic venues—churches, museums, and palace chambers—throughout Kraków.
	The second half of August sees the **International Festival of Highland Folklore** in Zakopane, which brings to the capital of the Polish Tatras highlanders from the world over—not only from Slovakia and Ukraine but also from more remote countries like Peru and Nepal.
FALL Sept.	For those ambitious music buffs curious about classical music today, the **International Competition of Contemporary Chamber Music** is held in Kraków.
	Łódź invites all the muses and art forms when celebrating the German, Jewish, Polish, and Russian cultures in the **Four Cultures Dialogue Festival.**
	Wratislavia Cantans is a great classical vocal music festival (founded in 1966) with concerts in various venues of Wrocław (usually in the first half of September) and Lower Silesia (usually in the second half of the month).

		Biskupin holds an **Archaeological Festival**, a chance to get a glimpse of life in prehistoric times.
		Since 1956, Poland's capital has hosted the **Warsaw Autumn International Festival of Contemporary Music** with an eclectic program of concerts, featuring 20th-century classical and avant-garde music.
	Nov.	Poles all over the country visit the cemeteries on **All Saints Day** (Nov. 1), and commemorate their ancestors with flowers and candles.
		Święty Marcin Day in Poznań commemorates the city's Patron Saint on November 11 (incidentally, Polish Independence Day), while the colorful pageant, fireworks, and the fair outside the castle constitute a major tourist attraction.
		The capital of the Lower Silesia hosts an international **Wrocław Guitar Festival**, usually in the last half of the month.
		Usually in late November the Łódź **Camerimage** festival starts rolling, an international event dedicated to the work of cinematographers.

Warsaw & Mazovia

WORD OF MOUTH

"There are so many new hotels in Warsaw, it is a bit hard to keep with the latest lists . . . my recommendation is to get something closer to Old City and not near Central Train Station. . . ."

—PeterB

"I think one needs to know Warsaw's history to really appreciate this very special city. The restored old town as well as a few other reconstructed parts are beautiful."

—Caroline 1

PERHAPS THE ONLY CONSTANT QUALITY OF WARSAW IS CHANGE. It is remarkable how often—and how quickly—Poland's capital rebuilds and reinvents itself over time. Though in the past this reinvention was involuntary, the city having been invaded and destroyed several times over the ages, Warsaw now continues to metamorphose quite well on its own. To today's young Varsovians—and visitors alike—World War II may seem like ancient history, but it is impossible to forget that some 85% of the city was utterly destroyed in the war. The "phoenix from the ashes" label fits no other modern European city more than Warsaw.

In decades immediately after World War II, Poland's capital was often—and rather unjustly—dismissed as "concrete jungle" or "a life-size model of a city." In the first decade of the 21st century, both these phrases simply no longer apply. Warsaw will consistently surprise you: you may find yourself in a beautiful park wondering whether you are in a city at all; but go just a bit farther, and you will be confronted by a brand-new, tech-and-chic skyscraper you would not necessarily expect in the country from the former Soviet bloc. Warsaw is a modern, thriving metropolis, with everything you'd expect in a bustling urban environment: plush five-star hotels, a thriving arts scene, top-notch contemporary architecture, gourmet restaurants, and upmarket shops. It's worthy of the label "European capital" as much as Berlin, Paris, or Rome.

And yet it is more than a fashionable modern city: it is a city with a memory—or rather with multiple, carefully preserved memories. Within today's Warsaw, you will find the city of Chopin's youth; and also the city that resisted the Nazis in 1944 during the heroic, tragic Warsaw Uprising. Fragments of the city that survived the war acquire a special poignancy in their isolation: odd rows of art nouveau tenements, such as those on the south side of the great square around the Pałac Kultury i Nauki (Palace of Culture and Science) and on ulica Wilcza; the elegant Aleje Ujazdowskie, now the Diplomatic Quarter, leading to the Belvedere Palace and the Łazienki Palace and Park. The reconstructed areas of the Polish capital—the historic Old Town area, rebuilt brick by brick in the 1950s; the Royal Castle; the Ujazdowski Castle—are moving tributes to the Poles' ability to survive and preserve their history.

There are many areas where the city slows down its pace. The right-bank district of Praga, until recently regarded as an "off-limits" area, is now a fashionable bohemian hangout. The wild, unregulated Vistula River is lined with surprisingly nice city beaches. The city's abundant

WARSAW'S TOP 5

- Łazienki Park, an oasis in the capital city, with historic monuments and the Center for Contemporary Art.

- Warsaw University Library, new Polish architecture at its finest, with a beautiful rooftop garden.

- The Museum of the 1944 Warsaw Rising, arguably the best museum in Poland.

- Żelazowa Wola, Chopin's birthplace and a typical old-Polish country dwelling.

- Łódź, often called "the Polish Manchester," a city of industrial heritage with a vibrant nightlife scene.

green space will allow you to walk the length and breadth of town practically from park to park. Warsaw is a city that deserves to be loved; it's definitely a city to enjoy.

EXPLORING WARSAW

It is very difficult to pinpoint where Warsaw city center is. Varsovians differ in its definition. Some would say it is the area around the Palace of Culture and Science (and the Central Railway Station), the former natural center of prewar capital, which is once again bustling with fashionable shops and hotels. Others would argue that plac Trzech Krzyży is the center—or plac Zbawiciela. For many, it would be the area around the Royal Castle and the Old Town square; after all, it was at this location that a fishing hamlet was founded and eventually grew into Warsaw town.

For the visitor, the question is, happily, not so important because all these places are not at all far from one another, and Warsaw is an easy city to navigate. The Palace of Culture and Science will certainly provide you with a useful orientation point: to its north lies the Royal Route, the Old Town, and the New Town; to its south, the Diplomatic Quarter and the Łazienki Park. West of the Old Town lie Muranów and Mirów, neighborhoods in the former Jewish district. All these sights are on the left bank of the Vistula River.

On the right bank is the Praga District, a poorer quarter of workers and artisans that emerged from the war fairly intact. Today, Praga is becoming increasingly fashionable, and many visitors find its galleries, bars, and unique "provincial" flavor well worth the trip across the Vistula.

About the Restaurants
Like everything else in Warsaw, the dining scene is changing rapidly. New restaurants serve ethnic cuisines (Korean, Japanese, Chinese, and Italian are particularly popular), while others spin hip variations on traditional cuisine like "Peasant Chic" and "Light Old Polish." Prices can be steep compared to most other places in Poland, and eating out in Warsaw is much more expensive than in any other Polish city. Restaurants in and around the Old Town square are particularly pricey, though some great places are found off the beaten track. Always check the price of the wine before ordering, as restaurants sometimes charge astronomical prices for an ordinary bottle. Reservations are always recommended and are noted where essential. Some restaurants are closed on public holidays.

About the Hotels
There is a good selection of luxury lodgings in Warsaw, provided by most major international chains and some interesting local establishments. Most hotels have a conveniently central location: around the Palace of Culture and Science, along Aleja Jana Pawła II, Marszałkowska, and Aleje Jerozolimskie; or away from the main route, but still fairly central, such as boutiques Le Regina and Rialto. Lower down the price scale, options remain more limited, and there is a shortage of affordable bed-and-breakfast accommodations of good quality.

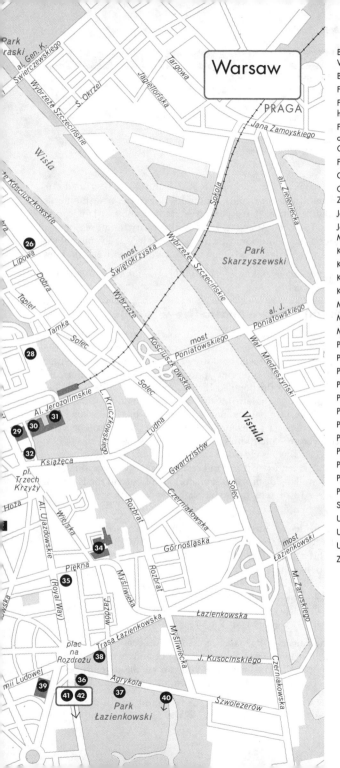

Warsaw

PRAGA

	WHAT IT COSTS In Polish złoty (zł)				
	$$$$	**$$$**	**$$**	**$**	**¢**
RESTAURANTS	over 70	50–70	30–50	15–30	under 15
HOTELS	over 800	500–800	300–500	150–300	under 150

Restaurant prices are per person for a main course at dinner. Hotel prices are for two people in a double room with a private bath and breakfast in high season.

Timing

The Polish capital is busy 365 days a year—and it can be visited during any season. If you enjoy parks and trips out of the city, summer is, of course, the best time. If temperatures are hot, the fast-lane capital city seems to slow down its pace. Łódź is also a city for all seasons—it has more indoor than outdoor attractions. Hotels in Warsaw target business travelers on weekdays, and tempt tourists with lower weekend rates.

Numbers in the margins correspond to numbers on the Warsaw and Warsaw City Center maps.

Stare Miasto (Old Town) & Nowe Miasto (New Town)

The rebuilding of Warsaw's historic Old Town, situated on an escarpment on the left bank of the Vistula, is a real phoenix-risen-from-the-ashes story. Postwar architects, who were determined to get it absolutely as it was before, turned to old prints, photographs in family albums, and paintings, in particular the detailed 18th-century views of Bernardo Bellotto (the nephew of Canaletto). Curiously, they discovered that some of Bellotto's views were painted not from real life but from sketches of projects that were never realized. Whatever your feelings about reproduction architecture—and there's a lot of it in Warsaw—it seems to have worked. The Old Town is closed to traffic, and in its narrow streets you can leave the 21st century behind and relax for a while. Everything here is within easy walking distance. Just a short stroll beyond the Barbakan gate is the New Town, which also has sights well worth seeing.

What to See

❸ Archikatedra św. Jana (Cathedral of St. John). Ulica Świętojańska, leading from the Rynek Starego Miasta to the Zamek Królewski, takes its name from this cathedral, which was built at the turn of the 14th century; coronations of the Polish kings took place here from the 16th to 18th centuries. The crypts contain the tombs of the last two princes of Mazovia, the archbishops of Warsaw, and such famous Poles as the 19th-century novelist Henryk Sienkiewicz, the Nobel Prize–winning author of *Quo Vadis?* ✉ *Świętojańska 8, Stare Miasto.*

❾ Barbakan. The pinnacled Barbakan, the mid-16th-century stronghold in the old city wall on ulica Freta, now marks the boundary between the Old Town and the New Town. From here you can see the partially restored wall that was built to enclose the Old Town. ✉ *Freta, Stare Miasto.*

❹ Kościół Jezuitów (Jesuit Church). On the left-hand side of the entrance to the Cathedral of St. John you'll find the early 17th-century Jesuit

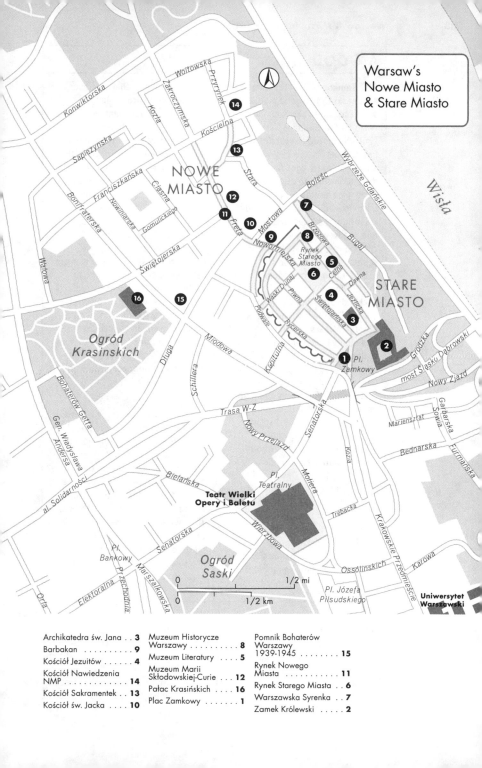

A GOOD WALK

Plac Zamkowy ❶ or the **Zamek Królewski** ❷ is a good place to start. Look up to see Zygmunt III Waza (or Sigismundus Vasa): the king who moved the capital of Poland from Kraków to Warsaw about 400 years ago. You can visit the interiors of the castle now or leave it for another day. Now, head north toward the Old Town and its extension, the "New Town." Long ago, the New Town was a separate city; today, it's not really even a separate neighborhood since many consider it to be just another part of the Old Town. Step inside **Archikatedra św. Jana** ❸ and continue to the bustling **Rynek Starego Miasta** ❹, where you will find plenty to explore. In the middle of the square, the **Warszawska Syrenka** ❼ is waiting, fully armed, her sword risen; the **Muzeum Historyczne Warszawy** ❽ on your left explains why this woman-warrior is a symbol of Warsaw. Don't miss a viewing of the museum's documentary about Warsaw's dramatic experiences during World War II—you will blink when you reemerge in the Old Town, which you had just seen as a sea of ruins in the film. In the northwestern corner of the square, find Nowomiejska Street, which will take you to the **Barbakan** ❾, the official border between the Old Town and New Town; this double

gate and the wall that extended from it used to protect the city against fire. If you want, you can take a little detour here; a pleasant walkway travels along the line of the old city wall, with views of the Vistula River to the east and a touching statue of a child in a military helmet (known as the "Little Soldier") to the west. Then return to the route of this tour, northwest of the Barbakan. Freta Street will take you to **Rynek Nowego Miasta** ⓫, where you can rest awhile before you climb up north toward the towering redbrick **Kościół Nawiedzenia Najświętszej Marii Panny** ⓮. You can sit on a bench outside and watch the Vistula and its riverbank below; in summer, this stretch of the riverbank turns into a stage for open-air concerts and other events.

TIMING & PRECAUTIONS

The Old Town is not large in area. If you are content to admire the exteriors of buildings, you can see it easily in half a day. But to take the area in fully, you will need a whole day. At the Zamek Królewski, give yourself about three hours if you want to explore all of the exhibits. The Rynek Starego Miasta, with its cafés and restaurants, is a good place to relax in the evening—but it is also one of the most expensive areas in town.

Church, founded by King Jan III Sobieski. Throughout the postwar years, a visit to this church at Eastertime was considered a must by Varsovians and its Gethsemane decorations always contained a hidden political message. (In 1985 the risen Christ had the face of Father Jerzy Popiełuszko, the Warsaw priest murdered the previous year by the Polish secret police.) ⊠ *On east side of Świętojańska, 1 block up from Plac Zamkowy, Stare Miasto.*

(14) Kościół Nawiedzenia Najświętszej Marii Panny (Church of the Annunciation of St. Mary). A picturesqure redbrick Gothic church—the oldest in the New Town—St. Mary's was built as a parish church by the princes of Mazovia in the early 15th century. It has been destroyed and rebuilt many times throughout its history. ⊠ *Przyrynek 2, Nowe Miasto.*

(13) Kościół Sakramentek (Church of the Sisters of the Blessed Sacrament). Built as a thanksgiving offering by King Jan III Sobieski's queen, Marysieńka, after his victory against the Turks at Vienna in 1683, this cool, white church stands on the east side of Rynek Nowego Miasta (New Town Square). ⊠ *Rynek Nowego Miasta 2, Nowe Miasto.*

(10) Kościół św. Jacka (St. Hyacinth's Church). This baroque Dominican church in the New Town was badly damaged in the aftermath of the 1943 uprising, when the adjoining monastery served as a field hospital for wounded insurrectionists. It was reconstructed in the 1950s. ⊠ *Freta 8–10, Nowe Miasto.*

(8) Muzeum Historyczne Warszawy (Warsaw Historical Museum). Four fine examples of Renaissance mansions can be found on the northern side of the Old Town Square (note the sculpture of a black slave on the facade of No. 34, the **Negro House**). These historical homes, some of which contain Renaissance ceiling paintings, now house the Warsaw Historical Museum. The museum screens a short documentary film on the history of Warsaw daily at noon in English. ⊠ *Rynek Starego Miasta 28–42, Stare Miasto* 🕿 *022/635–16–25* ⊕ *www.mhw.pl* 🎫 *zł 8* ☉ *Tues. and Thurs. 11–5:30, Wed. and Fri. 11–3:30, weekends 10:30–4.*

(5) Muzeum Literatury im. Adama Mickiewicza (Adam Mickiewicz Museum of Literature). Mickiewicz was Poland's greatest Romantic poet. He and other Polish writers are the focus of this museum of manuscripts, mementos, and portraits. The museum is closed on the first Sunday of each month. ⊠ *Rynek Starego Miasta 20, Stare Miasto* 🕿 *022/831–40–61* 🎫 *zł 5* ☉ *Mon., Tues., and Fri. 10–3, Wed., Thurs., and Sat. 11–6, Sun. 11–5.*

(12) Muzeum Marii Skłodowskiej-Curie (Marie Curie Museum). The house in which Marie Curie Skłodowska was born has a small museum inside dedicated to the great physicist, chemist, winner of two Nobel Prizes, and discoverer of radium. ⊠ *Freta 16, Nowe Miasto* 🕿 *022/831–80–92* 🎫 *zł 6* ☉ *Tues.–Sat. 10–4, Sun. 10–2.*

(16) Pałac Krasińskich (Krasiński Palace). This late-17th-century palace currently houses the historic-prints collection of Poland's National Library. Only scholars can visit by appointment to examine examples from the collections. ⊠ *pl. Krasińskich 5, Nowe Miasto* 🕿 *022/831–32–41 tours* 🎫 *zł 12* ☉ *By appointment only.*

OFF THE BEATEN PATH

KOŚCIÓŁ ŚWIĘTEGO STANISŁAWA KOSTKI – In October 1984 Polish secret police officers murdered the popular parish priest Jerzy Popiełuszko because of his sermons, which the Communist regime considered gravely threatening. Thereafter the martyred Popiełuszko's church became the site of huge and very moving Solidarity meetings. You can visit his grave on the grounds of this church north of the New Town. Take a taxi or Bus 116 or 122 from ulica Bonifraterska to plac Wilsona; then walk two blocks west along ulica Zygmunta Krasińskiego. ⊠ *Stanisława Hozjusza 2, Żoliborz.*

❶ Plac Zamkowy (Castle Square). Many visitors enter the Old Town through this plaza area on the southern border of the district. You can't miss the **Kolumna Zygmunt,** which honors King Zygmunt III Waza, king of Poland and Sweden, who in the early 17th century moved the capital to Warsaw from Kraków. ⊠ *Stare Miasto.*

⓯ Pomnik Bohaterów Warszawy 1939–1945 (Monument to the Heroes of Warsaw). Unveiled in 1989, this monument constitutes a poignant reminder of what World War II meant for the citizens of Warsaw. Massive bronze figures raise defiant fists above the sewer openings used by Polish resistance fighters in Warsaw's Old Town to escape the Nazis in 1944. ⊠ *pl. Krasińkich and Długa, Stare Miasto.*

⓫ Rynek Nowego Miasta (New Town Square). Warsaw's so-called "New Town" was actually founded at the turn of the 15th century. This part of the city, however, was rebuilt after World War II following popular 18th- and 19th-century styles and has a more elegant and spacious feel about it than the Old Town. The centerpiece of the district is the leafy New Town Square, slightly more irregular and relaxed than its Old Town counterpart. The houses on the square—and in such nearby streets as ulica Kościelna—have curiously stark and formalized wall paintings. ⊠ *Nowe Miasto.*

★ ❻ Rynek Starego Miasta (Old Town Square). This is the hub of life in Warsaw's Old Town. The earliest settlers arrived at this spot during the 10th and 11th centuries. Legend has it that a peasant named Wars was directed to the site by a mermaid named Sawa—hence the name of the city in Polish, Warszawa. (Sawa has been immortalized in Warsaw's official emblem.) In the 14th century Warsaw was already a walled city, and in 1413 its citizens obtained a borough charter from the princes of Mazovia. The present layout of the Old Town dates from that time, and traces of the original Gothic buildings still surround the Old Town Square. The appearance of today's square, however, largely dates from the 16th and early 17th centuries, when Warsaw's wealth and importance grew rapidly as a result of the 1569 Polish-Lithuanian union and Warsaw's new status as Poland's capital city.

The Old Town Square is usually very active, even though no traffic is allowed and there is no longer a formal market. Artists and craftspeople of all kinds still sell their wares here in the summer, but don't ex pect many bargains—tourists are their prime targets. Musical performances are often held here on weekends on a stage erected at the north end of the square. Horse-drawn cabs await visitors. To explore some of the square's beautiful and historic houses, visit the **Muzeum Literatury im. Adama Mickiewicza** (⇨ *above*) on the east side of the square and the **Muzeum Historyczne Warszawy** (⇨ *above*) on the north side. After being almost completely annihilated during World War II, these mansions were meticulously reconstructed using old prints, plans, and paintings. For some of the best Gothic details, look for No. 31, traditionally known as the House of the Mazovian Dukes. At night the square is lit up romantically. If you're after good food and atmosphere, this is one of Warsaw's best places to hang out after dark.

Krzywe Koło (Crooked Wheel Street) runs from the Old Town Square to the reconstructed ramparts of the city wall. From this corner you can see out over the Vistula and also over the New Town stretching to the north beyond the city walls. As you look out over the town walls and down the Vistula embankment, you will see the **Stara Prochownia** (Old Powder Tower), now a popular venue for poetry readings, music, and drama. ✉ *Stare Miasto.*

> **THURSDAY DINNER**
>
> In 18th-century Warsaw, Thursday-night dinners were the big event. Between 1770 and 1784, every Thursday, the last King of Poland, Stanislaus Augustus Poniatowski, invited artists, intellectuals, and statesmen to join him in the Royal Castle in Warsaw—and later in the Palace on the Isle (aka Pałac Łazienkowski)—to discuss current affairs, literature, art, and politics.

❼ Warszawska Syrenka (Warsaw Mermaid). The mermaid is the symbol on the crest of the city of Warsaw. This particular stone statue had been traveling around the city for more than 70 years before finding itself back home in 2000. It had originally been installed in 1855, in the center of a fountain in the Old Town Square. ✉ *Stare Miasto.*

★ **❷ Zamek Królewski** (Royal Castle). Warsaw's Royal Castle stands on the east side of Castle Square. The princes of Mazovia first built a residence on this spot overlooking the Vistula in the 14th century. Its present Renaissance form dates from the reign of King Zygmunt III Waza, who needed a magnificent palace for his new capital. Reconstructed in the 1970s, it now gleams as it did in its earliest years, with gilt, marble, and wall paintings. It also houses impressive collections of art—including the famous views of Warsaw that were painted by Canaletto's nephew Bernardo Bellotto (also known as Canaletto), which were used to rebuild the city after the war. Tours in English are available. ✉ *pl. Zamkowy 4, Stare Miasto* ☎ *022/657–21–70* 💲 *zł 14* ☉ *Daily 10–4.*

▌ **NEED A BREAK?** **Kawiarnia Literacka** (✉ Krakowskie Przedmieście 87/89, Stare Miasto ☎ 022/ 826–57–84), on the ground floor of the PEN club premises, is an airy café where you can listen to classic jazz on weekend evenings.

The Royal Route

All towns with kings had their "royal routes," and the one in Warsaw stretches south from Castle Square for 4 km (2½ mi), running through busy Krakowskie Przedmieście, along Nowy Świat, and on to the Park Łazienkowski (Łazienki Park). The route is lined with some of Warsaw's finest churches and palaces, but there are also landmarks of some of the city's most famous folk, including Frédéric Chopin. As a child Chopin played in the Kasimir Palace gardens, gave his first concert in the Radziwiłł Palace (now the Pałac Namiestnikowski [Presidential Palace]), then moved with his family to the building that now houses the city's

IF YOU LIKE

CONTEMPORARY ART

Warsaw has a good range of modern art galleries, with Galeria Zachęta and Zamek Ujazdowski Center for Contemporary Art at the lead. Many small private galleries are in the flourishing Praga district on the right bank of the Vistula. Among these are Galeria Luksfera and Fabryka Trzciny, which is also a performance space.

MODERN ARCHITECTURE

Don't miss Warsaw's landmark of Stalinist architecture, the Palace of Culture and Science. From the top, you can pick out other contemporary buildings to visit later. These should certainly include Daniel Libeskind's skyscraper (still under construction at this writing), Sir Norman Foster's Metropolitan Building in Plac Piłsudskiego, and Marek Budzyński & Zbigniew Badowski's Warsaw University Library.

FRYDERYK CHOPIN

Chopin's birthplace is at Żelazowa Wola, a charming country manor just outside of Warsaw. You will find many traces of the great Polish composer within Poland's capital as well, notably at the Pałac Ostrogskich, which houses the Chopin Museum; the Pałac Czapskich on Krakowskie Przedmieście, where Chopin once played regular concerts; and—on the same street—the Church of the Holy Cross, where the composer's heart is buried inside a pillar on the left side of the main aisle of the sanctuary. Every five years, Warsaw hosts the International Chopin Piano Competition (the 16th contest will be held in October 2010).

FINE DINING

Warsaw has some great restaurants. Biblioteka restaurant is right in the wonderful Warsaw University Library; admire the architecture, read a book, but don't miss your feast. The Zamek Ujazdowski Center for Contemporary Art houses Qchnia Artystyczna, which serves Polish and Mediterranean cuisine. And Fabryka Trzciny in Praga will serve you not only art and music but also "art-industrial" food.

CLASSY HOTELS

Warsaw has two lovely boutique hotels, the smooth Rialto with its consistent art deco style, and the serene Le Regina, an oasis at the top of the Old Town. Old-world charm can be found at the glamorous Bristol and the resurrected Polonia Palace. International chains also offer top standards; look for the popular and upscale Westin, InterContinental, or Marriott.

INDUSTRIAL HERITAGE

Warsaw's Praga District has some interesting industrial heritage. The redbrick complex of the Koneser vodka distillery is worth a visit; it now houses, among other establishments, the Luksfera art gallery. Also in Praga, Fabryka Trzciny is a former factory turned art center. The whole city of Łódź is a real gold mine of industrial heritage, along with fashionable clubs, art galleries, and shopping centers.

A GOOD WALK

The top floor of the **Pałac Kultury i Nauki** ㉝ (Palace of Culture and Science) is a perfect place to start a tour of the Royal Route. Get the preview of your walk while you enjoy the panorama and the breeze. After you descend to earth from the clouds, head north–via the busy Marszałkowska Street to Ogród Saski. Check out the allegorical statues before the approach to the memorial **Grób Nieznanego Żołnierza** ㉔. Look carefully: this is a gate that remained from the place that used to stand there before it was destroyed during the war–along with some 85% of the city. See what's currently on display at the **Galeria Zachęta** ㉑ across the street, directly south of the monument, and enter to see the exhibition if it takes your fancy. Then walk north on plac Piłsudskiego and east via Ossolińskich until you see Krakowskie Przedmieście Street and **Pałac Namiestnikowski** ⑲ just in front of you (you can't miss it–it's the one with the guards). If you turn right (facing the palace), you will get to **Kościół świętego Krzyża** ㉗, where the (literal) heart of Fryderyk Chopin now rests in peace. Retracing your steps a little, you will find the entrance to the **Uniwersytet Warszawski** ㉕. Follow the students walking across the campus, and then through the park toward the river–on Dobra Street you will find the brilliant **Biblioteka Uniwersytetu Warszawskiego** ㉖ (Warsaw University Library) with its millions of books and other attractions in a beautiful setting. You may be tempted to finish your walk here, or at least take a break in the rooftop garden or the gourmet restaurant downstairs. If you feel like taking a walk again, you can stroll down Dobra Street, turn right into Tamka to visit the Fryderyk Chopin Museum at **Pałac Ostrogskich** ㉘. Or if Chopin is not your cup of tea, take a taxi directly to the **former headquarters of the Polish Communist Party** ㉙, today's Centrum Bankowo-Finansowe. Today you can walk past the monolithic block without the fear that once sent a shiver down the spine of any sensible Pole passing by. Outside, in the middle of a roundabout, you will see a palm tree growing (though not exactly thriving) in the Polish climate; this is an art installation by Polish artist Joanna Rajkowska, entitled "Greetings from Aleje Jerozolimskie." Only a little farther to the east is Warsaw's **Muzeum Narodowe** ㉚, and you need to walk no farther if you want to see a varied collection of Polish art and other art objects across the ages. The upstairs gallery of Polish painting from the 17th through the 20th centuries is particularly interesting.

TIMING

There's a lot to see on the Royal Route, so you might also consider splitting your walk into two parts: a visit to the Palace of Culture and Warsaw University Library on one day, and the museums on the next. Check out museum opening times if you want to see the exhibitions, and know that most museums are closed on Monday.

Academy of Fine Arts. Today, the Chopin Society is headquartered in the Pałac Ostrogskich (Ostrogski Palace).

What to See

㉖ **Biblioteka Uniwersytetu Warszawskiego** (Warsaw University Library). A
FodorśChoice 10-minute walk toward the river from the main campus of Warsaw Uni-
★ versity is the relatively new (1999) Warsaw University Library, a sight not to be missed, even if you're not on a research trip. You'll find some shops and cafés (including noteworthy restaurant Biblioteka) on the ground floor, but it's the building's roof and its rooftop garden that are truly special and definitely worth the trip. The garden, open to the general public, is both vast and intimate, not to mention one of the most beautiful rooftop spaces in all of Europe. With its nooks, crannies, brooks, paths, lawns, and benches where you can hide with or without a book, the garden provides a perfect space for thought and inspiration. It is also full of surprises: look for various "reinterpretations" of Einstein's theory of relativity. In addition, you'll find a kaleidoscope of vistas of both the city and the library's interior. If you dare, cross the footbridge over the glass library roof—with the sky reflected under your feet, you literally walk in the clouds. ⊠ *Dobra 56/66, Powiśle* 🕾 *22/ 552–51–78* ⊕ *www.buw.uw.edu.pl* ✉ *Garden free* ☉ *Library Mon.–Sat. 9–9, Sun. 3–9; garden daily 9–8.*

㉙ **Former headquarters of the Polish Communist Party.** Anti-Communists love the irony of this once-despised symbol of oppression; for a decade after the Communist fall, until 2001, it was the seat of the Warsaw Stock Exchange (today, it's the Centrum Bankowo-Finansowe). This is not a tourist sight in a strict sense, but it is worth a peek for its monumental—even oppressive—architecture, a remainder of what the fallen system was like. ⊠ *al. Jerozolimskie and Nowy Świat, Royal Route.*

㉑ **Galeria Zachęta** (Zachęta Gallery). Built at the end of the 19th century by the Society for the Encouragement of the Fine Arts, this gallery has no permanent collection but organizes thought-provoking special exhibitions (primarily modern art) in high-ceilinged, well-lit halls. It was in this building in 1922 that the first president of the post–World War I Polish Republic, Gabriel Narutowicz, was assassinated by a right-wing fanatic. Admission costs to the exhibits vary. ⊠ *pl. Małachowskiego 3, Royal Route* 🕾 *022/827–69–09* ⊕ *www.zacheta.art.pl* ✉ *Most exhibitions zł 10–40* ☉ *Tues.–Sun. 10–6.*

⑳ **Grób Nieznanego Żołnierza** (Tomb of the Unknown Soldier). Built as a memorial after World War I, the Tomb of the Unknown Soldier contains the body of a Polish soldier brought from the eastern battlefields of the Polish–Soviet war of 1919–20—a war not much mentioned in the 45 years of Communist rule after World War II. Ceremonial changes of the guard take place at noon each Sunday; visitors may be surprised to see the Polish Army still using the goose step on such occasions. The memorial is a surviving fragment of the early 18th-century Saxon Palace, which used to stand here on the west side of plac Piłsudskiego. Behind the tomb are the delightful **Ogród Saski** (Saxon Gardens), which once belonged to the palace and were designed by French and Saxon landscape gardeners. ⊠ *pl. Piłsudskiego, Royal Route.*

CLOSE UP

More Than Books   1

THE NEW WARSAW UNIVERSITY LIBRARY, designed by architects Marek Budzyński and Zbigniew Badowski, opened in 1999 and is certainly one of the most exciting buildings ever built in Warsaw. The wealth of the collection is also impressive: nearly 3 million cataloged items and more than 3,000 readers per day. However, this library is not just a repository of inanimate objects, it is a living thing, accommodating popular cafés, a gourmet restaurant, a post office, a video-game parlor, and a couple of bookshops—and the whole compound is covered with a green roof that is landscaped into an elaborate, magical garden.

Symbolically designed as a meeting point for nature and culture, on the one hand, and heaven and earth, on the other, this is a dream library. I daresay even Umberto Eco wouldn't argue with that label. The design is not just visionary, but thoroughly pragmatic. The library is reader-friendly in every way, equipped with state-of-the-art facilities complete with free wireless Internet access to all comers, so this is one of the best places to go with your laptop if you want some quiet time to answer your e-mail. Sunlight penetrates inside spacious reading rooms, which remain cool in the summer and warm through the winter.

The building, decorated throughout with symbols and quotes from learned manuscripts, is itself a book to be read. Green-patinated bronze plates on the street facade carry texts in ancient languages: Sanskrit, Hebrew, Arabic, Greek, Old Russian, Old Polish, not to mention records in musical and mathematical notations, turning this library into a kind of reverse Tower of Babel. So it would seem from the library's maxim: a Latin inscription found at the entrance to the main building is a large open book that reads HINC OMNIA (literally, "hence all" as in, hence all the wisdom comes).

㉜ Kościół świętego Aleksandra (St. Alexander's Church). Built in the early 19th century as a replica of the Roman pantheon, St. Alexander's stands on an island in the middle of **plac Trzech Krzyży,** a name that is notoriously difficult for foreigners to pronounce and means "Three Crosses Square." One of the crosses is on the church itself. ⊠ *pl. Trzech Krzyży, Royal Route.*

㉗ Kościół świętego Krzyża (Holy Cross Church). The heart of Poland's most famous composer, Frédéric Chopin, is immured in a pillar inside this baroque church. Atop the church steps is a massive, sculpted crucifix. Across from the church is the **statue of Nicolaus Copernicus,** standing in front of the neoclassical Staszic Palace, the headquarters of the Polish Academy of Sciences. Like many other notable Warsaw monuments, this statue is the work of the 19th-century Danish sculptor Bertel Thorvaldsen. ⊠ *Krakowskie Przedmieście 3, Royal Route.*

⑰ Kościół świętej Anny (St. Anne's Church). Built in 1454 by Anne, princess of Mazovia, the church stands on the south corner of Castle Square. It was rebuilt in high-baroque style after being destroyed during the

Swedish invasions of the 17th century, and thanks to 1990s redecoration and regilding, it glows once again. A plaque on the wall outside marks the spot where Pope John Paul II celebrated mass in 1980, during his first visit to Poland after his election to the papacy. ⊠ *Krakowskie Przedmieście 68, Royal Route.*

㉓ Kościół Wizytek (Church of the Visitation Sisters). In front of this late-baroque church stands a statue of Cardinal Stefan Wyszyński, primate of Poland from 1948 to 1981. Wyszyński was imprisoned during the 1950s but lived to see a Polish pope and the birth of Solidarity. The fresh flowers always lying at the foot of the statue are evidence of the warmth with which he is remembered. ⊠ *Krakowskie Przedmieście 30, Royal Route.*

㉒ Muzeum Etnograficzne (Ethnographic Museum). On display here you'll find an interesting collection of Polish folk art, crafts, and costumes from all parts of the country. ⊠ *Kredytowa 1, Royal Route* ☎ *022/827–76–41* 🖰 *zł 4, free Wed.* ☉ *Tues., Thurs., and Fri. 9–4, Wed. 11–6, weekends 10–5.*

★ ㉚ Muzeum Narodowe (National Museum of Warsaw). In a functional 1930s building, the National Museum has an impressive collection of contemporary Polish and European paintings, Gothic icons, and works from antiquity. It's usually closed on the day after a major holiday. ⊠ *al. Jerozolimskie 3, Royal Route* ☎ *022/621–10–31* ⊕ *www.mnw.art.pl* 🖰 *zł 13, free Wed.* ☉ *Tues., Wed., and Fri. 10–4, Thurs. noon–5, weekends 10–5.*

㉛ Muzeum Wojska Polskiego (Polish Army Museum). If you're interested in all things military, you might want to visit this museum's exhibits of weaponry, armor, and uniforms, which trace Polish military history for the past 10 centuries. Heavy armaments are displayed outside. ⊠ *al. Jerozolimskie 3, Royal Route* ☎ *022/629–52–71* ⊕ *www.muzeumwp. pl* 🖰 *zł 10, free Wed.* ☉ *May–Sept., Wed.–Sun. 11–5; Oct.–Apr., Wed.–Sun. 10–4.*

NEED A
BREAK?
Blikle (⊠ Nowy Świat 35, Royal Route), Warsaw's oldest cake shop, has a black-and-white-tile café that serves savory snacks as well as Blikle's famous doughnuts.

㉔ Pałac Czapskich (Czapski Palace). Now the home of the Academy of Fine Arts, the Czapski Palace dates from the late 17th century but was rebuilt in 1740 in the rococo style. Zygmunt Krasiński, the Polish romantic poet, was born here in 1812, and Chopin once lived in the palace mews. ⊠ *Krakowskie Przedmieście 5, Royal Route.*

⑱ Pałac Kazanowskich (Kazanowski Palace). This 17th-century palace was given a neoclassical front in the 19th century. The courtyard at the rear still contains massive late-Renaissance buttresses and is worth a visit because of its plaque commemorating Zagloba's fight with the monkeys, from Sienkiewicz's historical novel *The Deluge*. In a small garden in front of the palace stands a **monument to Adam Mickiewicz**, the great Polish romantic poet. It was here that Warsaw University students gath-

CLOSE UP

40 Million Bricks

1

ONE OF THE MOST CHARACTERISTIC LANDMARKS of Warsaw, the Palace of Culture and Science produces mixed feelings. Varsovians used to hate this oversized wedding-cake, Stalin's "gift" to the city, which meant, "Big Brother is watching you." Adding insult to injury, the Palace landed—not unlike an alien spaceship—in the emptied center of the city, once Warsaw's social and commercial heart, which stopped beating during World War II.

At 231 meters the highest building in Poland, the 40-million-brick edifice turned 50 in 2005. While the atmosphere around it—both political and architectural—has changed dramatically, Varsovians seem to have forgiven and accepted the Palace. Placed atop the Palace in 2001, the (reputedly) largest clock in the world keeps ticking away with the current time in Warsaw, and the viewing platform on the 30th floor still offers the best views of the city.

ered in March 1968, after a performance of Mickiewicz's hitherto banned play *Forefathers' Eve,* which set in motion the events that led to the fall of Poland's Communist leader Władysław Gomułka, a wave of student protests, and a regime-sponsored anti-Semitic campaign. Unfortunately, you cannot visit the interior. ⊠ *Krakowskie Przedmieście 62, Royal Route.*

★ ☾ ㉝ **Pałac Kultury i Nauki** (Palace of Culture and Science). This massive Stalinist-Gothic structure looks like a wedding cake and is the main landmark in the city. From the 30th floor you can get a panoramic view. The old joke runs that this is Warsaw's best view because it is the only place from which you can't see the palace. To view all of urban Warsaw from 700 feet up, buy tickets at the booth near the east entrance. The building houses a number of facilities, including a swimming pool and the **Museum of Science and Technology.** Also in the palace is the **Teatr Lalek,** a good puppet theater (the entrance is on the north side). ⊠ *pl. Defilad 1, Royal Route* ☏ *022/620–02–11, 022/620–49–50 theater* ⊞ *zł 7.5* ⊙ *Daily 9–6.*

⑲ **Pałac Namiestnikowski** (Presidential Palace). This palace was built in the 17th century by the Radziwiłł family (into which Jackie Kennedy's sister Lee later married). In the 19th century it functioned as the administrative office of the czarist occupiers—hence its present name. In 1955 the Warsaw Pact was signed here; later the palace served as the headquarters for the Presidium of the Council of Ministers, and since 1995 it has been the official residence of Poland's president. In the forecourt is an **equestrian statue of Prince Józef Poniatowski,** a nephew of the last king of Poland and one of Napoléon's marshals. He was wounded and drowned in the Elster River during the Battle of Leipzig in 1813, following the disastrous retreat of Napoléon's Grande Armée from Russia. You can't visit the inside, unfortunately. ⊠ *Krakowskie Przedmieście 46–48, Royal Route.*

㉘ **Pałac Ostrogskich** (Ostrogski Palace). The headquarters of the To-warzystwo im. **Fryderyka Chopina** (Chopin Society) is in this 17th-century palace, which towers above Tamka. The best approach is via the steps from Tamka. In the 19th century the Warsaw Conservatory was housed here (Ignacy Paderewski was one of its students). Now a venue for Chopin concerts, it is also home to the **Muzeum Fryderyka Chopina** (Frédéric Chopin Museum), a small collection of mementos, including the last piano played by the composer. The works of Chopin (1810–49) took their roots from folk rhythms and melodies of exclusively Polish invention. Thanks to this composer, Poland can fairly claim to have been the fountainhead of popular music in Europe in the mid-19th century, when the composer's polonaises and mazurkas whirled their way around the continent. ⊠ *Okólnik 1, Royal Route* ☏ *022/827–54–71* ⊕ *www. nifc.pl* ⊠ *Free* ⊙ *Mon.–Sat. 10–2, Thurs. noon–6.*

NEED A BREAK? **Nowy Świat** (⊠ Nowy Świat 63, Royal Route), on the corner of Nowy Świat and ulica Świętokrzyska, is a spacious, traditional café, with plenty of foreign-language newspapers for those who want to linger over coffee.

㉕ **Uniwersytet Warszawski** (Warsaw University). The high wrought-iron gates of Warsaw University lead into a leafy campus with some beautiful buildings. The **Pałac Kazimierzowski** (Kazimierzowski Palace), which currently houses the university administration, is among the more historic campus buildings but also a focal point for the university. In the 18th century it was the Military Cadet School where Tadeusz Kościuszko studied. ⊠ *Krakowskie Przedmieście 26–28, Royal Route.*

OFF THE BEATEN PATH **GALERIA LUKSFERA –** In a 19th-century liquor factory in the right-bank Praga district, Luksfera displays works "painted" with light: artistic photography. The gallery exhibits, promotes, and even sells works by well-known contemporary Polish photographers. Sometimes the curators organize music and theater events. ⊠ *Warszawska Wytwórnia Wódek Koneser, Ząbkowska 27/34, Praga* ☏ *022/619–91–63* ⊕ *www.luksfera. pl* ⊠ *zł 5* ⊙ *Wed.–Fri. 2–7, weekends 11–5.*

Diplomatic Quarter & Park Łazienkowski

In the 19th century smart carriages and riders eager to be seen thronged the aleje Ujazdowskie. Today the avenue is a favorite with Sunday strollers. It leads to the beautiful Łazienki Park and the white Pałac Łazienkowski (Łazienki Palace), the private residence of the last king of Poland.

What to See

㊱ **Botanical Gardens.** These gardens, covering an area of roughly 3 acres, were laid out in 1818. At the entrance stands the neoclassical **observatory,** now part of Warsaw University. ⊠ *al. Ujazdowskie 4, Łazienkowski* ☏ *No phone* ⊠ *Free* ⊙ *Daily dawn–dusk.*

㊈ **Former Gestapo Headquarters.** The building that currently houses Poland's Ministry of Education was the Gestapo headquarters during World War II. A small museum details the horrors that took place behind its

CLOSE UP

He Left His Heart in Warsaw

1

"WHEN THE FIRST NOTES OF CHOPIN** sound through the concert hall, there is a happy sigh of recognition. All over the world men and women know his music. They love it; they are moved by it," said Arthur Rubinstein, the famed Polish pianist. While the music belongs to everyone in the world, Chopin's heart always belonged to Warsaw.

It is in Warsaw that Fryderyk Chopin spent his youth, certainly most of the first 20 years of his life. He was born in Żelazowa Wola in the region of Masovia in 1810, where his father Nicolas Chopin, a Frenchman of distant Polish ancestry, had moved from in 1787; Nicolas then married a Pole, Justyna Krzyżanowska.

The family moved to Warsaw in October 1810. A child prodigy of great musical talent, Fryderyk Chopin soon gained a reputation as a "second Mozart" who composed his first two polonaises by the age of 7; he performed his first piano concert at the age of 8. It was in Warsaw that he got his education, including music lessons from Wojciech Żywny and then Wilhelm Würfel. He attended the Warsaw Lyceum, where his father was a professor, and then the Warsaw Conservatory, where he was taught by composer Jozef Elsner. In Warsaw, Chopin first heard Paganini play; the city is also where he met his first love, a singing student Konstancja Gładkowska.

While giving concerts in Vienna in late 1830, Fryderyk learned about trouble at home: the November Uprising had begun. He decided not to return to Warsaw immediately but went on to Munich and Stuttgart (where news reached him of Poland's occupation by the Russian army), finally arriving in Paris—where most of the Polish political refugees had relocated—in 1831.

He never returned home. Chopin died in Paris in 1849 and is buried at Père-Lachaise Cemetery, where, according to legend, there has never been a day when flowers were not placed on his grave. At his own request, his heart was removed upon his death and sent in an urn to Warsaw, where it rests in the Church of the Holy Cross at Krakowskie Przedmieście.

---

peaceful facade. ✉ *al. Szucha 25, Łazienkowski* ☎ *022/629–49–19* 🎫 *Free* ☉ *Wed. 9–5, Thurs. and Sat. 9–4, Fri. 10–5, Sun. 10–4.*

㊶ Pałac Belweder (Belvedere Palace). Built in the early 18th century, the palace was reconstructed in 1818 in neoclassical style by the Russian governor of Poland, the grand duke Constantine. Until 1994 it was the official residence of Poland's president. Now the building is used for some gala state occasions and for some performances during the summer Chopin festival. Belvedere Palace stands just south of the main gates to Łazienki Park. ✉ *Belwederska 2, Łazienkowski.*

★ ㊵ Pałac Łazienkowski (Łazienki Palace). This magnificent palace is the focal point of the Park Łazienkowski. This neoclassical summer residence was so faithfully reconstructed after the war that there is still no electricity—be sure to visit when it's sunny, or you won't see anything of the interior. The palace has some splendid 18th-century furniture as well as part of the art collection of King Słanisław August Poniatowski. ⊠ *Agrykola 1, Łazienkowski* ☎ *022/621–62–41* ⌨ *zł 10* ☉ *Tues.–Sun. 10–3:15.*

┌─
│ OFF THE
│ BEATEN
│ PATH
│ ㊷

PAŁAC WILANÓW (Wilanów Palace) – A baroque gateway and false moat lead to the wide courtyard that stretches along the front of Wilanów Palace, built between 1681 and 1696 by King Jan III Sobieski. After his death, the palace passed through various hands before it was bought at the end of the 18th century by Stanisław Kostka Potocki, who amassed a major art collection, laid out the gardens, and opened the first public museum here in 1805. Potocki's neo-Gothic tomb can be seen to the left of the driveway as you approach the palace. The palace interiors still hold much of the original furniture; there's also a striking display of 16th- to 18th-century Polish portraits on the first floor. English-speaking guides are available.

Outside of the Pałac Wilanów, to the left of the main entrance, is a romantic **park** with pagodas, summer houses, and bridges as well as a lake. Behind the palace is a formal Italian garden from which you can admire the magnificent gilt decoration on the palace walls. There's also a gallery of contemporary Polish art on the grounds. Stables to the right of the entrance now house a poster gallery, the Muzeum Plakatu that is well worth visiting—this is a branch of art in which Poles have historically excelled. ⊠ *Wiertnicza 1, Wilanów* ☎ *022/842–81–01* ⊕ *www.wilanow-palac.art. pl* ⌨ *Palace zł 15; park zł 3, free Thurs.* ☉ *Palace Tues.–Sun. 9:30–2:30, Sun. until 6* PM *mid-June–mid-Sept. Park daily 9–dusk.*

☾ ㊲ **Park Łazienkowski** (Łazienki Park). The 180 acres of this park, commis-
Fodor's Choice sioned during the late 18th century by King Słanisław August Poniatowski,
★ run along the Vistula escarpment, parallel to the Royal Route. Look for the peacocks that wander through the park and the delicate red squirrels that in Poland answer to the name "Basia," a diminutive of Barbara. Of course, the best way to entice a squirrel to come near is to have some nuts in your hand. In the old coach houses on the east side of the park you'll find the **Muzeum Łowiectwa i Jeździectwa** (Museum of Hunting; ☎ 022/621–62–41), which contains a collection of stuffed birds and animals native to Poland. It is open Tuesday through Sunday from 10 to 3; admission is zł5. One of the most beloved sights in Łazienki Park is the **Pomnik Fryderyka Chopina** (Chopin Memorial), a sculpture under a streaming willow tree that shows the composer in a typical romantic pose. In summer, outdoor concerts of Chopin's piano music are held here every Sunday afternoon. ⊠ *al. Ujazdowskie, Łazienki.*

☾ ㉟ **Park Ujazdowski** (Ujazdów Park). At the entrance to this formal garden, there is a **19th-century weighing booth,** just inside the gate, still in operation. There is also a well-equipped **playground** for small children, with sand, swings, and slides. ⊠ *Corner of al. Ujazdowskie and Piękna, Diplomatic Quarter.*

㉞ **Sejm.** The Polish Houses of the Sejm (parliament) are housed in a round, white debating chamber that was built during the 1920s, after the rebirth of an independent Polish state. ⊠ *Wiejska 6, Diplomatic Quarter.*

NEED A BREAK?

Modulor Café (✉ pl. Trzech Krzyży 2, Diplomatic Quarter), up the street from the Sheraton, has great coffee and a variety of fresh-squeezed juices.

★ ㊳ **Zamek Ujazdowski** (Ujazdowski Castle). If you are interested in modern art, you will find it in the somewhat unlikely setting of this 18th-century castle, reconstructed in the 1980s. Now the home of the **Center for Contemporary Art**, the castle hosts a variety of exhibitions by artists from Poland and all over the world. ✉ *al. Ujazdowskie 6, Łazienski* ☎ *022/628–12–71* 🖅 *zł 4, free Thurs.* ☉ *Tues.–Thurs. and weekends 11–5, Fri. 11–9.*

Jewish Warsaw

The quiet streets of Mirów and Muranów, which are now primarily residential neighborhoods, once housed the largest Jewish population in Europe: about 380,000 people in 1939. The Nazis sealed off this area from the rest of the city on November 15, 1940, and the congested ghetto became rapidly less populated as people died from starvation and disease. Between July and September 1942, the Nazis deported about 300,000 Jewish residents to the death camp at Treblinka. On April 19, 1943, the remaining inhabitants instigated the Warsaw Ghetto Uprising. Children threw homemade bombs at tanks, and men and women fought soldiers hand to hand. In the end, almost all of those remaining died in the uprising or fled through the sewers to the "Aryan side" of Warsaw.

What to See

㊻ **Femina Cinema.** Before the war, this area was the heart of Warsaw's Jewish Quarter, which was walled off by the Nazis in November 1940 to isolate the Jewish community from "Aryan" Warsaw. The cinema is one of the few buildings in the district that survived the war. It was here that the ghetto orchestra organized concerts in 1941 and 1942. Many outstanding musicians found themselves behind the ghetto walls and continued to make music despite the dangers. ✉ *al. Solidarności 115, Muranów.*

㊸ **Fragment of ghetto wall.** In the courtyard of this building on Sienna Street, through the archway on the left, and just a little farther east, on Złota Street, are the only two surviving fragments of the infamous wall built by the Nazis to close off the Warsaw Ghetto in November 1940. Warsaw's was the largest Jewish ghetto established by the Germans during World War II. Between 300,000 and 400,000 people perished during the three years of its existence, from starvation, diseases (mostly typhoid), and deportation to Nazi death caps. It was the scene of the Warsaw Ghetto Uprising, led by Mordechaj Anielewicz, who died there at the age of 24. Among the hostages of history in the Warsaw Ghetto we find such memorable figures as Władysław Szpilman, "The Pianist" from Polański's movie, and Doctor Janusz Korczak, a pediatrician, pedagogue, and writer who ran an orphanage for Jewish children—who decided to accompany them all the way to the gas chambers of Treblinka. ✉ *Sienna 55, Muranów.*

49 **Jewish Cemetery.** Behind a high brick wall on ulica Okopowa you will find Warsaw's Jewish Cemetery, an island of continuity amid so much destruction of the city's Jewish heritage. The cemetery, which is still in use, survived the war, and although it was neglected and became badly overgrown during the postwar period, it is gradually being restored. Here you will find 19th-century headstones and much that testifies to the Jewish community's role in Polish history and culture. Ludwik Zamenhof, the creator of the artificial language Esperanto, is buried here, as are Henryk Wohl, minister of the treasury in the national government during the 1864 uprising against Russian rule; Szymon Askenazy, the historian and diplomat; Hipolit Wawelberg, the cofounder of Warsaw Polytechnic; and poet Bolesław Leśmian. To reach the cemetery, take Bus 107, 111, or 516 from Plac Bankowy. ⊠ *Okopowa 49–51, Muranów* 🖃 *zł 4* ☉ *Apr.–Oct., Mon.–Thurs. 10–5, Fri. 9–1, Sun. 11–4; Nov.–Mar., 10–sunset.*

45 **Jewish Historical Institute & Museum.** You'll find the institute behind a glittering new office block on the southeast corner of plac Bankowy—the site of what had been the largest temple in Warsaw, the Tłomackie Synagogue. For those seeking to investigate their family history, the institute houses the **Ronald S. Lauder Foundation Genealogy Project,** which acts as a clearinghouse of information on available archival resources and on the history of towns and villages in which Polish Jews resided. English-speaking staff members are available. The institute also houses a museum that displays a permanent collection of mementos and artifacts and periodically organizes special exhibitions. ⊠ *Tłomackie 3, Muranów* 🕾 *022/827–92–21* ⊕ *www.jewishinstitute.org.pl* 🖃 *Free* ☉ *Tues.–Fri. 10–6.*

47 **Pomnik Bohaterów Getta** (Monument to the Heroes of the Warsaw Ghetto). On April 19, 1943, the Jewish Fighting Organization began an uprising in a desperate attempt to resist the mass transports to Treblinka that had been taking place since the beginning of that year. Though doomed from the start, the brave ghetto fighters managed to keep up their struggle for a whole month. But by May 16, General Jürgen Stroop could report to his superior officer that "the former Jewish District in Warsaw had ceased to exist." The ghetto had become a smoldering ruin, razed by Nazi flamethrowers. A monument marks the location of the house at nearby **ulica Miła 18,** the site of the uprising's command bunker and where its leader, Mordechaj Anielewicz, was killed. ⊠ *al. Zamenhofa, between al. M. Anielewicza and al. Lewartowskiego, Muranów.*

50 **Powązki Cemetery.** Dating from 1790, Warsaw's oldest cemetery is worth a visit if you are in a reflective mood. Many well-known Polish names appear on the often elaborate headstones and tombs. There is also a recent memorial to the victims of the Katyń Massacre, when 4,000 Polish servicemen, who had been taken prisoner when the Soviets were still aligned with the Nazis, were murdered by the Soviet army on orders from Stalin in 1940 in the Katyń Forest. Enter from ulica Powązkowska. ⊠ *Powązkowska 43–45, next to Jewish Cemetery, Muranów* ☉ *Sun.–Thurs. 9–3, Fri. 9–1.*

44 Ulica Próżna. This is the only street in Jewish Warsaw where tenement buildings have been preserved on both sides of the street. The Lauder Foundation has instigated a plan to restore the street to its original state. No. 9 belonged to Zelman Nożyk, founder of the ghetto synagogue. ✉ *Muranów.*

48 Umschlagplatz. This plaza was the rail terminus from which tens of thousands of the ghetto's inhabitants were shipped in cattle cars to the extermination camp of Treblinka, about 100 km (60 mi) northeast of Warsaw. The school building to the right of the square was used to detain those who had to wait overnight for transport; the beginning of the rail tracks survives on the right. At the entrance to the square is a memorial gateway, erected in 1988 on the 45th anniversary of the uprising. ✉ *Stawki and al. Dzika, Muranów.*

> **TARGET: MUSEUM OBJECT**
>
> Many exhibits in the Warsaw Rising Museum were collected from the former insurgents and their families. A gentleman in his eighties brought a still-functioning gun, which he had used during the 1944 Rising and never again since— though he could never part with it, either. Needless to say, he did not have a permit to keep it, and— blameless as he was—Polish laws about gun possession are strict. After a short brainstorming session, guardians of the museum arranged for the gun to be left anonymously just outside the museum's door.

OFF THE BEATEN PATH

Fodor'sChoice ★

WARSAW RISING MUSEUM – One of the youngest and certainly one of the best museums in Poland tells the story of the 1944 Rising by means of interactive displays. The museum features a life-size plane, cobblestone streets, reconstructed sewers (vital transportation and evacuation lines during the battles), real objects, photographs, and also video footage and audio recordings. It is a day-by-day account of the heroic struggle of the insurgents, most of them twentysomething years old— often told in their own words. It is impossible not to be involved and moved by it. Allow a minimum of 2½ hours to see the exhibition with a guide. English-language guides are available, but to ensure that you have a guide, you should make a tour reservation on the museum Web site by e-mailing a request to the museum, especially in summer. It is possible to wander around on your own as well. Large groups (11-plus persons) must book their entry in advance. ✉ *Grzybowska 79, Mirów* ☎ *22/539–79–33* ⊕ *www.1944.pl* 🎫 *zł4, free Sun.* ۞ *Sept.–June, Wed.–Mon. 8–6 (Thurs. until 8); July and Aug., Wed.–Mon. 10–6 (Thurs. until 8).*

WHERE TO EAT

You'll find a great many restaurants around the Old Town Square and along the Royal Route, but many of these are expensive and priced for tourists and upscale business travelers. There are some great off-the-beaten track finds in the Diplomatic Quarter, Powiśle, and Praga neighborhoods.

The Warsaw Rising of 1944

ALTHOUGH THE WARSAW RISING OF 1944 is one of the key events to understanding modern Polish history, for a long time it received insufficient attention, particularly from the Western world. It was a common misconception to confuse the event with the 1943 Ghetto Uprising, a mistake (in)famously committed by both German Chancellor Herzog and the French newspaper *Le Figaro*.

The Warsaw Rising was an armed struggle by the Home Army (Armia Krajowa), the Polish resistance group, in an attempt to liberate Warsaw from German occupation and Nazi rule. It started on August 1, 1944. The date was not chosen at random: at the time, Allied troops were breaking through the Normandy defenses and the Red Army was approaching Warsaw.

Although the Rising failed, the Polish troops resisted the German-led forces for 63 days, until October 2. Losses on the Polish side amounted to 18,000 soldiers killed and 25,000 wounded; in addition, approximately 200,000 civilians were killed, mostly in mass executions conducted by advancing German troops. The German orders were to kill all the inhabitants of Warsaw and take no prisoners. More than 17,000 German soldiers were killed and 9,000 wounded.

During and after the Warsaw Rising—on Hitler's orders—the city was systematically bombed with as many as 123 sorties daily. The bombings were followed by a massive and organized looting campaign. Block after block, Poland's capital was burned to ruins, until 85% of it was destroyed. The fate of Warsaw was to be a grim "example" for Europe.

It all could have turned out differently. Warsaw could have been one of the first European capitals liberated but, as many argue, political miscalculations by its leaders—and even more so by global leaders Joseph Stalin, Winston Churchill, and Franklin D. Roosevelt—turned the tide against the Polish capital. Airdrops from the Allies were too little and too late, and the Soviet army stood before the city only a few hundred meters away, watching Warsaw burning from the other bank of the Vistula River.

Stalin did not want the Polish Home Army to have a victory over the German occupiers. His plans for Poland were different: he wanted to liberate it himself and make it into a Communist state. Although a tragic irony, it is perhaps not surprising that 1944 insurgents faced persecution from the Communists in postwar Poland.

$$$–$$$$
Fodor'sChoice
★

✕ **Biblioteka.** A university library may seem an unlikely location for a gourmet restaurant, but you are in for a delightful surprise. The menu is well-booked in terms of fine cuisine, including an exceptional saddle of deer in calvados sauce served with a layer of aubergine, and *branzino* (sea bass) with Pernod sauce. Good luck trying to decide which excellent dish to choose. The great food is accompanied by fine Italian wines imported directly from the producers. Don't forget dessert: how about a hot chocolate soufflé with mint ice cream? ⊠ *University of Warsaw*

GREAT ITINERARIES

As the capital of Poland and of Mazovia, Warsaw has the majority of the region's attractions, but Łódź, the region's second city, also has a lot to offer. Suggested day-trip destinations are all within easy access of Warsaw.

IF YOU HAVE 3 DAYS

On your first day, start with a trip to the top floor of the Palace of Culture and Science to enjoy an aerial view of the city. Descend and explore the Old Town and the Royal Route; include a stop to see the latest show at the Zachęta Gallery and a visit to the Royal Castle. Walk down through the Warsaw University campus toward the river to see a marvelous piece of contemporary Polish architecture, the Warsaw University Library. After exploring the beautiful garden on the green roof of the library, you can enjoy gourmet dinner in Biblioteka restaurant on the ground floor. On your second day, take a trip to Chopin's birthplace, Żelazowa Wola. In the afternoon, back in the city, stroll around Łazienki Park, where you will see the most famous Polish composer, though only in statue form. Then visit the Center for Contemporary Art at Pałac Ujazdowski (and don't miss the restaurant). On Day 3 head for the Warsaw Rising Museum and the former Jewish District. In the afternoon, visit the other bank of the river, where you can stroll through the Praga District and its fashionable art centers: Luksfera

Gallery at the old Koneser distillery and Fabryka Trzciny, where you can catch a play or a concert and a meal of "art-industrial" cuisine.

IF YOU HAVE 5 DAYS

Follow the three-day itinerary for Warsaw, above. Spend Day 4 visiting Łowicz, Nieborów, and Arkadia, returning to Warsaw for the night; be sure to get a good night's sleep so you can start early the next day. On Day 5, head for Łódź, 140 km (87 mi) southwest of Warsaw, stopping at the Tum Church on your way; this requires a bit of a detour from the most direct path to Łódź, but is definitely worth it. In Łódź, stroll down Piotrkowska Street and visit the Księży Młyn settlement and palace. If you are looking for good nightlife, this is the place, so you might consider spending a night here before moving on.

IF YOU HAVE 7 DAYS

Follow the five-day itinerary, but add an extra day in Warsaw, where you will have time to explore its sights and museums at leisure, and be sure to fit in a visit to the Wilanów Palace. Also, stretch your visit to Łódź into two days; there is plenty to see, and two days will give you time to explore the city's unique museums, particularly the Modern Art Museum and the Textile Museum. And spending the night gives you the opportunity to take in the city's vibrant nightlife scene.

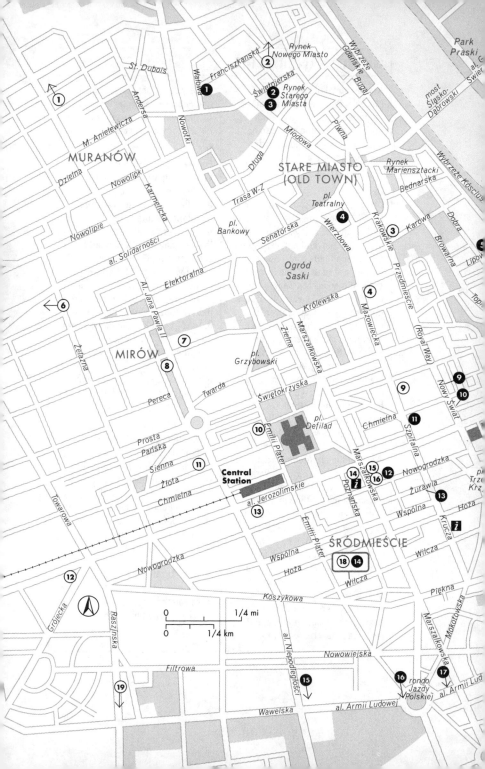

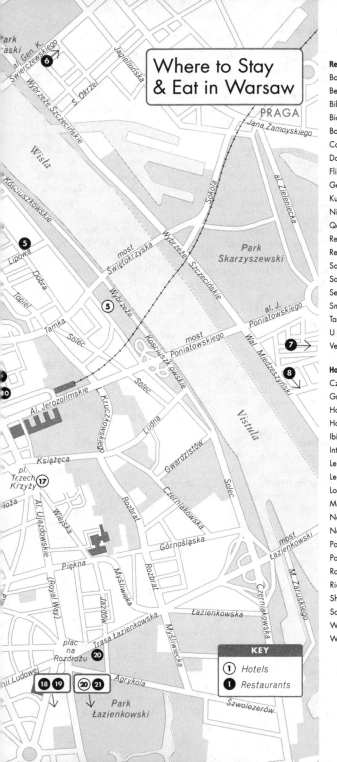

Where to Stay & Eat in Warsaw

KEY

① *Hotels*

❶ *Restaurants*

Library, Dobra 56/66, Powiśle ☎ *22/620–19–99* 🖃 *AE, DC, MC, V* ⊘ *Closed Sun.*

$$–$$$$ ✕ **Belvedere.** You could not find a more romantic setting for lunch or dinner than this elegant restaurant in the New Orangery at Łazienki Park. The lamp-lit park spreads out beyond the windows, and candles glitter below the high ceilings. The atmosphere can be quite formal, though, especially when official delegations arrive—and they do. Polish cuisine is a specialty, and many dishes are prepared with a variety of fresh mushrooms, including the very recommendable mushroom soup. Also recommended is the roast boar, served with an assortment of vegetables. ⊠ *Łazienki Park, Agrykola 1, enter from Parkowa or Gargarina, Łazienki* ☎ *022/841–48–06* 🏛 *Jacket and tie* ⌣ *Reservations essential* 🖃 *AE, DC, MC, V.*

$$–$$$$ ✕ **Boathouse.** This restaurant away from the city center serves great Mediterranean dishes. "Boathouse sole," a sole fillet stuffed with crabmeat in a crunchy potato crust with saffron sauce and wild-mushroom arancini (fried risotto cakes), served with fresh green asparagus, is really good. Boathouse is popular with expats and families with kids, especially for a Sunday brunch. It is particularly popular in summer. ⊠ *Wał Miédzeszyński 389a, Praga* ☎ *22/616–32–23* ⌣ *Reservations essential* 🖃 *AE, DC, MC, V.*

$$–$$$$ ✕ **Dom Polski.** The "Polish Home" restaurant is more of a manor, with
Fodor'sChoice several patrician, yet cozy, rooms and a conservatory. The service is suit-
★ ably courteous, the food is equally genteel. Although the Polish recipes are traditional Polish recipes, they are not as heavy as much of the country's cuisine and minimize the use of fat. Some good examples from the menu are veal liver with baked apple and caramel sauce and sheatfish (catfish) fillet with green pepper and spinach. ⊠ *Francuska 11, Śródmieście* ☎ *22/616–24–32* 🖃 *AE, DC, MC, V.*

$$–$$$$ **Gessler Karczma.** People flock here partly for the atmospheric setting: a warren of candlelit, bare-brick cellars and ground-floor rooms in one of the historic houses on the Rynek Starego Miasta (Old Town Square). The historical interiors are beautiful and help to set a romantic mood. The food can be pretty decent, for instance, duck in apples, an old Polish recipe, is quite tasty. The priceswell, the prices are less so, and the service is varied. On the whole, Gessler Karczma is a bit of a gamble given how much you have to pay for the privilege. ⊠ *Rynek Starego Miasta 19–21, Stare Miasto* ☎ *022/831–44–27* 🖃 *AE, DC, MC, V.*

★ **$$–$$$$** ✕ **Kurt Scheller's Restaurant.** The most prominent Swiss chef in Warsaw is still running strong with his signature restaurant in the Rialto Hotel. The food is excellent: interesting reinterpretations of both Polish and international dishes. The menu is always changing, but the cutlet of deer loin roasted in a mushroom crust with blackberry sauce on soft potato pancakes is an excellent example of Kurt Scheller's inspired skill. Both the setting—a beautiful art deco interior—and the service are impeccable. ⊠ *Rialto Hotel, Wilcza 73, Śródmieście* ☎ *22/584–87–71* ⌣ *Reservations essential* 🖃 *AE, DC, MC, V.*

$$–$$$$ **U Fukiera.** This long-established wine bar on the Old Town Square has been turned into a curious—though ultimately inviting—network of elaborately decorated dining rooms. There is a talking parrot in a cage here, and candles adorn all available shelf space (sometimes set dangerously close to diners' elbows). The decor is, admittedly, lovely; the food is okay but overpriced "Light Old Polish." Expect to find such standbys as oven-roasted carp, sautéed veal liver, and crabmeat crepes. As with most places in the Old Town, sadly, you don't really get you're money's worth. Nevertheless, there's no denying that this is still one of the most famous and popular restaurants in Warsaw. If you dine here, go in with your eyes open and your pocketbook full. ✉ *Rynek Starego Miasta 27, Stare Miasto* ☎ *022/831–10–13* ♿ *Reservations essential* ▭ *AE, DC, MC, V.*

¢–$$$$ ✗ **Sakana.** The fresh and tasty sushi does not come cheaply here, as you'll discover when you add up your seemingly inexpensive, individual pieces for a rather large final bill; however, your little bites arrive in fancy little boats in this floating interpretation of the "kaiten-sushi" (conveyor-belt–sushi) restaurant. Watch the chef at work: he definitely knows what he is doing, and it's like watching an artist work as he produces picture-perfect maki and nigiri. You don't even have to bother reading a menu: just grab the plates as they pass; and try to keep a running total in your mind so you are not so surprised when you get a hefty bill. Sakana has bar seating only. ✉ *Moliera 4/8, Śródmieście* ☎ *22/826–59–58* ♿ *Reservations essential* ▭ *AE, DC, MC, V.*

$$–$$$ ✗ **Restauracja Polska.** With a stylish room and some of the best food in the city, this basement restaurant is one of the more popular places to be in Warsaw these days. The tasteful main salon is furnished with antiques and decorated with large bouquets of fresh flowers. You can't go wrong here with the food, especially if you try the homemade pierogi or pike-perch fillet in white-leek sauce. For dessert, the homemade cakes are outstanding. ✉ *Chocimska 7, Śródmieście* ☎ *022/848–12–25* ▭ *AE, DC, MC, V.*

$–$$$ **Flik.** On a corner overlooking the Morskie Oko Park, this restaurant in Mokotów has a lovely geranium-frilled terrace. The dining room has well-spaced tables, light cane furniture, and lots of greenery. Try the fresh salmon starter followed by *zrazy* (rolled beef fillet stuffed with mushrooms). There is a self-service salad bar, and downstairs is a small, casual café. ✉ *Puławska 43, Morskie Oko Park* ☎ *022/849–44–34* ▭ *AE, DC, MC, V.*

$–$$$ **Nippon-kan.** Before Toshihiro Fukunaga opened the longest-standing
FodorśChoice Japanese restaurant in Warsaw (with the longest sushi bar in Europe),
★ he worked in the fashion industry and lived in South America. He moved to Poland in 1990, hoping to promote Polish fashion models in Japan; he ended up promoting sushi, tempura, and noodles to initially reluctant—and now enthusiastic—Poles. The menu is extensive to the point of overwhelming, but whatever you choose, you cannot go wrong. ✉ *Roma Office Center, Nowogrodzka 47a, Śródmieście* ☎ *22/585–10–28* ▭ *AE, DC, MC, V.*

★ $–$$$ ✗ **Qchnia Artystyczna.** This artsy place at the back of the Zamek Ujazdowski is not for the impatient. This is a busy restaurant—and deservedly so—and the result can be sometimes hectic, even rude service. However, all may be forgiven once you dig into your meal, which is always delicious and well-prepared. The creative menu, which is always freshly prepared and full of flavor, includes everything from potato pancakes to

Parma ham to pork in orange sauce. The location is simply unbeatable: in summer, outdoor tables overlook a magnificent view of the park. The best strategy is just to work yourself into a Zenlike state and go with the flow, but make reservations. ⊠ *Zamek Ujazdowski, al. Ujazdowskie 6, Łazienki* ☎ *022/625–76–27* ⚖ *Reservations essential* ☰ *AE, DC, MC, V.*

$–$$$ ✗ **Sense.** Its owners claim Sense is the first Asian fusion restaurant in Poland, and that may very well be. Good modern decor compliments the East-meets-West cuisine prepared in the open kitchen. The chefs have fun cooking up the names for the dishes, such as "stir crazy," "wok'n'roll" or "hurry curry." You can "go bananas!" for dessert. Of the Asian restaurants in Warsaw, this would have to be near the top of the list. ⊠ *Nowy Świat 19, Śródmieście* ☎ *22/826–65–70* ⚖ *Reservations essential* ☰ *AE, DC, MC, V.*

$–$$
Fodor'sChoice
★
✗ **Restauracja Fabryki Trzciny.** You'll find the atmosphere at this restaurant cozy and warm, which is surprising since the modern arts center that houses it was once an industrial warehouse. The cuisine here is classified as "art-industrial cuisine," but the truth is that the food served here is Polish—mostly Varsovian—with influences from the Mediterranean and other European cuisines. Many dishes may recall childhood favorites, such as *leniwe* (sweet cheese raviolis) or *pyzy* (a kind of dumpling popular in Mazovy). Among the many excellent dishes, don't miss horseradish soup or veal liver in mushroom sauce, both of which are unforgettable. If you feel indecisive, go with the six-course tasting menu and a shot of *żołądkowa* vodka to wash everything down. ⊠ *Fabryka Trzciny, Otwocka 14, Praga* ☎ *22/619–17–05* ☰ *AE, DC, MC, V* ⊘ *Closed Mon.*

¢–$$$
Fodor'sChoice
★
✗ **Banja Luka.** The best Balkan restaurant in Warsaw serves a mix of Croat, Serbian, Bosnian, and Jewish recipes, executed by Serb and Croat chefs. Meat dishes are the menu's core, although Thursday is fish day, and food comes in generous portions. Worthy choices include *dimljena vesalica* (sirloin smoked with cherrywood and then grilled very slowly), and *jareći kotleti* (mixed lamb cutlets in herbs). The decor is rustic, and in summer, the garden is one of the best places in town. ⊠ *Puławska 101, Stary Mokotów* ☎ *22/854–07–82* ☰ *AE, DC, MC, V.*

$–$$ ✗ **Casa to tu!** "To tu!" means "it's here!" but this casa can be easy to miss: the slightly uninviting entrance is through a courtyard and down steps to a cellar door; you'll see a sign. But once you find the restaurant, you'll be glad for the effort. The gazpacho, paella, and tapas are all excellent, and the setting very pleasant: calming ambient lighting, warm colors, and wood tables and chairs give the space a comfortable, cozy feel. Plus the service is as good as the prices are reasonable. ⊠ *Nowy Świat 54/56, Śródmieście* ☎ *022/828–00–66* ☰ *AE, MC, V.*

$–$$ ✗ **Sadhu Café.** In what was once a boiler room, healthy, primarily vegetarian food is served on wooden tables in a wood-paneled dining room. A full range of dishes is available, from simple to sophisticated, including "Monsoon" (zucchini marinated in olive oil with garlic, grilled with chili and served with yogurt sauce and basil), "Tomatos in Love" (baked tomatoes stuffed with a variety of vegetables and herbs, with soy-sauce-and-honey dressing) or "The Little Prince" (salmon fillet in cream-and-wine sauce with green peppers, served with spinach and fried potatoes). The combination of an interesting, varied menu plus great service means the restaurant is widely considered among the best vegetarian choices in Warsaw. ⊠ *Wałowa 3, Śródmieście* ☎ *22/635-81-39* ▤ *AE, DC, MC, V* ⊗ *No lunch weekdays.*

$-$$ ✕ **Smaki Warszawy.** You can't go wrong with any of the chef's recommendations, which are usually traditional Polish dishes with a twist. Both the duck breast in a sauce of apples, plums, and apricots; and the pappardelle with boletus mushrooms and freshly chopped parsley are truly delicious and among the highlights on the menu. ⊠ *Żurawia 47, Śródmieście* ☎ *022/621-82-68* ▤ *AE, DC, MC, V.*

$-$$ ✕ **Tandoor Palace.** This establishment is widely considered one of the best

Fodor'sChoice Indian restaurants in Poland—and not just by its owner, Charanjit

★ Walia. Tandoor Palace serves North Indian food, mostly tandoori dishes, as the name indicates—including excellent butter tikka masala, and a selection of *jalfrezi* (a vegetable curry), *biryani* (a sweet and spicy rice dish), and other recipes where green chilis, ginger, and coriander are used generously. Curries can be washed down with Kingfisher beer. The restaurant is the favorite haunt of foreign residents, who attend the monthly Curry Club and the Comedy Club. ⊠ *Marszałkowska 21/25, Śródmieście* ☎ *22/825-23-75* ▤ *AE, DC, MC, V.*

$-$$ ✕ **Vernix.** This is the only Belgian restaurant in Warsaw, though the own-

Fodor'sChoice ers say it serves "International cuisine with a Belgian touch." Behind a

★ beautiful, neobaroque facade (which remains from a prewar restaurant pavilion of Grand Hotel Garni) is a sleek, minimalist interior. The decor is elegant yet simple, and the patrons are similarly chic. The main draw is, not surprisingly, mussels (order them on Thursday and Friday, when they are at their most fresh), but all seafood is good, particularly the "chef's prawns." The food is accompanied by a good selection of Belgian beers. ⊠ *Chmielna 5 (enter from the patio), Śródmieście* ☎ *22/ 826-46-60* ▤ *No credit cards.*

★ **$** ✕ **Biosfeera.** At this fashionable, upscale vegetarian restaurant, you'll find no alcohol, cigarette smoke, or meat. The food is delicious, and the service friendly. Tortillas, pastas, pancakes, and salads are accompanied by freshly squeezed juices, and there is usually a nod to non-veg diners with a fish dish or two; however, most of the menu is vegan. You emerge from the orange glow of Biosfeera refreshed and energized. ⊠ *al. Niepodległości 80, Śródmieście* ☎ *22/898-01-55* ▤ *AE, DC, MC, V.*

WHERE TO STAY

Warsaw is beginning to deal with its shortage of luxury hotel rooms for business travelers, and you'll now find a good selection of luxury lodgings in the city, including both large international chains and interesting individually owned hotels. However, lower down the price scale, options still remain restricted. Bed-and-breakfast accommodations are difficult to find. In summer there are generally more options because student hostels rent out their spaces. Demand is high, so book well in advance.

Warsaw is a small city, and the location of your hotel is not of crucial importance in terms of travel time to major sights or nightspots. Many hotels are clustered in the downtown area near the Palace of Culture and along aleja Jana Pawła II, ulica Marszałkowska, and aleje Jerozolimskie. This is not an especially scenic area; nevertheless, the neighborhood doesn't exactly become a "concrete desert" after business hours, since there are many residences, restaurants, and nightspots. Note that with a rising crime rate in the city, it is best to be cautious when strolling downtown at night—although the greatest hazards usually turn out to be uneven pavement and inadequate lighting.

The hotels on plac Piłsudskiego, which is close to parks and within easy walking distance of the Old Town, offer more pleasant surroundings. Most of the suburban hotels have no particular scenic advantage, though they do provide immediate access to larger tracts of open space and fresh air.

$$$$
Fodor'sChoice
★
🏨 **Polonia Palace.** When this hotel opened in 1913, it was the best address in Warsaw. Following decades of faded glory—and a two-year-long complete restoration—it reopened in 2005 in a condition that is once again worthy of its name. Corner and front rooms have what is, perhaps, the coolest view in town: the socialist realist Palace of Culture and Science, which is right across the street. The rooms are spacious, although they differ in size and layout, with modern, muted decor and comfortable amenities. The breakfast is an adventure in itself, a full splash featuring caviar and champagne or vodka (yes, we mean *breakfast*); it is served in the grand Ludwikowska restaurant, embellished with crystal chandeliers, mirrors, and some six kilos of gold. ✉ *al. Jerozolimskie 45, 00–692, Śródmieście* ☎ *22/318–28–00* 🖷 *22/318–28–01* ⊕ *www. poloniapalace.com* ➾ *198 rooms, 8 suites* ♿ *Restaurant, café, in-room fax, in-room safes, minibars, cable TV, gym, massage, sauna, steam room, bar, in-room broadband, business services, meeting rooms, no-smoking floors* ➚ *AE, DC, MC, V* ⌷O⌷ *BP.*

★ $$$$
🏨 **Rialto.** Soft jazz plays in the lobby of this boutique hotel, which is completely in tune with its wonderfully consistent and tasteful art deco design, the work of architect Michał Borowski. Original period furniture was hunted down in antique fairs all over Europe, then lovingly restored by Polish artisans and supplemented with quality copies: a Charles Rennie Mackintosh lamp here, a Tamara de Lempicka painting there. While rooms are a bit on a small side because of the historical building's architectural quirks, their style is large enough that you won't mind. Each room is different, from cool, classy suite No. 65 (with slanted ceilings) to warm, wild African single No. 29. The hotel's fashionable restaurant is run by a renowned chef Kurt Scheller. ✉ *Wilcza 73, 00–670, Śródmieście* ☎ *22/584–87–00* 🖷 *22/584–87–01* ⊕ *www. rialto.pl* ➾ *33 rooms, 11 suites* ♿ *Restaurant, room service, in-room safes, minibars, cable TV, in-room DVD, in-room broadband, gym, hot tub, sauna, bar, library, laundry service, business services, meeting rooms, parking (fee)* ➚ *AE, DC, MC, V* ⌷O⌷ *BP.*

$$$–$$$$
🏨 **Holiday Inn.** Designed—and later franchised—by Holiday Inn, this gleaming six-story complex opposite Warsaw's Central Station avoids some of the standard chain-hotel impersonality. It's softly carpeted and furnished throughout in shades of gray and blue. A tree-filled, steel-and-

CLOSE UP

A Material Girl

1

"I LIVE LIFE IN THE MARGINS OF SOCIETY, and the rules of normal society don't apply to those who live on the fringe." These defiant words were spoken not by a notorious gangster but an acclaimed painter, Tamara de Lempicka, an extraordinary woman whose life could easily provide material for several novels. She was born in Warsaw as Maria Górska in 1895–or -96 or -98. (Later, she "corrected" the date to 1902.) Her father was a wealthy attorney, so she lived a comfortable life in Warsaw until her teens, when her parents divorced and Tamara was sent to school in Switzerland.

Around 1915, in Saint Petersburg, she married Tadeusz Łempicki, a Russian lawyer and socialite, with whom she had her only child, a daughter Kizette. Their *dolce vita* was interrupted by the Russian Revolution, when the Bolsheviks arrested Tamara's husband.

In 1918, the family fled to Paris, where Tamara studied painting at Académie de la Grande Chaumière and Académie Ranson, with such teachers as Maurice Denis and André Lhote. She quickly established a reputation as a painter of portraits, primarily of glamorous people in the fashionable social circles in which she moved.

While Tamara received considerable critical acclaim and became a social celebrity, famed for her aloof Garboesque beauty, her parties, and her love affairs (with women as well as men), Tadeusz Łempicki returned to Warsaw and filed for a divorce. Tamara came to Poland three times to stop him, but the damage to their marriage was beyond repair.

In 1939, she moved to the U.S. with her second husband, Baron Raoul Huffner. They settled first in Hollywood, where they bought King Vidor's mansion, moving later to New York, where they took a fashionable apartment on East 57th Street. She remained successful and socially adventurous; by the 1950s, however, her style of painting was going out of fashion. She tried to change to abstract painting and started using a spatula instead of a brush, but these experiments were not very well received. In the 1970s, interest in her earlier work began to revive, and by the 1990s she had again become something of a stylish icon, with her paintings in high demand, fetching record prices in auctions.

Her work remains controversial: some consider her a genius, others a fraud. Laura Cumming sarcastically credits Tamara's paintings with "lighting by Caravaggio, tubism by Legér, lipstick by Chanel, styling by *Esquire* out of Ingres." Love it or hate it, her distinctive work–precise and smooth, decadent and stylized–is believed to epitomize the art deco style better than almost anyone else's.

Tamara de Lempicka finally retired to Mexico, where she moved after her second husband's death. She died in her sleep in 1980. According to her last wish, her ashes were scattered over the crater of Mount Popocatépetl (El Popo). Today her paintings are owned by Jack Nicholson, Donna Karan, Madonna, and Barbra Streisand, but you won't find any of them in the galleries of Warsaw, her hometown.

glass conservatory fronts the building up to the third floor. The generously proportioned guest rooms have projecting bay windows that overlook the very center of the city. ☒ *Złota 48, 00–120, Śródmieście* ☎ *022/697-39-99* 🖷 *022/697-38-99* ⊕ *www.ichotelsgroup.com* ⤴ *365 rooms, 8 suites ♨ 3 restaurants, café, room service, in-room data ports, minibars, cable TV, gym, hot tub, sauna, 2 bars, shop, dry cleaning, laundry service, concierge, business services, parking (fee), some pets allowed* ▭ *AE, DC, MC, V* ⑩ *BP.*

$$$–$$$$ ▥ **InterContinental Warszawa.** One of Warsaw's tallest buildings is also one of its most prominent modern landmarks. The hotel's pride and joy—justly so—is a brilliant swimming pool on the 44th floor, which shares space with the Riverview Wellness Center. Guest rooms are spacious and comfortably furnished, while amenities include tea/coffeemakers. The views from upper floors are spectacular. Residential suites offer ultramodern trimmings for long-term guests (75 long-term apartments for zł 4,000–zł 12,000 per month). ☒ *Emilii Plater 49, Śródmieście* ☎ *022/ 328-88-88* 🖷 *022/328-88-89* ⊕ *www.warsaw.intercontinental.com* ⤴ *290 rooms, 36 suites ♨ 2 restaurants, 2 bars, room service, in-room safes, some kitchens, minibars, cable TV, in-room data ports, in-room broadband, indoor pool, fitness, gym, sauna, laundry service, concierge, business services, computer room, car rental, parking (fee)* ▭ *AE, DC, MC, V* ⑩ *BP.*

$$$–$$$$
Fodor'sChoice
★

▥ **Le Regina.** The latest addition to Warsaw's lineup of top-end hotels, this boutique, luxury establishment is an oasis within the busy capital. With a superb location at the north end of the Old Town, the hotel is a remodeled 18th-century palace that's rich in history, including a stint as the quarters of the U.S. Embassy in the 1950s. Rooms are spacious and serene, but the nicest suites are the "deluxe" category, which include private gardens or terraces; the fun and fashionable, black-and-white penthouse suite (number 303) is stunning. Nice touches include complimentary Internet access—uncommon in this class of hotel—and an umbrella in every closet. However, the sun always shines in Le Regina. ☒ *Kościelna 12, 00–218, Nowe Miasto* ☎ *022/531-60-00* 🖷 *022/531-60-01* ⊕ *www.leregina.com* ⤴ *58 rooms, 3 suites ♨ Restaurant, room service, in-room safes, minibars, cable TV, Wi-Fi, gym, pool, sauna, bar, laundry service, business services, Internet room, meeting rooms, parking (fee)* ▭ *AE, DC, MC, V* ⑩ *BP.*

★ $$$–$$$$ ▥ **Le Royal Méridien Bristol.** Built in 1901 by a consortium headed by Ignacy Paderewski—the concert pianist who served as Poland's prime minister from 1919 to 1920—the Bristol was long at the center of Warsaw's social life. Impressively situated on the Royal Route, next to the Pałac Namiestnikowski (Presidential Palace), the hotel survived World War II more or less intact. It continues to maintain a long tradition of luxury and elegance under the ownership of Le Méridien. Additionally, the hotel has one of the best cafés in town—no one can resist its pastries. ☒ *Krakowskie Przedmieście 42/44, 00–325, Royal Route* ☎ *022/ 625-25-25* 🖷 *022/625-25-77* ⊕ *www.bristol.polhotels.com* ⤴ *163 rooms, 43 suites ♨ 2 restaurants, café, in-room fax, in-room safes, minibars, cable TV, in-room broadband, indoor pool, gym, massage, sauna, steam room, bar, Internet room, business services, meeting rooms, no-smoking floors* ▭ *AE, DC, MC, V* ⑩ *BP.*

$$$–$$$$ ⌧ **Sheraton Warsaw Hotel & Towers.** Halfway down the Royal Route from the Old Town, this curved six-story building overlooks plac Trzech Krzyży, while behind it lie the parks that run along the Vistula embankment. The interiors are bright, the rooms generously sized, and the well-trained staff succeeds in making the Sheraton one of the friendliest of the big business-oriented hotels in Warsaw, one reason why it's also popular among leisure travelers. ✉ *Bolesława Prusa 2, 00–504, Śródmieście* ☎ *022/657–61–00* 🖷 *022/657–62–00* ⊕ *www.sheraton.pl* ⇄ *350 rooms, 20 suites* ♿ *3 restaurants, café, some in-room data ports, some in-room faxes, in-room safes, cable TV, health club, hair salon, massage, sauna, steam room, dry cleaning, laundry service, concierge floor, business services, parking (fee)* ⊟ *AE, DC, MC, V* ⑩ *BP.*

$$$–$$$$ ⌧ **Sofitel Victoria Warsaw.** Opened in the late 1970s, the Victoria was, until 1989, Warsaw's only luxury hotel, hosting a stream of official visitors and state delegations. The large and comfortably furnished guest rooms, which are decorated in tones of brown and gold, are what you might expect in a big business hotel. Health facilities include a basement swimming pool and three exercise rooms. All these features are good enough to draw business travelers, but it's really the location that will appeal most to tourists: the hotel is just across the street from the jogging (or walking) paths of the Ogród Saski (Saxon Gardens), Zachęta Art Gallery, and Teatr Wielki. ✉ *ul. Królewska 11, 00–065, Śródmieście* ☎ *022/657–80–11* 🖷 *022/657–80–57* ⊕ *www.sofitel.com* ⇄ *347 rooms, 13 suites* ♿ *3 restaurants, room service, in-room data ports, in-room safes, minibars, cable TV with movies and video games, pool, health club, bar, casino, nightclub, shops, dry cleaning, laundry facilities, business services, car rental, travel services, parking (fee), some pets allowed, no-smoking rooms* ⊟ *AE, DC, MC, V* ⑩ *BP.*

$$$ ⌧ **Hotel Jan III Sobieski.** Since it opened in 1991, this hotel's bright pink, blue, and yellow illusionist facade has startled more than a few Varsovians. Inside, however, the decor is more conventional, and the service is impeccable. The rooms are reasonably sized and warmly furnished in soft rosewood and flowered prints. This hotel is primarily devoted to caring for the needs of business travelers. ✉ *pl. Zawiszy 1, 02–025, Śródmieście* ☎ *022/658–44–44* 🖷 *022/659–88–28* ⊕ *www.sobieski.com.pl* ⇄ *377 rooms, 27 suites* ♿ *2 restaurants, café, room service, some in-room safes, minibars, cable TV, gym, hair salon, 2 hot tubs, massage, sauna, bar, shops, laundry service, business services, meeting rooms, parking (fee)* ⊟ *AE, DC, MC, V* ⑩ *BP.*

$$$ ⌧ **Novotel Warsaw Centrum.** This dun-color, 30-story, Swedish-designed metal cube (formerly the Forum) has been a fixture on the Warsaw skyline since 1974. Guest rooms are of average size, and those on the east side of the building have good views—but don't choose this hotel if you're counting on cheerful surroundings. Depressing tones of brown and green predominate, and the furnishings seem to have been chosen solely for function rather than comfort. The staff, used to dealing with rapid-turnover group tours, can be offhand. The hotel is in the middle of a heavily built-up area. On the plus side, it is within easy reach of the entertainment districts. Though impersonal, it's a perfectly adequate. ✉ *Nowogrodzka 24/26, 00–511, Śródmieście* ☎ *022/621–02–71* 🖷 *022/*

625–04–76 ⊕ *www.novotel.com* ⟿ *750 rooms, 13 suites* ♿ *2 restaurants, some in-room safes, some minibars, some refrigerators, cable TV, hair salon, bar, shops, dry cleaning, laundry facilities, some pets allowed* ⊟ *AE, DC, MC, V* ⦶ *BP.*

$$$ 🏨 **Warsaw Marriott.** Located in the high-rise Lim Center opposite Central Station, the Marriott currently has some of the city's best accommodations, particularly for the price. It's a classy hotel with a well-trained and helpful staff, of whom nearly everyone speaks some English. The views from every room—of central Warsaw and far beyond—are spectacular on a clear day. The Lila Veneda restaurant on the second floor hosts a special Sunday brunch, complete with Dixieland band. ⊠ *al. Jerozolimskie 65/79, 00–697, Śródmieście* ☎ *022/630–63–06* 🖷 *022/620–52–39* ⊕ *www.marriott.com* ⟿ *489 rooms, 34 suites* ♿ *3 restaurants, café, room service, in-room data ports, in-room safes, some kitchens, minibars, cable TV, indoor pool, gym, hair salon, hot tub, sauna, 3 bars, casino, nightclub, shop, laundry service, concierge, business services, car rental, parking (fee)* ⊟ *AE, DC, MC, V* ⦶ *BP.*

$$–$$$ 🏨 **Novotel Warsaw Airport.** You won't have to worry about getting a good night's sleep if you stay at this Novotel, as it is some distance away from the hustle and bustle of the city center. However, this is far from an ideal location if you are coming to Warsaw to see the sights. If your flight out is early in the morning, though, this is a perfect location for your last night: it's only five minutes from the airport (fortunately, *not* under any flight paths), and it's right across the road from a major area of gardens and parks. Though removed from the heart of the city, the hotel is on the main bus routes; Bus 175 will take you downtown in 15 minutes. The atmosphere is friendly, and the rooms are light, clean, and comfortable. ⊠ *1 Sierpnia 1, 02–134, Mokotów* ☎ *022/846–40–51* 🖷 *022/846–36–86* ⟿ *150 rooms* ♿ *Restaurant, minibars, pool, gym, bar, meeting rooms, airport shuttle* ⊟ *AE, DC, MC, V* ⦶ *BP.*

$$–$$$ 🏨 **Radisson SAS Centrum.** All the various room categories here are fitted with proper comforts, including an iron, tea/coffeemakers (as well as free use of espresso machines), and, last but not least, free broadband and wireless Internet throughout the hotel. The guests are a mix of business travelers and tourists. The pleasant and reliable hotel is within walking distance of many major sights. ⊠ *Grzybowska 24, Śródmieście* ☎ *022/321–88–88* 🖷 *022/321–88–89* ⊕ *www.warsaw.radissonsas.com* ⟿ *298 rooms, 13 suites* ♿ *Restaurant, café, room service, in-room safes, some kitchens, minibars, cable TV, in-room broadband, in-room data ports, Wi-Fi, indoor pool, gym, sauna, laundry service, concierge, meeting rooms, parking (fee)* ⊟ *AE, DC, MC, V* ⦶ *BP.*

★ $$–$$$ 🏨 **Westin Warsaw.** The pleasant, contemporary form of the Westin fits in well with the context of aleja Jana Pawła II, one of the most interesting streets in Warsaw in terms of new architecture. The elevators are fitted within the glass tower, so that you can admire the view while you ride up and down. The lobby, which has a spiral staircase, feels cozy for a big hotel, and you may notice echoes of Mies van de Rohe in the Fusion restaurant, which is famous for its Sunday brunch that even Varsovians often book in advance. Inside the comfortable rooms, Westin's trademark "Heavenly Bed" is not an empty promise. ⊠ *al. Jana Pawła II,*

00–854, Śródmieście ☎ *22/450–80–00* 🖷 *22/450–81–11* ⊕ *westin. com/warsaw* ⤳ *345 rooms, 16 suites* ♨ *Restaurant, minibars, cable TV, in-room safe, gym, massage, sauna, bar, in-room broadband, meeting rooms, laundry service* ▤ *AE, DC, MC, V* ⦿| *BP.*

$$ 🖻 **Gromada Dom Chłopa.** With an excellent location in the center of Warsaw, this white five-story hotel was built during the late 1950s by the Gromada peasants' cooperative and originally had a plant-and-seed store on the ground floor. The hotel, which was renovated in 2000, offers clean and reasonably priced accommodations; rooms are rather small, but the colors are lively, and the bathrooms have been updated. There is no air-conditioning, though. ✉ *pl. Powstańców Warszawy 2, 00–030, Śródmieście* ☎ *022/625–15–45* 🖷 *022/625–21–40* ⊕ *www.gromada. pl* ⤳ *282 rooms* ♨ *Restaurant, cable TV, bar, parking (fee); no a/c* ▤ *AE, DC, MC, V* ⦿| *BP.*

★ $$ 🖻 **Parkowa Hotel.** This 1970s-era hotel, reserved for official government delegations, frequently has rooms available to the general public. It is just south of the Pałac Belweder (Belvedere Palace) in a landscaped area adjacent to Łazienki Park (fresh air from the latter is free of charge). The hotel has been renovated since it was privatized in the late 1990s, most recently in 2003, and offers Western-style accommodations (including air-conditioning). In addition to standard hotel accommodations, Parkowa offers also suites in luxury villas for rental for suitably high prices. ✉ *Belwederska 46/50, 00–594, Łazienki* ☎ *022/694–80–00* 🖷 *022/41–60–29* ⊕ *www.hotelparkowa.pl* ⤳ *44 rooms* ♨ *Restaurant, minibars, cable TV, sauna, bar, business services, meeting rooms, free parking* ▤ *AE, DC, MC, V* ⦿| *BP.*

$–$$ 🖻 **Ibis Warszawa Centrum.** Part of the popular budget chain from Accor, this hotel in central Warsaw was built in 2000, providing convenient access to all places you need to visit. It's 2½ km (1½ mi) from Old Town, within convenient walking distance from the Old Town and the old Jewish District. The rooms are light, clean, reasonably spacious, and comfortable. And the hotel staff are friendly and helpful. ✉ *al. Solidarności 165, 00–876, Wola* ☎ *022/520–30–00* 🖷 *022/520–30–30* ⊕ *www. ibishotel.com* ⤳ *189 rooms* ♨ *Restaurant, in-room data ports, cable TV, bar, business services, parking (fee), some pets allowed (fee)* ▤ *AE, MC, V* ⦿| *BP.*

$–$$ 🖻 **Metropol Hotel.** This 1960s hotel is right on Warsaw's main downtown intersection. Most of the rooms are singles and are large enough to contain a bed, armchairs, and desk without feeling crowded. Bathrooms, though small, are attractively tiled and fitted. Each room has a balcony overlooking busy ulica Marszałkowska, and traffic noise can be very intrusive when the windows are open. There is no air-conditioning, but the hotel's exterior is getting a facelift at this writing. ✉ *Marszałkowska 99A, 00–693, Śródmieście* ☎ *022/629–40–01* 🖷 *022/ 625–30–14* ⊕ *www.syrena.com.pl* ⤳ *175 rooms, 16 suites* ♨ *Restaurant, cable TV, business services, meeting room, parking (fee); no a/c* ▤ *AE, DC, MC, V* ⦿| *BP.*

$ 🖻 **Czarny Kot.** This quirky hotel seems like something straight out of a David Lynch film: the gaudy decor—with plush draped curtains and a lot of gilded frames—is a bit surreal. However, it offers surprisingly good value, particularly if you can get one of the special rates. The rooms are comfortable, and some are equipped with rather sumptuous—though once again, quite gaudy—bathrooms. Although not strictly central, the location is not bad at all: right next to the fashionable Burakowska Street, Arkadia shopping mall, and the beautiful, historical Powázki Cemetery. Every wall seems to be adorned with mirrors, and they are for sale, so if you fancy taking one home . . . Unfortunately, the breakfast is rather disappointing, a buffet with limited choices that just parks there in the early morning and waits (and waits). ⊠ *Okopowa 65, 01–042, Muranów* ☎ *22/838–09–38* 🖷 *22/ 636–92–52* 🖅 *25 rooms* 🍴 *Restaurant, room service, cable TV, in-room broadband, laundry service, meeting rooms* ⊟ *AE, DC, MC, V* ⌾ *BP.*

¢–$ ⌨ **Logos.** This hotel is situated in Powiśle, across the road from the Vistula River and 10 minutes by foot (admittedly all uphill) from the Royal Route. Traffic noise can be a big problem in front-facing rooms, but courtyard-facing rooms are peaceful. The decor throughout is dull, with plenty of dark-wood paneling and chocolate-brown paint, and there is no air-conditioning. Needless to say, the main draw here is the low price. Only the 10 doubles have private bathrooms. ⊠ *Wybrzeże Kościuszkowskie 31/33, 00–379, Powiśle* ☎ *022/622–55–61* 🖷 *022/ 625–51–85* ⊕ *www.hotellogos.pl* 🖅 *137 rooms, 10 with bath* 🍴 *Restaurant, café; no a/c* ⊟ *AE, DC, MC, V* ⌾ *BP.*

NIGHTLIFE & THE ARTS

Nightlife

Like many large European cities, Warsaw offers a variety of options for activities after dark to meet the growing and changing needs of its population. Some Varsovians still prefer to meet for drinks in the evenings in the old central European style in *kawiarnie* (cafés), where you can linger for as long as you like over a cup of coffee or glass of brandy (well, almost as long as you like, since most cafés are open only until 10 PM). Others head directly to more cosmopolitan pubs, DJ-bars, and clubs, many of which stay open until the wee hours. Live music is fairly common, and there is a certain fashion these days for melding art and nightlife into a single multifunctional establishment: you will find more than one concert venue/pub/gallery, or bookshop-cum-café.

BARS & LOUNGES If you've got to know the score, **Champions** (⊠ Lim Center, al. Jerozolimskie 65/79, Śródmieście ☎ 022/630–40–33), a popular sports bar and restaurant, is a great (albeit pricey) place to watch American basketball, football, and motor sports.

Harenda (⊠ Krakowskie Przedmieście 4/6, enter from ul. Oboźna, Royal Route ☎ 022/826–29–00) occasionally hosts some good jazz and has an outdoor terrace that gets crowded in summer.

The **John Bull Pub** (⊠ al. Zielna 37, Śródmieście ☎ 022/620–06–56 ⊠ Jezuicka 4, Stare Miasto ☎ 022/831–37–62) is open until midnight and serves English draft beers at both its locations.

Brilliantly and eccentrically named **Łysy Pingwin** (bald penguin ⊠ Ząbkowska 11, Praga ☎ 022/628–91–32) is a relaxing pub run by a Swedish Buddhist (*sic!*) who settled in Warsaw's trendy Praga District.

Szpilka (✉ pl. Trzech Krzyży 18, Śródmieście ☎ 22/628–91–32) is perfect for insomniacs; it opens at 7 PM and stays open until 6 AM. Its sister club Szpulka, which shares the same address, closes as "early" as 3 AM.

CASINOS Warsaw's casinos have a fairly strict dress code of jacket and tie. You must be 18 or over to enter, and you will have to show your passport. Most casinos are affiliated with big hotels.

The **Casino Warsaw** (✉ al. Jerozolimskie 65/79, Śródmieście ☎ 022/830–01–78), on the second floor of the Marriott, is Warsaw's plushest and most sedate casino. The gamblers are often international businessmen or Polish jet-setters. It's open daily from 11 AM to 7 AM.

The **Victoria Casino** (✉ al. Królewska 11, Royal Route ☎ 022/827–66–33) is quite popular and open daily from 2 PM to 7 AM.

CLUBS & DISCOS The crowd at posh and pricey **Cinnamon** (✉ pl. Piłsudskiego 1, Śródmieście ☎ 022/323–76–00) leans toward businessmen in suits, fashionably dressed models and celebrities, and an international crowd (lots of expats). It's part bar, part lounge, part restaurant, and part club, with DJs playing on the weekend. More of a café-restaurant during the day, it's the hottest club in Warsaw on Thursday through Saturday nights.

Ground Zero (✉ al. Wspólna 62, Śródmieście ☎ 022/625–43–80), a former bomb shelter, is a large, crowded bi-level disco, probably the most popular in town. An upscale, younger crowd dances to mostly mainstream disco and pop. Ground Zero is one of the oldest of the "new" clubs to open in Warsaw after the Communist period (it turned 16 in October 2006).

Klubokawiarnia (✉ al. Czackiego 8, Śródmieście) is relaxed, with funky disco music among plaster busts of Lenin and 1950s propaganda posters. You dance to both DJs and live (mostly rock) music from local bands.

House music emporium **Piekarnia** (✉ Młocińska 11, Wola ☎ 022/323–76–00) might have become too popular for its own good—still, it is one of the uncontested leaders of the Warsaw night scene. Famous international DJs (Roger Sanchez, Barry Ashworth, etc.) are brought in for big events. If you like Ibiza, then you'll like this.

There is a well-established disco at the student club **Stodoła** (✉ Batorego 10, Ochota ☎ 022/25–86–25). Though it draws mostly students, it's open to everyone. Music spans from house to techno to R&B to hip-hop, and there are often live bands.

JAZZ CLUBS **Jazz Bistro Gwiazdeczka** (✉ Piwna 40, Stare Miasto ☎ 022/887–87–65) is brighter and more spacious than most smoky jazz clubs in Warsaw and has a glass-covered atrium.

Jazz Café Helicon (✉ Freta 45/47, Stare Miasto ☎ 022/635–95–05) is a smoky jazz club, with Latino music on some nights—it has an adjoining specialty record store.

Tygmont (✉ Mazowiecka 6/8, Śródmieście ☎ 022/828–34–09 ⊕ www. tygmont.com.pl) is a local legend, frequented by older and younger generations of musicians and audiences.

The Arts

You can find out about Warsaw's thriving arts scene in the English-language *Warsaw Insider* or *What's Up,* both of which are available at most major hotels. If you read Polish, the monthly *IKS* (*Informator Kulturalny Stolicy*) and *Activist* and the daily *Gazeta Wyborcza* have the best listings. Tickets for most performances are inexpensive, but if you want to spend even less, most theaters sell general-admission tickets—*wejściówki*—for a few złoty immediately before the performance. Wejściówki are often available for performances for which all standard tickets have been sold.

ZASP (✉ al. Jerozolimskie 25, Śródmieście ☎ 022/621–94–54), a ticketing agency, is also a good source for information on arts happenings.

Tickets for many events can be bought at **EMPiK** (✉ Nowy Świat 15/17, Śródmieście ☎ 022/627–06–50), a local chain of shops.

If you are planning in advance, you can buy tickets for many events from the Web site of **Warsaw Tour** (⊕ www.warsawtour.pl), which has an English-language option.

FILM   Since 1989, it seems every cinema in Warsaw has been showing foreign films—mainly U.S. box-office hits—nonstop. These are generally shown in the original language with Polish subtitles. In the year 2000, cineplexes burst onto the Warsaw scene, providing state-of-the-art cinematic environments, but there are also several independent cinemas with a more "ambitious" repertoire. There are a lot of outdoor screenings during **Filmowa Stolica** (⊕ www.filmowastolica.pl), the city's summer film festival. The screenings are held at venues all over town.

Don't count on seeing many Polish films while visiting Warsaw; only one cinema specializes in Polish features: **Iluzjon Filmoteki Narodowej** (✉ Narbutta 55A, Ochota ☎ 022/48–33–33).

Tiny **Kino.LAB** (✉ al. Ujazdowskie 6, Śródmieście) is a part of the Center for Contemporary Art at the Ujazdowski Castle, showing experimental art films, video art, and even kitschy 1950s science-fiction movies. In summer, the cinema goes open-air (the screen is moved to the castle's courtyard. You won't find box-office blockbusters at the stylish **Kino Muranów** (✉ Andersa 1, Śródmieście), the favorite choice of serious cinemaniacs.

Silver Screen (✉ Puławska 21/29, Centrum ☎ 022/852–88–88), close to the city center, is one of the newest cinemas in town specializing in U.S. films.

MUSIC   In summer, free Chopin concerts are held at the Chopin Memorial in Łazienki Park on Sunday and at Chopin's birthplace, Żelazowa Wola, outside Warsaw. The **Filharmonia Narodowa** (National Philharmonic; ✉ Sienkiewicza 10, Śródmieście ☎ 022/826–72–81) hosts an excellent season of concerts, with visits from world-renowned performers and orchestras as well as Polish musicians. Very popular concerts of classical music for children—run for years by Jadwiga Mackiewicz, who is herself almost a national institution—are held here on Sunday at 2; admission begins at zł 5.

CLOSE UP

Nocturne in C-Sharp Minor

1

ON SEPTEMBER 23, 1939, Władysław Szpilman was giving a performance for Polish Radio, where he worked as a pianist. He was playing Fryderyk Chopin's "Nocturne in C-Sharp Minor" in a live broadcast, when the music was interrupted by an explosion: the German invasion of Warsaw had begun.

Szpilman, a most versatile pianist and composer—he played both classical music and jazz and authored many popular songs in addition to serious orchestra pieces—refused to give up music when the world around him started to crumble. In 1940, he was imprisoned in the Warsaw Ghetto; two years later, his entire family was deported to the Nazi death camp Treblinka; his inability to do anything to help them continued to haunt him for the rest of his life. Szpilman escaped to the "Aryan" part of the city and spent two long years in hiding, assisted by his Polish friends. After the Warsaw Rising of 1944, he continued the life of a recluse, starving in the ghost of a town Warsaw had become. He must have felt like the last man alive among the ruins.

In one of his hiding places, he was found by a German officer of the Wehrmacht, Wilm Hosenfeld. When Szpilman played Chopin's "Nocturne" on an out-of-tune piano, not only did Hosenfeld not denounce the pianist, but he saved his life by helping him find a secure hiding place and providing food.

After the war, Szpilman published his account of what he himself calls his "miraculous survival." Initially his memoirs were issued only in a limited edition and were heavily censored—he was deemed politically incorrect in his description of goodness in varying shades of black, white, and gray. After all, Władysław Szpilman was rescued not only by a German but by a Jewish policeman, and by no less than 20 Poles who risked their lives to help him, and some of them were members of Polish Home Army, the wartime, anti-Communist Polish underground. For the Polish Communist government, his story touched on too many taboo subjects. Szpilman's book, *The Pianist*, was published in 1988, soon becoming a best seller; in 2002, it was made into an Oscar-winning film by Roman Polański.

After the war, Szpilman resumed his career at the Polish Radio (between 1945 and 1963 he held the title of Music Director). During these years he composed several symphonic works, film music, and hundreds of songs. He performed as a soloist and with the violinists Bronisław Gimpel, Roman Totenberg, Ida Haendel, and Henryk Szeryng. He also co-founded the Warsaw Quintet.

Władysław Szpilman did not see Polański's Oscar-winning movie based on his memoirs. He died on July 6, 2000, in Warsaw, at the age of 88. He left behind an amazing story of goodness in the times of evil. That story has a poignant coda: Szpilman opened the first postwar transmission of the Polish Radio in 1945 by playing, once again, Chopin's "Nocturne in C-Sharp Minor."

The **Studio Koncertowe Polskiego Radia** (Polish Radio Concert Studio; ✉ Woronicza 17, Mokotów ☎ 022/645–52–52), open since 1992, has excellent acoustics and popular programs of mostly classical and modern classical (and sometimes jazz).

The **Royal Castle** (✉ pl. Zamkowy 4, Stare Miasto ☎ 022/657–21–70) has regular concerts in its stunning Great Assembly Hall.

The Chopin Society, **Towarzystwo im. Fryderyka Chopina** (✉ Okólnik 1, Śródmieście ☎ 022/827–54–71), organizes recitals and chamber concerts in the Pałac Ostrogskich (Ostrogski Palace).

OPERA & DANCE Housed in a beautifully restored 19th-century theater, **Opera Kameralna** (✉ al. Solidarności 76B, Muranów ☎ 022/625–75–10), the Warsaw chamber opera, has an ambitious program and a growing reputation for quality performances.

Teatr Wielki (Opera House; ✉ pl. Teatralny 1, Śródmieście ☎ 022/826–32–88), Warsaw's grand opera, stages spectacular productions of the classic international opera and ballet repertoire, as well as Polish operas and ballets. The massive neoclassical house, built in the 1820s and reconstructed after the war, has an auditorium with more than 2,000 seats. Stanisław Moniuszko's 1865 opera *Straszny Dwór* (Haunted Manor), a lively piece with folk costumes and dancing, is a good starting point if you want to explore Polish music: the visual aspects will entertain you, even if the music is unfamiliar. Plot summaries in English are available at most performances.

THEATER You don't necessarily need to speak Polish to appreciate the theater scene in Warsaw. Globe Theater performs in English; Rozmaitości and Studium Teatralne are avant-garde theaters performing in Polish, but some performances might be interesting all the same (this is not to say that words are unimportant in these productions); the same is true of Teatr Wielki (which performs Polish classics); however, the majority of Teatr Wielki's repertoire is opera and ballet (no need to speak Polish in order to enjoy these). By the same token, Teatr Lalek's puppets speak a "universal" language.

The **Globe Theater Group** (✉ pl. Grzybowski 6/2, Śródmieście ☎ 022/620–44–29 ⊕ www.globetheatre.art.pl) performs American and British plays at various theater venues.

↻ **"Gulliwer" Teatr Lalek** (✉ Różana 16, Śródmieście ☎ 022/45–16–76 ⊕ www.teatrguliwer.waw.pl) is one of Warsaw's excellent puppet theaters.

Studium Teatralne (✉ Lubelska 30/32, Praga ☎ 022/833–43–60 ⊕ www.studiumteatralne.pl) is one of the city's avant-garde theater companies.

Teatr Narodowy (✉ pl. Teatralny, Śródmieście ☎ 022/826–32–88), adjoining the opera house and under the same management, stages Polish classics.

Perhaps the most creative avant-garde scene is at **Teatr Rozmaitości** (✉ Marszałkowska 8, Śródmieście ☎ 022/629–02–20 ⊕ www.trwarszawa.pl).

Warsaw's Jewish Theater, **Teatr Żydowski** (✉ Plac Grzybowski 12/16, Śród-mieście ☎ 022/620–70–25 ⊕ www.teatr-zydowski.art.pl), performs in Yiddish, but most of its productions are colorful costume dramas in which the action speaks as loudly as the words. Translation into English is provided through headphones.

SPORTS & THE OUTDOORS

Health Clubs

The best health club in Warsaw is the **Fitness Center at the Sheraton** (✉ Bolesława Prusa 2, Royal Route ☎ 022/657–61–00). Open to non-members, the center has the latest equipment, aerobics and other classes, and child care.

Hiking

In Warsaw the local branch of the PTTK (Polish Tourist Association) organizes daylong hikes in the nearby countryside on weekends. If you read Polish, you can watch the local papers for advertisements of meeting points and routes.

Horse Racing

You can reach Warsaw's atmospheric but seedy **racecourse** (✉ Puławska 266, Służewiec ☎ 022/843–14–41) by taking Tram 4 or 36 or one of the special buses marked WYŚCIGI, which run from the east side of the Pałac Kultury i Nauki (Palace of Culture and Science) on Saturday in season (May–October). Betting is on a tote system. Admission to the stands is zł 20.

Jogging

Along with dogs and bicycles, joggers are banned from Warsaw's largest and most beautiful park, Łazienki Park. The 9½-km (6-mi) trail through parkland and over footbridges from the Ujazdów Park to Mariensztat (parallel to the Royal Route) is a good route if you want to do a longer run. The Vistula embankment makes for a good straight run (the paved surface continues for about 12 km [8 mi]). Piłsudski Park has a circular route of about 4½ km (3 mi). You can jog in the center of town on the somewhat restricted pathways of the Ogród Saski (Saxon Gardens).

Soccer

Warsaw's soccer team, **Legia** (✉ Łazienkowska 3, Łazienski ☎ 022/621–08–96), plays at a field in Łazienki Park. Admission is from zł 20.

Swimming

Warsaw's indoor pools tend to be overcrowded, and some restrict admission to those with season tickets; it's best to check first. For a swim your best bet is the indoor pool at the **Le Royal Méridien Bristol** (✉ Krakowskie Przedmieście 42/44, Royal Route ☎ 022/625–25–25).

Klub Sportowy Warszawianka (✉ Dominika Merliniego 9, Mokotów ☎ 022/844–62–07) is an option if you are not afraid of crowded places. This pool is usually used by the Polish professional swimmers before all major international tournaments.

At the **Spartańska** (✉ Spartańska 1, Mokotów ☎ 022/48–67–46) you can usually persuade them to let you swim on a special one-day pass.

SHOPPING

In terms of shopping, Warsaw has it all—from big, sparkling shopping malls to tiny boutiques and specialty stores, as well as some decent street markets. Increasingly, international chains—such as Marks & Spencer—are appearing, which has meant that locally produced products are sometimes harder to find than expensive imported alternatives. Shopping hours are usually from 11 AM to 7 PM on weekdays and from 10 AM to 1 PM on Saturday, but shopping malls are open until 8 or even 10 PM. RUCH kiosks, which sell bus and train tickets, newspapers, and cosmetics, are usually open from 7 to 7.

Shopping Districts

Warsaw has four main shopping streets, all in Śródmieście. The larger stores lie on **ulica Marszałkowska** (from ulica Królewska to plac Zbawiciela) and **aleje Jerozolimskie** (from Central Station to plac Generała de Gaullea, in Śródmieście). Smaller stores and more specialized boutiques can be found on **ulica Nowy Świat** and **ulica Chmielna**. Another fashionable shopping street just a bit farther off is **ulica Burakowska**, while some smaller designer shops and ateliers are scattered around town.

Shopping Malls

Since the mid-1990s, shopping malls started sprouting like mushrooms in Poland's capital—and new ones continue to appear. Many of those are not far at all from the city center. Lately, one of the most popular shopping mall is **Arkadia** (✉ al. Jana Pawła II, Muranów ☎ 022/331–34–00 ⊕ www.arkadia.com.pl), where you can buy almost anything in more than 180 shops, grab a quick bite at a Japanese restaurant, and get your nails done, too.

♻ **Galeria Mokotów** (✉ Wołoska 12, Mokotów ☎ 022/541–30–00 ⊕ www.galeriamokotow.com.pl) is the big sister among the newer malls. Unceasingly popular, it is still the best destination for designer clothing. Plus it has a good selection of restaurants and snack bars, as well as a multiplex cinema, a play area for children, and a bowling alley.

Department Stores

Warsaw's oldest department store, **Arka** (✉ Bracka 25, Śródmieście ☎ 022/692–14–00), has a monumental staircase, art nouveau stained-glass windows, and stores selling clothing, jewelry, and household items.

At the **Galeria Centrum** (✉ Marszałkowska 104–122, Śródmieście ☎ 022/551–41–41) private boutiques sell mainly imported fashion items.

Street Markets

The largest Warsaw market—known as the Russian market, and composed largely of private sellers hawking everything from antiques to blue jeans—is at the **Tysiąclecia Stadium,** east of the river at Rondo Waszyngtona in Grochów. If you go, watch out for pickpockets. A smaller market (with mostly food vendors) can be found closer to the center—just outside the 19th-century covered markets of **Hala Mirowska.**

For treasures among the junk—and the general nostalgic ambience—try one of Warsaw's two flea markets on a Sunday morning: **Olimpia** (✉ Corner of Górczewska and al. Prymasa Tysiąclecia, Wola). **Koło** (✉ Corner of Obozowa and Ciołka, Wola).

Specialty Stores

ANTIQUES For fine antique furniture, art, and china try **Desa** (✉ Marszałkowska 34/50, Śródmieście ☏ 022/621–66–15), an auction house and gallery. Remember, however, that most antiques cannot be exported. You will also sometimes find antiques at the Olimpia and Koło flea markets.

ART GALLERIES For slightly conservative buyers, **Galeria Farbiarnia** (✉ Piękna 28/34, Śródmieście ☏ 022/621–72–35 ⊕ www.galeriafarbiarnia.pl) promises paintings for all tastes and pockets. There are many galleries in Praga, some seasonal and with "flexible" opening hours, but **Galeria Nizio** (✉ Inżynierska 3, Praga ☏ 022/618–72–02 ⊕ www.nizio.com.pl), which moved to Warsaw from New York in 2002, is one of the best established.

Galeria Sztuki Katarzyny Napiórkowskiej (✉ Świętokrzyska 32, Śródmieście ☏ 022/652–19–39 ⊕ www.napiorkowska.pl) holds one of the finest collections of contemporary Polish art in the world.

Raster (✉ Hoża 42/8, Śródmieście ☏ 022/869–97–81 ⊕ www.raster.art. pl) is definitely the most talked-about art gallery in town: showing exhibitions of independent art in a top-floor flat of an old tenement house. It sometimes also has film screenings and live concerts.

In the courtyard of Sir Norman Foster's Metropolitan building, **Yours** (✉ Plac Piłsudskiego 2, Śródmieście ☏ 022/313–19–00 ⊕ www.yours. pl) is where a renowned photographer Tomasz Gudzowaty exhibits and sells his work.

BOOKS **Czuły Barbarzyńca** (✉ Dobra 31, Powiśle ☏ 022/826–32–940) is Warsaw's most popular two-in-one establishment, a bookshop and a café. Most books are in Polish, but there is a good selection of English-language paperbacks and art books, and you can stock up on Moleskine notebooks and diaries since this is probably the only place in Poland where they are available.

Pałac Starej Książki Chimera (✉ Działdowska 8a, Wola ☏ 022/692–14–50) is the largest secondhand and antiquarian bookshop in town.

Traffic Club (✉ Bracka 25, Śródmieście ☏ 022/692–14–50) is five stories of books and records in a beautiful 18th-century building, an old-time department store. Open seven days a week, it offers comfy armchairs, a cafeteria, and free Wi-Fi Internet.

CLOTHING FOR CHILDREN **Endo** (✉ Mokotowska 51/53, Śródmieście ☏ 022/629–30–65) sells fun, colorful children's clothing (for ages 2 and up) and has a play area for ♻ the young customers.

CLOTHING FOR WOMEN　While you'll find outlets for all the famous international designers in Warsaw, it is much more exciting to look for creations of young and talented local designers, and their work is often a real bargain with prices somewhere between popular *prêt-à-porter* and true designer treasures. Warsaw has been blessed with quite a few local talents, and their studios are scattered around town, usually away from the main shopping streets.

The **First Class** (⊠ Jasna 1, Śródmieście ☎ 022/826–88–25) boutique showcases the designs of Maciej Zień.

Designer clothing by **Gosia Baczyńska** (☎ 048/501–520–589), which you can see by appointment only, is popular with Polish celebrities; her collection—modern and classically elegant at the same time—represented Polish fashion culture at the European Union accession ceremony.

Designer tandem **Paprocki & Brzozowski** (⊠ Krucza 17, Śródmieście ☎ 048/608–301–120)—that's Marcin Paprocki and Mariusz Brzozowski—have a shop to sell their fashions.

Pola La (⊠ Solec 85, Solec ☎ 022/622–89–00) is the handbag atelier of a talented Polish designer.

The **Polscy Projektanci** (⊠ Chmielna 30, Śródmieście ☎ 022/828–96–32) is a boutique that will clothe you from head to heals with locally designed, limited-edition fashions.

Ruta (⊠ Czerwonego Krzyża 2, entrance from Solec, Solec ☎ 048/601–851–420 bags, 048/501–087–002 hats) is the shop selling the fantastic hats, bags, and belts designed by Pracownia Kaletnicza and Marta Ruta. Liza Minelli owns one already.

FOLK ART & CRAFTS　**Cepelia** (⊠ pl. Konstytucji 5, Śródmieście ☎ 022/621–26–18 ⊠ Marszałkowska 99/101, Śródmieście ☎ 022/628–77–57), which has several branches in Warsaw, sells folk art, including wood carvings and silver and amber jewelry.

Modern Polish design for the home can be found in **Galeria Opera** (⊠ Freta 14, Stare Miasto ☎ 022/831–73–28).

Red Onion (⊠ Burakowska 5/7, Muranów ☎ 022/887–10–56) sells an international mix of Polish and international goods and has a strong Asian theme.

At **Studio Forma** (⊠ Skorupki 5, Śródmieście ☎ 022/583–68–58) you can find folk-inspired bright and cheerful wool rugs, made by young Polish artists from Moho Design, which won the owners a prize from *Wallpaper** magazine in 2006.

FOOD　If you are looking for more than just the sweets, **Blikle Delikatesy** (⊠ Nowy Świat 35, Śródmieście ☎ 022/826–45–68) sells traditional Polish products (such as natural honey or smoked meats) as well as delicious imports (olive oil, cheeses, and much more). Of course, if you *are* looking for sweets, then there is always something for your sweet tooth. After all, Blikle is best known in Poland as the maker of prize-winning *pączki* doughnuts.

Spiżarnia (⊠ Słomińskiego 19/501, enter on al. Dzika, Muranów ☎ 022/ 424–34–28) is a well-stocked deli with traditional homemade products to take away, and a small restaurant if you want to eat in.

To satisfy your chocolate craving, direct your steps toward **Wedel** (⊠ Szpitalna 8, Śródmieście ☎ 022/827–29–16). When Wedel first opened in 1851, it was a family-owned company; now it's part of the Cadbury candy conglomerate. But the charming old-fashioned shop, where the selection of sweets is impressive, is just as homey as it was when the company was just a local company. In the cafeteria you'll find the best cup of hot chocolate in town.

GLASS & CRYSTAL **A. Jabłonski** (⊠ Nowy Świat 52, Royal Route ☎ No phone) sells unique pieces of handblown glass and crystal.

Krosno (⊠ Arkadia Shopping Mall, al. Jana Pawła II, Muranów ☎ 022/ 331–25–55) sells glass from the famous Krosno factory.

Szlifierna szkła (⊠ Nowomiejska 1/3, Stare Miasto ☎ 022/831–46–43), next to the Old Town Square, custom engraves all kinds of crystal goods.

JEWELRY There are many *jubiler* (jewelry) stores clustered around the Old Town and ulica Nowy Świat. The **Art Gallery** (⊠ Rynek Starego Miasto 13, Stare Miasto) has a great selection of silver and amber, although much of it is somewhat overpriced.

Quadrat–Brodzińska Atelier (⊠ Marszałkowska 9/15, Śródmieście) sells jewelry in ultramodern designs.

One of the oldest and best-established jewelry stores in Poland is **W. Kruk** (⊠ pl. Konstytucji 6, Śródmieście ☎ 022/628–75–34).

Zielony Kot (⊠ Chmielna 26, Śródmieście ☎ 022/826–51–18), the "green cat" in English, is as fun and funky as the name promises.

LEATHER **JKM** (⊠ Krakowskie Przedmieście 65, Royal Route ☎ 022/827–22–62) is a small shop crammed with bags, suitcases, and gloves from the best Polish producers.

Pekar (⊠ al. Jerozolimskie 29, Śródmieście ☎ 022/621–90–82) carries a wide range of bags, gloves, and jackets.

TOYS **Kalimba** (⊠ Mierosławskiego 19, Żoliborz ☎ 022/869–97–81) sells ☾ lovely toys made of natural materials and houses a colorful "Kofifi" cafeteria for parents and their children.

☾ **Niebieskie Migdały** (⊠ Mokotowska 61, Śródmieście ☎ 022/629–11–92) sells cute child-size furniture and toys, including great dollhouses.

EXCURSIONS FROM WARSAW

Mazovia lies in the very middle of Poland and is the heart of the country. One of the first lands to be incorporated in the Piast territory in

Poland's beginnings, the historical Mazovian duchy was an independent domain from 1138 to 1526, and for a lot of that time it served as a battlefield for different forces. At the turn of the 17th century, Warsaw became Poland's capital, but there was no lasting peace: Swedish wars, insurrections, and then two world wars left their marks on the region.

Mazovia—like the whole of Poland—is full of polarities. The flourishing capital city of Warsaw and revitalized, fashionable Łódź contrast with underdeveloped, traditional agricultural regions, sleepy little villages, historical palaces, and churches in the smaller and less densely populated regions.

The most interesting sights within easy reach of Warsaw include Chopin's birthplace at Żelazowa Wola; the Radziwiłł country estate, which encompasses a palace and two wonderful parks at Nieborów and Arkadia; and Kampinoski National Park. Łowicz, with its colorful folk traditions, can be visited as a day trip from Warsaw. Better still, it can be a stop en route to Łódź, and on the way you can see the magnificent Tum basilica.

Numbers in the text correspond to numbers in the margin and on the Mazovia map.

Puszcza Kampinoska

🟢 *10 km (6.2 mi) west of Warsaw west of Warsaw.*

If you have an extra day in Warsaw, a trip to Kampinoski National Park, about an hour west of the city, makes a fun day trip, especially if you want to escape the capital bustle for a few hours in a more soothing natural environment. Officially established in 1959, this ancient kingdom of nature became a UNESCO-listed biosphere reserve in 2000. The area has a variety of landscapes and diverse habitats with dune belts separated by swampy areas and a mixture of forest types (bog-alder forest, ash-alder floodplain forest, pine-oak mixed forest, and low oak-lime-hornbeam forest). In addition to the many elk, which feature in the Park's logo, many other species live there, including lynx, rabbits, foxes, deer, European beaver, and wild boar. Some 121 different birds species have been observed here—either as residents or more temporary visitors—including black stork, herons, and cranes. The forest also has some 4,000 resident insect species and more than 1,100 plant species, including 60 protected varieties. In most years, between 500,000 and 1 million visitors hike the park's many trails.

There are many well-marked walking trails in the Kampinos National Park. The main trail of 55 km (34 mi) crosses the park from east to west (from Dziekanów Leśny to Brochów). The lower, green trail also begins in Dziekanów and travels 51 km (32 mi), ending at Żelazowa Wola, Chopin's birthplace. There are several short trails starting in Truskaw—notably the yellow trail of insurgents and partisans—and the blue folklore trail. If you are planning a true hiking trip rather than a short walk, it is worth the trouble to pick up the map of Kampinoski National Park in advance. You can easily spend an entire day in the area.

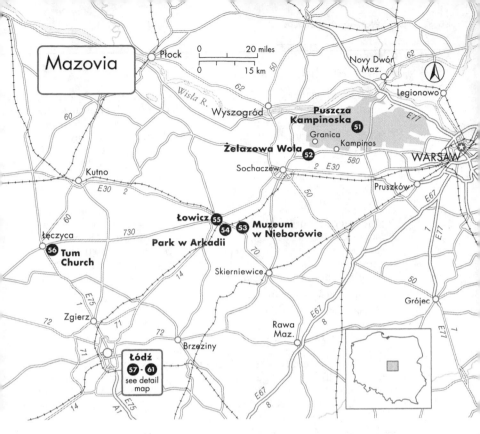

In the village of Granica, near Kampinos and Żelazowa Wola, you'll find the **Muzeum Puszczy Kampinoskiej** (Museum of Kampinos Forest; ⊠ Granica, near Kampinos ☎ 022/725–01–23). Admission to the museum, which is open Tuesday through Sunday from 9 to 4, is zł 3.30.

The most convenient starting points for day-hikers include Truskaw village (in the eastern corner of the park) or Kampinos (in its southwestern section). Both can be reached by PKS bus from Warsaw (⇨ By Bus *in* Warsaw & Mazovia Essentials, *below*). If you are driving from Warsaw, you can use one of the unguarded parking lots at the outskirts of the park These can be found in Truskaw, Wólka Węglowa, Granica, or Dąbrowa Stara.

Two of Warsaw's loveliest historic houses are in this area: the birthplace of Chopin in Żelazowa Wola and the Radziwiłł country estate in Nieborów. The best way to view these two sights quickly is to take one of the many available organized bus tours. However, both places can also be reached by public bus from Warsaw's main bus station.

⊠*Kampinoski Park Narodowy, Tetmajera 38, Izabelin* ☎*022/722–60–01* ⊕ *www.kampinoski-pn.gov.pl* ⊠ *Free* ☉ *Daily sunrise–sunset.*

Żelazowa Wola

★ ❺❷ *30 km (18 mi) west of Warsaw.*

A mecca for all Fryderyk Chopin lovers, the composer's birthplace is a small 19th-century manor house, still with its original furnishings and now a museum dedicated to telling the story of the composer's life. When Chopin was born here on February 22 (or March 1) 1810, his father was a live-in tutor for the children of the wealthy Skarbek family. Although the family soon moved to Warsaw, Fryderyk used to return many times for holidays, and the house—not to mention the sounds and sights of the Mazovian countryside—is said to have influenced him in his early years.

The manor is surrounded by a beautifully landscaped park that was planted in 1930s and designed by Franciszek Krzywda Polkowski. In summer, from May through September, concerts are held on the house's terrace every Sunday at noon and 3 PM. On weekdays, at noon, there are presentations of young artists and talented students playing Chopin.

If you are driving, take Route 2 (E30) west out of Warsaw, and at Sochaczew, turn north on Route 580. The house is also reachable by PKS bus and by private minibuses running from Warsaw's main bus station (⇨ By Bus *in* Warsaw & Mazovia Essentials, *below*), but several companies also offer guided tours that include both Żelazowa Wola and Nieborów, the estate of the Radziwiłł family (and sometimes Arkadia Park as well). (For information on tour companies, see ⇨ Tour Options *in* Warsaw & Mazovia Essentials, below.) ✉ *Żelazowa Wola* ☎ *046/ 863-33-00* 🖭 *zł 12* ◎ *May–Sept., Tues.–Sun 9:30–5:30; Oct.–Apr. 9:30–4.*

Muzeum w Nieborowie

❺❸ *83 km (52 mi) west of Warsaw, 30 km (19 mi) south/southwest of Żelazowa Wola.*

The stunning country estate of the Radziwiłł family includes an impressive baroque palace designed by Tilman van Gameren in the late 17th century. In 1945, the estate was taken over by the National Museum of Warsaw, and it still contains the home's original furnishings. When you walk around the museum, you can admire wooden panels, cobalt tiles, imposing stoves and fireplaces, and numerous paintings and sculptures—notably the ancient head of Niobe. The palace outbuilding houses temporary exhibitions of modern art. The regular, symmetrical baroque park, designed in the 16th century, is truly magnificent. The palace's hunting pavilion contains a number of limited-access guest rooms, where you can stay if you apply far in advance and have a valid reference from an associated artistic, scientific, or political organization. (Book far ahead; no children allowed.)

To get here from Żelazowa Wola, return to the 2 (E30) and drive west to Łowicz; then take Route 70 southeast about 10 km (6 mi). PKS buses run from Warsaw's main bus station in the direction of Łowicz, with stops at both Nieborów and Arkadia. Several guided tours starting in Warsaw include both Chopin's birthplace in Żelazowa Wola and Nieborów (and sometimes Arkadia Park as well).

✉ *Nieborów* ☎ *046/838–56–35* ⊕ *www.nieborow.art.pl* 🎟 *zł15 for palace and park, zł 6 for park only* ⊙ *Mar. and Apr., Tues.–Sun. 10–4; May and June, daily 10–4; July–Sept., weekdays 10–4, weekends 10–6; Oct., Tues.–Sun. 10–3:30. Park 10–sunset.*

Park w Arkadii

⑤④ *85 km (53 mi) from Warsaw, 5 km (3 mi) west of Nieborów.*

Arkadia Park is, like Nieborów, a part of the Radziwiłł family estate and was a noble obsession of Helena z Przeździeckich Radziwiłłowa, who devoted 20 years of her life to the making of it. The imaginary realm of happiness, the romantic park is landscaped in the English style and was designed by renowned landscape architects of the time (in the late 18th century and early 19th century). The 14-hectare parkland is filled with nooks and oases for contemplation and paths for strolling around, brooks and lakes, and fairy-tale construction: artificial ruins, grottoes, and the like. ✉ *Nieborów, 3 mi west of Nieborów Palace* ☎ *046/838–56–35* ⊕ *www.nieborow.art.pl* 🎟 *zł 6* ⊙ *Daily 10 AM–sunset.*

Łowicz

⑤⑤ *90 km (56 mi) from Warsaw, 19 km (12 mi) southwest of Nieborów.*

In Poland, the name Łowicz is synonymous with Mazovian folk traditions—arts and crafts, as well as colorful religious celebrations, notably the city's famous Corpus Christi procession, which was featured in *National Geographic* magazine at the beginning of the 20th century. Corpus Christi is a moveable feast of the Catholic Church, held exactly 60 days after Easter. The Host, figures of Virgin Mary and the Saints, as well as religious banners and symbols are carried through town to the accompaniment of music and prayers. The locals are dressed in traditional folk costumes while children throw petals of flowers, which make a carpet for the advancing procession. The most important sights in Łowicz are all around the perimeter of the Old Town square.

Łowicz Cathedral mixes Renaissance and baroque styles, but its history goes back to the 12th century. Buried under its floor are famous bishops and laypersons. Worth noting are the rococo altar, beautifully carved 17th-century stalls, and side chapels: especially the chapel of Saint Victoria, Łowicz's patron

THE DEVIL DID IT

According to a legend, it was demon Boruta who built the church at Tum. Of course, he was tricked into it—he thought it was a tavern that he was building. Using his supernatural powers, he managed to complete the task in a jiffy. However, when he discovered the scheme, he got angry as hell and tried to destroy his unwanted creation. He aimed at one of the towers, but was not able to tear it down. Nevertheless, his devilish paw left a mark, which can still be seen today.

saint. The latter chapel was designed in the 16th century by Jan Michałowicz of Urzędów, a renowned Polish Renaissance-era artist, who is also buried in the cathedral's crypt. ⊠ *Stary Rynek 24/30* ☎ *046/837–62–66.*

The **Muzeum w Łowiczu** (Łowicz Museum) displays folk crafts and traditions of the area, as well as Polish baroque art. Among the most interesting exhibits are local costumes with characteristic fabrics of colorful stripes, the coffin portraits of local burghers, and several good baroque sculptures. ⊠ *Stary Rynek 5/7* ☎ *046/837–39–28* 💳 *zł 5* ⊙ *Tues.–Sun. 10–4.*

Tum Church

★ ⑤⑥ *35 km (22 mi) north of Łódź, 3 km (2 mi) east pf Łęczyca.*

The Romanesque collegiate church in Tum, which is built of granite and sandstone, dates back to the 12th century and is one of the most magnificent churches throughout Poland—and it's well worth a detour from the main routes if you are traveling to Łódź or Toruń from Warsaw. Even though it was partly damaged and has been rebuilt periodically throughout its history, the church has retained its original shape and many of its original architectural details. At the main entrance, note the Romanesque portal, which is framed by adoring angels. Be sure to take a look at the crucifix in the main aisle and the surviving fragments of ancient frescoes in the western apse.

Today the church stands well off the beaten tourist path, so it's not often visited, though you should expect absolutely no tourist infrastructure in the small village. The church is usually open, but if it happens to be locked when you arrive, the keys can be collected from the priest at the parish house opposite the church (approximately 100 meters to the east). Admission is free, but contributions toward the restoration of the church are gratefully accepted. ⊠ *Tum.*

Łódź

140 km (87 mi) southwest of Warsaw, 45 km (28 mi) from Łowicz

Łódź (pronounced roughly as "wooch" or "woodge") is a relatively young city, which has grown up quickly in the last 200 years—from a small village to one of the largest cities in the country. Its development was the direct result of the textile industry boom in the 19th century, hence its nickname "the Polish Manchester." Łódź has also been dubbed "the Polish Hollywood"—or "Holly-Łódź"—as it is the location of the most famous Polish film school that educated Andrzej Wajda, Roman Polański, and Krzysztof Kieślowski.

The city hosts the **Camerimage Film Festival** (⊕ www.camerimage), which is usually in late November. Unique among Europe's major film festivals, this one focuses on the work of the cinematographer rather than the director.

Numbers in the text correspond to numbers in the margin and on the Łódź map.

Łódź

(map labels) Ogrodowa · Północna · Pomorska · Pl. Wolności · Rewolucji 1905r. · R. Mielczarskiego · Cmentarna · Zachodnia · Wschodnia · Sterlinga · Adama Próchnika · Stefana Jaracza · Legionów · aleja 1 Maja · S. Więckowskiego · Gabriela Narutowicza · Jana Kilińskiego · Składowa · Zielona · 28 Pułku Strzelców Kaniowskich · Kpt. S. Pogonowskiego · Lipowa · Stefana Żeromskiego · 6 Sierpnia · Wólczańska · Gdańska · R. Traugutta · L. Żeligowskiego · Andrzeja Struga · Piotrkowska · pl. Komuny Paryskiej · Henryka Sienkiewicza · Juliana Tuwima · Dowborczyków · Lipowa · Marii Skłodowskiej-Curie · L. Zamenhofa · Nawrot · Karolewska · Mikołaja Kopernika · Tadeusza Kościuszki · Roosevelta · aleja Marszałka Józefa Piłsudskiego · al. Adama Mickiewicza

0 ——— 1/2 mi
0 ——— 1/2 km

What to See

61 Księży Młyn. This model city within a city was founded by the Scheibler and Grohman industrialist families, who were initially competitors but who have been partners and owners since 1921 in the largest cotton mill in Europe. Księży Młyn (or Priest's Mill) was a model industrial village with production facilities, shops, a fire department, hospital, school, railway station, residential quarters for the workers, and the owner's palace surrounded by a park. The palace—called the Herbst Villa or **Rezydencja Księży** (Priest's Mill Residence)—is open to visitors, who can marvel at the fabulous and expensive taste of the early capitalists. ✉ *Przędzalniana 72* ☎ *042/674–96–98* 🎫 *zł 7* ☉ *Tues. 10–5, Wed. and Fri. noon–5, Thurs. noon–7, weekends 11–4.*

57 Muzeum Historii Miasta Łodzi (Historical Museum of Łódź). The Pałac Poznańskiego, another grand home of another of Łódź's major industrialist families, is now the city's main museum. The opulent neo-baroque residence itself is magnificent. Among the exhibits are memorabilia of famous Łódź citizens, including English-language writer Jerzy Kosiński (born in Łódź in 1933, died in New York in 1991). ✉ *Ogrodowa 15* ☎ *042/654–03–23* ⊕ *www.muzeum-lodz.pl* 🎫 *zł 7* ☉ *Tues. and Thurs. 10–4, Wed. 2–6, Fri.—Sun. 10–2.*

58 **Muzeum Sztuki** (Modern Art Museum). One of the best art collections in Poland specializes mostly in modern avant-garde and contemporary art—both Polish and international. It originated as an artists' museum in late 1920s. The present building is too small to exhibit the whole collection, so only a selection is shown. The museum is hoping to receive new facilities soon. ⊠ *Więckowskiego 36* ☎*042/633-97-90* ⊕*www.muzeumsztuki.lodz.pl* 🖾*zł 7* ☉ *Tues. 10-5, Wed. and Fri. 11-5, Thurs. noon-7, weekends 10-4.*

> ## PROMISED LAND
>
> *Ziemia Obiecana (Promised Land)* is a film about the making of Łódź—filmed by one of the leading Polish directors, Oscar-winning Andrzej Wajda. The movie is based on Władysław Reymont's novel of the same title. It tells the story of three friends: a Pole, a Jew, and a German, all entrepreneurs in the textile industry. Both Reymont and Wajda captured the spirit of this developing, multicultural city. Today the *Promised Land* is one of the classics of Polish cinema.

60 **Muzeum Włókiennictwa** (Textile Museum). This impressive collection of both machines and textiles is an important record of the industry that make Łódź the city it is today. The museum is housed in the Biała Fabryka Geyera (Geyer's White Factory). In this very building, in 1839, the first steam engine in Poland was launched. ⊠ *Piotrkowska 282* ☎ *042/683-26-84* 🖾*zł 6* ☉ *Tues., Wed., and Fri. 9-5, Thurs. 11-7.*

59 **Ulica Piotrkowska** is the main boulevard of Łódź, lined with shops, cafés, cinemas, galleries, bars, and clubs. And to think that in the mid-19th century it was a road leading through the woods. Today Piotrkowska is the longest street (with the longest uninterrupted line of buildings) in Europe, but if you get tired of walking, you can always take a rickshaw or a "retro streetcar." Along the street, you will find benches with life-size statues of famous Poles: poet Julian Tuwim, novelist Władysław Reymont, and pianist Artur Rubinstein.

Where to Eat

$–$$ **Anatewka.** The inspiration for this restaurant came straight out of Łódź's Jewish heritage. This can be seen both in the nostalgic decor and the rich menu: chicken in honey-and-ginger sauce or Rothschild's duck in cherries or lamb "Łódź style." All this comes with accompaniment of klezmer music—and it's just a stone's throw from Piotrkowska Street. ⊠ *6 Sierpnia 2/4* ☎ *48/630-36-35* ☐ *AE, DC, MC, V.*

$–$$ **Ciągoty i tęsknoty.** This restaurant's name is difficult to pronounce, even for a native Pole. What's not difficult is the accessible, mostly Mediterranean-influenced menu and the pleasant, warm interior. You'll find a good selection of starters and salads; especially good main courses include chicken with avocado cream sauce and beef tenderloin with spinach. ⊠ *Wojska Polskiego 144a* ☎ *042/650-87-94* ☐ *AE, DC, MC, V.*

Where to Stay

In addition to the hotels recommended below, you can also rent an apartment in Łódź. **Home Travel** (⊠ Piotrkowska 21 ☎ 042/633-80-80

CLOSE UP

1

The Artists' Museum of Art

THE "INTERNATIONAL COLLECTION OF MODERN ART" in the Łódź Museum was begun in 1929 by a group of artists led by Władysław Strzemiński, Katarzyna Kobro, and Henryk Stażewski. They had the idea of creating an international collection of the most recent art, for which they managed to gain the support of such renowned artists as Hans Arp, Max Ernst, Theo van Doesburg, Fernand Léger, Pablo Picasso, Kurt Schwitters, and others. Among Polish artists, they were pledged support by Leon Chwistek, Karol Hiller, and Stanisław Ignacy Witkiewicz.

The collection was actually quite revolutionary. From the beginning it represented—as no other contemporary European collection had done—the main movements of the avant-garde, from cubism, futurism, and constructivism to purism, neo-plasticism, and surrealism. The tradition of artists donating their works to the museum continues to this day. In 1981, Joseph Beuys gave to the museum part of his famous archive, a collection of more than a thousand works. In 1983, a group of American artists handed over to the museum the works they created as part of the *Échange entre artistes 1931–1982, Pologne–USA* project.

🏨 042/633–80–10 ⊕ www.hometravel.pl) rents simple but perfectly comfortable modern flats (40 to 60 square meters [430 to 646 square feet]), each of which has a kitchenette, TV, and Internet service. All are in the center of town. The company accepts most major credit cards.

$–$$ **Savoy.** Built in 1912, this historic hotel was immortalized by Joseph Roth, a famous Austrian writer whose 1923 novel took place in the Savoy. The hotel is within a short walk of both the Piotrkowska Street and the railway station. The rooms are varied but generally spacious and pleasant—ask for one of the "retro" rooms, which are more stylish than others. ⊠ *Traugutta 6* 🏨 *042/632–93–60* 🖷 *042/632–93–68* ⊕ *www. hotelsavoy.com.pl* ☞ *45 rooms, 2 suites* ⚏ *Restaurant, cable TV, meeting rooms; no a/c* ⊟ *AE, DC, MC, V* ¶⊙¶ *EP.*

$ **Déjà Vu.** This tiny boutique hotel with only six rooms (advance booking essential) occupies a grand 1925 villa. And the hotel remains true to the original style of the place: dark wood and stained-glass windows, along with a little magic and mystery. The rooms are beautiful and comfortable, and staying here is definitely an experience. ⊠ *Wigury 4* 🏨 *042/636–20–60* 🖷 *042/636–70–83* ☞ *6 rooms* ⚏ *Restaurant, cable TV, in-room broadband, meeting room; no a/c* ⊟ *AE, DC, MC, V* ¶⊙¶ *EP.*

Fodor'sChoice
★

Shopping

Ulica Piotrkowska has traditionally been the main downtown shopping street in Łódź. Today, you will still find plenty of shops here selling fashions, art, and other products, right next to the many clubs and cafés. The top shopping experience in Łódź can be found at **Manufaktura**

(✉ Between Ogrodowa and Zachodnia ☎ 042/664–92–89 ⊕ www.
manufaktura.com). Manufaktura is not just about shopping; it is, at this
writing, the largest revitalization project in Europe in the former textile area of Izrael Poznański (established in 1852). Covering an area of
150,000 square meters (about 37 acres), this city within a city has its
own Town Square and internal tramline. There are concert halls, movie
theaters, events, restaurants, cafés, and—not least—many great boutiques.
At this writing, museums and a four-star hotel were also in the works.

WARSAW & MAZOVIA ESSENTIALS

Transportation

BY AIR
If you are flying into Poland from abroad, it's mostly likely that you
will fly into Warsaw. The city's Okęcie Airport, also known as Fryderyka
Chopina International Airport, is the largest airport in Poland, with about
70% of all the air traffic into and out of the country. About 80 daily
international fights—as well as many charter flights—connect Warsaw
with the rest of the world. You can fly nonstop from Warsaw to Chicago,
Newark, New York–JFK, and Toronto. In addition, most European airlines connect Warsaw with the U.S. The new Etiuda Terminal serves most
of the "low-cost" airlines that operate flights within Europe. The flying time from New York to Warsaw is approximately 9 hours, from London approximately 2½ hours. For more information on airlines flying
to Poland, *see* By Air *in* Smart Travel Tips, at the back of this book.

A much smaller airport in Łódź is served by Ryanair; most other flights
here are domestic.

🔢 **Aer Lingus** ☎ 022/626–84–02. **Aeroflot** ☎ 022/628–25–57. **Aerosvit Airlines**
☎022/650–40–60. **Airberlin** ☎022/650–11–11. **Air Europa** ☎022/455–38–40. **Air France**
☎ 022/556–64–00. **Alitalia** ☎ 022/962–82–85. **American Airlines** ☎ 022/625–30–02.
Austrian Airlines ☎ 022/627–52–90. **Belavia** ☎ 022/650–23–14. **British Airways**
☎ 022/529–90–00. **CSA** ✉ Sobieski Hotel, pl. Zawiszy 1 Śródmieście ☎ 022/659–
67–99. **El Al** ☎ 022/630–66–16. **Finnair** ☎ 022/657–01–29. **KLM Royal Dutch Airlines**
☎ 022/556–64–44. **LOT** ☎ 022/95–7 in Warsaw. **Lufthansa** ☎ 22/338–13–00. **Malev**
☎ 022/697–74–72. **SAS** ☎ 022/850–05–00. **Sky Europe** ☎ 022/433–07–33. **SN Brussels Airlines** ☎ 022/575–71–00. **Swiss** ☎ 022/697–66–00. **Wizzair** ☎ 022/351–94–99.

AIRPORTS & TRANSFERS
Warsaw's Okęcie Airport, also known as Fryderyka Chopina International Airport, is 7 km (4½ mi) south of the city center and has the most
international flights into and out of Poland.

The direct route to downtown, where almost all the hotels are, is along
Żwirki i Wigury and Raszyńska streets. The AIRPORT–CITY bus leaves
from Platform 4 outside Terminal 1 every 20 minutes and stops at all
the major hotels as well as the Central Station. Tickets cost zł 6, and
the trip takes about 25 minutes. Alternatively, Bus 175 leaves Okęcie
about every 10 minutes (at night, Bus 611 is much less frequent). It also
runs past most major downtown hotels and is reliable and cheap, but

beware of pickpockets. Purchase tickets for zł 2.40 at an airport RUCH kiosk. If your immediate destination is not Warsaw, Polski Express has direct service from Okęcie to major Polish cities. Avoid at all costs the taxi hawkers and unmarked vehicles (which have no number at the top) outside the arrivals hall: not only are these cabs expensive but they can also be dangerous. Your best bet is to call radio taxi from one of the radio taxi kiosks in the arrivals area, or call your hotel in advance and have them pick you up. A cab ride into the city should cost about zł 25 (most hotel taxis have higher, fixed rates, of approximately zł 50).

Łódź Lublinek Airport is located southwest of the city center, about a 10-minute drive. It can be reached by public transportation (Bus L from the Main Railway Station; also bus number 55 via Piotrkowska Street and number 65 from Łódź Kaliska, the city's second railway station). A cab ride from the airport to the city center should cost about zł 20 to zł 25.

🛪 **Okęcie Airport** ✉ Żwirki i Wigury 1, Warsaw ☎ 022/650-42-20 ⊕ www.polish-airports.com. **Łódź Lublinek Airport** ✉ Gen. Maczka 35, Łódź ☎ 042/683-52-00 ⊕ www.airport.lodz.pl.

BY BUS

Warsaw's main bus station, Dworzec PKS Zachodni, 10 minutes from Central Station on Bus 127 or 130, serves most long-distance routes, both domestic and international. Domestic buses headed east leave from Dworzec PKS Stadion on the east bank of the Vistula. The private long-distance bus service Polski Express, which goes to most major destinations within Poland, arrives and departs from Jana Pawła II Station, between Central Station and the Holiday Inn. Polski Express also has a stop at the airport.

Łódź central bus station (Dworzec Centralny PKS) is connected to the Łódź Fabryczna train station; it's also within a 15-minute walk of Piotrkowska Street. Both regular buses and Polski Express buses stop there. The north bus terminal (Dworzec Północny) is approximately 1 km from the city center (tram number 5 will take you to the town center) and is served by regular buses only.

🚌 **Warsaw Buses Dworzec PKS Zachodni** ✉ al. Jerozolimskie 144, Śródmieście, Warsaw ☎ 022/822-48-11 ⊕ www.pks.warszawa.pl. **Dworzec PKS Stadion** ✉ Zamoyskiego 1, at Targowa, Praga, Warsaw ☎ 022/818-15-89 ⊕ www.pks.warszawa.pl. **Polski Express** ✉ Jana Pawła II, between Central Station and the Holiday Inn, Śródmieście, Warsaw ☎ 022/620-03-30 ⊕ www.polskiexpress.pl.
🚌 **Łódź Buses Dworzec Centralny PKS** ✉ pl. Sałacińskiego 1, Łódź ☎ 022/823-63-94 ⊕ www.pks.lodz.pl. **Polski Express** ✉ Łódź Fabryczna railway station, Łódź ☎ 042/205-56-30 ⊕ www.polskiexpress.pl.

BY CAR

Within the city, a car is more of a problem than a convenience. Particularly in Warsaw, traffic jams are frequent and parking problematic, with a significant threat of theft—of contents, parts, or the entire car—if you leave a Western model unattended. If you do bring your car, park it overnight in a guarded parking garage.

A car can be a useful independent means of transportation if you are planning to travel around Mazovia to explore the countryside and off-the-beaten track sights. For example, you may wish to follow the route from Warsaw to Łódź via Żelazowa Wola, Arkadia, Niebórow, Łowicz, and Tum.

Major international car-rental agencies have offices in both Warsaw's and Łódź's city center and at the airports as well.

🚗 **Avis** ✉ Marriott hotel, al. Jerozolimskie 65/79, Śródmieście, Warsaw ☎ 022/630–73–16 ✉ Okęcie Airport, Warsaw ☎ 022/650–48–72 ✉ Kilińskiego 59/63, Łódź ☎ 042/633–21–41. **Budget** ✉ Okęcie Airport, Warsaw ☎ 022/650–42–62. **Europcar** ✉ Okęcie Airport, Warsaw ☎ 022/650–25–64. **Five** ✉ Marriott hotel, al. Jerozolimskie 65/79, Śródmieście, Warsaw ☎ 022/629–75–15. **Hertz** ✉ Nowogrodzka 27, Śródmieście, Warsaw ☎ 022/621–13–60 ✉ Okęcie Airport, Warsaw ☎ 022/650–28–96 ✉ Hotel Światowit, Kościuszki 68, Łódź ☎ 042/636–46–39 ✉ Lublinek Airport, Łódź ☎ 042/686–60–01. **Mieszek** ✉ Obywatelska 191, ódź ☎ 022/629–75–15.

BY TAXI

In Warsaw, it is always best to use the services of radio taxi because these are the most reliable and because the operators usually speak English. This is also true in Łódź. The standard charge is about zł 5 to zł 7 for the first kilometer (½ mi) and zł 1.30 to zł 2 for each kilometer thereafter (about 50% more at night and during holidays). You do not need to tip taxi drivers, although you can round up the fare to the nearest złoty. Avoid unmarked Mercedes cabs as well as taxis that do not have a number and a name of a company you know on the top. Those "independent" taxis are likely to charge far more than the going rate.

🚕 **Warsaw Taxi Companies** Halo Taxi ☎ 022/96–23. MPT ☎ 022/91–91. OK! Taxi ☎ 022/96–28. Partner Taxi ☎ 022/96–69. Sawa Taxi ☎ 022/644–44–44. Super Taxi ☎ 022/96–22. Tele Taxi ☎ 022/96–27. Top Taxi ☎ 022/96–64. Taxi Wawa ☎ 022/96–44. 🚕 **Łódź Taxi Companies** Taxi Dwa Dwa ☎ 042/96–22. Euro Taxi ☎ 042/96–67. Merc Taxi ☎ 042/650–50–50. Taxi Nova ☎ 042/96–24.

BY TRAM & SUBWAY

In Warsaw, a trip on a city bus costs zł 2.40. There are also timed tickets: zł 3.60 for up to 60 minutes, zł 4.50 for up to 90 minutes, and zł 6 for up to 120 minutes. A 1-day pass is zł 7.20, 3-day pass, zł 12, and a 7-day pass, zł 24. There are additional charges for large pieces of luggage. Purchase tickets from RUCH kiosks or directly from bus drivers (zł 0.60 surcharge), and validate one in the machine on the bus for each ride. Buses that halt at all stops along their route are numbered 100 and up. Express buses are numbered from E-1 and up. Buses numbered 500–599 stop at selected stops. You can check details on the bus stop's information board. Night buses (numbered 600 and up) operate between 11 PM and 5:30 AM; the fare is three tickets. Buses can be very crowded, and you should beware of pickpockets.

Trams are the fastest means of public transport since they are not affected by traffic holdups but are also often crowded. Purchase tickets from RUCH kiosks or tram operators, and cancel one ticket in the machine on the tram for each ride. Trams run on a north–south and east–west grid system along most of the main city routes, pulling up automatically at all stops. Each tram has a diagram of the system.

Warsaw's underground opened in spring 1995. Although it has only one line, which connects the southern suburbs (Kabaty) and northern suburbs (Marymont) to the city center, it is clean and fast and costs the same as the tram or bus. Use the same tickets, canceling them at the entrance to the station.

In Łódź, the public transportation network of trams and buses is well developed, and there is a system of timed tickets (zł 1.70 up to 10 minutes, zł 2.40 up to 30 minutes, zł 3.60 up to 60 minutes, zł 4.80 up to 120 minutes, and zł 9.60 for a 24-hour pass). If you buy your ticket on the tram or the bus, there is a zł 0.50 surcharge. You can also buy tickets from a ticket machine (though not yet at every stop and only in some trams/buses) or from most newspaper kiosks around town (probably the easiest option). As in Warsaw, remember to validate your ticket on entering a bus or a tram.

🚌 **ZTM Warszawa** 📞 022/94–84 🌐 www.ztm.waw.pl. **MPK Łódź** 📞 042/672–11–11 🌐 www.mpk.lodz.pl.

BY TRAIN

As the name implies, Warsaw's Warszawa Centralna (Central Station) is right in the heart of the city, between the Marriott and Holiday Inn hotels, and next to the Palace of Culture. Beware of pickpockets and muggers who prey on passengers as they board or leave trains. Most trains from Warszawa Centralna stop on their way out in Warszawa Wschodnia, Warszawa Zachodnia, or Warszawa Gdańska, or Warszawa Wileńska—depending on their direction.

In Łódź, the main station is Łódź Fabryczna, within a 15-minute walk from the central Piotrkowska Street. Łódź Kaliska is a suburban station west of the city center.

You can purchase train tickets at the train station or at travel agencies, including Orbis. You can also buy tickets on the train (there is a small surcharge), but be warned: old-fashioned regulations require you to notify the train attendant before you actually get on that train if you need to purchase a ticket on board—otherwise you may have to pay a penalty. Tickets can also be bought online, and the full train timetable (*rozkład jazdy pociągów*) is available on the Web site of Polskie Koleje Państwowe, the Polish national rail company.

🚌 **Łódź Fabryczna** ✉ pl. Sałacińskiego 1, Łódź 📞 042/94–36. **Polskie Koleje Państwowe** 🌐 www.pkp.pl. **Warszawa Centralna** (Central Station) ✉ al. Jerozolimskie 54, Śródmieście, Warsaw 📞 022/94–36.

Contacts & Resources

BANKS & EXCHANGE SERVICES

To change money, head to any *kantor* (currency exchange)—or specifically, to *kantor wymiany walut*—which usually offer slightly better rates than hotels and banks. In Warsaw, there is a kantor in the main post office that is open 24 hours a day. TEBOS, in Warsaw's Central Station—at the foot of the staircase leading from the main hall to the access passage for platforms—is also open 24 hours a day. In Łódź, there are numerous kantors on ulica Piotrkowska.

Another option, not necessarily more expensive, is drawing cash directly from an ATM—there are plenty of these around Warsaw and Łódź.

☎ Kantor Wymiany Walut ✉ Main Post Office, Świętokrzyska 31, Śródmieście, Warsaw. **TEBOS** ✉ Central Station, al. Jerozolimskie 54, Śródmieście, Warsaw. **Western Union** ✉ Bank BPH, al. Jerozolimskie 27, Warsaw ☎ 0800-120-224.

EMERGENCIES

The general emergency number (when calling from a mobile phone) is 112; there are also separate numbers for ambulance, fire, and police (which are free if dialed from public phones). Falk is a private ambulance service.

☎ Emergency Services Ambulance ☎ 999. **Falk** Warsaw: ☎ 022/536-97-10 in Warsaw, 998 in Łódź. **Fire** ☎ 998. **Police** ☎ 997.

☎ Dentists Austria-Dent Center ✉ Żelazna 54, Śródmieście, Warsaw ☎ 022/654-21-16.

☎ Doctors Damian Medical Center ✉ Wałbrzyska 46, Warsaw ✉ Foksal 3/5, Warsaw ✉ Modlińska 310/312, Warsaw ☎ 022/566-22-22. **Lux Med Medical Clinics** ✉ Chmielna 85/87, Warsaw ✉ Kopernika 30, Warsaw ✉ al. Jerozolimskie 162, Warsaw ☎ 0801/80-08-08. **Medicover** ✉ Marszałka Piłsudskiego 3, Łódź ☎ 042/639-66-66 or 96-77.

☎ Hospitals Dzieciątka Jezus Hospital ✉ Lindleya 4, Warsaw ☎ 022/502-16-98. **Hospital of the Interior Ministry** ✉ Wołoska 137, Warsaw ☎ 022/508-20-00. **Kopernik Hospital** ✉ Pabianicka 62, Łódź ☎ 042/689-50-00 ⊕ www.kopernik.lodz.pl. **Pulsmed Private Hospital** ✉ P.O.W. 26, Łódź ☎ 042/633-32-75 ⊕ www.pulsmed.com.pl.

☎ 24-hour Pharmacies Apteka Beata ✉ al. Solidarności 149, Śródmieście, Warsaw ☎ 022/620-08-18. **Apteka Grabowskiego** ✉ Central Station, 1st fl., al. Jerozolimskie 54, Śródmieście, Warsaw ☎ 022/825-69-86. **Cito** ✉ Żeromskiego 39, Łódź ☎ 042/633-48-29. **Familia** ✉ Lutomierska 115a, Łódź ☎ 042/640-71-27.

INTERNET, MAIL & SHIPPING

Most hotels in Warsaw and Łódź offer Internet access (sometimes for a fee). There are also plenty of Internet cafés around, with rates between zł 3 and zł30 per hour for high-speed access. In Warsaw, you'll find several hot spots with free Wi-Fi access for those carrying laptops: in plac Zamkowy, ulica Nowy Świat, ulica Chmielna, plac Bankowy, Warsaw University Library, the Traffic Club, and even in some restaurants and cafeterias. In Łódź, the library of Łódź Polytechnics, among other places, offers free Wi-Fi.

In Warsaw, the main post office in Świętokrzyska Street, and in Łódź, the post office in Tuwima Street, are open 24 hours a day.

☎ Warsaw Internet Cafés Café Casablanca ✉ ul. Krakowskie Przedmieście 4/6, Warsaw ☎ 022/828-14-47 ⊕ www.casablanca.com.pl. **Courtyard by Marriott Cyber Café** ✉ Okęcie Airport, Courtyard by Marriott, Żwirki i Wigury 1, Warsaw ☎ 022/650-650-01-72. **Simple Internet Café** ✉ Marszałkowska 99, Warsaw ☎ 022/628-31-90 ⊕ www.simpleinternetcafe.com.

☎ Łódź Internet Cafés Café del Mundo ✉ Piotrkowska 53, Łódź ☎ 042/633-68-67. **Spadochronowa** ✉ Narutowicza 41, Łódź ☎ 042/631-91-57 ⊕ www.skydive.pl/kawiarnia.

☎ Post Offices Poczta Ğówna (Main post Office) ✉ Świętokrzyska 31/33, Warsaw ☎ 022/826-60-01. **Poczta No. 1** ✉ Tuwima 38, Łódź ☎ 042/632-58-16.

🚢 **Shipping Companies DHL** ✉ Wirażowa 35, Warsaw ☎ 0801–345–345 ✉ Kasprzaka 79, Łódź ☎ 042/634–21–96 ⊕ www.dhl.com. **EMS Pocztex** ✉ Central Railway Station, al. Jerozolimskie 54, Warsaw ☎ 022/825–77–18 ✉ Tuwima 38, Łódź ☎ 042/633–94–52 ⊕ www.pocztex.pl. **Stolica** (UPS) ✉ Prądzyńskiego 1/3, Warsaw ☎ 022/534–00–00 ✉ Traktorowa 111, Łódź ☎ 042/658–82–26 ⊕ www.stolica.pl.

TOUR OPTIONS

Tours of either city or the country can be booked at major hotels or through the agencies directly. Tourist Information Offices can provide contact for organized tours and suggest self-guided tours (ask for free booklets and maps).

ℹ **Information Warsaw Local Rent a Car Poland LTD** ✉ Marszałkowska 140, Śródmieście, Warsaw ☎ 022/826–71–00. **Mazurkas Travel** ✉ al. Wojska Polskiego 27, Śródmieście, Warsaw ☎ 022/536–46–00. **Our Roots—Jewish Information and Tourist Bureau** ✉ Twarda 6, Śródmieście, Warsaw ☎ 022/620–05–56. **Travpol** ✉ Kasprowicza 57, Śródmieście, Warsaw ☎ 022/847–80–40.

ℹ **Information Łódź Fabricum Travel Services** ✉ Wigury 7, Łódź ☎ 042/636–28–25 ⊕ www.fabricum.pl.

VISITOR INFORMATION

The Warsaw City Information & Promotion Center is open every day from 8 to 8 May through September, from 8 to 6 October through April. There are branches at the arrivals hall of Warsaw's airport and the Central Railway Station. In Łódź, the Tourist Information Office on Piotrkowska Street is open weekdays from 9 to 7 and on Saturday from 10 to 3. (These are opening hours for May through September; during the rest of the year the office closes an hour earlier.)

ℹ **Łódź Tourist Information Office** ✉ Piotrkowska 87, Łódź ☎ 042/638–59–55 ⊕ www. uml.lodz.pl. **Łódź Cultural Information Office** ✉ Narutowicza 20/22, Łódź ☎ 042/633–92–21 ⊕ www.cik.lodz.pl. **Łowicz Tourist Information Office** ✉ Stary Rynek 3, Łowicz ☎ 046/630–91–49 ⊕ www.um.lowicz. pl. **Warsaw City Information & Promotion Center** ✉ Krakowskie Przedmieście 89, Śródmieście, Warsaw ☎ 022/94–31 ⊕ www. warsawtour.pl. **Warsaw Tourist & Cultural Information Center** ✉ Palace of Culture & Science, Plac Defilad 1, Śródmieście, Warsaw ☎ 022/656–68–54 ⊕ www.e-warsaw. pl. **Warsaw Tourist Information** ✉ pl. Zamkowy 1, Stare Miasto, Warsaw ☎ 022/635–18–81.

Silesia

WORD OF MOUTH

"Wrocław is a grand city, on par with the beautiful towns . . . such as Kraków or Gdańsk."

—Caroline1

"The area southwest of Wrocław is very picturesque, with the Sudeten Mountains, natural mineral springs, [and] good hiking, although lacking the drama of the High Tatras."

—sights_soul

OCCUPYING THE SOUTHWEST corner of Poland, Silesia was an independent duchy ruled by the Polish Piast dynasty in the Middle Ages, but from the 14th century on it was claimed by a succession of monarchs, including rulers of the Holy Roman Empire, Austria, Bohemia, and Prussia. As if this weren't complicated enough, in the 18th century, Prussia and Austria actually fought over the rule of Silesia. Its more contemporary borders—closer approximations of the state as it exists today—were not set until the 20th century, first after World War I and then, finally, after World War II. The new map of Europe—which was finalized by Roosevelt, Churchill, and Stalin—placed most of Silesia within Poland, while Poland's western and eastern Polish borders shifted west. The majority of the pre-war ethnic German population were "repatriated" back to German territory. Some parts of southern Silesia were incorporated into Czechoslovakia (now the Czech Republic) and Germany; along the way, some border towns were divided in two and remain living remainders of the region's tumultuous history. Polish Zgorzelec faces the German Görlitz across the river Nysa, while the Olza River divides Polish Cieszyn from Czech Tešin.

History and geopolitics have left their respective marks upon Silesia, and the area has a different personality from the rest of the country. Local architecture displays strong German sensibilities, and an array of local dialects include both German and Czech influences. People here have strong local identity, and some would even present themselves as Silesians rather than Poles. However, today, the region's multicultural heritage is once again celebrated and enjoyed.

Exploring Silesia

The region is traditionally—if somewhat confusingly—subdivided into Lower Silesia, including Wrocław, and Upper Silesia, including Katowice. If you look at a map, you'll see that "Lower Silesia" is, in fact, in the northwestern corner of the Upper Silesia. The city of Wrocław is the uncontested cultural center of Lower Silesia. It has many attractions of its own and is also a good starting point for day trips into the mountains, smaller towns, and villages. Upper Silesia is mostly industrial, but the area also has some important sights. The Auschwitz concentration camp in Oświęcim (technically part of the Małopolska region) and Częstochowa (where you'll find the shrine of Black Madonna) are both within the easy reach of Katowice, the capital of

SILESIA'S TOP 5

- Wrocław, with its picturesque Old Town, islands, bridges, and gardens.
- The labyrinth of fantastic rock shapes in Góry Stołowe National Park.
- Częstochowa, with the shrine of Black Madonna, a famous pilgrimage site.
- The restored art deco Hotel Monopol in Katowice, an unlikely tourist attraction in the middle of an industrial region.
- The divided city of Cieszyn, on both sides of the border between Poland and the Czech Republic.

Upper Silesia. If your travels are not taking you to Katowice, both these important sights can also be visited as day trips from Kraków. A large part of what was historically called Cieszyn Silesia (to the south of Upper Silesia) is now part of the Czech Republic, with the international border dividing the charming town of Cieszyn.

About the Restaurants

Silesian cuisine displays some German and Czech influences, and there are some distinct regional dishes, like potato-based, round and soft *kluski śląskie* (Silesian dumplings), mostly found in Upper Silesia. These dumplings often accompany meat dishes with gravy; for example, a rolled piece of meat with stuffing in the middle (*rolada*) is often accompanied by kluski śląskie, but they can also be served on their own. Pickled "blue" cabbage (*modro kapusta*), which is actually red, is often served as a side dish in Silesia. *Wodzionka,* which is also called *broŧtzupa,* is a typical locally popular "peasant" food: garlic-flavored soup made of bread and meat stock; for the true peasants, who often lacked meat stock, water had to suffice.

Traditional Silesian fare an be found in many places throughout the region but especially in the Upper Silesia, while bigger towns offer more dining choices, including some truly gourmet restaurants, notably in Wrocław and Katowice.

About the Hotels

As in many other Polish regions, your choice of hotels is fairly broad in larger cities, which have choices at many different quality and price levels, but hotels in smaller towns are almost always very basic and are limited in number, giving you few real choices. In general, top-end lodging options remain scarce, but some true gems can be found, notably in Wrocław and Katowice. Throughout Silesia, some nice hotels are located in converted castles and palaces, but often they are not easily accessible by public transport. Most hotels introduce minor seasonal variation to their price lists (April through October is considered high season), and only few offer weekend rates.

WHAT IT COSTS In Polish złoty (zł)				
	$$$$	**$$$**	**$$**	**$**	**¢**
RESTAURANTS	over zł70	zł50–zł70	zł30–zł50	zł15–zł30	under zł15
HOTELS	over zł800	zł500–zł800	zł300–zł500	zł150–zł300	under zł150

Restaurant prices are per person for a main course at dinner. Hotel prices are for two people in a double room with a private bath and, usually, breakfast in high season.

Timing

The best time to visit Silesia is between May and October, when the weather is most pleasant. This is also when many cultural events and festivals are scheduled. Film fans might want to plan their trip in the last week of July, when Wrocław's "Era New Horizons" Film Festival takes place. Music fans might want to consider the schedules of the Great Symphony Orchestra of Polish Radio & TV at Katowice, or the Sile-

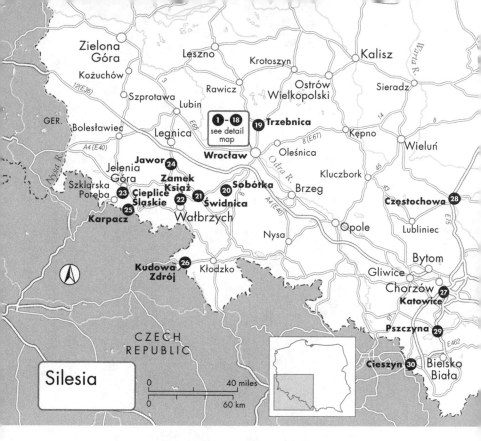

Silesia

0 ——— 40 miles

0 ——— 60 km

sian Opera in Wrocław. The latter city offers a seemingly never-ending string of interesting cultural festivals throughout the spring, summer, and early fall. Pilgrims arrive to Częstochowa throughout the year, but the gatherings of the faithful peak in August.

Numbers in the margins correspond to numbers on the Silesia map.

WROCŁAW

350 km (220 mi) southwest of Warsaw, 260 km (165 mi) northwest of Kraków.

Midway between Kraków and Poznań on the Odra River, Wrocław is the capital of Dolny Śląsk (Lower Silesia). The city was founded in the 10th century, when the Ostrów Tumski islet on the Odra became a fortified Slav settlement. There are now some 100 bridges spanning the city's 90-km (56-mi) network of slow-moving canals and tributaries, giving Wrocław its particular charm.

Wrocław—until after World War II known by its German name, Breslau—is an important piece in the jigsaw puzzle of European history. Although post-war Polish Communist authorities tried to erase its past, Wrocław was a German city for much of its existence. The Germanic

Wrocław

B. Drobnera

gen. Józefa Bema

Henryka Sienkiewicza

WYSPA BIELARSKA

WYSPA SŁODOWA

Ogród Botaniczny 17

Świętokrzyska

16

pl. Kościelny

Pomorska

most Uniwersytecki

mosty Pomorskie

most Grodzka

2 WYSPA PIASEK

św. Jadwigi

Katedralna 15

plac Uniwersytecki

1

OSTRÓW TUMSKI

Uniwersytecka

Nankiera

św. Ducha

Odra

Kiełbaśnicza

Odrzańska

Nożownicza

Więzienna

Kuźnicza

Łaciarska

plac Nowy Targ

W. Krasińskiego

Wzgórze Polskie

3

Kotlarska

Jana Ewangelisty Purkyniego

14

4

Rynek

5

6

Wita Stwosza

STARE MIASTO

K. Bernardyńska

obo

13

Park Juliusza Słowackiego

7

12

plac Solny

Ofiar Oświęcimskich

Szewska

Oławska

Biskupia

Krawiecka

plac Dominikanski

Aleja J. Słowackiego

11

Kazimierza Wielkiego

Oławska

9 10

Romualda Traugutta

Świdnicka

Mennicza

Wierzbowa

Piotra Skargi

Fosa Miejska

Zygmunta Krasińskiego

J. Hauke-Bosaka

plac Teatralny Teatralna

Park M. Kopernika

Fosa Miejska

S. Worcella

Podwale

Fosa Miejska

Podwale

Komuny Paryskiej

plac Tadeusza Kościuszki

Łąkowa

Strawowa

Hugona Kołłątaja

Tadeusza Kościuszki

Dworcowa

gen. K. Kniaziewicza

Gen. Kazimierza Pułaskiego

Marsz. Józefa Piłsudskiego

Gwarna

J. H. Dąbrowskiego

W. Bogusławskiego

plac Konstytucji 3 Maja

S. Małachowskiego

8

Swobodna

Sucha

| 0 | | 1/8 mi |

| 0 | | 1/8 km |

heritage can still be seen today, notably in the city's architecture and infrastructure.

Following the destruction that ravaged Wrocław during World War II, many of the city's historic buildings were restored. Wrocław's architectural attractions are its many brick Gothic churches, the majority of which lie in or around the Stare Miasto (Old Town) and Ostrów Tumski, an island in the Odra River. This area is small enough to explore easily on foot. Within a 15-minute drive (or a tram ride) to the east is the famous Centennial Hall by Max Berg and the charming Japanese garden, while the old Jewish cemetery lies within a similar distance, directly south of the old town center.

Wrocław is a convenient starting point for one-day trips to Mount Ślęża and Sobótka, Karkonosze National Park and Góry Stołowe, peace churches in Jawor and Świdnica, Cistercian monasteries in Lubiąż and Trzebnica, castles in Brzeg and Krobielowice, and many other places in Lower Silesia.

What to See

❾ Hala Ludowa (Centennial Hall). Featuring prominently in textbooks of
Fodor'sChoice architecture students around the world—and now recognized as a UN-
★ ESCO World Heritage Site—the Centennial Hall, also known as Jahrhunderthalle in German (the Polish name means "People's Hall"), was erected between 1911 and 1913 by Max Berg, who was the municipal architect in Breslau. With its amazing reinforced concrete structure, exposed and free from any redundant decorations, the Hall is considered a pioneering work of modern engineering and architecture of the early 20th century. This multipurpose recreational building sits in the middle of the Exhibition Grounds. It has a form of a symmetrical quatrefoil with a vast circular central space (65 meters around and 42 meters high) capable of seating 6,000. The dome is topped with a lantern in steel and glass. To improve the acoustics, the walls are covered with an insulating layer of concrete mixed with wood or cork. And the acoustics are amazing indeed. And if you cannot take in a concert or another performance here, try it yourself. Stand in the middle of the stage and clap your hands or sing a song. Throughout its near 100-year history, the Centennial Hall witnessed manifold events: industrial fairs, sports events, circus performances, 1930s speeches by Hitler, the World Intellectual Congress for Peace in 1948, and the Taizé Christian Youth meetings in 1990s. The adjoining concrete pergola, overgrown with vines and surrounding an artificial pond, was designed by architect Hans Poelzig. ✉ *Wystawowa 1, Szczytniki* 🎫 *zł 5* 🕙 *Daily 8–7.*

❿ Japanese Garden. Wrocław's Japanese Garden, designed by Fritz von
Fodor'sChoice Hochberg and Mankichi Arai, opened in 1913 as a part of the Centen-
★ nial Exhibition—and it was thoroughly restored in 1996 with the aid of Japanese experts. They gave it the name "Hakkōen" ("white and red"), in a reference to the national colors of Poland and Japan. Complete with ponds and waterfalls, a tea ceremony pavilion and arched wooden bridges, it is a lovely place to rest and meditate under the gingko and

katsura trees, cedars and cypresses, rare hornbeam maples, and over-100-year-old oaks. ⊠ *Park Szczytnicki, Szczytniki* ▦ *zł5* ☉ *Daily 9–7.*

❹ Jaś i Małgosia (Hansel and Gretel Houses). Just off the square to the northwest, these little houses are linked by a baroque arcade—holding hands, so to speak. ⊠ *ul. Odrzańska and ul. Wita Stwosza, Stare Miasto.*

★ **⓯ Katedra świętego Jana Chrzciciela** (Cathedral of St. John the Baptist). The 13th-century cathedral, with its two truncated towers, is the focal point of Cathedral Island. Its chancel is the earliest example of Gothic architecture in Poland. The cathedral houses the largest organ in the country, with 10,000 pipes. On the southern side of the cathedral is **St. Elizabeth's Chapel**; a bust of Cardinal Frederick above the entrance, along with numerous other sculptures and frescoes, came from the

> **LIGHTING THE LANTERNS**
>
> Wrocław's Ostrów Tumski is the only place in Poland with functioning gas lighting. Ninety-one lanterns are lit manually every evening at dusk—the perfect time to stroll around the cathedral island in the orange glow.

studio of Gian Lorenzo Bernini. The **Elector's Chapel,** in the northwestern corner of the cathedral, dates from the early 18th century and was designed by the baroque architect Johann Fischer von Erlach of Vienna. As these chapels are often closed, check at the sacristy for an update as well as for admission fees to climb to the top of the towers. ⊠ *pl. Katedralny, Ostrów Tumski* ▦ *zł 5 for Tower* ☉ *Cathedral daily 10–7; Tower Apr.–Oct., daily 10–5:30.*

❸ Kościół świętej Elżbiety (Church of St. Elizabeth). The 14th-century brick church was ravaged by fires in 1975 and 1976 and reopened only in the late 1990s. You can brave the 302-step climb to the top of the **tower** and look inside at the magnificent organ. The church can be reached through the arcade linking the Hansel and Gretel houses. ⊠ *ul. Kiełbaśnicza, at św Elżbiety, Stare Miasto.*

★ **❼ Kościół świętej Marii Magdaleny** (St. Mary Magdalene's Church). The massive 14th-century church has a 12th-century **Romanesque portal** on the south wall that is considered the finest example of Romanesque architecture in Poland. ⊠ *Corner of ul. Szewska and ul. Łaciarska, 1 block east of market square, Stare Miasto.*

❽ Main Railway Station. The year 1842 saw the opening of the first railway line in lands of modern Poland, linking Wrocław with Oława. The castle-like, mock-Tudor-Gothic building of Wrocław's main train station was constructed between 1854 and 1856 and was designed by Wilhelm Grapow. When it opened, it was hailed as one of the biggest and finest stations of the 19th century. A 1960s renovation only added to its charm, and the neon signs and mirrors added during that renovation have survived to this day. In addition to food stalls and newspaper stands, you will find a rare railway station amenity of a cinema, which has operated here since 1947. ⊠ *Piłsudskiego 105, Stare Miasto.*

16 **Muzeum Archidiecezjalne** (Archdiocesan Museum). The small museum, north of the Cathedral of St. John the Baptist, houses a collection of medieval Silesian art. ✉ *ul. Kanonia 12, Ostrów Tumski* ☎ *071/322–17–55* 🖱*zł 4* ⊙ *Tues.–Sun., 10–3.*

12 **Muzeum Architektury we Wrocławiu** (Museum of Architecture in Wrocław). Since 1965, the only architectural museum in Poland has occupied the Gothic halls of an old Bernardine monastery. The building itself merits a visit, but there are more reasons to stop by. Always interesting are the temporary exhibitions on offer—focusing primarily on contemporary Polish architecture and design. ✉ *Bernardyńska 5, Stare Miasto* ☎ *No phone* ⊕ *www.ma.wroc.pl* 🖱 *zł 7* ⊙ *Wed.–Sat. 11–5; Sun. 10–6.*

> **CHRISTMAS ALL YEAR ROUND**
>
> One of the side chapels, to the right of the main aisle of St. Mary's church, is dedicated to persons with disabilities, particularly those who are hard of hearing. Holy Masses in sign language are held there. The special attraction of the chapel is a very unusual nativity scene. Charming and rather bizarre, it is filled with kitsch objects and toys, not all of which are related to Christmas.

14 **Muzeum Narodowe we Wrocławiu** (National Museum in Wrocław). Nearly everything from medieval to contemporary art can be found in this rather overwhelming museum. The oldest exhibits are on the ground floor, while the top floor is an exhibition of Polish modern and contemporary artworks. Some exhibitions are temporarily closed due to a renovation in progress, but you'll still have plenty to see; in fact, it's more than most visitors can take during a single museum visit. ✉ *pl. Powstańców Warszawy 5, Stare Miasto* ☎ *No phone* 🖱 *zł 15* ⊙ *Wed., Fri., Sun 10–4, Thurs. 9–4, Sat. 10–6.*

11 **Muzeum Poczty i Telekomunikacji** (Museum of Post & Telecommunications). The only postal museum in Poland is aptly located in the former Main Post Office building. Exhibits tell the story of Polish postal services since its beginning in the 16th century. Exhibits include examples of historical post boxes, mail coaches, postage stamps, old telephones, radios, and TV sets. ✉ *ul. Krasińskiego 1, Stare Miasto* ☎ *No phone* 🖱 *zł 4.50* ⊙ *Mon., Wed.–Sat. 10–3, Sun. 11–2:30.*

★ **18** **Ogród Botaniczny** (Botanical Garden). Behind the cathedral and through a narrow lane to the north is Wrocław's botanical garden, established in the early 19th century. Scattered around the garden among beautiful plants you will find some interesting artworks and monuments—one of them commemorating Brahms, who once visited the garden. (He would be happy to hear that there are classical music concerts in the Botanical Garden every Sunday throughout the summer.) The best time to visit is perhaps late spring: azaleas bloom in the second half of May, peonies and lilies in June. The latter bear fantastic names such as Bacon Gold Nugget, Sometimes Alleluia, or Muscle Man. ✉ *Sienkiewicza 23, Ostrów Tumski* ☎ *No phone* 🖱 *Free* ⊙ *Apr.–Oct 8–6.*

Spot the Dwarves

IN THE 1980s, the walls and fences of Wrocław (and other Polish cities) provided a handy communications forum for the opposition, whose members would paint on them their anti-Communist slogans, which were subsequently erased by the militia. A group called Orange Alternative in Wrocław started decorating the fresh coats of paint with absurd graffiti: pictures of harmless yet subversive dwarves in pointed hats, which soon became their trademark.

Partly inspired by the Provo Movement of playful but nonviolent anarchists in Amsterdam in the 1960s, the Orange Alternative was distinctly Polish in its irony and mockery of the system. The nonviolent resistance of Orange Alternative, which grew to include thousands of members, became particularly famous in the later 1980s. The events and performances they organized in the streets of Wrocław–

which included the free distribution of much-coveted tampons to passersby and the promotion of the the the unofficial state holiday "Undercover Agent Day"–parodied the current Polish political situation. They both heartened the public undermined the system. As the movement's leader, Waldemar "Major" Fydrych had said, "Can you treat a police officer seriously when he is asking you the question, 'Why did you participate in an illegal meeting of dwarves?'"

Today the Orange Alternative has its own monument on Świdnicka Street in Wrocław, and not surprisingly, it takes the form of a dwarf. He is not the only one: you can find them all over town. You must keep your eyes peeled–they're tiny. If you look closely (and low) enough, you might spot the entrance to the Dwarves Museum in the Market Square.

---

⑬ Racławice Panorama. Today, this panoramic war portrait, 15 meters high and 114 meters long, is the city's biggest and most visited painting, the joint work of Wojciech Kossak and Jan Styka. After World War II the painting came to Wrocław from Lviv, which ceased to be a Polish city and was incorporated into the Soviet Union (now independent Ukraine). For Poles, the Panorama is deeply symbolic in many ways since it depicts the legendary victory of General Tadeusz Kościuszko over the Russians in 1794. With more than 1,500 visitors per day, you have to queue to get in (it would be smart to book your ticket in advance) and admire this circular painting with a crowd of other tourists. ⊠ *Purkyniego 11, Stare Miasto* ⊕ *www.panoramaraclawicka.pl* 🖼 *zł 20* ⊙ *May–Sept., daily 9–4; Oct.–Apr., Tues.–Sun. 9–4.*

❻ Ratusz (City Hall). The magnificently ornate city hall is the highlight of the market square. Mostly Gothic in style, with a dash of Renaissance and baroque thrown in, the town hall was under continuous construction from the 14th to the 16th centuries as Wrocław grew and prospered. In the center of the spired, pinnacled, and gabled east facade is a Renaissance **astronomical clock** from 1580; the **Gothic portal** was the main entrance of the Ratusz until 1616. The lavish south facade, dating from the 15th and 16th centuries, swarms with delicately wrought sculptures, friezes, reliefs, and oriels. Today the town hall houses the **Historical Museum of Wrocław**, which is well worth visiting for its interiors. ⊠ *Sukiennice 9, Stare Miasto* ☎ *071/344–36–38* ✉ *Museum zł 6* ⊙ *Museum Wed.–Fri. 10–4, weekends 10–5.*

❺ **Rynek** (Market Square). Together with the adjoining plac Solny (Salt
Fodor'sChoice Square), Wrocław's two main squares form the heart of the Old Town,
★ which stretches between the Fosa Miejska moat and the Odra River. This market square is almost as grand as Kraków's. In the summer it is filled to the brim with sidewalk cafés and street performers. ⊠ *Stare Miasto.*

❶ **Uniwersytet Wrocławski** (Wrocław
Fodor'sChoice University). Wrocław's university
★ district lies between ulica Uniwersytecka and the river. First attempts to establish a university in Wrocław date back to 1505, but it wasn't until the 17th century—some 200 years later—that the higher educational institution was founded thanks to the generous support of the Habsburgs and efforts of the Jesuits. The university's main building, which dates from the 18th century, was built by Emperor Leopold I on the site of the west wing of the former prince's castle. Behind the fountain and up the staircase is the magnificent assembly hall, **Aula Leopoldina**. The Aula is decorated with illusionist frescoes and life-size sculptures of great philosophers and patrons of learning, and allegories of arts and sciences. Climb further up to the **Mathematical Tower** (sometimes called Astronomers' Tower) for great views of Wrocław's rooftops. ⊠ *pl. Uniwersytecki 1, Stare Miasto* ☎ *No phone* ✉ *zł 4.50* ⊙ *Oct.–Apr., Thurs.–Tues. 10–3:30; May–Sept., Mon., Tues., Thurs. 10–3:30, Fri.–Sun. 11–5.*

NOBEL EFFORTS

The impressive list of Wrocław University professors who have won the Nobel Prize includes Theodor Mommsen (literature, 1902), Philipp von Lenard (physics, 1905), Eduard Buchner (chemistry, 1907), Paul Ehrlich (medicine, 1908), Fritz Haber (chemistry, 1910), Friedrich Bergius (chemistry, 1931), Erwin Schrödinger (physics 1933), Otto Stern (physics, 1943), and Max Born (physics, 1954). The list of famous scientists who didn't make it to the Swedish podium features Robert Bunsen, Alois Alzheimer, and Ferdinand Cohn.

NEED A BREAK

Café Uni (⊠ pl. Uniwersytecki 11 ☎ No phone), with its outdoor patio and frequent recitals, is a good place to sip coffee and admire the 565-foot facade of the university.

❷ **Wyspa Piasek** (Sand Island). North of the university district, the Most Piaskowy (Sand Bridge) connects the left bank of the Odra with this river island. On the island directly across from the Sand Bridge is a former Augustinian monastery used as Nazi headquarters during World War II; the building is now the **University Library**. The 14th-century **Kościół Najświętszej Marii Panny** (St. Mary's Church) is in the middle of the island. The church's Gothic interior was restored after World War II; it

IF YOU LIKE

20TH-CENTURY ARCHITECTURE

Wrocław holds some magnificent examples of early 20th-century architecture, and Max Berg's Centennial Hall is a must-see for anyone with a serious interest in the history of architecture. The city center has further examples of architecture of that period, particularly the city's department stores—look for elegant, simplified expression of facades often reminiscent of ocean liners of old. Don't miss current exhibitions at the Muzeum Architektury we Wrocławiu, Poland's only architecture museum. Further afield are suburban housing developments of the 1920s—the most interesting of which is the model community of Sępolno to the west of the city center.

CANALS & BRIDGES

While it might not be immediately apparent, Wrocław encompasses 12 islands and is surrounded by rivers and canals. This is supplemented with beautiful antique infrastructure: the oldest Municipal Canal was built between 1859 and 1897, and the city has more than 100 bridges, notably Most Grunwaldzki, Most Zwierzyniecki, Most Uniwersytecki, and Most Tumski. The best way to explore Wrocław's waterways is, of course, by boat; most cruises depart from one of three marinas: on Zwierzyniecka Street, on Włostowica Boulevard, or at Hala Targowa Harbor.

MOVIES

Every summer, for the last 10 days of July, Wrocław hosts an international film festival called "Era New Horizons." Hundreds of movies are subdivided into a panorama of contemporary cinema, international and Polish movies' competitions, documentaries, and animated films; there are also retrospectives of great artists of the silver screen. Silent movies with live accompaniment by top modern bands are the icing on the cake. Cinematic traditions of Wrocław are strong and long standing—there is even a small movie theater in the city's railway station.

GARDENS

The Japanese Garden near the Centennial Hall is a great example of landscape architecture—constructed in 1913 as one of the displays of the Garden Art Exhibition, part of the Centennial Exhibition. Park Szczytnicki, where the garden is located, is also worth noting, particularly for the artificial lake surrounded with a concrete pergola. Don't miss the Botanical Garden (in Ostrów Tumski), established as a scientific institution of Wrocław University in 1811.

UNIQUE SPAS

The capital of Lower Silesia boasts the historical Wrocław Indoor Bathing Resort, a two-story swimming hall built in the end of the 19th century by Wilhelm Werdelmann. The building's interior is covered with quotes and references to antiquity—including marvelous mosaics. Restored in 2005, it now houses the Wrocław Spa Center (see ⇨ Spas, below). Head there for a swim while you're in town. Perhaps more unique still is the Tołpa Spa; fantastically relaxing and rejuvenating, it may very well be the only peat-based spa in the world.

has a lofty vaulted ceiling and brilliant stained-glass windows. ⊠ *Wyspa Piasek, Stare Miasto.*

Where to Eat

Most restaurants in Wrocław, including those listed here, are concentrated in the Market Square or one of the streets immediately surrounding it. Whether you choose Polish or Spanish, Japanese, or French cuisine, you won't have to walk far—different establishments are virtually door-to-door.

$–$$$$
Fodor'sChoice
★
✕ **JaDka.** The interior of this elegant restaurant is comfortably luxurious: vaulted ceilings, red-brick walls, tables covered with white linen, white candles, and fresh white flowers. The waitstaff are super-attentive and efficient, so the service is excellent. On the menu is mix of traditional Polish dishes and their Mediterranean cousins: Spanish gazpacho as well as Polish *barszcz* (borscht) and saddle of deer with Silesian dumplings alongside typical Italian pasta dishes. This is a good place to sample venison—or anything else that takes your fancy. ⊠ *Rzeźnicza 24/25, Stare Miasto* ☎ *071/343–64–61* ▭ *AE, DC, MC, V.*

$$–$$$
Fodor'sChoice
★
✕ **Sakana.** This mini-universe revolves around the sushi conveyor. You can chat with the chefs and watch your food take form and sail—very fresh—toward you in little boats. The concept is simple: grab what you like, and then your plates are counted (there are different prices for different colors, listed in the menu). Happily, you can also order a tailor-made sushi or sashimi—or ask the friendly chefs to suggest a dish for you. For dessert, try excellent ginger- or green-tea ice cream. ⊠ *Odrzańska 17/1a, Stare Miasto* ☎ *071/343–37–10* ▭ *AE, DC, MC, V.*

$–$$$
✕ **Gospoda Wrocławska.** This popular, traditional Polish restaurant is right in the heart of Wrocław. The interior is wood-clad and medieval-looking, and while the food is heavy, it is also tasty. At the core of the menu you will find roasts, pork chops, pig's feet, steaks, venison, and other meat dishes. Adjoining the restaurant is a shop where you can buy take-out sandwiches and other products, mostly made on the premises. ⊠ *Sukiennice 6 Stare Miasto* ☎ *071/342–74–56* ▭ *AE, DC, MC, V.*

$–$$
✕ **Karczma Młyńska.** This pleasant, unpretentious restaurant serves traditional, no-frills Polish food: soups, meat dishes, and desserts. The wooden interior is cozy, and in the summer, the terrace offers splendid river views. The food is solid and wholesome, if not terribly inspiring, and it comes in generous portions. ⊠ *Wyspa Słodowa 10, Stare Miasto* ☎ *071/322–60–77* ▭ *AE, DC, MC, V.*

$–$$
✕ **Le Bistrot Parisien.** Head for this quiet bistro when you are tired of the bustle of the Rynek—it's just a block farther north but a world away in terms of atmosphere. You can grab French crepes—sweet or savory—and a salad, or just sip your coffee or beer in this laid-back, cozy café. The walls are decorated with French posters and photographs; look for other interesting objects, including a great prewar cigarette vending machine in the corner. ⊠ *Nożownicza 1d, Stare Miasto* ☎ *071/343–76–98* ▭ *AE, DC, MC, V.*

★ ¢–$$
✕ **Taverna Española.** The terrace of this Spanish Tavern is a good place to sit and watch the incessant action in the Rynek, Wrocław's Market

Swan Song

TIME-DARKENED WOOD, worn plush carpets covering creaking parquet floors, a candelabra and chandeliers, the bittersweet taste of fading grandeur. This description is not from a time-worn movie script. It's what you'll find in the art-nouveau Hotel Monopol, designed by architect Karl Grosser. The hotel, which opened in 1892, has endured through two world wars and other upheavals, including state management during the 50 years of Communism. If you take a look in its registration book, you'll see such names as Marlene Dietrich, Pablo Picasso, and Adolf Hitler—the front porch was added especially for him and his infamous speeches.

Some rooms retain their original furnishings: a 100-year-old desk here, a whole bedroom suite there; others date from more contemporary times. The bar is one of the best examples of art deco in the city. Alas, grandfather Monopol has been sentenced to death: it still welcomes visitors at this writing but is scheduled for liquidation and waiting for the end.

Square. In the summer, you can really relax and cool down over their excellent gazpacho. Tasty paellas, *tortillas* (thin omelets that are popular in Spain), and other typical Spanish favorites come at very affordable prices, especially considering their quality and the "expensive" location of this eatery. Best of all, the friendly staff keep smiling even when it gets really busy and hot. ⊠ *Rynek 53/55, Stare Miasto* ☎ *071/344-65-62* ▤ *AE, DC, MC, V.*

Where to Stay

Most good hotels—and that includes different price categories—are located in Wrocław's Old Town, within easy walking distance of major sights and restaurants. Surprisingly, even those on the busy central streets are usually peaceful and quiet. As in the rest of Poland, air-conditioning is not a given, so if it is important to you, be sure to ask before making reservations.

$$ 🏨 **Art Hotel.** The charming Art Hotel is true to its name. Located in a

Fodor'sChoice carefully restored, furnished and decorated series of combined 14th- and

★ 15th-century tenement houses, it hides some amazing original pieces: fragments of wall paintings and coats of arms, wooden beams, decorated doors and stairways. The rooms are tasteful and warm, and each is a little different. Nice service touches include homemade cookies as you check in. Works by contemporary Polish artists are displayed in the hallways (in keeping with the theme), and the in-house restaurant is justly considered one of Wrocław's best. ⊠ *Kiełbaśnicza 20, 50–110, Stare Miasto* ☎ *071/787-71-00* 🖷 *071/342-39-29* ⊕ *www.arthotel.pl* ⇱ *75 rooms, 3 suites ↻ Restaurant, minibars, cable TV, in-room broadband, gym, bar, meeting rooms* ▤ *AE, DC, MC, V* ⏍ *BP.*

$$ 🏨 **Hotel Patio.** This hotel is a remodeled old tenement house. Its simple but perfectly adequate rooms surround a central covered courtyard. The inner courtyard is multifunctional, housing the hotel's restaurant, a travel agency, a jazz bar, and some shops. The location on one of the streets leading out of the Market Square is very convenient for seeing the sights, and plugging into the Internet is free. ⊠ *Kiełbaśnicza 24, 50–110, Stare Miasto* ☎ *071/375–04–00* ⌂ *071/343–91–49* ⊕ *www. hotelpatio.pl* ⇗ *50 rooms* ⌂ *Restaurant, minibars, in-room broadband, cable TV, meeting rooms; no a/c* ⊟ *AE, DC, MC, V* ⊘❘ *BP.*

★ $$ ⊞ **HP Park Plaza.** The characteristic green block of the HP Plaza Hotel (also green-lit at night) overlooks Wrocław's islands across the water. It is worth asking for a room with river view. While the rooms are quite comfortable, the hotel's fitness center and the adjoining casino might tempt you to leave your room. In the summer, you will appreciate the summer terrace by the water and a nice walkway leading across a footbridge to another bridge, providing an excellent shortcut into the Old Town. ⊠ *Drobnera 11–13, 50—257, Stare Miasto* ☎ *071/320–84–00* ⌂ *071/320–84–59* ⊕ *www.beph.pl* ⇗ *175 rooms, 2 suites* ⌂ *Restaurant, minibars, cable TV, Wi-Fi, gym, sauna, bar, casino, meeting rooms* ⊟ *AE, DC, MC, V* ⊘❘ *BP.*

★ $-$$ ⊞ **Hotel Tumski.** This hotel has a picturesque location on the island of Wyspa Słodowa, just across the bridge from Ostrów Tumski, another of Wrocław's many islands. Although the rooms are pretty standard, the hotel building itself has a long history; in the 1920s, it was the seat of the Rheno Palatia, the German students' corporation. It's only been a hotel since 2000; still, it draws a wide range of travelers looking for decent accommodations at fair prices. Every year the hotel management and staff organize a truly impressive series of events, including a punting regatta on the Oder and picnics in the Botanical Garden. Hotel Tumski also organizes standard and specialized tours throughout the region. ⊠ *Wyspa Słodowa 10, 50—077, Stare Miasto* ☎ *071/322–60–88* ⌂ *071/322–61–13* ⊕ *www.hotel-tumski.com.pl* ⇗ *55 rooms, 2 suites* ⌂ *Restaurant, minibars, cable TV, Wi-Fi, bar, meeting rooms, parking (free); no a/c* ⊟ *AE, DC, MC, V* ⊘❘ *BP.*

★ $ ⊞ **Hotel Europeum.** Property of Krzyżowa Foundation for Mutual Understanding in Europe, this modern B&B rises to a very comfortable standard in its 20 rooms, although officially the hotel carries only a modest 2 stars. Europeum has an excellent location: a five-minute walk from the Market Square and one minute from a nine-screen Helios cinema. Although it is on a busy street, the windows are soundproof, and the a/c (certainly not a given in local hotels) is super efficient. Some rooms overlook a lovely zen-like terrace covered with river stones. ⊠ *Kazimierza Wielkiego 27a, 50—077, Stare Miasto* ☎ *071/371–45–00* ⌂ *071/371–44–01* ⊕ *www.europeum.pl* ⇗ *20 rooms* ⌂ *Restaurant, refrigerators, cable TV, in-room broadband, bar* ⊟ *AE, DC, MC, V* ⊘❘ *BP.*

$ ⊞ **Hotel Zaułek.** This small hotel, which belongs to Wrocław University, offers pleasant, good-value rooms in the center of the Old Town. Incidentally, Zaułek was awarded the Connecticut University certificate for exceptional quality and service—check out the diploma left to the reception desk. The staff are genuinely hospitable, very friendly, and helpful, which tends to make staying here a pleasure, even if it's not a four-star hotel. Your stay comes with a bonus of complimentary Wi-Fi

The Bridges of Wrocław

AT THE CONFLUENCE OF FIVE RIVERS —which branch out into numerous rivulets and canals that are spanned by well over a hundred bridges and viaducts large and small— Wrocław is among the select club of European cities famous for their many waterways, a group that includes Venice, Amsterdam, and St. Petersburg. Wrocław's "Polynesia" is made up of 12 islands connected by a multitude of bridges. Various sources around the city enumerate the bridges differently. Some sources say there are around 100 bridges, others tell you that the number is more like 220; what is certain is that before World War II, exactly 303 bridges were meticulously counted; many of these were destroyed during the war and never rebuilt.

Most Tumski (Cathedral Bridge) was originally built in the 13th century, but the steel structure you see today was built between 1888 and 1889. This blue-painted bridge is for pedestrians only and it is guarded by Saint Hedwig, the Patron Saint of Silesia, and by Saint John the Baptist.

Most Uniwersytecki (University Bridge), originally made of wood (the current incarnation is made from iron), was for years the city's longest bridge. It has an observation platform affording a panoramic view of Wyspa Piaskowa and Wyspa Słodowa (Sand and Malt Islands).

Most Zwierzyniecki, near the Centenary Hall, used to be the primary entrance of the city. It was first built as a wooden bridge around 1655, and during the plague of 1704 it was the control point for passage into the city, hence its old German name of Paßbrücke. The stylish art-nouveau structure you see today was built between 1895 and 1897 by Karl Klimm. Until 1945, the bridge bore a poetic inscription, but it was removed after World War II, when all German-language signs were taken away. The plaque said: "Hölzern ruht ich Jahrhunderte lang über trägem Gewässer / Jetzt aus Eisen und Stein schmück ich den schiffbaren Strom" ("For centuries I rested wooden, over the quiet river / Today I adorn the waterway with steel and stone").

Wrocław's equivalent of the Eiffel Tower, **Most Grunwaldzki**, is a steel suspension bridge designed by Richard Plüddelmann. It was constructed between 1908 and 1910 to connect the city center with new residential neighborhoods to the northeast. Initially called Kaiserbrücke (the Emperor's Bridge), its name was later changed to the Freiheitsbrücke (the Freedom Bridge). It was unveiled on October 10, 1910, in the presence of Kaiser Wilhelm II. Legend has it that the bridge's chief engineer cracked under the pressure of opening the structure for the Kaiser and committed suicide a day before the inauguration, fearing the structure would collapse; no such thing happened.

service, and a free entry ticket to the Wrocław University Museum, which is right next door and not to be missed. ⊠ *Garbary 11, 50—115, Stare Miasto* ☎ *071/341–00–46* 🖷 *071/375–29–47* ⊕ *www.hotel.uni.wroc. pl* 🛏 *12 rooms* ⚹ *Restaurant, fans, minibars, cable TV, Wi-Fi, bar; no a/c* ➡ *AE, DC, MC, V* ⊠ℿ *BP.*

CLOSE UP

The Power of Peat

BELIEVE IT OR NOT, peat is the latest craze in health and beauty, and Wrocław's Tołpa Spa is probably the only peat spa in the world. Along with a range of peat-based cosmetics, it was named after Professor Tołpa, who for many years had been researching the benefits of peat. He became famous in the 1980s, when the media prematurely hailed him for inventing a "cure for cancer," which consisted of a peat-derived formula. While the cure for cancer remains to be found, the professor was able to prove that peat has many beneficial properties. A visit to Tołpa Spa is not only good for your health but it's also very pleasant. Smiling English-speaking staff usher you into an elegant, serene environment. From cotton bathrobes to beautiful mosaics in the steam room, this is a great place to relax. The highlight is a blissful, 50-minute peat mud massage.

2

Shopping

Souvenir shops, bookshops, and galleries are scattered around the Old Town, especially in the vicinity of the Market Square and Kiełbaśnicza, Świdnicka, and Oławska streets. Most shops are open from Monday through Saturday, from 10 AM to 6 PM. **Galeria Dominikańska** (⊠ pl. Dominikański 3 🕾 71/344–95–17) is a conveniently located department store/mall with a selection of fashion, cosmetics, and food stores, and it is even open on Sunday.

Spas

Fodor'sChoice
★
Tołpa Spa (⊠ ul. Oławska 27/29 🕾 071/344–41–56 ⊕ www.tolpaspa.pl) is the only peat spa in Poland—and perhaps the world. This elegant city spa furnished in a style of a subtle, discreet luxury, offers blissful treatments such as peat mud massages and thermal treatments from which you re-emerge feeling healthier, younger, and calmer. Advance booking is essential. The spa is open from 10 to 10 Tuesday through Sunday, and from noon to 10 on Monday.

The **Wrocław Spa Center** (⊠ ul. Teatralna 10-12 🕾 071/344–16–56 ⊕ www.spa.wroc.pl) has as its slogan "Sanus per aquam" (healthy through water). Here, you can practice swimming and take fitness classes, and schedule massages or balneology treatments. All this is done in the magnificent, fin-de-siècle interiors complete with two-story arcades and intricate mosaics. The spa center is open weekdays from 7 AM to 11 PM, Saturday from 8 AM to 10 PM, and Sunday from 9 AM to 9 PM.

Nightlife & the Arts

Wrocław hosts a great number of festivals, many of them throughout the summer. The city's municipal Web site (see ⇨ Visitor Information *in* Silesia Essentials, below) lists all local festivals and current events in English as well as Polish. **Era New Horizons** (⊕ www.eranowehoryzonty.pl) is a

CLOSE UP

Movie Marathon

THE CITY OF WROCŁAW—which was called Breslau until the mid-20th century—served as a perfect backdrop for Friedrich-Wilhem Murnau's silent film, *The Phantom*. Some sets, like the Market Square with its characteristic town hall, are recognizable today, but other movie images are only that—movie stills.

Movies are alive and kicking in the "Phantom's" town. Whether you like early black-and-white classics or the latest independent cinema, you will find it all in Wrocław. Each year, film buffs arrive here to attend the Era New Horizons International Film Festival, which takes place during the last eleven days of July. You won't find many blockbusters among the approximately 200 features, but if you like different and so-called "difficult" cinema, this festival is for you.

Two competitions are held as a part of the festival: one for new movies from all around the world, and the other for the latest Polish productions. In addition, you can see a number of the best recent movies, feature-length documentaries, shorts, and animated films, as well as retrospectives of great auteurs of 20th-century cinema. Movies are always shown in their original languages, most often with both Polish and English subtitles.

And that is not all. Every night there is a concert of contemporary music accompanying a silent movie show at Opera Wrocławska (the Wrocław opera house). Live music continues until the wee hours at the Festival Club, starting with a band gig and ending with a DJ and dancing. You can party all night, but don't miss 10 AM show every morning.

---

great film festival, held typically in the last week of July. One of the most renowned of Wrocław's festivals is **Jazz on the Odra** (⊕ www.jnofestival. pl), a summertime event that has attracted an international group of performers for over 40 years. **Wratislavia Cantans** (⊕ www.wratislavia.art. pl) is a series of concerts (usually a week in June and a week in September) featuring Gregorian chants, German oratorios, operas, cantatas, and other choral performances. Concerts take place at different points in the city.

If you get tired of the bars around the market square try the **Kalambur** (✉ ul. Kuźnicza 29A, Stare Miasto ☎ 071/343–26–50). This art nouveau-esque café-bar is attached to a small, well-known theater, where you can sometimes hear live music. The **Pasaż Niepolda** (✉ between Ruska, św. Antoniego, and Kazimierza Wielkiego) is not so much a "passage" as a large and colorful courtyard filled with bars, clubs, and cafés on some 10,000 square meters, situated only 300 meters from the Rynek. This is the place to head in the evening for live music, loud conversation, drinking, or dancing. Most of these clubs open at around 5 or 6 PM and stay open until 2 AM (longer on Saturday nights).

Wrocław's **Opera Wrocławska** (✉ ul. Świdnicka 35 ☎ 071/344—57–79 ⊕ opera.wroclaw.pl) performs in a recently restored, beautiful old-fashioned opera house; "super-productions" are staged at Hala Ludowa (⇨ What to See, *above*). The box office is open on Monday from 10 to 6, Tuesday through Friday from 9 to 7, and on Saturday from 10 to 2 and then again one hour before the performance.

Teatr Polski (✉ ul. G. Zapolskiej 3, Stare Miasto ☎ 071/343–86–53) is the occasional home of the Wrocław Pantomime Theater. **Wrocławski Teatr Lalek** (✉ pl. Teatralny 4, Stare Miasto ☎ 071/344–12–17) is widely regarded as the best puppet theater in Poland.

> **MEDIEVAL AMNESTY**
>
> When wife of Silesian Duke Henryk Brodaty (Henry the Bearded) founded the Cistercian convent in 1202, he suspended executions of death penalty throughout his land. The offenders had to work at the construction instead, and thus earn their pardon.

2

The **Wrocław Philharmonic** (✉ ul. Piłsudskiego 19, Stare Miasto ☎ 071/342–20–01 ⊕ www.filharmonia.wroclaw.pl) hosts classical performances several times each week.

TRZEBNICA

⑲ *24 km (15 mi) north of Wrocław.*

This small town is famous for its **Cistercian Abbey,** founded in the late 12th century, as one of the first Cistercian establishments throughout Poland. In the same location, in 1202, the wife of the Duke of Wrocław (Henryk Brodaty), Princess Jadwiga (Hedwig in English)—today known as the Patron Saint of Silesia—founded the first Cistercian convent to match. Upon her husband's death she entered the convent herself. She died in 1243, at about age 70, and only 24 years later Pope Clement IV proclaimed her Saint Jadwiga Śląska. Since then—and for seven centuries thereafter—Trzebnica became a major pilgrimage destination, and the following of Saint Jadwiga spread throughout central Europe.

Today the abbey's church is a combination of the original Romanesque structure and later interpolations, as the church was several times rebuilt, notably in the baroque period. The oldest surviving elements of the original church include two portals and the crypt. Make sure that you see Kaplica Świętej Jadwigi (Chapel of St. Jadwiga), which has a Gothic vaulted ceiling, and a baroque tomb of the Saint herself. The funerary monument of black and pink marble is impressive both in size and degree of ornament—very unusual for a female saint.

SOBÓTKA

⑳ *35 km (22 mi) southwest of Wrocław.*

The small town of Sobótka is the starting point for climbing **Mount Ślęża** (718 meters), dubbed the "Silesian Mount Olympus." Between the 5th century BC and 11th century AD, this was the holy place of ancient pagan tribes for whom the sun was the ruling god. Today the area is protected as a landscape and archeological reserve. Mysterious stone statues—which some archaeologists believe may be Celtic in origin—can still be found along the path. Some depict bears, and one is called a "Maiden with a fish." *Grzyb* (the mushroom) can be found within the town itself, next to St. Anne's church, and *Mnich* (the monk) is further up. The **hike** up the mountain starts at the end of Garncarska street (on a clearly-labeled trail with red markings), and it takes about one hour.

ŚWIDNICA

㉑ *50 km (31 mi) southwest of Wrocław.*

Once a rival of Wrocław, a wealthy capital of one of the Silesian princedoms, contemporary Świdnica is a rather sleepy, provincial town. It is best known as the hometown of famous World War I flying ace, Manfred von Richthofen, more popularly known as the Red Baron (who even found his way to the Peanuts cartoon).

The most noteworthy sight in Świdnica is the **Church of Peace** (Kościół Pokoju; ✉ pl. Pokoju 6 ☎ 074/852–28–14), which is open Monday through Saturday from 9 to 1 and 3 to 5, and from 3 to 5 only on Sunday. The Protestant temple was erected after the Peace of Westphalia of 1648, which ended the Thirty Years' War. This wood-and clay structure has 28 doors but not a single nail. It is two stories tall, with inner galleries and balconies; the walls and ceiling are covered with paintings. Note the ornate, late-baroque pulpit with an hour glass to time the sermons—a sensible invention. The church can accommodate up to 7,000 people for services, 3,000 of them seated!

Other noteworthy sights of Świdnica include Rynek (the Market Square), the Town Hall, and the kosciol Świętych Stanisława i Wacława (parish Church of Saints Stanislaus and Wenceslas).

ZAMEK KSIĄŻ

㉒ *60 km (37 mi) southwest of Wrocław.*

Zamek Książ (Książ Castle) was built in the late 13th century by Prince Bolko I of Świdnica; it has been remodeled and extended many times since. The central section, which is marked by a series of arcades and is lighter in color than the rest of the castle, is the oldest; the right (easterly) wing is from the late-baroque period; and the left (westerly) wing, dates from early 20th century and was built in a neo-Renaissance style. The largest and most interesting room of the castle is the 18th-century Maximilian Hall, which has mythological scenes painted upon the ceiling. The castle is surrounded with terraced gardens and woodlands. The complex, which is in a suburb of modern-day Wałbrzych, houses a museum, a restaurant, and a hotel. ✉ *Piastów Śląskich 1, Wałbrzych* ☎ *074/840–58–62* ⊕ *www.zamekksiaz.pl* 🎫 *zł 9* ⏱ *May–Sept., Tues.–Sun. 10–5; Apr. & Oct., Tues.–Sun. 10–4; Nov.–Mar., Tues.–Sun. 10–3.*

Where to Stay

$ 🏨 **Hotel Zamek Książ.** The hotel, which is in one of the castle outbuildings and not the main structure itself, is far from palatial, unfortu-

Ephemeral and Lasting

THE THIRTY YEARS' WAR (1618–1648) was more about power than about religion. Although the war started as a conflict between Protestants and Catholics, it became primarily a rivalry between the Habsburg Empire and France (paradoxically, Catholic France supported the Protestant side). The war ended with the Peace of Westphalia (often used by historians to mark the beginning of the modern era). The impact of the war was devastating for all of Europe but especially for the Silesian Protestants, who lost all their churches. However, in an exceptional act of tolerance, Austrian Emperor Ferdinand III (Holy Roman Emperor from the House of Habsburg) allowed them to build three new churches: in Jawor, Świdnica, and Głogów. This was done under the conditions that Protestant communities had only one year to

complete the construction, churches were to be built away from the center, and they could not resemble traditional religious structures. Perhaps most important, only ephemeral materials were allowed in their construction, such as wood, straw, sand, and clay–the churches weren't meant to last. Paradoxically, those constraints inspired pioneering constructional and architectural solutions. And two of the three churches have proved lasting indeed. While the church in Głogów burned down, having been struck by lightning, the other two–Jawor and Świdnica–have survived to the present day. The largest timber-framed religious buildings in Europe, today they are considered architectural masterpieces, impressive in scale and complexity. In 2001, both churches were added to the list of UNESCO World Heritage Sites.

nately. The rooms—last redecorated in 2002—are pretty basic, and the decor uninspiring. However, if you choose to stay here, inspiration awaits you in the immediate surroundings: the castle itself and the lovely park around it. ⊠ *Piastów Śląskich 1, Wałbrzych 58–306* ☎ *074/ 664–38–90* 🖶 *074/664–38–92* ⊕ *www.zamekksiaz.pl* ⟳ *43 rooms, 2 suites* ⚭ *Restaurant, café, cable TV, meeting rooms; no a/c* ▤ *AE, DC, MC, V* ❏❘ *EP.*

CIEPLICE ŚLĄSKIE

㉓ *100 km (62 mi) west of Wrocław.*

Cieplice Śląskie (or Cieplice Zdrój), which is a suburb of modern-day Jelenia Góra, is one of the oldest spa towns in the region. The health benefits of the local mineral waters became famous in the 18th century, but the sulfurous hot springs had been used much earlier than that (the first spa-house was constructed by the 13th century). The 18th-century **parish church** is worth visiting. At the center of town you'll find a **Park Zdrojowy** (Spa Park) with the outdoor **Teatr Zdrojowy** (Spa Theater). Mineral waters can be sampled at the historic *pijalnia* (pump room).

Where to Eat

¢–$ ✕ **Restauracja Pokusa.** The restaurant's name translates as "temptation," and the best temptations here are of the traditional Polish variety. The menu includes everything from barszcz to *szarlotka* (apple pie). The location in one of the arcaded houses of the Town Hall Square is at its best in the summer, when you can enjoy your meal al fresco on the outdoor terrace. ⊠ *pl. Ratuszowy 12, Cieplice Śląskie* ☎ *075/752–53–47* ▭ *AE, DC, MC, V.*

JAWOR

❷❹ *40 km (25 mi) west of Wrocław.*

The history of Jawor goes back over 1,000 years. During the 13th and 14th centuries it was even a capital city (of a Piast Duchy). Famous citizens include Nicolas Magnus (dean of the Prague and Heidelberg universities at the turn of 15th century, and Christopher Rudolph (author of one of the first algebra textbooks in the 16th century). The town went into a decline after the Thirty Years' War, but following the Peace of Westphalia it gained what is considered its most valuable historic building. The famous **Church of Peace** is located some 400 meters west of the main train station, in the Park of Peace, and looks not unlike an over-sized barn from the outside. The interior, however, is striking and enchanting. An abundance of decorations includes 143 painted scenes from the Bible. The scale is also impressive: the church can accommodate up to 6,000 worshippers. ⊠ *Park Pokoju 2* ☎ *076/870–32–73* ⊙ *Mar.–Oct., daily 10–1 and 2–5.*

KARPACZ

❷❺ *100 km southwest of Wrocław.*

Karpacz lies in the Karkonosze Mountains, at the foot of Śnieżka (the highest peak of the Sudeten range, at 1602 meters). The region is a popular holiday destination, with exceptional skiing in the winter.

Approximately 2,000 dolls and other toys from all over the world are displayed in the small **Doll Museum.** Among the most interesting exhibits are dolls' houses complete with miniature furniture and doll-size utensils. The collection was started by Henryk Tomaszewski, the founder of Wrocław Mime Theater. ⊠ *Karkonoska 5* ☎ *075/761–85–23* 🎫 *pł 5* ⊙ *Tues. 9–4:30, Wed.–Fri. 9–3:30, Sat. 10–3:30, Sun. 10–4:30.*

If you want to ski or simply look at the view, you can take chair lift to **Kolej Liniowa na Kopę** (Mt. Kopa Chair Lift), from which you get a panoramic view of the region year-round. In the winter, this is a popular local ski slope. ⊠ *ul. Turystyczna* ☎ *075/761–92–84* 🎫 *chair lift zł 17 one-way, zł22 round-trip* ⊙ *Daily 8:30–5.*

The **Wang Temple** is a pine church that was originally built in Norway at the beginning of the 13th century. Prussian king Friedrich Wilhelm IV brought it here to serve the local Protestant community. The church is a unique example of old Nordic (Viking) style and is the only building of its kind in Poland. It is also a rare gem throughout Europe: of the original 400 churches in this particular style, only 24 have survived until our times. ⊠ *Na Śnieżkę 8* ☎ *075/752–82–90* ⊠ *pl 3* ☉ *Mid-Apr.–Oct., Mon.–Sat. 9–6; Nov.–mid-Apr., Mon.–Sat. 9–5.*

2

┌─────────────┐
│ NEED A
│ BREAK?

Rustic and just a wee bit kitschy, **Jaśkowa Izba** (⊠ Konstytucji 3 Maja 39 ☎ 075/761–85–27), serves traditional, stomach- and heart-warming mountain fare on wooden plates, by a fireplace.

KUDOWA ZDRÓJ

㉖ *100 km south of Wrocław.*

Kudowa Zdrój, a spa town long known for its mineral springs, is where the Góry Stołowe (Table Mountains), part of the Sudeten range, begin. As the town grew, it eventually encompassed—and now incorporates—the former village of Czermna.

Kudowa Zdrój's unmissable—if rather morbid—local attraction can be found within the 14th-century **Kościół świętego Bartłomieja** (Church of St. Bartholomew). The church's **Chapel of Skulls,** which dates from 1776, is the only such chapel in Poland and one of only three in Europe. (A more famous example may be the Kostnice in Sedlec, outside of Prague.) The decoration—and indeed some of the construction material—of the chapel is several thousand human skulls, remainders of 18th-century wars and plague. ⊠ *Kościuszki 42* ☎ *075/866–17–54* ⊠ *pl 4* ☉ *May–Sept., daily 9:30–1 and 2–5:30; Oct.–Apr., daily 10–1 and 2–4.*

Park Narodówy Gór Stołowych encompasses the beginnings of the Góry Stołowe, which begin approximately 10 km (6.2 mi) northeast of Kudowa Zdrój. The mountains are filled with rocky terraces and other formations of varied, fantastic shapes. Paths lead hikers through what seems like a labyrinthine city of rocks. ⊠ *Słoneczna 31* ☎ *074/866–14–36* ⊠ *pl 5* ☉ *May–Oct., daily sunrise–sunset.*

Where to Eat

$–$$ ✕ **Zagroda W Starym Młynie.** The "Old Mill restaurant is indeed in an old mill—the water mill was built to produce energy for the spa resort in 1910. The legend goes that the late owner of the mill hid a treasure in it somewhere, but it is yet to be found. The restaurant's specialty is fish, especially trout and carp, all freshly caught. ⊠ *Fredry 10* ☎ *074/866–36–01* ⊟ AE, DC, MC, V.

Where to Stay

¢ ▦ **Willa Sanssouci.** In a quiet area of Kudowa Zdrój, this beautiful 19th-century villa has been turned into a welcoming and comfortable small hotel. The rooms are spacious, and the garden is lovely. The local spa park is only 200 meters away, and the "Water World" water park 300 meters. ⊠ *Buczka 3, 57–350* ☎ *074/866–13–50* ⊟ *074/866–44–90*

⊕ *www.sanssouci.info.pl* ⇥ *24 rooms* ♨ *Restaurant, minibars, cable TV, in-room broadband, meeting rooms; no a/c* ☰ *AE, DC, MC, V* ⦿*EP.*

KATOWICE

㉗ *200 km (124 mi) southeast of Wrocław, 100 km (62 mi) west of Kraków.*

Katowice is the main city of Upper Silesia, and the center of the Upper Silesian Industrial District. The region is certainly more than coal mines and steelworks; there are several important sights, including the Auschwitz concentration camp in Oświęcim (part of the Małopolska region, *see* Chapter 7, Małopolska & the Tatras); Częstochowa, where you'll find the famous shrine of Black Madonna; and Pszczyna Castle. All of these are within the easy reach of Katowice, making it a decent spot to base yourself when exploring the region. In the town itself, you'll find some noteworthy historic sights, good museums, and other cultural institutions.

Exploring Katowice

FodorśChoice
★
One of the country's best art collections can be found in the **Silesian Museum**, which has an especially strong collection of Polish paintings dating from 1800 to 1939. The galleries will take you through classicism, realism, symbolism, art nouveau, impressionism, and all the major movements, with examples of Polish contributions to each. Some names to look out for include Piotr Michałowski ("Blue Boy" and "Amazon"), Henryk Rodakowski, Józef Chełmoński, Aleksander Gierymski ("Jewish Woman with Lemons"), Aleksander Kotsis ("Summer"), Stanisław Wyspiański, Jacek Malczewski, and Olga Boznańska. ⊠ *al. Korfantego 3* ☎ *032/258–56–61* ⊕ *www.muzeumslaskie.pl* 🖾 *pł 9* ◷ *Tues.—Fri. 10—5, weekends 11–5.*

Cathedral of Christ the King (Katedra Chrystusa Króla), constructed between 1927 and 1955, is one of the biggest churches in Poland. The adjoining **Archdiocesal Museum** has a collection of religious art, including several beautiful medieval Madonnas. ⊠ *Jordana 39* ☎ *032/608–14–52* 🖾 *pł 4* ◷ *Museum Tues. and Thurs. 2–6, Sun. 2–5.*

OFF THE
BEATEN
PATH
★
GISZOWIEC – Seven kilometers (4 mi) north from the center of Katowice lies a progressive—utopian even—coal miner's settlement constructed between 1906 and 1910 based on the concept of a garden city. The city was designed by the Zillman brothers, architects from Charlottenburg. The colony—initially called Gieschewald—was meant to serve the workers of the "Giesches Erben" coal works. This model settlement was built on prime land surrounded with woodland and orchards, and there is plenty of space, air, and light for the tenants to enjoy; the founders spared no expense to create the best design. The colony was organized around a central square, with schools, shops, a post office, an inn, administrative buildings, public baths, and other modern public infrastructure. Residential houses—none taller than two stories—were designed for two or more families. Each had a lovely garden and was modeled on a traditional Upper-Silesian cottage. In 1914, Giszowiec was connected to Janów and a similar, new settlement of Nikiszowiec by a narrow-gauge

rail, which was humorously dubbed "The Balkan Express"; the rail line operated until 1970s.

Where to Eat

$–$$$ ✕ **Cristallo.** Even if you do not stay at the Hotel Monopol, do sample
Fodor'sChoice the taste and atmosphere of its Italian restaurant, which is in the ele-
★ gant and wonderfully spacious inner courtyard under a glass roof. The menu changes according to season, and the dishes are skillfully and imaginatively prepared. For your main course, try the pheasant with foie-gras cream sauce and roasted apple, or the veal with couscous and vegetables. Although it is really hard to ignore the starters, remember to leave some room for desserts: how does apple tart with Gorgonzola ice-cream sound? ⊠ *Dworcowa 5* ☎ *032/782–82–82* 🖷 *071/3782–82–83* 🖃 *AE, DC, MC, V.*

★ ¢ ✕ **Złoty Osioł.** This lovely place (in English, the "Golden Donkey") serves great vegetarian dishes and plenty of good karma. The menu includes an excellent choice of quiches, salads, lasagnas, and pies—all homemade and healthy. And your food can be accompanied by healthy juices and smoothies. The walls are painted in all the colors of the rainbow, and each tablecloth is a different pattern. The happy, smiling staff make you feel at home. ⊠ *Mariacka 1* ☎ *048/502–518–224 or 048/501–465–690* 🖃 *No credit cards.*

Where to Stay

$$$ 🏨 **Hotel Monopol.** Even if you don't have another purpose in visiting
Fodor'sChoice Katowice, a sojourn at the excellent Hotel Monopol will suffice for a
★ reason to stop over. This 19th-century palace has served as a hotel since early 1900s, but the 1930s were its golden age, and its art-deco spirit has been renewed with a complete renovation. Reopened in 2003, the Monopol is a beauty clad in marble, exotic wood, luxurious fabrics, and oriental carpets. Note the excellent black-and white photos of old Katowice—you'll find them in every room and hallway. Each room is different: 515 has canopy beds, and the corner room (102) is where famous prewar Polish tenor Jan Kiepura stayed on the night of his wedding with Marta Eggert. Today, the hotel is favored both by businesspeople and famous musicians (Pat Metheny Group, Krzysztof Penderecki, Adam Makowicz, and Deep Purple, among many others). The hotel has a lovely viewing platform on the top floor. ⊠ *Dworcowa 5, 40–012* ☎ *032/782–82–82* 🖷 *071/3782–82–83* ⊕ *www.hotel.com. pl* 🛏 *105 rooms, 3 suites* 🖧 *2 restaurants, minibars, cable TV, in-room broadband, gym, hair salon, sauna, bar, shops, business services, meeting rooms* 🖃 *AE, DC, MC, V* ¶⊙¶ *EP.*

$–$$ 🏨 **Hotel Diament.** Pleasant and modern, the Hotel Diament sits near the railway station, so it is as well located as the Monopol next door. It is, however, decidedly less sophisticated. The rooms are fairly standard, and simply yet comfortably furnished. In the lobby and restaurant, fragments of warm redbrick walls contrast nicely with gray modern concrete and light-colored plywood. The hotel is part of a regional chain of contemporary business hotels throughout the Upper Silesia. ⊠ *Dworcowa 9,*

40–012 ☎ 032/253–90–41 🖷 032/253–90–43 ⊕ *www.hoteldiament.
pl* ⇨ *43 rooms* ⚬ *Restaurant, minibars, cable TV, in-room broadband, meeting rooms; no a/c* ⊟ *AE, DC, MC, V* ¶❶ *EP.*

CZĘSTOCHOWA

❷❽ *90 km (56 mi) north of Katowice, 130 km (81 mi) from Kraków.*

Częstochowa is known to all Poles as place of residence of the "Queen
of Poland," as Virgin Mary has been called since the 18th century. The
icon of the Black Madonna is believed to be miraculous, and it attracts
thousands of pilgrims every year. The monastery complex, where the painting is kept, is best visited as a day or half-day trip from Kraków or Katowice—just as well, because there's not much to see here otherwise.

Fodor'sChoice An estimated five million pilgrims a year make their way—some on foot—
★ to the town of Częstochowa. They come to visit the 14th-century **Klasztor Paulinów** (Pauline Monastery) at the Jasna Góra (Hill of Light). The
town itself grew with the monastery, and there is little else to draw visitors here. Although the Communist government planted industry here
in the hope of overshadowing the cult, it didn't work. There's still but
one reason why masses of people come to this city. Inside the monastery
is Poland's holiest shrine, home to the *Black Madonna of Częstochowa,*
a wood-pane painting of a dark-skinned Madonna and child, the origins of which are uncertain (legend attributes the work to Luke the Apos-
tle himself, but it may have been painted anytime between the 6th and
14th centuries, anywhere between Byzantium and Hungary). The Black
Madonna has a number of miracles attributed to it, including the re-
pulsion of invading Swedish forces in the 16th century, and its designation as savior of Poland dates from those turbulent days. To see the Black
Madonna up close, you have to join the faithful and walk on your knees
round the chapel and behind a screen, where the eyes, according to believers, will fix directly on you. There are often times during the day
when the icon is veiled, but these are irregular and hard to predict. The
monastery was rebuilt in baroque style during the 17th and 18th centuries, as was the interior of the Gothic church. The **Monastery Treasury** holds an important collection of manuscripts and works of art. ⊠ *al.
Najświętszej Marii Panny 1* ☎ *No phone* 🖃 *Free* ☉ *Basilica daily 5
AM–9:30 PM (icon unveiled at 6 AM). Treasury daily 11–1 and 3–5.*

Where to Eat

★ **$–$$** ✕ **Pod Aniołami.** A mere 100 meters down from the main gate of the
monastery, "Under the Angels" serves unsophisticated yet tasty traditional Polish dishes in a pleasant wooden interior with a fireplace. Meat
with Silesian dumplings accompanied by fresh and pickled salads is a
good choice, and the chicken soup with homemade noodles is excellent.
⊠ *7 Kamienic 21* ☎ *034/322–93–08* ⊟ *AE, DC, MC, V.*

¢–$ ✕ **Wiking.** You can take in the local color at this crowded restaurant,
which offers Polish, Swedish, and Chinese food—or at least a local version. The specialties are mostly meat dishes, notably the beef with asparagus. ⊠ *Nowowiejskiego 10/12* ☎ *034/324–57–68* ⊟ *No credit cards.*

Where to Stay

$$–$$$ 🏨 **Hotel Noma Residence.** This 19th-century shooting lodge—now a luxury hotel with character—is hidden away in the woods about 30 km south of Katowice on the way to Pszczyna and Cieszyn. Lovely wooden ceilings, creaking floors, and winding stairs will take you back in time, and the furnishings are suitably antique and romantic, with a pinch of kitsch. In the surroundings, you will find sights and sounds of nature to accompany a pleasant walk, sail, or ride. ✉ *Kobiór k Tychów, 34-210* 🕿 *032/219–46–78* 🖷 *071/219–54–75* 🌐 *www.promnice.com.pl* 🛏 *13 rooms* ♿ *Restaurant, minibars, cable TV, Internet, hot tub, sauna, some pets allowed; no a/c* 🚫 *AE, DC, MC, V.*

$$ 🏨 **Mercure Patria Częstochowa.** This six-story 1980s hotel, which is owned by Accor's Mercure group and managed by Orbis, offers predictable cuisine and accommodations close to the Jasna Góra Monastery. Rooms are brightly furnished and comfortable, the staff cheerful and friendly. ✉ *Popiełuszki 2, 42–200* 🕿 *034/324–70–01* 🖷 *034/324–63–32* 🌐 *www.mercure.com* 🛏 *90 rooms, 12 suites* ♿ *2 restaurants, Wi-Fi, tennis court, volleyball, bar, meeting rooms; no a/c* 🚫 *AE, DC, MC, V* ❙◉❙ *BP.*

$ 🏨 **Hotel Inter.** This modern hotel is privately owned and reasonably priced. Every room has satellite TV, and there's a small fitness center. ✉ *Marszałka E. Rydza-Śmigłego 26–34, 42–225* 🕿 *034/366–02–67* 🖷 *034/366–04–57* 🛏 *17 rooms* ♿ *Cable TV, gym; no a/c* 🚫 *AE, DC, MC, V* ❙◉❙ *EP.*

A NAME GAME

On March 7, 1953, just a day after comrade Joseph Stalin died, passengers who took the train to Katowice arrived in Stalinogród (Stalintown) instead. The decision of the Polish Communist Party to change the city's name had been even more sudden than the death of the Revolution Leader. People say that the first choice to receive the honorary name change was Częstochowa, but apparently the idea of religious pilgrimages to "Our Lady of Stalintown" caused party leaders to rethink the plan. The new name did not last, though; since 1956, trains began arriving in Katowice station again.

PSZCZYNA

㉙ *40 km (25 mi) south of Katowice.*

The little town of Pszczyna, one of the oldest in Silesia, is well worth a visit for its magnificent castle and park. The history of the **Castle,** also known as Château Pless, goes back to the 12th century. Between 1548 and 1765, both the town and castle were owned by the Promnice family, then the princes of Anhalt-Köthen; during this time, the family renovated and expanded the castle, turning it into more of a palace, first in Renaissance and then baroque style. The family—by then known as Anhalt-Köthen-Pless—owned the castle for another hundred years, expanding the park surrounding it and building more structures, including a neoclassical parts of the manor house that you see today. When the family line died off, only the Pless name endured. From the mid-19th century until World War II, the estate was owned by the Hochberg family of Prussia—one of the wealthiest aristocratic clans of Europe at the time. The interiors we see today largely reflect the (rather expensive) taste of the Hochbergs and reflect a never-subtle sense of 19th-century glamour. Save time to explore the park, which has lakes, gardens, memorials, graves, and pavilions hidden among ancient trees. ⊠ *Brama Wybrańców 1* ☎ *032/210–30–37* ⊕ *www.zamek-pszczyna.pl* 🖃 *pł 12* ☉ *Jan.–Mar. and Nov.–Dec., Tues. 11–3, Wed. 9–4, Thurs.–Fri. 9–3, Sat. 10–3, Sun. 10–4; Apr.–June and Sept.–Oct., Mon. 11–3, Tues. 10–3, Wed. 9–4, Thurs.–Fri. 9–3, Sat. 10–4, Sun. 10–5; Jul.–Aug., Mon. 11–3, Tues. 10–3, Wed. 9–4, Thurs.–Fri. 9–3, weekends 10—6.*

> ### POLISH CONCERTS
>
> Between 1704 and 1707—every summer—Georg Philipp Telemann came to Pszczyna as the "in-house" composer of the Promnice family. It is here that he composed his "Polish concerts." In his autobiography, he recalls listening to Polish folk music, which, as he remarks, "within a week would equip a careful listener with musical ideas for life."

CIESZYN

30 *90 km (56 mi) southwest of Katowice.*

The town of Cieszyn lies on the border of Poland and the Czech Republic. In fact, since 1920 it has been divided into two towns, one Polish the other Czech, separated by the river Olza. Legend has it that the town was founded in AD 810 by three brothers—Leszko, Bolko, and Cieszko—to commemorate their meeting after a long separation. They celebrated their reunion by calling the place "Cieszyn," which is derived from the Polish word *cieszyć się* (to rejoice). In reality, the town was probably founded somewhat later—in all likelihood in the 10th century as a stronghold built to defend Poland's southern marches, although traces of much earlier human settlements have been found on Castle Hill. Cieszyn town—and the Cieszyn region of Silesia—are distinguished by their multicultural character and strong traditions of religious diversity, which have endured since the Reformation. In addition to ethnic Poles, Germans, Czechs, Hungarians, and Slovaks live here, and the town has a small Jewish community.

Cieszyn has preserved its medieval urban plan and may be the most pleasant and best-preserved small town in Silesia. The town hosts several interesting festivals, including the "On the Border" Theatre Festival in May, and the Organ, Choral, and Chamber Music Decade in November.

Cieszyn's **Rynek** (Town Square), which was built at the end of the 15th century, is the favorite hangout for the people of Cieszyn. The fountain in the middle of the square is a popular meeting point; people will sit in one of the cafés surrounding it to socialize, making it a truly local gathering spot. The square is surrounded with representative tenement houses, not to mention the Town Hall, which takes up the whole south side of the square. Leading out of the Rynek towards Castle Hill is ulica Głęboka, the town's main shopping street, with more interesting building fronts.

Góra Zamkowa (Castle Hill) is a great area for a stroll and a reflection upon Cieszyn's history. It is here that archaeologists found first traces of the region's first human inhabitants—dating from the 5th century BC. The Romanesque St. Nicholas' Rotunda and two stone towers have survived from the medieval Castle of Cieszyn Piasts. In the 19th century, a Habsburg residence in classicist style was built on the old castle's ruins. The Habsburg Palace (or Hunting Lodge) and the surrounding romantic park were designed by a renowned Viennese architect Kornhäusel. Today the palace houses the institution called Silesian Castle of Art and Enterprise and a music school. Remaining from the original Piast castle, the **Piast Tower** (⊠ Castle Hill, uphill from Zamkowa, northwest of the Town Sq.) offers the best views of the town and its surroundings. The tower (free admission) is open from April through September, daily 9:30 to 6:30, from October through March, daily 9:30 to 3.

Muzeum Śląska Cieszyńskiego (Museum of Cieszyn Silesia), which was established in 1802, is one of the oldest museums in Europe. After a long renovation, it reopened in 2002 to host temporary exhibitions related to the history of the area as well as a permanent collection of art, archaeological artifacts, and ethnographic exhibits. One of the most famous pieces in the museum is a beautiful Gothic stone sculpture of the Madonna from the workshop of Peter Parler of Prague. Another wonderful artwork is Breughel-Franken's painting of *Christ and John the Baptist with Mary and St Anne.* ⊠ *Regera 6* ☎ *033/851–29–32* ⊕ *www.muzeum-cieszyn. ox.pl* ⊠ *zł 5* ☉ *Tues., Thurs., Sat. 10–2; Wed. and Fri. 12–4; Sun 11–3.*

The **Three Brothers' Well** is linked to the legend of Cieszyn's founding in AD 810 (the reunion of three brothers, sons of Polish ruler Leszek III, was supposed to have taken place beside the well). In reality, the well probably dates to a later period—most likely the 14th century—and belonged to different "brothers," namely friars of the Dominican Order. Up to the 19th century, the water from the well was used by town brewery on Śrutarska Street and made excellent beer. A few steps down from the well is the lovely area called the **Wenecja Cieszyńska** (Cieszyn's Venice) by the Młynówka Brook, which is all that remains from the old quarter of tanners and weavers; you'll see a working water mill on the brook. ⊠ *Trzech Braci.*

The **Kościół Jezusowy** (Church of Jesus), founded in 1709, is the main Protestant (Evangelical) church in Cieszyn. In this five-aisle temple, the central rococo-style altarpiece includes a painting of "The Last Supper" by Adam Friedrich Oser. In the two-story choir, a late-baroque pipe organ is decorated with figures of angels. Masses are held Sunday year-round at 8 and 10 AM. ⊠ *pl. Kościelny* ☎ *No phone* ☉ *May–Sept., Sun.–Fri. 10–12 and 1–3; Oct.–Apr., open only for mass on Sun. at 8 and 10 AM.*

Where to Eat

★ ¢ ✗ **Spaghetteria Toscana.** Chef Marcello, a native of Italy, serves a range of authentic pastas, lasagnas, soups, pizzas, and salads, and you'll always find a great-value "dish of the day" as well as a prix-fixe option.

Hacquetia Epipactis

THE FLOWERING PLANT
Cieszynianka wiosenna (Spring Cieszynian), which is more formally known as *hacquetia epipactis*, its scientific name, is unique to this region of Poland. Green and yellow, the *Cieszynianka* is one of the first plants to awaken after the winter. It can be seen in early March or even as early as late February—before the first leaves start sprouting on the trees. Not technically a flower, it is an inflorescence of the *umbellate* (palmate) family. What looks like green corolla petals are, in fact, a false perianth of green stipules, which are transformed leaves, growing on a long, leafless stem. *Hacquetia epipactis* can be found in municipal nature reserves—by the River Olza, for instance—as well as in the private gardens of Cieszyn citizens, who are proud to cultivate their own unique flora.

The restaurant also offers Italian conversation classes for beginners and more advanced students. ☒ *Szersznika 1* ☎ *048/668–270–353 or 048/501–465–690* ▤ *No credit cards* ☉ *Mon.–Sat. 12–5:30.*

Where to Stay

¢   🏨 **Dworek Cieszyński.** This restored 19th-century country manor house is hidden away in a lovely corner of town, which is undoubtedly the most picturesque, called "Cieszyn Venice." With its shingle roof, white walls, and flowers in the windows, the hotel has a welcoming and cheerful look, and the rooms are comfortably furnished. An on-site restaurant serves wholesome Polish-European cuisine. ☒ *Przykopa 14, 43–400* ☎ *033/858–11–78* 📠 *033/857–82–65* ⊕ *dworek.cieszyn.com.pl* ☞ *6 rooms, 1 suite* ᕖ *Restaurant, cable TV, bar, meeting rooms; no a/c* ▤ *AE, DC, MC, V* ❢ *EP.*

Fodor'sChoice ★

¢   🏨 **Kora Guest House.** This small guest house in the middle of the Old Town has a homey feel. Two of the four rooms have en-suite bathrooms, and the other two have shared facilities. There is a pleasant common area with a living room, a kitchen, and a dining room. This is a simpler and more low-key option than Dworek Cieszyński. Breakfast is available for an extra charge. ☒ *Wyższa Brama 19, 43–400* ☎ *033/851–22–99* 📠 *033/857–81–52* ⊕ *www.domgoscinny-kora.com.pl* ☞ *4 rooms, 2 with bath* ᕖ *Cable TV; no a/c* ▤ *AE, DC, MC, V* ❢ *EP.*

BREUGHEL'S MAGNOLIAS

Cieszyn prides itself on its magnolias. The most famous bloom in town is found in Muzeum Śląska Cieszyńskiego, in a painting from 17th-century Antwerps signed by Franz Frank and Bluhmen Breughel. The museum itself was founded in 1802 by a Jesuit priest Leopold Jan Szersznik, who brought magnolia trees to Cieszyn around the same time. Back then it was an exotic plant, which had only just begun to be grown in Europe. Today, every spring, magnificent magnolias bloom in the gardens of Cieszyn.

SILESIA ESSENTIALS

TRANSPORTATION

BY AIR

There are two international airports in Silesia. The larger is the Katowice (Pyrzowice) Airport (33 km/20 mi north of the city), the smaller one in Wrocław (approximately 10 km/6 mi west of the city center). Both serve domestic and international (intra-Europe, but not intercontinental) flights. Some airlines—notably Lufthansa and Wizzair, for whom Katowice is the main Polish base—fly to Katowice year-round; several other airlines offer only seasonal service; and some charter companies also fly into Katowice. Lufthansa, Lot, Norwegian, Ryanair, and Wizzair fly directly into Wrocław.

TRANSFERS There is regularly scheduled bus service between Katowice and its airport via the Lotnisko Airport Bus, which also serves some smaller towns in the area. Regular shuttles operated by Matuszek in coordination with Wizzair go into Kraków.

City buses numbers 406 and 117—as well as an Airport Shuttle—operate between the airport and railway station in Wrocław.

🛈 **Katowice-Pyrzowice International Airport** ✉ Wolności 90, Ożarowice ☎ 032/392-73-85 ⊕ www.gtl.com.pl. **Matuszek** ☎ 032/236-11-11 ⊕ www.matuszek.com.pl. **Copernicus Airport Wrocław** ✉ Skarżyńskiego 36, Wrocław ☎ 071/358-10-00 ⊕ www.Airport. Wroclaw.pl.

BY BUS

Buses are usually slower and less convenient than trains, but they are often indispensable for local travel, especially to smaller towns and villages. The PKS Katowice bus station is about 500 meters north of the main railway station and has local, domestic, and international bus connections. The Wrocław Bus Terminal is at the back (south side) of the Main Railway Station.

🛈 **PKS Cieszyn** ✉ Korfantego 23 ☎ 033/477-99-99 ⊕ www.pkscieszyn.pl. **PKS Katowice** ✉ Piotra Skargi ☎ 032/258-94-65 ⊕ www.pkskatowice.bip.jur.pl. **Wrocław Bus Terminal** ✉ Sucha 1 ☎ 0300-300-122 ⊕ www.polbus.pl.

BY CAR

The A4 motorway connects Kraków with Katowice and Wrocław (via Opole). From Katowice, National Route 1 will take you north to Cieszyn or south to Pszczyna and Bielsko-Biała, from where you must turn west towards Cieszyn. Most car-rental companies are located at the airports.

🛈 **Avis** ☎ 601/354-812 in Katowice, 601/354-811 in Wrocław. **Budget** ☎ 032/284-50-11 in Katowice, 071/353-77-50 in Wrocław. **Europcar** ☎ 032/284-50-86 in Katowice, 071/358-12-91 in Wrocław. **Hertz** ☎ 032/284-51-03 in Katowice, 071/353-77-43 in Wrocław.

BY TAXI

Calling a taxi is usually cheaper than catching one in the street. Beware of private taxis outside stations and airports; their rates can be exorbitant. It is wise to stick to well-known taxi companies with four-digit phone numbers preceded by the right city code. Be aware that many taxi companies have the same four-digit number in several cities, where the only difference is the city code (and since some street names occur all over the country, you might end up calling a Katowice company while you are in Cieszyn).

🛈 **Cieszyn Taxis Halo Taxi** ✉ Cieszyn ☎ 033/852-19-19. **MPT** ✉ Cieszyn ☎ 033/9191. 🛈 **Częstochowa Taxis Echo Taxi** ✉ Częstochowa ☎ 34/9625. 🛈 **Katowice Taxis Karolina** ✉ Katowice ☎ 032/9622. 🛈 **Wrocław Taxis Radio Taxi Blues** ✉ Wrocław ☎ 071/9661. **Super Taxi** ✉ Wrocław ☎ 071/9663. **City Radio Taxi** ✉ Wrocław ☎ 071/9662.

BY TRAIN
Several daily trains connect Wrocław and Katowice, and most of these continue to Kraków. From Katowice you can also go up to Częstochowa or down to Cieszyn. Wrocław also has good connections with Warsaw (some via Łódź) and Poznań.

🛈 **Cieszyn Główny** ✉ Hajduka 10, Cieszyn ☎ 033/94-36 ⊕ www.rozklad.pkp.pl. **Katowice Dworzec Główny** ✉ pl. Szewczyka 1, Katowice ☎ 032/94-36 ⊕ www.rozklad.pkp. pl. **Wrocław Główny** ✉ Piłsudskiego, Wrocław ☎ 071/94-36 ⊕ www.rozklad.pkp.pl.

Contacts & Resources

BANKS & EXCHANGE SERVICES
Currency exchange services are available at all banks and at special exchange offices (called *kantor*). ATMs can be found in all towns, although not always in smaller villages, and they accept most international credit cards.

EMERGENCIES
Emergency phone numbers should be preceded by an area code—71 for Wrocław, 32 for Katowice, 33 for Cieszyn, and 34 for Częstochowa.

🛈 **Emergency Services Ambulance** ☎ 999. **Fire** ☎ 998. **Police** ☎ 997. 🛈 **Hospitals & Clinics Medicover** ✉ Grabiszyńska 165, Wrocław ☎ 071/781-81-42 ⊕ www. medicover.com. **Szpital Śląski** ✉ Bielska 4, Cieszyn ☎ 033/852-05-11 ⊕ www.szpital. netus.pl. **Szpital Kliniczny Śląskiej Akademii Medycznej** ✉ Medyków 14, Katowice ☎ 032/789-40-00. 🛈 **24-hour Pharmacies Apteka Całodobowa** ✉ Tyska 3, Katowice ☎ 032/252-00-53. **Apteka Magiczna** ✉ Traugutta 105, Wrocław ☎ 071/341-34-50.

INTERNET, MAIL & SHIPPING
🛈 **Internet Cafés Bit** ✉ Pokoju 1, Cieszyn ☎ 033/858-24-43. **Cyber Tea Tavern/Pod Kalamburem** ✉ Kuźnicza 29a, Wrocław ☎ 071/372-35-71. **Eurocafé** ✉ Katowice Dworzec Główny, Katowice ☎ 032/257-53-61. **Galaxy** ✉ Kazimierza Wielkiego 55, Wrocław ☎ 071/374-61-14. **Xtreme Internet Café** ✉ Al. NPM 65a, Częstochowa ☎ 034/368-36-89. 🛈 **Post Offices Cieszyn** ✉ Rynek 13, Cieszyn ☎ 033/852-03-00 **Częstochowa** ✉ Orzechowskiego 7, Częstochowa ☎ 034/360-64-49. **Katowice** ✉ Pocztowa 9, Katowice ☎ 032/359-45-00. **Wrocław** ✉ Rynek 28, Wrocław ☎ 071/347-19-38.

VISITOR INFORMATION
🛈 **Cieszyn Visitor Information** ✉ Rynek 1, Cieszyn ☎ 033/852-30-50 ⊕ www.cieszyn. pl. **Częstochowa-Jasna Góra Information Center** ✉ Kordeckiego 2, Częstochowa ☎ 034/365-38-88 ⊕ www.jasnagora.pl. **Katowice City Information Office** ✉ Młyńska 2, Katowice ☎ 302/259-38-08 ⊕ www.um.katowice.pl. **Wrocław Tourist Information** ✉ Rynek 14, Wrocław ☎ 071/344-31-11 ⊕ www.wroclaw.pl.

Wielkopolska

WORD OF MOUTH

"As for Poznań, if you are there at noon, be sure to see the clock tower on the town hall. Metal goats come out and knock heads twelve times."

−gggsal

"Biskupin . . . we found amazing. It is an archae-ological reserve of an early Slav settlement which has been reconstructed. . . .Some of the original wooden buildings go back 2,500 years. . . . Fas-cinating if you are into that kind of thing."

−joegri

HISTORICALLY, WIELKOPOLSKA (GREAT POLAND), which neighbors Dolny Śląsk (Lower Silesia) on the south, and Kujawy and Pomorze on the north, is the oldest part of the Polish state. Gniezno, the first capital of Poland, is worth visiting for its cathedral and, together with the nearby early settlement at Biskupin, could be a day trip from Poznań. Toruń, the birthplace of Nicolas Copernicus, is already "abroad" (at the border between Kujawy and Pomorze), but due to its proximity to Poznań, it is convenient to include it in your Wielkopolska itinerary.

Wielkopolska's capital, Poznań, was the seat of the first Polish bishopric (AD 968), while three of the region's towns—Poznań, Ostrów Lednicki, and Gniezno—each claim that it was in their city that the first Polish ruler, Mieszko, embraced Christianity in 966. Several other historical distinctions are less disputed. In Gniezno, near the tomb of Saint Adalbert (Wojciech), the famous Congress of Gniezno took place in the year 1000, during which Holy Roman Emperor Otto III crowned the Polish prince Bolesław Chrobry as King Bolesław I, thus Poland's autonomous role in the empire. After Poland's capital was moved from Gniezno to Kraków in 1039, Wielkopolska lost some of its importance but regained it in the period of feudal fragmentation (approximately 1138–1320), when it was the seat of the local line of the Piast Dynasty. The reunification of the Polish lands in the 14th century nurtured further growth of Wielkopolska, and in the 15th century Poznań became an important commercial hub in the trade routes that connected Lithuania with western Europe. During the first and second partition of Poland (1772 and 1793), Wielkopolska was under the rule of Prussia until the successful Wielkopolska Uprising of 1794 made it possible for the region to join Księstwo Warszawskie (the Warsaw Duchy) created by Napoleon Bonaparte. After Napoleon's defeat, Wielkopolska was again under Prussian rule and remained a part of Prussia until Poland regained its independence in 1918.

During Poland's long partition, the people of the region resisted the intensive Germanizing policy; yet the period has left its mark in the architecture of the cities and the specific regional dialect, easily recognizable by Poles from other regions. The Poles of Great Poland are affectionately mocked by their countrymen for having absorbed the archetypal German habits of cleanliness, order, and thrift. The region, which includes both fertile plains and numerous glacial lakes, has a well-developed agricultural

WIELKOPOLSKA'S TOP 5

- Poznań has both a sense of history and a vibrant present, a university town that is also a business center.

- The 10th-century Gniezno Cathedral, with its famous doors and the tomb of Saint Adalbert, is worthwhile even for nonpilgrims.

- The palaces at Kórnik and Rogalin are stately, historic homes.

- Wielkopolski National Park offers a break from history, with lovely walking trails through scenic woodlands.

- Toruń, the birthplace of Copernicus, is one of the most beautiful Polish cities.

CLOSE UP

Saint Adalbert and the Congress of Gniezno

THE FIRST YEARS of every new state—when it is often surrounded by not-so-friendly neighbors—are a test of survival. Sometimes a haphazard event, cleverly used, can establish a country's importance for centuries. For Poland, such an event might have been the martyrdom of a missionary named Wojciech (Adalbert). He lived from 956 to 997, and his story is a curious one. He had been named bishop of Prague but left his own diocese after witnessing the public lynching of the unfaithful wife of one of the lords there. In spite of bishop's mediation, the woman was dragged out of the church and murdered, and thus the holy right of asylum was broken. The bishop cursed the offending parishioners and left Prague for Rome.

A bishop's curse in those days was a terrible thing and had serious repercussions: it precluded administration of any sacraments, including the last sacrament, and according to the dogmas of the Middle Ages, this meant eternal damnation for the parishioners. Therefore, the Mainz Council ordered the future saint to return immediately to the diocese he had abandoned. But Pope George V, who was well-disposed toward Adalbert—and who was influenced by Emperor Otto III, Adalbert's friend— gave the bishop an alternative: he would be allowed to go on a Christian mission instead. Adalbert embraced that opportunity and set off, via Poland, to Baltic Prussia. Most probably the Prussians thought he was an envoy from Poland who would

attempt to annex their lands, and not a priest. They expelled him and escorted him to the border; when he returned, breaking the prohibition of entry to a holy wood where he performed a Mass, Adalbert was killed.

His dead body was ransomed by the Polish ruler, Bolesław Chrobry (Boleslaus the Brave), who paid its weight's equivalent in gold; Bolesław buried the bishop in Gniezno. Only two years later, Adalbert was proclaimed a saint by Pope Silvester II. In the year 1000, Chrobry received Emperor Otto III, who most probably wanted to take the relics of his friend and bury them in Aachen (Aix-la-Chapelle), in Gniezno.

The emperor's visit, which Polish history has dubbed the Conference (or Congress) of Gniezno, had far-reaching consequences: although Otto got no more of the relics—except for the saint's arm, he was received with a truly imperial welcome. Otto then crowned Bolesław Chrobry with his diadem as Bolesław I, and gave him the gift of a copy of the Spear of St. Maurice as the sign of ruling power. In this manner, Poland was included in the domain of the Holy Roman Empire, as an autonomous province. However, only two years later the young emperor Otto died, perhaps from poison. His successor, Henry II, soon waged war on Bolesław I. The blessings of the Conference were lost immediately, and stability which the young Polish state needed, was endangered.

3

base, with large, well-managed farms, which have always driven its prosperous economy.

Exploring Wielkopolska

Poznań, the capital of Wielkopolska, is a good place to start and also a good anchor for exploring the rest of the region, but it would be a mistake to linger there too long: there are major sights waiting farther afield. The good news is, they are all within easy reach of Poznań: Kórnik and Rogalin are only 20 km (12 mi) away; Gniezno is about 50 km (31 mi). A visit to Wielkopolska, the cradle of Polish state, will be mostly about history, which goes back more than 1,000 years. However, from Poznań, nature is also easily accessible: there are lakes even within the city, as well as a national park and a meteorite reserve just past the city limits. Toruń, about 200 km (124 km) from Poznań, is another must-see city in the area, although technically—and historically—it does not belong to Wielkopolska but to the Kuyavia and Pomerania (Kujawy i Pomorze) region.

About the Restaurants
Wielkopolska's culinary traditions are a result of combined German and Silesian influences on one hand, with traditional, simple, village dishes on the other. A local classic is roast duck served with *pyzy* dumplings and gravy; the pyzy are round and soft pieces of steamed dough the size of small apples. The difficulty of country living in centuries past has left its mark in a dish called *pyry z gzikiem* (boiled and then roasted potatoes with a sauce of white cottage cheese, cream, garlic, and spring onions). The soup called *żurek* (which can also be found in other regions) has a base of sour flour.

About the Hotels
Poznań and Toruń have a good selection of international-standard hotels; in smaller towns you can expect no more than basic comforts, with an exception of a few interesting castle hotels. Therefore, many visitors to the region base themselves in one or the other city and then see the countryside on day trips. In Poznań, finding accommodations can be tricky during the International Trade Fairs, which occur throughout the year; it's always a necessity to make reservations in Poznań.

WHAT IT COSTS In Polish złoty (zł)				
	$$$$	**$$$**	**$$**	**$**	**¢**
RESTAURANTS	over zł70	zł50–zł70	zł30–zł50	zł15–zł30	under zł15
HOTELS	over zł800	zł500–zł800	zł300–zł500	zł150–zł300	under zł150

Restaurant prices are per person for a main course at dinner. Hotel prices are for two people in a standard double room with a private bath; most hotels include breakfast in their quoted rates.

Timing
For those who like cheerful commotion and seasonal, outdoor festivals, June will be the best time to visit Poznań. Jarmark Świętojański, which encompasses the feast days of Poznań's patron saints, Peter and Paul,

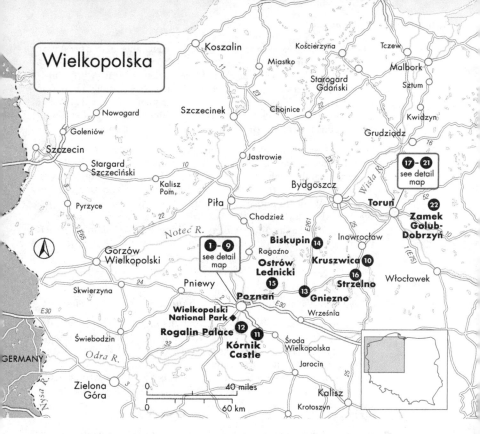

means numerous concerts and festivals (including the Malta International Theatre Festival) that draw thousands of tourists. You may even have difficulty finding accommodations at this time; hotels certainly increase prices for the season. For those who like to relax in the country, summer is the best time to visit. On hot days you can sit by one of many lakes, hike in the Wielkopolski National Park, or go horseback riding in one of several stables in the immediate vicinity of Poznań. Sightseers may wish to wait until September, when the tourist traffic lessens and moderate temperatures are more appropriate for urban exploring. Another reason to wait is that many hotels cut their prices after mid-September by as much as 30%.

Numbers in the margins correspond to numbers on the Wielkopolska map.

POZNAŃ

300 km (186 mi) west of Warsaw, 170 km (105 mi) north of Wrocław.

Halfway between Warsaw and Berlin, in the middle of the monotonously flat Polish lowlands, Poznań has been an east–west trading center for more than 1,000 years. In the Middle Ages, merchants made a great point of bringing their wares here on St. John's Day (June 23), and the annual tradition has continued, though the markets have now been superseded by the International Trade Fairs, which have been held here since 1922. Until the 13th century, Poznań was, on and off, the capital of Poland, and in 968 the first Polish bishopric was founded here by Mieszko I. It still remains the capital of the Wielkopolska (Great Poland) region.

Despite its somewhat grim industrial outskirts, Poznań has one of the country's most charming Old Towns; consider making a trip through western Poland, if only to visit the city's majestic market square. While Poznań may be only the fifth-largest city in Poland, to a tourist, it may feel larger. While the majority of sights are near the Old Town's impressive Stary Rynek (Old Market Square), other attractions are off in the sprawling maze of ancillary streets. Walking is not recommended here. Invest in some tram tickets and a city map with the transit routes marked; your feet will thank you.

What to See

Numbers in the margin correspond to numbers on the Poznań map.

⑥ Biblioteka Raczyńskich (Raczyński Library). On plac Wolności (Freedom Square) is the beautiful library built in 1829 by the aristocratic Raczyń'ski family. It remains a working library with a special collection of old manuscripts; otherwise, it's the facade that is remarkable, and you won't be nearly as impressed with the interior. This is a good place to head after visiting the Muzeum Instrumentów Muzycznych and/or Muzeum Narodowe. ⊠ *pl. Wolności 19, Stare Miasto* ☎ *061/852–94–42* ⌨ *Free* ☉ *Daily 9–5.*

★ ⑧ Katedra św. Piotra i Pawła (Cathedral of Saints Peter and Paul). Poznań's cathedral, which was rebuilt after World War II in pseudo-Gothic style, was originally constructed between the 10th and 11th centuries. Those remains can be seen in some interior details and in the cellars. The design for the current three-aisle church dates to the 15th century. The Gothic interior reveals, among other treasures, a beautiful late-Gothic **altar** with Saints Mary, Catherine, and Barbara, as well as 15th-century **bronze tombstones** from the famous Nuremberg workshops of the Vischers. (These were removed by the Germans during World War II and discovered in the Hermitage in Saint Petersburg in the 1990s.) Directly behind the main altar is the heptagonal **Golden Chapel,** worth seeing for the sheer opulence of its romantic Byzantine decor. Within the chapel is the **mausoleum** that contains the remains of the first rulers of Poland, Mieszko I and Bolesław the Great. ⊠ *ul. Mieszka I, Ostrów Tumski.*

③ Kościół Farny (Parish Church). A former Jesuit temple, the parish church, which is dedicated to Saints Stanislaus and Mary Magdalene, was consecrated in 1705 (though the construction started as early as 1649). The

FodorsChoice
★

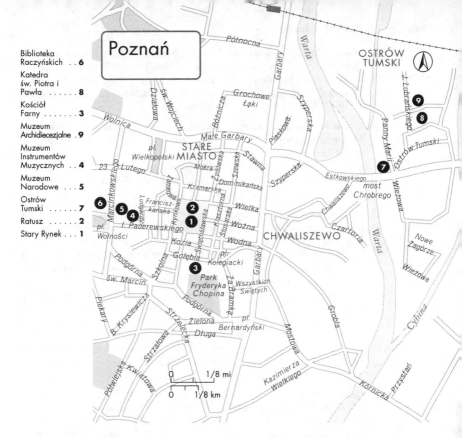

baroque building—the finest example in the city and one of the best in the entire country—was designed by Bartłomiej Nataniel Wąsowski, the facade by Giovanni Catenacci, and the beautiful archway by Pompeo Ferrari. The interior, in the style of Roman baroque, is decorated with wall paintings by Karol Dankwart, and in the main altar is the painting of Saint Stanislaus by Szymon Czechowicz. One of the most valuable objects inside the church is the pipe organ built between 1872 and 1876 by Friedrich Ladegast, the most famous European organ-builder of the age. There is a curious story connected with the organ. Half of the enormous sum necessary to build this intricate—and expensive—instrument was donated by an anonymous, elderly lady. Through the years, as many a witness claims, her ghost has supervised the gift she made before her death; and she appears in the choir and the gallery, which is hardly accessible to humans, during all repair or conservation work. She was last seen in 2002, when the pipe organ was thoroughly renovated. ⊠ *At the end of Świętosławska, Stare Miasto.*

⑨ Muzeum Archidiecezjalne (Archdiocese Museum). If you find yourself in Ostrów Tumski and wish to explore the holdings of the diocese, this museum is available for a nominal charge, but it's a dusty little museum with few really good pieces. ✉ *ul. ks. Posadzego 2, Ostrów Tumski* ☎ *061/852–61–95* 🖹 *zł 3* ⊙ *Mon.–Sat. 9–5.*

④ Muzeum Instrumentów Muzycznych (Museum of Musical Instruments). The tiny, arcaded shopkeepers' houses in the Old Market Square date to the mid-16th century. Some of them now house this museum, where you can see Chopin's piano and a plaster cast of the maestro's hands. ✉ *Stary Rynek 45, Stare Miasto* ☎ *061/856–81–78* 🖹 *zł 6* ⊙ *Tues.–Sat. 11–5, Sun. 10–3.*

⑤ Muzeum Narodowe w Poznaniu (National Museum in Poznań). A few blocks west of the Old Market Square is the national art museum, which has a good collection of Polish art (in the new building) and Western European paintings (in the old building; both buildings are connected). You'll see interesting examples of paintings by Dutch masters, in addition to examples of early Polish impressionism, more accurately described as works by artists who were inspired by the French impressionism. Represented artists include Wojtkiewicz, Malczewski, and, above all, Pankiewicz; his painting Flower Market, which was painted when Pankiewicz returned from Paris, is considered the first work of Polish Impressionism. ✉ *al. Marcinkowskiego 9, Stare Miasto* ☎ *061/856–80–00* ⊕ *www.mnp.art.pl* 🖹 *zł 10* ⊙ *Tues. 10–6, Wed. 9–5, Thurs. and Sun. 10–4, Fri. and Sat. 10–5.*

⑦ Ostrów Tumski (Cathedral Island). This islet in the Warta River—about 15 minutes by foot east of the Old Town—is the historic cradle of Poznań. The oldest part of city, it's where the Polanie tribe built their first fortified settlement and their first basilica in the 10th century. During the reign of Poland's first ruler, Mieszko I, the island hosted both the city's lay and ecclesiastical governments. When walking around Ostrów Tumski, you can see the Archbishop's Palace, the tiny, 15th-century church of Saint Mary's, and the former Lubrański Academy, a college that was established in 1512 (and which was, until 1991, home to the Archdiocese Museum). ✉ *Ostrów Tumski.*

⎸OFF THE BEATEN PATH

MORASKO METEORITE RESERVE – Just north of Poznanis the Morasko Meteorite Reserve, seven craters that were formed about 5,000 years ago as a result of a meteorite shower. The largest of the craters is 100 meters (300 feet) in diameter, and the meteorite "chunk" that produced it was the largest of all, weighing some 4,500 tons. The site is one of 150 meteorite fields in the world, but it is the only one in Poland. In the 1930s, the largest piece of meteorite was found here, weighing over 75 kilos (165 pounds). Between the craters, you can follow a marked interpretive trail (alas, it is in need of repair). Access the reserve by bus number 88, or by your own transportation: take Route 11 in the direction of Koszalin, past the railway bridge to Sprzeczna Street. ✉ *ul. Meteorytowa, off ul. Sprzeczna.*

★ **② Ratusz** (Town Hall). Poznań residents will proudly tell you that the imposing Renaissance Town Hall at the center of the Old Market Square

Stary Licheń

CLOSE UP

IN A MERE 10 YEARS, Stary Licheń, a small village some 120 km (75 mi) east of of Poznań, has been transformed from a modest center for the cult of Saint Mary Dolorous into a huge, national pilgrimage site that every Pole has heard about. Spiritual motivations notwithstanding, many pilgrims head for Licheń also to see the most astonishing religious architectural project in many years, the St. Mary Dolorous Basilica in Licheń.

The construction of the church was started in 1994 and completed 10 years later. What is unusual about this basilica is above all its gigantic dimensions: it is the largest church in Poland and 12th-largest in the world. It has five aisles, and the sanctuary is 139 m long and 77 m wide (456 feet by 252 feet). By design, everything in this church is superlative: it has the largest pipe organ in Poland, the largest bells, the tallest tower, the biggest dome. Unfortunately, it is also the

greatest imaginable example of architectural kitsch. The size, not to mention the "monumental" quality of the church, doesn't inspire respect and admiration as much as they overwhelm. The architect meant to portray the church as a golden, wavy cornfield by adding hundreds of vertical lines against the golden background of the walls, window ornaments, and amber tint of glass. The whole is more like a mad pasty chef's dream about the most complicated layer cake in the world than a temple to St. Mary. The otherwise spacious interior overflows with gold, and excess replaces nonexistent harmony. No wonder that for many, this building is a symbol of bad taste and scandal rather than of religious sentiment. The architect herself admits that she was only passively implementing the vision by the real author of this improbable project, Marian priest Eugeniusz Makulski.

is the most splendid building in Poland. The building, which dates to the mid-16th century, was designed by Giovanni Battista Quadro. Every day at noon, hundreds of tourists look up to watch the clock tower, where two billy goats butt heads before disappearing back inside the tower. Legend has it that the clock-maker who installed the timepiece planned a party on the occasion. He ordered two goats for the feast, but the goats escaped and started fighting on the tower. The mayor was so amused by the event that he ordered the clock-maker to construct a mechanism to reenact the goat fight. The town hall now houses a **Muzeum Historii Miasta Poznania** (Museum of City History), which contains a room dedicated to Chopin. ⊠ *Stary Rynek 1, Stare Miasto* ☎ *061/852–56–13* ☜ *Museum zł 5.5* ☽ *Mon.–Tues. and Fri. 9–4, Wed. 11–6.*

❶ **Stary Rynek** (Old Market Square). Today's, Poznań's Old Town is a result of the "new" town charter of 1253, which was granted by prince Przemysł I. Other than the urban layout, not much survived from those days. The present-day main square dates primarily from the 16th century and has a somewhat cluttered feeling, since the center is occupied with both 20th-century additions and Renaissance structures. But this is where you'll find the Ratusz, where everyone gathers to watch the famous clock. ⊠ *Stare Miasto.*

OFF THE BEATEN PATH

WIELKOPOLSKI NATIONAL PARK – This beautiful national park is 19 km (10 mi) southwest of Poznań on Route 430. The pine forests are punctuated with 16 lakes, two of which, Lake Rusałka and Lake Strzeszynek, have long beaches, tourist accommodations, and water-sports equipment for hire. There are several interesting legends associated with the park; for example, at the bottom of Lake Góreckie there is supposed to be a submerged town, and on still nights you can hear the faint ringing of the town bells. ⊠ *Rte. 430 Jeziory, Mosina* ☎ *061/813–22–06.*

Where to Eat

Poznań´ offers a good variety of dining choices, many of which are clustered around the Old Town, in and around the Stary Rynek (Old Market Square); quite a few restaurants will be found on św. Marcin. Your choice is usually between a European gourmet menu and regional Polish cuisine.

$$–$$$ ✕ **Bażanciarnia.** You'll find top-notch Old-Polish specialties at Bażanciarnia, which is owned by Magda Gessler, perhaps the best-known Polish restaurateur (or, rather, *restauratress*). In two rooms in a town house on Old Town Square, guests are served in impeccable, high style. The menu includes excellent poultry and venison dishes, which are prepared according to 18th- and 19th-century Polish recipes, some of which are from the collection of the Gessler family. It is one of the most expensive restaurants in Poznań but worth every penny. ⊠ *Stary Rynek 94, Stare Miasto* ☎ *061/855–33–58* ⊕ *www.bazanciarnia.pl* ⚞ *Reservations essential* ⊟ *AE, MC, V.*

$–$$$ ✕ **Kresowa.** On the main town square, this popular restaurant specializes in cuisine from the *kresy* (Poland's former eastern territories of Lithuania, Ukraine, and Belarus). The interior may be a bit unexciting, but the friendly service and tasty food make up for that particular deficiency. Excellent soups include borscht and mushroom, both with a slightly sweet taste. (This can be surprising to the contemporary palate, but it's perfectly proper as far as historical recipes go.) For a main course, try *cepeliny* ("Zeppelin"), potato dumplings stuffed with meat and seasoned with marjoram. ⊠ *Stary Rynek 2* ☎ *061/853–12–91* ⊟ *AE, DC, MC, V* ☺ *No dinner Sun.*

$–$$$ ✕ **Piano Bar.** The upper floor of this huge, post-industrial space—it was once a brewery—has been reinvented as a hip restaurant. Chefs Sławomir Domiński and Roop Lal Balu serve international, mostly Mediterranean, dishes from pizza and pasta, to seafood and grilled meats, as well as excellent desserts. Live music and other events (such as fashion shows) are an additional draw. The Browar Pub is downstairs. ⊠ *Słodownia, ul. Półwiejska 42* ☎ *061/859–65–70* ⊟ *AE, MC, V.*

$–$$

Fodor'sChoice

★

✕ **Brovaria.** This hotel restaurant boasts its own microbrewery. Excellent food—a kind of European fusion cuisine—borrows from what is best in various Continental cuisines. The beer is always fresh, having been produced on the spot. The interior is decorated with brewery machinery and utensils. You can pick and choose from a widely varied menu;

IF YOU LIKE

GOLF

While remaining an exclusive sport, the game of golf enjoys increasing popularity in Poland—and in Wielkopolska in particular. The same natural conditions that make the region perfect for horseback riding make this terrain ideal for teeing the ball, and there are some great golf courses and clubs around.

HISTORY

Historical sights and monuments are the real highlights of Wielkopolska. If you have the time, you can journey to the places that witnessed the beginning of the Polish state: to Gniezno, Ostrów Lednicki, Poznań, and Kruszwica. These four cities will take you back 1,000-some years. But you can travel even further, into prehistoric times: in Biskupin you can see archaeological excavations going back about 2,700 years.

HORSEBACK RIDING

Wielkopolska has many excellent stables and riding clubs. In addition to famous centers, you will find countless smaller stables as you drive through the countryside. Natural conditions here are perfect for horseback riding, as vast plains, woods, and fields invite more experienced riders to venture out into the open. Beginners will find great horses and instructors, and the lessons are cheaper than in other European countries.

WATER SPORTS

In order to practice water sports in Wielkopolska, you don't even have to leave Poznań. The city has several large lakes and reservoirs where you can rent canoes, water bikes, and small sailboats. More advanced sailors should try Jezioro Maltańskie, which has the best regatta course in Poland; it is where that European rowing and canoeing championships take place.

on offer are everything from beer snacks (such as prunes wrapped in bacon, or Brie rolled in sesame seeds) to full-fledged main courses (such as sirloin steak or lamb chops). There is a separate dining room, for "proper" diners, to supplement the lounge, where you can still get a casual meal. ⊠ *Stary Rynek 73–74, Stare Miasto* ☎ *061/858–68–68* 🖃 *AE, MC, V.*

$-$$ ✕ **Wielkopolska Zagroda.** If you want to try regional specialties like *pyry z gzikiem* (pork knuckle simmered in beer) or pork roulade with barley, this is a good place to go. The menu here has an extensive selection of traditional Polish dishes typical of the Wielkopolska region. The decor is pleasant and rustic, creating an impression you are in a country cottage rather than a restaurant in a large town. Note that you will need to order your garnish and/or side dishes separately; they are not included in the main courses and are separately priced. ⊠ *ul. Fredry 2, Stare Miasto* ☎ *061/665–88–02* 🖃 *AE, MC, V.*

★ ¢-$$ ✕ **Da Luigi.** This tiny pizzeria in a cellar is near the Old Town Square. The Italian owner also acts as the chef. The atmosphere is a wholly unpretentious, the food tasty and inexpensive. In addition to great pizzas, there is a selection of pastas and desserts. The place closes relatively early (8 PM on weekdays, 7 PM on weekends) and is always busy. ⊠ *ul. Woźna 1, Stare Miasto* ☎ *061/852–73–11* ▤ *No credit cards.*

¢–$ ✕ **Cocorico.** Mere meters from the facade of the Poznań town church and
Fodor'sChoice a one-minute walk from the Old Town Square, this lovely café looks not
★ unlike a traditional Parisian bistro, decorated with French prints on the walls and furnished with cushioned sofas. There's even a lovely garden in the courtyard. It's a perfect stop for coffee and/or cocktails, but you can also get light snacks such as toasts and salads, though the excellent hot cherry sundae is the real treat. ⊠ *ul. Świętosławska 9, Stare Miasto* ☎ *061/665–84–67* ⌂ *Reservations not accepted* ▤ *AE, MC, V.*

Where to Stay

In Poznań's hotels, you will find high standards as well as high prices. It is virtually impossible to find accommodation during the International Trade Fairs (Międzynarodowe Targi Poznańskie), which occur throughout the year; hotels invariably raise prices by at least 30% during each Trade Fair. The prices quoted here are for the high tourist season and do not apply during the Trade Fair periods (you can see a calendar of Trade Fairs at www.mtp.pl).

If you want a different kind of accommodation, you can also rent a serviced apartment. **Domina Poznań Residence** (⊠ ul. św. Marcin 2, 61–808 ☎ 61/859–05–90 ⊕ www.dominapoznanresidence.com) offers luxury serviced apartments with a 24-hour reception desk in the very center of town. Each flat comes with a fully equipped kitchen and a bathroom, cable TV, broadband Internet access, and a/c. You don't have to make your own meals; there is a restaurant on the site for breakfast and lunch only, and the building offers hotel-style amenities, including daily maid service. A flat for two persons costs between zł 360 and zł 560.

$$–$$$ ▦ **Hotel Royal.** On Poznań's main street, this small hotel with just 55 beds in a 19th-century tenement house has a long-standing, if not exactly continuous, tradition of hospitality. The building became a hotel in the 1920s and served in that capacity through much of the 20th century; it was restored to its current status in the late 1990s. The classy interior design—some rooms have wood paneling, some bay windows, some richly pattern fabrics—gives the hotel plenty of character, further enhanced by friendly and efficient service. The restaurant serves breakfast only (included in the room rates). ⊠ *ul. św. Marcin 71, 61–808* ☎ *061/ 858–23–00* 🖷 *061/858–23–06* ⊕ *www.hotel-royal.pl* ⇔ *30 rooms, 1 suite* ⌂ *Some kitchenettes, some minibars, cable TV, bar, laundry service, Internet room, meeting rooms, parking (free)* ▤ *AE, MC, V* ⦿❘ *BP.*

$$–$$$ ▦ **Hotel Trawiński.** A great location in the heart of the city's largest park lends the Cytadela a peaceful and quiet air, even though it is close to the city center. This is a good choice if you want to do more than just sleep: use of a fitness center, Jacuzzi, and sauna are included with all accommodations. And if you feel the sudden need to get a new haircut or facial, you won't even have to leave the hotel. Rooms are comfortable and bright, well up to international hotel standards. The hotel also

GREAT ITINERARIES

Traveling beyond the region's capital is obligatory, although Poznań is a good place to start. Everything else is within the easy range, including the earliest monuments of the Polish state at Gniezno and Ostrów Lednicki, and the prehistoric site of Biskupin. The city of Toruń is at the far northeastern end of the itineraries suggested here, but you could always reverse direction and use it as a starting point.

IF YOU HAVE 3 DAYS

You can see a few of the highlights of Great Poland in three packed days. On Day 1, leave Poznań and head toward Gniezno on Route 5, stopping along the way to see the Wielkopolski Park Etnograficzny, which includes more than 50 samples of wooden folk architecture on the shore of Lednickie Lake. Then take the ferry to Ostrów Lednicki itself, where you can see the remains of an early-Romanesque bishopric before continuing to Gniezno. Spend the rest of your afternoon walking around the Old Town and doing some sightseeing. Spend the night here. On Day 2, head out to Strzelno to see the Holy Trinity Church and the nearby Saint Prokop rotunda. Continue on to Kruszwica for a bit more sightseeing before setting off for Toruń. An obligatory itinerary through one of the loveliest Polish towns must include places connected with Mikołaj Kopernik (Copernicus). Spend the night here. On Day 3, after coffee, head off toward Biskupin to see the open-air archaeological museum. Return to Poznań via Gniezno.

IF YOU HAVE 5 DAYS

With five days, you should certainly devote Day 1 to some sightseeing in Poznań. Both the Stare Miasto and Ostrów Tumski neighborhoods are worth your time, and you can easily spend a day exploring here. Head out from Poznań on Day 2 to see Strzelno and Kruszwica (as outlined in Day 2 of the itinerary above), but end your day in Gniezno. On Day 3, visit Biskupin's open-air archaeological museum; end the day in Toruń, where you should do some sightseeing in the afternoon. On Day 4, head out to Kruszwica; spend the night in the palace in Kobylniki. On Day 5, head out to Strzelno and then finally back to Poznań via Gniezno if you have time.

IF YOU HAVE 7 DAYS

With a week to explore Great Poland, you can get a good sense of what the region is like. Spend Day 1 in Poznań, as on the five-day itinerary. On Day 2, visit Wielkopolski National Park and the two manor houses there (Rogalin and Kórnik); you should still have some time to do a bit of hiking on one of the easy trails before touring the manor houses, ending your day back in Poznań. For Day 3, follow the first-day plan of the three-day itinerary, above, ending in Gniezno. On Day 4, visit Biskupin on the way to Toruń. On Day 5, relax and soak in the atmosphere in Toruń, or take an optional short trip to visit the castle in Golub-Dobrzyń. End your week by following the suggestions for Days 4 and 5 in the five-day itinerary, above.

3

has conference facilities. ⊠ *ul. Żniwna 2, 61–663* 🖀 *061/827–58–00* 🖷 *061/827–57–81* ⊕ *www.hoteltrawinski.com.pl* ⮡ *57 rooms, 1 suite* ⟁ *Restaurant, minibars, cable TV, in-room broadband, gym, hair salon, hot tub, sauna, bar, dance club, business services, meeting rooms, parking (fee)* ▤ *AE, MC, V* ⵔ *BP.*

$$–$$$ 🏨 **Hotel Vivaldi.** This pleasant, new hotel not far from the center is surrounded by greenery and perfect for a quiet night's sleep followed by a morning jog. Frequented by business travelers arriving for the Trade Fairs, it's also a pleasant and reasonably priced option for leisure travelers. The hotel restaurant—named, somewhat predictably, the Four Seasons—serves Polish and Italian cuisine. ⊠ *ul. Winogrady 9, 61–663* 🖀 *061/858–81–00* 🖷 *061/853–29–77* ⊕ *www.vivaldi.pl* ⮡ *47 rooms, 1 suite* ⟁ *Restaurant, minibars, cable TV, in-room broadband, pool, sauna, bar, meeting rooms, parking (fee)* ▤ *AE, MC, V* ⵔ *BP.*

$$–$$$ 🏨 **Mercure Poznań.** This five-story, glass-front hotel is an Orbis product from the 1960s, now part of the French Mercure chain. Identical brown doors lead from long corridors into nearly identical rooms that are furnished in dark shades but have the usual Mercure standard of comfort. This is a typical, but perfectly adequate, business hotel, so you won't get any surprises here, either positive or negative. Its strong suit is convenience: an excellent location (the best for the Poznań Trade Fair) and good parking facilities. ⊠ *ul. Roosevelta 20, 60–829* 🖀 *061/855–80–00* 🖷 *061/855–89–55* ⊕ *www.orbisonline.pl* ⮡ *227 rooms, 1 suite* ⟁ *Restaurant, café, minibars, cable TV, in-room broadband, bar, gym, sauna, meeting facilities, parking (fee)* ▤ *AE, DC, MC, V* ⵔ *BP.*

$$–$$$ 🏨 **Novotel Poznań Centrum.** This charmless high-rise in the city center next to the railway station has the familiar Orbis touch: rooms decorated in government-regulation brown with slightly outdated bathrooms. It's now part of Accor's Novotel chain, though still managed by Orbis. ⊠ *pl. Andersa 1, 61–898* 🖀 *061/858–70–00* 🖷 *061/852–26–31* ⊕ *www.orbisonline.pl* ⮡ *470 rooms, 10 suites* ⟁ *Restaurant, room service, minibars, in-room broadband, sauna, bar, nightclub, playground, car rental* ▤ *AE, DC, MC, V* ⵔ *BP.*

$$–$$$ 🏨 **Sheraton.** This is the newest hotel of the Sheraton network in Poland; it opened in November 2006 as one of the more expensive hotel building projects in this part of the country. Here, you'll find the highest standard of service and plush rooms with all conceivable comforts. The location—across from the Trade Fair Grounds and within easy walking distance of the main train station, is a strong selling point. ⊠ *ul. Bukowska 3/9, 60–813* 🖀 *061/655–20–00* 🖷 *061/655–20–01* ⊕ *www. starwoodhotels.com* ⮡ *168 rooms, 13 suites* ⟁ *3 restaurants, minibars, in-room safes, in-room broadband, Wi-Fi, cable TV, indoor pool, sauna, gym, bar, shops, dry cleaning, laundry service, meeting rooms, parking (fee)* ▤ *AE, MC, V* ⵔ *EP.*

$–$$ 🏨 **Brovaria Hotel.** If you want to be near the center of Poznań, it's impossible to get any closer than this small, cozy hotel on the Old Town Square. If one is available, ask for a room overlooking the square. The hotel is located over a great microbrewery restaurant-cum-bar. The rooms are a smooth and happy marriage between classic and contemporary style. ⊠ *Stary Rynek 73/74, 61–772* 🖀 *061/858–68–68* 🖷 *61/*

858–68–69 ⊕ www.brovaria.pl ↪ 16 rooms, 1 suite ⚅ Restaurant, cable TV, in-room broadband, bar ▤ AE, MC, V ⵌ⊙ⵜ BP.

$–$$ ⵌⵝⵜ **Hotel Rzymski.** Prewar traditions combined with modern comforts add up to a true "Poznań bourgeois" atmosphere (in the best sense). What you get are pretty standard hotel rooms—nothing noteworthy, but comfortable nonetheless, though few services or facilities beyond a business center. The hotel has a central location right next to the National Museum, but because of this rooms in the front can get a bit noisy. Prices can vary considerably, with the cheapest rates being offered on weekends and the highest during one of the many Trade Fairs. The De Rome restaurant serves Polish and European food. ⊠ *al. K. Marcinkowskiego 22, 61–827* ☎ *061/852–81–21* ⧉ *061/852–89–83* ⊕ *www.hotelrzymski. pl* ↪ *82 rooms, 5 suites* ⚅ *2 restaurants, cable TV, in-room broadband, Wi-Fi, bar, business services, meeting rooms, no-smoking rooms, some pets allowed* ▤ *AE, MC, V* ⵌ⊙ⵜ *BP.*

$ ⵌⵝⵜ **Dom Turysty PTTK.** This hotel has only 18 rooms (singles, doubles, and triples), but if you can get in, you'll like its location, right at the center of the Old Town. Expect no luxuries, but the place has character. Rooms are quite spacious and comfortably furnished, with Polish folk touches, and interesting eclectic elements. The staff is friendly and well-informed. ⊠ *Stary Rynek 91, 61–001* ☎☎ *061/852–88–93* ⊕ *www.domturysty. naszemiasto.pl* ↪ *18 rooms, 10 with shared bath* ⚅ *Restaurant, café, cable TV; no a/c* ▤ *AE, DC, MC, V* ⵌ⊙ⵜ *BP.*

$ ⵌⵝⵜ **Hotel Lech.** This older hotel near the university is a good base for exploring Poznań on foot. Rooms are on the small side but comfortably furnished. There is no restaurant service apart from breakfast, and the hotel bar sometimes attracts a rather rowdy crowd in the evening. ⊠ *Św. Marcin 74, 61–809* ☎ *061/853–08–79* ⧉ *061/853–08–80* ⊕ *www.hotel-lech.poznan.pl* ↪ *78 rooms, 1 suite* ⚅ *Restaurant, cable TV, in-room broadband, laundry service; no a/c* ▤ *AE, DC, MC, V* ⵌ⊙ⵜ *BP.*

Nightlife & the Arts

If you want to get out for a drink, consider the Brovaria restaurant, which has its own microbrewery (⇨ Brovaria *in* Where to Eat, *above*), or the Browar Pub (closed Monday), a lively pub with a music stage as a bonus (⇨ Piano Bar *in* Where to Eat, *above*).

The **Filharmonia Poznańska** (Poznań' Philharmonic; ⊠ ul. Św. Marcin 81 ☎ 061/852–47–08 ⊕ www.filharmonia.poznan.pl) holds concerts in Wrocław University's beautifully restored Aula, where the acoustics are excellent.

Stefan Stuligrosz's Boys Choir (⊠ Teatr Wielki, ul. Fredry 9 ☎ 061/852–82–91)—the Poznań Nightingales—is one of Poznań's best-known musical attractions.

Sports & the Outdoors

Golf

Approximately 20 km (12 mi) north of Poznań, **Villa Mon Repos** (⊠ Wojnowo 1, Murowana Goślina ☎ 061/647–75–22 or 061/811–30–82

⊕ www.villamonrepos.pl), built in the first half of the 19th century, houses a hotel, the gold club quarters, and the Mon Repos Association, whose mission is the promotion of tolerance. The 9-hole course has lovely surroundings, and there are six guest rooms and four suites for rental on the premises. The golf club features an *Akademia Golfa* for the promotion of the sport. The course is easy to reach from Poznań via Route 196 (go toward Wałgrowiec); 5 km (3 mi) after Murowana Goślina, turn left toward Rogoźno. You should make prior arrangements by phone.

Water Sports

If you would like to get out on the water—particularly if you would like to rent a small sailboat—there are several places that are convenient to Poznań. **Jezioro Maltańskie** is approximately 2 km (1 mi) east of the Old Town Square. There are even three large lakes within the city limits, all northwest of the center: **Rusałka, Strzeszynek,** and **Kierskie (Kiekrz)** are all popular destinations for locals to get out on the water. Kiekrz is the city's largest lake, and is also the most popular with sailors. All three can be accessed by public transportation—take any bus to Ogrody terminal, and then take Bus 95 toward Kiekrz. By car, head to Koszalinłska Street (for Rusałka, Strzeszynek) or onto the A2 highway (direction: Słwiecko), turning toward Szamotuły (Rte. 184).

KRUSZWICA

❿ *110 km east of Poznań via Rtes. 5, 15, and 62*

According to a legend found in the 11th-century *Polish Chronicle* by Gall Anonim, Piast—who was called Kołodziej (the Wheelwright)—and became the legendary progenitor of the Piast dynasty, who ruled in Kruszwica. The story goes that he was chosen by the people after the death of cruel monarch Popiel, who committed fratricide and was subsequently gnawed to death by mice (in the "Mice Tower," which to this day looms over lake Gopło). To separate fact from the legend, Kruszwica was indeed one of the most important centers of power in the early days of Poland and was inhabited by the Goplanie tribe, who were incorporated into the state founded by the Polanie tribe shortly before the Mieszko I embraced Christianity. The tower that we call the **Mice Tower** today is actually the only remaining portion of a Gothic castle that dates to the mid-14th century (much later than the era of Popiel). In addition to that tower, the Romanesque collegiate **Church of Saints Peter and Paul** and Kruszwica's Old Town are also worth a visit.

Where to Stay

¢ 🏨 **Pałac w Kobylnikach.** The French neo-Renaissance–style Kobylniki Palace is now a hotel and conference center. Situated in a beautiful park on the shores of Lake Gropło (which has mosquitoes in summer), the setting is peaceful and lovely. Regrettably, the inexpensive rooms do not have much of a palatial style or atmosphere, and there are few creature comforts (the cheapest room categories have shared bathroom facilities). There is a kind of restaurant—a cantina, really—on the premises, serving inexpensive, basic meals (zł30–zł 40 for a full meal). Guests are mostly organized groups, coming for training sessions and conferences, but individuals can book rooms if they are available. ✉ *Kobylniki 2, 88–150* ☎ *052/351–54–21* 🖶 *ending 24* ⊕ *www.kom-rol.pl* ⇆ *25 rooms* ⏃ *Restaurant, meeting rooms* ▭ *No credit cards* 🍽 *EP.*

KÓRNIK CASTLE

⑪ *20 km (12 mi) southeast of Poznań on Rte. 42.*

Kórnik's biggest draw is an 18th-century neo-Gothic **Kórnik Castle,** which houses a museum full of antique furnishings and a magnificent library of rare books (including manuscripts by Mickiewicz and Słowacki); you may also notice the magnificent wood-inlay floors. Originally the castle was a Gothic fortified structure, but in the 18th century it was remodeled into a baroque palace and rebuilt again in the 19th century in its current neo-Gothic style by the most eminent German architect of the time, Karl Friedrich Schinkel. The 19th-century project was commissioned by Tytus Działyński, who founded the castle library (which today counts some 400,000 volumes, including more than 30,000 rare prints); Tytus also started the adjoining **arboretum** by bringing and planting rare species; the arboretum is Poland's largest, with more than 3,000 trees and shrubs. The work was continued by Tytus's son, Jan Działyński. Today, the library and the arboretum are under the care of the Polish Academy of Sciences. ✉ *Kórnik* ☎ *061/817–00–81* 🖃 *zł 4* ⊙ *May–Sept., daily 9–5; Oct.–Apr., daily 9–3.*

ROGALIN PALACE

⑫ *20 km (12 mi) south of Poznań, 12 km (7 mi) west of Kórnik.*

For centuries, **Rogalin Palace** was the ancestral home of the Raczyński clan, one of the most long-standing of the landed gentry in the Wielkopolska region. The magnificent, part-Baroque, part-classicist palace, park, and coach house were built in the 18th century. Each generation of the family added to the interior furnishings and treasures, and with time the palace became a wonderful gallery of European and Polish painting. Near the palace, the **Chapel of Saint Marcelin,** styled in the fashion of Roman antiquity, is the mausoleum of the Raczyński family, where nearly all most-eminent family members are buried. Nearby is the English-style landscaped park of Dęby Rogalińskie (Oaks of Rogalin), with three 700-year-old oak trees named Lech, Czech, and Rus; they are some of the oldest living oaks in Europe. The entire complex is now a branch of the National Museum of Poznań. ✉ *Rogalin* ☎ *061/813–80–30* 🖃 *zł 4* ⊙ *Tues.–Sun. 10–4.*

Horseback Riding

An hour of individual instruction with a licensed coach in a good riding center costs between zł 75 and zł 150, depending on the level of advancement; group riding trips are cheaper (between zł 30 and zł 40 per hour). Group rides at **Centrum Hipiki** (✉ Jaszkowo 16, Brodnica ☎ 061/

Three Men Called Edward Raczyński

THE RACZYŃSKI FAMILY—of Nałęcz coat of arms—produced many an outstanding member; however, when considering the entire line, we most remember three men called Edward: Edward Raczyński (1786–1845), his grandson Edward Aleksander (1847–1926), and his great-grandson Edward Bernard (1891–1993).

Edward Raczyński was politically and socially active; he established the Rogalin library and became famous for the creation of the first city waterworks in Poznań (in 1841) and for his other grand philanthropic projects. However, he is perhaps most remembered for the tragic history of the construction of Mieszko I and Bolesław Chrobry's mausoleum in the Poznań's cathedral (the Golden Chapel), which he initiated. Raczyński was accused (although most probably he was innocent) of embezzlement and committed suicide by shooting himself with . . . a cannon.

His grandson, Edward Aleksander, was an art lover and connoisseur. Within decades, he enriched the Rogalin collection with the best works of Polish painters and interesting examples from throughout Europe. In total, he purchased more than 450 paintings of great quality, and today still more than 350 of those remain in the palace. As the president of the Kraków's Society of Friends to Fine Arts (Towarzystwo Przyjaciół Sztuk Pięknych), he maintained contact with artists' circles and supported them financially.

Edward Bernard Count Raczyński, great-grandson of Edward, son of Edward Aleksander, was an outstanding diplomat and politician. He was Poland's Ambassador to London, and after World War II was an important figure in the circles of Polish emigrants there. It is there that he became the President of Poland in exile—the head of the war-time government of Poland, which continued to meet in exile but was never recognized by the government of communist Poland. He died in London at the age of 102; his body was laid in the mausoleum of the Raczyński family. He was the last male descendant of his line and the last heir of the Rogalin Palace, which now belongs to the people of Poland.

283–75–56 ⊕ www.centrumhipiki.com) are led by an excellent jockey and trainer, heir to the most respected family clan in Wielkopolska, Antoni Chłapowski. The center is also regarded as one of the best riding schools for children throughout Poland.

GNIEZNO

⑬ *54 km (34 mi) northeast of Poznań via Rte. 5 (E261).*

Lying along the Piast Route—Poland's historic memory lane running from Poznań to Kruszwica—Gniezno is the original capital of Poland and is surrounded by towns whose monuments date as far back as the origins of the Polish state. Legend has it that Lech, the legendary founder of the country, spotted some white eagles nesting on the site; he then named the town Gniezno (Nesting Site) and proclaimed the white eagle the nation's emblem. On a more historical note, in AD 1000, Gniezno became the seat of the country's first archbishopric, a couple of years after St. Wojciech (Adalbert) was buried in Gniezno Cathedral. In that same year, by St. Adalbert's tomb, the famous conference took place during which Holy Roman Emperor Otto III crowned Bolesław Chrobry as Bolesław I, the ruler of Poland. Since 1419, the archbishop of Gniezno has also been the primate of Poland, making him the head of all Polish Catholic clergy.

★ The town's first cathedral, the **Gniezno Cathedral,** was built by Prince Mieszko I before AD 977. The present 14th-century building is the most imposing Gothic cathedral in Poland. At the back of the church the 12th-century bronze-cast **Doors of Gniezno** have intricate bas-relief scenes depicting the life of St. Wojciech (Adalbert), a Czech missionary commissioned to bring Christianity to the Prussians in northern Poland. Not everyone appreciated his message: he was killed by pagans. It is said that his body was bought from his murderers by Bolesław I of Poland for its weight in gold, which the Poles paid ungrudgingly. The saint was then laid to rest in the Gniezno church, which was soon promoted to the rank of cathedral. On the altar a silver sarcophagus, supported by four silver pallbearers, bears the remains of St. Wojciech. ⊠ *Łaskiego 9* 🎟 *Doors of Gniezno zł 3* 🕙 *Mon.–Sat. 10–5, Sun. 1:30–5:30.*

Muzeum Archidiecezji Gnieźnieńskiej (Museum of Gniezno Archdiocese) is a typical church museum, a bit dusty and old-fashioned. It features a plaster copy of the Doors of Gniezno (but *do* see the real thing), religious art, and some documents. If you have a spare half-hour, why not? But if you don't have the time, this can be safely skipped. ⊠ *ul. Kolegiaty 2* ☎ *061/426–37–78* ⊕ *www.muzeum.gniezno.net* 🎟 *zł 3* 🕙 *May–Sept., Mon.–Sat. 9–5:30, Sun. 9–4; Oct.–Apr., Tues.–Sat. 9–4 (Oct. also Sun. 9–4).*

Housed in a characterless concrete school building in Gniezno, the **Muzeum Początków Państwa Polskiego** (Museum of the Polish State Origins) has multimedia exhibitions in five languages, including English, that describe medieval Poland. ⊠ *Kostrzewskiego 1* ☎ *061/426–46–41* 🎟 *zł 3* 🕙 *Tues.–Sun. 10–5.*

Where to Stay & Eat

Gniezno is lamentably short of good dining options. Although there are many small roadside snack bars and food stands if you are looking for a quick bite, it is probably safer to head for Hotel Pietrak to fill both your dining and lodging needs.

$-$$ ✕🏨 **Hotel Pietrak.** This hotel in Gniezno's Old Town has lovely views of the cathedral, good rooms, and decent restaurants ($-$$$). It is here that heads of European states stayed during the celebration of the 1,000th anniversary of the Gniezno Conference—evidence that this is by far the best option in a town with few other acceptable lodging options. The three dining rooms serve Polish and Continental cuisine, and the food in each is fine, though a little bland. ⊠ *ul. Chrobrego 3,*

CLOSE UP

The Doors of Gniezno

THE DRZWI GNIEŹNIEŃSKIE, or the Doors of Gniezno, which cover the original southern entrance to the Gniezno Cathedral, are the greatest treasures of Romanesque art preserved anywhere in Poland, dating to approximately 1170. The left wing, 328 x 84 cm (10.7 x 2.7 feet), was cast as a single, large piece of bronze, while the right wing is slightly smaller, at 323 x 83 cm (10.6 x 2.7 feet), and it is composed of 24 bronze fragments joined together. The doors are covered by 18 plaques depicting scenes from the life and martyrdom of Saint Adalbert and are surrounded with ornamental border plaques featuring floral elements and animal scenes taken straight from early medieval bestiaries. The authors and designers of this unique work are unknown, while the style suggests both German and French inspirations. The size and splendor of the doors is astounding, but we should not be surprised since in the Middle Ages, church doors were considered symbols of passage between the earthly and heavenly worlds. Wedding ceremonies took place in front of the doors and were then completed with a Mass inside the church. Courts were often held outside the doors of important churches, where local magistrates ruled on small matters of the day. The doors were considered as an external altar, which extorted sobriety and acted as a remainder: of both the significance of the temple and of the inevitable death and man's passage to the new, spiritual, reality.

62–200 🏨 *061/426–14–97* ⊕ *www.pietrak.pl* ➦ *48 rooms, 8 suites* ♨ *3 restaurants, minibars, cable TV, in-room broadband, gym, sauna, bar, parking (fee)* ▤ *AE, MC, V* ⦿ *BP.*

BISKUPIN

⓮ *30 km (18 mi) north of Gniezno on Rte. E261, toward Bydgoszcz.*

Step back in time by wandering along the wood-paved streets and peering into the small wooden huts at the fortified settlement at Biskupin. This 100-acre "Polish Pompeii" is one of the most fascinating archaeological sites in Europe. It was discovered in 1933, when a local school principal and his students noticed some wood stakes protruding from the water during an excursion to Lake Biskupieńskie. The lake was later drained, revealing a settlement largely preserved over the centuries by the lake waters. Dating to 550 BC, the settlement was surrounded by defensive ramparts of oak and clay and a breakwater formed from stakes driven into the ground at a 45-degree angle. A wooden plaque at the entrance shows a plan of the original settlement. The museum holds a yearly festival in the last week of September that includes historic reenactments. ⊠ *Biskupin* ☎ *052/302–50–55* ⊕ *www.biskupin. pl* 💶 *zł 4* ⊙ *May–Sept., daily 8–6; Oct.–Apr., daily 8–dusk.*

OSTRÓW LEDNICKI

⓯ *36 km (22 mi) east of Poznań via Rte. 5.*

Next to Lednogóra village are the remains of an early medieval settlement on a small island in Lednickie Lake. The islet was likely already inhabited in the 8th century, but the mid-10th century was its golden age. It is then that the chapel was built with baptismal fonts (basins) that were excavated in the 1980s; there was also a palatium (a manor house), and the foundations and some walls of those structures survive to this day. According to a perfectly feasible theory, the palatium was the first seat of bishop Jordan, and the adjoining chapel may have hosted the christening of Mieszko I, the first Christian ruler of Poland, in the year 966. In the 10th century, the islet was connected to the mainland by two wooden bridges of unprecedented length; the longer of the wooden bridges was as much as 440 meters (1,443 feet). Today the only access to the archaeological site is by ferry, which departs at 30-minute intervals (from mid-March to late October). A few minutes' walk away is the Wielkopolski Park Etnograficzny (Ethnographic Park, an open-air museum) in Dziekanowice—a part of the Biskupin site—where interesting examples of historical folk architecture of the region can be seen. ⊠ *Lednogóra* ☏ *61/427–50–10* ⊕ *www.lednicamuzeum.pl* ⊠ *zł 10* ⊘ *May–June, Tues.–Sun. 9–6; July–Oct., Tues.–Sun. 9–5; mid-Feb.–mid-Apr., Tues.–Sun. 9–3; mid-Apr.–late Apr., Tues.–Sun. 9–5.*

STRZELNO

⓰ *101 km (63 mi) northeast of Poznań, via Rtes. 5 and 15.*

Strzelno is worth visiting for its two most valuable Romanesque monuments: **Holy Trinity Church** and the **Rotunda of St. Prokop** (St. Procopius). The unique features of the first building (which dates to the 13th century) are the amazing, carved columns that separate the main aisle from the side aisles; their decoration depicts personified virtues and vices. Similar carved columns from this period can be found in only two other places throughout the world: St. Jack Basilica in Santiago de Compostela in Spain, and in St. Mark's Basilica in Venice. Fewer than 100 meters (325 feet) from the church, the Rotunda of St. Prokop is the largest Romanesque round church in Poland, dating to the 12th century.

TORUŃ

★ *210 km (130 mi) northwest of Warsaw, 150 km (93 mi) east of Poznań.*

The birthplace of Nicolaus Copernicus, the medieval astronomer who first postulated that the earth travels around the sun, Toruń´ is a beautiful medieval city. It is also one of the few Polish cities to have survived World War II relatively unscathed. The Stare Miasto (Old Town) brims with ancient churches, civic buildings, and residences. Its Gothic burgher

The Baptism of Poland

WHEN MIESZKO I, THE RULER of the Polanie tribe, embraced Christianity, it was a milestone that marked the beginning of Poland as a modern state. The period of Mieszko's rule, however, is filled with question marks and enigmas, as surviving historical resources are scarce. Among the most interesting of those enigmas is the exact place of Mieszko's christening. Only the date has been established beyond doubt: Easter Saturday of the year 966. We know the time, but do we know the place?

The answer remains the subject of animated dispute between the proponents of Gniezno and those of Poznań, the two cities which are considered to be the first capitals of Poland. Poznań-based archaeologists firmly argue that the relics surviving in the vaults of the cathedral and results of archaeological excavations indicate that Poznań is the place where Mieszko became a Christian; but the followers of the Gniezno hypothesis recall that their city was described in the oldest existing documents as the first Polish capital, and, therefore, Gniezno is most likely where the ruler was christened.

However, there is a third option: the actual place was neither Gniezno nor Poznań. Upon careful examination of the remains of the interconnected rotunda, palatium, and church in Ostrów Lednicki, archaeologists now believe that the compound was built soon after the first half of the 10th century. And at the very focal point of the rotunda they have discovered two baptismal fonts. The layout of the rotunda is similar to those of churches in northern Italy (so-called Episcopal compounds) and is unique in this part of Europe; it is also the first significant architectural "project" of the Polish state. Therefore, a new hypothesis has emerged: perhaps Ostrów Lednicki was the location of Mieszko's christening, and the residence of missionary bishop Jordan, who answered directly to the Pope and who arrived here to perform the christening ceremony of the monarch as well as his marriage to the Czech princess Dobrawa.

This new hypothesis did not reconcile the two disputing parties. And it is unlikely that we will ever know for certain the location of the most important event in the early history of Poland—the precise location where Poland's first ruler embraced Christianity.

houses and town hall blend harmoniously with the Renaissance and baroque of its later patrician mansions.

Numbers in the margin correspond to numbers on the Toruń map.

What to See

🔀 Kościół świętego Jana (St. John's Church). Toruń's most historic church was built in the long period from the 13th through 15th centuries. This is where Copernicus was baptized. The **tuba Dei**, a 15th-century bell in the church's tower, is one of the largest in Poland. ⊠ *ul. Żeglarska, south of Old Town Sq.*

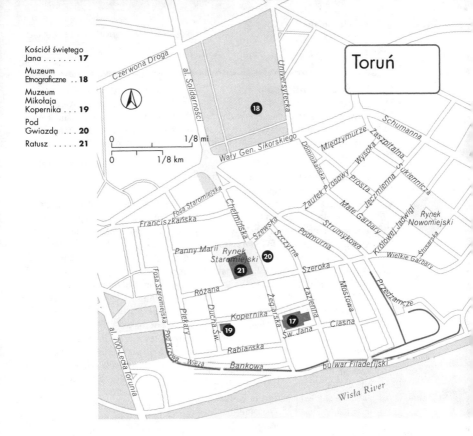

Toruń

⑱ Muzeum Etnograficzne (Ethnographic Museum). In a pleasant park northeast of Toruń´'s Old Town stands the city's ethnographic museum. Outside the museum are brightly decorated farmhouses that have been restored and filled with antique furnishings. The grounds have been designed to replicate life as it might have been lived in the Bydgoszcz region (west of Toruń) in the 19th and early 20th centuries. ⊠ *Wały Sikorskiego 19* ☎ *056/622–80–91* ✉ *zł 4* ☉ *Mon., Wed., and Fri. 9–4; Tues., Thurs., and weekends 10–6.*

★ **⑲ Muzeum Mikołaja Kopernika** (Nicolaus Copernicus Museum). Toruń's most important museum is one block south of the Rynek Staromiejski (Old Town Square) and dedicated to the city's most famous native son, who in 1617 wrote *De Revolutionibus Orbium Coelestium* (*On the Revolutions of the Celestial Spheres*), explaining his theory of a heliocentric universe. The museum consists of two houses: the house at ulica Kopernika 17, where Copernicus was born (in 1473) and lived until he was 17 years old; and the adjoining historic town house. The rooms have been restored with period furnishings, some of which belonged to the Copernicus family. There is also a scale model of Toruń, which is accompanied by a sound-and-light show (available in English) that tells the history of the city. ⊠ *Kopernika 15/17* ☎ *056/622–67–48* ✉ *zł 4* ☉ *Sept.–Apr., Tues.–Sun. 10–4; May–Oct., Tues.–Sun. 10–6.*

Mikołaj Kopernik

HE WAS THE AUTHOR of the heliocentric theory, and an outstanding astronomer. Everyone knows this much about Nicolaus Copernicus. But is that true? And is it the whole truth?

Mikołaj Kopernik (1473–1543) was born to a family of merchants. After his parents death, his uncle, Łukasz Watzenrode, became his guardian, and soon thereafter that uncle was chosen to be Bishop of Warmia. It was he who introduced Copernicus into the clergyman's career, a move that enabled him to study first in the Kraków Academy (Akademia Krakowska, today's Uniwersytet Jagielloński), and later, already as a priest-canon, in Bologna, where his subject was law.

Indeed, in Ferrara, Copernicus became the doctor of canonical (church) law; later, he studied medicine in Padua. Eventually, Copernicus became the personal physician of Warmia's bishop, his uncle. In his time he was famous not for his work in astronomy but for his contributions on economics and the theory of money. He formulated the principle of "bad" money driving the "good" money out of the market, today known as the Copernicus-Gresham law. His astronomical observations were therefore only a private pursuit, a mere pastime, of a Warmia canon devoted to public service.

Did Copernicus discover that the Earth revolves around the Sun? Certainly not. That view had been known much earlier; in the first chapter of his *De revolutionibus Orbium Coelestium*, Copernicus presented a "summary of knowledge to date" in which he mentions Aristarchus of Samos, a Greek philosopher from 3rd century BC, who claimed that Earth was circling the sun. Copernicus himself did not develop a compact, proper theory; in his work, for instance, planets revolve around the sun along regular, circular paths rather than elipsoidal courses, which we know now is the proper orbit. Copernicus's real and unquestioned merit, though, was the breakthrough in disproving the Ptolemaic paradigm that was prevalent in his day (which held that the Earth was the center of the universe) to develop a more modern theory of science: that in science, dogmas are not valid and what is needed instead are hypotheses, which can be either proven or disproven.

㉚ Pod Gwiazdą (House under the Star). On the eastern side of the Old Town Square, this 15th-century town house was remodeled in the 17th century in the baroque style. It is now the **Far Eastern Art Museum,** which is worth visiting to see the interior of the house, especially the carved-wood staircase. ✉ *Rynek Staromiejski 35* ☎ *056/622–67–48* 💶 *zł 6* ⊙ *Tues.–Sun. 10–4.*

㉛ Ratusz (town hall). The Old Town Square is dominated by the 14th-century town hall, one of the largest buildings of its kind in northern Poland. It has 365 windows, and its four pinnacles are meant to represent the four seasons of the year. Built in 1274, the town hall's **tower** is the oldest in Poland, although it did receive some later Dutch Renaissance additions. You can go up into the tower to enjoy a spectacular view. Inside the town hall, the **historical museum** houses a collection of painted glass, paintings, and sculptures from the region's craftsmen. Look for the gingerbread molds, which have been used since the 14th century to create the treats for which Toruń is famous. ⊠ *Rynek Staromiejski 1* ☎ *056/622–70–38* ⌑ *Museum zł 4* ⊙ *May–Oct., Wed.–Sun. 10–6; Sept.–Apr., Wed.–Sun. 10–4.*

NEED A BREAK? Inside the town hall, around the corner from the historical museum, the atmospheric café **Piwnica Pod Aniołem** (⊠ Rynek Staromiejski 1) serves great coffee. The "Cellar under the Angel" doubles as an art gallery/club, with changing exhibitions and live music nearly every night.

3

Where to Eat

In addition to the restaurant listed here, the hotels Heban and Spichrz have creditable restaurants serving traditional Polish cuisine, and these are your best options in Toruń.

$$–$$$$ ✕ **Restauracja Staromiejska–La Farfalla.** The double name of this restaurant reflects its double dedication: to Italian and Polish food, well-cooked and well-served. In the old wine cellar of a 4th-century building, this place has polished wood and stone floors, white-washed walls, and redbrick-ribbed, vaulted ceilings. ⊠ *ul. Szczytna 2–4* ☎ *056/622–67–25* ▱ *AE, DC, MC, V.*

Where to Stay

$$ ✕⌸ **Hotel Heban.** Opened in the year 2000 in two converted burghers' houses dating to 17th and 19th centuries, the Heban has plenty of history. Just look at the fancy, black-front, Renaissance-style facade. Inside, check out the original wall paintings revealed during the restoration. Although Samuel Bogumił Linde, author of an early Polish-language dictionary, was born in one of the houses, the hotel staff aren't limited to their native tongue; they are fluent in English. The rooms are comfortable and bright. The hotel's restaurant ($–$$$) is considered one of Toruń's best, and the food is mostly traditional Polish, with some culinary journeys into other European cuisines. The food is served in a nice and elegant setting of a large hall with a wooden ceiling and fireplace. ⊠ *Małe Garbary 7, 87–100* ☎ *056/652–15–55* ⌑ *056/652–15–65* ⊕ *www. hotel-heban.com.pl* ⇴ *19 rooms* ⌂ *Restaurant, refrigerators, cable TV, in-room broadband, Wi-Fi, billiards, meeting room* ▱ *AE, MC, V* ⓘⓞⓘ *BP.*

$–$$ ✕⌸ **Hotel Spichrz.** The name (*spichrz* is Polish for granary) may be unpronounceable, but the hotel is well worth considering if you are planning to stay over in Toruń. It's a historic, 18th-century structure (known as the Swedish Granary of 1719), next to the Bridge Gate. The granary was reconstructed and adapted as a hotel, but many details are reminiscent of its past. Note the original timber construction and the newer grand, glass elevator. Wood features prominently also in the decor of comfortable and warm guest rooms. The restaurant—with an even more advanced, tongue-twisting name—Karczma Spichrz (pronounced, roughly, carrr-tchma spee-h-shhh)—has a good reputation in town; it serves regional cuisine in an interior reminiscent of a hunting lodge, often accompanied by live music. Befitting the setting, venison and grilled meats are the specialty. ✉ *Mostowa 1, 87–100* ☎ *056/657–11–40* 📠 *056/657– 11–44* ⊕ *www.spichrz.pl* ⇱ *17 rooms, 2 suites* ⚒ *Restaurant, refrigerators, in-room safes, some in-room data ports, cable TV, meeting rooms* ▤ *AE, MC, V* ¶◎¶ *BP.*

$–$$ ⊞ **Hotel Pod Czarną Różą.** The charming Black Rose Hotel was created from two buildings, one dating from the 19th century and one brand-new, connected by a patio. The older building was once an inn, but the present management launched hotel operation in 1992, after a thorough renovation that saved the historic house from complete dilapidation. The new section, with a modern glass facade, was added later. The rooms and facilities have a lot of character and nice touches, with tasteful antique furnishings and traditional interior decor. The hotel prides itself on being environmentally friendly and has policy of waste segregation. ✉ *Rabiańska 11* ☎ *056/621–96–37* 📠 *056/621–96–47* ⊕ *www. hotelczarnaroza.pl* ⇱ *14 rooms, 1 suite* ⚒ *Some kitchenettes, Wi-Fi, bicycles, bar* ▤ *AE, MC, V* ¶◎¶ *BP.*

$–$$ ⊞ **Mercure Helios Toruń.** This friendly, medium-size Orbis-owned Mercure hotel in the city center has typical network hotel rooms (comfortable but plain). It also has a decent restaurant called Solaris, offering Polish and European food. Frescoes on the wall are fragments of Copernicus's treaty on the solar system. ✉ *Kraszewskiego 1/3, 87–100* ☎ *056/ 619–65–50* 📠 *056/622–19–64* ⊕ *www.orbis.pl* ⇱ *105 rooms, 5 suites* ⚒ *Restaurant, some minibars, cable TV, some in-room broadband, nightclub, meeting rooms, shop, parking; no a/c* ▤*AE, DC, MC, V* ¶◎¶*BP.*

¢–$ ⊞ **Hotel Pod Orłem.** The Pod Orłem is a pleasant, medium-size hotel with a history of more than 100 years in the hospitality business. It has a rather old-fashioned simplicity and charm, and it doesn't strive to be fashionable or contemporary. The restaurant serves Polish food. Breakfast costs an additional zł 15. ✉ *ul. Mostowa 17, 87–100* ☎📠 *56/622–50–25* ⊕ *www.hotel.torun.pl* ⇱ *52 rooms, 1 suite* ⚒ *Restaurant, cable TV, meeting room, parking (fee)* ▤ *AE, MC, V* ¶◎¶ *EP.*

GOLUB-DOBRZYŃ CASTLE

㉒ *40 km (25 mi) east of Torú.*

The castle in Golub-Dobrzyń is famous for knights' tournaments organized by amateurs of history and these medieval "sports." Part Gothic, part Renaissance, Golub Castle was once the seat of Knights of the Cross (the Teutonic Order); during its tumultuous history the castle has changed owners many times. Its shape and outer appearance it is particularly impressive, though the courtyard and interiors are not very interesting. What is worth noting is the so-called "horse-stairway," a wide and not too steep set of steps that enabled knights in full attire to arrive in the upper floor of the castle on horseback. A local legend says that any person who turns back while walking up those stairs will neigh like a horse in the least expected and least appropriate situation for an entire year. The knights' tournaments, organized by modern knightly fraternities since the mid-1970s, are quite a sight. The meetings are usually held in the second weekend of July, but you are better off checking the dates in advance to be sure. ⊠ *Golub-Dobrzyń* ☎ *056/638–24–55* ⊕ *www.golub-dobrzyn.pttk.pl* ⊠ *Museum zł 7* ☉ *Castle daily 9–8, museum daily 9–4.*

WIELKOPOLSKA ESSENTIALS

3

Transportation

BY AIR

Poznań's Ławica Airport is to the west of the city in the Wola district. Currently the following airlines operate to/from Poznań: Air Lingus, Ryanair, Wizzair, LOT, Lufthansa, and SAS. Express bus line "L" runs regularly between the airport and the main railway station (also regular Bus no. 59 and night Bus 242 will take you to the airport); allow about an hour for the journey.

🛪 **Port Lotniczy Poznań-Ławica** Poznań Airport ☎ 061/84-92-343 ⊕ www.airport-poznan.com.pl. **LOT office Poznań** ⊠ ul. św. Marcin 69, Poznań ☎ 058/852-28-47.

BY BUS

In Poznań the PKS bus station is a short walk from the train station. Frequent bus service is available to and from Kórnik and Gniezno. Toruń's PKS bus station is east of the Old Town; take local Bus 22 to and from the station.

🛪 **Dworzec PKS Bus Station Poznań** ⊠ ul. Towarowa 17/19, Poznań ☎ 061/664-25-25 ⊕ www.pks.poznan.pl. **PKS Bus Station Toruń** ⊠ ul. Dąbrowskiego 8-24, Toruń ☎ 056/655-53-33 ⊕ www.pks.torun.com.

BY CAR

Poznań, on the main east–west route from Berlin to Moscow, is easily accessible by car. Route 2 (E30), which leads from the border at Frankfurt/Oder through Poznań and Warsaw to the eastern border at Terespol/Brest in Belarus, is still mostly a two-lane road and is considered—because of its curves and lack of shoulders—one of the most dangerous roads in Europe.

CAR RENTAL Car rental in Poland is relatively expensive, particularly with large international car-rental companies. Nevertheless, it's much easier to explore the Wielkopolska with your own vehicle. Prices vary within the range of zł 150 to zł 500 per day (24 hours), and some companies have a two-day minimum for rentals. Some companies require an additional credit-card deposit of zł 1,500 to zł 3,000, depending on the class of the rented car. All the major firms have offices in the Poznań city center as well as at PoznanŁawica airport.

🛪 **Avis** ⊠ ul. Bukowska 12, Poznań ☎ 061/849-23-35. **Budget** ⊠ ul. Roosevelta 18, Poznań ☎ 061/845-14-89. **Express Rent a Car** ⊠ ul. Kościuszki 118, near the Ikar Hotel, Poznań ☎ 61/857-67-07. **Hertz** ⊠ ul. gen. Andersa 1, Poznań ☎ 61/868-41-77.

BY TAXI
As anywhere else in Poland, using a radio taxi company is recommended; it is both cheaper and safer than a private taxi.
🚖 Selected Toruń Radio Taxi Companies ☎ 056/9191, 056/9192, 056/9193, 056/9194, 056/9195, or 056/9667. Selected Poznań Radio Taxi Companies ☎ 061/9661, 061/9667, 061/9622, 061/9623, 061/9624, 061/9625.

BY TRAIN
All trains arriving in Poznań stop at Dworzec Główny (Central Station), located in the center, next to the Poznań Trade Fair grounds. Trains run frequently from the modern Poznań Główny to Szczecin (3 hours), Toruń (2½ hours), Wrocław (3 hours), Kraków (8 hours), and Warsaw (4 hours). International destinations include Berlin (4½ hours), Budapest (15 hours), and Paris (20 hours).

Toruń's PKP train station lies south of the city, across the Vistula River, and is connected to town by Bus 22. There is daily service to and from Poznań (3 hours), Gdańsk (4 hours), Warsaw (3 hours), and Kraków (9 hours).
🚆 PKP train station Toruń ✉ ul. Kujawska 1, Toruń ☎ 056/621-30-44 ⊕ www.pkp.
pl. Poznań Główny ✉ ul. Dworcowa 1, Poznań ☎ 061/863-38-14 ⊕ www.pkp.pl.

Contacts & Resources

EMERGENCIES
🚑 Emergency Services Ambulance Service Poznań ✉ ul. Chełmońskiego 20, Poznań ☎ 061/866-00-66 or 999. Ambulance Service Toruń ✉ ul. Konstytucji 3 Maja 40a, Toruń ☎ 056/648-65-25 or 999.
🏥 Hospitals Certus private hospital ✉ ul. Grunwaldzka 156, Poznań ☎ 061/860-42-00 ⊕ www.certus.med.pl. Citomed ✉ ul. Skłodowskiej-Curie 73, Toruń ☎ 056/658-44-60 ⊕ www.citomed.pl.
💊 24-hour Pharmacies Apteka im. J. Korczaka ✉ ul. Łyskowskiego 29/35, Toruń ☎ 056/648-56-64. Galenica ✉ Plac Wiosny Ludów, ul. Strzelecka 2/6, Poznań ☎ 061/852-99-22. Panaceum ✉ os. Przyjaźni 149, Poznań ☎ 061/820-16-42. Magiczna ✉ ul. Głogowska 118, Poznań ☎ 061/865-19-00.

INTERNET, MAIL & SHIPPING
💻 Internet Cafés Bajt ✉ ul. Zamkowa 5/2, Poznań ☎ 061/853-18-08. Klub Internetowy Jeremi ✉ Rynek Staromiejski 33, Toruń ☎ 056/633-51-00. Tunel ✉ Main Railway Station, ul. Dworcowa 1, Poznań.
📮 Post Offices Poznań Main Post Office ✉ ul. Kościuszki 77, Poznań ☎ 061/869-73-00. Toruń Main Post Office ✉ Rynek Staromiejski 15, Toruń ☎ 056/619-43-00.
📚 Bookstores EMPiK Megastore Poznań ✉ Ratajczaka 44, Poznań ☎ 061/852-66-90. EMPiK Toruń ✉ Wielkie Garbary 18, Toruń ☎ 622-48-95.

VISITOR INFORMATION
ℹ️ Gniezno Tourist Information ✉ Tumska 12 ☎ 061/428-41-00. IT Toruń ✉ Rynek Staromiejski 25, Toruń ☎ 056/621-09-31 ⊕ www.it.torun.pl. Poznań City TI ✉ Ratajczaka 44, Poznań ☎ 061/851-96-45 ⊕ www.cim.poznan.pl. Wielkopolska Region TI ✉ Stary Rynek 59/60, Poznań ☎ 061/852-61-56 ⊕ www.city.poznan.pl.

The Baltic Coast & Pomerania

WORD OF MOUTH

"You'll not be bored in Gdańsk! Also, don't miss Sopot while you're visiting the Tri-Cities."

—Caroline 1

"I went . . . and was delighted. It is just so beautiful. We walked from the castle to the other side of the river to get some stunning pictures."

—qqqsal

POLAND'S BALTIC COAST STRETCHES for 400 km (249 mi) from the isle of Wolin in the west to the Mierzeja Wiślana (Vistulan Sandbar) in the east. It is mostly a gentle and friendly shore with pine forests leading to sandy beaches, incorporating two national parks and several nature reserves (and more further inland) that are the habitats to many rare species of fish and fowl. The region is also a source of precious amber. But there is more to Pomerania than the Baltic beaches and nature: the bustling city of Gdańsk attracts visitors to the birthplace of the Solidarity Movement; it is also perhaps Poland's most attractive historic city after Kraków and a convenient gateway to Poland's castle country.

Until World War II, most of this area of northwestern Poland was included in Prussia and was referred to as "the sandbox of the Holy Roman Empire." It is indeed sandy, but it contains some startling landscapes and magnificent historic sites, such as the fortress of the Teutonic Knights at Malbork (close to and easily accessible by train from Gdańsk) and Frombork, where Copernicus lived and worked, and where he is buried.

Gdańsk, the capital of this region, is linked with two smaller neighboring towns, Gdynia and Sopot, in an urban conglomeration called the Trójmiasto (Tri-City), on the western bank of the Bay of Gdańsk. These cities operate as a single organism (if taken as one, they would make the third-largest city in Poland) and form one of Poland's most exciting and vibrant places. Szczecin, often underrated as a tourist destination, is another interesting city in the region, and a good starting point for further exploration.

Exploring the Baltic Coast & Pomerania

This chapter focuses on the highlights of the Baltic Coast and destinations farther inland in the area called Pomerania. Tourists will be most interested in the Tri-City area (in and around Gdańsk, Gdynia, and Sopot), Wolin Island (in the western part of the Baltic coast), Szczecin (south of Wolin, on the sea proper, but on the bay that cuts through inland), and the Drawskie Lake District (inland, approximately 100 km east of Szczecin, and twice that far from Gdańsk). Historic towns such as Malbork (with its castle) and Frombork (with its cathedral) can be easily seen on day trips from Gdańsk, while Szczecin is a good starting point for exploring Wolin Island and the lakes. For a relaxing holiday, spiced up with a bit of history, head to Wolin or Pojezierze Drawskie; in both the Tri-City and Szczecin you will find history, culture, and entertainment, but also beaches and pleasant sea breezes.

About the Restaurants

Fresh and smoked fish is one of the favorite regional foods. You will often find fresh local fish served in the simplest variety possible: fish-and-chips, perhaps with a bit of salad on the side. More sophisticated seafood dishes may be found in the fancier restaurants of Gdańsk and other cities. For dessert, grab a typical seaside holiday delicacy: *gofry* (sweet soft wafers with a choice of fruit and/or other toppings, with or without whipped cream). If you like to catch your own food, there are certified fishing spots in the lakes and in the bay. In autumn the pine-

and-oak forests abound with wild mushrooms and berries.

About the Hotels

Larger cities—especially Gdańsk, Gdynia, and Sopot—offer a good range of luxury accommodations, including some of the best hotels in the country. Both the prices and the number of options vary depending on the season; many small summertime resorts virtually close down for the winter.

During the summer, in smaller towns and villages, a pleasant if fairly basic lodging option is a room in a private home—*pokoje do wynajęcia*—usually very simply furnished, with an en suite or shared bathroom and, sometimes, a kitchenette. Bed linens are usually provided, but towels aren't. Most rooms will be equipped with portable wind shelters or beach umbrellas. Breakfast is ordinarily not included, the idea being that you will make your own. The price for these rooms is usually around the equivalent of $15 to $20 per person per night.

THE BALTIC & POMERANIA'S TOP 5

- The Tri-City: historic Gdańsk, Gdynia and its seaport, and Sopot and its holiday resorts.
- Kamień Pomorski, a small and dreamy medieval town, is famous for its summer Festival of Organ Music.
- Malbork, a picture-perfect castle of Teutonic Knights.
- The Pojezierze Drawskie Lake District, with flocks of birds, lakes full of fish, and woods full of mushrooms.
- Wolin Island, for its Woliński National Park and the fashionable seaside resort of Międzyzdroje.

WHAT IT COSTS In Polish złoty (zł)				
	$$$$	**$$$**	**$$**	**$** ¢
RESTAURANTS	over zł70	zł50–zł70	zł30–zł50	zł15–zł30 under zł15
HOTELS	over zł800	zł500–zł800	zł300–zł500	zł150–zł300 under zł150

Restaurant prices are per person for a main course at dinner. Hotel prices are for two people in a standard double room with a private bath and breakfast in high season.

Timing

Many of the seaside villages and resorts become overcrowded in summer, yet there are still parts of the region that remain relatively quiet and unspoiled, and these spots always retain a remote and mellow feel. If you are craving peace and quiet, head farther inland: the lakes are always serene.

In July and August most beaches get crowded. (On the other hand, most festivals and other entertainment are concentrated in those two summer months.) June or September can be nice: while it may be cooler, the experience will be no less—and in some places considerably more—enjoyable. Even busy resorts such as Międzyzdroje and Sopot have a quaint "vintage" atmosphere.

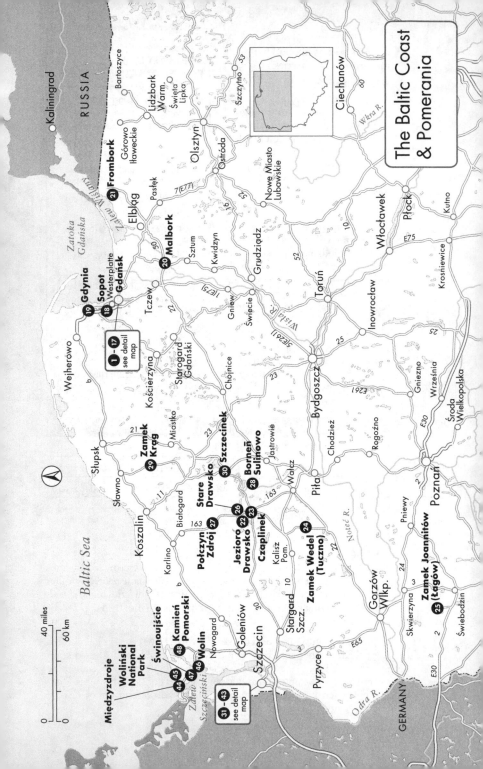

The Baltic Coast & Pomerania

THE TRI-CITY (GDAŃSK, SOPOT & GDYNIA)

The so-called Trójmiasto (Tri-City) is comprised of the ancient Hanseatic city of Gdańsk, the historic resort of Sopot, and the much newer town and port of Gdynia, which was created in the 1920s and '30s. You can get a taste of the three cities in two days. They are conveniently joined together by a commuter train: the SKM (Szybka Kolej Miejska, which translates as Fast City Rail).

A stroll down the pristine cobbles of Gdańsk's Old Town is to a walk through history, while Sopot is enchanting with the hedonistic atmosphere of a seaside resort filled with neon-lighted bars hidden inside rambling, pre-war villas. Gdynia is again different, with a special climate of a 1930s harbor city.

> **CAUTION** ⚠
>
> Even in the middle of the summer, good weather may not necessarily be a part of your holiday package. Nights can be cool, and water will never be really warm. Along with swim trunks and sun lotion, you should bring a warm sweater and rain gear. Cool weather does not provide protection from the sun, so don't forget sunblock, whatever the weather!

Numbers in the margins correspond to numbers on the Baltic Coast & Pomerania and Gdańsk maps.

Gdańsk

350 km (219 mi) north of Warsaw, 340 km (215 mi) east of Szczecin.

Maybe it's the sea air, or maybe it's the mixture of the city's cultural importance and political tumult. Whatever the reason, Gdańsk is special to Poles—and to Scandinavians and Germans, who visit the region in great numbers. From 1308 to 1945, this Baltic port was an independent city-state called Danzig, a majority of whose residents were ethnic Germans. When the Nazis fired the first shots of World War II here on September 1, 1939, they began a process of systematic destruction of Poland that would last for six years and leave millions dead. Nevertheless, in 1997 Gdańsk celebrated its 1,000th year as a Baltic city.

It remains well-known as the cradle of the workers' movement that came to be known as Solidarność (Solidarity). Food-price increases in 1970 led to the first strikes at the (former) Lenin Shipyards. The Communist authorities put down the protest quickly and brutally, killing 40 workers in December of that year. Throughout the 1970s, small groups of anti-Communist workers and intellectuals based in Gdańsk continued to organize. By August 1980, they had gained sufficient critical mass to form an organization that the government was forced to recognize eventually as the first independent trade union in the former Soviet bloc. Although the government attempted to destroy Solidarity when it declared martial law in December 1981, union activists continued to keep the objectives of democracy and independence from the Soviet Union alive. After the collapse of the Soviet bloc in 1989, Solidarity leader Lech Wałęsa

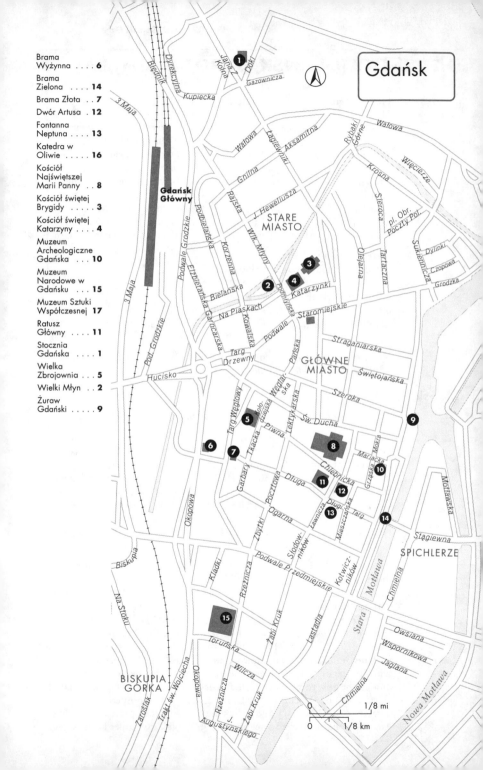

Gdańsk

IF YOU LIKE

AMBER
In Baltic beaches—especially after a storm—pieces of amber can be found. These are usually little crumbs, but every now and then you may come across a larger chunk. Some areas, like Mierzeja Wiślana, are better for amber hunting than others. And don't worry if you don't find any: souvenir stores in cities have plenty of nice amber jewelry and other artifacts.

CASTLES
If you ever dreamed about living in a castle, northwestern Poland is a place to make your dream come true. You can choose between a medieval or Renaissance castle. Most castles with hotels are situated in appealing surroundings, either on a lakeside or between two lakes, neighboring forests, or nature parks. Head for Łagów Castle, which was owned by the medieval Knights Hospitallers, or to the Krąg Castle of the Podewils family.

MARITIME HISTORY
Don't miss the Maritime Museum in Gdańsk and the Naval Museum in Szczecin, both rich with model ships and historic maritime instruments. Perhaps even better than museums, visit real ships: including the freighter MS *Sołdek* in Gdańsk, and the frigate *Dar Pomorza* and the battleship *Błyskawica* in the docks

of Gdynia (in the Southern Pier). There are also the shipyards: in Szczecin (the largest Polish port in terms of tonnage) and Gdańsk. The latter is famous for more than shipbuilding—it was the cradle for the Solidarity Movement.

ORGAN MUSIC
Many churches throughout Pomerania boast great pipe organs, but the most famous instruments are to be found in Kamień Pomorski, in Gdańsk-Oliwa, and in Frombork. The rococo Oliwa organs are really three sets of instruments complementing each other. Inaugurated in 1672, the organs at Kamień have more than 2,500 pipes, and their decoration is nearly as breathtaking as their sound. The Frombork organ, in the city's Gothic cathedral, is the best of its kind in Poland; the city even hosts a summer festival of organ music.

WATER SPORTS
In the Baltic Sea, you can swim, sail, or surf. Both Sopot and Międzyzdroje have good infrastructure for water sports. The region's lakes—notably in Pojezierze Drawskie—offer further possibilities for splashing. Practically every establishment, from an elegant hotel to a simple wooden hut for rental, has boats or kayaks or other similar equipment for rent.

became president of Poland in the nation's first free elections since World War II.

The historic core of this medieval city can be explored easily on foot. Although Gdańsk was almost entirely destroyed during World War II, the streets of its Główne Miasto (Main Town) have been lovingly restored and still retain their historical and cultural richness. North of the Main Town, the Stare Miasto (Old Town) contains many newer hotels and shops, but several churches and the beautifully reconstructed Old Town Hall justify its name. At the north end of the Old Town sit the shipyards. This site, which captivated world attention during the many clashes between workers and militarized police units during the 1970s and '80s, has now settled back into its daily grind, and the shipyards struggle to make the adjustment to the free market.

Having come to Gdańsk, it would be a crime not to explore the Tri-City further, particularly when it is so easy. Just hop on a commuter train and head northwest to Gdańsk's suburb of Oliwa, which has an amazing cathedral; farther north is Sopot, with its high-life resort atmosphere, and Gdynia, which has some wonderful ships moored in its docklands.

What to See

★ ❻ **Brama Wyżynna** (High Gate). The historic entrance to the Old Town of Gdańsk is marked by this magnificent Renaissance gate, which starts the so-called "Royal Route," along which the king passed through the city on his annual visit. The gate is adorned with the flags of Poland, Gdańsk, and the Prussian kingdom. Its builder, Hans Kramer of Saxony, erected it as a link in the chain of modern fortifications put up to frame the western city borders between 1574 and 1576. The brick gate was renovated and decorated in 1588 by Flemish sculptor Willem van den Blocke, whose decorations you can still see today. ⊠ *Off Wały Jagiellońskie, at ul. Długa, Stare Miasto.*

❶❹ **Brama Zielona** (Green Gate). At the water's edge is the eastern entrance to the medieval city of Gdańsk. Before this elegant structure was erected, the site had been occupied by the oldest gate in town, the 14th century Cog Gate. Pulled down in 1564–68, it made room for the current Mannerist building. The construction works, supervised by Regnier of Amsterdam and Hans Kramer from Dresden, lasted from 1568 to 1571. This 16th-century gate killed two birds with one stone, doubling as a royal residence. Unfortunately, the name no longer fits: the gate is now painted brown. ⊠ *At eastern end of Długi Targ, Stare Miasto.*

❼ **Brama Złota** (Golden Gate). Just behind the Brama Wyżynna, the Golden Gate was the second through which the king passed on the Royal Route. This structure dates from 1614 and combines characteristics of both the Italian and Dutch Renaissance. It was built to the design of Abraham van den Blocke. The stone figures (by Pieter Ringering) along the parapet (on the Wały Jagiellońskie facade) represent allegories of citizen's virtues, that is Caution, Justice, Piety, and Concord. On the Długa Street facade, there are allegories of Peace, Freedom, Wealth, and Fame—the pursuits of Gdańsk city over the centuries. Next to the Golden Gate squats the house of **St George's Brotherhood** that was erected by Glotau between 1487 and 1494 in the late-Gothic style. ⊠ *Off Wały Jagiellońskie, at western end of ul. Długa, Stare Miasto.*

★ ❶❷ **Dwór Artusa** (Artus Mansion). Behind the Fontanna Neptuna on Długi Targ, one of the more significant of the grand houses was constructed over a period from the 15th through the 17th centuries and is now a museum. The mansion was named for mythical King Arthur, who otherwise has no affiliation with the place (alas, there are no traces of Ex-

GREAT ITINERARIES

Pomerania is a vast area to explore in a few days: the Baltic coast itself is 400 km (249 mi) long, not to mention areas further inland. The most famous tourist attractions, however, are clustered within 60-km (37-mi) radius of Gdańsk, the region's biggest city. The second-largest city, Szczecin, is a good starting point for trips to the Wolin Island and Kamień Pomorski, about 70 km (43 mi) north. Between Gdańsk and Szczecin, there are areas of great natural beauty, sandy beaches, forests, and lakes.

IF YOU HAVE 3 DAYS

Spend your first day in Gdańsk walking around the Old Town and the Gdańsk shipyards to take in some 1,000 years of Polish history in one day—from the Middle Ages to much more recent times. In the Old Town, don't miss St. Mary's Church, the Harbor Crane, and the Artus Mansion; if you are interested in contemporary history, have a look at the shipyards, and see the "Roads to Freedom" exhibition. Around sunset head for a pier in Gdynia-Orłowo or the one in Sopot, where you can also take an evening stroll on the beach. On Day 2, head southeast to see one of the greatest castles in Poland: UNESCO-listed Malbork, built by Teutonic Knights in the late 13th century. Then continue to Frombork, where Copernicus lived and died—look for his epitaph in the cathedral overlooking the Vistulan Lagoon. On Day 3, head for Oliwa Cathedral in the morning, then to Gdynia's docklands around noon; in the afternoon, move on to Sopot to celebrate your last night in Tri-City in style.

IF YOU HAVE 5 DAYS

Try to squeeze the above itinerary into two days: Gdańsk Old Town, the shipyards, and Oliwa on Day 1, and then Malbork and perhaps Frombork, with an evening in Sopot, on Day 2. On Day 3, prepare for a 5½-hour train ride to Szczecin (ideally, bring a good book and a lunch box; alternatively, take the whole day to drive down. The best option would be to take an early train so you can enjoy the afternoon sightseeing in Szczecin's Old Town, including one of its museums; spend that night in Szczecin. On Day 4, head for the Wolin Island to visit Woliński National Park, then spend the night in the fashionable resort of Międzyzdroje. Save Day 5 for a real gem of Kamień Pomorski (the town's name literally means "the Pomeranian Stone"), before returning to Szczecin.

IF YOU HAVE 7 DAYS

Follow the itinerary above for the first two days. On Day 3, head toward Pojezierze Drawskie and spend two days visiting Szczecinek, Borne Sulinowo, and Czaplinek. You can easily spend the two days sightseeing, but why not just moor by Drawsko Lake in any place that takes your fancy to enjoy the peace of nature. On the morning of Day 6, continue to Szczecin, where you can spend the afternoon sightseeing; on Day 7, head for Kamień Pomorski and Wolin National Park (you can stay overnight in Międzyzdroje).

4

calibur or Merlin). This and the other stately mansions on the Długi Targ are reminders of the traders and aristocrats who once resided in this posh district. The Court's elegant interior hides a huge, 40-foot-high Renaissance tiled stove, possibly the world's largest, a mid-16th-century masterpiece by George Stelzener. The decorative tiles were painted by master Jost, who used this opportunity to portray the eminent European rulers of the times. The likenesses are interspersed with coats of arms, personifications of virtues, and drawings of the planets. The mansion's collection also includes Renaissance furnishings, paintings, and holy figures. The building was the meeting place of the Gdańsk city nobles. ⊠ *Długi Targ 43, Stare Miasto* ☎ *058/346–33–58* 🖃 *zł 5* ☉ *Tues.–Sat. 10–4, Sun. 11–4.*

Ⓒ ⑬ **Fontanna Neptuna** (Neptune Fountain). One of the city's most distinc-
Fodor's Choice tive landmarks is the elaborately gilded, 17th-century fountain at the
★ western end of Długi Targ. Every day after dusk, it is illuminated, adding a romantic glow to the entire area. Around the fountain, vendors selling amber jewelry and souvenirs maintain a centuries-old tradition of trade at this point. The fountain itself is perhaps the best-known symbol of Gdańsk, emphasizing its bond with the sea. The initiative to erect it came from the City Mayor Bartłomiej Schachmann. It was sculpted by Peter Husen and Johann Rogge, and the cast, moulded in 1615, was commissioned from Augsburg. The general conceptual design was developed by Abraham van den Blocke. The magnificent surrounding fencing was added in 1634. Between 1757 and 1761 Johann Karl Stender remade the fountain chalice and plinth in the rococo style and added a whole array of sea creatures. ⊠ *ul. Długa, east of Wały Jagiellońskie, Stare Miasto.*

⑯ **Katedra w Oliwie** (Oliwa Cathedral). The district of Oliwa, northwest
Fodor's Choice of the Old Town, is worth visiting if only for its magnificent cathedral
★ complex. Originally part of a Cistercian monastery, the church was erected during the 13th century. Like most other structures in Poland, it has been rebuilt many times, resulting in a hodgepodge of styles from Gothic to Renaissance to rococo. The cathedral houses one of the most impressive rococo organs you're ever likely to hear—and see. It has more than 6,000 pipes, and when a special mechanism is activated, wooden angels ring bells and a wooden star climbs up a wooden sky. Demonstrations of the organ and a brief narrated church history are given almost hourly on weekdays in summer (May through September), less frequently on weekends and the rest of the year. Don't miss a proper fullfledged concert if there is one. The Oliwa District is best reached by train; get off at Gdańsk–Oliwa and walk west up ulica Piastowska to ulica Opacka; or take Tram 2 or 6 toward Sopot. ⊠ *ul. Cystersów 10, Oliwa.*

⑧ **Kościół Najświętszej Marii Panny** (St. Mary's Church). The largest brick
Fodor's Choice church in the world—and the largest church of any kind in Poland—
★ St. Mary's is on the north side of ulica Piwna. The sanctuary can accommodate 25,000 people. Often referred to by the abbreviated Kościół Mariacki, this enormous 14th-century church underwent major restoration after World War II. Although it originally held 22 altars, 15 of them have been relocated to museums in Gdańsk and Warsaw. The highlight

of a visit is the climb up the hundreds of steps to the top of the church tower. Although you must pay zł 3 to climb, the cost is significantly cheaper than an aerobics class, and the splendid panorama is spectacular. The church also contains a 500-year-old, 25-foot-high astronomical clock that has only recently been restored to working order after years of neglect. It keeps track of solar and lunar progressions, and it displays the signs of the zodiac, something of an anomaly in a Catholic church. ⊠ *Pod-kramarska 5, at ul. Piwna, Stare Miasto* ☷ *Tower zł 3* ☉ *Daily 9–5.*

❸ **Kościół świętej Brygidy** (St. Brigitte's Church). The monument in the Gdańsk Shipyards clearly symbolizes the fundamental link in the Polish consciousness between Catholicism and political dissent; another example is this church, a few blocks north of the shipyards. After the Communist government declared martial law in 1981 in an attempt to force Solidarity to disband, the union's members began meeting here secretly during celebrations of mass. A statue of Pope John Paul II can be seen in front of the church. ⊠ *ul. Profesorska 17, near Old Town Hall, Stare Miasto.*

❹ **Kościół świętej Katarzyny** (St. Catherine's Church). The former parish church in Gdańsk's Old Town, near the corner of ulica Podmłyńska and ulica Katarzynki, is supposedly the oldest church in the city. Its construction was begun in 1220s; the tower was constructed in the 1480s; the carillon of 37 bells was added in 1634. The 17th-century astronomer Jan Hevelius is buried in the presbytery of the church, below which lies what's left of the town's oldest Christian cemetery (which dates from the 10th century). ⊠ *Wielki Młyn, Stare Miasto* ☎ *058/301–15–95.*

❿ **Muzeum Archeologiczne Gdańska** (Gdańsk Archaeological Museum). Gdańsk's small archaeological museum displays Slavic tribal artifacts, including jewelry, pottery, boats, and bones. ⊠ *ul. Mariacka 25–26, Stare Miasto* ☎ *058/301–50–31* ☷ *zł 3* ☉ *Tues.–Sun. 10–4.*

★ ⓖ **Muzeum Narodowe w Gdańsku** (National Museum in Gdańsk). The former Franciscan monastery just south of the old walls of the Main Town is now a branch of the national museum. Exhibits include 14th- to 20th-century art and ethnographic collections. Hans Memling's triptych *Last Judgment* is the jewel of the collection. ⊠ *ul. Toruńska 1, off ul. Okopowa, Stare Miasto* ☎ *058/301–70–61* ☷ *zł 5, free Sun.* ☉ *Daily 10–3.*

⓱ **Muzeum Sztuki Współczesnej** (Modern Art Museum). Two museums can be found in a beautiful park surrounding the cathedral in Oliwa in the former Abbots' Palace. The Modern Art Museum has a large collection of works by Polish artists from the inter-war period onward, and not just paintings: there's a good collection of sculpture, ceramics, fabrics, and tapestry, as well as samples of works for the theater (mise-en-scène). Some names to look out for are Jan Tarasin, Henryk Stażewski, and Jan Sawka. Connected to the Modern Art Museum, administratively and physically, is the **Muzeum Etnograficzne** (Ethnographic Museum; ⊠ ul. Opacka 12, Oliwa ☎ 058/552–12–71), in the former Abbots' Granary. The museum displays many has fine examples of local crafts from the 19th century and also has an interesting display of amber folk jewelry. It has a separate entrance from the Modern Art Museum and a separate admission fee (zł 9), but the hours and other contact information are the same for both museums. The Oliwa District is best reached by train; get off at Gdańsk-Oliwa and walk west up ulica Piastowska to ulica Opacka; or take Tram 2 or 6 toward Sopot. ⊠ *Pałac Opatów, Cystersów 15A, Oliwa* ☎ *058/552–12–71* ⊕ *www.muzeum.narodowe. gda.pl* ᗏ *zł 8* ☉ *Tues.–Sun. 9–4.*

★ ⑪ **Ratusz Główny** (Old Town Hall). Although Gdańsk's original town hall was completely destroyed during World War II, a careful reconstruction of the exterior and interior now re-creates the glory of Gdańsk's medieval past. Inside, the **Muzeum Historii Miasta Gdańska** (Gdańsk Historical Museum) covers more than five centuries of Gdańsk's history in exhibits that include paintings, sculptures, and weapons. ⊠ *ul. Długa 47, Stare Miasto* ☎ *058/301–48–72* ᗏ *Museum zł 4* ☉ *Tues.–Sun. 11–4.*

❶ **Stocznia Gdańska** (Gdańsk Shipyard). Three huge and somber crosses
Fodor's Choice perpetually draped with flowers stand outside the gates of the former
★ Lenin Shipyards, which gave birth to the Solidarity Movement. The crosses outside the entrance to the shipyards are the **Monument to Fallen Shipyard Workers** (Pomnik Poległych Stoczniowców), as well as plaques that commemorate the struggle, and a quotation by Pope John Paul II inspired by his visit to the monument in 1987: "The Grace of God could not have created anything better; in this place, silence is a scream." Formerly inside the shipyard gates (and now a bit further away), the **Roads to Freedom** exhibition once consisted of a number of symbolic gates, which until recently led to a multimedia exhibition in the historic BPH room on Plac Solidarności, where the Gdańsk Agreements were signed. The BPH room is now closed for renovation and was expected at this writing to reopen in March 2007; the exhibition had moved temporarily to Wały Piastowskie Street. The exhibition itself is really interesting, as it traces the beginning and development of the Solidarity movement, taking you on a virtual tour through 1980s Poland. ⊠ *Wały Piastowskie 24, Stare Miasto* ☎ *058/308—47–12* ⊕ *www.fcs.org.pl* ᗏ *zł 6* ☉ *Oct.–Apr., Tues.–Sun. 10–4; May–Sept., Tues.–Sun. 10–5.*

❺ **Wielka Zbrojownia** (Great Armory). Two blocks west of St. Mary's Church, the armory is a good example of 17th-century Dutch Renaissance architecture. The ground floor is now a trade center, and the upper floors house an art school. ⊠ *Piwna, near Targ Węglowy, Stare Miasto.*

❷ **Wielki Młyn** (Great Mill). On a small island in the canal just north of St. Catherine's Church, the largest mill in medieval Europe operated from the time of its completion in 1350 until 1945. It was the largest Teutonic investment in Gdásk. The structure combined three functions: flour mill, granary, and bakery. It was equipped with 18 overshot waterwheels, each 15 feet in diameter, and the works represented a great technical achievement for the time. Today, it's filled with shops and boutiques, which are open weekdays from 11 to 7, Saturday from 11 to 3. ⊠ *Intersection of Podmłyńska and Na Piaskach, Stare Miasto.*

❾ **Żuraw Gdański** (Harbor Crane). Built in 1444, Gdańsk's crane was medieval Europe's largest; it's also Europe's oldest crane. It used to play the double role of a port crane and city gate. The structure was given its present shape between 1442 and 1444. Inside, a huge wooden wheel was set in motion by men walking inside it. The crane was used to unload cargo and also to put up ships' masts. Today, it houses the **Muzeum Morskie** (Maritime Museum), with a collection of models of the ships constructed in the Gdańsk Shipyards since 1945. At the museum ticket office, inquire about tickets for tours of the *Sołdek*, a World War II battleship moored nearby on the canal. ✉ *Ołowianka 9–13, Stare Miasto* ☎ *058/301–86–11* 🎟 *zł 8* ◷ *Oct.–June, Tues.–Sun. 10–4; July–Sept., daily 10–4.*

OFF THE BEATEN PATH

WESTERPLATTE – Ten kilometers (6½ mi) north of the Old Town, the peninsula of Westerplatte is home to a branch of the **National Museum.** World War II broke out here, at the entrance to the northern port. On September 1, 1939, a German warship, the *Schleswig Holstein*, began a bombardment of the Polish army positions here. A **monument** to the men who attempted to defend the Westerplatte for seven days against impossible odds was erected in the 1960s. Westerplatte can be reached by Bus 106 or 158 from ulica Okopowa, just outside the Main Town wall, or by water bus. ✉ *Majora Sucharskiego 1* ☎ *058/343–69–72* 🎟 *Museum zł 5* ◷ *Museum May–Oct., daily 9–4.*

Where to Eat

Because the parts of the Tri-City (Gdańsk, Sopot, and Gdynia) are linked by good public transit, it's quite easy to dine in any of the three regardless of where you are staying. Be sure to consider restaurants in the other parts of the Tri-City as viable alternatives.

$$–$$$$ ✕ **Euro.** Euro serves up the closest thing to nouvelle cuisine in Gdańsk, in a prime location, and in a lavishly decorated interior. Specialties include the veal escallopes with fettuccine in cream sauce and the substantial steak Madame Walewska with croquettes, prunes, and sausage in red wine. Fish dishes, notably eel and salmon, are also well worth a try. ✉ *Długi 79/80, Stare Miasto* ☎ *058/301–23–83* 🍴 *AE, DC, MC, V.*

$$–$$$$
Fodor'sChoice
★
✕ **Pod Łososiem.** "The Salmon" is certainly the most famous restaurant in Gdańsk, with a long-standing reputation. It is memorable for its elegant baroque-era dining rooms, well-oiled maître d', attentive service, and excellent seafood (the menu also extends to game and fowl dishes). Try the salmon or smoked eel to start, followed by flounder or grilled trout. You may want to try the famous Goldwasser vodka—after all, this is its original source. ✉ *ul. Szeroka 52/53* ☎ *058/301–76–52* 🍴 *AE, DC, MC, V.*

$$–$$$$ ✕ **Tawerna.** A scale-model sailing ship outside leads you into a series of wood-paneled dining rooms overlooking the Motława Canal. This is a pleasant place to linger over lunch or dinner. Tawerna's fresh trout is always reliable, but ask the polite, multilingual waitstaff about the fish of the day. The only complaints most diners have regard the price of the meal. Be aware, though, that this is a very touristy spot. ✉ *ul. Powroźnicza 19–20, off Długi Targ* ☎ *058/301–41–14* 🍴 *AE, DC, MC, V.*

$–$$$ ✕ **Czerwone Drzwi.** Behind the red door (that's what "Czerwone Drzwi" means in Polish) is a very elegant café-cum-restaurant, a favorite with Gdańsk's fashionable people (with well-stocked wallets). The atmosphere is a little posh but cozy all the same. The menu changes with seasons. Marinated herring is served in a variety of ways, and beefsteak with pepper in brandy is one of the trademark dishes. ⊠ *ul. Piwna 52/53. Stare Miasto* ☎ *058/301–57–64* ▤ *AE, DC, MC, V.*

★ $–$$ ✕ **Barracuda.** Although the interior may be rather simple—even a little dull—most people agree that this is one of the best restaurants in Gdańsk. The menu offers a tempting array of seafood dishes, which are the specialties of the house. Examples from the menu include pike-perch in dill sauce, or a sole-salmon duo served with spinach. No matter which you choose, you won't go wrong. Of course, there are also nonfish dishes, but who wants to eat chicken in a fish restaurant in a sea port? ⊠ *ul. Piwna 61/63, Stare Miasto* ☎ *058/301–49–62* ▤ *AE, DC, MC, V.*

Where to Stay

If you do not insist on staying in Gdańsk's Old Town, there are some great options of really classy hotels in beautiful surroundings in Gdańsk-Oliwa, Sopot, or Gdynia-Orłowo, all of which are covered in subsequent sections of this chapter. The city transportation system makes it easy enough to travel between the important sights of the three cities, using the combination of convenient commuter trains and fairly inexpensive taxis.

★ $$$$ 🏨 **Hotel Podewils.** This luxurious hotel is located on the edge of the Old Town, opposite the Gdańsk Główny train station. Rooms are stylishly furnished and decorated, the staff are uniformly pleasant, and the facilities are up-to-date; each room includes such extras as a trouser press, a hair dryer, and a DVD player. Each bathroom is equipped with a Jacuzzi tub. ⊠ *ul. Szafarnia 2, Stare Miaso 80–755* ☎ *058/300–95–60* 🖷 *058/300–95–70* ⊕ *www.podewils-hotel.pl* ↻ *8 rooms, 2 suites* ⚴ *Restaurant, minibars, in-room safes, cable TV, in-room broadband, sauna, bar* ▤ *AE, DC, MC, V* ⎰ *BP.*

$$–$$$$ 🏨 **Dwór Oliwski.** This is easily one of the best hotels in Poland. A peaceful oasis of low, thatched buildings surround a renovated manor and **FodorsChoice** are surrounded by lovely gardens, ponds, and vast woods (ask at the ★ reception for a map of walking trails through Lasy Oliwskie). Large rooms are furnished with luxurious simplicity, and some ground-floor rooms come with porte-fenêtres opening directly onto the garden. The hotel has its own spa facilities and an excellent French restaurant. ⊠ *ul. Bytowska 4, Oliwa 80–328* ☎ *058/554–70–00* 🖷 *058/554–70–10* ⊕ *www. dwor-oliwski.com.pl* ↻ *32 rooms, 8 suites* ⚴ *Restaurant, minibars, cable TV, in-room broadband, pool, gym, hot tub, sauna, spa, bar, meeting rooms, free parking* ▤ *AE, DC, MC, V* ⎰ *BP.*

★ $$–$$$ 🏨 **Hotel Hanza.** This hotel has the best location in town in a spanking new building set right on the Motława Canal. Though modern, the Hanza blends in with its surroundings nicely. All rooms are air-conditioned for those few weeks in summer when cooling off is really necessary. If you want to stay here, make your reservation as far in advance as possible, especially in peak season. ⊠ *ul. Tokarska 6, Stare Miasto 80–888* ☎ *058/305–34–27* 🖷 *058/305–33–86* ⊕ *www.hanza-hotel.com.pl* ↻ *53 rooms, 7 suites* ⚴ *Restaurant, minibars, cable TV, in-room data ports, Wi-Fi, gym, hot tub, sauna, bar, laundry service, meeting rooms, free parking* ▤ *AE, DC, MC, V* ⎰ *BP.*

Nightlife & the Arts

Although Sopot is where the Tri-City really goes to have fun, there's also good nightlife in Gdańsk. On summer nights, the Old Town teems with street musicians, families, and high-spirited young people. Look for the English-language publication *The Visitor* for information on more timely events.

The **Cotton Club** (⊠ al. Złotników 25, Stare Miasto ☎ 058/301–88–13) draws a mixed crowd to two levels of laid-back drinking and pool tables. The **Jazz Club** (⊠ Długi Targ 39/40, Stare Miasto) has regular live jazz concerts and the best bar staff in town. **Kamienica** (⊠ ul. Mariacka 23, Stare Miasto) is a popular bar decorated in murals showing the street outside.

Local and international performers take to the stage at Gdańsk's **Opera i Filharmonia Bałtycka** (Baltic Opera & Philharmonic; ⊠ al. Zwycięstwa 15, Stare Miasto ☎ 058/341–05–63). Gdańsk has a well-known theater company, **Teatr Wybrzeże** (⊠ św. Ducha 2, Stare Miasto ☎ 058/301–70–21).

Shopping

The Tri-City is not a shopping destination. Nevertheless, Gdańsk and also Sopot are good places to look for amber jewelry. You'll find souvenir shops and stores specializing in amber everywhere in town. In fact, they can't be missed they are so ubiquitous.

Sopot

18 *12 km (7½ mi) north of Gdańsk.*

Sopot is one of Poland's leading seaside holiday resorts, with miles of sandy beaches—in theory now safe for swimming (efforts are being made to deal with the Baltic's chronic pollution problems). Sopot enjoyed its heyday in the 1920s and '30s, when the wealthy flocked here to gamble and enjoy the town's demure, quiet atmosphere. Once the most elegant seaside resort in Poland, Sopot got a little too popular for its own good in the 1980s, when it began to look more down-at-heels. Today it is restoring its Riviera-like atmosphere. Much of Sopot's life transpires close to the Grand Hotel, which was once—and after the recent restoration, again—*the* place to stay in the area. Sopot's marvelous 19th-century pier is the longest on the Baltic.

What to See

The street of Bohaterów Monte Cassino (The Heroes of Monte Cassino), popularly referred to as **Monciak,** which stretches along the main urban axis of Sopot is one of the most important streets in town. The original German name, Seestrasse (Sea Street) tells you everything you need to know about its purpose. Monciak is lined with numerous pubs, shops, restaurants, cinemas, and galleries as well as countless 19th- and 20th-century houses. In summer, it becomes a venue for itinerant street theaters, musicians, and artists.

When you're walking on Monciak, heading east toward the water, you'll pass through the pleasant **Plac Zdrojowy,** which is filled with out-

The Rise and Fall (and Rise) of the Polish Riviera

SOPOT WAS ESTABLISHED in the 13th century as a small fishing village by Cistercians of Oliwa. Its transformation into a stylish resort had already begun in the time of the Renaissance, when wealthy residents of Gdańsk started visiting the place for recreation. Development almost ground to a halt when a surgeon from Napoleon's army by the name of Jean George Haffner settled in Sopot. Enchanted by the beauty and the magic atmosphere of Sopot, he decided to build the pier, the park, and the baths—and clashed with the locals. Although the fishermen grew to like the merry French doctor, they did not approve of all his fancy ideas. In those days, bathing in the sea was considered unhealthy and immoral. Nevertheless, in 1823 Haffner started the construction of a bathing institution with six faience bathtubs. Water was supplied directly from the sea and heated. In 1827, thanks to Haffner's efforts, construction began on the famous Sopot pier.

Sopot maximized its seaside resort potential in 1870s, when it became a stop on the railroad connecting Gdańsk and Szczecin. In those days, Sopot was inhabited by a population of almost 10,000; in summer, several thousand more people would arrive from the adjacent Polish territory that had been annexed by Prussia, as well as from "abroad." (In those days, Warsaw and Kraków were considered abroad). On 8 October 1901, Kaiser Wilhelm II (who also had his summer residence here) signed Sopot's civic charter. After World War I, it became part of the Free City of Gdańsk under the Treaty of Versailles. In the early 20th century, the city became one of the most popular holiday destinations on the Baltic Sea coast. The town enjoyed its heyday in the 1920s and 1930s, when the wealthy flocked here to gamble and enjoy the town's demure, quiet atmosphere.

Sopot survived WWII without much major damage (Hitler actually stopped for a week's holiday at the Grand in September 1939, as his army marched toward Warsaw). Some of the seafront promenade and a few of the magnificent hotels were destroyed in March 1945. In 1950s Sopot became an important cultural center, hosting Poland's first jazz festival. Even during the deepest and bleakest years of communism, people would still come to Sopot to have fun.

In the 1980s, the once-elegant resort became a bit down-at-the-heels. But its Riviera-like atmosphere and sense of luxury are back now—not least in the form of the freshly renovated Grand Hotel.

door cafés, flowers, fountains, and plenty of places to grab *lody* (ice cream). The **sculpture of a fisherman** is a reminder of Sopot's past as a small fishing village.

You can't miss the **Krzywy Dom** (Crooked House), which is almost in the middle portion of Monte Cassino (aka Monciak). Its eccentric and wobbly (and arguably, rather kitschy) shape is vaguely based on the style of the Spanish architect Antonio Gaudí. Inside you'll find a little shopping mall with some restaurants. Love it or hate it, it is the most photographed object in Sopot. Although it's a working office building—and arguably the interesting part is outside rather than in—you can pop into the lobby during business hours. ⊠ *Haffnera 6, corner of Monte Cassino 53* ☎ *No phone.*

The **Molo** (Pier) is at the very end of Monte Cassino. A simple wooden jetty was built in this spot in the late 1820s and was repeatedly extended through the first half of the 20th century. The current pier is 1,693 feet long and 33 feet wide and is longest such structure in Europe. In summer this is a focal point for exhibits, events, and commerce. The lower and upper decks are used by passenger ships and yachts. This is a favorite place for romantic walks. At the end of the pier, a viewpoint allows you to look out at the Grand Hotel, the panorama of Sopot, and the Bay of Gdańsk. This is where you catch ferries, water taxis, and harbor cruises. ⊠ *End of Monte Cassino* ⊕ *www.molo.sopot.pl* ☒ *zł 1.50 May–Oct., 8 AM–10 PM* ☉ *24 hrs.*

The **Muzeum Sopotu** (Museum of Sopot) is situated by the seaside promenade, very close to the beach, between the Southern Baths and Bar Przystań, in an early-20th-century villa. A permanent exhibition of early-20th-century decorative arts and furniture is on the ground floor, with temporary exhibitions upstairs and museum workshops in the attic. In the cellar is a restaurant. Concerts are held throughout the year, outdoors in the summer. ⊠ *ul. Poniatowskiego 8* ☎ *058/551–22–66* ☒ *zł 5* ☉ *Tues.–Fri., 9–4, Sat. 11–5.*

Ⓒ The reconstructed, medieval-era **Grodzisko** (Fortress) is Poland's only city-center open-air museum of this kind. Lying on a postglacial hill, 400 yards from the sea, it has steep slopes and is separated from the neighboring hills by deep ravines. ⊠ *ul. Haffnera 63* ☎ *058/301–52–28* ☒ *zł 4* ☉ *May–Oct., Tues.–Sun. 10–4; July–Aug. until 6.*

Where to Eat

Because the parts of the Tri-City (Gdańsk, Sopot, and Gdynia) are linked by good public transit, it's quite easy to dine in any of the three regardless of where you are staying. Be sure to consider restaurants in the other parts of the Tri-City as viable alternatives.

$–$$$ ✕ **Klub Wieloryb.** The one thing that stands out at "The Whale" is the gaudy and rather bizarre maritime decor. If you can get past that, the restaurant serves both seafood and meat, though the seafood usually wins out. Consider trying either the mussels or shrimp. There is usually a good vegetarian selection, for instance an omelet with four kinds of cheese. ⊠ *ul. Podjazd 2* ☎ *058/551–57–22* ▤ *AE, MC, V.*

$–$$ ✕ **Baola II.** The restaurant, which has a blue interior to evoke the sea, is in a former fishing cottage. In summer, the lovely and leafy garden terrace, though small, is very inviting. Duck in raspberry sauce and other excellent dishes are complemented with a decent wine list. ⊠ *ul. Grunwaldzka 27* ☎ *058/550–27–32* ▤ *AE, MC, V.*

Ⓒ **$–$$** ✕ **Tivoli.** This restaurant opened in 2000 in a renovated, 19th-century building. Good Italian food—everything from pizza and pasta to meat and fish—is served in an elegant interior decorated with the colors of Italian flag. There is a special children's menu, and yes it does include French fries. ⊠ *Bohaterów Monte Cassino 14/16* ☎ *058/555–04–10* ▭ *AE, MC, V.*

$–$$ ✕ **Złoty Ul.** In the "Golden Beehive," cuisines of many different countries buzz about. You'll find Tex-Mex, Brazilian grilled meats, Mediterranean seafood dishes, and Spanish paella. With so many different cuisines, it comes as a bit of a surprise that the food is actually okay, and often quite a bit more than simply "okay." The great location on the Monciak promenade makes this a particularly attractive place in the summer, when you can sit on the terrace and watch a never-ending show. ⊠ *Bohaterów Monte Cassino 31/35* ☎ *058/555–14–81* ▭ *AE, MC, V.*

Where to Stay

There are also great accommodation options in Gdańsk and Gdynia-Orłowo, all of which are covered in other sections of this chapter. The city transportation system makes it easy enough to travel between the important sights of the three cities, using the combination of convenient commuter trains and fairly inexpensive taxis.

★ **$$$–$$$$** 🏨 **Grand Sopot by Sofitel.** The Grand is not only Sopot's best-known hotel, it's also one of its best-known landmarks. Designed in the late 1920s, this spectacular neo-baroque structure used to house a casino, which in the mid-war period won the hotel both popularity and ill fame as well. Rumors of gamblers committing suicide both in the hotel itself and outside were willingly—and widely—spread. The hotel was completely renovated from top to bottom in 2006 and has regained much of its prewar splendor. Some renovation work continued at this writing. Rooms are furnished in a combination of modern and period style, but the result is very promising. ⊠ *pl. Powstańców Warszawy 8–12, 81–718* ☎ *058/551–00–41* 🖷 *058/551–61–24* ⊕ *www.orbis.pl* ⚲ *127 rooms* ♿ *Restaurant, coffee shop, room service, cable TV, gym, hair salon, sauna, steam room, beach, billiards, 2 bars, casino, nightclub, dry cleaning, laundry service, business services, meeting rooms, some pets allowed* ▭ *AE, DC, MC, V* ❏ *BP.*

★ **$$$–$$$$** 🏨 **Hotel Rezydent.** This classy art nouveau hotel in the heart of Sopot is reminiscent of the grand old days, when Sopot was known as the Riviera of Poland. The rooms have all the expected modern amenities and are beautifully decorated: marble floors, crystal chandeliers, and flower-patterned upholstery on stylish furniture. ⊠ *pl. Konstytucji 3 Maja 3, 81–704* ☎ *058/555–58–00* 🖷 *058/555–58–01* ⊕ *www.hotelrezydent. pl* ⚲ *62 rooms, 3 suites* ♿ *Restaurant, café, room service, pub, in-room broadband, Wi-Fi, minibars, in-room safes, laundry service, gym, sauna, spa, meeting rooms, parking (free)* ▭ *AE, DC, MC, V* ❏ *BP.*

$$$ 🏨 **Haffner Hotel.** If you like brushing against famous sports champions, movie stars, and models (albeit mostly European ones), the Haffner will be your scene. (Alas, the aura of fame may be in this case contagious—the staff can sometimes be as diffident as the movie stars.) Decor tends toward the rich and heavy (a lot of dark green and dark wood). There is a nice swimming pool, which incidentally does not smell of chlorine. The hotel bar, the Charlie Pub, does smell strongly of cigars, though. The restaurant offers a different, seasonal menu each month. ⊠ *ul. Haffn-*

era 59, 81–715, Sopot ☎ 058/550–99–99 🖷 058/550–98–00 ⊕ *www.
hotelhaffner.pl* ↩ *100 rooms, 6 suites* ♿ *Restaurant, bar, room service, minibars, cable TV, Internet, gym, pool, hair salon, dry cleaning,
laundry service, business services, meeting rooms, parking (fee)* ☰ *AE,
DC, MC, V* ⁺◎⁺ *BP.*

$$ ⌧ **Zhong Hua.** First things first: the hotel is a little—to say the least—
shabby and in need of a major renovation. It opened in 1996 and has
had no investment since. Still, it has a marvelous location directly on
the beach (the only beachfront hotel in Sopot) and is not without a cer-
tain charm. This curious place was once the Southern Baths, (Łazienki
Południowe), and its architectural features display Norwegian influence.
It is a Polish-Chinese joint venture, with the Chinese theme through-
out. The owners quote feng shui philosophy as the inspiration to the
decor—and indeed, there is a pleasant simplicity to the rooms even if
they are dated. In keeping with the theme, the hotel has a Chinese
restaurant. In summer there are jazz concerts on the hotel's terrace
every Thursday. ✉ *pl. Powstańców Warszawy 8–12, 81–718* ☎ *058/
551–00–41* 🖷 *058/551–61–24* ⊕ *www.hotelchinski.pl* ↩ *37 rooms,
12 suites* ♿ *Restaurant, room service, cable TV, Wi-Fi; no a/c* ☰ *AE,
DC, MC, V* ⁺◎⁺ *BP.*

Nightlife & the Arts

Stroll down ulica Bohaterów Monte Cassino to find the café, pub, or
nightclub of your choice. In August, the **Międzynarodowy Festiwal Piosenki**
(International Song Festival) is held in the open-air concert hall (Mus-
zla Koncertowa) in Skwer Kuracyjny in the center of town near the pier.

BARS & CLUBS Sopot has a reputation as a rather extravagant and decadent nightlife
scene. Especially in summer, the parties go on long into the night, per-
haps until the early morning. The crowds are mostly young, and the par-
ties are mostly cheerfully loud and chaotic (more like a Spring-Break
scene). If this is not your style, then you should avoid the beachside lo-
cations in the summer.

Mandarynka (✉ ul. Bema 6 ☎ 058/550–45–63) is a fashionable bar-cum-
club with plenty of comfy sofas where you can simply chill out.

Model types tend to congregate at **Number 5** (✉ Bohaterów Monte
Cassino 5 ☎ 058/550–49–44).

Viva Club (✉ al. F. Mamuszki 2 ☎ 058/551–53–23) is a giant, two-level
club on the beach with six bars, two dance floors, a stage with catwalk,
and a beach terrace for warm weather. It tends to draw a young crowd,
particularly for the frequent student parties.

Sfinks (✉ pl. Powstańców Warszawy 18 ☎ 058/550–48–79) is a mod-
ern, avant-garde club. During the summer season there are many live
concerts, and when the music is not live, there's always a DJ. It's closed
Monday–Wednesday.

With a strong Asian theme, the **Siouxie 9** (✉ Bohaterów Monte Cassino
9 ☎ 048/508–128–281) begins the day as a quiet coffee bar, but as night
falls, it turns into a popular bohemian hangout.

CAFÉS An atmospheric but modern, **Vanilia Café** (✉ Bohaterów Monte Cassino 36/2 ☎ 058/550—76–67) is a small, cozy café offering an excellent choice of coffees and cakes.

If you want to relax in a place where time seems to have stood still, stop in at **Art Deco** (✉ Bohaterów Monte Cassino 91 ☎ 058/555–01–60), a retro but stylish spot with a fireplace, sentimental photos on the wall, and grandma's armchairs for relaxing.

OPERA The **Opera Leśna** (Forest Opera; ✉ Moniuszki 12 ☎ 058/555–84–00) produced a series of famous Wagner concerts during the interwar period, garnering Sopot the title of "Little Bayreuth." The open-air amphitheater (the seating area is partially covered by a roof), is one of the most beautiful outdoor performing arts venues in Europe and has excellent acoustics. The theater complex, which covers nearly 10 acres, can seat 4,400; the orchestra pit alone can accommodate 110 musicians. Both classical and popular music concerts are given throughout the summer, but the theater also hosts many of Sopot's performing arts festivals. This is the venue for the **Sopot Festival**—a fixture on the Sopot summer calendar since the 1960s—and the **Opera Festival**, which was organized to continue the Wagner series. The theater also hosts the International Song Festival.

Sports & the Outdoors

HORSEBACK The **Hipodrom Sopot Plc** (Sopot Hippodrome; ✉ Polna 1 ☎ 058/551–78–96
RIDING & HORSE ⊕ www.hipodrom.sopot.pl) extends 100 beautifully landscaped acres be-
RACING tween Polna, Łokietka, and Rybacka streets in the region between the city limits of Sopot and Gdańsk. The most convenient street access is from Sopot—and the nearness of the railway station Sopot-Wyścigi (literally: the Races) makes it easy to visit. There are horse-riding schools, stables, break-in rooms, and training yards, a bar, and a restaurant. The grounds have a beautifully restored, 19th-century grandstand for watching frequent horse races, and it's the venue for numerous festivals, open-air events, and concerts throughout the summer season. Among the artists who have performed here is Tina Turner, who sang in front of a crowd of 70,000. In 1999, Pope John Paul II celebrated mass for 700,000 here. Entrance to the grounds, which are open from 7 AM to 9 PM, is free, but there are admission charges for the races and other events.

SAILING & The **Sopocki Klub Żeglarski** (Sopot Sailing Club; ✉ ul. Hestii 3 ☎ 058/
WINDSURFING 555–72–00 for club, 058/503–114–384 for Navigo Sopot ⊕ www. katamaran.sopot.pl) is one of the largest and most modern windsurfing centers in Poland. It's directly on Sopot Beach, close to the famous pier, drawing well-known competitive windsurfers. It is one of the few European clubs that has its own instructional programs for all ages, from seven-year-olds to senior citizens. The club also operates a gym and sauna. In the summer season, you can rent windsurfing equipment and catamarans, or buy sports or windsurfing gear from the seasonal shop, or take lessons in windsurfing (from the resident windsurfing club) or sailing (from the Navigo Sopot, the resident catamaran club) for zł 30 to zł 50 per hour. The center operates a restaurant and a small hotel, Pokoje Gościnne (zł80–zł 380; all rooms have private bath, satellite TV, and broadband Internet). In summer, there's also an open-air bar.

Gdynia

⑲ *24 km (14 mi) north of Gdańsk, 12 km (7½ mi) north of Sopot.*

The northernmost member of the Tri-City, Gdynia has less to offer the visitor than its southern neighbors. In 1922 it was only a tiny fishing village, but by 1939 it had grown into one of the Baltic's biggest ports. In addition to housing the shipyards and docks that dominate this industrial area, Gdynia has a beautifully landscaped promenade.

All the major tourist attractions in Gdynia are on the waterfront. Ulica 10 Lutego (10 February Street) leads you from the railway station up to Kościuszko Square and the Southern Pier. This is the most interesting and representative part of a modern Gdynia, where you'll see numerous public buildings with architecturural characteristics of the 1920s and '30s. Kościuszko Square (Skwer Kościuszki) is the sightseeing center of Gdynia, and moored in the dockyards that are right off the square are several historic ships that testify to the great ambition of mid-war Poland to become a maritime power.

If you're in Gdynia, it would be a shame not to take a walk along the **Bulwar Nadmorski** (Seaside Promenade) or visit the nearby Contrast Café for a beer. You can enjoy the beautiful panorama of the harbor and of the city from the top of **Kamienna Góra** (Stone Mount), easily recognizable by the large cross on its top. On your way to the mountain, you will pass the **Teatr Muzyczny** (Musical Theater).

Near the harbor, the **Muzeum Oceanograficzne-Akwarium Morskie** (Oceanographic Museum and Aquarium) is in the building formerly housing the Sea Station. In a glazed rotunda a model of the Baltic Sea bottom is on display; the museum also displays a rich collection of sea flora and fauna. You can see piranhas, barracudas, sharks, and other tropical and freshwater fish from around the world. The largest aquarium is the 16,000-liter (4,200-gallon) turtle tank, the home of loggerhead and green sea turtles. You might also spot a blacktip reef shark (the kind that has been known to attack swimmers). ⊠ *al. Zjednoczenia 1* ☎ *058/621–70–21* 🖃 *zł 11* ☉ *Tues.–Sun. 9–7, July–Aug. until 8.*

Near the *Błyskawica,* the three-masted frigate **Dar Pomorza** is moored and on display. The ship was built in 1909 in the Hamburg shipyards and was bought with public subscription money in 1929 to serve the Maritime School as a training ship. It visited 383 ports and traveled more than 800,000 km (almost 500,000 mi) during its life at sea. Just before the ship was officially retired in 1982, it had taken part in numerous sailing competitions, winning the Cutty Sark Trophy in 1980. Visitors can tour the engine rooms, officers' quarters, and kitchens. ⊠ *Nadbrzeże Pomorskie, al. Jana Pawła* ☎ *058/620–23–71* ⊕ *www.cmm.pl* 🖃 *zł 6* ☉ *Tues.–Sun. 10–4.*

In keeping with the nautical tradition of the town, Gdynia's **Muzeum Marynarki Wojennej** (Naval Museum), south of the pier on Bulwar Nadmorski, traces the history of Polish sea life from Slavic times to the present. Moored near the Naval Museum is the World War II battleship, the *Błyskawica,* (⊠ al. Zjednoczenia at Skwer Kościuszki ☎ 058/626–

The Youngest City on the Baltic

THE ORIGINS OF GDYNIA, originally a small fishing village, go back to the 13th century, but in truth the Gdynia you see today didn't really exist until the 1920s. In the aftermath of World War I, when the newly born Free City of Danzig (Wolne Miasto Gdańsk) no longer represented Polish interests, Poland still needed its own direct access to the sea, so the Polish government decided to build a new port at Gdynia. The construction of the temporary port began in 1921, and in only 10 years Gdynia became the largest and most modern port on the Baltic. The city was granted a town charter in 1926. The construction and extension of Gdynia harbor was one of the major projects of mid-war Poland.

36–58), which was built in Cowes in the U.K., was the fastest pre-war ship of its class in the Baltic Sea. Poland once had four destroyers in its navy, but *Błyskawica* is famous for the part it played in the battles of Narvik and Dunkirk (1940), in convoy duty across the Atlantic (throughout the war), and in the invasion of Normandy (1944). The crew sunk two enemy destroyers and various other escort vessels, damaged three submarines, and shot down three aircraft. A plaque commemorates its role in the defense of Cowes during a German strike in 1942. Renovated in 2004, and now sporting the natty winter camouflage it wore in 1941–42, this is by far the most famous naval vessel in Poland's history. The guides are bona fide sailors, who will show you the ship's bell (dating from 1937), a three-barreled torpedo launcher, a torpedo cross-section, scale models of other naval vessels, weapons, uniforms, and the Virtuti Militari medal that was awarded to the ship's crew for its outstanding service. ⊠ *Skwer Kościuszki 15* ☎ *058/626–35–65* ⊕ *www.mw.mil.pl* ⊠ *Naval Museum zł 3. Błyskawica zł 4* ⊙ *Museum mid-May–Oct., Tues.–Sun. 10–5; Nov.–Apr., Tues.–Sun. 10–4. Błyskawica mid-May–Oct., Tues.–Sun. 10–1 and 2–5.*

Where to Eat

Compared to the other two cities of the Tri-City, Gdynia does not have as many good restaurants. If you don't want to eat at your hotel, consider going to Sopot or Gdańsk for your meals—good public transit and relatively inexpensive taxis make it easy.

¢–$$　✕ **Etnica.** Bar, bistro, and restaurant in one, Etnica serves dishes from China, Cuba, France, Georgia, Greece, Hungary, India, Indonesia, Italy, Turkey—a perfect place for the undecided? The interior is really pleasant, spacious, and nicely decorated, with comfortable chairs and sofas. ⊠ *Abrahama 46, enter from Władysława IV* ☎ *058/661–91–26* ⊟ *AE, MC, V.*

Where to Stay

There are also great accommodations options in Gdańsk and Sopot, all of which are covered in other sections of this chapter. The city transportation system makes it easy enough to travel between the important sights of the three cities, using the combination of convenient commuter trains and fairly inexpensive taxis.

$$ ✗🖼 **Willa Lubicz.** In a lovely location in Orłowo, the leafy district of Gdynia that was developed in the 1930s, this small hotel (once the private home of sea captain Władysław Zalewski) is a short walk from the quiet little bay and the charming Orłowo pier. It's a stylish hotel with clean lines, and the interior has been restored to its original 1930s-era appearance; however, you'll find all the modern conveniences you would expect. The hotel's restaurant ($$–$$$) is excellent and worth a trip even if you don't stay here. The beautiful space has a real fireplace and serves such delicacies as sole fillets in sesame and saffron sauce, or wild boar stuffed with chanterelles. If you want to try something more avant-garde, try the strange-sounding but delicious onion ice cream with caramel and pistachios. ✉ *ul. Orłowska 43* ☎ *058/668–47–40* ⊕ *www.willalubicz.pl* 🛏 *16 rooms, 1 suite* △ *Restaurant, minibars, cable TV, in-room broadband, meeting rooms, free parking; no a/c in some rooms* 🖃 *AE, MC, V* ⦿ *BP.*

$$–$$$ 🖼 **Nadmorski Hotel.** In an area between the sea and a woodland nature reserve, this hotel feels far away but is actually about 1 km (½ mi) away from the center of Gdynia. It has great facilities, including excellent health and wellness programs (massage, fat reduction, oxygen therapy, etc.). Rooms are large and bright, decorated in a modern, simple style. ✉ *ul. Ejsmonda 2, 81–409* ☎ *058/699–33–33* ⊕ *www.nadmorski.pl* 🛏 *90 rooms* △ *4 restaurants, minibars, cable TV, in-room broadband, gym, spa, 2 bars, convention center, parking (free)* 🖃 *AE, MC, V* ⦿ *BP.*

$–$$ 🖼 **Hotel Spa Faltom.** The Faltom is as much a spa and sports center as a hotel, with a bowling alley, sauna, and even water slides in the swimming pool. It offers great wellness packages. Because it is fairly distant (8 km [5 mi]) from the center of Gdynia, the hotel offers particularly large rooms, with plenty of room to spread out. The lobby is all marble, and rooms—otherwise unremarkable—have pleasant peach-color scheme and comfy armchairs. But the real reason to come is the spa center, and this is where the real luxury is seen and felt. ✉ *ul. Grunwaldzka 7, 84–230* ☎ *058/671–57–11* ⊕ *www.hotel-faltom.com.pl* 🛏 *110 rooms, 3 suites* △ *2 restaurants, in-room broadband, cable TV, pool, gym, spa, bowling, 3 bars, dance club, meeting rooms, parking (fee)* 🖃 *AE, MC, V* ⦿ *BP.*

Nightlife & the Arts

The **Municipal Theater** (Teatr Miejski) (✉ Bema 26 ☎ 058/620–88–01 ⊕ www.teatrgombrowicza.art.pl) also operates a great Summer Stage (Scena Letnia) on the beach in Orłowo, where all shows are accompanied by the gentle humming of the waves.

Jazz artists from all over the world often perform in the **Sax Club** (Teatr Miejski, ✉ Bema 26 ☎ 058/621–02–26), which is located in the main building of the Municipal Theater.

Elypse (✉ Waszyngtona 21 ☎ 058/669–51–15) is a fashionable bar (with decent food, too), where you can often hear live music.

MALBORK CASTLE

★ ⑳ *45 km (28 mi) southeast of Gdańsk.*

One of the most impressive strongholds of the Middle Ages, the huge Zamek w Malborku (Malbork Castle) is the central feature of the quiet town of Malbork (the former German city of Marienburg). In 1230, the Teutonic Knights arrived on the banks of the Vistula River and settled here, aiming to establish their own state on these conquered Prussian lands. The castle passed into Polish hands after the second Toruń Treaty in 1466 concluded the 13-year war between the Poles and the Order of Teutonic Knights. For the next three centuries, Malbork served as the royal residence for Polish kings during their annual visit to Pomerania. The castle was half-destroyed during World War II, after which the building underwent a major renovation. Two-hour guided tours offer the best way to see the castle; tours are available in English, and there's an English-language guidebook in the gift shop. You can easily see the castle on a day trip from Gdańsk, but there is a hotel on the castle grounds if you want to spend the night. ✉ *Rte. 50, Malbork* ☎ *055/647–09–78* ⊕ *www.zamek.malbork.pl* 🎫 *zł 25* ⊙ *May–Sept., Tues.–Sun. 9–7; Oct.–Apr., Tues.–Sun. 9–3.*

┌─────────
│ OFF THE
│ BEATEN
│ PATH

GNIEW – Located 67 km (42 mi) south of Gdańsk on Route 1 (E75), the restored castle of Gniew specializes in medieval-style festivals. Staff stage realistic reenactments of jousting tournaments and sword fights, followed by wild boar roasts, in the town square and in the castle. The castle has a museum and a hotel. ✉ *pl. Zamkowy 2, Gniew 83–140* ☎ *058/535–35–29* ⊕ *www.zamek-gniew.pl* 🎫 *Museum zł 8, English-language guide zł 25* ⊙ *Museum May–Sept., Tues.–Sun. 9–4:30; Oct.–Apr. by appointment only.*

Where to Stay

$-$$ 🏨 **Hotel Zamek.** The hotel in Malbork's Lower Castle opened in 1993 in a restored medieval building. It's perhaps not as exciting as you might expect given the magnificent surroundings. The decor makes an attempt at re-creating "old-style" rooms, but unfortunately, the faux-Medieval look ends up not being very authentic or stylish. Having said that, dark wood and slightly gloomy atmosphere somehow fit in the context, and of course the location is unbeatable. ✉ *ul. Starościńska 14, 82–200* ☎ *055/272–33–67* ⊕ *www.hotel-zamek.e-tur.com.pl* 🛏 *42 rooms* ♿ *3 restaurants, café, cable TV, meeting rooms, parking (free).*

FROMBORK

㉑ *80 km (50 mi) east of Gdańsk, 64 km (40 mi) northeast of Malbork.*

Frombork (*Frauenberg* in German), overlooking the Vistula lagoon, was originally a Prussian settlement before it became the capital of the diocese of Warmia. The town's most famous citizen was Nicholas Copernicus, canon of the Chapter of Warmia, who lived here between 1510 and his death in 1543; he died here on May 21 and is buried at the Frombork Cathedral.

CLOSE UP

All Through the Knights

THE ORIGIN OF CHRISTIAN military orders—the medieval fighting monks—is linked with the Crusades, when these groups set off to protect and propagate the Christian faith but over time built their own mighty kingdoms. The "Knights of the Cross" left marks of their presence throughout the northern part of Poland.

The Teutonic Knights (Order of the Teutonic House of Saint Mary in Jerusalem; *Krzyżacy* in Polish) were founded in Palestine in the 12th century. They were enlisted by Duke Konrad of Mazovia in 1226 to help defend his northern borders against the Prussians (and spread Christianity). The order had its own agenda, establishing an independent, monastic state within Poland. The awe-inspiring sight of Malbork Castle gives you a sense of their power. They were defeated finally at the Battle of Grunwald in 1410, but the order's military powers weren't extinguished until 1809, when Napoleon put them out of the military business for good.

The Knights Templar, or the Poor Fellow-Soldiers of Christ and of the Temple of Solomon (*Templariusze* in Polish) were founded in late 11th or early 12th century to defend Christian pilgrims to Jerusalem. While members took vows of obedience, chastity, and poverty, the order itself grew quite wealthy and became the medieval bankers who protected transfers of gold between the Holy Land and Europe. The order was dissolved in 1312 by Pope Clement V, and their master, Jacob de Molay, was burned at the stake on charges of heresy. Most of the French templars were arrested or killed on Friday the 13th on orders of King Philip IV; hence, the origin of the superstition. The Knights Templar were active in the area of present-day Poland at the invitation of Duke Władysław Odonic and Barnim I, who sought protection from attacks by Brandenburg. Eventually, the Knights Templar controlled, among others, Chwarszczany—near Kostrzyn, Rurka, and Tempelburg (Czaplinek), among some 15 fiefdoms.

In the 1960s—decades before *The Da Vinci Code*—Polish writer Zbigniew Nienacki wrote a series of gripping young-adult novels that featured a crusading art historian and detective, a precursor of Indiana Jones. He traveled, mostly through northern Poland, to save treasures of art and history from the ruthless and greedy hands of art dealers. Every Polish child has read *Pan Samochodzik and the Templar Knights*.

After the destruction of the Templar order in 1312, the surviving members were incorporated into the Knights Hospitallers (*Joannici* in Polish), who were also known as Knights of Malta, Knights of Rhodes, or the Order of St. John of Jerusalem. Of the three major Christian orders, this one has survived the longest. The order emerged in 1070 in Jerusalem, where they ran hospitals for pilgrims. They took their name from Hospital of St. John the Baptist and only became a military order in the 12th century. Like the Templars, they were powerful and controlled vast properties all over Europe. After the collapse of the Kingdom of Jerusalem in 1291, they moved to Cyprus, then to Rhodes, and later to Malta. Eventually, the order made Western Pomerania their stronghold. They built numerous fortified settlements, only a few of which survive, including the castle in Łagów, and ruins of Drahim in Stare Drawsko.

4

Looking at today's dreamy town, who would have guessed that Frombork's history was so stormy, although the fact that the cathedral looks a bit like a fortress might provide a clue. Raided and looted during the wars with the Teutonic Knights, and then during wars with the Swedes, Frombork emerged from World War II severely injured; in fact, the city lost its official charter. The numbers tell the story: in 1945, there were just 250 people living here (compared to some 3,000 today). Between 1966 and 1973, the Polish Scouts Association ran a volunteer campaign called "Frombork 1001," and it is chiefly as a result of these efforts that the city of Frombork regained its splendor for the 500th anniversary of Copernicus's birth in 1973.

> ## THE FROMBORK ORGAN
>
> The Frombork organ is one of the best instruments of this kind throughout Poland. Its playing table has six keyboards, five manual and one pedal keyboard. The keys are made of Japanese rosewood, polished to a dark violet color, while the casing is of amaranth. The sound is deep and powerful, and the acoustic properties of the cathedral enhance it further. The sound carries for a full six seconds. Each July and August, it's the star of the International Organ Music Festival.

The Cathedral compound (*zespół katedralny*) contains all of Frombork's main attractions. It looks rather like a fortified castle. The silhouette of cathedral hill is visible from afar, whether you arrive by land or by water. The entrance to the compound is from the south, through the Main Gate (while admission to the courtyard is free, there are fees to enter each particular sight). Żegluga Gdańska operates cruises on the Vistula (⇨ Tour Options *in* Baltic Coast & Pomerania Essentials, *below*).

Fodor'sChoice
★ Frombork's **Katedra pw. Najświętszej Marii Panny i św. Andrzeja** (Cathedral of Most Holy Virgin and St. Andrew), an impressive Gothic structure, was erected in stages between 1329 and 1388, with further annexes gradually added in the centuries that followed. Most of the interior decorations and furnishings you see today, including the main altar, date from the baroque era. One exception is a late-Gothic (1504) polyptych, a gift of Copernicus's uncle, the Bishop of Warmia. It is now found in a side altar in the northern aisle (left-hand side), but until mid-18th century, it served as the main altar. At its center is a wonderful sculpture of Virgin Mary and Child, both smiling gently. The pipe organ, which was constructed by the master organ-maker Daniel Nitrowski, was fitted in 1683 to replace one destroyed by the Swedes; it has been reconstructed several times since then. Note the seven hats suspended under the presbytery vault: they are the hats of seven cardinals from different periods. Curiously enough, although we know that Copernicus was buried in the Frombork Cathedral, the exact spot of his tomb remains a mystery. ✉ *ul. Katedralna 8* ☎ *055/244–00–75* 💲 *zł4* ☉ *Daily 9–4 (restricted admission during Sun. masses).*

Muzeum Mikołaja Kopernika (Nicholas Copernicus Museum), in the former bishops' palace, tells the story of astronomer's life and work, and it also has a collection of telescopes, field glasses, and more general exhibitions of archaeological findings and stained-glass windows. ✉ *ul. Katedralna 8* ☎ *055/244–00–71* ⊕ *www.frombork.art.pl* ⌂ *zł 4* ☉ *Tues.–Sun. 9–4.*

In the **Dzwonnica** (Belfry), which is also called the Wieża Radziejowskiego (Radziejowski's Tower), you will find a Foucault's pendulum, which demonstrates the rotation of the Earth, a planetarium, and temporary exhibitions of modern art. ✉ *ul. Katedralna 8* ☎ *055/244–00–70* ⊕ *www.frombork.art.pl* ⌂ *zł 4* ☉ *Daily 9–4.*

The former **Szpital Ducha Świętego** (Hospital of the Holy Ghost), which dates from the 15th century, was destroyed and abandoned in 1945. After a renovation in the 1970s, it was turned into the **Museum of the History of Medicine**. Note the impressive 15th-century *Last Judgment* fresco in St. Anne's Chapel, part of the former hospital compound. There's also a natural "pharmacy" (i.e., an herb garden) on the southern side. ✉ *ul. Stara* ☎ *055/243–75–62* ⊕ *www.frombork.art.pl* ⌂ *zł 4* ☉ *Tues.–Sat. 10–4.*

NEED A BREAK?

Globus in the Water Tower (✉ ul. Elbląska 2, just down from the cathedral toward the Vistula lagoon ☎ 055/243–75–00) is a pleasant cafeteria, with tourist information and a souvenir shop.

Where to Eat

$–$$ ✗ **Restauracja Stara Gorzelnia.** The Old Distillery is easily the best restaurant within close proximity to Frombork. The chef will serve you a pepper steak "as you like it" prepared on a hot stone, with rich, blue-cheese sauce, homemade French fries, and steamed carrots with a pinch of cinnamon. Or perhaps you can persuade your dinner companions to share the farmer's fondue of tender neck of pork, bacon, ribs, and cheese. In addition to such sophisticated oeuvres, the restaurant offers also simple country dishes such as homemade blood sausage. While you can usually get a table without much of a wait, we strongly recommend reservations because the restaurant hosts many large-group functions. ✉ *Kadyny Country Club, Tolkmicko* ☎ *055/231–65–20* ⌂ *Reservations essential* ▭ *AE, MC, V.*

Where to Stay

$ ▦ **Hotel Kadyny Country Club.** Snuggled between a woodland landscape

Fodor'sChoice
★
reserve and the water of Vistula Lagoon, Kadyny is a most romantic location, though that's not a secret in these parts. Emperor William II made it his summer residence at the end of the 19th century. His summer palace (which was built in 1720 in the baroque style) is now a hotel, which was remodeled in the early 20th century. It still has a lot of old-time charm. Surrounded by what may be the most ancient oak forest in Poland, the Dąb Jana Bażyńskiego at some 700 years old, it's an oasis of comfort and luxury in this part of the country. The rooms are comfortably furnished, with modern fittings in stylish interiors, featuring lovely details such as wooden beams and large, arched windows. It also has

the finest restaurant in the region. ⊠ *Tolkmicko, 82–340, 15 km (9 mi) southwest of Frombork* ☎ *055/231–65–20* ⊕ *www.kadyny.com.pl* ⟿ *43 rooms* ⚹ *Restaurant, minibars, cable TV, in-room broadband, indoor pool, outdoor pool, gym, hot tub, sauna, steam room, miniature golf, bicycles, bar, meeting rooms* ⊟ *AE, MC, V* ⟨○⟩ *BP.*

¢–$ 🏠 **Dom Familijny Rheticus.** This pleasant, informal B&B (which the owners call a "family home") opened in 1997 in a historical building called the House of St. Joseph. All the simply furnished suites have private bathrooms and full-equipped kitchens, but you can also order breakfast made to order for zł 7 per person. One of the suites (#11) is a two-level studio with a cozy attic bedroom; another has a faux-fireplace (#7). A planned expansion (which was scheduled to open in the summer of 2007 at this writing) will add 10 more suites, a restaurant, and a meeting room. ⊠ *ul. Kopernika 10, 14–530* ☎ *055/243–78–00* ⊕ *www.domfamilijny.pl* ⟿ *10 suites* ⚹ *Kitchens, cable TV, bicycles, parking (free)* ⊟ *AE, MC, V* ⟨○⟩ *EP.*

POJEZIERZE DRAWSKIE

Jezioro Drawsko is 100 km east of Szczecin, approx. 200 km (124 mi) southwest of Gdańsk.

Imagine a square with a blue corner encompassing about 10% of its surface. While that might seem to be a rather small amount of blue if it were concentrated in a single part of the square, it would be a different story entirely if the blue were spread all over the square; even such a small amount of blue would influence its overall color. The same happens in the Pojezierze Drawskie (Drawsko Lake) District, where 10% of the total region is water, formed into lakes and rivers, shaping weather, plants, landscape, and maybe even human character. It is said that the people here are slow and dreamy, despite the sometimes fierce winds. In Pojezierze Drawskie you may quickly sober up when you see the scenery of the region that is often called the Szwajcaria Połczyńska (Połczyn Switzerland), a hilly and woody oasis amid flatter, sandier, and sunnier surroundings. The irresistible beauty of gigantic Drawsko Lake is known to have persuaded thousands of couch potatoes to become keen sailors, and send city-bound fashionistas out to hunt mushrooms in the nearby forests instead of designer bargains in Berlin.

The region takes its name from the river Drawa, whose capricious curves have made it a legendary route for Polish *kajak* (kayaking) fans.

㉒ **Jezioro Drawsko** (Lake Drawsko) is the 12th-largest but second-deepest lake in the country (262 feet deep). A withdrawing glacier left an area of some 4,500 acres sculpted with numerous bays, narrow straits, and 14 islands, providing a dreamlike dynamic space for sailing, canoeing, and kayaking. Drawsko is an oligotrophic lake, which means that its edges are overgrown with grass and water plants, and its fertile waters provide an ideal habitat for numerous species of fish. In the deepest part of the lake, you can find an ancient species of crab that has survived from the Diluvial era.

On its western side lies a 102,375-acre **landscape park** protecting some of the splendid glacier-formed terrain. It is full of low hills and valleys, grown over with beech, pine, and fir trees, little lakes, and unexpected stones left by the retreating glacier. The area is the habitat for a number of rare plants, with almost unpronounceable names—strange even for Poles—include wawrzynek wilczełyko (daphne mezereum, which is strongly poisonous), rosiczka okrągłolistna (drosera rotundifolia, round-leaved sundew, which is a carnivorous plant), and marzanka wonna (woodruff, gallium odoratum). There are also many beautiful blooming flowers, including species of orchids and lilies, throughout the reserve.

Czaplinek

㉓ *200 km (124 mi) southwest of Gdańsk, 100 km (62 mi) southeast of Szczecin.*

Czaplinek is the only town at the shore of Drawsko Lake. During the summer season, it is pleasantly filled—but not overcrowded—with sailors, surfers, fishermen, and other water-sports enthusiasts. The abundance of herons (Polish: *czapla*) is incorporated into the name, but the town's German name, Tempelburg, alludes to its medieval foundation. In 1286, prince Przemysł II presented the land to the Order of the Templars, who were supposed to defend the nearby border against assaults from Brandenburg. The Templars built a castle and founded the town under the Magdeburg charter. Later, control of Czaplinek frequently changed: the town passed between the Joannites (more popularly known as the Knights of Malta or Knights Hospitallers), Brandenburg, Poland, and Prussia. Its career as a tourist destination began after World War II (during which it was not greatly damaged), when tourists discovered the beauty of the region and began to have more leisure time to enjoy it.

Strolling around the little town is particularly pleasant, since you can see one of the two nearby lakes—Drawsko or Czaplino—from almost every street. Narrow strips of blue glitter at the ends of paths appear unexpectedly behind the chaotic courtyards of tiny tenement houses, and reveal themselves fully when you'll finally descend from the center to the promenade in the park along the bigger lake.

The picturesque **Rynek** (market square), with a statue of a fisherman in the middle, is the heart of Czaplinek. There are several interesting 19th- and early-20th-century houses overlooking it, and in the northwest corner, tourist information and a tiny museum, where a charming regional bricolage waits for visitors. It's easiest to see the old-fashioned small-town atmosphere if you stroll down ulica Studzienna, which extends from the southern edge of the square. A 2-km (1-mi) **promenade** extends along the lakeshore; it's here you'll find the open-air **amphitheater** where you might be able to take in a summer concert of classical music. In July, the town loses a great deal of its serenity as Harley-Davidson fans from all over Europe meet in Czaplinek for their annual get-together, filling the streets with joy, noise, and petrol fumes.

NEED A BREAK? If you need to rest after walking around Czaplinek, take a break in the pleasant **Caffe Bar** (✉ ul. Sikorskiego 17).

The **Kościół Podwyższenia Krzyża Świętego** (Church of the Exaltation of the Cross) was built in 1829. Karl Friedrich Schinkel, the architect of most of the important public buildings and churches in 19th-century Berlin, designed it along the rarely used plan of a Greek cross, in the Romanesque-revival style. Its majestic white shape is aided by well-planned steps and is free of unnecessary ornamentation. Inside, do not miss the original wooden gallery and interesting wall paintings that date from the 1950s. ⊠ *Rynek*.

Most of the visible parts of **Kościół Marii Panny** date from the end of 14th century, though the foundations include the remains of an older Templars' castle and chapel that date from the town's founding in the 13th century. The small, one-nave church underwent a major renovation after a fire in 1725. The present result is a genuine, noble mixture of severe stone outside with a lavishly decorated interior, spiced with exquisite furnishings: an 18th-century altar with a picture of the Coronation of St. Mary and six wildly beautiful white-and-gold spiral columns carrying a carved golden *baldaccino* (canopy) with triumphant Christ, which would not seem out of place even in a baroque church in Rome. Next to the church stands a wooden 18th-century bell tower; the bell inside was made in the Kołobrzeg workshops in 1730. ⊠ *ul. Moniuszki 20* ☎ *094/375–52–35.*

Where to Eat

Don't come to the Pojezierze Drawskie looking for gourmet dining. If your hotel or pension offers food, you'd be advised to take advantage of the offer or eat in the many simple places that serve unsophisticated and unassuming—though often quite tasty—local food.

¢–$$ ✕ **Elektor Restaurant.** One restaurant in Czaplinek—the one in the Hotel Elektor—stands above the town's simple eateries. It specializes in game and fish dishes, which are usually complemented by skillfully prepared produce from the local forests. Some of the best include local mushrooms—try *kurki* (chanterelles) in summer and *rydze* (agaric) in September—and a variety of berries. ⊠ *Hotel Elektor, ul. Rynek 4* ☎ *094/ 375–50–86* ▤ *AE, MC, V.*

Where to Stay

Although the Pojezierze Drawskie region is not bursting with tourist facilities, you can certainly find decent and even interesting accommodations. You may find a mansion glued to a post-Communist hostel, a pension in the middle of a forest, or even a little wooden hut with a view on a lake (⇨ Boating & Kayaking *in* Sports & the Outdoors, below).

$–$$ ⊞ **Elektor.** The most luxurious hotel in the Pojezierze Drawskie region is in Czaplinek. The modern building is unfortunately out of sync with the town's market square. The comfortable rooms do seem to belong to a better, more glittering world than what you'll see elsewhere in town, and the staff are very professional and genuinely kind, helpful, and obliging. Popular with tourists and female business travelers, the in-house spa offers both a fitness center and advanced beauty treatments. The hotel's restaurant, which serves excellent fresh fish and venison, is also recommended. ⊠ *Rynek 4, 78–550* ☎ *094/375–50–86* ☎ *094/375–*

50–87 ⚮ *27 rooms* ⚭ *Restaurant, minibars, cable TV, gym, spa, billiards, meeting rooms, bar* ▤ *AE, MC, V* ⓘ◎ *BP.*

$ ▦ **Drawtur.** If you are seeking proximity to the lake, you can't get any closer than one of the wooden huts of the holiday settlement called Drawtur. Among the offerings are cabins directly on the edge of the lake, so close that you can feed the fish or swans from your terrace. These simple, two-bedroom cabins—called *Brda* ("Tramp" in English)—are right on the lake, but you must reserve them a few months in advance. Note that if you reserve one of these cabins, you do have to pay for electricity use in addition to the nightly rental charge. ⊠ *ul. Pięciu Pomostów 1, 78–550* ☎ *094/375–54–54* ⊕ *www.drawtur.com* ⚮ *40 cabins* ⚭ *Restaurant, kitchens, sauna, beach, boating, fishing, bar, playground, parking (fee)* ▤ *No credit cards* ☽ *Nov.–Apr. by special arrangement only* ⓘ◎ *EP.*

¢–$ ▦ **Stare Kaleńsko.** If you have a weakness for unusual settings—and don't mind a simpler standard of accommodations—consider staying in a princely seclusion in the deepest woods with an entire, beautiful lake for your own use. The holiday resort Stare Kaleńsko is just a few kilometers southwest of Czaplinek, but the way through the forest is hard to find. The surroundings are superb; the main building has a lot of charm, and the nicest accommodations are inexpensive, two-room apartments, which have been renovated and provided with a fully equipped little kitchen. A restaurant on-site is open only in the summer season (or if there are enough guests present to open the kitchen). ⊠ *Stare Kaleńsko, 78–550* ☎ *094/375–52–56* ⊕ *www.starekalensko.com.pl* ⚮ *28 cabins* ⚭ *Restaurant, kitchens, gym, billiards, parking* ▤ *No credit cards* ☽ *Mid-Sept.–Apr. by special arrangement only.*

Sports & the Outdoors

BIKING   If you would like to travel around the lake or town on two wheels, you can arrange bicycle rentals from **Czaplinek Bicycle Rental** (⊠ Wałecka, at corner of Kościuszki ☎ 094/375–30–14).

BOATING &   **Biuro Turystyczne Mrówka** (⊠ ul. Wałecka 3 ☎ 094/375–50–67 ⊕ www.
KAYAKING   mrowka.pl) has kayaks for rent and organizes canoeing trips on the Drawa and Piława rivers and arranges yacht rentals on Drawsko Lake.

Jadwiga and Jerzy Grabowiec, the proprietors of **Czaplinek Yacht Charter** (⊠ ul. Żuławska 10 ☎ 094/375–42–83 or 048/692–747–459 ⊕ www.czarterczaplinek.com) can arrange for yacht rentals of Drawsko Lake for zł 90 to zł 190 per day.

HIKING   The easiest way to explore the area around Jezioro Drawsko is to get out and hike a bit in the surrounding area. There are two good nature walking routes, which have been designed specially to allow you to see some of the region's rare plant and animal species. The **Bielawa Trail**, on the biggest island in Jezioro Drawsko (197 acres), is marked with a cormorant symbol and is about 4 km (2½ mi) long. It takes at least 90 minutes to hike the trail at a steady pace, especially if you take the time to stop at the many marked observation and information points along the way. Particularly thrilling is the opportunity to see a cormorant colony on a neighboring island. To reach Bielawa Island, take the ferry from Czaplinek (⇨ Boat & Ferry Travel *in* Baltic Coast & Pomerania Essentials, *below*).

Zamek Wedel

㉔ *120 km (75 mi) southeast of Szczecin, 45 km (28 mi) south of Czaplinek on Rte. 177*

Although the origins of the Wedel Castle in Tuczno date back to 1338, it was completely rebuilt by its owner Stanisław Tuczyński between 1542 and 1581, when its main two wings were added as a beautiful example of Renaissance style. Note the characteristic *sgraffito* decoration—a black-and-white polychrome imitating the texture of a stone wall, the imposing Renaissance *attic,* and capricious proportions of the three wings with round towers "glued" to them. One of the wings was added in the 17th century. During World War II the castle was almost completely destroyed: included as a part of German defense line, it was blown up by the Soviet Army in 1945. It existed as a frightening ruin until 1957, when a complicated reconstruction process started. It was meticulously redesigned and rebuilt by the SARP (Polish Association of Architects); the process continued until 1976, when it was awarded a prize by the Minister of Art & Culture. Today the castle still belongs to SARP, which influences its not-so-strictly hotel-like atmosphere. After you have enjoyed nearby lakes, a peaceful old park, and gorgeous panoramas from the castle situated on high, you can venture on a short trip to see Drawski Park Narodowy, 10 km (6 mi) away, protecting surroundings of the Drawa River and its unique flora. The castle is now strictly a hotel and conference center, as are many such castles in Poland, so the only way to see the inside is to stay here. ✉ *ul. Zamkowa 1* ☎ *067/259–31–17* ⊕ *www. zamek-tuczno.pl.*

Where to Stay & Eat

★ $ ▦ **Hotel Zamek Wedel.** The simple, tasteful—mostly modern—double rooms at this hotel hold 80 beds. On special request, you can stay in the relatively luxurious "White Lady" suite (apartament Biała Dama), which has an illusionist wall painting. The restaurant ($–$$) will prepare traditional rich Polish dishes (lots of meats, poultry, etc.), elegantly served. The management of Tuczno castle can organize a surprising variety of activities: roasting a boar on the fire, *via kulig* (nighttime winter sleigh rides with torches), canoeing, cross-country driving, and "survival" trips into local woods, though these group activities are mostly offered for conference attendees. ✉ *ul. Zamkowa 1, 78–640* ☎ *067/259–31–17* ⊟ *067/259–31–12* ⊕ *www.zamek-tuczno.pl* ⟱ *40 rooms, 2 suites* ♻ *Restaurant, meeting rooms* ▤ *AE, DC, MC, V* ⦿ *EP.*

Zamek Joannitów

㉕ *150 km (93 mi) south of Szczecin, 130 km (81 mi) west of Poznań.*

The Castle of Knights Hospitallers in Łagów balances on a narrow spit of ground between two lakes in a lovely little town known more these days as a holiday resort and the site of a summer film festival. The surrounding landscape park offers dreamlike, shady forests, lakes, very clean air, and a pleasantly relaxed, albeit touristy, atmosphere (it never gets to be too much). The castle dates back to 14th century, when it was owned by the Knights Hospitallers. As seems to be the lot of nearly every castle, it has undergone several architectural changes, but what is exceptional is that these basically stopped in the 17th century. After that period, the building has managed to survive numerous wars without being seriously damaged or destroyed, and in Poland, that makes it a decided exception to the rule.

The castle consists of four two-story wings that form a spacious courtyard, and a tower. The courtyard of the castle is now covered by a glass roof, so it can serve as a ballroom or an additional restaurant in summer. The complex is surrounded by a park that offers access to a lake and a floating, boatlike pier. Since it has now been turned completely into a hotel and conference center, so the only way you can see the interior is to stay the night or eat in the cafeteria. ⊠ *ul. Kościuszki 3, 4 km (2½ mi) off E30* ☎ *068/341–20–10* ⊕ *www.zamek-lagow.pl.*

Were to Stay & Eat

$ ▣ **Hotel Zamek Joannitów.** The hotel offers both regular rooms and suites, including the fancily arranged Pokój Komtura (Commander's Room), with three windows and three different views, bright yellow walls, and a huge fireplace; the Katownia (Torture Room) is arranged like a medieval torture chamber with gloomy iron chains and tools, contrasting with the modern conveniences of a phone and TV. One thing that makes the rooms in the castle hotel stand out among their peers is that they are decorated and furnished to evoke the period castle atmosphere: expect oak herringbone-patterned parquet floors, massive wood antiques, and fireplaces. A restaurant ($–$$) in the castle's west wing has vaulted ceilings, chandeliers, and a vast fireplace. It specializes in old-style Polish food with a focus on wild game; but don't ignore the deliciously simple sirloin in juniper marinade. For a fancy dessert, head for Kawiarnia, a café hidden in the old refectory. ⊠ *ul. Kościuszki 3, 66–220* ☎ *068/341–20–10* ⊕ *www.zamek-lagow.pl* ⟿ *14 rooms* ⌂ *Restaurant, café, cable TV, meeting rooms; no a/c* ▤ *AE, MC, V* ⦶ *BP.*

Fodor'sChoice
★

Stare Drawsko

㉖ *5 km (3 mi) north of Czaplinek.*

Stare Drawsko is a charming little village on a narrow strip of land between Drawsko and Żerdno lakes. Its beautiful setting and ruins of 14th-century Joannite (Knights Hospitallers') Castle make it a favorite tourist stop. Much of Drahim Castle, built between 1360 and 1366 has been in ruins since the fire of 1758. What remains are parts of the 6-foot-thick walls and cellars. The castle was built to protect salt caravans that had to pass through the narrow Drawsko Lake on their way from Wielkopolska to Pomerania. As a border defense, it was frequently the site of military actions. In the 1960s, a shameful treasure was found in its dungeons: a collection of counterfeit Medieval coins and the tools with which they were produced (the tools had been stolen from the local mint); the find suggests that the Joannites were involved in serious forgery. ⊠ *Stare Drawskie* ☎ *048/504–150–817 mobile phone of owner*

Zbigniew Mikiciuk ⊕ www.drahim.pl ⊠ zł 5 ☉ May–Sept., daily 10–6; Oct.–Apr., knock loudly at gate or call owner for an appointment.

█ NEED A BREAK? If you feel like having a little something to eat while you're exploring the ruins of Drahim Castle, have a meal in a simple and inexpensive bar **Gospoda Podzamcze** (⊠ Stare Drawsko 4 ☎ 094/375–88–85), where you can get fresh fish and other wholesome, uncomplicated meals.

Where to Eat

¢–$ ✗ **Gospoda Podzamcze.** This simple restaurant serves good venison, fresh lake fish, and homemade pierogi in a very simple, unsophisticated interior. ⊠ *Stare Drawsko 4* ☎ *094/375–88–85* ▱ *No credit cards.*

Where to Stay

¢ ▦ **OWK Legnica-Pałac.** A secret retreat for in-the-know travelers in the Pojezierze Drawskie is Lake Siecino and this faux–Renaissance-style palace with a 16-acre English-style park on its southeastern side. The palace itself is now a hotel offering moderately priced rooms. You'll find plenty of ways to occupy your time at the hotel, including a private beach on the lake—the only one on this side of the lake, where the shore soon turns into lovely high cliffs. You may never forget the dramatic entrance hall lined with dark wood, a huge staircase, fireplace, and chandelier. A second 1960s-era annex is less attractive, and there are a few cabins in the park, but these don't disturb the dramatic views, though many people also camp in the park during high season. ⊠ *Cieszyno Drawskie 34, Złocieniec* ☎ *094/367–11–70* ▤ *094/367–29–82* ⊕ *http://oit.pl/okwlegnica* ⟿ *20 rooms, 2 apartments* ⟡ *Restaurant, in-room refrigerators, cable TV, tennis court, gym, sauna, beach, billiards, bar, meeting room* ▱ *AE, MC, V* ☉ *Sometimes closes Nov.–Mar.*

Sports & the Outdoors

HIKING & BIKING The **Spyczyna Góra–Prosino Lake Trail,** marked with the sign of a heron, can provide a fascinating full-day hike, as the full route is 16.5 km (10.3 mi) long. It starts in Stare Drawsko (5 km [3 mi] north of Czaplinek), near the ruins, and leads through Spyczyna Góra, the highest point in the area, and then to Kuźnica Drawska, where there is a heron observation point, and finally to the avian reserve around Prosino. The return trail is a straight route back to Stare Drawsko. Even if you have no interest in a full-day hike, it's worth it to hike even a portion of the trail. It's also possible to bike through most of the trail, instead of walking.

Bikes can be rented from **Zajazd Drahim** (⊠ Stare Drawsko 24 ☎ 094/375–88–12 ⊕ www.drahim.com.pl).

KAYAKING The shore of Żerdno Lake in Stare Drawsko is the point where a well-known kayak route on the Drawa River begins. It is called "Szlak Papieski" (the Pope's route), since Pope Jan Paweł II used to sail it as a young man in the 1950s. All the lakeshore holiday centers and resorts have kayaks for rent, including Biuro Turystyczne Mrówka (⇨ Where to Stay, *above*). **Ośrodek Nad Srebrnym** (✉ Stare Drawsko ☏ 094/375–88–21), a large resort on the lakeshore, rents kayaks and other water-sports equipment.

Połczyn Zdrój

㉗ *28 km (17 mi) north from Stare Drawsko.*

Połczyn Zdrój is the oldest and most important health resort area in north-west Poland. The healing properties of its waters were discovered as early as 1688, after which numerous hotels and spa lodges were built in the town. It has charming, small-scale architecture, similar to most spa towns. You'll find an amphitheater, a fountain, a concert shell, and even a gigantic outdoor chess-board. The main *corso* of the town consists of two streets: Grunwaldzka and Mariacka. Around the central **Rynek** (market square), you'll find the Kościół Najświętszej Marii Panny (St. Mary's Church), a Medieval church whose contemporary look was shaped mostly in late 19th century. South of the Rynek is a castle, nowadays the town library. Above all you'll find the architecture of nu-merous spa lodges, grouped in the vicinity of the park, with nice, though slightly outdated, cafés and restaurants.

If you want to discover the town's nostalgic atmosphere, with streets and alleys still filled with patients, the best place to head is Park Zdro-jowy. The garden was designed and created between 1836 and 1839 in a French geometric style. In the early 20th century, a spacious English-style garden was added, and the park today covers some 198 acres, all scenically arranged on the banks of the small Wogra River. Among its rare decorative trees, the most unusual is Jodła Jeffersona (Jefferson's fir), which has foot-long needles. ✉ *Enter from ul. Zdrojowa, at the end of ul. Kościuszki* 🎟 *Free* ☉ *24 hrs.*

NEED A BREAK? Take a break in the art nouveau **Café Parkowa** (✉ ul. 5 Marca 24 ☏ 094/366–22–48).

Where to Stay & Eat

Given the scarcity of good restaurants in the region, you would be ad-vised to dine at your hotel whenever possible. The restaurant in the **Hotel Polanin** (✉ ul. Wojska Polskiego 50 ☏ 094/266–21–58), which serves simple, traditional Polish food is an acceptable choice if you want to get away from your hotel.

$ 🏨 **Willa Hopferówka.** If you like health resorts with a nostalgic atmos-phere, consider a stay in Połczyn Zdrój, the main spa center of north-west Poland. Next to the park stands a villa that for many years served as housing for the spa's doctors. In 2002 it was fully renovated and turned into a pleasant pension offering rooms and, on request, even full board in the lovely dining room with a winter garden. The staff can help you arrange your treatments at the spa center. ✉ *ul. Solankowa 8* ☏ *094/366–61–88* 🖷 *094–366–61–87* ⊕ *hopferowka.ovh.org* ⚭ *Restaurant, cable TV, in-room broadband* ⊟ *AE, MC, V* ⦿ *BP.*

Sports & the Outdoors

BIKING If you like biking, there is a marvelous bike path leading from Połczyn Zdrój, 26 km (16 mi) south to Złocieniec, along the disused railway route. It reaches its peak at the level of Cieszyno Drawskie, where it passes by a wonderful clean Lake Siecino, a mecca for Polish divers, surrounded by opulent forest, and an presently absurd, but lovely, 19th-century railway station in Cieszyno Drawskie.

HIKING A few kilometers south of Połczyn you can walk through the amazing **Dolina Pięciu Jezior** (Valley of Five Lakes), with the lakes Małe, Głębokie, Okrągłe, Długie, and Górne placed like beads on a string of the Drawa River. To get to the start of the trail, take the bus from Połczyn Zdrój or Czaplinek, and get off at the Leśniczówka Czarnkowie stop. Walk back the way you came until you reach a parking lot (you will see a board with the description of the trail near the first of the trail markers). The easy, self-guided trail takes about two hours.

Borne-Sulinowo

㉘ *20 km (12 mi) east from Czaplinek*

Twenty years ago, the little town of Borne-Sulinowo couldn't be found on a map. Not because it did not exist. It did—and even flourished—but under a supervision of the Soviet army, as one of its main bases, the town was surrounded by a vast military polygon. After the Soviets withdrew in 1992, a unique site emerged for the grey-haired residents of the nearby village. The military town was built by Hitler's government in 1934–38 as a schooling base for the Wermacht artillery Grossborn; it was part of a complicated defensive line called the Wał Pomorski along the former borders of Poland and Prussia. Above ground is a regularly spread heap of elongated rectangular buildings with steep, tiled roofs, all set in a middle of a pine forests. The new inhabitants, mostly elderly people from ecologically damaged Upper Silesia region, went about their business, picking mushrooms in their gardens and watching wild animals wander through the streets at nights.

The town now has two star attractions. First is a series of mysterious underground town of bunkers, until now mostly inaccessible and unexplored, with underground streets large enough to fit small trucks and a complicated system of chambers, paths, and unexplored emergency exits. Second is the large, beautiful **Jezioro Pile** (Lake Pile), where the unexplained collapse of part of an island—perhaps due to old military experiments—has created an unbelievable underwater forest, with miraculously preserved trees still standing several meters deep in the water. To explore the secrets of Borne Sulinowo, including its numerous fortifications, bunkers, missile launchers, and unique heather fields, you should hire an experienced guide, though few speak English. Start with the owner of the local private military ethnographical museum, whose name is **Andrzej Michalak** (✉ ul. Orła Białego 25 ☎ 094/373–47–10).

━━━
■ NEED A
BREAK?

In **Sacha Café** (✉ ul. Bolesława Chrobrego 3 ☎ 094/373–37–44) you will find authentic Russian and Ukrainian food and drinks, including vodka imported from the east and tea from a real samovar.

ZAMEK KRĄG

29 *56 km (35 mi) north of Biały Bór, 85 km (53 mi) north of Szczecinek, via Rte. 205.*

The massive, Renaissance-era Krąg Castle was owned for many centuries by the Podewils family. It's a jewel that is practically in the middle of nowhere. With parklike grounds at an edge of a lake, the whiteness of its walls are brightly reflected in water. According to a legend, the castle possesses as many windows as there are days in a year, rooms as many as the weeks, gates as many as the months, and four high towers representing four seasons. Counting busily, do not forget to pay attention to Renaissance attics of this impressive building. Its shape today is heavily marked by changes that were made in the 19th century: an extra wing in Renaissance-revival style, as well as a new upper floor and a spacious terrace with an impressive staircase. After World War II, the castle was devolving slowly into a ruin until 1995, when new owners renovated it and turned it into a three-star hotel. And as with most of these castle hotels, the only way you get to see the interior is to stay here.

4

Where to Stay & Eat

$–$$ Fodor'sChoice ★ **Podewils Hotel Krąg.** The Podewils castle is gigantic, so it offers a lot of space and facilities to its guests. Hotel rooms are conservatively decorated in a rather cool style; though perhaps not evoking the period, the rooms do evoke a comfortable elegant country manor. They have all the modern comforts as well. Six suites are in the towers, and these all have particularly beautiful views. A favorite with large groups, the hotel hosts frequent seminars and meetings (there are five well-equipped conference rooms). For individual guests the castle has attractive packages to help you discover what the region has to offer. The restaurant ($–$$$) serves upscale Polish cuisine. ✉ *Krąg 16, 76–010* ☎ *094/347–05–16* 🖷 *094/316–91–11* 🌐 *www.podewils.pl* *38 rooms, 12 suites* *Restaurant, café, minibars, cable TV, in-room broadband, gym, sauna, bicycles, wine bar meeting rooms, parking (fee)* *AE, MC, V* *BP.*

SZCZECINEK

30 *18 km (11 mi) northeast of Borne Sulinowo.*

If the wind is blowing right, your first sensory impression of Szczecinek will be all-present scent of wood. It will accompany you wherever you go, reinforcing the point that this town is ruled by the trees. At its heart, you'll find Lake Trzesiecko, surrounded by a park. The town's streets run right along the water, the squares filled with flowers and trellises; the town's pier and lanterns may remind you of Zürich and the banks of Züricher See, only smaller in scale.

Szczecinek has always been torn between its competing identities of military and industrial center and tourist destination. Founded as a medieval fortress—which no longer exists—it received its official charter in 1310.

It was given the name Nowy Szczecin (Neustettin), and only in the 19th century has the present name ("Small Szczecin") prevailed. Its strategic location made the town an object of constant diplomatic ambushes and military actions. Through the centuries, control has passed between the princes of Pomerania, the Order of the Knights of the Cross, and various Polish kings. In the 19th century, the town was a center for cloth manufacturing, famous for the lovely sash belts (*pasy kontuszowe*), which were worn by the gentry. Another major business was the Meyer & Schumacher bell foundry. Later in the 19th century, it became a resort town.

Much of the life of the town centers on the market square, called **Plac Wolności**. The size of the local railway station may surprise you, with exaggerated proportions for the needs of a provincial town of 45,000. Though a bit shabby, the beautiful 19th-century details in the woodwork is complemented by stylish additions in the 1960s.

The **Ratusz** (Town Hall) is a two-level brick building with a massive, centrally placed tower. The style of the building is Romanesque revival, and it dates back to 1852. Try to see the interior, which has interesting stained glass in the hall on the first floor that shows scenes from a life of town. On the facade you can find a threatening sign: a mark of the water level during a big flood in 1888. ⊠ *pl. Wolności* ☉ *Weekdays 9–5.*

The **Muzeum Regionalne** (Regional Museum) is a permanent exposition of archaeological and historical artifacts found place in a tower of a medieval church that was destroyed many years ago. In addition to a collection of European baroque silver, it has one stunning object: on the second floor stands a statue of a pagan god Belbuk, which was fished out of Lake Lubicko, near Łubowo, in 1925. According to a local legend, during the Christian mission of Saint Otto, the local peasants took away the stone statue from its temple and threw it to the lake. ⊠ *ul. Księżnej Elżbiety 7* ☏ *094/374–09–77* ⊕ *www.muzeum.szczecinek.pl* 💶 *zł 2* ☉ *Sept.–June, Wed.–Sun. noon–4, July–Aug., Wed.–Sun. 11–5.*

The **Kościół Mariacki** is a brick Gothic-revival church that was consecrated in 1908. Its three-nave main sanctuary is supplemented by a transept, decorative stained-glass windows, and a high tower. The interior is consequently kept in the same style, with the exception of baroque lamps at the entrance, and the confessionals and epitaph in the northern nave, which were transferred from the now-destroyed Gothic church św. Mikołaja. ⊠ *ul. 3 Maja.*

┌▬▬
OFF THE
BEATEN
PATH

CERKIEW GRECKOKATOLICKA POD WEZWANIEM NARODZENIA PRZENEJŚWIĘTSZEJ BOGURODZICY (Greek Catholic church of the Birth of the Holiest Mother of God; ⊠ ul. Dworcowa) – Some 30 km (19 mi) north of Szczecinek, Biały Bór is one of the most hideous little towns we've ever come across, but on its dingy ulica Dworcowa stands this holy treasure of united architecture and painting. In 1992 the most famous living Polish painter, Jerzy Nowosielski (along with architect Bogdan Kotarba) designed a church for the local Greek Catholic community. Painted and decorated according to Nowosielski's plan—and in large part painted by the artist himself—the small church offers surprises both within and without. The exterior has a sophisticated white-burgundy and carmine-red coloring, with sacred figures painted on the facade. The interior offers unforgettable lessons about what power color, enhanced by the play of light and dark, can have. The few simple but stunning painted figures of Mary, Christ, and several saints have a truly magnetic character.

If you make the detour to Biały Bór, you might want to take part in the other unforgettable local experience, horseback riding. The town has **STADO OGIERÓW,** – one of the most famous stables in Poland. You can rent horses at Hubertus Pension (⊠ ul. Dworcowa 22 ☎ 094/373–90–66 ⊕ www.hubertus.pensjon.pl), where an hour of riding costs zł 25–zł 35, and a half-hour individual lesson costs zł 30.

Where to Eat

You should not expect to find a gourmet feast in Szczecinek, but if you look for simple places serving local food, you will not be disappointed. Most people choose to eat in their hotels; as in many parts of the Polish countryside, these usually have the best restaurants. There are a couple of decent pizzerias on the Market Square. The town has a few simple restaurants, none of which is expensive or is likely to take credit cards.

Bar Zameczek (⊠ pl. Wolności 15 ☎ 094/372–43–53) specializes in tender beef sirloin. If you are looking for dessert, line up at the locally famous **Cukiernia "Oleńka"** (⊠ pl. Wolności 18 ☎ 094/372–88–76), at the southeast corner of the market square. It sells delicious cakes called *jagodzianki* (sweet rolls filled with blueberries) and delicious homemade ice cream. One alternative to hotel dining is **La Paz** (⊠ ul. Ordona 4 ☎ 94/372–59–69), which serves Italian food. If during your stay in Poland you developed certain inclination or curiosity toward *pierogi,* **Pierogarnia Primavera** (⊠ pl. Wolności 18 ☎ 094/372–38–53) is a must. It's almost hidden, along a small path to left off ulica Zamkowa. In addition to pierogis, the bar serves tasty soups. **Restaurant Tawerna** (⊠ ul. Ordona 30 ☎ 094/712–82–90), which is on the lake in the city park, specializes in fish and sometimes has a bonfire and live music on Friday and Saturday night.

Where to Stay

$ 🏨 **Hotel Resiedence.** The small hotel is right next to the city park and 80 feet from the shore of Lake Trzesiecko. It offers a somewhat more luxurious—albeit less intimate—environment than the nearby Żółty Dom. Most of the rooms are spacious and pretty, and the hotel has laptops for loan if you need a computer to check your e-mail. The owners do not shrink from helping you plan your free time and will help you organize mushroom-picking, horseback riding, and tennis, and will even arrange transportation if you want to go into Germany. The restaurant serves traditional Polish cuisine but its atmosphere lacks warmth, thanks primarily to the interior design. ⊠ *ul. Lelewela 12* ☎ *094/372–88–50* 🖶 *094/372–88–52* ⊕ *www.resiedence.szczecinek.pl* 🛏 *15 rooms* ⚹ *Restaurant, cable TV, in-room broadband, massage, sauna, parking (fee)* ▤ *AE, MC, V* ¶◉¶ *BP.*

CLOSE UP

Under the Lindens

TRAVELING INLAND through this part of Poland can be bliss. The roads are lined with old trees—lindens, oaks, chestnuts—whose connecting branches create delightful shady tunnels, making each prosaic drive a leafy adventure into an opulent and friendly natural environment. The trees date back to the 1920s, when they were planted in volunteer campaigns by (then German) schools of the region. Regrettably, the alleys are today threatened with extinction; in this case, a law of European Union is against them, forcing the practical to compete against the beautiful. In the EU's opinion, the trees, which grow at the edges of many roads, are regarded as a potential danger to drivers and therefore they have been sentenced to death. Environmentalists have filed an appeal, and they continue to lobby for the preservation of this unique feature of the Pomeranian landscape. However, the future of the trees remains uncertain—so enjoy them before they fall.

$ 🏠 **Pensjonat Żółty Dom.** The "Yellow House," which was built in the 19th century, is on the prettiest street of town, overlooking the lake and the park. The villa has been thoroughly modernized, and a few of the rooms have either a balcony or terrace overlooking the park. The rooms, full of light streaming through big windows, are kept in pale yellowish or cream tones, with blue upholstery. There is a friendly little restaurant downstairs. It's considered among the best pensions in the area. ⊠ *ul. Ordona 11, 78–400* ☎ *094/372–34–82* 🖷 *094/372–34–81* ⊕ *www. zoltydom.com.pl* ⇗ *8 rooms* ⌂ *Restaurant, cable TV, parking (fee)* ▭ *AE, MC, V* ⦿ *EP.*

¢ 🏠 **Hotelik Orzeł.** If you are looking for a more economical option—assuming you are traveling by car—the Eagle Hotel is in the rather uninteresting motel in the suburbs of Szczecinek. The modestly furnished double rooms are so immaculately clean that together with the no-carpet policy you can recommend this hotel even to travelers with serious allergies. Huge tasty breakfasts are served personally by the owners at a long common table in the dining room. There is no restaurant, but it's possible to barbecue in the summer, and there is free parking for guests. ⊠ *ul. 1 Maja 74* ☎ *094/372–39–75* ⊕ *www.orzel.net.pl* ⇗ *6 rooms* ⌂ *Kitchenettes, cable TV, in-room broadband, parking (free)* ⦿ *BP.*

Sports & the Outdoors

The real draws of Szczecinek for most tourists are the surrounding lakes. Lake Trzesiecko's forested banks encompass 680 acres; the deepest point is 30 feet. On the southwest, Trzesiecko is connected, through a stream, with the smaller Lake Wilczkowo (225 acres). These lakes are the center of the region's activities.

HIKING   Several walking trails can be found in the region. The **yellow route** leads around the perimeter of the bigger lake. Another path leads through Las Klasztorny (Cloister Woods), which lie between Trzesiecko and Wilczkowo; the trail starts on Marientron (Świątki) Hill, where remains of a medieval settlement and Augustine cloister can be seen. If you want to admire the view, go to the nearby stone tower, which has a viewing platform. From here, you can see the south shore of Lake Wilczkowo, where an old-growth oak forest is protected in the Dęby Wilczkowskie reserve.

KAYAKING & WINDSURFING Four kilometers (2½ mi) north of Szczecinek lies moraine **Lake Wielimie,** the second-biggest lake in the Pojezierze Drawskie region. Despite its large surface area of 4,045 acres, significant shoreline, inviting islands, and shallow waters (the typical depth is just 18 feet)—making the water pleasantly warm in summer—it is still not overcrowded by tourists. Strong and ever-changing winds do make it a paradise for windsurfers. If you want to hike there, a trail to Lake Wielimie starts at Lake Trzesiecko in Szczecinek, running along the Niezdobna River. By car, take Route 20 northeast.

A river with a name which is impossible to pronounce (even for a Pole), the **Gwda River** flows through Lake Wielimie, to the delight of kayakers, who usually enjoy the relative vastness of the lake after the narrow, whimsical river.

OSIR (⊠ ul. Piłsudskiego 3 ☎ 094/372–10–91) rents water-sports equipment, including kayaks (z4 per hour, zł 15 per day), and organizes trips.

SZCZECIN

340 km (215 mi) west of Gdańsk, 515 km (325 mi) northwest of Warsaw, 240 km (150 mi) north of Poznań.

If you were to describe Szczecin in three words, the words would probably be green, aqueous, and industrial. Above all the city is green and lush, with civilized city parks in tune with Szczecin's superb urban design. It also has an untamed side: wild groves and meadows, numerous little islands only birds can reach that spread along the endless little streams, channels, lakes, and ponds. In the north, the town melts into the woods of Las Arkoński; from all sides on the other three sides, it is surrounded with forests: Puszcza Bukowa, Puszcza Goleniowska, and Puszcza Wkrzańska.

Though not directly on the Baltic, Szczecin is formed and exists in connection with water. The Odra (Oder), the second-largest Polish river, divides into two parts shortly before it reaches Szczecin, creating the unique landscape preserved in the Park Krajobrazowy Dolnej Odry. The divided river reaches the city as the Odra Zachodnia on the west and the Odra Wschodnia (or the Regalica) on the east. Numerous channels, tiny lakes, and even another short river called the Parnica cut through Szczecin, and farther north many merge into the Jezioro Dąbie, the city's largest lake. This area, although partly inaccessible, hosts Port Szczeciński, the harbor that impedes nature with industrial flair. The best point to admire this landscape is from Wały Chrobrego, the main town promenade, which is perched high above and along the river. The promenade is surprisingly peaceful even during tourist season.

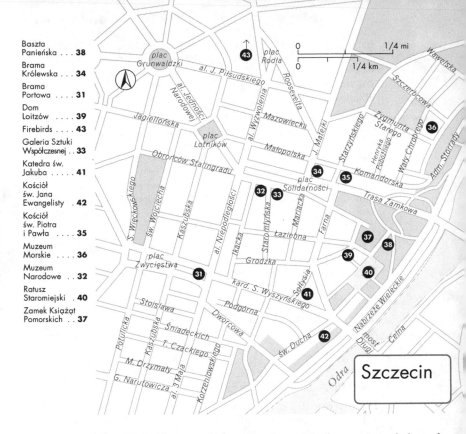

Szczecin

The port landscape, which creates Szczecin's characteristic skyline of
cranes, is supported in its industrial glory by a network of roads and
highways (particularly the Trasa Zamkowa, which was finished in
1996) that cut through and cross the peaceful land and water. It's supplemented by the buildings of Stocznia Szczecińska, one of the two
biggest Polish shipyards, a steel plant, and numerous other factories. The
urban, industrial look of Szczecin was created chiefly in the 19th and
early 20th centuries. The vast, gloomy, brick or concrete public buildings, reminders of the past Prussian glory, are knitted into a complex
unity that also includes a net of steel tramway lines, knots of railways,
and bows of steel bridges.

Despite its monuments, interesting 19th-century architecture, good museums, theaters, opera, and outdoor opportunities, Szczecin is not a typical tourist destination, and most tourist traffic bypasses the city. It is,
however, an excellent starting point for further explorations of northwestern Poland. To paraphrase Jack London's description of Oakland:
"Szczecin is a town from which one starts to see the world!"

Numbers in the margins correspond to numbers on the Szczecin map.

Szczecin: A Mirror of Pomeranian History

CLOSE UP

THE CHRONICLES OF SZCZECIN reflect the history of Pomorze (Pomerania): its changing owners, fields of influences, wars, and times of prosperity and collapse. The town existed already in the 11th century, although it didn't receive an official designation until the Magdeburg Charter of 1243. The town had been Christianized—relatively peacefully—by Otto von Bamberg in the 1224 and 1228—inspired by Polish king Bolesław Krzywousty. In 1278, Szczecin joined the Hanseatic Union, which, thanks to superb trade privileges that followed, improved its economic situation.

Until the 17th century, Szczecin was ruled by the dynasty of Piastowie Gryficcy, whose mighty princes favor various influences: Polish kings, the German Kaiser, and even the Danes. Accordingly, the inhabitants were a colorful mixture of nationalities and languages: Polish, German, Danish, Swedish, Dutch.

Szczecin's golden age peaked in 1478, when prince Bogusław X named Szczecin the capital of the recently united Pomorze Zachodnie (Northern Pomerania). Under his reign, Pomerania stretched from Stralsund and the island Rugien (now Vorpommern, in Germany) all the way to Łeba in the east. The last of the Piastowie Gryficcy line died in 1637, and control of Szczecin passed to the Swedish; cut off from its previous

commercial base, 17th-century Szczecin slowly changed its character, from a trading to a military center. Sold in 1720 by Eleonora, a sister of the Swedish king, to Prussia, it was turned almost into a fortress, a living proof of Prussia's military inclinations.

Looking at Szczecin today, you can see its modern roots in the 19th century, having been turned into an industrial hub by the Germans. It became the largest German shipyard in the this era. During this second golden age, Baron Hausmann, the architect who laid out Paris, redefined a vast part of Szczecin, adding a series of roundabouts and a system of streets arranged in starlike structures connecting into a larger necklace.

World War II proved disastrous for Szczecin. About 90% of its old harbor and 50% of the rest of the town were destroyed. It moved from Germany to Poland in 1945, after the Yalta conference. An influx of new inhabitants came mostly from central Poland, and the city was quickly rebuilt. Modern buildings replaced the bombed ruins, concrete settlements of block of flats expanded the town borders. However the character of Szczecin, a town of 420,000 inhabitants, did not change. The Szczecin Shipyard, one of the biggest in Europe, still produces up to 20 large ships per year.

What to See

38 **Baszta Panieńska** (Lady's Gate). This defensive tower was previously a part of the Medieval city fortifications that were otherwise destroyed in the 18th century. The responsibility of its defense belonged to the guild of tailors, who realized a difficult task by providing seven coats for princess

Anne. In honor of that deed, it was called "Baszta Siedmiu Płaszczy" (a tower of seven coats). ⊠ *Panieńska 47.*

㉞ Brama Królewska (Royal Gate). The magnificent gate was built shortly after Szczecin fell under the rule of Prussia, and its purpose was basically to show off Prussia's power. The gate, designed by Gerhard Cornelius von Wallrave and built between 1725 and 1728, shows a shield with the Prussian eagle, the chain of the Black Eagle Order, and a crown. Next to the gate, on the same square, a lone mast belonging to the steamship *Kapitan Maciejewicz,* from 1929, is a favorite photo opportunity. ⊠ *pl. Żołnierza Polskiego.*

㉛ Brama Portowa (Port Gate). Known previously as "Berlin gate" (Berliner Tor), this structure dates back to the years 1724 to 1740, when Szczecin was defended by a complicated system of fortifications. It is decorated with the personifications of Glory, and they are blowing their trumpets towards coats of arms of Friedrich Wilhelm I, king of Prussia. ⊠*pl. Brama Portowa, off ul. Niepodległości.*

㊴ Dom Loitzów. The Loitz family was a mighty banking family, who traditionally sympathized with Polish kings, sometimes with unfortunate results. They never recovered the borrowed sums for a Royal Navy project of King Zygmunt August, due to his sudden death. Nowadays, an art school occupies their town house, which was built in the style of the late Renaissance. ⊠ *ul. Kurkowa 1.*

㊸ Firebirds. This sculpture was created in 1975 by one of the most famous Polish sculptors, Władysław Hasior. It was originally planned to sit near the castle, but it caught fire just as it was supposed to be inaugurated. Years later, forgotten and falling apart in the park, the artwork was saved by fans from Wrocław, who collected and "arrested" the broken parts and agreed to give them back on the condition, that the town of Szczecin would take better care of the masterpiece. ⊠ *Park Kasprowicza, next to Teatr Letni.*

㉝ Galeria Sztuki Współczesnej (Gallery of Modern Art). The third branch of the National Museum in Szczecin occupies an 18th-century palace called the Pod Głowami (literally, "Under the Heads"). Unfortunately, the interior shows nothing of its original splendor, instead, it offers somewhat cold design from the 1960s. White walls, geometrical iron crates, and smooth, ornament-free solid woodwork (softened by 40-some years of patina) create a stylish, though forlorn, space to enjoy modern art. Although the gallery owns an exquisite collection of modern Polish paintings and sculptures, including works by Malczewski, Wyspiański, Krzyżanowski, and painters belonging to "Grupa Krakowska," the collection is not on permanent display. Instead, different temporary exhibitions take place. ⊠ *ul. Staromłyńska 1* ☎ *091/431–52–42* ▱ *zł 6* ⊙ *Tues.–Fri. 10–5, weekends 10–4* ⊕ *www.muzeum.szczecin.pl.*

㊶ Katedra Św. Jakuba (The Cathedral of St. Jacob). The cathedral's first incarnation was built on this spot in the late 12th century (it was then outside the city walls). A Gothic, three-aisle church was built between the 13th and 14th centuries. In 1456, the 390-foot tower and the vaults collapsed, probably due to miscalculation by medieval architects. The present tower, only 220 feet high, dates back to late 15th century and holds one of the biggest Polish bells, the baroque "Saint Jacob." Each of the church's three aisles is of equal height, so light fills the vast, homogenous space. Although partly rebuilt after World War II, the modest, white-walled interior of the cathedral already calls for further renovations. Artistic highlights include a 14th-century triptych from Ciećmierz and a 15th-century Pietà from Lubniewice. Do not miss the biggest stained-glass window in Pomerania; you'll see it in the eastern wall of the cathedral. It depicts St. Mary with Christ and the Holy Ghost, accompanied by various saints. In the main altar, a small box contains relics of St. Otto, one of the patrons of Pomerania. ✉ *ul. św. Jakuba 1* ☎ *091/433–05–95.*

4

㊷ Kościół Św. Jana Ewangelisty (Church of Saint John the Evangelist). This 19th-century Gothic church hides remains of one from the 15th century—include its beautiful wall frescos—and a beautiful 18th-century pipe organ. The church once belonged to the Franciscan order; when they lost their holdings as a result of the Reformation in 1527, their buildings were turned into a hospital and a shelter for the poor. They retained that function until 1957, when the buildings were returned to the Catholic church. ✉ *ul. św. Ducha 9* ☎ *No phone.*

㉟ Kościół Św. Piotra i Pawła (Saints Peter and Paul's Church). The parish church of Szczecin was built between 1425 and 1440 on the spot where the city's very first church was built. Built of brick, with a simple white interior, it was remodeled at the end of the 17th century and turned into a late-baroque structure. On the ceiling, a fresco depicts the Holy Trinity. The church is situated next to a busy road, so it's filled with traffic noise and has, to be honest, seen better days. Outside, notice the Pomeranian tracery (brick ornamental decoration) and terra-cotta late-Gothic portraits of town burgers on the facade between the windows. Curiously, the church belongs to the Polish Catholic (as opposed to the prevalent Roman Catholic Church of Poland) congregation. ✉ *pl. św. Piotra i Pawła 4/5* ☎ *091/433–85–32* ⊞ *Free.*

㊱ Muzeum Morskie (Naval Museum). This branch of the National Museum was created in 1950 and occupies a building designed in 1909 by Wilhelm Meyer-Schwartau. From its windows one can admire the splendid view of the port and the bank of the Odra. Given the museum's contents and the view, your curiosity for everything water-connected—sailing, shipping, and the sea—may be enhanced. Behind the main building is an open-air *skansen morski* (maritime museum); the old retired ships or their parts enjoy prolonged lives on the grass, far from water. Inside, the Naval Section presents several permanent exhibitions, but the highlights may very well be almost 250 ship models, including the *Mayflower*. There's also a collection of 18th- and 19th-century maps, navigation tools, anchors, and steam engines. ✉ *ul. Wały Chrobrego 3* ☎ *091/433–60–02* ⊞ *zł 6* ☉ *Tues.–Fri. 10–5, weekends 10–4* ⊕ *www.muzeum.szczecin.pl.*

㉜ Muzeum Narodowe (National Museum). Housed in a baroque palace—and in an annex across the street—the branch of the National Museum in Szczecin is devoted mainly to art: older paintings, sculpture, and an-

Born in the U.S.A.

THE KOŚCIÓŁ Polskokatolicki (Polish Catholic Church) arrived in Poland only in the 1920s, brought to the shores of their homeland by returning former Polish emigrants to the United States, where the church was first established in the late 1800s. The founder and the first bishop of the Polish National Catholic Church (PNCC) was Franciszek Hodur, an immigrant to the United States and a Polish Roman Catholic priest. The main impulse behind the foundation of the new church was to be able to celebrate Masses in Polish and to break through the domination of German and Irish prelates in America at the time. The new church rejected several Roman Catholic dogmas, and (since 1921) their clergy are allowed to get married. Back in Poland, history of the PNCC is not a happy one. After 1945, the communist authorities were reluctant to accept it as legal, mostly because Bishop Hodur was a U.S. citizen. Finally, in 1951, the authorities—who arrested some of the priests—forced the Polish diocese to separate from the PNCC proper, and they renamed it the Polish Catholic Church. Until communist rule ended in the early 1990s, the authorities exercised their power to control the church, and manipulated it to their own ends.

tiques (most 13th- to 16th-century Pomeranian), and some other Polish pieces from the 17th century. The building itself is a palace of the former regional parliament, Sejm Stanów Pomorskich, built between 1726 and 1727 and designed by Gerard Cornelius von Walrawe. The highlights of the museum include an 18th-century oak cross from the cathedral in Kamień Pomorski, richly sculpted 13th-century columns from the Cistertian cloister in Kołbacz, a portrait of Prince Filip I by Lucas Cranach the Younger from 1541, and a set of 16th- and 17th-century gold jewelry and robes, a stunning treasure found in 1946 in the crypt of the castle. At the time of this writing, the museum was closed for refurbishment but was scheduled to reopen sometime in 2007 or early 2008. ⊠ *ul. Staromłyńska 27/28* ☏ *091/433–50–66* ⊕ *www.muzeum.szczecin. pl* 🎫 *zł 6* ☉ *Tues.–Fri. 10–5, weekends 10–4.*

40 **Ratusz Staromiejski.** The Old Town Hall dates back to the turn of 15th century. It was rebuilt in the 18th century, which has created a charming architectural puzzle of styles. Since 1975, the building has hosted the **Museum of History of Town.** In addition to a permanent exhibition on the history of Szczecin, you can also admire a treasure found in the Podzamcze (Lower Castle) in 1999, a vast collection of 14th- and 15th-century coins and about 300 pieces of burgers' silver as well as some gold jewelry. An interesting complement to the exhibition is music, played from metal records on an original 19th-century jukebox. ⊠ *ul. Mściwoja 8* ☏ *091/431–52–55* ⊕ *www.muzeum.szczecin.pl* 🎫 *zł 6* ☉ *May–Sept., Tues.–Fri. 10–5, weekends 10–4; Oct.–Apr., Tues.–Sun. 10–4.*

37 **Zamek Książąt Pomorskich** (Pomeranian Princes' Castle). Szczecin is rapidly regaining some of its former prominence as a Baltic port because of its close proximity to Berlin. In fact, the city still carries many reminders of its Medieval heritage, including the grandiose castle, built on the left bank of Odra, which, due to its favorable defensive position, was inhabited as early as the 8th or 9th century. The first buildings of the current stone-and-brick castle, Stary Dom (the Old House) and St. Otto's chapel, date back to the 14th century and the reign of prince Barnim III, whose father Bogusław II decided to move the family residence from Kamień Pomorski to Wieża Zegarowa. The clock tower dates from the beginning of the 16th century; later in that century, the castle grew in magnificence during a grand extension project started by prince Barnim X; the expansion was continued by Jan Fryderyk. Eventually, the castle grew to have four wings and a courtyard decorated with picturesque loggias, reminiscent of Wawel in Kraków. Szczecin even received Italian interior decoration, designed by Giovanni Perini and Ottavio Amati, just like the royal seat. In the 17th century a fifth wing was added, creating a second narrow courtyard and a second tower (the bell tower, which, incidentally, offers the best panoramic view of the city). Since the death of prince Bogusław XIV in 1637, the castle fell into slow decline since he had no heirs to carry on the family building projects. The past 300 years have not been kind to the castle, which fell into the hands of the Swedes, Prussians, and French, only to be ruined by carpet bombing near the end of World War II. Today the reconstructed castle is a cultural center housing art exhibits, an opera and concert hall, the music department of the university, and a restaurant. Incidentally, you can also get married here. ⊠ *ul. Korsarzy 1* ☎ *091/434–02–92* ▣ *Castle museum zł 6, bell tower zł 3* ☉ *Tues.–Sun. 10–4.*

Where to Eat

$$–$$$$ ✕**Columbus.** If you are looking for a beautiful view while you dine, consider this one in a nice wooden pavilion on Wały Chrobrego. The interior may remind you of an old ship or battered port tavern. Unlike many places in Szczecin, the menu concentrates on meat rather than fish, offering hearty steaks with different additions. Beware that it's often noisy. ⊠ *ul. Wały Chrobrego 1* ☎ *091/489–34–01* ▤ *AE, MC, V.*

$–$$$$
Fodor'sChoice
★
✕**Chief.** According to Piotr Bikont, one of Poland's renowned food experts, Chief is the best fish restaurant in Poland. Owner Andrzej Boroń is an ichthyologist and fervent admirer of the sea. In the cellar, a pool holds live crayfish for the specialty of the house, crayfish boiled with dill. Fresh fish from all over the world is on the menu. This is not a hidden gem; it's well known, so book your table as far in advance as possible. ⊠ *ul. Rayskiego 16* ☎ *091/488–14–17* ⌕ *Reservations essential* ▤ *AE, MC, V.*

$–$$$$ ✕**Chrobry.** The faux-Medieval interior decor may be kitschy, but this restaurant has the most beautiful terrace in Szczecin, so it's a must when the weather is warm. Food comes in huge portions, particularly when you order the Knight's Trophy, which includes three kinds of meat served on a sword. ⊠ *ul. Wały Chrobrego 1B* ☎ *091/488–41–83* ▤ *AE, MC, V.*

$–$$$ ✕**Bombay.** If you tire of Polish cooking, consider a visit to this excellent Indian restaurant. Owned by Anita Agnihotri, Miss India of 1973, it serves a wide range or traditional Indian delicacies in a lovely and warm space. The service is excellent, too. ⊠ *ul. Partyzantów 1* ☏ *091/488–49–32* ▭ *AE, MC, V.*

¢–$$$ ✕ **Konik Morski.** This small, cozy modest restaurant is the local place to go if you want to eat fish that can honestly be called a "catch of the day." Everything you get here is really fresh and served in a simple way. ⊠ *Nowy Rynek 2* ☏ *091/482–60–88* ▭ *AE, MC, V* ☉ *Closed Mon.*

$–$$ ✕ **Na Kuńcu Korytarza.** The restaurant in the castle, which is decorated with vintage posters, is a favorite meeting spot of true Szczecinians. A strong point is extremely nice and helpful service. The imaginatively named dishes show culinary imagination as well; for instance, Dracula's Aphrodisiac is a black soup that is actually made using blood from the poultry served with dumplings, while Goose Temptation features foie gras. ⊠ *Zamek Książąt Pomorskich, ul. Korsarzy 34* ☏ *048/601–732–300 mobile* ⚠ *Reservations not accepted* ▭ *AE, MC, V.*

$ ✕ **Cafe Pravda.** The most fashionable place in Szczecin offers a deliciously sophisticated mixture of style and excellent coffee. The range of food and beverages emphasizes light, healthy food. The food choices include fancy salads, filled baguettes, a few kinds of pasta, and homemade red-beet chips. But this is a good place to go for delicious coffee and milk shakes. If you are dieting, a very practical "half-portion policy" involves paying an extra fee of zł 2.5 to order a half-portion of any meal. ⊠ *ul. Wielka Odrzańska 20* ☏ *091/812–22–89* ▭ *AE, MC, V.*

Where to Stay

In Szczecin, location is important, and we recommend you find a hotel in the vicinity of Kasprowicza Park, a green, charming, and quiet villa district within walking distance to the heart of town. This excellent location will allow you to explore the city and its green surroundings, and you will also get a taste of what a daily life is like since this is also an upscale residential area.

$$–$$$$ ⛉ **Radisson SAS Hotel Szczecin.** If you want real five-star luxury in Szczecin, you will have a limited number of choices in hotels. The Radisson, hidden in a modern skyscraper downtown, is the best large upscale hotel in town. Its good design offers comfort and all the modern amenities travelers—either business or leisure—will want. The location is on a noisy and busy square in the city center, but it's a good and convenient location. ⊠ *pl. Rodła 6, 70–419* ☏ *091/359–51–11* ⊕ *http://szczecin.radissonsas.com* ⮿ *369 rooms* ♨ *3 restaurants, minibars, cable TV, in-room broadband, Wi-Fi, indoor pool, hair salon, health club, 2 bars, nightclub, business services, meeting rooms, parking (fee)* ▭ *AE, MC, V* ¶◎❙ *BP.*

$$ ⛉ **Hotel Atrium.** This huge villa has been thoroughly renovated to provide all the modern comforts, including air-conditioning, an elevator, and an underground car-park. Although the updates took away a lot of the building's original charm, the rooms are spacious and cozy, with modern, solid-wood furniture and large, pretty bathrooms. The apartment has a large balcony, the only one in the building, as well as a direct entrance to the hotel sauna, with the priority of usage. Internet use is free. A spacious,

high-ceiling restaurant on the ground floor specializes in Italian cuisine at rather moderate prices. ⊠ *al. Wojska Polskiego 75, 70–481* ☎ *091/424–35–32* 🖷 *091/422–10–96* ⊕ *www.hotel-atrium.pl* 🖙 *30 rooms, 1 apartment* ⚖ *Restaurant, minibars, in-room safes, cable TV, in-room broadband, sauna, bar, meeting room, parking (fee)* ⏹ *AE, MC, V.*

$$ 🏨 **Park Hotel Szczecin.** This newly opened hotel in Żeromskiego Park, near the river, has a peaceful but central location that is perfect for exploring the city. With a traditional, mansion-house interior from the early 20th century, you may feel you're staying in a private country house rather than a hotel. There's also a lovely winter garden and a small but good spa complex. The traditional look of the rooms is complemented by flat-screen TVs. A big attraction is the indoor pool decorated with mosaic tiles and roof that reflects the delicate waves running across the surface of the water. An adjoining spa is especially soothing and welcoming. The hotel has no elevator. ⊠ *ul. Plantowa 1, 70–527* ☎ *091/434–00–50* 🖷 *091/434–45–03* ⊕ *www.parkhotel.szczecin.pl* 🖙 *32 rooms* ⚖ *Restaurant, minibars, cable TV, in-room broadband, indoor pool, health club, spa, meeting rooms, parking (fee)* ⏹ *AE, MC, V* ⏹ *BP.*

¢ 🏨 **Schronisko Młodzieżowe.** If you are on a budget but still want a decent room with a view, do not hesitate and reserve room 207 or 208 in the local youth hostel. Both of these doubles are freshly renovated, furnished with pine pieces (and TVs), and share a brand-new bathroom. The real draw is that both have their own huge terraces overlooking the garden and a small, quiet street. ⊠ *ul. Monte Cassino 19A, 70–467* ☎ *091/422–47–61* ⊕ *www.ptsm.home.pl* 🖙 *2 rooms with shared bath, 130 dorm beds (most rooms with 4–12 beds)* ⚖ *Cable TV* ⏹ *No credit cards* ⏹ *EP.*

WOLIN ISLAND

Poland's biggest island is a bit like a bear: it hibernates through the winter, only to wake up in late spring, live intensely through the buzzing, hectic summer season, and calm down again as soon as the school year starts in early September. Little remains from its early medieval origins, when the Wolinianie tribe ruled over the Baltic, impressing friends and foes alike with their might and wealth.

Today's Wyspa Wolin is a place of contrasts: swarming mass of tourists but also a peaceful nature reserve of beautiful, empty forests and meadows. Exclusive hotels and elegant prewar villas contrast with appalling concrete apartment blocks that violate the serene panoramas of most of the small towns. But the island's greatest treasure will not disappoint and has no contrasting counterpart: a beautiful coast of white, sandy beaches, cliffs overgrown with grass, and pine forests clinging to the cliff-sides, offering breathtaking panoramas of the changing sea and a kaleidoscope of sunrises and sunsets.

Wolin has two major resorts on the island, and both are worthy destinations. Where you decide to base yourself will depend on your own preferences. Międzyzdroje has the lion's share of the island's hotels, and it is a much more centrally located jumping-off point for exploring

Woliński National Park. Świnoujście has one particularly nice lodging option.

Międzyzdroje

 112 km (66 mi) northwest of Szczecin.

Międzyzdroje was a small fishing village surrounded by forests until the 19th century, when it was developed into a spa and vacation refuge for citizens of nearby Szczecin and Berlin. Nowadays, it is one of the best-known and most expensive holiday destinations in Poland, partly due to its film festival, which brings visiting stars in summer. If you search for fishermen's huts these days, you will search in vain. Międzyzdroje is no longer about old-fashioned simplicity. However, a few of the historic remnants remain, including the old villa quarter in the northwestern section of town and a lovely park and pier.

The main promenade is called **Bohaterów Warszawy,** and it leads along the beach, hidden from view at points by dunes overgrown with grass. From the beach you can admire the distant sight of Świnoujście with its huge lighthouse. The main entrance to the beach is marked with funny little white towers, and it faces the **molo** (pier). Originally a wooden structure, it was rebuilt and enlarged in 2004 and is now a favorite—and often crowded—spot for sunset walks. The **villa quarter** is on the outskirts of town.

East of the pier is a small **nudist beach,** so do not be alarmed by the sight of naked sunbathers. (Passing through this section of beach does not oblige you to get rid of your own clothes.) West of the pier is the original spa park, with a water-cure building from the turn of 20th century, nowadays hosting a pleasant café with a large terrace overlooking the park.

Farther west are the big modern hotels, where the name of the street changes to **Promenada Gwiazd** (Promenade of the Stars). Here, in the Hollywood manner, famous Polish actors leave imprints of their palms. If you feel like perpetuating the stardust atmosphere, visit a small **Muzeum Figur Woskowych** (Wax Museum). ✉ *ul. Bohaterów Warszawy 20* ☎ *091/328–25–70* 💶 *zł 10* ⊙ *Daily 10–4, later in summer.*

If crowds and noise of the main promenade affect your nerves, or if you encounter a rainy day, you may wish to visit a place dedicated to nature, the **Muzeum Przyrodnicze Wolińskiego Parku Narodowego** (Natural History Museum of the Wolin National Park). Instead of wandering in the national park itself, you can study the abundance of its flora and fauna under a roof. The highlights of the well-designed modern exhibition include a model of a sea-eagle's nest, a collection of 130 stuffed male *bojownik batalion* (ruff) in their mating colors, and a collection of amber. ✉ *ul. Niepodległości 3* ☎ *091/328–07–37* 💶 *zł 5* ⊙ *May–Aug., Tues.–Sun. 9–5; Sept.–Apr., Tues.–Sat. 9–3.*

Where to Eat

The best food you'll find on Wolin will be fish, the freshest of which will be obtained directly from fishermen each morning. You can buy fish freshly smoked or fried for you in one of the chaotic but friendly *budki* (fish stands) that you'll find right by the port on each town on the island. If you can find it, smoked bellona, a curious, elongated fish with a spike and a skeleton of fluorescent green, is excellent.

$$-$$$ ✕ **Chopin.** The most famous and expensive restaurant in Międzyzdroje is in the Amber Baltic Hotel. You'll find flickering candles on every table and live piano accompanying your meal. The menu of traditional Polish cuisine with cosmopolitan flair changes with the seasons and always includes both meat and fish choices. Roast duck is a specialty. The summer terrace overlooks the Promenade of Stars. ⊠ *Amber Baltic Hotel, Promenada Gwiazd 1* ☎ *091/322–85–00* ⊟ *AE, MC, V.*

🕊 **¢-$$** ✕ **Atlantis.** Specializing in fish, Atlantis offers a classical combination of Polish cooking with some Italian touches. The simple, cheerful interior sets a relaxed but refined mood. The specialty of the house is *fish shashlik* (fish kebabs), which is made from three kinds of fish. There's also a simpler menu of dishes suitable for children. ⊠ *Hotel Nautilus, Bohaterów Warszawy 25* ☎ *91/328–09–99* ⊟ *AE, MC, V.*

Where to Stay

$$-$$$ 🏨 **Hotel Amber Baltic.** If you love luxury and comfort or golf, or if you simply wish to impress your Polish business partners, choose the Amber Baltic, the most luxurious hotel on Poland's Baltic coast. The Austrian-owned high-rise, which has never learned the meaning of the word understatement, is a popular getaway for Germans. Rooms are slightly on the small side, but the outstanding views and immaculate service compensate. The hotel's restaurant is the best in town. ⊠ *Promenada Gwiazd 1, 72–500* ☎ *091/322–85–00* 🖶 *091/328–10–22* ⊕ *www. hotel-amber-baltic.pl* ↘ *191 rooms* ♿ *2 restaurants, café, minibars, cable TV, golf privileges, 2 pools (1 indoor), sauna, beach, bowling, beach bar, bar, parking (fee), some pets allowed (fee), spa, no-smoking floors* ⊟ *AE, MC, V* ⦿ *BP.*

$$ 🏨 **Villa Modiva.** Standing directly on Międzyzdroje's main promenade, this 1920s-era villa has direct access to both the beach and a lively tourist neighborhood. The stylish two-story building is a study in whites and neutral colors—no chaos of colors here! The result is comfortably cozy and serene rooms furnished with white-wood furniture made especially for the hotel. Decor includes black-and-white photos by Peter Lindbergh, spiced with dark-chocolate woodwork. ⊠ *ul. Bohaterów Warszawy 2, 72–500* ☎ *091/ 328–18–15* ⊕ *www.villamodiva.pl* ↘ *9 rooms, 4 suites* ♿ *Restaurant, cable TV, sauna, parking (fee); no smoking* ⊟ *AE, MC, V* ⦿ *BP.*

$-$$ 🏨 **Hotel Nautilus.** On the main promenade, the villa that houses this small hotel was built in 1913, and has beautifully restored woodwork. Comfortable, bright rooms have grey and navy upholstery, and most rooms have balconies and a fridge and tea-making facilities. Some rooms have particularly fancifully arranged curtains. ⊠ *ul. Bohaterów Warszawy 25, 72–500* ☎ *091/328–09–99* ⊕ *www.hotel-nautilus.pl* ↘ *12 rooms* ♿ *Restaurant, café, refrigerators, cable TV, in-room broadband, some pets allowed, parking (fee)* ⊟ *AE, MC, V* ⦿ *BP.*

$ 🏨 **Hotel Rybak.** An eight-story, modern building from the 1960s, the Rybak offers wonderful views of the sea and the nearby nature park from its balconies, which are a feature of most of the rooms. If you can get a room on the seventh floor, you'll get a choice of the best range of fully renovated rooms. The spa offers a relatively extensive selection of services. If you can't get a room here, a sister hotel, the low-rise Merlin, is also available and connected to the larger hotel. ⊠ *ul. Promenada Gwiazd 36* ☎ *091/328–11–21* ⊕ *www.hotelrybak.pl* ⏎ *100 rooms* ⚑ *Restaurant, café, sauna, spa, meeting rooms* ⊟ *AE, MC, V* ⦿ *EP.*

Sports & the Outdoors

If you are a keen golfer, you may wish to visit the **Amber Baltic Golf Club** (⊠ Bałtycka 13, Kołczewo ☎ 091/326–51–10 ⊕ www.abgc.pl/english/), the best golf course in Poland. It's 12 km (7½ mi) northeast of Międzyzdroje. The property of the Amber Baltic Hotel, it was designed by H. G. Erhardt.

Woliński National Park

45 *1 km (½ mi) east of Międzyzdroje.*

Just beyond the national park museum in Międzyzdroje, at the edge of the town line, a green route leads directly into **Woliński Park Narodowy** (Woliński National Park). At 42 square mi, it's one of the smallest national parks in Poland, but it's also one of the most splendid. The area is mostly covered by a mixed forest overgrowing green hills, with steep cliffs overlooking the Baltic sea to the north. Just after leaving Międzyzdroje are two excellent viewpoints: **Kawcza Góra,** which is 195 feet above sea level, and **Wzgórze Gosań,** which is 305 feet above sea level. The park offers protection to an enormous number of rare plants, including the *wiciokrzew pomorski* (European honeysuckle), *mikołajek nadmorski* (sea holly), and 16 kinds of orchids, which live in symbiosis with beech. Please remember that it is forbidden to pick any plant in the national park, even fruits and mushrooms. Among various rare animals and birds in the park are sea-eagles, which are present on the Polish coats arms. There's also a bison reserve on the path to Warnowo, which has beautiful gardens in summer. The park has two information points, where you can also get maps and brochures. One is in the Natural History Museum of the Woliński National Park (see ⇨ Międzyzdroje, *above*), and the others at the Bison Preserve (see ⇨ Zagroda Żubrów, *below*). ⊠ *Międzyzdroje* ⊕ *www.wolinpn.pl* ⚐ *Free* ☉ *Daily dawn–dusk.*

The two original bison in Wolin National Park's **Zagroda Żubrów** (Bison Preserve) were imported to the island 1976, from their birthplace in Borki, near Augustów. The happy couple soon provided several offspring, and today there are 10 bison who roam free in their fenced home. The information center here can give you maps and brochures on Woliński National Park. ⊠ *Leśna 15, Warnowo* ☎ *091/328–04–68* ⊡ *zł 5* ☉ *May–Sept., Tues.–Sun. 10–6; Oct.–Apr., Tues.–Sat. 8–4.*

Jezioro Turkusowe (Lake Turkusowe), which is at the southern end of Wolin National Park, has an unusual, deep turquoise tint, owing to calcium compounds from its existence as a chalk mine; it was accidentally flooded in 1945. Nevertheless, it's one of the most beautiful lakes on the island. You can't swim in the lake. ⊠ *Wapnica, 6 km [3½ mi] south of Międzyzdroje.*

Wolin

 15 km (9 mi) southeast of Międzyzdroje.

The town of Wolin at the southeastern tip of the island is at its best during the busy summer Międzynarodowy Festiwal Słowian i Wikingów (International Slav & Viking Festival). Thousands of early medieval history fans from all over Europe gather her to dress up like Vikings, simulate fights, demonstrate forgotten crafts, play music, and cook strange meals for the enchanted audience. Be sure to take a walk to picturesque **Wzgórze Wisielców** (Hangman's Hill) at the south edge of town, which has an ancient *kurhan* (burial mound) that dates back to the 9th or 10th century and a beautiful view from the top of the town and the bay. On the island of Ostrów Recławski a gigantic **Skansen** (open-air museum) is being developed at this writing. It is expected to cover 10 acres and represent a complete early-medieval wooden town. Part of the settlement is open already, and you can now see various crafts being demonstrated. There's a smithy, a pottery house, and even music workshops; you can also sail on a replica of a medieval wooden ship, called *Światowid* (after the deity Światowid / Svetovid).

Świnoujście

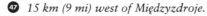 15 km (9 mi) west of Międzyzdroje.

With one of the island's most important harbors, the health resort of Świnoujście, which is on the far western tip of Wolin, is actually split between two different islands. The eastern half is on Wolin itself; but western part of the resort area is on the far eastern tip of Uznam (Usedom), most of which is German territory. The river Świna—from which the name of the town is derived—meanders between Wolin and Uznam before it finds its way to the sea; the gentle bay rewards with a splendid view of the seashore, as well as the distant German towns of Ahlbeck and Heringsdorf to the west, and Międzyzdroje to the east. Nearby is Karsibór Island, which has a small village with a modest but beautiful Gothic church but is mostly a nature preserve for birds and other animals.

The main train and bus stations are on the east (Wolin) side of Świnoujście, but there are only a couple of noteworthy sights on this side of town. A bike path leads from the ferry terminal to the most famous sight in this part of Świnoujście, the **Latarnia Morska,** which was built in the early 19th century. At 223 feet in height, it is the tallest lighthouse on the Polish coast. Climb up to the top for the marvelous view, or visit the little lighthouse museum in the base. In summer there's also the pleasant Pod Latarnią (Under the Lighthouse) for a drink or light refreshments. ✉ *Warszów* ☎ 091/321–61–03 ☞ zł 3 ☉ *Daily 10–6.*

Fort Gerharda is immediately north of the lighthouse. Running 1.5 km (1 mi) from the fort down the shore is the stunning **Falochron Wschodni** (Eastern Breakwater), a stunning, 19th-century Prussian engineering masterpiece that provides excellent views of the passing ferries and ships. Depending on the strength of the wind, you may be tempted to spend a great deal of your free time here, just admiring the view. At the end of the breakwater is a *wiatrak* (windmill); it's been a navigation signpost since 1823. ✉ *Warszów* ☎ *048/503–741–307 appointments to visit Fort* 🎫 *zł 5* ⏱ *Fort open irregularly, or by appointment.*

A ferry connects the Wolin and Uznam sections of town, and the inhabitants use it matter-of-factly as one would use a tram in any other city. The center of town—with almost all of the interesting sights—is on the Uznam side. Next to the ferry terminal, **Wybrzeże Władysława IV,** the main promenade, flows along the bank of the Świna. Going west, the promenade ends at Plac Rybaka, where you'll find an interesting little fishing museum with an almost unpronounceable name.

The **Muzeum Rybołówstwa Morskiego** (Museum of Sea Fishery) was founded in 1973 in the former town hall. Its permanent exhibitions teach about the variety of fish in the Baltic and display examples of the abundance of equipment necessary to catch them. There's also an extensive collection of rather beautiful seashells. A portion of the museum is dedicated to the stormy and capricious history of the town. ✉ *pl. Rybaka 1* ☎ *091/321–23–26* 🎫 *zł 5* ⏱ *Tues.–Sun. 10–6.*

North of plac Rybaka is the one of the town old market squares, plac Kościelny, where you'll find the **Kościół Chrystusa Króla** (Church of Christ the King), the town's most distinctive church. The main body of the church dates from the late 18th century, while the tower wasn't built for another 100 years. Inside hangs a 6-foot-long model of a sailing ship. ✉ *pl. Kościelny.*

At 100 acres, **Park Zdrojowy,** which has both English- and French-style formal gardens, is one of the biggest city parks on the Polish coast. It was built in 1827, and the designer, Peter Joseph Lenne of Berlin, was one of the most famous European landscape architects of the 19th century.

North and west of Park Zdrojowy lies the old sanatorium and villa district, the most beautiful part of town; it is divided from the beach by a green, parklike area. In this part of the city you'll find the Muszla Koncertowa, which frequently hosts summer open-air concerts. The beach itself is long, broad, and beautiful, but it is interrupted at each end—on the east by the river mouth, and on the west by the German border-crossing. From here you can see the Wolin part of town, including the lighthouse, Fort Gerharda, and the breakwater and its windmill.

The island of **Karsibór** is 6 km (4 mi) away from Świnoujście by ferry. Most of the island encompasses the **Karsiborska Kępa,** a wildlife reserve with 150 different bird species, just north of the main village. It's the home of rare eagles and kingfishers. The primary sight on the island is **Kościół Nawiedzenia NMP** (Church of Annunciation of Virgin Mary), which is in the main village. The Gothic church has a 19th-century Gothic-revival tower. Inside, take a close look at the main altar, which has a splendid late-Gothic triptych of scenes from Christ's Passion and the life of Mary.

Where to Eat

¢–$$ ✕ **Centrala.** This jazz club and restaurant is almost an institution in town, famous for good concerts and for its artsy atmosphere. The menu offers good choice of dishes including good breakfasts. For lunch, try boar goulash served in a bread bowl, or *sandacz,* pike-perch in caper sauce. ⊠ *ul. Armii Krajowej 3* ☎ *091/321–26–40* ▤ *AE, MC, V.*

¢–$ ✕ **Restauracja Antykwariat.** The warmly decorated restaurant, furnished with antiques in an old-fashioned style (the name means "antique shop" in Polish) serves traditional, simple dishes such as *pomidorowa* (tomato soup), *kapuśniak* (dense cabbage soup), steak and other grilled meats, goulash, and great sweet pancakes and hot chocolate for dessert. ⊠ *ul. Paderewskiego 14* ☎ *091/321–39–47* ▤ *AE, MC, V.*

Where to Stay

Although Świnoujście does not have the most fashionable of resorts on the island, it does have one particularly lovely boutique hotel.

☾ ¢–$$ ▦ **Kamienica Pod Kasztanami.** In the peaceful villa quarter of Świnoujście, this small gem is not directly on the beach, but it's within easy walking distance to both the beach and the park. The building is a carefully renovated, early-20th-century villa, and each of the rooms and suites is named after a sign of zodiac. For a real treat, take large "Capricorn" suite, which has an original wood floor, gigantic windows that flood the room with light, and a built-in fireplace to provide ambiance and warmth. The hotel offers romantic weekend packages that include a candlelight dinner and massages, but this is also a child-friendly hotel. There's a small art gallery, spa, and a good restaurant. ⊠ *ul. Paderewskiego 14/1, 72–600* ☎ *091/321–39–47* ⊕ *www.pod-kasztanami.pl* ⤳ *7 rooms, 3 suites* ⅃ *Restaurant, cable TV, in-room broadband, sauna, spa, parking (fee)* ▤ *AE, MC, V* ⦿ *EP.*

KAMIEŃ POMORSKI

48 *90 km (55 mi) north of Szczecin.*

Once a member of the powerful Hanseatic Union, the small town of Kamień Pomorski sits on the mainland across the mouth of the bay from Świnoujście. Its quiet streets may offer a welcome respite from the touristy coast. The town's name (which means Pomeranian Stone) comes from the huge boulder in the water outside Wyspa Chrząszczewska. The old walls that once encircled the town are no longer complete, but portions have survived, including the gateway, Brama Wolińska, on the west end of the Rynek (market square). Also on the square is a well-preserved town hall, but the town's most impressive structure is its late-Romanesque cathedral, with a splendid baroque organ. Frequent organ concerts take place in the cathedral, and there's a yearly International Organ and Chamber Music Festival in June and July. Regular bus service connects Szczecin, Kamień Pomorski, and Międzyzdroje.

At one point, the bishop of Pomerania resided in Kamień Pomorski. The late-Gothic **Bishops' Palace,** which dates to the 16th century is today a Catholic Cultural Centre. A stroll through the market square will reward you with a sight of elegant Gothic **town hall,** which has abundant tracery decoration of its western facade, contrasting with sad and grey concrete communist-era housing.

Fodor's Choice The most noteworthy sight in Kamień Pomorski is the grand, Ro-
★ manesque-Gothic **Katedra św. Jana Chrzciciela** (Cathedral of Saint John
the Baptist), which is surrounded by majestic old trees. Its construction
took 300 years, from the 13th through 15th centuries, and bridged together various architectonic styles, from Romanesque to baroque. It's organ
is the best in Poland, and perhaps one of the very best in all of Europe.

While admiring the architecture of the cross-shape sanctuary, notice such
details as a **chapel** on the presbytery side with a Romanesque arch that
is decorated with a animals on the sides and frescos with dragons on
the vault of the chapel. Look also at the **main altar,** which was created
in the early 16th century and shows the Assumption of Mary in the late-
Gothic style. The Gothic **baptismal font** in the north part of transept is
surrounded with a charming Pomeranian-style baroque grating from 1685.
On the northern wall of presbytery hang two paintings from the workshop of Lucas Cranach the Elder. A **baroque painting of Jesus** on the
cross with Mary is believed to have miraculously shed drops of blood
after it was brought from Brzostowice to the cathedral after the World
War II by those "relocated" from Eastern Galicia. The cathedral's famous **pipe organ** was commissioned by Prince Ernest Bogusław von Croy
and built by Friedrich Breyer of Stralsund; it was decorated by Martin
Edelber and Johan Grundmann, who praised organ music as a perfect
heavenly treat worshipping God.

The loveliest part of the cathedral is its **cloister,** the only medieval-era
garden that has survived in Pomerania. You will find there 500-year-
old thuja trees in addition to 350-year-old oaks. A subtle, arched gallery
surrounds the garden, with medieval, Renaissance, and baroque grave-
stones set into the walls. The beautiful play of light and shadow may
encourage you to linger. In summer, it's worth climbing the **Tower** to
enjoy the marvelous views. ⊠ *pl. Katedralny* ☎ *No phone* ⌕ *Cathedral free, Cloister & Tower al 2* ⊙ *Daily 10–6.*

Close to the Cathedral, the Brama Wolińska, a part of the 14th-century
fortifications, houses a small but interesting Muzeum Kamieni (Museum
of Precious Stones), which has a good collection of amber. ⊠ *ul. Słowackiego 1* ☎ *091/382–42–43* ⌕ *zł 5* ⊙ *Daily 10–6.*

**NEED A
BREAK?** The best restaurants in Kamień Pomorski are in the hotels. If you want to venture out on your own, consider trying the fish filet cooked in beer or the stuffed
perch at the very simple tavern **Magellan** (⊠ ul. Wysockiego 5 ☎ 091/382–
14–54).

**OFF THE
BEATEN
PATH** **TRZĘSACZ –** About 20 km (12½ mi) northeast of Kamień Pomorski, you
can visit the ruins of a Gothic church that has been partly swallowed
by the sea between the villages of Trzęsacz and Pobierowo. Originally,
this church was built 2 km (⅔ mi) from the shore, but during the centuries the water steadily washed away sand, pushing the drop-off farther and farther inland. Finally, in 1874, the last service was held and
the church decorates evacuated, though the building didn't collapse
until just after the turn of the 20th century. Nowadays, only one wall

with high Gothic arches remains, and even this may soon disappear, as the sea approaches further.

If you like horseback riding, consider popping into **OŚRODEK WCZASOWO-JEŻDZIECKI W TRZĘSACZU** (⊠ ul. Kamieńska 9, Rewal ☎ 091/386–27–00 ⊕ www.palac-trzesacz.pl), which has an active stable. While you might be tempted to stay overnight in the old mansion house, which is now a hotel, the rooms here are very basic and somewhat less palatial than you might expect from a hotel described as a "mansion."

Where to Stay & Eat

There are few good choices in Kamień, but the hotels that do exist match the town's size and atmosphere wonderfully. During the International Organ Music Festival in summer (mid-June to late August), hotels often fill up on the days of famous concerts.

¢ ✕▦ **Pod Muzami.** The best hotel in Kamień occupies a lovely 18th-century house. A thorough renovation in 1994 preserved and protected the beautiful old woodwork, windows, and uneven texture of the walls. The interior design doesn't take full advantage of the building's potential and is mostly—and blandly—modern, but the rooms are bright and clean, with exposed wood beams and pine furniture. The restaurant (¢–$$) serves traditional Polish cuisine of the region, and it's also the town's best. ⊠ ul. Gryfitów 1, 72–400 ☎ 91/382–22–41 ⊕ www.podmuzami.pl ⤴ 30 rooms ⚹ Restaurant, cable TV, meeting room ▤ MC, V ¶◎¶ EP.

¢–$ ▦ **Hotel Staromiejski.** The biggest advantage of this hotel is its great location right in the heart of town. You have a beautiful, panoramic view of the waters of the Zalew Kamieński and of Wyspa Chrząszczewska. ⊠ ul. Rybacka 3 ☎ 91/382–26–44 ⊕ www.hotel-staromiejski.pl ⤴ 36 rooms ⚹ Restaurant, café, cable TV, meeting room ▤ AE, MC, V ¶◎¶ EP.

BALTIC COAST & POMERANIA ESSENTIALS

Transportation

BY AIR

Gdańsk has the main airport in northeastern Poland with regular service, both domestic and international (LOT, Direct Fly, Lufthansa, Norwegian, SAS, and Wizzair flights). The airport is expanding, and the number of connections is growing.

Szczecin is served by LOT, Ryanair, and Centralwings flights, connecting the city to Warsaw, London Stansted, and Dublin.

🛪 Airlines **Centralwings** ⊕ www.centralwings.com. **Direct Fly** ⊕ www.directfly.pl. **LOT** ☎ 058/348-12-60 in Gdańsk. **Lufthansa** ⊕ www.lufthansa.com. **Norwegian** ⊕ www.norwegian.no. **Ryanair** ⊕ www.ryanair.com. **SAS** ☎ 058/348-12-38 in Gdańsk. **Wizzair** ⊕ www.wizzair.com.

AIRPORTS Gdańsk's airport is 16 km (10 mi) out of town in Rębiechowo and can be reached by Bus B (night Bus N3) from the center of Gdańsk, or Bus 510 from Gdynia, or by taxi (about 40 zł to Gdańsk, 70 zł to Gdynia).

The bus to Szczecin airport is operated by Interglobus Tour. Taxi fare to Szczecin from the airport is an exorbitant 120 zł.

🏢 Gdańsk Lech Wałęsa Airport ✉ Słowackiego 200, Gdańsk-Rębiechowo ☎ 058/ 348-11-63 ⊕ www.airport.gdansk.pl. **Interglobus Tour** ☎ 091/485-04-22 ⊕ www. interglobus.pl. **Szczecin-Goleniów Airport** ✉ Glewice, Goleniów ☎ 091/481-74-00 ⊕ www.airport-lotnisko.szczecin.pl.

BY BOAT & FERRY

Ferries travel daily from Gdańsk and Gdynia to Karlskrona and Nynashamn, Sweden. You can (operated by Polferries and Stena Line), Gdynia being the main international port for cruise ships. In summer there are pleasure cruises on the Motława River and the Baltic, and an hourly water-bus service links Gdańsk with Sopot and Gdynia, via Westerplatte and Hel. Polferries and Unity Line operate also between Świnoujście and Ystad (Sweden) and Copenhagen (Denmark).

Stateczek Europa operates the ferries on Drawsko Lake from the Czaplinek to Bielawa Island on Wednesday, Saturday, and Sunday at 11:30 and 2:30. Tickets are zł 12; on other days, the small ship is available for private rentals at zł 100 per hour.

🏢 Gdańsk Water-Bus Station ✉ Długie Pobrzeże, near Brama Zielona, Gdańsk ☎ 058/301-49-26. **Gdynia Water-Bus** ✉ al. Zjednoczenia 2, Gdynia ☎ 058/620-21-54. **Polferries** Small Terminal ✉ Nowy Port Przemysłowa 1, Gdańsk ☎ 058/343-00-78 ⊕ www.polferries.pl ✉ Main terminal ✉ Portowa 3, Gdynia ☎ 058/620-87-61 ✉ Wolin Island Ferry Terminal ✉ Dworcowa 1, Świnoujście ☎ 091/322-61-40. **Sopot Water-Bus** ✉ Sopot Pier, Sopot ☎ 058/551-12-93. **Stateczek Europa** ✉ Rnd of ul. Młyńska, Czaplinek ☎ 094/375-55-76. **Stena Line** ✉ Kwiatkowskiego 60, Gdynia ☎ 058/665-14-14 ⊕ www.stenaline.pl. **Unity Line** ✉ Dworcowa 1, Świnoujście ☎ 091/ 359-55-92 ⊕ www.unityline.pl.

BY BUS

Gdańsk is the major gateway for the Baltic coast and northeastern Poland. Gdańsk's PKS bus station is right next to the main train station. Buses may be useful for those who want to venture to small towns off the beaten track since PKS buses link all the small towns of the region; otherwise, trains are more frequent and more comfortable.

A regular service runs throughout the Tri-City area, taking you from Gdańsk through Oliwa and Sopot to Gdynia. The whole trip takes about 1¾ hours. The buses run from 5 AM to 11 PM; after 11 PM there is an hourly night-bus service.

🏢 Gdańsk PKS Bus Station ✉ ul. 3 Maja, Gdańsk ☎ 058/302-15-32 ⊕ www.pks. gdansk.pl. **Szczecin PKS Bus Station** ✉ pl. Grodnicki,. Szczecin ☎ 091/434-64-28 ⊕ www.pks.szczecin.pl.

BY CAR

From Warsaw, Route 7 (E77), a two-lane road for part of its length, goes directly to Gdańsk. From the west, the quickest route to the coast from the border crossing at Frankfurt/Oder is to take Route 2 (E30) to Poznań and then Route 5 (E261) via Gniezno and Bydgoszcz to Świecie, where it becomes Route 1 (E75) and continues via Tczew to the coast.

The road network in this part of Poland is relatively well-developed, and there are plenty of gas stations. Although Gdańsk's Stare Miasto (Old Town) and Główne Miasto (Main Town) areas are easily walkable, a car is useful if you wish to visit other parts of the Tri-City region, such as Sopot and the museums and cathedral at Oliwa, or sights farther afield, though all of these are linked by the Gdańsk area transit system.

Smaller villages, beaches and lakes of Pomerania are best accessed by car, especially out of season, when the number of bus connections decreases.

⊞ Avis Gdańsk Airport ⊠ ul. Słowackiego 200, Gdańsk-Rębiechowo ☎ 058/348-12-89 ⊕ www.avis.pl ⊠ Gdańsk City Center ⊠ ul. Podwale Grodzkie 9, Gdańsk. **Budget Gdańsk Airport** ⊠ ul. Słowackiego 200, Gdańsk-Rębiechowo ☎ 058/348-12-98 ⊕ www.budget.pl. **Hertz Gdańsk** ⊠ ul. Brygidki 14b, Gdańsk ☎ 058/301-40-45 ⊕ www.hertz.com.pl. **Joka Rent-a-Car** ⊠ Mercure Hevelius Hotel, ul. Heweliusza 22, Gdańsk ☎ 058/320-56-46 ⊕ www.joka.com.pl. **Sixt** ⊠ Neptune Hotel, ul. Matejki 18, Szczecin ☎ 091/488-38-83 ⊕ www.e-sixt.com. **Europcar** ⊠ Saczecin Novotel Hotel, al. 3 Maja 31, Szczecin ☎ 091/480-14-08 ⊕ www.car-rental.europcar.com.

BY TAXI

Just as in any other Polish city, it is always better to use a network radio taxi—they are cheaper and more reliable. There are few, if any, taxis, in smaller towns and resorts.

⊞ Taxis in Gdańsk & Vicinity ☎ 058/9624, 058/9686, 058/306-00-00, or 058/9195 **Taxis in Szczecin** ☎ 091/9627, 091/9660, 091/9455, or 091/9662

BY TRAIN

The main station in the Tri-City area is Gdańsk Główny. Many daily trains leave here for Warsaw (four hours), Kraków (eight hours), Poznań (four hours), and Malbork (take the train to Warsaw, which stops in Malbork; local trains can take ages). All the towns of the region can be reached by train. Within the Tri-City area, a fast electric-train service runs every 15 minutes from Gdańsk Główny via Oliwa, Sopot, and Gdynia to Wejherowo. The service operates from 4 AM to 1 AM.

There is a direct train connection between the Tri-City and Szczecin, a "fast" connection—but not an express (more than five hours); and there is a direct slow train from Szczecin, via Drawsko Pomorskie and Czaplinek, to Szczecinek (three hours from Szczecin to Szczecinek).

⊞ Gdańsk Główny ⊠ ul. Podwale Grodzkie 1, Gdańsk ☎ 058/94-36. **Szczecin Główny** ⊠ ul. Kolumba 1, Szczecin ☎ 091/94-36. **Tri-City Fast City Rail** PKP Szybka Kolej Miejska w Trójmieście ☎ 058/721-21-70 ⊕ www.skm.pkp.pl.

Contacts & Resources

EMERGENCIES

⊞ Emergency Services Ambulance ☎ 999.

⊞ 24-hour Pharmacies Apteka Dworcowa Gdańsk ⊠ Gdańsk Główny, main train station, ul. Podwale Grodzkie 1, Gdańsk ☎ 058/346-25-40. **Apteka Kuracyjna Sopot** ⊠ al. Niepodległości 861, Sopot ☎ 058/551-31-58. **Apteka Pod Gryfem Gdynia** ⊠ ul. Starowiejska 34, Gdynia ☎ 058/620-19-82. **Apteka Pod Wagą** ⊠ ul. Bolesława Krzywoustego 7a, Szczecin ☎ 091/433-66-73.

INTERNET, MAIL & SHIPPING
🏿 **Internet Cafés Bondi** ✉ ul. Jedności Narodowej 1, Szczecin ☎ 091/812-20-28 **Crist@l Internet** ✉ ul. Armii Krajowej 13 Gdynia ☎ 048/504-666-993. **Internet café Międzyzdroje** ✉ ul. Norwida 17a, Międzyzdroje ☎ 091/328-04-21. **J@zz** ✉ ul. Monte Cassino 35, Świnoujście ☎ 091/321-03-09. **Jazz 'n' Java** ✉ ul. Tkacka 17/18, Gdańsk ☎ 058/305-36-16. **Netcave** ✉ ul. Pułaskiego 7a, Sopot ☎ 058/555-11-83.
🏿 **Post Offices Gdańsk Main Post Office** ✉ ul. Długa 23/28, Gdańsk ☎ 058/301-80-49. **Gdynia Main Post Office** ✉ Wybrzeże Władysława IV 43, Gdynia ☎ 058/620-43-04. **Sopot Main Post Office** ✉ ul. Kościuszki 2, Sopot ☎ 058/551-08-24. **Świnoujście Main Post Office** ✉ ul. Piłsudskiego 1, Świnoujście ☎ 091/3210-30-40. **Kamień Pomorski Post Office** ✉ ul. Pocztowa 1, Kamień Pomorski ☎ 091/382-01-05. **Międzyzdroje Post Office** ✉ ul. Gryfa Pomorskiego 7, Międzyzdroje ☎ 091/32-80-140. **Szczecin Main Post Office** ✉ al. Niepodległości 41/42, Szczecin ☎ 091/440-11-03.

TOUR OPTIONS
Żegluga Gdańska operates between Tri-City, Westerplatte, and Hel peninsula, and arranges sightseeing trips through the port the Bay of Gdańsk. A branch of Żegluga Gdańska based in Frombork runs cruises on hydrofoil and regular boats between Frombork and Krynica Morska (in the Vistulan Sandbar), Elbląg, and Kaliningrad (Russia).

Odra Queen offers short boat tours of Szczecin harbor.
🏿 **Gdańsk Ticket Sales** ✉ Brama Zielona, at eastern end of Długi Targ, Gdańsk ☎ 058/301-49-26. **Gdynia Ticket Sales and Pier** ✉ al. Zjednoczenia 2, Gdynia ☎ 058/620-26-42. **Odra Queen** ✉ ul. Jana z Kolna, opposite Wały Chrobrego, Szczecin ☎ 091/434-57-00 ⊕ www.statki.net.pl. **Sopot Ticket Sales and Pier** ✉ Sopot Pier, Sopot ☎ 058/551-12-93. **Żegluga Gdańska Main Office** ✉ ul. Pończoszników 2, Gdynia ☎ 058/301-63-35. **Żegluga Gdańska Frombork** ✉ ul. Portowa, Frombork ☎ 055/243-72-31 Apr.-Oct., 048/604-646-962 mobile year-round ⊕ www.zegluga.pl.

VISITOR INFORMATION
🏿 **Agencja Infomacji Turystycznej Gdańsk** ✉ ul. Długa 45, Gdańsk ☎ 058/301-93-27.

Informacja Turystyczna Szczecin ✉ al. Niepodległości 1, Szczecin ☎ 091/434-04-40. **Kamień Pomorski Tourist Information** ✉ ul. Szpitalna 9, Kamień Pomorski ☎ 091/382-50-42.

Malbork Tourist Office ✉ ul. Piastowska 15, Malbork ☎ 091/273-49-90. **Międzyzdroje Tourist Information** ✉ ul. Niepodległości 3a, Międzyzdroje ☎ 091/328-07-27. **Tourist Information Szczecinek** ✉ pl. Wolności 7, Szczecinek ☎ 094/372-37-00. **Świnoujście Tourist Information** ✉ Wybrzeże Władysława IV, by ferry crossing, Świnoujście ☎ 091/322-49-99.

Mazury & Eastern Poland

WORD OF MOUTH

"My Polish friends insist that the number one site to visit is, Łańcut, pronounced *Wine-soot*."

—GSteed

"Zamość is on the Unesco World Heritage list, and it is supposedly the most perfect example of a true Renaissance town layout outside of Italy."

—Caroline1

EASTERN POLAND is not a homogenous entity as it is comprised of several very distinct regions, each with its own geographical, historical, and cultural traits. The lands along the Polish eastern border—a border that shifted several times over the country's long history—have been marked and enriched with the presence of different cultures: Prussians, Lithuanians, Belarusians, Tartars, Jews, and Ukrainians.

With approximately 350,000 inhabitants, Lublin is the biggest city in eastern Poland. Historically, Lublin used to be in the heart of the country, serving as a crossroads between east and west. Following World War II, when Poland's borders shifted westward, Lublin found itself near the Soviet border.

The location near the border actually protected Lublin and much of eastern Poland from the influences that have swept the country since it opened to the West in 1989. Visitors here can get a peek at the old Poland—which is decidedly less prosperous and more traditional than anything you will find in Warsaw or Kraków.

The east has a lot to offer, from the popular Mazury Lake District, through Poland's poorest corner near the Belarusian border, to the virgin forest of Białowieża, to historical towns and villages such as Lublin, Zamość, and Kazimierz Dolny, to the remote and wild Bieszczady mountains. Northeastern Poland has been dubbed the "Green Lungs" of the country. Indeed, the pristine, unspoiled natural environment is the region's main draw; as many as seven national parks and numerous nature reserves have been set aside in the belt of land along the border.

Those looking for treasures of art and monuments of history will not be disappointed. The romantic palace and park at Puławy, the beloved artists' town of Kazimierz Dolny, the model Renaissance town of Zamość, and the baroque palace and grounds of Łańcut are some of the region's highlights.

Exploring Mazury & Eastern Poland

Both the Mazury and Suwalskie lake districts are located in the northeastern corner of Poland and are described in the first part of this chapter. Head there for kayaking and sailing. Olsztyn will be a good starting point; you can easily head east from this northern Polish city, from which there are good connections to the capital, Warsaw. To reach the southern part of the country, the most convenient connection is always via Warsaw, whether you are driving or taking public transportation. South and east of Warsaw, you will find many lovely, small cities and towns, including the historical and cultural gems such as Kazimierz Dolny and Zamość. These locations farther south are described in the second part of the chapter. Lublin is the biggest city in the area and the main communications and transportation hub.

About the Restaurants

With a couple of exceptions, you will find few upscale restaurant in eastern Poland. In the countryside, simple home cooking is definitely the best deal, and in many holiday resorts you will find *obiady domowe* (home cooking) prepared by a local land-lady. Many small hotels offer the same kind of wholesome, tasty meals. In small- and mid-size towns (there aren't any big towns in the region), there are restaurants, of course, but the sophistication is nothing at all like what you will find in the larger cities. This is not always a bad thing: you may be pleasantly surprised by a simple (and inexpensive) meal in a small provincial town.

About the Hotels

In general, infrastructure in Eastern Poland is a little underdeveloped, but more and more small hotels and country club–style resorts—with spas, fitness centers, golf, tennis, and perhaps sailing—can be found in the area. In popular tourist destinations such as Mikołajki in the Mazury Lake District and in Kazimierz Dolny you will find a wide selection of comfortable accommodations, but remember these places are really popular, and book up far in advance, particularly in summer and on weekends, so reservations are essential in the busier parts.

EASTERN POLAND'S TOP 5

■ Kazimierz Dolny, a historic town on Vistula River, is so picturesque it became a living studio to many generations of artists.

■ The Krutynia River, near Klasztor Starowierców, which meanders through Mazurian lowlands, through forests and lakes filled with rare flora and fauna.

■ The Augustów Canal, which was built in the 1820s, is a masterpiece of engineering.

■ Several statues of Lenin are enjoying their retirement in a grand aristocratic palace: the Museum of the Art of Socialist Realism in Kozłówka.

■ The "ideal city" of Zamość is a textbook example of Renaissance town planning.

5

WHAT IT COSTS In Polish złoty (zł)				
$$$$	**$$$**	**$$**	**$**	**¢**
RESTAURANTS Over zł70	zł50—zł70	zł30–zł50	zł15–zł30	Under zł15
HOTELS Over zł800	zł500—zł800	zł300–zł500	zł150–zł300	Under zł150

Restaurant prices are per person for a main course at dinner. Hotel prices are for two people in a standard double room with a private bath and, most cases, breakfast in high season.

Timing

Many areas of Eastern Poland—especially destinations like the Mazurian Lakes that are popular for their natural beauty and outdoor activities—are mostly visited during the summer season. Autumn and winter weather usually do nothing but make traveling treacherous, and cold winds do not add to their charms. But in many of the historical towns, including Kazimierz Dolny, Zamość, and Łańcut, you'll find most attractions open year-round and far less crowded streets out of season.

Numbers in the margins correspond to numbers on the Eastern Poland map.

**Mazury &
Eastern
Poland**

IF YOU LIKE

BIRD-WATCHING

The northeast corner of Poland is the perfect place for ornithological voyeurism. Lake Łuknajno Reserve is home to the largest colony of mute swans in Europe (approximately 1,500 birds). This and other lakes and rivers offer a multitude of rare and common water birds: herons, ducks, and cormorants. Just BYOB (bring your own binoculars).

CHARMING OLD TOWNS

Two of the regions towns are particularly enchanting: Kazimierz Dolny and Zamość. The first is a favorite among bohemians, who hail its picturesque qualities; the latter is admired as a completely planned, "ideal" city, a masterpiece of renaissance town planning. They are both small, sleepy, and very beautiful towns, which comes alive in summer when they fill with aesthetically minded tourists and holiday makers.

GETTING AWAY FROM IT ALL WITHOUT ROUGHING IT

Eastern Poland hides some great and hidden luxury hotels. In the northeast, Młyn Klekotki is a great cozy hotel and spa in a converted historical water mill, right by the lake and in the middle of the woods. Farther south, Kazimierz Dolny has two great spa hotels: Spa Kazimierz and Hotel Król. All offer opportunities to indulge in a range of beauty and wellness treatments.

GRAND MANORS

Eighteenth-century Kozłówka was the seat of the Zamoyski family, while 17th-century Łańcut owes its beauty to the Lubomirski, and then Potocki clans. Both palaces are now museums filled with artworks and memorabilia and are surrounded by beautiful parks. Although the golden days of those grand manors are a thing of the past, both museums successfully summon up at least some of their former glory.

KAYAKING

Meandering along the Krutynia, the wild Rospuda, or the civilized Augustów Canal—some of the loveliest and most rewarding waterways in Europe—can be a great active holiday, but also an encounter with nature and culture. There are different trail options of varying lengths and difficulties, and experienced local tour operators are at hand to assist less experienced boaters.

MONUMENTS OF CIVIL & MILITARY ENGINEERING

The Wolf's Lair in Gierłoż is more than 20 acres—almost an entire city of bunkers and other infrastructure—from which Hitler planned to command his eastern conquest, and although the retreating German army destroyed it upon their departure, a lot still remains that will be of interest not only to military historians and engineers. The Augustów Canal, which connects the Neman with the Vistula, was a state-of-the-art structure when it was first built in 1820s, and it still astounds visitors today. The remains of the fortifications at Zamość are another fascinating marriage of architecture and engineering, a system that proved itself efficient throughout the city's history.

OLSZTYN

❶ *130 km (81 mi) southeast of Malbork, 150 km (93 mi) southeast of Gdańsk, 215 km (133 mi) north of Warsaw.*

A city where Polish and Prussian influences overlap, Olsztyn lies in the southernmost corner of Warmia, and it serves as a capital of the modern Warmia and Mazury region (historically, two separate entities). Although it is not strictly in the east, Olsztyn is a gateway to the Mazury region in the northeast corner of Poland. It makes a nice stopover and a convenient jumping-off point for the lakes, whether you are traveling from Gdańsk or from Warsaw.

Olsztyn itself is set amid scenic lakes and woodlands. In fact, there are 15 lakes within the administrative borders of the city, accounting for more than 8% of its total area; woodland covers more than 20% of the city, and various green areas in total count for as much as 50% of Olsztyn.

The Gothic **Brama Wysoka** (High Gate) marks the entrance to Olsztyn's Old Town and the main square. Southeast of the square is the 15th-century Katedra świętego Jakuba. East of the Old Town is one of the town's main attractions, the Planetarium, and the Astronomical Observatory.

The Gothic **Katedra świętego Jakuba** (St. James's Cathedral) was built in the second half of the 14th century, while the 200-foot tower was added in the end of 16th. Crystalline vaults in the aisles are worth noting, but the pearl of the church is the altar in the right aisle: the triptych, when closed, reveals a scene of Annunciation. In 1807, during the Napoleonic wars, the French locked 1,500 Russian prisoners of war inside the cathedral. It was winter, a time of severe frosts, and the prisoners burned almost everything they could find inside the church just to keep warm, which is why not many wooden pieces of the original interior have survived. ✉ *ul. Staszica 12* 🎫 *Free* 🕐 *Mon.–Sat. 9–5, Sun. 3–5.*

The **Zamek** (Castle), with its ethnographic and historical **Museum of Warmia & Mazury** stands just to the west of the town's square. Once again, Copernicus, that Renaissance man who really got around in Poland, is featured in an exhibit. He successfully directed the defense of the castle from 1516 to 1521 against the Teutonic Knights while serving as an administrator of Warmia Province. ✉ *ul. Zamkowa 2* ☎ *089/527-95-96* ⊕ *www.muzeum.olsztyn.pl* 🎫 *Museum zł 6* 🕐 *Museum June–Sept., Tues.–Sun. 9–5; Oct.–May, Tues.–Sun. 10–4.*

Obserwatorium Astronomiczne (Astronomical Observatory) is arranged in the former water tower (from 1897). You should make a reservation for either a daytime visit or one of the nighttime shows. You can observe the sun at anytime during the daytime hours; on Monday, Wednesday, and Friday, at 8 and 9 PM, you can watch the night sky. The terrace also offers a nice panorama of Olsztyn town. ✉ *ul. Zamkowa 2* ☎ *089/*

GREAT ITINERARIES

Eastern Poland is a vast area, stretching along the country's eastern border, which is nearly 1,000 km (625 mi) long. The east is the least densely populated and most remote part of Poland and therefore a favorite destination for relaxing, long holidays (rather than strict sightseeing itineraries). The Poles will tell you that you need at least two weeks for such a holiday—whether you are planning on going sailing, kayaking, or just being lazy. If your time is limited, it is probably wise to concentrate your exploring in the lakes of the northeast, or the cities—including Lublin, Kazimierz Dolny and Zamość—in the southeast, rather than trying to do it all.

IF YOU HAVE 3 DAYS

Start in Kazimierz Dolny and relax there for a day and a night. Wander around the old town: you don't really need a plan, as you're bound to come across all the important sights as you walk, including the main square and churches. Take one of the hourly cruises on the river and enjoy an evening of good food and good music. On Day 2 start early and head to Kozłówka to see the aristocratic residence of the Zamoyski family, which incorporates a museum of socialist realism. Then

head for Lublin, where you can spend the afternoon sightseeing (don't miss the castle and the old town with its cathedral). On Day 3, move farther east to Zamość to spend at least one day in the "ideal" Renaissance town.

IF YOU HAVE 5 DAYS

Spend two days in Kazimierz Dolny, with perhaps a longer river trip and/or a walk into Kazimierz Landscape Park to see the loess ravines. On Day 3, follow the second day of the three-day itinerary. On Day 4, spend more time sightseeing in Lublin, visiting the old Jewish cemetery and the former Majdanek Concentration Camp. Save Zamość for your last day in the area.

IF YOU HAVE 7 DAYS

Spend two days in and around Krutynia River, either kayaking or walking. The two most original places to stop along the Krutynia Trail would be the Old Believers Monastery in Wojnowo and the "Under the Dog" Auberge (Oberża Pod Psem) in Kadzidłowo. Before heading southeast toward Lublin, you will probably need to stop in Warsaw (⇨ Chapter 1). You can be in Kazimierz Dolny early on Day 4 and take it from there (as in the first itinerary suggests above).

527–67–03 ✉ *zł 6* ⊙ *Mon.–Sat. 9–3; Mon., Wed., and Fri. at 8 and 9* PM *by appointment only.*

Under the same management as the nearby Astronomical Observatory, the **Planetarium,** which opened in 1975, has shows in a number of languages, including English. The shows are on the hour, the first at 9 AM, and the last at 2 PM. ✉ *al. Piłsudskiego 38* ☎ *089/533–49–51* ⊕ *www.planetarium.olsztyn.pl* ✉ *zł 7.50, shows zł 3.50* ⊙ *Mon.–Sat. 9–3.*

Kresy—Poland's Eastern Borderlands

THE CONCEPT OF THE EASTERN BORDERLANDS, or Kresy, is very much alive in the Polish psyche, and yet it is not easy to define the region in concrete, physical, and geographical terms. The Kresy do encompass the eastern parts of the Podlaskie, Lubelskie, and Podkarpackie regions; on the other hand, in strictly historical terms *Kresy* also denotes what remained *behind* Poland's eastern frontier, within the former Soviet Union, after World War II. Today, parts of the old Polish kingdom are now incorporated into Ukraine, Belarus, and Russia. When they were instigated, these demarcations were very disruptive to the people living there, and the 20th century was a time of many enforced migrations, when many people—not just those in this region—had to leave their homes across various new regional borders never to return. It should be no wonder that phrases including the noun "kresy" or the adjective *kresowy* have a resident ring of nostalgia. Today, kresy has come to mean something even broader, referring to the transborder regions of Poland with Western Belarus, Western Ukraine, and Lithuania. With so much in common—historically and culturally—these lands and their people could and perhaps even should be more together than apart. There may be more opportunities for cross-border cooperation now that democracy is slowly but surely returning to Poland's neighbors across the eastern border, and with the future further expansion of the European Union; new chapters may be appended to the legend of the Eastern Borderland.

Where to Eat

$–$$$$ ✕ **Karczma Jana.** The word *karczma* denotes a roadside inn, but this is an upmarket one, located right in the Old Town, near St. John's bridge (hence Jana—John's—in the name). The menu is extensive, and you might be tempted to indulge in a multicourse meal. Start with *matjas* (herring) with cream, apple, and onion dressing, and end with baked apples with honey, flavored with *żubrówka* vodka. For a main course, there's an excellent selection of fish, at least some of which is freshly caught in the local lakes (e.g., fried pike-perch with cherry tomatoes), but you can also get poultry and red meats (including sophisticated tournedos Rossini served with *foie gras*, truffles, and green asparagus, in Madeira sauce). On top of that is a selection of vegetarian dishes and a couple of no-nonsense options for kids. ⊠ *ul. Kołłątaja 11* ☎ *089/522–29–46* ▭ *AE, MC, V.*

$–$$ ✕ **Różana Café.** Roses, roses are everywhere, including on the pink walls and on the tables. But you'll also find crisp, white tablecloths, crystal mirrors, old photographs, and a pleasant garden for the summer. Although the restaurant opened in 2003, it seems to evoke the spirit of the interwar period. The menu is truly eclectic, with everything from homey potato pancakes to exotic tiger prawns. The owners label some dishes female and others male (pancakes versus steak), but you should feel free to break through these gender stereotypes. Rabbit in cream sauce served with hot beets or veal ravioli with crispy pork and chanterelles are truly delicious. The dessert menu is tempting as well: how about ice cream with hot raspberry sauce? ⊠ *Targ Rybny 14* ☎ *089/523–50–39* ⊟ *AE, MC, V.*

Where to Stay

$–$$ 🏨 **Hotel Pod Zamkiem.** This hotel is right under the castle, as the name promises. What is more, the place itself has an interesting history. This turn-of-the-19th-century villa used to belong to the Sperl family (one of the clan was head of the Olsztyn's freemasons' lodge). Details, including the original wooden staircase, wooden beams, and door frames are absolutely lovely. The room decor is a bit of a mishmash of questionable taste but paradoxically rather cozy and comfy all the same. ⊠ *ul. Nowowiejskiego 10, 10-162* ☎ *089/535–12–87* 🖨 *089/534–09–40* ⊕ *www.hotel-olsztyn.com.pl* ↝ *16 rooms, 1 suite* ⌂ *Cable TV, meeting room, parking (fee); no a/c* ⊟ *AE, MC, V* ⧈ *BP.*

$–$$ 🏨 **HP Park.** This comfortable if blandly modern hotel sits in parkland 4 km (2.5 mi) away from the city center, but only 1 km (½ mi) from a lakeside beach and with direct access to walking and riding trails. HP Park offers horseback riding and bicycles for rent, and access to tennis courts (2 km [1 mi] away) and a golf course (8 km [5 mi] away). ⊠ *ul. Warszawska 119, 10–701* ☎ *089/524–06–04* 🖨 *089/524–00–77* ⊕ *www.beph.pl* ↝ *100 rooms* ⌂ *Restaurant, room service, cable TV, bicycles, horseback riding, bar, shop, laundry service, business services, some pets allowed, no-smoking rooms* ⊟ *AE, DC, MC, V* ⧈ *BP.*

$ 🏨 **Villa Pallas.** This stylish residence from the early 20th century is east of the town center in pleasant, green surroundings. The rooms are perfectly neat and comfortable, but the decor is not particularly imaginative, especially when compared to the much grander lobby and restaurant space, presided over by the statue of Greek goddess, Pallas Athena (the hotel's namesake). ⊠ *ul. Żołnierska 4, 10–557* ☎ *089/535–01–15* ⊕ *www.villapallas.pl* ↝ *30 rooms, 2 suites* ⌂ *Restaurant, cable TV, Wi-Fi, spa, bar, meeting room, parking (fee); no a/c* ⊟ *AE, MC, V* ⧈ *BP.*

LIDZBARK WARMIŃSKI

② *46 km (28½ mi) north of Olsztyn.*

This was originally a Prussian town called Lecbark, but it was "conquered" by the Teutonic Knights in 1241. Ten years later, it was ceded to the bishops of Warmia. If you decide to make the detour to see the castle, then it might also be worth making an even further detour to the village of Godkowo (53 km [33 mi]) to stay overnight in the Młyn Klekotki Resort & Spa; the only problem is that you may not want to leave the next day.

Lidzbark Warmiński's 14th-century **castle** survived World War II only because the local population refused to help the Germans demolish it. Fantastically angular and sharp-edged, this powerful castle has an arcaded courtyard, and a square tower at each corner. It is nearly all surrounded with water: the Lyna River and its tributary, the Synsarna, feed the castle moat. One of the best-preserved Gothic castles in Poland today, it is home to the Warmia Museum, and has a café in the medieval cellars. Buses run to Lidzbark from Olsztyn and Gdańsk. ✉ *pl. Zamkowy 1* ☎ *089/767–29–80* 🎫 *zł 6* ⊙ *May–Sept., Tues.–Sat. 9–6; Oct.–Apr, Tues.–Sat. 9–4.*

Where to Stay & Eat

$$
FodorśChoice
★

✗🍴 **Młyn Klekotki Resort & Spa.** On a lake in the woods, this spa resort was once a 17th-century water mill, though the building has been rebuilt several times. Abandoned and neglected after World War II, it was renovated and turned into a hotel in 1999. The water mill itself still works and helps provide power for the hotel. Many of the original architectural elements have been lovingly restored, which leads to the charming irregularity of the rooms: each of which is individually styled and tastefully furnished and decorated. Comforts continue beyond the rooms, with extensive sports and spa facilities. On top of everything, an excellent restaurant ($$–$$$$) serves contemporary food based on old regional recipes. Some of the most popular dishes include eel soup, Polish *kulebiak* (a pastry shell filled with chanterelles), carp stuffed with bacon, and Lithuanian dumplings with meat, pepper, marjoram, garlic, and onion. ✉ *Godkowo, 14-407* ☎ *055/249–00–00* 🖨 *055/249–00–08 Ext. 230* ⊕ *www.hotelmlynklekotki.pl* 🛏 *36 rooms, 6 suites* ⚘ *Restaurant, room service, refrigerators, in-room safes, cable TV, tennis court, gym, hot tub, sauna, spa, bicycles, Ping-Pong, billiards, bar, laundry service, meeting rooms, business services, Internet room, parking (free)* ▭ *AE, MC, V* 🍽 *BP.*

THE MAZURY LAKE DISTRICT

The Mazury Lake District is one of the most popular holiday regions of Poland, particularly favored by those who prefer active leisure, including excellent sailing and kayaking. If you don't like the water, this is the part of Poland to avoid: the area contains some 2,700 large lakes, and countless little "lakelets," connected by a network of rivers, streams, and canals, which splash, spill, and spread through the region's meadows and marshlands. At the center of the region is the area of 1,700 square km (656 square mi) called the Mazurian Great Lakes (Kraina Wielkich Jezior Mazurskich); nearly a third of this area is covered by water. The "great lakes" include two of Poland's largest (Śniardwy and Mamry), as well as the popular resort of Mikołajki, which is more or less in the middle. The Suwalskie Lake District (Pojezierze Suwalskie), which includes Augustów, lies to the east of Mazurian Great Lakes, in the far northeastern corner of Poland.

Mikołajki

❸ *85 km (53 mi) east of Olsztyn.*

Mikołajki derives its name from the patron saint of the local chapel, St. Nicholas (the name in Polish means "the little Nicks"). Once a medieval fishing hamlet, today it is one of the most popular—if not *the* most popular—resort in the Mazurian Lakes region, referred to as "the Boating Capital of Poland." In fact, in the summer months the small town gets a little too popular for its own good. Mikołajki is situated on the shores of Lake Tałty and Lake Mikołajskie, with Lake Śniardwy nearby. A nature preserve surrounds Lake Łuknajno, 4 km (2½ mi) east of Mikołajki.

Four kilometers (2½ mi) east of Mikołajki lies Łuknajno Lake, which covers a little more than 2¾ square mi. The lake is an bird sanctuary, with the largest colony of Mute Swan (*Cygnus olor*) in Europe (approximately 1,500 birds), and many other water birds: Montagu's harrier (*Circus pygargus*), little bittern (*Ixobrychus minutus minutus*), little crake (*Porzana parva*), common crane (*Grus grus*), and ducks such as wigeon (*Anas penelope*), or northern shoveler (*Anas clypeata*). There are observation towers (*wieża widokowa*) around the lake. Bring your binoculars—or a camera with a good zoom—and indulge in innocent voyeurism, also called bird-watching. Don't forget good walking shoes (or galoshes) because the track can get a little muddy. The reserve's management office is actually in Krutyń, which is 25 km (16 mi) from the reserve. Most tourists skip that and follow the trail marked P1, which follows Spacerowa and Leśna streets in Mikołajki, or the biking route marked R2, which also starts in the center of town on Łabędzia. ✉ *4 km east of Mikołajki* ☎ *089/742–14–05* 🎫 *Free* 🕙 *Daily dawn–dusk.*

5

Wolf's Lair

❹ *8 km (5 mi) east of Kętrzyn, 30 km (19 mi) north of Mikołajki.*

Hitler's onetime bunker, at Gierłoż, called Wolfsschanze or Wilczy Szaniec (Wolf's Lair), was built during World War II as his East Prussian military command post. Its massively fortified concrete bunkers were blown up, but you can still climb in and among the remains and get a feel for his megalomania. Wolf's Lair was also where a small group of German patriots tried—and failed—to assassinate Hitler on July 20, 1944. ✉ *Gierłoż* ☎ *089/752–44–29* ⊕ *www.wolfsschanze. home.pl* 🎫 *zł 8, English-language tour zł 50* 🕙 *Daily 9–sunset.*

Klasztor Starowierców

❺ *Wojnowo is 20 km (12 mi) south of Mikołajki.*

The Old Believers Monastery in Wojnowo is on the Krutynia River trail, south/southwest of Mikołajki. The village was founded by the Old Believers (of the Russian Orthodox Church). Also called the Philipons (after Philip the Hermit), Raskolniks, or Schismatics, the Old Believers did not adopt Patriarch Nikon's reforms in the 17th century and were forced to emigrate in order to escape persecution. Initially, they settled in the area around Suwałki, but after refusing military service and the registration of their marriages, they ran afoul of the laws there. They were pardoned and exempt from the military obligation, in return for their help in colonizing the Puszcza Piska forest. In the 1820s and '30s, the Old Believers settled in this area, and Wojnowo is one of several villages they founded. The present monastery was founded in 1836 by a pious elder Ławrientij Rastropin. The hermitage was expanded and turned into a full-fledged monastery, and in the mid-19th century it was changed to a convent. The last nun died in April 2006. Today, the monastery (with its prayer room/chapel) can be visited and remains under the loving care of private owners who want to preserve this place without turning it into a museum; they want to keep it alive. The chapel serves people of every faith, and there are several rooms to rent in the monastery building. ⊠ *Wojnowo 76, Ukta, 18 km (11 mi) southwest of Mikołajki* ☎ *087/425–70–30* ⊕ *www.klasztor.pl* ⊠ *Free* ⊙ *Hours are irregular, but open most days by request.*

Where to Stay & Eat

In addition to mid-range, comfortable hotels, there are a growing number of luxury accommodations, hotel-spas, and out-of-the-ordinary guesthouses in the region. If you like the bustle of a lively resort, try Mikołajki, but if you find the fashionable flurry too overwhelming, escape to one of the smaller villages nearby—for instance, south into the forest of Puszcza Piska. Since the region's hotels are spread out all over the place, we've grouped them here for more easy perusing. Not all hotels listed here are actually in Mikołajki.

Rural tourism, self-catering accommodation, camping, and kayak and yacht holidays are very popular forms of holiday-making in Mazury, and there are plenty of opportunities out there. **EuroMasuren** ⊕ www. euromazury.pl represents a wide range of homes and villas for rent throughout the region. Unfortunately, like most of the Web sites and agencies that represent these rural accommodations, the information is available only in German or Polish.

There are hardly any independent restaurants in the region, but you certainly won't starve: hotels, pensions, seasonal bar-stands, or local landladies who advertise *obiady domowe* (home cooking) in their homes will feed you well, and usually inexpensively too.

¢–$ ✕▣ **Oberża Pod Psem.** The Under the Dog Auberge, run by artist

Fodor'sChoice Krzysztof Worobiec and his wife Danuta, is a very special place, per-

★ fect if you want to get away from it all. The owners are set on preserving local traditions, and their hotel is part of a culture park of renovated traditional wooden houses that also includes a private ethnographical museum. The cheeky name should put you on notice to expect a rather remote and relaxed place, with no crisp white tablecloths, but plenty of old wooden furniture and rooms decorated in all the colors of the rainbow. There are few traditional creature comforts, but it's the rusticity that is the draw. Even if you are staying elsewhere, Auberge is worth a trip for a meal given that it has one of the best restaurants ($–$$) in the entire Mazury region. The owners cook their so-called slow food using regional recipes supplemented by their own imagination. Try *kwaśnica* (a dense soup made with mushrooms and cabbage) or *wereszczaki* (pork in beetroot, served with buckwheat). The hosts make many ingredients, including excellent goat cheese, themselves. They will guide you around their private museum (zł 5), generally open daily from 11 to 5, which includes a typical Mazurian cottage and a re-created schoolroom of old. ⊠ *ul. Kadzidłowo 1, Ukta 12–20* ☎ *048/425–74–74*

⊕ *www.oberzapodpsem.com* ✑ *5 rooms* ⚭ *Restaurant, sauna* ▭ *No credit cards* ⓘ *EP.*

$$ ▦ **Hotel Gołębiewski.** Set right on a lake, this is a popular summer resort. This enormous hotel has just about everything you might want, including a water park and ice rink (free for hotel guests), horseback riding, and even access to a nearby golf. The spa offers a range of health and beauty treatments. The interiors are bland, international-hotel style, but with so many attractions, you are not likely to spend a lot of time in your room. ⊠ *ul. Mrągowska 34, Mikołajki 11–730* ☏ *087/429–07–00* 🖷 *087/429–04–44* ⊕ *www.golebiewski.pl* ✑ *652 rooms, 13 suites* ⚭ *3 restaurants, 2 cafés, cable TV, in-room broadband, 4 tennis courts, 3 indoor pools, 1 outdoor pool, spa, horseback riding, ice-skating, marina, bar, convention center, parking (fee)* ▭ *AE, DC, MC, V* ⓘ *BP.*

★ $ ▦ **Pensjonat Kipnick.** This pleasant pension is located along the Krutynia River canoeing trail, at the edge of the village of Spychowo. It is an alternative to the fashionable Mikołajki resort; compared to the latter, it feels like nirvana. In fact, even without any comparisons, it is an oasis of peace, and with no shortage of luxury either. Rooms are cheerful and comfortable, the lounges rich and snug, inviting you to take a book from the hotel library and read it by the fire. And there are countless options for outdoor activities in the splendid natural environment surrounding the hotel from every direction. If you could review this hotel in a single word, it would be "mellow." ⊠ *ul. Leśna 4, Spychowo 12–150* ☏ *048/ 602–175–896 mobile* 🖷 *089/622–52–37* ⊕ *www.kipnick.pl* ✑ *10 rooms* ⚭ *Restaurant, cable TV, sauna, badminton, volleyball, basketball, playground, Internet room, meeting room* ▭ *AE, DC, MC, V* ⓘ *EP.*

¢ ▦ **Klasztor Starowierców** (Old Believers Monastery). If you would like to get a small taste of what monastic life might have been like (or rather get a glimpse and then use your imagination), you can rent a cell at this monastery. The rooms are spotlessly clean and cheerful, but very simple, low-key, and modest, and they seem permeated with mystic aura of the place. This is by no means a typical accommodation, but it is very special and has a definite charm about it. Bathroom facilities are shared, as is a kitchenette, but you can also order prepared meals. Guests can use boats, kayaks, and mountain bikes free of charge. The lakeside location is ideal. ⊠ *ul. Wojnowo 76, Ukta 12–210, 18 km (11 mi) southwest of Mikołajki* ☏ *087/425–70–30* ⊕ *www.klasztor.pl* ✑ *5 rooms with shared bath* ⚭ *Kitchen, boating, bicycles, parking (free); no room phones, no TV, no a/c* ▭ *No credit cards* ⓘ *EP.*

Sports & the Outdoors

KAYAKING
Fodor$Choice
★

The Krutynia River is considered one of the loveliest lowland kayaking trails in Poland, perhaps even in Europe. It crosses—or rather meanders through—the ancient forest of Puszcza Piska as well as through numerous picturesque lakes. It was the Prussians that gave the river its name: in the old Prussian dialect *Krutina* means "meandering." The infrastructure for tourists (equipment rental, simple dining and lodging establishments) is relatively well developed. The total length of the river is 116.5 km (72 mi), and the entire route takes about seven or eight days. The Krutynia is an easy river to traverse, not too strenuous for a beginner; however, there are four spots where kayaks have to be carried over land,

and 44.5 km (28 mi) of the route is on still water. Trips usually start in the PTTK Marina in Sorkwity (where you can rent a kayak), and then set off for the village of Zyndaki on the northern shore of Zyndackie Lake. The kayak trail ends in Nidzkie Lake, in the PTTK Marina in Ruciane-Nida.

Perkun (✉ ul. Krutyń 4, Piecki ☎ 089/742–14–30 or 048/600–427–868 ⊕ www.krutynia.com.pl), which is the popular name for the Perkun Association of Water Guides on Krutynia, organizes boat trips from April through November. The basic rate is zł 24 per person per day, but individual tailor-made options may be priced differently. The organization can also put together a short, several-hour kayaking trip for those who don't have time to do the whole route. Boat trips start from the quay next to the bridge in Krutyń, 15 km (9 mi) south of Mikołajki.

Stanica Wodna PTTK-Sorkwity (✉ ul. Zamkowa 13, Sorkwity ☎ 089/642–81–24 ⊕ www.sorkwity.pttk.pl) is 30 km (19 mi) west of Mikołajki, near Mrągowo and is open from May through the end of September.

Stanica Wodna PTTK Ruciane-Nida (✉ al. Wczasów 17, Ruciane-Nida ☎ 087/423–10–12 ⊕ www.uandrzeja.pl) is about 20 km (12 mi) south of Mikołajki and is open from May through mid-September.

SAILING   There are numerous popular sailing routes along the region's many lakes, and you can easily start in Mikołajki. For instance, the trips from Mikołajki to Ruciane Nida (19 km [12 mi]), Mikołajki to Giżycko (37 km [23 mi], via Lake Niegocin), Mikołajki to Pisz (25 km [16 mi], via Lake Śniardwy), and Mikołajki to Ryn (20 km [12 mi]) are all popular routes. Many variations and circular routes are possible, and it's quite easy to use Mikołajki as your base.

The **Wioska Żeglarska** (Sailors' Village ✉ ul. Kowalska 13 ☎ 087/421–60–40 ⊕ www.wioskazeglarskamikolajki.pl) is a good place to rent a boat. Bareboat yacht charters range from zł 130 to zł 250 per day, and the marina has full facilities.

If you aren't an experienced sailor, **Żegluga Mazurska** (Mazurian Sailing Company ✉ Port Mikołajki ☎ 097/421–61–02 ⊕ www.zeglugamazurska.com) offers sailing scheduled pleasure cruises, running between Mikołajki, Ruciane-Nida, and Giżycko, as well as a round-trip itinerary from Mikołajki to Lake Śniardwy. Cruises are scheduled from May through September only and are more frequent in July and August.

POJEZIERZE SUWALSKIE

The Suwalskie Lake District is a less-visited but no less beautiful region than the Mazurian Great Lakes. Huddled in the northeastern corner of Poland, this region sets many national records: the lakes here are the country's deepest, their water is the cleanest, and winter temperatures are the lowest. Although larger sailboats are restricted, the region has some of the best waterways for canoeing.

Augustów

❻ *110 km (68 mi) from Mikołajki.*

Built in the 1820s and designed by General Ignacy Prądzyński, the Kanał Augustowski (Augustów Canal) connects the rivers Biebrza and Czarna Hańcza (and through them the water systems of the Vistula and Neman). When the Prussians effectively blocked the traditional overland Vistula Trail in 1823 by charging prohibitively high tariffs on the export of key goods passing through Gdańsk, the canal gave the Kingdom of Poland a transportation alternative (all this was happening before the railways). Today, it is one of the main tourist attractions in the region.

The canal is an engineering masterpiece. It is 102 km (63 mi) long, with 80 km (50 mi) within the current borders of Poland. The highest point of the canal is at 407 feet above see level, which is 49 feet above the level of Biebrza and 128 feet above the level of Neman River. These differences in elevation are corrected with 18 locks (14 of them within Poland), including a two-chamber and a three-chamber lock. The biggest difference of heights is at the Paniewo lock (21 feet).

The canal can be navigated by a kayak, canoe, or a boat (partly also by cruise boats operated by Żegluga Augustowska). There are also walking and cycling trails along the banks from Augustów to Mikaszówka, a distance of nearly 40 km (25 mi).

Sports & the Outdoors

There are several places to rent canoes and other water-sports equipment in Augustów. The average price for a kayak or a canoe rental is between zł 20 and zł 30 per day, with separate charges for the canoe's transportation to and from the departure/arrival points (usually an additional zł 100 to zł 200 each way, depending on the distance).

Kanu (✉ Zarzecze 8a ☎ 087/643–25–30) has canoes, rowing boats, and water bikes for rent; the company can also organize your trip for you.

Necko (✉ Portowa 1 ☎ 087/644–56–39) offers full-day or multiday canoeing trips.

Szot (✉ Konwaliowa 2 ☎ 087/644–67–58) organizes both kayaking and biking trips of various length.

Żegluga Augustowska (✉ Augustów Wharf, 29 Listopada 7 ☎ 087/643–28–81) runs scheduled boat cruises to the surrounding lakes and sections of the Augustów Canal.

Wigry

❼ *45 km (28 mi) north of Augustów.*

Wigry, a village on a peninsula in Lake Wigry, was a settlement of Yotvingians (Sudovians), an ancient Baltic tribe—now extinct—that was conquered by the Teutonic Knights in the 13th century. Remote and protected by woods and water, Wigry was one of the last hiding places of the Yotvingians. In the 15th century, this area became one of the most popular hunting grounds for Polish and Lithuanian royals. But Wigry is most famous for the monastery of the Camadolese monks and their very strict monastic rule. In 1667, King Jan Kazimierz endowed the *Eremus Insulae Wigrensis*, or the Hermitage of Wigry Island. Camadolese monks extended the monastic compound, where they lived their life of work, contemplation, and prayer. They avoided any excess, maintained a vegetarian diet, slept little, and spoke even less. They worked hard to develop the surrounding area, inviting and assisting settlers in the region and founding new farms and factories.

> **A GREEN HIGHWAY**
>
> Greenpeace is campaigning to save the Rospuda River by lobbying against the planned construction of a motorway junction, part of the future Via Baltica Highway, in the area. The organization argues that the planned ring road for Augustów should not only redirect traffic from the city but also avoid cutting through the Rospuda Valley, with its unique and fragile natural environment. The more ecological version of the traffic plan is also more expensive, but it is hoped that environmental values will prevail over strict financial considerations.

In 1800, the Wigry monastery was dissolved by the Prussian authorities. Neglected, it fell into disrepair, and two world wars added even more damage. In the 1960s, the monastery was rebuilt and turned into a hotel—intended primarily for writers and artists seeking a quiet refuge for their intellectual and creative work, though it is open to the public. In 1999, Pope John Paul II visited the monastery for a quiet day.

The lake and the area surrounding Lake Wigry, including 41 smaller lakes in the region, is now **Wigry National Park.** The region is home to 1,000-some species of plants (75 of them protected) and more than 1,700 species of animals (nearly 300 of them protected). Among the inhabitants of the national park are the European beaver (*Castor fiber*), black cormorant (*Phalacrocorax carbo*), and four species of dragon flies.

Where to Stay & Eat

¢-$ ✕📷 **Dom Pracy Twórczej w Wigrach.** The former Camadolese monastery is now the Wigry Home for Creative Work, a hotel that is meant for writers and artists but also open to the public when rooms are available. There are a variety of options. The best accommodation is in one of eight *erems* (hermitages), each with two double rooms, and an individual garden/terrace. The *erems* in the lower terrace have en-suite bathrooms, in the upper terrace, the bathroom is shared by two rooms. Although there are TVs in these rooms, try to ignore them and instead enjoy the blissful silence, the same holy silence the Camadolese monks observed in this place. There are also more beds in the Papal House dormitories and a couple of en-suite doubles in the Royal House. The Dom Wigierski Restaurant serves meals from 1 to 8 PM daily. The menu includes such local specialties as boiled crayfish, buckwheat blini with salmon, and excellent fresh fish from the lake, including tench (*lin*), powan (*sieja*), and whitefish (*sielawa*). ✉ *Lake Wigry, Stary Folwark, 16–412*

☎ *087/563–70–00* 🖨 *087/563–70–19* ⊕ *www.wigry.org* ⇥ *20 rooms, 8 with shared baths, 40 dormitory beds* ♻ *Restaurant, cable TV* ▭ *No credit cards* ⅋⊙⅋ *BP.*

Sports & the Outdoors

The **Rospuda River** is a fairly advanced kayaking route, actually one of the loveliest in all of Poland. Its charm is that it varies from a fast river with high banks and stony bed, to a river that runs and turns through woodlands, to a slow lowland river with muddy banks overgrown with rushes. The total route is 68 km (42 mi) and traversing the entire route will take about four to five days. The route can be divided into two main parts: the **Upper Rospuda** (Km 0–35) is mostly easy, though some spots are of medium difficulty and a few sections are a little strenuous due to stony shoals; the **Lower Rospuda** (Km 35–68) is slightly more difficult and strenuous, and there is one stretch where kayaks have to be carried overland. A full 21 km (13 mi) of the route is on still water, but you may encounter some obstacles (windfallen tress and rushes/reeds). The trail starts on the southeast bank of Jezioro Czarne (Black Lake), also called Polskie or Filipowskie Lake. At the far southeastern end of the lake is an entrance—overgrown with reeds and rushes—to the Rospuda River. The kayaking route ends in Jezioro Białe (White Lake) in the Augustów marina.

Przedsiębiorstwo Turystyczne Rospuda (✉ ul. Wita Stwosza 1, Raczki ☎ 604/18–00–83 mobile phone of Marcin Sidor ⊕ www.rospuda.pl) organizes kayaking tours and other activities, including windsurfing and paintball—not just on the Rospuda River but also in Czarna Hańcza, Drawa, Brda, and other locations in the region. The company runs both large student-oriented kayaking trips and also tailor-made tours for small groups and individual tourists. Raczki is 24 km (15 mi) northwest of Augustów.

LUBLIN

160 km (100 mi) southeast of Warsaw, 360 km (224 mi) southeast of Olsztyn.

Lublin was once at the very heart of the Polish-Lithuanian empire. In fact, it was here that the Union treaty was signed between the two states in 1569. Then history swept through the land, shifted the borders, and places Lublin far in the east of Poland, far from the heart of the things and somewhat in the corner. Although Lublin is one of Poland's largest cities (the ninth-largest, in fact, with about 350,000 inhabitants), you'll probably see it as a peaceful, quiet, and very romantic town. Lublin's pride is its walled Old Town, which was built between the 13th and 16th centuries. The city is rich in parks, offering wild, lush green spaces in summer and golden yellow colors in autumn.

Lublin makes a good hub for exploring the villages and countryside of the eastern parts of the country. In less than an hour visitors can travel to Puławy to enjoy a picnic on the palace grounds or to the village of Kazimierz Dolny for a walk along the banks of the Vistula. It's also pos-

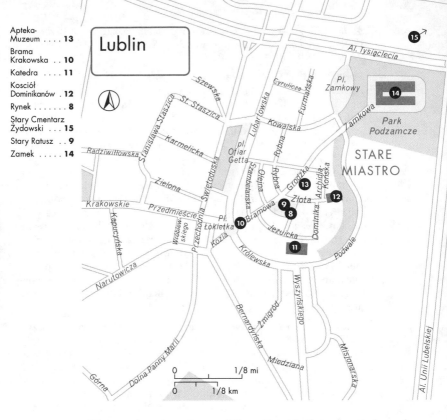

sible to make a day-trip out of Zamość and Łańcut, though these places also make nice stopovers if you have the time.

The tourist attractions in Lublin are in three distinct regions of the city. The Stare Miasto (Old Town) is a medieval walled city at the eastern end of Krakowskie Przedmieście, the main street. The castle and nearby Jewish cemetery are just outside the old city wall, to the northeast. The Catholic and Marie Skłodowska-Curie universities and the adjacent Saxon Gardens are on the western edge of the city, off aleje Racław-ickie (take a bus west from Krakowskie Przedmieście).

Numbers in the margins refer to the Lublin map.

What to See

⓭ Apteka–Muzeum (Museum of Pharmacy). In one of the recently recon-structed medieval tenements you can visit the small ground-floor mu-seum, which is a reproduction of an early chemist's shop. The café behind it is a good place to stop for a cup of coffee or other refreshments. ⊠ *ul. Grodzka 5A* ☎ *081/532—88–20* ✉ *Free* ◷ *Weekdays 8–4.*

⓾ Brama Krakowska (Kraków Gate). Situated at the eastern end of Lublin's main shopping street, Krakowskie Przedmieście, is the structure that served as the main entrance to the medieval city of Lublin. Today, it separates modern Lublin from the Old Town, and its characteristic silhouette is the city's "logo": a redbrick Gothic corpus, with Renaissance elements in the upper octagonal section, and a green baroque helmet. It's quite a cross-section of centuries and styles. The gate houses the **Muzeum Historii Miasta Lublina** (Lublin History Museum), where you can learn about the area's history. Among the museum objects you will find a 16th-century bronze bell cast during the reign of King Stefan Batory. The top-floor windows open to a panoramic view of Lublin. Each day at noon a tune is played from the tower. The passage through the gate is also a gallery of sorts, where young artists and amateurs exhibit and sell their works. ☒ *pl. Łokietka 3* ☏ *081/532–60–01* ☞ *zł 3.50* ☉ *Wed.–Sat. 9–4, Sun. 9–5.*

⑪ **Katedra** (Lublin Cathedral). Outside the old city wall, just around the corner from Kraków Gate, stands the cathedral that was founded by the Jesuits in 1625. It now bears later neoclassical features, the result of a thorough remodeling by the Italian architect Antonio Corazzi. You can reach the **Kaplica Akustyczna** (Whispering Chapel) by a passage to the right of the high altar. Watch what you say here—a whisper in one corner can be heard perfectly in another. Next to the chapel is the **treasury,** holding what remains of the original illusionistic frescos that decorated the church interior: the images were painted so skillfully that they appear almost three-dimensional. Next to the cathedral, the impressive belfry, or **Wieża Trynitarska** (Trinitarian Tower) is the tallest historical building in Lublin (138 feet); today it houses the Archdioceseal Museum, with a display of religious art, and a viewing platform. ☒ *ul. Królewska 10* ☏ *081/532–11–96* ☞ *Cathedral free, whispering chapel and treasury zł 4, museum (tower) zł 5* ☉ *Cathedral, daily dawn–dusk; whispering chapel and treasury, Tues.–Sun. 10–2 and 3–5; museum, Apr.–Oct., daily 10–5, Nov.–Mar., weekends 10–5.*

★ ⑫ **Kościół Dominikanów** (Dominican Church & Monastery). Dating from 1342, this church is the jewel of Lublin's Old Town. The original Gothic interior was renovated in rococo style in the 17th century. Two of its 11 chapels are particularly noteworthy: the **Kaplica Firlejowska** (Firlej Family Chapel) from the late-Renaissance period and the **Kaplica Tyszkiewskich** (Tyszkiewski Family Chapel) from the early baroque. Circling the walls above the chapels are paintings depicting the transport of a piece of the True Cross—the cross on which Jesus was crucified—to Lublin and the protection the relic has given the city through the ages. Unfortunately, this protection did not extend to the relic itself, which was stolen from the church in 1991. ☒ *ul. Złota 9* ☏ *081/532–89–90* ⊕ *www.dominikanie.lub.pl* ☞ *Free* ☉ *Weekdays 9–noon and 3–6, weekends 3–6.*

★ ❽ **Rynek** (Market Square). Part of Lublin's tremendous success as a Medieval trading center stemmed from a royal decree exempting the city from all customs duties. As a result, huge fortunes were made and kept, and the town's merchants were able to build the beautiful 14th- and 15th-century houses—complete with colorful frescoed facades—that surround the city's original market square. The Rynek's unusual trapezoidal shape is the result of medieval builders adapting the construction of the town to the outline of the protective walls surrounding Lublin.

⑮ Stary Cmentarz Żydowski (Old Jewish Cemetery). Starting in the 16th century, Lublin was an important center of Jewish culture; indeed, the city was often called the "Jerusalem of the Polish Kingdom" or the university the "Jewish Oxford." The city was famous for its Hasidic school, and for two zaddikim in particular: Rabbi Yaacov Yitzchak, the Chozeh (Seer) of Lublin; and Reb Yehuda Lejb Eiger, the "Crying Tzadik"; as well as for many expert Talmudists. The hill behind Lublin Castle is the site of the city's original Jewish cemetery. The cemetery was destroyed during World War II by the German SS, which used the rubble from the headstones to pave the entryway to the Majdanek Concentration Camp. The park at the base of the castle hill was the site of the Jewish ghetto, where Nazis imprisoned the Jewish population of Lublin until April 1943, when they were sent to Majdanek. ⊠ *Grodzisko hill, between ul. Kalinowszczyna and ul. Sienna. Key to cemetery is kept by Mr. and Mrs. Honig, at Dembowskiego 4/7* ☎ *081/747–86–76.*

⑨ Stary Ratusz (Old Town Hall). Filling the center of the Rynek is the reconstructed town hall, which was built in the 16th century and rebuilt in the neoclassical style in the 1780s by the Italian architect Domenico Merlini. Here, a royal tribunal served as the seat of the Crown Court of Justice for Małopolska, beginning in 1579; records of its activities can be seen in the town hall's history museum (a branch of the Lublin History Museum). On Saturday the hall fills with young couples waiting to be married. ⊠ *Rynek 1* ☎ *081/532–68–66* ▦ *Museum zł 4* ☉ *Wed.–Sun. 9–4.*

★ **⑭ Zamek** (Lublin Castle). During the late 14th century, King Kazimierz the Great ordered the construction of the castle, as well as the defensive walls surrounding the city, to protect the wealthy trading center from invasion. Most of the castle was rebuilt in mock-Gothic style during the 19th century, when it was converted to a prison. Run at various times by the Russian czar, the German Gestapo, and the Communist secret police, the castle prison witnessed its largest number of deaths during World War II, when the Nazis murdered more than 10,000 political prisoners here. Most recently, the Communist government kept the members of the Polish Home Army (AK) prisoner here. The oldest part of the castle is the 13th-century *donjon* (round tower). Next to it is the **Kaplica Trójcy świętej** (Chapel of the Holy Trinity), which has been restored in a decades-long project, and is justly considered the most outstanding attraction in Lublin. The 14th-century chapel is covered with magnificent Byzantine-style murals: In 1418, King Władysław Jagiełło commissioned Rusyn artists to paint the whole interior. You can see scenes from the Old and New Testament, a gallery of Eastern saints and fathers of the church, and even two portraits of the king himself. The **Castle Museum** houses historical exhibits and an art gallery, which displays Jan Matejko's *Unia Lubelska* (1869), depicting the signing of the Lublin Union by the king of Poland and Grand Duke of Lithuania exactly three centuries earlier. ⊠ *ul. Zamkowa 9* ☎ *081/532–50–01* ⊕ *www.zamek-lublin.*

pl 🖾 *zł 6.50* ⊙ *June–Aug., daily 10–6; Sept.–May, Tues. and Thurs.–Sat. 9–4 and Wed. and Sun. 9–5. Access to Chapel of Holy Trinity has a limit of 30 people per hour.*

OFF THE BEATEN PATH

MAJDANEK CONCENTRATION CAMP – Reminders of the horrors of World War II are never far away in Poland, and 5 km (3 mi) southeast of Lublin's city center lie the remnants of the Majdanek Concentration Camp, second in scope only to Auschwitz. Established in July 1941, it grew to 1,235 acres, although the original plan was to make it five times as large. From 1941 to 1944, more than 230,000 people lost their lives here, either by direct extermination or through illness and disease. Standing at the camp entrance is one of two monuments designed for the 25th anniversary of the liberation of Majdanek. The **Monument of Struggle and Martyrdom** symbolizes the inmates' faith and hope; the **mausoleum** at the rear of the camp marks the death of that hope. Of the five fields constituting the original camp, only the gas chambers, watchtowers, and crematoriums, as well as some barracks on Field Three, remain. The **visitor center,** to the left of the monument at the entrance, shows a movie about the camp (in English) and has a bookstore as well as a restaurant. To reach the camp from Lublin, take Bus 153 or 156 from Krakowskie Przedmieście. Children under 14 years of age are not admitted. ⊠ *Droga Męczenników Majdanka 67* ☎ *081/744–26–47* ⊕ *www.majdanek.pl* 🖾 *Free* ⊙ *May–Sept. 8–6; Oct.–Apr. 8–3 PM.*

Where to Eat

$–$$ ✕ **Club Hades.** Hades is a local legend. The walls that contain it date back to the 18th century, when it was a convent, but the building's modern history started in 1984, when it became a popular cafeteria. Extended and updated in the 1990s, it is now a bar, restaurant, live music venue, exhibition space, sometime dance club, and a place to gather to talk. Locals consider this is the best place to dine in Lublin. Specialties include onion soup and all kinds of traditional meat dishes: for instance, *golonka* (pork knuckle), as well as chicken liver with apples. ⊠ *al. Peowiaków 12* ☎ *081/532–56–41, 081/536–00–27 concert and disco reservations* ⊟ *AE, DC, MC, V.*

★ **$–$$** ✕ **Oregano.** You'll find a mix of serious Italian–Mediterranean cuisine, with lasagna next to moussaka next to *gambas* (large prawns). The chef is inventive, and he has introduced some fusion dishes to the menu (e. g., tilapia with ginger, shiitake mushrooms, and soy sauce). Leave some room for dessert, which might include crème caramel with rosemary, or a baklava. The interior is nice and simple, with a Tuscan theme. This is probably the best restaurant in all of Lublin. ⊠ *ul. Kościuszki 7* ☎ *081/442–55–30* ⊟ *AE, DC, MC, V.*

¢–$$ ✕ **Więzienie.** Highly stylized and true to its name, Jailhouse is properly fitted with bars, beds of boards, and skeletons. A very unusual setting for the restaurant, which serves simple, traditional Polish fare, from *pierogi* and *placki* (potato pancakes) to pork cutlets and beef steaks. Accidental prisoners seem to be having fun, and the food is tasty, which is hardly a painful punishment. ⊠ *ul. Narutowicza 27* ☎ *081/411–59–10* ⊟ *AE, DC, MC, V.*

Where to Stay

$$–$$$ ☒ **Grand Hotel Lublinianka.** Built at the turn of the 20th century, this elegant building served as Chamber of Commerce headquarters in the early 1900s, and as a tourist hotel in 1950s. Revamped and reopened in 2002, the Grand Hotel Lublinianka, run by the Spanish IBB group, offers the best and most stylish accommodations in town. Comfortable and elegant rooms, palatial bathrooms, and some great facilities (including a Turkish bath and sauna) make a stay here a pleasure. ☒ *ul. Krakowskie Przedmieście 56, 20–002* ☎ *081/446–61–00* ☒ *081/446–62–00* ⊕ *www. lublinianka.com* ↪ *72 rooms* ⚴ *Restaurant, café, minibars, cable TV, in-room broadband, gym, hair salon, sauna, Turkish bath, bar, laundry services, meeting rooms, parking (fee)* ⊟ *AE, DC, MC, V* †◎† *BP.*

$$ ☒ **Hotel Europa.** Built between 1865 and 1867 in the Renaissance-revival style, the Europa was modeled on Warsaw's Hotel Europejski. It was the most elegant hotel in town for more than 50 years, but then was purchased by the Lublin Charitable Society. The building was badly damaged during World War II. Although it became a hotel again after the war, it wasn't properly renovated until after 2000, when it received a cheerful and comfortable look, becoming a member of Polish Prestige Hotels. Although not much remains from the original interiors, the designers have tried to re-create the spirit of the past, quite successfully. Presidential suites have a private Jacuzzi and more than 1,000 square feet of space and are the pride of the hotel. ☒ *ul. Krakowskie Przedmieście 29, 20–002* ☎ *081/535–03–03* ☒ *081/535–03–04* ⊕ *www.hoteleuropa. pl* ↪ *73 rooms, 2 suites* ⚴ *Restaurant, minibars, cable TV, in-room broadband, bar, club, shops, meeting rooms, parking (fee); no a/c in some rooms* ⊟ *AE, DC, MC, V* †◎† *BP.*

$$ ☒ **Mercure-Unia Hotel.** This six-story, Orbis-managed hotel is just off the main road outside the Old Town. Most of the public spaces are fairly cramped, but the rooms are reasonably spacious, comfortably furnished, and and have a fresh, contemporary look. The chain hotel caters primarily to business travelers. ☒ *al. Racławickie 12, 20–037* ☎ *081/ 533–20–61* ☒ *081/533–30–21* ⊕ *www.orbis.pl* ↪ *110 rooms* ⚴ *Restaurant, café, minibars, cable TV, Wi-Fi, gym, bar, casino, laundry facilities, meeting rooms; no a/c* ⊟ *AE, DC, MC, V* †◎† *BP.*

KOZŁÓWKA CASTLE

⑯ *41 km (25 mi) north of Lublin.*

In a beautiful and well-tended park, this 18th-century palace was built for the Zamoyski family and is one of a handful of palaces in Poland whose interiors has remained intact. The halls, drawing rooms, studies, and bedrooms are filled with high-quality furniture from many different periods and styles, from neo-rococo to Empire. The collection of paintings and sculptures includes great examples of Meissen and Sevres porcelain, as well as rare stoneware and goldware. The chapel, which was built at the beginning of 20th century, was modeled after the royal chapel in Versailles (as were some other elements of the compound, including the garden). Housed in the palace annex is a fascinating relic of the Stalinist era, the **Museum of the Art of Socialist Realism,** with samples of propaganda posters, beefy busts of the revolution leaders, and kitschy statues of happy Socialist workers. Occasional temporary exhibitions in the coach house supplement a permanent display there about travel in the old days; these have a separate charge. The coach house also has a café, open during museum hours. The palace is reachable by bus from Lublin. If you are driving, take Route 19 north of Lublin to Lubartów (29 km [18 mi]); then head west for 12 km (7 mi). ⊠ *Kozłówka* ☎ *081/852–83–00* ⊕ *www.muzeumkozlowka.lublin.pl* ▨ *Palace and chapel zł 15, museum zł5, coach house zł 4, park and grounds zł2, all-inclusive ticket zł 24, parking zł 4* ⊙ *Mar. 15–Dec. 15, Tues.–Sun. 10–4 (Nov. until 3, July and Aug. until 5); coach house Apr.–Oct., Tues.–Sun. 10–4.*

NEED A BREAK? You can get a tasty and reasonably priced lunch at a nearby **Cooking School** (⊠ Kamionka, 1 km (½-mi) from Kozłówka ☎ 081/852–70–09). If you want to eat lunch at the cooking school, you should make a reservation 48 hours in advance.

5

PUŁAWY

⓱ *40 km (25 mi) northwest of Lublin, 130 km (70 mi) southeast of Warsaw.*

The 18th-century **Puławy Palace** in the town of Puławy is worth a brief stop. The palace was originally the residence of the Czartoryski family, a patriotic, politically powerful clan. Prince Adam Czartoryski was one of the most educated men of his day and a great patron of the arts and culture. He attracted so many prominent Poles to Puławy that by the late 18th century it was said to rival Warsaw as a cultural and political capital. Today the yellow-and-white neoclassical building houses an agricultural institute.

Modeled on the Vesta Temple in Tivoli, **Świątynia Sybilli** (Sybil's Temple), completed in 1809, was Poland's first museum. The museum's collection was donated by the Czartoryski family to the Polish state and can now be seen at the Czartoryski Museum in Kraków. ⊠ *ul. Czartoryskich 6A* ☎ *081/887–86–74* ▨ *Palace grounds free, Sybil's Temple zł 4* ⊙ *May.–Oct., Tues.–Sun. 10–2.*

KAZIMIERZ DOLNY

★ ⓲ *12 km (7 mi) south of Puławy, 40 km (25 mi) west of Lublin, 130 km (80 mi) southeast of Warsaw.*

This small town is so pleasing to the eyes that it has thrived for more than a century as an artists' colony and vacation spot. It sits on a steep, hilly bank of the placid Vistula River, and whitewashed facades and steeply pitched red-tile roofs peek out over the treetops. Although the first settlement existed here in the 12th century, the town was formally founded by King Kazimierz the Great, after whom it was named. This Kazimierz received the nickname Dolny (the Lower) to distinguish it from another newly founded Kazimierz upriver, now part of Kraków. Kazimierz Dolny prospered as a river port during the 16th and 17th centuries, but the partitioning of Poland left it cut off from the grain markets of Gdańsk. Thereafter, the town fell into decline until it was rediscovered by painters and writers during the 19th century. Today both artistic and nonartistic visitors can still enjoy the Renaissance architecture along the village's dusty cobblestone streets or hike through the nearby hills and gorges.

On the southeast corner of the town's market square lie the **Kamienice Przybyłów** (Przybyła Brothers' Houses), left behind by one of the most powerful families in Kazimierz Dolny, the Przybyłas. The ornate houses were built in 1615, and their facades are adorned with the two-story bas-relief figures of St. Nicholas (left) and St. Christopher (right), the brothers' patron saints. ⊠ *Rynek.*

The **Kamienica Celejowska** (Celej Family House), seat of a powerful Kazimierz clan, stands one block toward the river from the main square, and it is embellished with griffins, dragons, and salamanders. The former residence now houses one of the five sections of the **Muzeum Nadwiślańskie** (Vistula Valley Museum) telling the history of Kazimierz town, and presenting works of the many artists who lived, visited, and worked here, starting from the shaping of the "Kazimierz artists' colony" phenomenon (late 19th century to 1920s), to its flourishing between the world wars, and its post-war and contemporary periods. Some names to look out for include Władysław Ślewiński, Tadeusz Pruszkowski, Antoni Michalak, Teresa Roszkowska, Eugeniusz Arct, Władysław Skoczylas, Jan Cybis, and Artur Nacht-Samborski. ⊠ *ul. Senatorska 11* ☎ *081/ 881-01-04* 🖱 *zł 5* ⊙ *Oct.–Apr., Tues.–Thurs. and Sun. 10–3, Fri. and Sat. 10–5; May–Sept., Tues.–Thurs. and Sun. 10–5, Fri. and Sat. 10–7.*

A covered passageway off ulica Senatorska leads up to the walled courtyard of the **Kościół i klasztor Reformatów** (Church and Monastery of the Reformati), which stands on the southern hill overlooking the town's market square. The Reformati were the reformed Franciscan Order. In the late 18th century an encircling wall was built to protect the monastery's buildings. A plaque inside the passageway memorializes the Nazis' use of the site as a house of torture during World War II. The climb up to the courtyard is worthwhile just for the spectacular view it affords of the town. ⊠ *ul. Klasztorna, off ul. Senatorska.*

On the north side of the main square is the **Kościół Parafialny** (Parish Church), initially built in Gothic style but remodeled in the so-called Lublin-Renaissance style. The original Gothic structure was badly damaged by fire in 1561, and remained in the state of near-ruin for the next 25 years, just long enough to benefit from the "fashion" for Renaissance architecture in Poland. The result of the combination of styles—Gothic slenderness with Renaissance ornament—is striking. An Italian resident of Poland, Jacob Balin, was the author of the new design for the presbytery. Note the Renaissance stalls, the rococo confessionals, an ornate

17th-century organ and pulpit, and an unusual chandelier made from stags' antlers. ⊠ *Rynek, north side.*

The ruins of the 14th-century **Zamek** (Kazimierz Castle), which served as a watchtower to protect the Vistula trade route, stand on a steep hill to the northeast of the town's market square. From here there is a grand view over the town and the Vistula Valley. Good exercise for imagination: try to see the powerful stronghold of Kazimierz Wielki, then an elegant Renaissance palace in today's romantic ruin left to its own devices. Resident ghosts roam undisturbed . . . most of the time. In the summer, the ruin sometimes becomes illuminated to serve as a backdrop to an open-air concert.

The **Góra Trzech Krzyży** (Three Crosses Mount) lies to the east of the market square. The crosses were constructed in 1708 to commemorate the victims of a plague (cholera) that ravaged the town. This vantage point affords perhaps the best view of the town.

5

OFF THE BEATEN PATH

The village of Janowiec, 6 km (4 mi) west of Kazimierz Dolny, on the other side of the Vistula, is most famous for the ruins of **FIRLEJ CASTLE** – The castle was built on the high left bank of the Vistula between 1526 and 1537 by Piotr Firlej, and in its time it rivaled the Kazimierz castle across the river. King Sigismundus the Old attended the opening of this magnificent residence, which was built in late-Renaissance style by a renowned Italian architect Santi Gucci. (The story goes that Santi Gucci fell in love with a local girl and remained in Janowiec for the next 20 years.) The castle served as the home of influential families of Firlej, Tarło, and then Lubomirski. Badly damaged during the Swedish raids in 1656, it was repaired and rebuilt in the baroque style, according to a design by Tylman van Gameren. With Kazimierz Dolny and Janowiec losing their significance, the castle suffered from neglect. Abandoned in 1790, it fell into ruin. It came under the care of the museum authorities in the 1970s, and now the picturesque ruin has been partly restored. A museum displays an architectural and ethnographic exhibition. Summer concerts are the castle's great attraction (May through August; check the program at the tourist information in Kazimierz Dolny). ⊠ *ul. Lubelska 10, Janowiec* ☎ *081/881–52–29* ☞ *zł 8* ☉ *Oct.–Apr., Tues.–Fri. 10–3, weekends 10–4; May–Sept., Mon. 10–2, Tues.–Fri. 10–5, weekends 10–7.*

Where to Eat

In addition to the one recommended below, the hotels Bohema and Król Kazimierz both have good restaurants.

★ $ ✕ **U Fryzjera.** "At the Barber Shop" commemorates the previous tenant of the house, a barber. The owners' mission is to serve food to the hungry and joy to the sad, and it's a perfect venue to enjoy some excellent klezmer music on Saturday nights (one of the owners is a musician in a klezmer band). Traditional Jewish dishes served here include trout with almonds, *szlajmzupe* (soup with chicken livers, buckwheat, and beans), and marinated goose (the latter must be ordered in advance, and costs zł 130 for the whole goose). The restaurant is also open for breakfast, but it closes at midnight sharp on most days, and at 2 AM on Friday and Saturday. Reservations are not accepted for weekends or holidays. ⊠ *ul. Witkiewicza 2* ☎ *081/881–04–26* ⊟ *AE, DC, MC, V.*

Where to Stay

$$$ ⊞ **Hotel Król Kazimierz.** The newest and most plush hotel in Kazimierz, which opened in November 2006, is hoping to offer a new standard of modern comforts combined with traditional Polish hospitality. The hotel is a converted granary just outside the center of town that has been transformed with a contemporary design. The luxury Kanebo Spa offers holistic body treatments and wellness programs, including yoga and purifying diets. ⊠ *Puławska 86, 24–120* ☎ *081/880–99–99* ☎ *081/880–98–98* ⊕ *www.krolkazimierz.pl* ⟳ *107 rooms, 8 suites* ⚭ *Restaurant, café, minibars, cable TV, Wi-Fi, pool, spa, bowling, 2 bars, night club, laundry service, meeting rooms, parking (free)* ⊟ *AE, MC, V* ⦿ *BP.*

$$ ⊞ **Bohema.** This elegant and comfortable hotel draws visitors not only with its stylish, simple, and chic rooms—which have custom-made furniture—but also with its beauty treatments and massages in its small spa. In tune with the wellness theme, the restaurant offers light and subtle dishes, a departure from traditional Polish cuisine, and gives a much strong nod toward a sophisticated European menu. ⊠ *Małachowskiego 12, 24–120* ☎ *081/882–10–88* ☎ *081/881–07–56* ⊕ *www.spakazimierz.pl* ⟳ *15 rooms, 2 suites* ⚭ *Restaurant, minibars, cable TV, in-room broadband, pool, hot tub, sauna, spa, meeting room* ⊟ *AE, DC, MC, V* ⦿ *BP.*

$–$$ ⊞ **Dom Pracy Twórczej Architekta SARP.** This ideally located hotel is right on a corner of the main town square. Although it caters primarily to the Architects' Association, the hotel will accept other guests if there is space available. The rooms are large and irregular in shape, with simple but adequate furnishings. The restaurant is usually packed with intellectuals. ⊠ *Rynek 20, 24–120* ☎☎ *081/881–05–44* ⊕ *www.kazimierz-news.com.pl/sarp.html* ⟳ *35 rooms, 2 suites* ⚭ *Dining room, cable TV, meeting rooms, parking (free)* ⊟ *No credit cards* ⦿ *BP.*

Sports & the Outdoors

Boat Tours

During the summer season (May through October), you can take boat rides on the Vistula. The most popular, half-hour ride takes you south to Janowiec and its Firlej Castle ruins.

Rejsy po Wiśle (⊠ ul. Nadwiślańska ☎ 081/881–01–35 ⊕ www.rejsystatkiem.com.pl) has six boats, each able to carry from 120 to 240 people. The company offers rides across the river to Janowiec, where you can pick up a 14-km (9-mi) trail to Puławy, and a 50- to 60-minute round-trip cruise on the river for zł 12 per person. You can purchase tickets right at the quayside.

Right outside the **Dziunia** (⊠ ul. Nadwiślańska ☎ 081/723–50–06) botel (a boat-hotel), you will find small wooden boats (seating up to 20 people) that sail on itineraries to Janowiec and also on hour-long round-trip river cruises, but these boats specialize in sunset sailing trips for zł 10 per person.

Hiking

If you take one of the numerous marked trails, ranging in length from 2 km to 6 km (1 mi to 4 mi), you can easily explore the hilly landscape around Kazimierz (now protected as Kazimierz Landscape Park) on foot. All these walking trails converge on the market square. Tourist tracks lead north (marked red) and south (marked green) along the river from the square, along streets and cart paths, through orchards and quarries. Many of these trails take you through the ravines that are characteristic for this area. In one densely "populated" (or rather, "perforated") section, you'll find 10 km of ravines in every square kilometer.

ZAMOŚĆ

19 *87 km (54 mi) southeast of Lublin, 318 km (198 mi) northeast of Kraków.*

Perhaps the most perfect realization of the ideal city—both refined in its beauty and rational in its composition—the fortified town of Zamość has a wonderfully preserved, Renaissance-era central square, wide boulevards, and neat rows of colorful houses with brightly painted facades. The town was conceived in the late 16th century by Hetman Jan Zamoyski as an outpost along the thriving trade route between Lublin and Lwów (now Lviv, Ukraine). He commissioned Italian architect Bernardo Morando, who created a masterpiece of Renaissance urban planning. Zamość became the administrative center of the region and, since 1594, home to Akademia Zamojska, the third Polish university after Kraków and Vilnius (though the Akademia was disbanded in 1784, following the city's decline).

Having welcomed Armenian, Greek, and Jewish settlers (and later also German, Dutch, Scottish, and other merchants and artisans), the town was thriving, and its strong fortifications spared it from destruction during the Cossack invasions, as well as the Swedish onslaught of the 17th century. In the 18th century, as the result of Poland's partitions, Zamość found itself under Austrian rule, and then in the 19th, it passed to the Russians. The Polish victory over the Bolsheviks near Zamość in 1920 kept the way clear for the coun-

---

THE BODY POLITIC

The city design by Bernardo Morando followed anthropomorphic principles; that is, Zamość was composed as if it were a human body. The "head" was the Zamoyski family palace, residence of the town's creator and owner. Grodzka Street was the city's "spine." The academy and the cathedral were the vital organs: Zamość's heart and lungs. The perpendicular artery with three city squares was the city's "belly," while the bastions, its "hands" and "feet," served as its protection. This layout has survived practically unchanged to this day and remains a textbook example of urban planning of the time.

try's restored independence. World War II saw the town renamed Himmlerstadt, with thousands of its residents (45% of the town was Jewish) deported or exterminated to make way for German settlers. Today the well-preserved city is a UNESCO World Heritage site.

FodorsChoice
★

Zamość's **Rynek** (Market Square) is a breathtaking arcaded plaza of 1,000 square feet, surrounded by the decorative facades of homes built by local merchants during the 16th and 17th centuries. Dominating the square is the impressive baroque **Ratusz** (Town Hall), topped by a 164-foot spire. It is placed unusually: not in the center, but in the corner of the square (to indicate that was less prominent than the palace of the city's founders and owners). The distinctive staircase, which renders the building more imposing, was added later, in the 17th century.

The **Muzeum Zamojskie** (Zamość Museum) is housed in four charming town houses next door to the town hall (at the north end of the square). These were called the Armenian houses after their original 16th-century tenants. The interiors themselves—with stucco decorations, wooden ceilings, and arcaded courtyards—are worth a visit, and the collection features paintings of the Zamoyski clan, Polish kings, and a scale model of Zamość. ✉ *ul. Ormiańska 24* ☏ *084/638–64–94* ⊕ *www.muzeum-zamojskie.one.pl* 🎫 *zł 5* ☉ *Oct.–Apr., Tues.–Sun. 9–4; May–Sept., Tues.–Sun. 9–5.*

The Renaissance cathedral, former **Kolegiata** (St. Thomas Collegiate Church), one of Poland's most beautiful Renaissance churches, stands near the southwest corner of the market square. It was built according to the design of Bernardo Morando, just as all other major structures of his "ideal city." In the presbytery are four 17th-century paintings ascribed to Domenico Robusti, Tintoretto's son. The church is also the final resting place of Jan Zamoyski, who is buried in the **Zamoyski Chapel** to the right of the high altar. ✉ *ul. Kolegiacka.*

The **Pałac Zamojskich** (Zamoyski Palace), home of the founding family of Zamość, lies in the western, or "top" end of the Old Town, near the Market Square beyond the Collegiate Church. The palace was turned into a military hospital in the 1830s; now it serves as a courthouse. ✉ *ul. Zamkowa.*

Behind the Zamoyski Palace is the **Arsenał** (Arsenal Museum), which houses a collection of Turkish armaments and rugs, as well as a model of the original town plan. ✉ *ul. Zamkowa 2* ☏ *084/638–40–76* 🎫 *zł 5* ☉ *Oct.–Apr., Tues.–Sun. 10–4; May–Sept., Tues.–Sun. 10–5.*

Near the northwest corner of the main square, behind Town Hall, is the **Akademia** (Old Academy), a distinguished center of learning during the 17th and 18th centuries and once the third-largest university after those in Kraków and Vilnius. It is now a high school. ✉ *ul. Akademicka.*

The old Synagoga (Synagogue), east of the Academy, was built in 1620 in late-Renaissance style; the two women's galleries were added later. Inside, architectural elements such as the cradle vault with lunettes and stucco decorations are worth noting. It was misused by the Germans during Word War II, when it housed a carpentry workshop; renovated

The Zamoyskis of Zamość

TODAY, THE TOWN OF ZAMOŚĆ, established in 1580 by Hetman Jan Zamoyski (the commander of the Polish army), is again "ruled" by the member of the Zamoyski clan. Marcin Zamoyski, son of the last heir to the *ordynacja* (estates) of Jan Zamoyski the 16th, was elected town mayor in 1990. Afterward, he served as a president of the city council and, in 2002, was reelected as the mayor of Zamość. The family–still the largest landowners in Zamość, though no longer the "owners" of the town–had been dispossessed of their estates after the Communist takeover following World War II, in what was then called the "agricultural reform of the People's Republic of Poland." The current mayor's father, Jan, was then forbidden to live anywhere within a 30-km radius of his former family property. Because he dared to enter this forbidden zone, Jan was imprisoned for seven years by the Communist government. The family's

property was never returned, though the Marcin Zamoyski, when not performing his official mayoral duties, has leased some of the land that once belonged to his family estate and operates it as a farm.

The family crest of the Zamoyski family is called the *Jelita*–bowels or guts–though this is happily just a symbolic name. The family emblem's bloody roots came from a battle, when nobleman Florian Sariusz–the precursor of the Zamoyskis–fought against the Teutonic Knights in the Battle of Płowce in 1331. In the course of the battle, he defended Polish King Władysław Łokietek with his own body, or more specifically with his own abdominal region, which was pierced with three spears, so that his bowels spilled out. The King ennobled the fatally wounded hero and the Jelita was borne: three spears against a red background.

in the 1960s, it is now a modest museum with plans for further expansion. At the time of this writing, it was recommended that you announce your visit in advance. ✉ *ul. Pereca 14* ☎ *048/608–409–055 or 048/693–124–572* 🎫 *zł 2* ☉ *May–Sept., weekdays 10–3, weekends 10–5; Oct.–Apr., weekends 10–2.*

The oldest entrance to Zamość, the **Brama Lubelska** (Lublin Gate) is to the northwest of Market Square, across the road from the Old Academy. In 1588, Jan Zamoyski triumphantly led the Austrian archduke Maximilian into town through this gate after defeating him in his attempt to seize the Polish throne from Sigismund III. He then bricked up the gate to commemorate his victory. ✉ *ul. ukasińskiego.*

What's left of Zamość's fortifications are at the bottom of ulica Staszica. This is the **Bastion i Brama Lwowska** (Lwów Gate and Bastion). With defenses like these—three stories high and 20 feet thick—it is easy to understand why Zamość was one of the few places to escape ruin in the Swedish attack. ✉ *ul. ukasińskiego 2* ☎ *084/627–07–48* 🎫 *zł 2* ☉ *Weekdays 9–5, weekends 9–3.*

South of the town's marketplace is the **Rotunda**, a monument to a tragic era in Zamość's history. From 1939 to 1944 this fortified emplacement served as an extermination camp, where tens of thousands of Poles, Jews, and Russians were brutally killed, some even burned alive. Now it serves as a memorial to the victims of Nazi brutality in the region. ⊠ *Droga Męczenników Rotundy* ☎ *084/638–52–06 or 048/606– 952–433* 🖹 *Free* ☉ *May–Sept., weekdays 7 AM–8 PM, Sat. 8–8, Sun. 8 AM–10 PM; Oct.–Apr., weekdays 7–3.*

Where to Eat

¢–$$ ✕ **Muzealna.** In the cellars underneath the main town square, the "Museum" restaurant specializes in Polish food. While the menu offers nothing too adventurous, everything is perfectly edible and served in a nice environment. At the lower end of the price range, try the homemade pierogi; more sophisticated—and expensive—meat dishes are also available. ⊠ *ul. Ormiańska 30* ☎ *084/638–73–00* ▤ *AE, DC, MC, V.*

¢—$ ✕ **Padwa.** Padwa is two-in-one: a restaurant (in the cellar) and a café (on the ground floor, with an entrance opposite the Zamość Town Hall on the main square). The restaurant offers a tasty and reliable, if not terribly imaginative, menu featuring cutlets and goulashes, which is reasonably priced, even almost unreasonably low. At the café, try the hot chocolate. ⊠ *ul. Staszica 23* ☎ *084/638–62–56* ▤ *AE, DC, MC, V.*

Where to Stay

$–$$ 🏨 **Hotel Zamojski.** This Orbis hotel is arranged in several historic tenement houses adjoining Market Square. All interiors have been thoroughly renovated, respecting their historical form and style, and the interior decor successfully captures the spirit of the place. The rooms are comfortable and well-equipped, and the service is professional. ⊠ *ul. Kołłątaja 2/ 4/6, 22–400* ☎ *084/639–25–16* ↜ *50 rooms, 4 suites* ⚭ *2 restaurants, room service, minibars, cable TV, in-room broadband, gym, hair salon, sauna, bar, meeting rooms, parking (free); no a/c* ▤ *AE, DC, MC, V* ⑩ *EP.*

$ 🏨 **Hotel Senator.** The hotel's name bears an appendix, "The Romantic Place." Indeed, the location couldn't be more romantic: in a tenement house in the heart of the Old Town, on a small square just off the main square. The decor continues on the romantic note, though the attempt to create an antique (or faux-antique) chivalric theme meets with mixed success and is slightly, well, overdone. Nevertheless, with comfortable rooms and friendly service, the Senator remains one of the best places to stay in town. ⊠ *Rynek Solny 4, 22–400* ☎ *084/638–99–90* ⊕ *www. senatorhotel.pl* ↜ *21 rooms, 2 suites* ⚭ *Restaurant, café, minibars, cable TV, in-room broadband, tennis court, meeting room, parking (free); no a/c* ▤ *AE, DC, MC, V* ⑩ *BP.*

¢–$ 🏨 **Hotelik Arkadia.** This tiny hotel is located right in the heart of the city, on the main square. Although the decor and fittings are a bit outdated, an excellent location, a certain laid-back charm, and a friendly atmosphere make up for it. The restaurant ($) serves tasty and cheerful dishes such as chicken wings in honey, turkey breast in sesame, and a selection of potato pancakes with various fillings. From May to September, umbrella-shaded tables spill out onto the square. ✉ *Rynek Wielki 9, 22–400* ☎ *084/638–65–07* ⊕ *www.arkadia.zamosc.pl* ⇝ *7 rooms* ⚒ *Restaurant, cable TV, billiards, parking (free); no a/c* ⊟ *AE, DC, MC, V* ⦿ *BP.*

ŁAŃCUT

⑳ *130 km (81 mi) southwest of Zamość on Hwy. 4(E40).*

Łańcut, a regional center with some 18,000 inhabitants, would most probably be completely unknown to tourists if it weren't for the palace compound in the eastern part of town, recognized as one of the most popular and magnificent aristocratic residences in Poland. It wasn't always as ornate as what you see today: the original building was commissioned by Stanisław Lubomirski as a fortified castle (*palazzo in fortezza*), but it acquired a lighter, brighter and much more grandiose form in the second half of the 18th century. As the story goes, the owner at the time, Izabela Lubomirska, was unhappy in her marriage. Rather than give in to despair, she decided to spend her energy on beautifying and expanding her residence in the rococo style. (This wasn't her only preoccupation: one of the most progressive women of her time, she was actively involved in politics, and she supported the arts and social reforms. She was called the "Blue Marchioness" as she liked to wear blue crinolines.)

★ The neo-baroque **Łańcut Palace,** situated within a 76-acre park, is the main attraction in town. Built during the 17th century, the palace is one of the most grandiose aristocratic residences in Eastern Europe. In the 19th century it was willed to the Potocki family, who amassed an impressive art collection here. Count Alfred Potocki, the last owner, emigrated to Liechtenstein in 1944 as Russian troops approached, escaping with 11 train cars full of art objects and paintings. Much was left behind, however, and after the war a **museum** was established in the palace (which had survived intact). Today you can see the family collection of art and interior decorations, including Biedermeier, neoclassical, and rococo furnishings. Of particular interest are the intricate wood-inlay floors, the tiny theater off the dining hall, and the hall of sculpture painted to resemble a trellis of grapevines. More than 40 rooms are open to the public, including the Turkish and Chinese apartments, which reflect the 18th-century fascination with the Near and Far East. Outside, a moat and a system of bastions laid out like a five-point star separate the inner Italian and rose gardens from the rest of the park. The **Carriage Museum** in the old coach house outside the main gates contains more than 50 vehicles and is one of the largest museums of its kind in Europe. ✉ *ul. Zamkowa 1* ☎ *017/225–20–08* ⊕ *www.zameklancut.pl* 🎫 *Castle zł 19–zł 21, exhibitions zł 3–zł 6* ⊗ *Museums Tues.–Sat. 8–2:30, Sun. 9–4; park daily dawn–dusk.*

Where to Stay & Eat

¢–$ ▦ **Hotel Zamkowy.** Although the rooms in this 18th-century palace have 1970s furnishings, they are cozy and overlook the palace courtyard. There are only 42 beds, so reservations are imperative. Also bear in mind that only some rooms have en-suite bathroom facilities and that these are almost three times more expensive than those with shared baths. The restaurant is no frills, but it serves decent traditional meals, from *pierogi* to pork cutlets. ⊠ *ul. Zamkowa 1, 37–100* ☎ *017/225–26–71* ⟁ *20 rooms, 13 with shared bath* ♦ *Restaurant; no a/c* ⊟ *AE, DC, MC, V* ⋈ *BP.*

★ ¢ ▦ **Pensjonat Pałacyk.** The name of this hotel-pension is the "Little Palace," yet it is decidedly more palatial than the accommodations offered to tourists in the "Big Palace," the Hotel Zamkowy. The rooms are cozy and cheerful. The restaurant (¢–$) uses locally made, ecological products to concoct simple but healthy and tasty traditional dishes, be it herring, borscht, or steak. ⊠ *ul. Paderewskiego 18, 37–100* ☎ *017/ 225–20–43* ⊕ *www.palacyk-lancut.pl* ⟁ *6 rooms, 1 suite* ♦ *Restaurant, cable TV, in-room broadband; no a/c* ⊟ *AE, DC, MC, V* ⋈ *BP.*

MAZURY & EASTERN POLAND ESSENTIALS

Transportation

BY AIR

The most convenient international airport for the lakes and northeast Poland would be Gdańsk (⇨ The Baltic Coast & Pomerania Essentials *in* Chapter 4). An international airport in Lublin is being developed at the time of this writing; for the time being, Warsaw remains the main aerial gateway to the area, and from Warsaw you can easily head southeast to Lublin.

BY BUS

From Olsztyn (which has a reasonably good connection both with Warsaw and Gdańsk—about 4 hours each), buses go east toward the lakes, to Mrągowo (1½ hours), Mikołajki (another 40 minutes), and Augustów (2½ hours direct, or 4 hours via Suwałki). The station is northeast of the Old Town. Bus services are more frequent in summer, and it's always a good idea to check schedules in advance.

Lublin is the gateway to the southeastern region. Lublin's main station, Dworzec Główny, is just north of the Stare Miasto (Old Town) near the castle and has regular buses to Warsaw (3 hours). There are regular buses to Puławy (1 hour), Kazimierz Dolny (1½ hours), and Zamość (1¾ hours). ▐ **Dworzec Główny PKS** ⊠ pl. Konstytucji 3 Maja 2a, Olsztyn ☎ 089/539–17–76 ⊕ www.pks.olsztyn.pl. **Dworzec Główny PKS** ⊠ al. Tysiąclecia 4, Lublin ☎ 081/747–89–22.

BY CAR

From Warsaw, you can reach Olsztyn by national Route 7 (E77) to Olsztynek, then national Route 51 (it then continues to Lidzbark Warmiński). Alternatively, Route 61 leads straight north from the capital, and it forks above Pułtusk. Route 61 turns northeast toward Augustów and Wigry, while Route 57 continues straight north to Szczytno. From there, you can turn northwest to Olsztyn (Route 53) or into Route 58 toward the Great Masurian Lakes.

From Warsaw, Route 17 (E372) takes you to Lublin and Zamość (with a convenient detour to Puławy and Kazimierz Dolny if you turn from the main road at Kurów, west into Route 44). From Kraków, the Tarnów-Rzeszów Route 4 (E40) will bring you farther south, close to Łańcut. A car can be useful if you wish to visit some of the smaller towns in this part of Poland and stay independent of bus and railway timetables.

🚘 **Hertz** ✉ ul. Dąbrowszczaków 1, Olsztyn ☎ 089/552-06-40 ⊕ www.hertz.com.pl **Sixt** ✉ ul. Unicka 3, Lublin ☎ 081/743-30-05 ⊕ www.sixt.pl.

BY TRAIN

Olsztyn's main railway station is northeast of the Old Town, and next to the town's bus station. From Olsztyn, it takes about 1 hour and 15 minutes by train to get to Mrągowo, and another 40 minutes to Mikołajki. Augustów has a direct train connection to Warsaw (4½ hours). There is no convenient train connection between Olsztyn and Augustów.

Lublin's main station, Lublin Główny, is about 4 km (2½ mi) south of the city center; take Bus 13 or 158 between the center and the station. Frequent train service connects Lublin with Warsaw (2½ hours) and Kraków (4½ hours). Trains run regularly between Lublin and Zamość (3 hours). A coach-class ticket costs about the same as the bus.

🚆 **Olsztyn Główny** ✉ pl. Konstytucji 3 Maja 3, Olsztyn ☎ 089/538-54-53 ⊕ www.pkp.pl. **Lublin Główny** ✉ pl. Dworcowy, Lublin ☎ 081/531-56-42 ⊕ www.pkp.pl.

Contacts & Resources

EMERGENCIES

🚨 **Emergency Services Medical Emergencies** ☎ 999
🚨 **24-hour Pharmacies Apteka** ✉ ul. Bramowa 8, Lublin ☎ 081/532-05-21 ✉ ul. Krakowskie Przedmieście 49, Lublin ☎ 081/532-24-25.

INTERNET, MAIL & SHIPPING

🌐 **Internet Cafés Internet Café** ✉ ul. Lubelska 4a, Kazimierz Dolny. **Internet Café** ✉ Rynek Wielki 10, Zamość ☎ 084/639-29-32. **Kawiarnia.net** ✉ ul. Okopowa 23, Olsztyn ☎ 089/527-22-90. **Piwnica Internetowa** ✉ ul. Szkolna 3d, Mikołajki. **www Café** ✉ Rynek 8, Lublin ☎ 081/442-35-80.
📮 **Post Offices Main Post Office Olsztyn** ✉ ul. Pieniężnego 21, Olsztyn ☎ 089/527-90-01. **Post Office Lublin** ✉ ul. Grodzka 7, Lublin ☎ 081/532-07-60. **Post Office Kazimierz Dolny** ✉ ul. Tyszkiewicza 2, Kazimierz Dolny ☎ 081/881-05-00. **Zamość Post Office** ✉ ul. Kościuszki 9. Zamość ☎ 084/639-20-48.

VISITOR INFORMATION

ℹ️ **Centrum Informacji Turystycznej w Lublinie** ✉ ul. Krakowskie Przedmieście 78, Lublin ☎ 081/532-44-12. **Centrum Informacji Turystycznej w Kazimierzu Dolnym** ✉ Rynek 27, Kazimierz Dolny ☎ 081/881-00-46 ⊕ www.kazimierz-dolny.com.pl.

Mrągowo Tourist Information ✉ ul. Warszawska 26, Mrągowo ☎ 089/743-34-68 ⊕www.it.mragowo.pl. **Mikołajki Tourist Information** ✉pl. Wolności 3, Mikołajki ☎087/ 421-68-50 ⊕ www.mikolajki.pl. **Regionalne Biuro Informacji Turystycznej w Olsztynie** ✉ ul. Staromiejska 1, Olsztyn ☎ 089/535-35-65 ⊕ www.warmia-mazury-rot.pl. **Zamojski Ośrodek Informacji Turystycznej** ✉ Rynek Wielki 13, Zamość ☎ 084/639-22-92 ⊕ www.osir.zamosc.pl.

Kraków

WORD OF MOUTH

"Da Vinci's *Lady with an Ermine* is in the [Arsenał Miejski, the] fantastic, small museum [that displays the] Czartoryski Collection (write it, don't try to pronounce it, if you need directions and don't speak Polish!) in the Old Town, and for the quality of the works displayed, I don't know if "undiscovered" is an accurate description, but we had the da Vinci to ourselves for at least 20 minutes . . . when 2 other people arrived. What a difference from *Mona Lisa* in the Louvre . . . push-shove!"

—delor

MANY FIRST-TIME VISITORS TO KRAKÓW are surprised at how quickly they feel at home there. Those who fall in love with the city at the first sight and claim it as their own are fully justified in their sentiment: since 1978 Kraków has been on the UNESCO World Heritage list, and as such, it "belongs to all the peoples of the world."

Kraków, once the ancient capital of Poland (before finally relinquishing the honor to Warsaw in 1609), has enchanted visitors for a thousand of years. It is often called a "magical city" and even the official municipal Web site calls it, fondly, "Magical Kraków." Krakovian air is composed of hefty doses of oxygen, nitrogen, history, and mystery. Here each stone tells a story; and—be warned!—a song or a sonnet may be lurking round the corner.

Despite Kraków's—and the region's—turbulent past, a wealth of treasures of art and architecture remain almost intact in one of the few Polish cities that escaped devastation by Hitler's armies during World War II. Some will tell you that it is due to Kraków's *chakhra,* a mystic stone that radiates energy from Wawel Hill, thus protecting the city against evil.

The marvels of Kraków include the Royal Castle of Wawel, Rynek Główny (the largest medieval square in Europe), several ancient synagogues in the old Jewish quarter of Kazimierz, some 150 churches, and 2.5 million works of art, including Leonardo da Vinci's famous portrait of *Cecilia Gallerani* as the jewel in the crown.

The seat of Poland's oldest university, Kraków is Poland's most important seat of higher learning, having educated Copernicus and Pope John Paul II. Today it is home to 20 universities, and some 200,000 students comprise about a fifth of the city's population, filling the city Kraków with their contagious energy.

Kraków has always inspired artists, and these include the Nobel Prize–winning poet Czesław Miłosz, the playwright Tadeusz Kantor, the composer Krzysztof Penderecki, and the American film director Steven Spielberg. Arts continue to thrive in the city of countless galleries, theaters, and concert halls; the list of annual festivals and cultural events is impressive.

Last but not least, this lively yet unhurried city is famous for its evergreen cafés, gourmet restaurants, and hip bars. Kraków may not be the seat of government any more, but it certainly is Poland's "time-out capital."

EXPLORING KRAKÓW

Starting as a market town in the 10th century, Kraków became Poland's capital in 1037. Until as recently as the 19th century walls encircled the Old Town; these have been replaced by the Planty, a ring of parkland, in the 1820s. Throughout the 19th and early 20th centuries, the city expanded, and many interesting examples of architecture from that period can be found within the second ring, marked by Aleje and Dietla streets. In late 20th century another phase of the city's development began farther out, and it will most probably continue well into the 21st century.

Most major historical attractions are within walking distance in the compact Old Town, but you'll also find very interesting sights further outside the city center, including Kościuszko's Mound, to the west, and Nowa Huta, to the east of the city center. The Wawel Hill—with the Royal Castle and cathedral—is perched between the south end of the Planty Ring and the Vistula River.

To the immediate southeast of the Old Town is the old Jewish quarter of Kazimierz. This was once a separate town, chartered in 1335 by its founder, King Kazimierz the Great. In 1495 Kraków's Jews were expelled from the city by King John Albert, and they resettled in Kazimierz. The Jewish community there came to an abrupt and tragic end during World War II. In 1941, the Jews of Kazimierz were moved first to a Jewish ghetto across the Vistula River in Podgórze, then to the Płaszów concentration camp. Most who survived Płaszów were transported to their deaths in the much larger concentration camp at Auschwitz–Birkenau. The story of the few Jews who escaped Płaszów through the help of businessman Oskar Schindler formed the basis of Thomas Kenneally's book (and Steven Spielberg's film) *Schindler's List*.

> ## KRAKÓW'S TOP 5
>
> - Kraków's Rynek is the largest medieval square in Europe, alive with history, pigeons, and people.
> - Wawel, which includes the Royal castle and cathedral, is the spiritual center of Poland.
> - The Jewish Culture Festival, held every July in Kazimierz, is one of the country's top events.
> - Nowa Huta, the model workers town built around the former Lenin steelworks, is a snapshot right out of the communist era.
> - The Muzeum Czartoryskich in the Arsenal Miejski displays the National Museum's most famous painting, Leonardo's *Lady with an Ermine*.

About the Restaurants

People of many different nationalities and traditions have left their marks in Kraków's cuisine. Dishes now considered "typically Polish" are often a mixture of Russian, German, Ukrainian, Italian, Jewish, Lithuanian, Turkish, French; many of these recipes were brought to Kraków and happily assimilated upon the addition of a pinch of the famed *genius loci*. Today international influence has entered the Krakovian culinary scene. The last 15 years or so not only have witnessed the arrival of French, Italian, Japanese, Chinese, Indian, Greek, and Mexican chefs, but also many creative interpretations of traditional fare.

Some traditional local specialties include cold meats such as tender cured ham (*polędwica* or *szynka wędzona*), and *kiełbasa* (sausage), preferably the *lisiecka* variety, which is made in a village of Liszki, near Kraków. In the same village they bake wonderful square loafs of dark bread (*ciemny chleb*). *Maczanka po krakowsku* (Kraków-style sippet) is pork stewed with onion and cumin seed, served in a sauce-filled bread-roll. You won't, however, find these dishes in most gourmet Krakovian restaurants today. The dining scene has become much more sophisticated, offering lighter, creative versions of traditional dishes, and often fusing local recipes with international tastes. A mixture of Polish and Mediterranean culinary traditions is particularly *en vogue*.

In high season, it is a good idea to make a reservation for most popular restaurants, which fill up around lunchtime (between 1 and 3) and again in the evening (after 6). The trend toward Mediterranean cuisine does not extend to Mediterranean opening hours, alas, and it is difficult to find a hot meal after 10 PM. Even then, if the restaurant stays open, the kitchen may have already closed. Krakovians do not tend to dress up much when they go out to dinner unless it is a very special celebration, so smart casual attire is perfectly proper even in top-end restaurants.

Prices are typically quoted inclusive of V.A.T. and service charge. (If an extra service charge is added, which is very rare, this should be stated on the menu.) Tipping is at your discretion; if you are happy with the service, it is customary to leave a tip of about 10% or just round up the bill.

About the Hotels

Although Kraków's range of accommodations is growing at an amazing rate, so are the numbers of visitors. It is a good idea to book well in advance—even in winter, when many tourists stay home but when the city plays host to many business conferences, and hotels often fill up. High season runs from April through October, and prices go down slightly between November and March. Few hotels offer lower weekend rates. In addition to reliable international chain hotels, such as the Sheraton and Radisson SAS, you will now find some charming high-quality boutique hotels, such as Amadeus and Copernicus. If you're staying in the Old Town, rooms facing the street can be noisy at night, so request a quiet room.

WHAT IT COSTS In Polish złoty (zł)				
$$$$	**$$$**	**$$**	**$**	**¢**
RESTAURANTS over 70	50–70	30–50	15–30	under 15
HOTELS over 800	500–800	300–500	150–300	under 150

Restaurant prices are per person for a main course at dinner. Hotel prices are for two people in a standard double room with a private bath and breakfast in high season. Prices include V.A.T., but do not include a small municipal fee of about zł 1.60 [50¢] per person per night.

Timing

With the arrival of low-cost airlines and continued expansion of the local airport, the number of visitors to Kraków is increasing. Although tourists now arrive in great numbers all year-round, the peak season to visit Kraków is between June and September. In terms of weather, May and September are probably the most pleasant months to visit the city, but Kraków has something to offer for each season.

Temperatures can get very cold in the winter, down to –20°C (–4°F), and summer days are reliably hot, with temperatures of up to 35°C (95°F).

GREAT ITINERARIES

The best way to explore Kraków is to slow down the pace of your steps in tune with this unhurried city, so reserve some time for just sitting in those wonderful cafés and watching life go by. Remember that most museums are closed on Monday, the synagogues of Kazimierz are closed on Saturday, and in high season, advanced booking is advisable for the Wawel Castle and Wieliczka Salt Mine (⇨ Chapter 7).

IF YOU HAVE 3 DAYS

Start Day 1 at the Market Square, the very heart of Kraków. Listen to the bugle call on the hour and explore all the sights within and around the Rynek: Sukiennice, Kościół Mariacki and other churches, the old university quarter with the Collegium Maius, and the Muzeum Czartoryskich (in the Arsenał Miejski) with its famous Leonardo. Climb Wawel Hill to visit the Zamek Królewski and cathedral and descend through the dragon's den to the river. For a memorable evening, book opera tickets at the historic Teatr im. Juliusza Słowackiego, catch a classical music concert in the Filharmonia im. Karola Szymanowskiego or a jazz gig in one of the clubs. On Day 2, go out of town to see the medieval Wieliczka Salt Mine, and visit the memorial museum at the former German concentration camp of Auschwitz–Birkenau (for both these attractions, ⇨ Chapter 7). Each is half-day trip, or they may be combined into one rather long day of sightseeing. On Day 3, explore the Jewish heritage of the Kazimierz District. Continue to the Christian part of Kazimierz, through the Pauline monastery garden to the

river, and across to the Manggha Center for Japanese Art & Technology.

IF YOU HAVE 5 DAYS

Again start with the Old Town as in the three-day itinerary, but leave Wawel for the morning of Day 2. In summer, take a boat trip on the Wisła River (⇨ Tour Options *in* Kraków Essentials). On Sunday, the boat will take you all the way to a Benedictine monastery in Tyniec (it can also be reached by road). If you get there in late afternoon, you may be able to catch an organ recital or an evensong. On the way back, stop at the Kościuszko Mound for a view of Kraków at sunset. On Day 3, marvel at the "model socialist town" of Nowa Huta, and then visit the Wieliczka Salt Mine. Take a trip to Auschwitz on your fourth day, and then go back to the Old Town. Visit Kazimierz on Day 5, and continue to the former ghetto in Podgórze, where Oskar Schindler's factory was memorialized in Steven Spielberg's movie. Enjoy an evening of traditional Yiddish music and the famous nightlife scene of Kazimierz.

IF YOU HAVE 7 DAYS

Follow the itinerary above. If you wish to explore more of the region, head for Zakopane (⇨ Chapter 7), a resort in the Tatra Mountains, where you can stay overnight. Or visit the Ojców National Park (⇨ Chapter 7) with its fantastic rock formations and hidden valleys. You could also take "The Pope's Express" (⇨ Chapter 7), which takes you to places connected with the life of John Paul II, between Kraków and his birthplace, Wadowice.

6

Kraków
Stare Miasto

The weather is often unpredictable and can turn very rapidly; therefore, it is advisable to bring an umbrella and a jacket even when you are traveling in the summer, just in case.

Krakovians love any opportunity for a celebration, and no matter when you come to town, you are almost sure to stumble upon some kind of cultural festival of music, theater, film, or dance. Some of the most famous include the *Shanties* sea songs festival in February; the *Misteria Paschalia* in April, a Polish Lent and Easter festival; the Jewish Culture Festival, Street Theatre Festival, and Summer Jazz Festival, all of which are in July; the Music in the Old Kraków festival in August; an Organ Music Festival throughout the summer; *Sacrum Profanum* in September, combining "sacred" and "profane" musical traditions; and the All Souls' Jazz Festival at the end of October and early November.

Numbers in the margins correspond to numbers on the Kraków Stare Miasto map.

Stare Miasto (Old Town)

Kraków's streets are a vast and lovely living museum, and the Stare Miasto (Old Town) in particular is a historical gold mine. Its ancient houses, churches, and palaces can overwhelm visitors with only a few days to see the sights. The heart of it all is Kraków's "drawing room"— the Rynek Główny, or Main Market Square.

What to See

4 **Arsenał Miejski** (Municipal Arsenal). The surviving fragment of Kraków's Fodor's Choice city wall opposite the Barbakan, where students and amateur artists hang ★ their paintings for sale in the summer, is the **Muzeum Czartoryskich**, a fantastic small museum that is a part of the National Gallery. The collection includes such celebrated paintings as Rembrandt's *Landscape with the Good Samaritan*. The prize—and to many observers the most beautiful portrait ever painted—is Leonardo da Vinci's *Cecilia Gallerani*, also known as the *Lady with an Ermine*. ⊠ *ul. św. Jana 19, Stare Miasto* ☎ *012/422–55–66* ⊠ *zł 7* ☉ *Tues. and Thurs. 9–3:30, Wed. 11–6, Sat. 10–3:30.*

1 **Barbakan.** Only one small section of Kraków's city wall still stands, centered on the 15th-century Barbakan, one of the largest strongholds of its kind in Europe. ⊠ *ul. Basztowa, opposite ul. Floriańska, Stare Miasto.*

12 **Collegium Juridicum.** This magnificent Gothic building, built in the early 15th century to house the Jagiellonian University's law students, lies on one of Kraków's oldest streets. ⊠ *ul. Grodzka 53, Stare Miasto.*

FIRST-TIME AMERICA

Among the University treasures and memorabilia in the Jagiellonian University Museum, you will find an early-16th-century Jagiellonian Globe—actually a mechanical sphere with a small globe inside. It's the very first globe that shows the newly discovered North America, with the inscription AMERICA TERRA NOVITER REPERTA (America, a newly discovered land).

A GOOD WALK

The **Barbakan** ❶, part of the medieval city fortification, and a traditional starting point of the "royal route," is a good place to start your tour. Most of the walls, which once included 47 city towers and eight tower gates, were pulled down at the beginning of the 19th century to make space for the growing metropolis, but a northern section with early 14th-century **Brama Floriańska** on **ulica Floriańska** ❷ survives. The Barbakan and the gate used to be connected, offering a number of impediments to prospective invaders. The Barbakan was equipped with arrow slits and "murder holes" (openings in the floor used for pouring boiling water or simmering pitch onto the enemy below), while the gate uses faith and persuasion: an icon of Madonna, St. Florian (patron saint of Kraków and of firemen), the Piast Dynasty eagle, and an inscription, which translates as follows: "The eagle in the gate under towers three, With wide open wings, kind guest, welcomes thee. Whilst adjudging discreetly as the city's guard, Who shall be admitted and who debarred." Entering through the gate, you will see Kraków's first McDonald's, which you can note with pleasure or try to avoid. On Floriańska, you'll find the **Dom Jana Matejki** ❸, which is now a museum showing the 19th-century artist's work.

Leave the Golden Arches behind, turn right onto Pijarska Street, and walk under the covered bridge above the street. Around the corner on your left, you will see the entrance to the Czartoryski Museum

in the **Arsenał Miejski** ❹. After you pay a visit to the most famous Krakovian lady, Leonardo's *Cecilia Gallerani*, continue along św. Jana Street to **Rynek Główny** ❺ (Main Market Square). When you reach the square, turn left and head for **Kościół Mariacki** ❻. Enter the church to see the famous altar, and check out the little square at the back. Wait for the trumpet call played on the hour, and cross the square to the other side. It may take a while, considering the number of attractions and distractions it offers: more sights, including the Renaissance **Sukiennice** ❼, countless terrace cafés, endless shopping opportunities, and street performances. Head for the southeast corner of the square, where you'll find the **Wieża Ratuszowa** (Town Hall Tower) and a sculpture of an oversized head—*Eros Bound* by Igor Mitoraj—and enter św. Anny Street; take the first left, onto Jagiellońska. Here on your right you will find the entrance to Kraków's oldest surviving university building, the **Collegium Maius** ❽. Here you can visit the museum or just meditate in the courtyard. When you continue, travel along Jagiellońska, left to Gołębia, and right into Bracka—which will take you directly to the **Kościół Franciszkanów** ❾ (Franciscan Church & Monastery) and the breathtaking stained-glass windows and exuberantly colored murals by Wyspiański. Opposite the church, in the Archbishop's Palace, is the famous window where Pope John Paul II used to appear (and where Pope Benedict XVI now appears) to great thousands who came to pray with him and serenade him. Facing the window, turn right and return to the royal route then take the first turn to the right onto Grodzka Street.

About halfway up on your left you will see two churches next to one another: the grand, baroque **Kościół świętego Piotra i Pawła** ➓ (Churches of Sts. Peter and Paul) and the smaller, cozy 11th-century **Kościół świętego Andrzeja** ⓫ (Church of St. Andrew). Opposite the church, check out another collegiate building, the **Collegium Juridicum** ⓬, its courtyard affording a welcome retreat from the busy street and hiding another curious statue by Mitoraj, the contemplative *Lights of Nara*.

Cross the little św. Marii Magdaleny Square and turn left into fairy-tale-ish **ulica Kanonicza** ⓭, which will take you to the foot of the Wawel Hill, where you will find **Katedra Wawelska** ⓮ and **Zamek Królewski** ⓯. Descending from the Wawel Hill toward the river, you can cross Grunwaldzki Bridge and visit **Manggha: Centrum Sztuki i Techniki Japońskiej** ⓰, a beautiful Japanese collection in a beautiful building by Arata Isozaki. Take another look at the castle and the river from Manggha's terrace, which frames the view perfectly.

TIMING & PRECAUTIONS
While this walk is perfectly manageable, you won't have time to stop in all the museums if you want to cover the entire Stare Miasto, so this is a better route if you just want an orientation tour; come back another day to visit the museums and sights that particularly interest you. It is probably better to see the Wawel Hill sights on a separate walk—the castle and cathedral alone require a whole morning or afternoon. You must buy a timed-entry ticket for the castle, so it is advisable to book that in advance. You need at least a day to explore the rest of the Old Town at leisure, and more than a day if you enter museums and other sites of interest.

6

★ **❽** **Collegium Maius.** Jagiellonian University was another innovation of Kazimierz the Great. Established in 1364, it was the first university in Poland and one of the earliest ones in Europe. The Collegium Maius is the oldest surviving building of the university, though historians are undecided where the very first one stood. Jagiellonian's most famous student, Nicolaus Copernicus, studied here from 1491 to 1495. The first visual delight is the arcaded Gothic courtyard. On the second floor, the **museum** and rooms are a must for all visitors to Kraków. They can only be visited on a guided tour (call in advance for an English guide). On the tour you see the treasury, assembly hall, library, and common room. The museum includes the so-called Jagiellonian globe, the first globe to depict the American continents. ⊠ *ul. Jagiellońska 15, Stare Miasto* ☏ *012/422–05–49* ⌨ *Courtyard free, museum zł 8* ◔ *Museum Mon.–Thurs. 11–3, Sat. 11–1:30.*

❸ **Dom Jana Matejki** (House of Jan Matejko). The 19th-century painter Jan Matejko was born and died in this house, which now serves as a museum for his work. Even if you don't warm to his painting, Matejko was a prodigious collector of everything from Renaissance art to medieval weaponry, and this 16th-century building is in wonderful condition. ⊠ *ul. Floriańska 41, Stare Miasto* ☏ *012/22–59–26* ⌨ *zł 5* ◔ *Tues. and Thurs. 9–3:30, Wed. 11–6, Sat. 10–3:30.*

★ **⑭** **Katedra Wawelska** (Wawel Cathedral). Wawel Hill, a 15-acre rocky limestone outcropping on the banks of the Vistula, dominates the old part of the city. The hill was a natural point for fortification on the flat Vistula Plain. During the 8th century it was topped with a tribal stronghold and since the 10th century has held a royal residence and served as the seat of the bishops of Kraków. Construction on the present Wawel Cathedral—the third cathedral in this very place—was begun in 1320, and the structure was consecrated in 1364. Little room for expansion on the hill has meant the preservation of the original austere structure, although a few Renaissance and baroque chapels have been crowded around it. The most notable of these is the **Kaplica Zygmuntowska** (Sigismund Chapel), built in the 1520s by the Florentine architect Bartolomeo Berrecci and widely considered to be the finest Renaissance chapel north of the Alps.

From 1037, when Kraków became the capital of Poland, Polish kings were crowned and buried in the Wawel Cathedral. This tradition continued up to the time of the partitions, even after the capital had been moved to Warsaw. During the 19th century, only great national heroes were honored by a Wawel entombment: Tadeusz Kościuszko was buried here in 1817; Adam Mickiewicz and Juliusz Słowacki, both great romantic poets, were also brought back from exile to the Wawel after their deaths; and Marshal Józef Piłsudski, the hero of independent Poland between the two world wars, was interred in the cathedral crypt in 1935.

The cathedral also has a treasury, archives, library, and museum. Among the showpieces in the library, one of the earliest in Poland, is the 12th-century *Emmeram Gospel* from Regensburg. After touring at ground level, you can climb the wooden staircase of the **Sigismund Tower,** entering through the sacristy. The tower holds the famous Sigismund Bell,

CLOSE UP

Mysterious Mounds

A PERFECT DESTINATION for a Sunday walk is Kraków's Mounds. Distant relatives of Stonehenge and Newgrange, Kopiec Krakusa (the Krakus Mound) and Kopiec Wandy (the Wanda Mound) are prehistoric man-made hillocks, each about 50 feet high and almost 6 mi apart. Like their British and Irish siblings, they constitute an astronomical calendar of a kind. Looking from the Krakus Mound on the eve of the Celtic celebration of the sun (May 1), you can see the sun rising exactly above the Wanda Mound. The Sikornik Mountain overlooks the sunrise above the Krakus Mound on the Celtic New Year, November 1.

According to the Medieval chronicler of Kraków, Jan Długosz, the mounds were erected to commemorate the first, legendary ruler of Kraków—Krak, from whom the city derives its name—and his daughter Wanda, who chose to jump into the Vistula River rather than marry a foreigner, as another legend tells us. Historians and scholars have given differing interpretations of the intriguing

humps in the skyline. So are they burial sites, fortifications, pagan temples?

Between 1813 and 1820, during the Austrian occupation, the people of Kraków erected another mound in the Sikornik Hill to commemorate the very Tadeusz Kościuszko who fought first for the freedom of Poland, and then supported the American War of Independence. Finally, near Kopiec Kościuszki, the fourth mound, Kopiec Piłsudskiego was erected between 1934 and 1937 to commemorate Marshal Piłsudski, the leader of the revived Polish state.

On a Sunday afternoon, as well as on major holidays, you will see a distinctly Krakovian ritual: families complete with grandparents and toddlers—more often than not in their Sunday best—majestically strolling along the walking path that follows the gentle slope of Sikornik Hill. A slightly more fit pedestrian can take the path farther: to Lasek Wolski and the Kraków Zoo, or to Przegorzały, and Bielany Monastery.

6

which was commissioned in 1520 by King Sigismund the Old and is still tolled on all solemn state and church occasions. ⊠ *Wawel Hill, Stare Miasto* ▨ *Museum zł 5* ☉ *Tues.–Sun. 10–5:30.*

❾ Kościół Franciszkanów (Franciscan Church & Monastery). The mid-13th-century church and monastery are among the earliest brick buildings in Kraków. The art nouveau stained-glass windows and wall decorations by Stanisław Wyspiański are true masterpieces. ⊠ *pl. Wszystkich Świętych 1, Stare Miasto.*

OFF THE
BEATEN
PATH

KOPIEC KOŚCIUSZKI (Kościuszko's Mound) – This mound on the outskirts of Kraków was built in tribute to the memory of Tadeusz Kościuszko in 1820, three years after his death. The earth came from battlefields on which he had fought; soil from the United States was added in 1926. The best place from which to get a panoramic view of the city, the mound presides above a 19th-century Austrian fort. Take Tram 1 or 6 from plac Dominikański to the terminus at Salwator and then walk up aleja

Waszyngtona to the mound. ✉ *al. Waszyngtona, Salwator* ☯ *Daily 10–dusk.*

★ ❻ **Kościół Mariacki** (Church of Our Lady). Dominating the northeast corner of Rynek Główny is the twin-towered Church of Our Lady, which is also known as St. Mary's Church. The first church was built on this site before the town plan of 1257, which is why it stands slightly askew from the main square; the present church, completed in 1397, was built on the foundations of its predecessor. You'll note that the two towers, added in the early 15th century, are of different heights. Legend has it that they were built by two brothers, one of whom grew jealous of the other's work and slew him with a sword. You can still see the supposed murder weapon, hanging in the gate of the Sukiennice. From the higher tower, a strange bugle call—known as the "Hejnał Mariacki"—rings out to mark each hour. It breaks off on an abrupt sobbing note to commemorate an unknown bugler struck in the throat by a Tartar arrow as he was playing his call to warn the city of imminent attack. The church's main showpiece is the magnificent wooden altarpiece with more than 200 carved figures, the work of the 15th-century artist Wit Stwosz (*Veit Stoss*). The panels depict medieval life in detail; the figure in the bottom right-hand corner of the Crucifixion panel is believed to represent Stwosz himself. ✉ *Rynek Główny, entrance from side of plac Mariacki, Stare Miasto* ⊡ *Church free, altar zł3* ☯ *Altar Mon.–Sat. 11:30–6, Sun. 2–6.*

⓫ **Kościół świętego Andrzeja** (Church of St. Andrew). The finest surviving example of Romanesque architecture in Kraków is this 11th-century fortified church. Local residents took refuge in St. Andrew during Tartar raids. The interior, remodeled during the 18th century, includes a fanciful pulpit resembling a boat. ✉ *At midpoint of ul. Grodzka, on east side, Stare Miasto.*

❿ **Kościół świętego Piotra i Pawła** (Church of Saints Peter and Paul). The first baroque church in Kraków was commissioned for the Jesuit order. It is one of the most faithful and successful examples of transplanting the model of the famous del Gesu Church (the "prototype" Jesuit church in Rome) to foreign soil. At the fence are the figures of the 12 apostles. ✉ *At midpoint of ul. Grodzka, on the east side, next to St. Andrew's Church, Stare Miasto.*

⓰ **Manggha: Centrum Sztuki i Techniki Japońskiej.** The "Manggha" Center for Japanese Art and Technology houses a magnificent collection of woodblock prints, pottery, Samurai armor, netsuke (small sculptures worn on the sash of a kimono), and more. The collection was the gift of an eccentric bohemian named Feliks Jasieński, who became caught up in the fashion of collection Japanese artifacts in fin de siècle Paris. Jasieński's admiration and obsession with all things Japanese earned him the nickname "Manggha." *Manggha* are picture books containing famous prints of old Japan (not exactly the same as today's manga, which are popular graphic novels). Jasieński actually donated the collection to the Kraków National Museum, but there was no space to properly display it. The present museum opened in late 1994. ✉ *ul. M. Konopnickiej 26, Dębniki* ☎ *012/267-27-03* ⊕ *www.manggha.krakow.pl* ⊡ *zł5, free Sun.* ☯ *Tues.–Sun. 10–6.*

CLOSE UP

The Japanese Connection

POLISH COLLECTOR FELIKS JASIEŃSKI was a great collector of Japanese art, but when he donated his collection to the Kraków Museum, it could be seen only in temporary exhibitions. It was at one such exhibition during World War II that Polish film director Andrzej Wajda—then a 19-year-old art student—saw the Jasieński collection for the first time. Wajda recalls that in the midst of the wartime chaos, the Japanese prints and drawings oozed harmony, clarity, and hope for him. Years later, he became the collection's protector.

When Wajda was awarded the prestigious Kyoto Prize for Achievement in the Arts in 1987, he decided to donate the prize money for the creation of "a beautiful Japanese building" in Kraków, which would house the Jasieński collection. Many others, including the Workers' Union of East Japan Railways, contributed to the project. When the construction committee ran out of funds to complete the project in 1992, money was collected in railway stations all over Tokyo, some 138,000 Japanese responding to Wajda's plea for donations.

The leaf- (or wave-) shape museum overlooks the Wawel Castle from the banks of the Vistula River and was designed by Japanese architect Arata Isozaki. Recently, a Japanese language school was added to the museum complex, another gift of Japanese railway workers. In front of the museum entrance is a sculpture by Aiko Miyawaki that looks like a lightly penciled drawing of the air and water.

Some of the treasures of the collection include ancient samurai swords and the helmets the samurai wore to inspire terror in the enemy—one of the outfits looks very much like a Japanese Darth Vader. In the dimly lighted gallery, the frowns on these helmets can still send a shudder down your spine. Other items on display include beautifully woven silk kimonos and screens and solid yet sophisticated bronze vessels. Light lacquer and elaborate enamel brush against ivory in tiny netsuke, which were once worn on the sashes of kimonos in Japan; the objects take forms of hilarious—but also sometimes spiteful—faces and grotesque creatures.

Looking at the color-saturated, clear impressions of woodblock prints from famous series by Hokusai, Toyokuni, Hiroshige, Utamaro, and other artists, one can hardly believe that they were once considered common enough to wrap fish. Now, these wonderful and refined works are considered high art.

Japan has always figured strongly in the Polish imagination. Japanese art—the fleeting world of famous beauties, endless yet ever-changing views of Mount Fuji, and the painted grimaces of kabuki actors—freeze and defy laws of time, as Krakovian Nobel Laureate Wisława Szymborska wrote in her beautiful poem about Utagawa Hiroshige's *People on the Bridge*. Another Polish Nobel Laureate, Czesław Miłosz, confessed in one of his poems that he came to consider himself " . . . one of the many merchants and artisans of Old Japan / Who arranged verses about cherry blossoms, / Chrysanthemums and the full moon."

6

⑤ Rynek Główny (Main Market Square). Europe's largest medieval mar-
Fodor'sChoice ketplace is on a par in size and grandeur with St. Mark's Square in Venice.
★ It even has the same plague of pigeons, although legend tells us the ones
here are no ordinary birds: they are allegedly the spirits of the knights
of Duke Henry IV Probus, who in the 13th century were cursed and turned
into birds. This great square was not always so spacious. In an earlier
period it contained—in addition to the present buildings—a Gothic
town hall, a Renaissance granary, a large weighing house, a foundry, a
pillory, and hundreds of traders' stalls. A few flower sellers under colorful umbrellas and some portable souvenir stalls are all that remain of
this bustling commercial activity. Above all, Rynek is Kraków's largest
outdoor café, from spring through autumn, with more than 20 cafés scattered around the perimeter of the square.

A pageant of history has passed through this square. From 1320 on, Polish kings came here on the day after their coronation to meet the city's
burghers and receive homage and tribute in the name of all the towns
of Poland. Albert Hohenzollern, the grand master of the Teutonic
Knights, came here in 1525 to pay homage to Sigismund the Old, King
of Poland. And in 1794 Tadeusz Kościuszko took a solemn vow to over-
throw czarist Russia here.

The square is surrounded by many historic buildings. The **Dom pod Je-
leniami** (House at the Sign of the Stag), at No. 36, was once an inn where
both Goethe and Czar Nicholas I found shelter. At No. 45 is the **Dom
pod Orłem** (House at the Sign of the Eagle), where Tadeusz Kościuszko
lived as a young officer in 1777; a little farther down the square, at No.
6, is the **Szara Kamienica** (Gray House), which he made his staff headquarters in 1794. In the house at No. 9, the young Polish noblewoman
Maryna Mniszchówna married the False Dymitri, the pretender to the
Russian throne, in 1605. (These events are portrayed in Pushkin's play
Boris Godunov and in Mussorgsky's operatic adaptation of it.) At No.
16 is the **14th-century house** of the Wierzynek merchant family. In
1364, during a "summit" meeting attended by the Holy Roman Emperor, one of the Wierzyneks gave an elaborate feast for the visiting royal
dignitaries; today the house is a restaurant.

At the southwest corner of Rynek Square, the **Wieża Ratuszowa** (Town
Hall Tower) is all that remains of the 16th-century town hall, which was
demolished in the early 19th century. The tower houses a branch of the
Muzeum Historyczne Miasta Krakowa (Kraków History Museum) and
affords a panoramic view of the old city. Although the museum and tower
are closed during the winter, it's possible to organize a group visit.
✉ *Rynek Główny, Stare Miasto* ☎ *012/422–15–04* 💰 *zł 4* ⊙ *Apr.–Oct.,
daily 10–5.*

★ **⑦ Sukiennice** (Cloth Hall). A statue of Adam Mickiewicz sits in front of
the eastern entrance to the Renaissance Cloth Hall, which stands in the
middle of the Main Market Square. The Gothic arches date from the
14th century, but after a fire in 1555 the upper part was rebuilt in Renaissance style. The inner arcades on the ground floor still hold traders'
booths, now mainly selling local crafts. On the first floor, in a branch

CLOSE UP

A Sane Argument

THE SURVIVING NORTH fragment of Kraków's old city wall narrowly escaped destruction thanks to clever arguments set forth by Professor Feliks Radwański of the Jagiellonian University. When arguments regarding the historical importance of the walls failed, he appealed to the reluctant City Senate by saying that, should the walls be pulled down, the northern winds would blow in "utmost violence" throughout the city, threatening its inhabitants—particularly, he said, "ladies and children of delicate breeding" with frequent "flushes, rheumatic diseases, and perhaps even paralyses." Moreover, walking would be made strenuous in such strong winds: "It would be a task of exceeding difficulty merely to remain on one's own two feet . . ." Last—but certainly not least—was the threat of immodesty, and that argument pushed the Senate over to the side of preservation: just imagine, he asked, what dreadful things would happen to the skirts of respectable ladies.

6

of the National Museum, you can view a collection of 19th-century Polish paintings. The gallery closed in late 2006 for a major renovation and is scheduled to reopen in 2009; until then, part of the collection will be exhibited in the Niepołomice Castle in Niepołomice (⇨ Chapter 7). ⊠ *Rynek Główny 1–3, Stare Miasto* ☏ *012/422–11–66.*

NEED A BREAK?

One of the oldest cafés in town, **Kawiarnia Noworolski** (⊠ Rynek Główny 1, Stare Miasto) next to the entrance to the National Museum in the Cloth Hall, is a wonderful café, where you can sit and watch the goings-on in the square while enjoying a coffee. This is also a good spot from which to observe the hourly trumpet call from the tower of the Church of Our Lady.

In the art nouveau café **Jama Michalikowa** (⊠ ul. Floriańska 45, Stare Miasto ☏ 012/422–15–61), the walls are hung with caricatures by late-19th-century customers, who sometimes paid their bills in kind.

② **Ulica Floriańska.** The beautiful **Brama Floriańska** (Florian Gate) was built around 1300 and leads through Kraków's old city walls to this street, which was laid out according to the town plan of 1257. The Gothic houses of the 13th-century burghers still remain, although they were rebuilt and given Renaissance or neoclassical facades. The house at No. 24, decorated with an emblem of three bells, was once the workshop of a bell founder. The chains hanging on the walls of the house at No. 17 barred the streets to invaders when the city was under siege. The **Dom pod Murzynami** (Negroes' House), standing where ulica Floriańska enters the market square, is a 16th-century tenement decorated with two rather fancifully imagined African tribesmen—testimony to the fascination with Africa entertained by Europeans in the Age of Discovery. The house was also once known as Dom pod Etiopy (House under the Ethiopians). ⊠ *Stare Miasto.*

★ ⑬ **Ulica Kanonicza.** This street, which leads from almost the center of town to the foot of Wawel Hill, is considered by some the most beautiful street in Europe. Most of the houses here date from the 14th and 15th centuries, although they were "modernized" in Renaissance or later styles. The street was named for the many canons of Wawel Cathedral who have lived here, including Pope John Paul II, who lived in the Chapter House at No. 19 and later in the late-16th-century Dean's House at No. 21. The Chapter House is now the **Muzeum Archidiecezjalne** (Archdiocesan Museum) (✉ ul. Kanonicza 19, Stare Miasto ☎ 012/421–89–63), displaying 13th-century paintings and other art belonging to the archdiocese, not to mention Pope John Paul II's former room. Admission is zł 5 and the museum is open Tuesday–Thursday 10–4 and weekends 10–3. ✉ *Stare Miasto.*

⑮ **Zamek Królewski** (Royal Castle). The castle that now stands here dates
Fodor'sChoice from the early 16th century, when the Romanesque residence that stood
★ on this site was destroyed by fire. King Sigismund the Old brought artists and craftsmen from Italy to create his castle, and despite baroque reconstruction after another fire in the late 16th century, several parts of the Renaissance castle remain, including the beautiful arcaded courtyard. After the transfer of the capital to Warsaw at the beginning of the 17th century, the castle was stripped of its fine furnishings, and later in the century it was devastated by the Swedish wars. In 1905, a voluntary Polish society purchased the castle from the Austrian authorities and began restoration. It narrowly escaped destruction in 1945, when the Nazis almost demolished it as a parting shot. Today you can visit the royal chambers, furnished in the style of the 16th and 17th centuries and hung with the 16th-century Arras-style tapestries from the Low Countries. Counted among the most valuable treasures of the Polish people, the tapestries were evacuated to Canada by Jan Polkowski (who had been appointed their guardian) during World War II in order to protect them against the invaders, and returned to Poland in 1961. The Royal Treasury on the ground floor contains a somewhat depleted collection of Polish crown jewels; the most fascinating item displayed here is the *Szczerbiec,* the jagged sword used from the early 14th century onward at the coronation of Polish kings. The Royal Armory houses a collection of Polish and Eastern arms and armor. The west wing holds an imposing collection of Turkish embroidered tents.

For many Poles, the castle's importance extends beyond its history. Hindu esoteric thinkers claim it is one of the world's mystic energy centers, a *chakhra.* Some believers—and there have been many over the last few decades—think that by rubbing up against the castle wall in the courtyard they will absorb vital energy.

Ⓒ Every Polish child knows the legend of the fire-breathing dragon that once terrorized local residents from his **Smocza Jama** (Dragon's Den), a cave at the foot of Wawel Hill. Follow the signs to the ticket office opposite the castle, in the direction of the river. The dragon threatened to destroy the town unless he was fed a damsel a week. The king promised half his kingdom and his daughter's hand in marriage to any man who could slay the dragon. The usual quota of knights tried and failed.

IF YOU LIKE

ART

Artworks of all kinds in record-breaking numbers are found in Kraków—not only in museums, but also in their natural surroundings: in the royal castle, in churches, and even in restaurants, cafés, and on the street. Highlights include the Wit Stwosz altarpiece in Kościół Mariacki, the *arras* tapestries in the Wawel castle, Leonardo's *Lady with an Ermine.* in the Czartoryski Museum, and Stanisław Wyspiański's stained-glass windows and wall paintings in the Franciscan church. More than 100 years ago, Polish artists decorated Jama Michalika café, a gem of art nouveau style. Modern art can be found in numerous galleries, located mostly in and around the Rynek and in Kazimierz quarter.

TRAVELING "ROYAL STYLE"

It's certainly possible to live like a king or queen in the royal city of Kraków, where you'll find a number of luxury hotels with truly regal fixtures and fittings: the Gródek Copernicus, Grand, and Amadeus hotels can all be recommended highly. Monarchs often choose the Sheraton Hotel, perhaps due to its location at the banks of the river, near the Wawel Royal Castle. To dine in style, head for Wierzynek, which was the site of a famous feast of European monarchs in 1364. Royal pleasures could include a concert in the castle (in the series called *Wieczory wawelskie*) or an opera in the historic Słowacki Theater—choose a box seat to feel like a VIP.

JEWISH HISTORY

If you are interested in Jewish History, try to plan your journey around the Jewish Culture Festival, which usually takes place in the first week of July, when dozens of events are scheduled. The Kazimierz District was the traditional home of Kraków's Jewish community; check out its synagogues, particularly Remuh, Isaac's, and Tempel, and visit the cemeteries, especially the one next to the Remuh Synagogue. You can stop for some Jewish dishes and tunes in one of the restaurants on Szeroka Street.

CLASSICAL MUSIC

Kraków's time is measured by the tune played from the tower of St. Mary's on the hour, and you will find music everywhere: in the streets, bars, churches, and concert halls. Check the schedule of musical events—regular concerts are held from September through June, while most (but not all) festivals are clustered in the summer months. You can listen to classical music at the philharmonics and catch a concert by Sinfonietta Cracovia; look for organ music and religious theme concerts in Kraków's historic churches.

NIGHTLIFE

If you ask Warsaw's elites to name their favorite places to go out in the weekend, they will tell you to visit some of Kraków's clubs and pubs—after all, they are just a 2½-hour train ride away from the capital. In the winter, social life descends underground—many bars are hidden in the vaulted cellars around the Old Town. In summer, the Market Square becomes the country's largest open-air café.

6

But finally a crafty cobbler named Skuba tricked the dragon into eating a lambskin filled with salt and sulfur. The dragon went wild with thirst, rushed into the Vistula River, and drank until it exploded. The Dragon's Den is still there, however, and in warmer months smoke and flame belch out of it every 15 minutes to thrill young visitors. A bronze statue of the dragon itself stands guard at the entrance. The den is open May–September, Monday–Thursday and weekends 10–3; admission is zł 5. To reach the castle, go to the end of Grodzka or Kanonicza streets, and then walk up Wawel Hill.

The number of visitors to the royal chambers is limited, and entry tickets are timed; therefore, you should always try to book your tickets in advance to avoid disappointment. Phone to make the reservation, and then collect your tickets from the Tourist Service Office (BOT) located opposite the Sigismund Chapel (the one with the golden dome).

> **A TRANSATLANTIC MEDIEVAL LEGEND**
>
> Every hour, the trumpet call from the tower of Kościół Mariacki comes to a sudden halt. The story goes that the melody was interrupted, when a Tartar arrow pierced the throat of the guard while he attempted to warn his fellow Krakovians. As with every legend, there must be some truth in it, but it's a fact that we owe its present and popular version to Eric P. Kelly, an American who came to Kraków with an aid mission after World War I. He recounted the famous legend in his book *The Trumpeter of Cracow*, published in 1928.

✉ *Wawel Hill, Wawel* ☎ *012/422–16–97* 🎫 *Royal chambers zł 15, royal private apartments zł 15, treasury and armory zł 15. Free Mon., but portions of the exhibit restricted.* ☯ *Royal chambers, treasury, and armory Mon. 9:30–noon, Tues.–Sat. 9:30–3 (Fri. until 4), Sun. 10–3. Closed Mon. Oct.–Mar.*

Kazimierz

As Rafael Sharf, founder of London's Jewish Quarterly and himself a Krakovian Jew once remarked, Kraków's Kazimierz is the only place in the world where you will find the street of Corpus Christi crossing the street named after Rabbi Meisels. Kazimierz was founded by King Kazimierz the Great as a separate city in 1335. By the end of 15th century, it had come to house a growing Jewish district at a time when industrious and enterprising Jews escaping persecution in Western Europe were welcomed by the Polish kings. Thus, Kazimierz became one of the most important centers of the Jewish diaspora in Europe. Here they thrived until World War II.

What to See

㉑ **Kościół Bożego Ciała** (Corpus Christi Church). This 15th-century church was used by King Charles Gustavus of Sweden as his headquarters during the Siege of Kraków in 1655. ✉ *Northeast corner of pl. Wolnica, Kazimierz.*

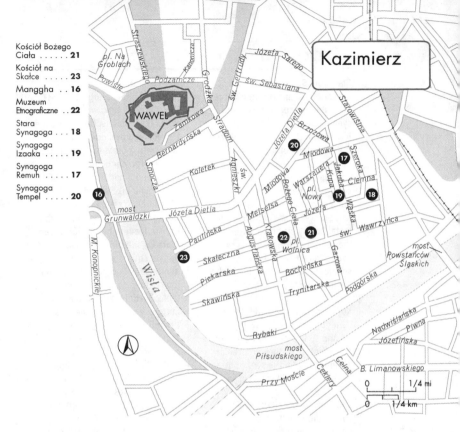

❷❸ Kościół na Skałce (Church on the Rock). Standing on the Vistula embankment to the south of Wawel Hill, this church is the center of the cult of Saint Stanisław. The bishop and martyr was beheaded and dismembered by order of the king in the church that stood on this spot in 1079—a tale of rivalry similar to that of Henry II and Thomas à Becket. The story goes that the saint's body was miraculously reassembled, as a symbol of the restoration of Poland's unity after its years of fragmentation. Beginning in the 19th century, the church also became the last resting place for well-known Polish writers and artists; among those buried here are the composer Karol Szymanowski, the painter and playwright Stanisław Wyspiański, and poet Czesław Miłosz. ⊠ *Between uls. Paulińska and Skałeczna on the Vistula embankment, Stare Miasto.*

❷❷ Muzeum Etnograficzne im. Seweryna Udzieli w Krakowie (Ethnographic Museum). Kazimierz's 15th-century Ratusz (Town Hall) stands in the middle of plac Wolnica. It is now the Ethnographic Museum, displaying a well-mounted collection of regional folk art. ⊠ *pl. Wolnica 1, Kazimierz* ☎ *012/656-28-63* 🖃 *zł 5* 🕑 *Mon. 10–6, Wed.–Fri. 10–3, weekends 10–2.*

❶❽ Stara Synagoga (Old Synagogue). The oldest surviving example of Jewish religious architecture in Poland, this synagogue was built in the 15th century and reconstructed in Renaissance style following a fire in 1557.

A GOOD WALK

Start from **Synagoga Remuh** ⑰ on Szeroka, a street that is more accurately a square. Next to the synagogue is one of the oldest Jewish graveyards in Europe, with the tombstone of the famous Rabbi Moses Isserles, famed for his wisdom and learning. His tomb is believed to possess special powers, and pilgrims from all over the world leave prayers and requests in the metal box by his grave. After visiting the historical display in **Stara Synagoga** ⑱ at the far end of the square, turn left and back, finding the entrance to Józefa Street. If you take the next right turn, you'll be on Kupa Street, which will take you to **Synagoga Izaaka** ⑲, well worth visiting so you can watch a short documentary feature on prewar Kazimierz. From the synagogue, walk straight to Plac Nowy, which you have just seen in the movie, and observe the changes. Today the square, lined with cafés and bars, is one of the most popular destinations for Kraków youth (of all ages) and visitors alike. On Sunday mornings, it is a scene of a crowded vintage clothing market, and every day you can find some stalls selling fruit, vegetables, and flowers—just like in the old days.

Leave the square from its northern end, by Estery Street, leaving the famous Alchemia, which is a popular café by day and a bar by night; it will be on your left. You will come upon lovingly restored, magnificent **Synagoga Tempel** ⑳ at the corner of Miodowa and Podbrzezie Streets. Don't miss the Bagelmama behind it, a cozy bagel shop with a great story. Walk back to plac Nowy and find Meiselsa Street in the middle of its western end—it will take you to the ubiquitous crossing with ulica Bożego Ciała—the street of Corpus Christi, leading to **Kościół Bożego Ciała** ㉑ and plac Wolnica, once the market square and the administrative center of Kazimierz town. The former town hall holds the collection of the **Muzeum Etnograficzne im. Seweryna Udzieli w Krakowie** (Ethnographic Museum) ㉒. End your walk with yet one more church. Head to the end of Paulińska; there you will find a door in the wall: it is a back entrance to **Kościół na Skałce** ㉓ (Church on the Rock). Walk across the Pauline monastery garden and exit through the elaborate wrought-iron gate to Skałeczna Street.

TIMING

Allow at least half a day to explore Kazimierz, and you might also want to return in the evening to sample the area's famous nightlife. Synagogues are closed on Saturday and Jewish holidays. The week of the Jewish Culture Festival (usually in early July) is a particularly good time to be in Kazimierz.

It was here in 1775 that Tadeusz Kościuszko successfully appealed to the Jewish community to join in the national insurrection. Looted and partly destroyed during the Nazi occupation, it has been rebuilt and now houses the **Museum of the History and Culture of Kraków Jews**. It's always closed on the first weekend of the month. ✉ *ul. Szeroka 24, Kazimierz* ☎ *012/ 422–09–62* 💰 *zł 5* ⊙ *Wed., Thurs., and weekends 9–3, Fri. 11–6.*

NEED A BREAK? **Alef Café** (✉ ul. Szeroka 17, Kazimierz ☎ 012/421-38-70) is as close as you can get to a glimpse of the lost world of Kazimierz. Traditional Eastern European Jewish (but not kosher) dishes are served daily, and musical performances are often given here.

⑲ Synagoga Izaaka. Isaac's Synagogue was named after its founder, Izaak Jakubowicz (reb Ajzyk reb Jekeles). One of the most famous Hasidic legends is connected with this pious Jew, who lived in Kazimierz. One day he had a dream about a treasure hidden in Prague, near the Charles Bridge. Without thinking twice, Isaac went to Prague and found the bridge he had seen in his dream. The bridge was filled with soldiers, and Isaac was unsure what to do next when one of the soldiers approached him and asked what he was doing there. When Isaac told the soldier about his dream, the man laughed: "Only a naive fool would come so far for a dream! I myself keep having this dream that in a house of a Krakovian Jew named Isaac, son of Jacob, there is a treasure hidden under the furnace, but I'm not so foolish as to go to Kraków and check it out. After all, every second Jew is named Isaac, and every third, Jacob!" Isaac thanked him, returned home, dismantled the furnace, and found a great treasure, becoming one of the wealthiest citizens of Kazimierz—wealthy enough to found a magnificent synagogue. Today the early baroque building with a beautiful, stucco-decorated vault and marvelous arcades in the women's gallery houses an exhibition on the history of Polish Jews. Don't miss the short documentaries (which date between 1936 and 1941) that were created by a German cameraman showing prewar Kazimierz and the removal to the ghetto. ✉ *ul. Kupa 18, Kazimierz* ☎ *12/430–55–77* *zł 7* ☉ *Sun.–Fri. 9–7.*

⑰ Synagoga Remuh. This 16th-century synagogue is still used for worship and is named after the son of its founder, Rabbi Moses Isserles, who is buried in the **cemetery** attached to the synagogue. Used by the Jewish community from 1533 to 1799, this is the only well-preserved Renaissance Jewish cemetery in Europe. (The so-called new cemetery on ulica Miodowa, which contains many old headstones, was established in 1800.) ✉ *ul. Szeroka 40, Kazimierz* *zł 2* ☉ *Weekdays 9–6.*

⑳ Synagoga Tempel. The 19th-century Reformed Tempel Synagogue has a striking decor complete with stained-glass windows. Under the care of the local Jewish Community, it is the main venue of the famous Jewish Culture Festival. ✉ *Corner of Miodowa and Podbrzezie, Kazimierz.*

NEED A BREAK? **Bagelmama** (✉ ul. Podbrzezie 17, Kazimierz ☎ 012/431-19-42) is a cozy little bagel shop. It's also the only bagel shop in Kraków (or for that matter the whole country).

Nowa Huta

Fodor'sChoice ★ A story goes that when Fidel Castro visited Kraków, he refused to see the famous royal castle and the largest medieval square in Europe: "Take me to the steelworks," he commanded instead. Although we don't propose to follow the Comandante's example to the letter, a visit to **Nowa Huta** is definitely worth your while.

The Bagel Returns Home

IN AN INTERESTING CAPRICE of culinary history, Bagelmama in Kraków's Kazimierz District is the only bagel shop in Poland. And to think that bagels were probably invented here! The 1610 community regulations of Kraków report that bagels were presented to women in childbirth. Legend has it that the bagel was popularized in Vienna, where it was baked to commemorate the Polish King Sobieski's 1683 triumph over the Turks. It was then named after *beugel,* (German for stirrup). Around 1900, Polish-Jewish immigrants brought this great bread to New York City, where it continues to thrive. Yet the bakery Pan Beigel ("Mr. Bagel" in English), the original bagel bakery in Kraków's Kazimierz District, which opened in 1915, has long since closed and disappeared. What a coincidence to find that its newly minted successor, Bagelmama, which is owned by Nava, an American expat, musician, and caterer, has opened up in exactly the same location. And so the history of the bagel has come full circle (with a hole in the middle).

Even for Kraków natives, a trip to Nowa Huta is something of an adventure. Though officially part of Kraków—and only a 20- to 30-minute tram ride from the city center—it is quite a different world. You'll feel the change not just in the sweeping scale of urban planning but also in the spirit of the place. Always the workers town—and designed as such by rulers of the obsolete Communist Bloc—it remains mostly proletarian, although the area is also increasingly popular with students and bohemians. Although you could look at the neighborhood as a living museum of the former era, this is not to suggest that Nowa Huta doesn't have an interesting present and (hopefully) brighter future.

Regrettably, its past is bleak indeed. In the 1950s, several villages outside Kraków were razed to build a huge steelworks and a steelworkers' town on the fertile farmland. The location of this "experiment" wasn't random: the "model socialist town," with its healthy social structure, was meant to counterbalance traditionally aristocratic and intellectual Kraków.

In June 1949, the foundations were laid for the first residential block of Nowa Huta. Nearly a year later, construction of the steelworks began. The steel factory reached its apogee in 1970s, when it employed 38,000 and produced 6.7 million tons of steel annually, not to mention fantastic volumes of pollution, which nobody seemed to control. (Now it has been privatized—and modernized—with production down to 1 million tons per annum and the environmental impact greatly reduced.) Next to the factory, the workers' town grew where authorities hoped to build "a modern socialist society."

Its ideological heritage notwithstanding, Nowa Huta is an interesting example of urban planning and architecture—so interesting that it was proclaimed a historical monument by the Polish government. The Central Square was modeled on that of Versailles, and the buildings that surround it are replete with echoes of the Renaissance and classicism. The street plan of the original residential areas of Nowa Huta is based on an American concept of "neighborhood units" first developed for New York City in the 1920s. Each block of Nowa Huta was equipped with all the necessary facilities to help the neighborhood function—shops, a school, a kindergarten, and so forth.

One thing was missing, however: as a model socialist town, Nowa Huta was not supposed to have churches, so none were built. Yet faith and tradition were stronger than the enforced model, and people of Nowa Huta erected an "illegal" crucifix around which they gathered to pray. When authorities ordered its removal in 1960, the citizens came to defend their cross, and hundreds were injured in a battle with the government militia. The struggle continued off and on until the first church in Nowa Huta was consecrated in 1977. Shaped like Noah's Ark, it was a powerful symbol in the political context at the time.

Paradoxically, the "model workers' town" played a key role in the downfall of communism, and became a stronghold of the Solidarity movement. Wide alleys of Nowa Huta were perfect for more than just May Day parades: in the 1980s, local residents people marched through them in antigovernment demonstrations.

It is not easy to cover Nowa Huta sights by walking—it is better to use a bike, tram, or car.

The **Plac Centralny** (Central Square) is a good place to start. Take a walk around the square, and check out the showcase Cepelia shop along the way. Then take a stroll through the residential neighborhoods on either side of the wide alleys leading from the square.

Although you won't find the famous statue of Lenin that used to stand on **Aleja Róż** (Boulevard of Roses), some original establishments remain, including Stylowa restaurant and the most authentic milk bar in town.

From plac Centralny, any tram going up aleja Solidarności will take you to **Centrum Administracyjne** (Central Administration Building), the impressive castlelike entrance and offices of the former Lenin Steelworks. Unfortunately, these days it is next to impossible to enter the steelworks as a visitor, but even a peek from outside can you some idea of the scale of this operation.

MILK BARS

The *Bar mleczny* ("milk bar") is an old-fashioned Polish self-service restaurant invented by the communist authorities in Poland in the 1960s. The purpose was to provide cheap, hearty meals to everyone—and workers in particular. The meals served at these restaurants were mostly dairy-based (hence "milk" bars), as meat was scarce, expensive, and at one point, even rationed (during the martial law in early 1980s). Today, milk bars are definitely more rare, but they remain an important alimentary institution, unceasingly popular with poorer citizens, pensioners, university students . . . and professors.

A 10-minute drive or ride west of the steelworks is the **Arka Pana** (The Lord's Ark), an amazing modern church with facade made of round river stones. These were brought by the people of Nowa Huta to the building site when authorities cut the supplies in yet another effort to stop the church's construction. Needless to say, the government's efforts failed, and the Ark sailed above the sea of communism.

To get to Nowa Huta, take tram numbers 4 or 15 from Kraków Główny, the city's main railway station. You need two to four hours to get a flavor of Nowa Huta, but bear in mind that there are considerable distances to cover if you really want to see the town. The company Crazy Guides (⇨ Tour Options *in* Kraków Essentials) offers tours to Nowa Huta in grand style—in an authentic Trabant car, a true wonder of the communist automotive industry.

WHERE TO EAT

Kraków's best restaurants can primarily be found in the Old Town, within walking distance of the main tourist sights. Most restaurants are located in the Market Square and the streets around it; some are also in the Kazimierz Quarter. Cheap fast-food joints may be found next door to upmarket establishments. The streets most densely populated with restaurants include Poselska, Szewska, św. Tomasza, and Sławkowska. At all but the most touristed restaurants, the custom in Kraków is to make a reservation, even if you do it just a few hours in advance.

$$$–$$$$ ✕ **Wierzynek.** This restaurant's history goes back to 1364, when a wealthy Krakovian merchant named Wierzynek treated a party of European monarchs to a truly royal feast. Following the fame of the only upscale restaurant in Kraków during the gray days of "real socialism"—and leaving behind the period of postcommunist slump—Wierzynek is now a private enterprise where customers (and their dollars) are once again kings. Traditional offerings on the menu include trout with almonds, roast duck with apples, and saddle of deer in juniper sauce. Dining rooms on upper floors are stylishly furnished and decorated with historical paintings, armor, and clocks. The new addition of a grill garden is rather tacky. ⊠ *Rynek Główny 15, Stare Miasto* ☎ *012/424–96–00* ⌕ *Reservations essential* ▤ *AE, DC, MC, V.*

$$–$$$$ ✕ **Wentzl.** The owners of this elegant and posh establishment have reincarnated Jan Wentzl's restaurant, which opened in the same building in 1792. On the menu, Old Polish cuisine meets the whole world in the wine list. You'll see saddle of deer marinated in lemongrass with aromatic cinnamon bark and red currant sauce, which you may wish to pair with a Rioja Muga Reserva or a Chianti classico. Not only your tastebuds will enjoy this experience, as Wentzl also offers a feast for the eyes: the restaurant is like a small gallery of École de Paris paintings, and there is a great view down to the Market Square. ⊠ *Rynek Główny 19, Stare Miasto* ☎ *012/429–57–12* ⌕ *Reservations essential* ▤ *AE, DC, MC, V.*

$–$$$$ ✕ **Metropolitan.** The smooth and sleek Metropolitan could be mistaken for something straight out of Manhattan. The atmosphere is elegant yet relaxed, and the food would be best summarized as "fusion," from tuna

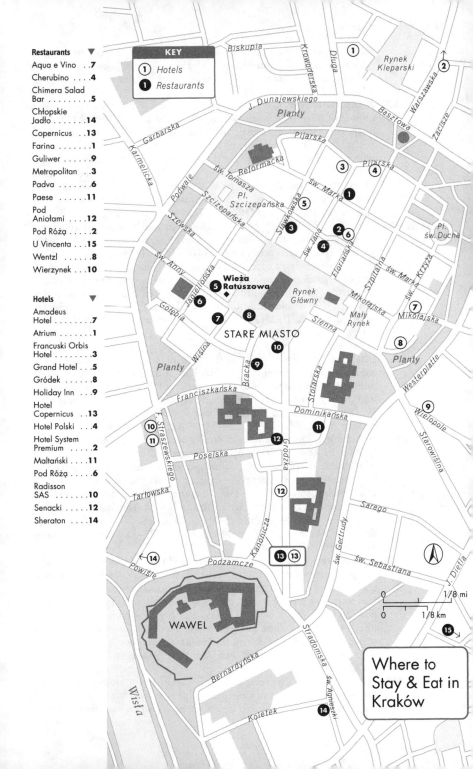

Restaurants ▼

Aqua e Vino . .**7**

Cherubino **4**

Chimera Salad
Bar **5**

Chłopskie
Jadło **14**

Copernicus . .**13**

Farina **1**

Guliwer **9**

Metropolitan . .**3**

Padva **6**

Paese **11**

Pod
Aniołami **12**

Pod Różą . . .**2**

U Vincenta . .**15**

Wentzl **8**

Wierzynek . . .**10**

Hotels ▼

Amadeus
Hotel **7**

Atrium **1**

Francuski Orbis
Hotel **3**

Grand Hotel . .**5**

Gródek **8**

Holiday Inn . . .**9**

Hotel
Copernicus . .**13**

Hotel Polski . .**4**

Hotel System
Premium **2**

Maltański **11**

Pod Różą **6**

Radisson
SAS **10**

Senacki **12**

Sheraton **14**

Where to Stay & Eat in Kraków

carpaccio served with green apple slices and lime olive oil dressing, to pork tenderloin in plum alcohol. All the dishes are both full of flavor and beautifully presented. ✉ *ul. Sławkowska 3, Stare Miasto* ☎ *012/ 421–98–03* ▭ *AE, DC, MC, V.*

$$$ ✕ **Copernicus.** This top-class restaurant in one of the city's top hotels is on one of Kraków's loveliest corners, at the foot of Wawel Hill. The imaginative menu is made up of classic Polish dishes—albeit the dishes you might find on the table of a typically aristocratic table—enriched with a cosmopolitan twist. Try the venison paté with marinated forest mushrooms or sea bass with couscous. In the summer you can dine on the rooftop terrace, with some of the best views in the city. ✉ *Hotel Copernicus, ul. Kanonicza 16, Stare Miasto* ☎ *012/431–10–44* ⚞ *Reservations essential* ▭ *AE, DC, MC, V.*

★ $$–$$$ ✕ **Farina.** True to its logo (a sack of flour and a fish), this relatively young restaurant offers consistently good fish, seafood, and homemade pasta. A special selection of seafood is offered Thursday through Sunday. Whatever you order, first you will get Farina's trademark appetizer of an excellent truffle-and-mushroom pâté to spread on scrumptious little rolls. There is a good selection of wines, including a great dry Prosecco that would stand up to any Champagne. ✉ *Św. Marka 16, Stare Miasto* ☎ *012/422–16–80* ⚞ *Reservations essential* ▭ *AE, DC, MC, V.*

★ $$–$$$ ✕ **Guliwer.** When you step into Guliwer, you may think you've stepped into a French country inn. You're still firmly planted on Polish soil, but the cuisine here is definitively Gallic. The food is simple yet tasty, in tune with the decor. The menu features excellent fish soup, liver Provençale, and crème brulée. Guliwer has many faithful followers, including poet Wisława Szymborska and film director Andrzej Wajda. ✉ *ul. Bracka 6, Stare Miasto* ☎ *012/430–24–66* ▭ *AE, DC, MC, V.*

★ $$–$$$ ✕ **Pod Różą.** Built in the converted courtyard of a tenement house, "Under the Rose" is airy, spacious, elegant, and contained under a glass roof. A seasonally changing, contemporary menu is matched by impeccable service; there is nightly live piano music. Pheasant with foie gras in a French pastry crust is just one of many mouthwatering options. The chefs make their own pastas, ice cream, and bread. Adjoining sister restaurant Amarone serves slightly cheaper, but no less delicious, Italian cuisine. ✉ *ul. Floriańska 14, Stare Miasto* ☎ *012/424–33–81* ⚞ *Reservations essential* ▭ *AE, DC, MC, V.*

★ $–$$$ ✕ **Aqua e Vino.** Venetian owners Roberto and Francesco believe in a hands-on approach to running their restaurant, so they are nearly always present: taking orders, chatting with customers, and checking to make sure that everything is okay. In fact, the homemade pastas, tiramisu, and sgroppino cocktails (made with Prosecco and lemon sorbet) are more than okay—they are excellent. Frequent visitors include Cardinal Dziwisz and conductor John Axelrod, and the Italian community in Kraków call it their second home. ✉ *ul. Wiślna 5/10, Stare Miasto* ☎ *012/421–25–67* ▭ *AE, DC, MC, V.*

$–$$$ ✕ **Padva.** Kraków's premier Italian restaurant is propitiously located just opposite the courtyard of Collegium Maius. It is certainly hard to argue with Padva's comprehensive Italian menu featuring excellent antipasti and pastas. The extra effort pays off in seafood that is flown in directly from Italy twice a week. ⊠ *ul. Jagiellońska 2, Stare Miasto* ☎ *012/292–02–72* ☐ *AE, DC, MC, V.*

$–$$$ ✗ **Paese.** The only Corsican restaurant in Poland—and one of the first memorable restaurants of the new post-communist era—Paese was an immediate success, and it remains just as nearly 20 years later. The restaurant consists of a series of pleasant, simple, tavernlike rooms. The menu is extensive enough that you're bound to find something appetizing—perhaps Calvi tenderloin, served in blue-cheese sauce and best accompanied by dumplings. Should you decide to sample the excellent tarte tatin, order it at the beginning of your meal, as it is always freshly prepared from scratch. Despite their essential constancy, both the interior and the menu get subtle face-lifts every now and again. ⊠ *ul. Poselska 24, Stare Miasto* ☎ *012/421–62–73* ⚑ *Reservations essential* ☐ *AE, DC, MC, V.*

$–$$ ✗ **Cherubino.** Cherubino must have one of the most intriguing menus in Kraków, serving a combination of Tuscan cuisine and lighter, more contemporary interpretations of Polish cuisine. Next to traditional gnocchi, carpaccio, and cannelloni, the menu features pierogi, roast duck, and buckwheat soup. The decor is also memorable: you can choose to dine under a winged boat or in one of four beautifully restored 19th-century carriages. ⊠ *ul. św. Tomasza 15, Stare Miasto* ☎ *012/429–40–07* ⚑ *Reservations essential* ☐ *AE, DC, MC, V.*

$–$$ ✗ **Pod Aniołami.** Legend has it that this downstairs cellar was once an alchemist's lab. These days, Under the Angels is one of the more tastefully furnished restaurants in Kraków, with excellent interpretations of Polish cuisine. Try smoked sheep's-milk cheese warmed under the grill, then the delectable Mr. John's ribs. Patrons crowd the upstairs courtyard when the weather is warm. ⊠ *ul. Grodzka 35, Stare Miasto* ☎ *012/421–39–99* ⚑ *Reservations essential* ☐ *AE, DC, MC, V.*

★ ¢–$$ ✗ **Chłopskie Jadło.** This restaurant's name means "Peasant Kitchen," but this is the most upscale interpretation of that theme imaginable. For a starter try the *żurek* (stone soup) made from soured barley; then indulge in the very traditional main course of cabbage rolls stuffed with sauerkraut and grits in a mushroom sauce. All meals come with complimentary bread and lard, and the menu is an artery-clogging cross section of traditional Polish peasant cuisine. ⊠ *Św. Agnieszki 1, Stare Miasto* ☎ *012/421–85–20* ⚑ *Reservations essential* ☐ *AE, DC, MC, V.*

¢–$ ✗ **Chimera Salad Bar.** Be prepared for some difficult choices at Kraków's most popular salad bar: the selection of nourishing salads and other savory staples is almost overwhelming. In winter, you can pick baked potatoes (free of charge) from an open fireplace in the cozy downstairs cellar. In summer, garden seating opens in the shaded inner courtyard. ⊠ *ul. św. Anny 3, Stare Miasto* ☎ *012/429–11–68* ☐ *No credit cards.*

¢–$ ✗ **U Vincenta.** This is paradise for the connoisseurs of pierogi, the Polish cousins of Italian ravioli and Japanese gyoza. In a tiny interior with no room to twist a cat, young and friendly staff serve your pierogi in some two dozen variations, traditional and novel, savory and sweet. ⊠ *ul. Józefa 11, Kazimierz* ☎ *012/430–68–34* ☐ *AE, DC, MC, V.*

6

WHERE TO STAY

To experience and enjoy Kraków to the fullest, you should try to stay in the Old Town, which will put you within walking distance of major attractions, cafés, and restaurants. The downside, of course, is that the best places to stay are rather expensive, and the streets surrounding the Market Square can be noisy at night. If you do not mind paying the price, try to find a room in one of the hotels next to the Planty Park, or facing the hotel's inner courtyard. Cheaper options tend to have a little less character and are farther away from the center.

A viable alternative to a higher-price hotel in Kraków is a short-term apartment rental. Many of these apartment rentals can be made for just a few days time and are usually considerably cheaper than a hotel room. **Affinity Flats** (⌧ ul. Karmelicka 7 ☏ 12/430–08–18 ⊕ www.affinityflats.com) rents 18 apartments in various locations around Kraków (including the Karmelicka location, where the office is based); prices range from zł 300 to zł 640 per night. Flats are classed "standard," "deluxe," "executive," or "Italian," and most of them are furnished with a certain flair (slightly bordering on kitsch sometimes)—a lot of color. **Apartment Cracow** (⌧ ul. Floriańska 39 ☏ 48/607–237–647 ⊕ www.apartmentskrakow.pl) offers 10 simple, no-frills standard, neat apartments in the heart of Kraków's Old Town. Prices range from zł 160 to zł 220 double. **Orient Express** (⌧ ul. Stolarska 13 ☏ 12/422–66–72 ⊕ www.pokoje.krakow.pl) has four types of accommodations: a single for zł 150 per night, a double for zł 165, and two larger apartments for zł 195–zł 340 per night. Simple and bright, the excellent location in the Old Town, opposite the Dominican church. All apartments are equipped with satellite TV, a fridge (the larger apartments have kitchenettes). The flats are located over a French restaurant; it is possible to get breakfast or dinner for a good price in a package; prices are negotiable for stays longer than one week.

$$$$ ▦ **Holiday Inn.** The Holiday Inn Kraków occupies a newly refurbished and extended block of historic tenement houses. Although the rooms are very nice, they are also business-hotel standard and not terribly unique or atmospheric. The hotel is next to the Main Post Office, just outside the Planty Ring, within walking distance to both the Market Square and the main railway station. ⌧ *ul. Wielopole 4, Stare Miasto 31–072* ☏ *012/ 619–00–00* 🖷 *012/619–00–05* ⊕ *www.krakow.globalhotels.pl* ⇥ *154 rooms, 10 suites* ♢ *Restaurant, café, room service, minibars, gym, sauna, laundry service, Internet, meeting rooms* ▤ *AE, DC, MC, V* ⓞ BP.

$$$$ ▦ **Radisson SAS.** Across the street from the Kraków's Philharmonic Hall, the Radisson hotel facade mirrors the pattern on the concert hall—although the lines of the former are decidedly more contemporary and sober than those of the latter. The location—at the edge of the leafy Planty, a mere two minutes' walk from the Market Square—is superb. A musical theme continues in the restaurant, which was named Solfeż (as in solfeggio vocal exercises). ⌧ *ul. Straszewskiego 17, Stare Miasto 31–101* ☏ *012/618–88–88* 🖷 *012/618–88–89* ⊕ *www.krakow. radissonsas.com* ⇥ *196 rooms, 10 suites* ♢ *Restaurant, café, room ser-*

vice, minibars, gym, sauna, laundry service, Internet, meeting rooms, business center ▤ *AE, DC, MC, V* ⍾◎⍾ *BP.*

$$$$ 🖾 **Sheraton.** This luxury business hotel is located at the bank of the Wisła River, in the immediate vicinity of the Royal Castle. It seems a popular choice for royals—this is where Earl and Countess of Wessex stayed during their journey to the region (not surprisingly, they occupied the Wawel Suite). Although Krakovians frown upon the building's not-too-handsome facade, inside the Sheraton offers all the comforts and the quality of service that can be expected of a five-star establishment. ✉ *ul. Powiśle 7, Stare Miasto 31–101* ☏ *012/662–10–00* 🖷 *012/662–11–00* ⊕ *www.starwoodhotels.com* ☜ *224 rooms, 8 suites* ⍾ *Restaurant, 2 bars, room service, minibars, in-room broadband, Wi-Fi, fitness center, pool, dry cleaning, meeting rooms, business services, babysitting, some pets allowed* ▤ *AE, DC, MC, V* ⍾◎⍾ *BP.*

★ $$$–$$$$ 🖾 **Hotel Copernicus.** Hotel Copernicus is a tastefully adapted medieval tenement house on the oldest and, arguably, the most charming street in Kraków. A story goes that Copernicus himself (a graduate of the Kraków University) stayed here once. Whether that's true or not, traces of history can still be seen throughout the hotel in the Renaissance portals, wall paintings, and floor mosaics. The rooms are happily modern: air-conditioned and equipped with minibars, TV, and jetted bathtubs. ✉ *ul. Kanonicza 16, Stare Miasto 31–002* ☏ *012/424–34–00* 🖷 *012/424–34–05* ⊕ *www.hotel.com.pl* ☜ *29 rooms, 8 suites* ⍾ *Restaurant, café, room service, in-room hot tubs, minibars, cable TV, indoor pool, gym, sauna, laundry service, Internet room, meeting room* ▤ *AE, DC, MC, V* ⍾◎⍾ *BP.*

★ $$$ 🖾 **Amadeus Hotel.** A stone's throw from the Rynek, this small hotel is among Kraków's newest. In style and ambience, it claims inspiration from Wolfgang Amadeus Mozart. This cozy and elegant establishment has hosted such celebrities as Mikhail Baryshnikov and Mrs. Vladimir Putin. Its international restaurant, in addition to the standard menu, features a selection of dishes from a different country each month. ✉ *ul. Mikołajska 20, Stare Miasto 30-027* ☏ *012/429–60–70* 🖷 *012/429–60–62* ⊕ *www.hotel-amadeus.pl* ☜ *20 rooms, 2 suites* ⍾ *Restaurant, café, room service, minibars, cable TV, in-room broadband, gym, sauna, bar, laundry service, meeting rooms* ▤ *AE, DC, MC, V* ⍾◎⍾ *BP.*

$$$ 🖾 **Francuski Orbis Hotel.** The "French" hotel—one of Kraków's oldest and classiest—is just across the street from Czartoryski Museum, where Leonardo Da Vinci's *Cecilia Gallerani* resides. A sweeping spiral staircase leads up from the large, high-ceiling lobby to rooms decorated in faux fin-de-siècle grandeur. This hotel may not be all new and shiny, but the slight patina only adds to its old-time charm. ✉ *ul. Pijarska 13, Stare Miasto 31–015* ☏ *012/422–51–22* 🖷 *012/422–52–70* ⊕ *www.orbis.pl* ☜ *27 rooms, 15 suites* ⍾ *Restaurant, room service, minibars, cable TV, in-room broadband, bar, dry cleaning, laundry service, business services, meeting room, some pets allowed, no-smoking rooms; no a/c in some rooms* ▤ *AE, DC, MC, V* ⍾◎⍾ *BP.*

★ $$$ 🖾 **Grand Hotel.** Without question this hotel around the corner from Kraków's main square is the most elegant address for visitors to the city and the one most accessible to the major sights. The decor is Regency inspired, though most of the furnishings are reproductions. Suite 11 has two large bathrooms, a gilded ceiling, and a bedroom fit for a potentate. The banquet room has its own miniature hall of mirrors. ⊠ *ul. Sławkowska 5–7, 31–016* ☎*012/421–72–55* 🖷*012/421–83–60* ⊕*www. grand.pl* ⇝ *50 rooms, 6 suites* ⚖ *Restaurant, café, minibars, cable TV, bar* ▤ *AE, DC, MC, V* ⚑⧉ *BP.*

$$$ 🎬 **Gródek.** Hidden away from the noise in a cozy cul-de-sac next to the
Fodor'sChoice   Planty Park and the Dominican convent, this boutique hotel is certainly
★   one of Kraków's finest. Each of the plush and tasteful rooms is furnished in a different style (you can check them out on the Web site), such as the Chinese room (No. 309). Hotel facilities include a library-cum-bar, a winter garden with a gourmet restaurant, with a small but exciting archaeological display. It is a noble and comfortable place with a lot of personality. ⊠*ul. Na Gródku 4, Stare Miasto 31–028* ☎*012/431–90–30* 🖷 *012/431–90–40* ⊕ *www.donimirski.com* ⇝ *21 rooms, 2 suites* ⚖ *Restaurant, café, room service, minibars, sauna, laundry service, Internet room, meeting rooms* ▤ *AE, DC, MC, V* ⚑⧉ *BP.*

$$$ 🎬 **Maltański.** This is a pleasant and quiet hotel on the west side of the Planty, a member of the same chain as Gródek but several years its senior. Once part of the Potocki family mansion, the building was confiscated after the war by Communist authorities. After the building was returned to its owners in 1990, it was restored and turned into a hotel a few years later. Friendly staff make sure that the atmosphere is homey. While the restaurant usually serves only breakfast, guests can order dinner for a minimum of six persons with 48 hours advance notice. ⊠ *ul. Straszewskiego 14, Stare Miasto 31–101* ☎*012/431–00–10* 🖷*012/431–06–15* ⊕ *www.donimirski.com* ⇝ *16 rooms* ⚖ *Dining room, café, room service, minibars, laundry service, Internet room, meeting rooms; no a/c in some rooms* ▤ *AE, DC, MC, V* ⚑⧉ *BP.*

★ $$$ 🎬 **Pod Różą.** The management is still proud that both Chopin and Czar Alexander I have slept here. More recently, the hotel has welcomed presidents and royals. Housed in a 14th-century building, the hotel offers guests spacious, high-ceiling rooms on the fashionable shopping street Floriańska. The first-class Italian restaurant and 15th-century wine cellar add to the hotel's attractions. ⊠*ul. Floriańska 14, Stare Miasto 31–021* ☎ *012/424–33–00* 🖷 *012/424–33–51* ⊕ *www.hotel.com.pl* ⇝ *51 rooms, 3 suites* ⚖ *2 restaurants, café, minibars, cable TV, wine bar, meeting rooms* ▤ *AE, DC, MC, V* ⚑⧉ *BP.*

$$$ 🎬 **Senacki.** Senacki is in a historic building along the Royal Route, halfway between the Market Square and the castle. You would be hard pressed to find a more central location. From the rooms on the Grodzka Street side of the hotel, you'll find stunning views of the churches of Saints Peter and Paul and of Saint Andrew, but the back rooms are quieter. ⊠*ul. Grodzka 51, Stare Miasto 31–001* ☎*012/421–11–61* 🖷*012/422–71–34* ⊕ *www.senacki.krakow.pl* ⇝ *20 rooms* ⚖ *Restaurant, café, room service, minibars, in-room broadband, laundry service, meeting rooms; no a/c* ▤ *AE, DC, MC, V* ⚑⧉ *BP.*

$$ 🎬 **Atrium.** This neat hotel is less than fashionably located, being just outside the green girdle of the Planty. However, it is still quite near the Main Square—a mere five-minute walk away, and the train station is also within

a walking distance. Rooms are spacious, though simply furnished, and they are a good value in expensive Kraków. ⊠ *ul. Krzywa 7, Kleparz 31–149* ☎ *012/430–02–03* 🖷 *012/430–01–96* ⊕ *www.hotelatrium. com.pl* ⟿ *47 rooms, 4 suites, 3 apartments* ⚭ *Restaurant, cable TV, meeting rooms, parking (fee), some pets allowed; no a/c* ⊟ *AE, DC, MC, V* ⍢ *EP.*

$$ 🏨 **Hotel Polski (Pod Białym Orłem).** Located within the medieval city walls—opposite the open-air art gallery by the Floriańska gate, "Under the White Eagle" is simple and unpretentious. An inn of the same name existed here in the 18th century; today the hotel is again the property of the Czartoryskis, the same family who founded the famous museum next door. Compared to the plush suites pictured on the Web site, the standard rooms are pretty basic, but they remain among the more affordable accommodation options within the Old Town. ⊠ *ul. Pijarska 17, 31–015* ☎ *012/422–11–44* 🖷 *012/422–15–29* ⊕ *www.podorlem. com.pl* ⟿ *50 rooms, 3 suites* ⚭ *Café, cable TV, some in-room broadband* ⊟ *AE, DC, MC, V* ⍢ *BP.*

$ 🏨 **Hotel System Premium.** This solid business hotel is located outside the center, but not too far out, so it's a perfect choice if you are traveling to Kraków by car. The location is also very handy for both the airport and the railway station. A swimming pool, fitness center, and free Internet are thrown into the bargain, making it one of Kraków's best values. ⊠ *29 Listopada 189, Czerwony Prądnik 31–241* ☎ *012/614–48–00* 🖷 *012/634–05–08* ⊕ *www.krakow.hotelsystem.pl* ⟿ *159 rooms, 2 suites* ⚭ *Restaurant, café, room service, cable TV, minibars, in-room broadband, gym, sauna, swimming pool, laundry service, meeting rooms; no a/c* ⊟ *AE, DC, MC, V* ⍢ *EP.*

NIGHTLIFE & THE ARTS

Kraków has a lively tradition in theater and music. You can buy a copy of *Karnet*, which gives detailed cultural information in Polish and English, at most newsstands and most local bookstores. A similar publication called *Miesiąc w Krakowie (This Month in Kraków)* is also available on newsstands and in bookstores. Also be on the lookout for a handy, free miniguide with map called *Cracow-life.com* (the publishers run a Web site as well).

Nightlife

Bars

We tried to count Kraków's bars, but we gave up. They are like mushrooms, new ones sprouting up every summer (and often going away again just as quickly). While reputations of Kraków's many bars is a moveable feast, as fashions come and go, some legends rise and some fall. But the thirst in Kraków never seems to be quenched completely, and the city's nightlife scene grows stronger all the time. While Kraków has not yet become a major destination for hard-drinking stag parties (it's certainly not in the same class as Prague and Talinn), you may see an occasionally raucous group.

Many of Kraków's pubs are located in medieval cellars, which make perfect wintertime hangouts. In the summer season, terrace cafés are the best place to sip a cold beer. The highest concentration of drinking establishments will be found in and around the Market Square, in Kazimierz, and in and around plac Nowy.

Just like anywhere else in Poland, you are more likely to find good beer or vodka (or vodka-based cocktails) than good wine in an average bar—although the first specialized wine bars have already arrived in Kraków.

Opening hours are very flexible. Few bars close at midnight, and most stay open while there are customers around, often until 3 or 4 AM.

The mysterious **Alchemia** (⊠ ul. Estery 5, Kazimierz) is a great bar in the plac Nowy area. Coffee and beer rule the drinks menu, but you can sometimes get decent wines by the glass. In winter, try to get the table by the fireplace; in summer, when Alchemia spills out onto the pavement, try to grab a seat outside—but be prepared for fierce competition.

Les Couleurs (⊠ ul. Estery 10, Kazimierz) is the address to seek out if you want a Parisian atmosphere along with your drinks. A lazy café during the day, it becomes a frantic bar at night. Choose between great coffee, beer, freshly squeezed orange juice, cocktails, and excellent homemade cakes.

O'Morgan's Irish Pub (⊠ ul. Garncarska 5, Stare Miasto) is headquarters for Kraków's English-speaking community. There is a good selection of beers—you will find stout and bitter in addition to omnipresent lager. The most crowded night of the year, not surprisingly, is March 17.

At trendy **Paparazzi** (⊠ ul. Mikołajska 9, Stare Miasto) you can observe Kraków's beautiful people in action and sip the best cocktails in town: mojitos in the summer, and bloody Marys in the winter. You can also grab a cold or hot snack, like a sandwich or a pasta.

Singer (⊠ ul. Estery 20, Kazimierz) is a good, though smoky, bar in Kazimierz; the first one to open here in the early 1990s. It was named after the famous brand of sewing machines, which are recycled here into coffee tables and candleholders.

Stalowe Magnolie (Steel Magnolias; ⊠ ul. św. Jana 15, Stare Miasto) is an elegant faux fin-de-siècle music club (smart attire required). The selection of cocktails is impressive, but the prices are steep.

Cabaret & Live Music
Like many restaurants in Kazimierz, **Alef** (⊠ ul. Szeroka 17, Kazimierz) is a place where klezmer music is on hand every night.

Harris Piano Jazz Bar (⊠ Rynek Główny 28, Stare Miasto), in Old Town, is a good spot for jazz.

At **Jama Michalika** (⊠ ul. Floriańska 45, Stare Miasto), popular musical and comedic cabarets take place in a café that has remained essentially the same for a century.

The underground venue **Klub Indigo** (✉ ul. Floriańska 26, Stare Miasto) often has live music—primarily jazz.

Loch Camelot (✉ ul. św. Tomasza 17, Stare Miasto) is a traditional Polish café that holds regular cabaret performances in its basement. The cabaret at **Pod Baranami** (✉ Rynek Główny 27, Stare Miasto) was founded in 1956 by the late Kraków theater legend Piotr Skrzynecki. Jazz sessions are regularly held at **U Muniaka** (✉ ul. Floriańska 3, Stare Miasto).

BILLY WILDER

Screenwriter, producer, and director Billy Wilder was born in 1906 in the village of Sucha Beskidzka, but it was in Kraków where he saw the first movies in his life. Years later, in Hollywood, he made several classics, including *Some Like It Hot*, *Sunset Boulevard*, and *Stalag 17*. His final project was to be *Schindler's List*, but Steven Spielberg had already bought the rights.

The Arts

Film

Kraków Cinema Centre ARS (✉ ul. św. Jana 6, Stare Miasto ☎ 012/421-41-99) shows movies from Hollywood and Europe, almost always in the original language with Polish subtitles. All Polish cinemas show movies in their original versions, in contrast with Polish TV channels, where monotonous dubbing prevails.

Kino Pod Baranami (✉Rynek Główny 27, Stare Miasto ☎012/423-07-68) is another pleasant "city-plex" with three screens in the upper floors of the "Under the Rams" Palace (the entrance is through the courtyard on the left). It often becomes a showcase of world cinema, showing both early and contemporary moving pictures from around the globe.

Classical Music

If you're a fan of chamber music, there are occasional performances in the great hall of the Zamek Królewski (Royal Castle) on Wawel Hill, at the Municipal Arsenal, or at the Sukiennice Art Gallery. You can check the schedule in *Karnet* monthly or ask at the Cultural Information Office on św. Jana Street. Smart attire is preferable but not mandatory for classical music concerts.

Kraków's symphony, **Filharmonia im. Karola Szymanowskiego** (✉ Philharmonic Hall, ul. Zwierzyniecka 1, Stare Miasto ☎ 012/422-94-77 tickets), gives frequent concerts.

Look out for the performances of **Sinfonietta Cracovia** (☎ 012/416-70-75 schedule and tickets); Kraków's young and brilliant city orchestra performs in different venues all over town.

Organ recitals can be found in many of Kraków's churches throughout the summer season. The **Summer Organ Concerts** (☎ 012/420-49-50) rate among the best.

FODOR'S FIRST PERSON

John Neal Axelrod
Conductor, Sinfonietta Cracovia

When American conductor John Neal Axelrod is leading Sinfonietta Cracovia, their conjoined energy sparkles to create a great thunderstorm of music. Maestro Axelrod, who was born in Houston, Texas, is considered one of the most talented, creative, and unconventional conductors of his generation. Since 2001, he has been the Principal Guest Conductor of the Sinfonietta Cracovia.

How did it all begin? "My first exposure with Sinfonietta Cracovia, much like my first impression of Kraków, was love at first sight," says the Maestro. "The musicians were so passionate about making music, so free of union restrictions, so hungry from post-communism, and so incredibly talented." Six years since that first encounter, Sinfonietta has become one of Poland's best orchestras.

Axelrod calls Kraków his "home away from home" for more than one reason: "My first experience in Kraków was personal, not only professional," he confesses. "I was able to trace my Polish roots to both sides of my family (I am third-generation) and I visited Auschwitz. Who knew that five years later the orchestra and I would be the first ensemble to play on the grounds of Auschwitz–Birkenau since the war ended, as part of a BBC film?"

Although Sinfonietta has a primarily classical repertoire, the Maestro believes that "the orchestra can play anything; they are that good." For three years now, Axelrod and Sinfonietta Cracovia have been successfully celebrating American Music in the annual "Rhythm and Swing" concerts: "I think the energy and optimism of American music—whether Bernstein or Barber, Gershwin or Ellington—is always fresh and fun for the orchestra and public."

Although the Maestro says that all of Kraków impresses him, as a musician he speaks with particular fondness of the trumpet call that sounds each hour from the tower of the Mariacki Church in Market Square: "The fact that this cultured city celebrates its freedom from invading Tartars in the 14th century by memorializing the trumpeteer—and exactly when, in the melody, he is hit by an arrow—is something that will never cease to impress me."

Any dining recommendations? "I adore Italian food, and I can very much recommend authentic Italian cuisine at Padua, near the Jagiellonian University and Aqua e Vino. Both have terrific tiramisu and homemade pasta. For visitors interested in art, Wentzl is the most interesting. And the restaurant in Hotel Copernicus is gourmet Polish. And the hotel itself, along with Hotel Amadeus, are the real way to stay in Kraków. The Likus Concept Store, also on Market Square, is part of the chain [that owns the] Kraków Hotel Pod Różą and Hotel Copernicus, so here quality is assured."

According to Axelrod, Kraków is "like Prague, only smaller and better." He noticed that it has become busier and more commercialized since he first arrived. "But it does not take away any of its beauty," he adds quickly.

Opera & Dance

At this writing, Kraków is awaiting the completion of a brand-new opera house in Rondo Mogilskie, though this venue is not expected to be open until at least mid-2007 or even 2008. For the time being, performances are still held at the Słowacki Theater. Although casual dress will not be frowned upon, this elegant old-timer theater is a perfect excuse to put on your Sunday best, as many Krakovians would, when going to the opera.

The stunning **Teatr im. Juliusza Słowackiego** (Słowacki Theater; ⊠ pl. św. Ducha 1, Stare Miasto ☎ 012/422–43–22) hosts traditional opera and ballet favorites as well as dramatic performances.

Dance performances are often held at the **Nowohuckie Centrum Kultury** (Nowa Huta Cultural Center; ⊠ al. Jana Pawła II 232, Nowa Huta ☎ 012/644–02–66), which is also home to the Kraków Ballet. Near Nowa Huta's Central Square, the Center is a 20- to 30-minute tram ride or a 10-minute taxi ride from Kraków's Old Town.

Theater

Kraków has a long-standing tradition of classical drama, but most performances are in Polish. English-language performances are advertised in the *Karnet* or at the Cultural Information Office.

Every summer in July, Kraków hosts the **Street Theatre Festival** (☎ 012/633–89–47) with performances all around town, but mostly at Kraków's biggest outdoor stage, Rynek Główny.

☾ The popular **Bagatela** (⊠ ul. Karmelicka 6, Stare Miasto ☎ 012/422–45–44) is a venue for children's theater as well as adult drama and farce.

Scena pod Ratuszem (⊠ Wieża Ratuszowa, Stare Miasto ☎ 012/421–16–57), a tiny theater in the cellar of the Town Hall Tower, stages small-scale dramas in front of a bare-brick backdrop.

The **Stary Teatr** (⊠ ul. Jagiellońska 5, Stare Miasto ☎ 012/422–85–66) is Kraków's oldest and most renowned theater, staging mostly Polish and international classical dramas—in the Polish language.

SHOPPING

Kraków's Old Town is a friendly ground for shoppers—and any time you need to take a break from retail therapy, you can easily find a place to refuel with a cup of coffee, a snack, or a beer. Popular souvenirs to take home include folk crafts such as wooden toys or chess boxes, pottery, and glass, Easter eggs and Christmas ornaments, designer amber jewelry, and Polish-made vodkas and liqueurs. Most shops are open weekdays from 10 to 6, Saturday from 9 to 2.

Shopping Neighborhoods & Malls

In Kraków's Old Town, you will find a mix of crafts and specialty shops next to department stores and brand-name fashion and leisure-wear stores.

For regionally produced goods, head to the middle of the Rynek Główny, the main Market Square. At the booths in the Sukiennice (Cloth

Hall), you'll find tooled leather goods, wood carvings, regional costumes, amber jewelry, and the embroidered felt slippers made in the Podhale region. Unexpectedly for such a central location, the prices at Cloth Hall are good.

Kraków abounds with galleries, where you can buy—or simply look at—contemporary Polish art. When walking around the Old Town or Kazimierz, you will stumble upon an art gallery every 100 meters or so.

In the streets leading out of the Market Square—notably Floriańska, Szewska, and Grodzka—you will find bookshops, small clothing boutiques, more jewelry and souvenir shops, and some delicatessens. Local brands are often disguised behind an English-sounding names, such as a popular fashion chain called **Reserved** (both women's and men's clothing), the more upmarket **Simple** and **Solar** (ladies' attire only) and **5-10-15** for kids. For a more concentrated shopping experience, head for one of Kraków's shopping malls. **Galeria Kazimierz** (☒ ul. Podgórska 34, Kazimierz ☎ 012/433–01–01 ⊕ www.galeriakazimierz.pl) is the most pleasant and most centrally located shopping mall in the city. It's within walking distance of the heart of Kazimierz and the river and is open seven days a week. Galeria **Krakowska** (☒ Pawia 5) opened in fall 2006, right next to Kraków's main railway station.

Specialty Stores

Accessories
If you happen to have a weakness for fashion accessories, Kraków has two very good choices. **Gorseletka** (☒ ul. Szpitalna, Stare Miasto ☎ 012/423–04–37) specializes in handmade corsets. Old-fashioned and fancy as they are, these tailor-made undergarments can prove surprisingly comfortable.

Pracownia Kapeluszy (☒ ul. św. Tomasza, Stare Miasto ☎ No phone) is a hatmaker that will take you for a journey back in time to the days when it was unthinkable for a lady not to own a hat—or several hats, for that matter.

Arts & Crafts
The **Galeria Przedmiotu AB** (☒ Rynek Główny 1/3 ☎ 012/429–23–40), on the northern side of the Cloth Hall, sells beautiful everyday objects and affordable artworks.

The **Sukiennice** (☒ Rynek Główny 1/3, Stare Miasto ☎ No phone) is the best place to buy your souvenirs—anything from amber jewelry to leather slippers, Kraków-theme T-shirts to toy dragons, embroidered tablecloths to hand-crafted wooden chess sets.

Books
You'll find a selection of English-language paperbacks in most large bookshops, but for the English-speaking readers, **Massolit** (☒ ul. Felicjanek 4, Stare Miasto ☎ 012/432–41–50) is the real thing. The converted apartment contains a little café that will tempt you with coffee and cakes, and several rooms filled to the brim with book-laden shelves offering endless browsing opportunities.

Food

Among the city's delicatessens, you'll find the best selection of international gourmet food and wine in the **Likus Concept Store** (✉ Rynek Główny 13, downstairs, Stare Miasto ☎ 012/617–02–12), Kraków's newest and finest food store—but it comes at a price! **Naturalny Sklepik** (✉ ul. Krupnicza 8, Stare Miasto ☎ 012/422–96–83), a health foods store, sells both food and a selection of natural cosmetics—local as well as imported. Fresh fruit, vegetables, cheese, and meat can be found in **Stary Kleparz** (✉ ul. Basztowa, Stare Miasto), a market located just outside of Planty Ring behind the LOT office.

Jewelry

Mikołajczyni Amber (✉ Rynek Główny 1/3, Stare Miasto ☎ 012/423–10–81) is one of the best shops in Kraków for amber jewelry in luxurious settings.

KRAKÓW ESSENTIALS

Transportation

6

BY AIR

Although many people fly into Warsaw from the U.S., there are direct air connections on LOT, the Polish airline, between Kraków and Chicago, Newark, and New York (JFK) several times weekly, and the city can be reached by direct flight from most major (and some minor) European cities. With the arrival of low-cost airlines to Kraków, the number of flights is on the increase. EURO-LOT flies several times daily between Kraków and Warsaw (40 minutes), while Direct Fly offers a nonstop connection to Gdańsk (75 minutes). Many other airlines offer daily or at least regularly scheduled service within Europe. LOT's Kraków office is open weekdays 9–6, Saturday 9–3. Many airlines have offices at the airport. Orbis Travel is also a good source for long-haul tickets, while tickets for low-cost airlines are best bought online, and booked well in advance for the best prices.

🛪 **Aer Lingus** ⊕ www.aerlingus.com. **Alitalia** ☎ 012/431-06-21. **Austrian Airlines** ☎ 012/629-66-66. **British Airways** ☎ 012/529-90-00. **Centralwings** ⊕ www.centralwings.com. **ČSA** ☎ 012/639-34-26. **Easy Jet** ⊕ www.easyjet.com **Finnair** ☎ 012/639-34-23. **Germanwings** ⊕ www.germanwings.com. **LOT** ☎ 0801-703-703 **Norwegian** ⊕ www.norwegian.no. **Ryanair** ⊕ www.ryanair.com. **Sky Europe** ⊕ www.skyeurope.com. **Swiss** ☎ 012/639-34-24.

AIRPORTS & TRANSFERS

The Pope John Paul II Kraków–Balice Airport, 11 km (7 mi) west of the city, is the region's only airport. In spring and fall fog can cause frustrating delays.

In summer 2006, a fast train connection finally opened between Balice Airport and Kraków's main railway station. The train stops some 200 meters from the airline terminal; from there you can walk or use the airport shuttle bus, free of charge. The train runs approximately every 40 minutes, the journey takes about 15 minutes, and the tickets (zł 3.80) can be bought on board.

Bus 208 runs between the airport and Nowy Kleparz (north from the city center), and Bus 192 between Rondo Mogilskie, the main station, and the airport. The basic fare is zł 2.50 with an extra charge for luggage. Tickets can be bought from newspaper kiosks at the terminal, or from the driver (when buying from the driver, there is a surcharge). Taxis are available from outside the terminal, and the fare into the city center is approximately zł 60.

⌖ Pope John Paul II Kraków-Balice Airport ☎ 012/411-19-55 ⊕ www.lotnisko-balice.pl.

BY BUS

Express bus service to Kraków runs regularly to and from most Polish cities. Most buses arrive at the main PKS station, located just to the east of the railway station. From here you can transfer to buses headed for other destinations in the region.

⌖ Kraków Main PKS Station ⊠ pl. Wita Stwosza ☎ 0300-300-120 ⊕ www.pks.krakow.pl.

BY CAR

A car will not be of much use to you in Kraków, since most of the Old Town is closed to traffic and distances between major sights are short. Elsewhere in the city, traffic jams are frequent and parking space insufficient, therefore an automobile may be a bit of a liability. A car will be useful if you set out to explore the region; but even then it is a good idea to consider a train or a bus first. You can approach Kraków either on the E77 highway (from Warsaw and north) or via the E40 (from the area around Katowice). Use the parking facilities at your hotel or one of the attended municipal parking garages (try plac Szczepański or plac świętego Ducha). On the whole, parking space in Kraków is rather scarce and expensive—between zł 5 and zł 10 per hour.

⌖ Avis ⊠ ul. Lubicz 23 ☎ 012/629-61-08 ⊠ Balice Airport ☎ 012/639-32-89. **Europcar** ⊠ ul. Szlak 2 ☎ 012/633-21-00 ⊠ Balice Airport ☎ 012/285-50-45. **Hertz** ⊠ Balice Airport ☎ 012/633-21-00.

BY TAXI

There is no shortage of taxis in Kraków, and there are several taxi ranks just outside the Platy Ring—for instance, on plac Szczepański, plac Wszystkich Świętych, or on Sławkowska Street. It is okay to hail a taxi in the street, and it will stop if it is free, but that would be unusual—most people either dial a cab or walk to the taxi rank. Phone rates are slightly cheaper than street rates, and it is definitely cheaper to take a taxi belonging to a reputable radio taxi company than a private taxi. Radio taxi companies are listed below.

⌖ Mega Taxi ☎ 012/9625. **Taxi Partner** ☎ 012/9633. **Taxi Dwójki** ☎ 012/9622.

BY TRAIN

Nonstop express trains from Warsaw take just under three hours and run throughout the day. All trains arrive at Kraków Główny Station, the city's main railway station, on the edge of the Old Town.

⌖ Kraków Główny Station ⊠ pl. Dworcowy 1 ☎ 012/9436.

Contacts & Resources

EMERGENCIES

There are plenty of health centers, hospitals, and pharmacies in Kraków, including private clinics and ambulance service in addition to public health care. A list of English-speaking doctors is available from the **US Consulate Department of Citizen Services** (✉ ul. Stolarska ☎ 012/429–66–55).

⚡ Emergency Services **Ambulance** ☎ 012/999 **Falck** ☎ 012/9675 has a private ambulance service and does house calls.

⚡ Late-night Pharmacies **Apteka 24** ✉ ul. Mogilska 21 ☎ 012/411-01-26 is open until 10 PM nightly. **Nonstop** ✉ Dunajewskiego 2 ☎ 012/422-65-04 is open until 9 PM nightly.

INTERNET, MAIL & SHIPPING

You can collect your *poste restante* at the **Main Post Office** (✉ Westerplatte 20), where the full range of postal services is available. A **24-Hour Post Office** (✉ pl. Kolejowy) is in front of the main railway station.

There are a number of Internet hotspots around the Old Town, including in the Market Square and on Szeroka in Kazimierz. Most four- and five-star hotels offer Internet access to their guests free of charge. Internet cafés are in abundance.

⚡ Shipping Companies **DHL** ✉ Zawiła 61 ☎ 012/261-60-60 ⊕ www.dhl.com. **Pocztex** ✉ pl. Kolejowy, inside the post office building next to the main railway station ☎ 0804-104-104 ⊕ www.pocztex.pl.

⚡ Internet Cafés **ARS Internet Café** ✉ ul. św. Jana 6 ☎ 012/421-41-99 ⊕ www.ars.pl is huddled in the Kraków Cinema Centre ARS. **Internet Café** ✉ Rynek Główny 23 ☎ 012/432-94-94 ⊕ www.cafe.studencki.pl is open 24 hours a day. **U Luisa Cyber Café** ✉ Rynek Główny 13 ☎ 012/617-02-22 ⊕ www.uluisa.com has flat-screen monitors and high-speed connection.

MEDIA

English-language newspapers and magazines can be bought from the **EMPiK Megastore** (✉ Rynek Główny 13 ☎ 012/617–02–22).

⚡ Bookstores The **Jarden Jewish Bookshop** ✉ ul. Szeroka 2 ☎ 012/421-71-66 has a good selection of books on the history of Polish Jews. The **Massolit Books & Café** ✉ ul. Felicjanek 4 ☎ 012/432-41-50 tempts the reader with coffee, cakes, and endless browsing opportunities.

TOUR OPTIONS

All major hotels will arrange tours of the city as well as surrounding attractions. There is a lot on offer, so it is a good idea to shop around a little. Some standard tours may be just a little bland, so consider alternative options: a bike tour, or an adventure with Crazy Guides. The Orbis hotel, through its subsidiary Cracow Tours, organizes tours by bus, minibus, or limousine—both within Kraków and to neighboring attractions. There are also plenty of smaller operators who provide well-informed, friendly guide services for both individuals and groups.

Crazy Guides are just great fun. The tours are informal, and everything done by individual arrangement. Most important, this company knows what good customer service is about, and the historic information they provide is reliable. Their tour of Nowa Huta in a Trabant is an absolute hit, but there are many other tours offered.

Emerson Lumico is a friendly and competent travel agency, catering to both groups and individual customers. Clients come from all over the world. The agency's English-speaking staff will help you book a hotel or a holiday apartment; they can also organize a tailor-made tour in Kraków or farther afield.

Jarden Tours specializes in tours of Jewish Kraków. Guides take you around the Kazimierz District, to the former Jewish ghetto in Podgórze, and on a *Schindler's List* tour. There is a specialty bookshop in the Jarden Tours headquarters.

Kraków Bike Tours offers daytime bike tours of Kraków from March through mid December, as well as nighttime tours from May through October.

Orbis Cracow Tours has been in the business the longest and can be a bit blasé—it all depends on the person who will be your guide.

From May through September, Żegluga krakowska operates short, one-hour cruises Monday through Saturday on the Wisła River aboard the boat *Nimfa* from the wharf below the Wawel castle near the Grunwaldzki Bridge; these cruises cost zł 10. On Sunday, three-hour round-trip cruises go to Tyniec Abbey at 10, 1, and 4 for zł 20. **🚩 Crazy Guides** ⊠ Lublańska 22/9 ☎ 048/5000–91–2000 ⊕ www.crazyguides.com. **Emmerson Lumico** ⊠ul. Karmelicka 29 ☎012/623–40–90 or 048/602–299–800 ⊕ www.lumico.pl. **Jarden Tours** ⊠ ul. Szeroka 2 ☎ 012/421–13–74 ⊕ www.jarden.pl. **Kraków Bike Tours** ☎ 012/663–731–515 ⊕ www.krakowbiketour.com. **Orbis/Cracow Tours** ⊠ Rynek Główny 41 ☎ 012/422–11–57 ⊕ orbis.krakow.pl. **Żegluga krakowska** ⊠ Wawel Wharf ☎ 012/422–08–55.

VISITOR INFORMATION

The Cultural Information Center is open weekdays 10–6, Saturday until 4. To check the transportation schedules and purchase air, train, and bus tickets, head to Orbis, which is open weekdays 9–5 and Saturday 9–2. The Tourist Information Point, in the Planty, between the main railway station and Słowacki Theater, is open weekdays 8–8, weekends 9–5. **🚩 Cultural Information Center** ⊠ ul. św. Jana 2 ☎ 012/421–77–87 ⊕ www.karnet.krakow2000.pl. **Orbis** ⊠ Rynek Główny 41 ☎ 012/422–11–57. **Tourist Information Point** ⊠ ul. Szpitalna 25 ☎ 012/432–01–10 or 012/432–00–60.

Małopolska & the Tatras

WORD OF MOUTH

"If you want to spend a night in Zakopane (recommended if you have time), I would recommend Belvedere Hotel."

—Caroline1

"I would suggest you book a tour . . . [Auschwitz] is quite complex and needs some explanation, and you will get a lot more out of the experience with a guide who can explain things as you go along."

—USNR

JUST TO THE SOUTH OF KRAKÓW, Poland's great plains give way to the gently folding foothills of the Carpathians, building to the High Tatras on the Slovak border. The fine medieval architecture of many towns in the Małopolska (Little Poland) region comes from a period when the area prospered as the intersection of thriving trade routes. In the countryside, wooden homesteads and strip-farmed tracts tell another story: of the hardships and poverty that the peasantry endured before the 20th century brought tourists to the mountains. During the 19th century, when this part of Poland was under Austrian rule as the province of Western Galicia, hundreds of thousands of peasants fled from the grinding toil of farm life to seek their fortune in the United States; it sometimes seems as if every family hereabouts has a cousin in America.

A visit to Kraków and Małopolska is incomplete without trips to at least two nearby destinations: the Wieliczka Salt Mine, where salt has been mined for a thousand years, and Auschwitz and Birkenau, sites of the Nazis' most gruesome and brutal concentration camps. Both Ojców National Park and Zakopane offer first-rate hiking in unadulterated natural surroundings. This is also Poland's main winter sports area. Zakopane is the self-styled winter capital of Poland, and the spa towns of Szczawnica, Krościenko, and Krynica are good bases for cross-country skiing.

Małopolska remains intensely Catholic and conservative, and the traditional way of life in the countryside is relatively intact. Folk crafts and customs are still very much alive in the mountains and foothills of *Podhale*. Carved-wood beehives stand in mountain gardens, and worshipers set out for Sunday church in embroidered white-felt trousers.

Exploring Małopolska & the Tatras

About the Restaurants

You will find good restaurants serving regional food everywhere in Małopolska, and these restaurants never seem to go out of fashion. Most menus follow a similar pattern of wholesome, simple fare: nutritious soups, meat dishes, and trout from local farms. Few restaurants offer a more refined version of traditional dishes—with recipes deriving from the king's, rather than commoner's table. Outside Kraków (Małopolska's capital)— and other than pizza or Big Macs— international cuisine is almost nonexistent. Some justly celebrated regional specialties include *oscypek* (smoked sheep cheese) in Zakopane and throughout Podhale; *kwaśnica* soup made of sauerkraut, bacon,

---

MAŁOPOLSKA'S TOP 5

- The underground labyrinths of Wieliczka Salt Mine, with its magnificent salt carvings.

- Taking in the Tatras—either easy way by cable car or the hard way by foot.

- The unspeakably sad but essential visit to Auschwitz-Birkenau, an unforgettable history lesson.

- A ride on the "Pope's Express" that travels between Kraków and Wadowice, the birthplace of John Paul II.

- The intersection of nature and culture in Ojców National Park.

and a variety of other ingredients; and Karol Wojtyła's favorite, *kremówka,* a cake made in Wadowice.

About the Hotels

Outside Kraków, it may be difficult to find upscale accommodations, but some reasonable mid-range and very decent budget options are available. You'll find a number of inexpensive bed-and-breakfast accommodations in private pensions. Pensions (generally small hotels) usually offer full board and hearty meals. The only exception is Zakopane, where the number of top-end establishments has been increasing over the last decade.

In addition to more traditional hotels, also look for signs in windows advertising POKOJE (rooms). Rural (or agro-) tourism is also popular—in farms converted or partly converted into pensions (*gospodarstwa agroturystyczne* in Polish). In most cases, you are just a guest on the farm, but a few places will give you the option of actually helping out with the work.

Wakacje Agro (⊕ www.wakacje.agro.pl) is a nationwide agro-tourism booking service with an English-language version that allows you to book places online.

Wrota Małopolski (⊕ www.wrotamalopolski.pl) has information on agro-tourism in the Małopolska region, but it is only in Polish.

WHAT IT COSTS In Polish złoty (zł)				
$$$$	**$$$**	**$$**	**$**	**¢**
RESTAURANTS over zł 50	zł 35–zł 50	zł 20–zł 35	zł10–zł 20	under zł10
HOTELS over zł 800	zł 400–zł 800	zł 200–zł 400	zł100–zł 200	under zł100

Restaurant prices are per person for a main course at dinner. Hotel prices are for two people in a standard double room with a private bath and breakfast in high season.

Timing

For sightseeing and hiking, late spring to early autumn is the best time to visit the Małopolska region. November and March can be rainy and cold, and temperatures will drop to freezing or below during the winter. Most attractions and places of interest, however, remain open year-round. A winter visit to Wieliczka Salt Mine has many advantages: the temperature in the mine is always the same (around 15°C/60°F), making it feel pleasantly warm during the winter months; the mine is also much less crowded in the winter than during the busy summer months. During summer vacations, spa towns, holiday resorts in the mountains, and the hiking trails tend to become crowded, and this is especially true of Zakopane and the Tatra Mountains. Winter is ski season, when mountain resorts again get busy—particularly during weekends. In winter, some hiking trails are closed, and only experienced mountaineers should try to ascend to the upper trails and mountaintops. Nevertheless, many trails remain perfectly accessible to all, especially in the valleys, and the cable-car ride to Gubałówka also runs year-round.

Numbers in the margins correspond to numbers on the Małopolska map.

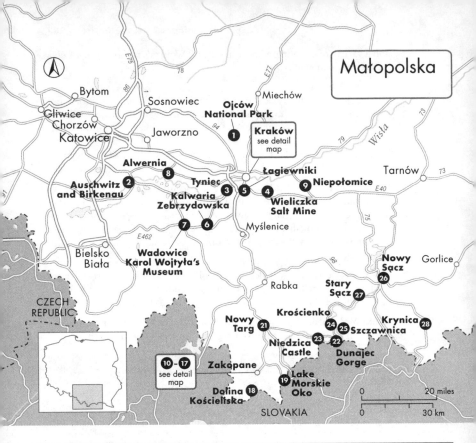

OJCÓW NATIONAL PARK

★ ❶ *48 km (30 mi) northwest of Kraków.*

Ojców National Park (aka Ojcowski Park Narodowy)—the smallest national park in Poland—encompasses the limestone gorge of the Prądnik River and its immediate surroundings. Easy walking trails take you through ravines and beech forests to fantastic Jurassic-era rock formations and caves. Most marked trails start from the parking lot next to the Park's management building and the Hotel Kazimierz. From this point south, the valley is closed to motorized traffic. In the parking lot, you'll find an information booth, where you can buy maps and arrange for a guided tour—but it is easy enough to walk around on your own. A good strategy is to begin by going south toward the rock formation of **Brama Krakowska** (aka Kraków's Gate).

One of the trails to the right will take you to **Władysław the Short's cave** (☎ 012/419–08–01). A legend has it that Władysław the Short, a medieval Polish king, escaped his German pursuers with the help of a spider that spun a web over the mouth of the cave in which he was hiding. Admission is zł 6.50, and it is open from mid-April through mid-Octo-

IF YOU LIKE

HIKING

The Tatras are crisscrossed with trails of varying difficulty, with Zakopane as a starting point. You'll experience everything from easy valley walks where you hardly have an incline to the seriously difficult Rysy or Orla Perć trails, which utilize chains and elements of rock climbing. The Pieniny, Gorce, and Beskidy ranges have plenty of trails that are easier than those in the Tatras, and there are great opportunities for easy recreational hiking in Ojców National Park.

WOODEN ARCHITECTURE

At harmony with nature, traditional wooden architecture blends in with the landscape of southern Poland. Interesting examples of regional styles can be found in nearly every town and village of the region: Zakopane, Krynica, Niedzica-Czorsztyn, and so forth. Four of the region's churches—including Dębno Podhalańskie—are listed on the UNESCO List of World Cultural and Natural Heritage. Open-air museums, such as the ones in Wygiezłów and Nowy Sącz, present the history of wooden architecture in a nutshell.

INDUSTRIAL HERITAGE

One of the most-visited sights of Małopolska—and indeed all Poland—is the amazing medieval salt mine in Wieliczka, with its miles of subterranean corridors, lakes, and chambers, including several chapels carved in salt. Other special-interest sights include the railway museum in Chabówka, Alwernia's Firefighting Museum, and the Apiculture Museum in Stróże.

FOLK ART & TRADITIONS

You will find folk arts, crafts, and traditions throughout the region. The village of Zalipie is famous for colorful paintings of flowers adorning everything from wooden houses to wooden spoons. In Krynica, memory of Nikifor lives on—he was a naif-style artist of Lemko origin; his works can be seen in the museum in Krynica. In Zakopane, locals often parade in traditional costumes, for their own sake as much as for the pleasure of tourists. Locally produced crafts are for sale around town, and probably no visitor has left Zakopane without a pair of sheepskin slippers, an embroidered tablecloth, or a carved wooden box.

CHURCHES & PILGRIMAGE SITES

Kalwaria Zebrzydowska, with its baroque church and monastery, is a major pilgrimage site year-round, but particularly at Easter, when pilgrims reenact the Mystery of Christ's Passion. Nearby Wadowice is the birthplace of Karol Wojtyła (who became Pope John Paul II), and you can get there on the special "Pope's Express" from Kraków, stopping also at Kalwaria and Łagiewniki for a visit to the Sanctuary of the Divine Mercy. Last but not least, there are countless wooden churches and chapels around Podhale (a region anchored by the town of Nowy Targ), where religious faith mixes with local folklore to a rather wonderful result.

7

ber, daily from 9 to 3:30 (until 4:30 in October, 5:30 in September, and 6:30 May through August).

Go back to the main road; directly north from the parking lot next to the Park's management building are several interesting sights to see, whether you are walking or driving up the valley. The first is the **Chapel of Saint Joseph the Worker,** also called the Chapel on the Water. This lovely wooden church, built on a bridge above the swift-running water, has elements of both Alpine and the so-called "Zakopane" style, a vernacular trend in the turn-of-the-century architecture. Further up the road is a famous rock called **Hercules' club,** and that is exactly what it looks like; there is no way you can miss it.

On the ridge above the gorge is a Renaissance-era castle called **Pieskowa Skała** (✉ Sułoszowa ☎ 012/389–60–04 ⊕ www.wawel.krakow.pl). This is one of a series of castles—most of them ruins today—that once guarded the trade route from Kraków to Silesia. The whole of the so-called Eagles' Nest Trail (aka Szlak Orlich Gniazd) is about 160 km (100 mi) long and comprises 25 castles between Kraków and Częstochowa (two of them—one of which is just a ruin—are found within the borders of the National Park). Today, Pieskowa Skała is a branch of the Wawel Museum and displays part of its art collection. The courtyard with arcades is among the most picturesque to be found in any Polish Renaissance residence. To the east, looking down from the outside loggia, you'll have a marvelous view down into the garden at the foot of the castle and further to the Prądnik Valley. Admission to the museum is zł 10, and it's open Tuesday through Thursday from 9 to 3:15, Friday from 9 to 12, and weekends from 10 to 5:15. The castle is on a side road that branches off from the main Olkusz–Kraków route; it's 22 km (13 mi) from Olkusz, 25 km (15 mi) from Kraków.

The gorge is lovely in spring for all its lush green, but the national park is probably at its best in autumn, when shades of gold and red stand out against the white limestone. To reach the park from Kraków, take the E40 northwest and turn off at Jerzmanowice for Pieskowa Skała. For the cave, park at Czajowice and walk from there. PKS buses leave regularly from the bus station on plac Kolejowy in Kraków. (✉ Ojców 9 ☎ 012/389–20–05 ⊕ www.ojcow.pl).

Where to Eat

¢–$ ✕ **Grill Bar "Kamienny Ogród."** This wholly unpretentious, very casual restaurant serves simple bar fare. The best bet is grilled (or fried) trout, fresh from the fish ponds next door. The food is served in an idyllic garden setting when the weather is nice. ✉ *Ojców 18* ☎ *012/389–20–54* ▤ *No credit cards.*

AUSCHWITZ & BIRKENAU

★ ❷ *60 km (38 mi) west of Kraków.*

Between 1940 and 1945 more than 1.5 million people, 90% of them Jews from Poland and throughout Europe, died here in the Nazis' largest

GREAT ITINERARIES

Many important sights in the Małopolska region—including Wieliczka Salt Mine, Auschwitz Memorial Museum, Ojców National Park, John Paul II's birthplace of Wadowice, and the sanctuary at Kalwaria Zebrzydowska—can be done easily as day trips from Kraków, so it's feasible to explore the region using that city as a base. If you decide to head south toward the mountains it is definitely worth staying overnight or longer for a really relaxing and proper holiday.

IF YOU HAVE 3 DAYS
On Day 1, visit Wieliczka Salt Mine in the morning (book your tickets in advance or plan to spend time in line). Head for Zakopane in the afternoon. If you are well organized—and if you arrive in Zakopane early enough—you can still take a cable car to Gubałówka and afterward visit the wooden church and Cmentarz na Pęksowym Brzyzku at dusk. In the evening, stroll down Krupówki, Zakopane's main promenade, and then listen to folk music while you have your supper in one of the many regional restaurants. On Day 2, choose a trail to follow, depending on the kind of mountain walking you like and how fit you feel, then relax and rest in the evening to prepare yourself for an early start on Day 3. On your last day in the region, head northwest via Wadowice to Oświęcim. In Wadowice, you can briefly visit the birthplace of Karol Wojtyła, better known as Pope John Paul II. Spend the afternoon in Oświęcim, at the Auschwitz-Birkenau museum in the former Nazi concentration camps.

IF YOU HAVE 5 DAYS
Follow the first two days of the three-day itinerary above. On Day 3, go straight to Oświęcim without stopping in Wadowice. Return to Kraków in the late afternoon/ evening, and if you are not too tired, try to catch evensong in Tyniec Abbey. On Day 4, take the "The Pope's Express" to Wadowice, stopping in Łagiewniki and Kalwaria Zebrzydowska on your way. On Day 5, enjoy the peaceful beauty of Ojców National Park, where you can take one of the hiking trails in the valley, then visit the castle at Pieskowa Skała.

IF YOU HAVE 7 DAYS
With a full week in Małopolska, start off in Zakopane and thoroughly explore the sights. Do some hiking on Day 2. On Day 3, head to Czorsztyn Lake via Nowy Targ, stopping to visit the old wooden church in Dębno. Stay overnight in Niedzica Castle or the Osada Turystyczna "Czorsztyn" in Kluszkowce. On Day 4, take a rafting trip through the Dunajec Gorge in the Pieniny Mountains; in the afternoon, go to Krynica Zdrój via Stary and Nowy Sącz, then spend the night in Krynica. On Day 5, explore the historical spa town, including the Nikifor Museum, and set off early in the afternoon for Wieliczka to visit the salt mine. Stay in Kraków overnight (⇨ Chapter 6), and on Day 6, start early on the "Pope's Express" to Kalwaria Zebrzydowska and Wadowice. In early afternoon, continue from Wadowice to Oświęcim by bus (the trip takes about an hour) to visit the Auschwitz complex, then return to Kraków by train for the night. On Day 7, head for Ojców National Park (⇨ If You Have 5 Days).

7

death-camp complex. The camp in the small town of Oświęcim (better known by its German name, Auschwitz) has come to be seen as the epicenter of the moral collapse of the West, proof of the human capacity for tremendous evil. The gas chambers at nearby Brzezinka (Birkenau) could exterminate thousands in a single day. The first inmates were Polish political prisoners, and the first gas victims were Russian POWs; the dead eventually included Poles, Jews, Romanies (Gypsies), homosexuals, Jehovah's Witnesses, and so-called criminals.

The *Konzentrationslager* (concentration camp) had three parts: Auschwitz, Birkenau, and Monowitz (where a chemical plant was run by prison labor). The bar-

> ## STILL WATERS RUN DEEP
>
> From the early 19th century until the end of World War I, this part of Małopolska was officially part of Tsarist Russia, as a result of the country's partitions by its three then not-so-friendly neighbors (Russia, Prussia, and Austria). The border between Austria and Russia was roughly half-way between Kraków and Ojców. Tsarist government issued a ban on building any churches on the Ojców land, but the clever, always technically obedient Poles built one anyway—on the water. As Polish history indicates, Poles seem to have a talent for such subtle subversiveness.

racks at Auschwitz have been completely restored and made into the **Państwowe Muzeum Auschwitz-Birkenau w Oświęcimiu** (Auschwitz-Birkenau State Museum), which has been described by one survivor, the author Primo Levi, as "something static, rearranged, contrived." With that in mind, begin with the heart-rending movie filmed by Soviet troops on January 27, 1945, the day they liberated the few prisoners left behind by the retreating Germans. The English version runs a few times a day, although narration isn't really necessary. Purchase a guidebook in English (most exhibits are in Polish or German), and walk through the notorious gate marked ARBEIT MACHT FREI (Work Brings Freedom). The most provocative exhibits are the huge piles of belongings confiscated from victims, as well as the two tons of human hair intended for use in the German textile industry. The execution wall, the prison block, and the reconstructed crematorium at the end of the tour are harshly sobering.

Far more affecting than the restored Auschwitz are the unaltered barracks, electric fences, and blown-up gas chambers at the enormous **Birkenau** camp, which is 3 km (2 mi) away. More prisoners lived and died here than at Auschwitz, including hundreds of thousands who went directly to the gas chambers from boxcars in which they had been locked up for days. The camp has been preserved to look much the way it did after the Nazis abandoned it. A walk to the back area brings you to the Monument to the Glory of the Victims, designed by Polish and Italian artists and erected in 1967. Behind the trees to the right of the monument lies a farm pond, its banks still murky with human ashes and bone fragments. To hear the tape on the camp's history in English, ask the reception staff in the main guardhouse. There are regularly scheduled, guided tours in English for an additional fee (inquire at the museum). To reach the camps from Kraków, take the E22a or the train or bus from plac Kolejowy. You can park at either camp; from April 15 to October 31 a shuttle bus runs between them once an hour. ☒ *Więźniów Oświęcimia 20, Oświęcim* ☎ *033/843–20–22* ⊕ *www. auschwitz-muzeum.oswiecim.pl* ✉ *Auschwitz and Birkenau free, film zł 2, guided tours in English zł 174* ⊙ *Auschwitz museum daily 8–6, Birkenau daily 9–4.*

OFF THE BEATEN PATH **NADWIŚLAŃSKI PARK ETNOGRAFICZNY** (aka Nadwiślański Ethnographic Park) – shows folk culture of the regions situated west of Kraków all the way to the old Silesian frontier on Przemsza River. The area of approximately 10 acres was filled with over 20 wooden buildings accompanied by exhibits of small details such as chapels, wells, and beehives. The exhibits are grouped in three sections: town homes, religious buildings, and rural architecture. There is also a restaurant arranged in a typical country cottage. ☒ *Podzamcze 1, Wygiełzów* ☎ *032/613–40–62* ⊕ *www.muzeum.chrzanow.pl/htm* ✉ *zł 6* ⊙ *May–Sept., daily 8–6; Oct.–Apr., daily 8–3.*

Where to Eat

★ ¢–$ ✕**Karczma Zagroda.** Located within the Nadwiślański Ethnographic Park, this restaurant has a great wooden interior decorated with hunting trophies; a roaring fire burns in the fireplace in winter. Very busy during summer weekends, it is mostly empty during the low season. The food is traditional Polish, with a variety of meat dishes and excellent *placki po myśliwsku* (hunter-style potato pancakes, with meat and vegetable goulash). ☒ *Podzamcze 2 67, Wygiełzów* ☎ *032/613–45–56* ▭ *No credit cards.*

TYNIEC ABBEY

★ ❸ *43 km (27 mi) east of Oświęcim, 12 km (7½ mi) southwest of Kraków.*

The Benedictine Abbey at Tyniec is perched high on a cliff above the Vistula River. Benedictine monks had settled at Tyniec as early as the 11th century, though the oldest remaining portions of today's abbey were not begun until the 12th century, and most of the buildings that stand today were begun in the 16th century. From this fortified cloister, the Confederates of Bar set off in 1772 to raid Kraków; as a result, the abbey was destroyed later that year by the Russian army; it was rebuilt, and it is those buildings that you see today. In 1817 the Benedictine order was banned, and the monks disbanded. It was not until 1939 that the order recovered the land and not until the late 1960s that it again became an abbey and the work of reconstruction began in earnest. From May to September recitals of organ music are held in the abbey church.

To get to the abbey from Kraków, take Highway 7 (E77) south to Highway A4, then take A4 about 4 km (2½ mi) to Tyniec; or take Bus 112 from most Grunwaldzki, near the Forum Hotel. On summer weekends, Żegluga krakowska runs boat trips to the abbey from Kraków (⇨ Tour Options *in* Kraków Essentials, Chapter 6). ☒ *Tyniec* ⊕ *www.tyniec. benedyktyni.pl* ✉ *Free* ⊙ *Daily 9–4.*

FODOR'S FIRST PERSON

Tadeusz Smreczyński
Auschwitz survivor

Mr. Tadeusz Smreczyński, an Auschwitz survivor and retired Polish physician, recalls: "One early morning in June 1944, I was walking from block number 2 to the kitchens where I was then working, when I heard, from the block right next to the ARBEIT MACHT FREI gate, someone singing Cavaradossi's aria from *Tosca*. In the scenery of the concentration camp, this was very striking indeed . . ."

"Later I found that the singer was the tenor from the Brussels Opera, a Belgian Jew, who had lost all his family to the gas chambers in Birkenau, while he himself was 'delegated' to the camp orchestra. This song at dawn was his private rebellion against all this impossible, unbearable drama. I saw SS officers run towards him, pulling him out of the window, and I can only guess that he was killed on that same day."

"If you've ever heard *Tosca*, you may recall the circumstances in which Cavaradossi sang that aria—in San Angelo castle in Rome—he was aware that these were the last moments before he died. It was this parallel that made the scene so powerful, so moving . . . Every time I hear that aria now—in the Philharmonic Hall, or on the radio—I recall that scene—it so vivid as if it were only yesterday."

Hard as it may be to believe, music was a part of daily life in the horror of Auschwitz. The Nazis organized orchestras made up entirely of prisoners, professional—often first-class—musicians. They were ordered to perform marching music when the prisoners set off to work in the morning and might be called for day or night to entertain the bored officers. For those incarcerated, the music was, in Primo Levi's words, "the perceptible expression of the camp's madness." For the surviving orchestra players, music was their salvation. In the evenings, there were concerts for prisoners, again. Among the audience, some hated the concerts as a reminder of oppression, depravity, and abuse, but many found encouragement and consolation in the music. The concerts also provided a way to pass information secretly. For instance, whenever a John Philip Sousa piece was played, this was a clue that the allied forces had won another battle. There were several orchestras and bands in the two camps, all made up entirely of inmates. One of the most famous was the women's orchestra directed by Alma Rosé, the niece of Gustav Mahler himself. The story of the women's orchestra was told in the U.S. television film *Playing for Time*.

WIELICZKA SALT MINE

4 *12 km (7½ mi) southeast of Kraków on the E40.*

Fodor'sChoice
★ Visiting the over 700-years-old mines of Wieliczka is a good way to spend half a day, combining the aesthetic pleasure of contemplating these

marvelous underground salt chambers with a lesson in history and geology. As an added bonus you can gulp as many breaths of the healthy balsamic air, famous for its medicinal properties, as your lungs can take. Famous fans of the Wieliczka Salt Mine included Polish kings, Nicolaus Copernicus, Johann Wolfgang von Goethe, Tsar Alexander I, and Austro-Hungarian Emperor Franz Josef. If all these arguments were not enough, in this first-rate tourist attraction, a Heritage Site recognized by UNESCO. And yes, you are allowed to lick the walls.

The salty underground labyrinth stretches and meanders for hundreds of miles. Old maps show 26 shafts starting at the surface, and more than 180 smaller underground shafts joining two or more neighboring levels. The mines have nine levels in total, and more than 2,000 chambers where excavation has now been abandoned. The tourist route, starting at the Daniłowicz Shaft, takes you through a small stretch of this fascinating underworld, a mere 1½-mi walk between levels 1 and 3.

The following legend attempts to explain the discovery of the salt deposits at Wieliczka. Thirteenth-century princess Kinga (also called Kunegunda), daughter of the Hungarian King Bela IV of the Árpád dynasty, married Bolesław Wstydliwy (Boleslaus the Bashful), Duke of Kraków and Sandomierz. She brought with her to Poland a large dowry, which helped rebuild the country destroyed during the Mongol raids. Boleslaus and Kinga were highly respected by the subjects for their piety and goodness. Legend has it that Kinga has given Poland yet another, very precious dowry. When touring the land of her father, she came to the salt mines of Maramures. Seized with sudden inspiration, she asked King Bela to give her one of the shafts as a present. Her Father consented, and Princess Kinga threw a gold ring off her finger into the pit as a sign of her ownership. Back in Poland, when the salt mines were founded, some say that it was Kinga who showed the miners where to dig. When they unearthed the first nugget of salt, they found inside it the very same ring that the Princess had thrown into the shaft in Hungary. In those days, salt was as precious as gold.

The underground itinerary takes you to several chapels that have been carved from the salt; huge, fantastically shaped multilevel chambers; and salty subterranean lakes that send off fantasmagorical reflections of light. Look especially for the 17th-century **Chapel of St. Anthony's**, with the saints' expressions softened with the moisture coming through the shaft. The colossal **Chapel of the Blessed Kinga** is rather like a cathedral hewn out of salt. Along the way you will notice powerful and ancient timber beams conserved with salt, mosslike saline deposits called "salt flowers," and even grandiose chandeliers made entirely of salt crystals. You will meet many salt-loving sprites and gnomes, along with and the most powerful

BENEDICTINE IKEBANA

In front of the main altar in the Tyniec church, observe the highly accomplished and refined flower arrangement of blooms and leaves of the season. It is the work of one of the monks, father Hieronimus, who has studied the Japanese art of ikebana for many years.

of all the spirits of the mine, the Treasure Keeper—all carved out of salt, of course.

After finishing your sightseeing tour, if you are not too tired of walking, you can visit the underground **Museum** that shows the history of salt mining at Wieliczka, as well as the archaeology and geology of the salty region.

You can get to Wieliczka by a slightly rickety suburban train (*przewozy regionalne*): the journey takes only 20 minutes (but you need to walk a little to the mine). There are also minibuses (both tour buses and regular connections by private companies) leaving from the Kraków train station. ⊠ *Daniłowicza 10, Wieliczka* ☎ *012/278–73–02* ⊕ *www. kopalnia.pl* ✉ *zł 46* ⊙ *Mine Apr.–Oct., daily 7:30–7:30; Nov.–Mar., 8–5. Museum daily 8–4.*

THE POPE'S EXPRESS

FodorsChoice *Wadowice is 48 km (30 mi) southwest of Kraków.*
★

The *Pope Express*, which commemorates the late John Paul II, is a modern train connecting Kraków—where Karol Wojtyła was a student, a young priest, and then a bishop—with his birthplace in Wadowice. The train makes stops on the way in places connected with the Pope's life and Catholic faith. The most interesting and significant stops are those in Łagiewniki and Kalwaria Zebrzydowska, two very important sanctuaries and pilgrimage sites. The journey between Krakow and Wadowice takes 1 hour 15 minutes, but you can get off at any stop along the way, do some sightseeing, and get back on the next train. Footage from Pope's speeches and his pilgrimages to Poland is shown on screens during the journey. Your best bet is to make this a half-day trip and go back to Kraków for lunch (or bring a picnic to enjoy on the train); there are few good options for lunch in Wadowice.

❺ Once you get off the train in Łagiewniki, one of the trails to the right will take you to the **Sanktuarium Bożego Miłosierdzia** (Sanctuary of the Divine Mercy) (⊠ Łagiewniki ⊕ www.milosierdzie.pl). Between the world wars, in the redbrick nunnery, lived Saint Faustyna Kowalska, who started the cult of the Divine Mercy, which, as the faithful believe, was communicated to her by Jesus himself. She described him as he appeared to her—and that vision is depicted in the famous painting, to be found in the new Łagiewniki church today. The modern church was designed by a renowned Polish architect, Witold Cęckiewicz. In the bright church,

CAUTION

Visitors usually descend into the Wieliczka Mine on foot (378 stairs, 210 feet) and return by elevator, but it is possible to take the lift down for an additional fee. It is a long walk, so make sure you wear comfortable walking shoes. The temperature in the mine is 14C (57F) year-round, so dress accordingly. Facilities down the mine include a post office, gift shops, and cafés/snack-bars.

which accommodates about 5,000 pilgrims, note the beautiful simplicity of the main altar, and the round tabernacle. Take the lift installed inside the characteristic tower and go up to the viewing platform.

6 The Pope's Express stops at the major pilgrimage site of **Kalwaria Zebrzydowska** (✉ Kalwaria Zebrzydowska ⊕ www.kalwaria.ofm.pl) on the UNESCO World Heritage List since 1999. South of the Kalwaria Zebrzydowska town center, atop the Calvary Mount lies a baroque church and monastery of Saint Bernard. The pilgrimage site encompasses also 42 chapels, Stations of the Cross, and Stations of Virgin Mary's, scattered to the south and east of the monastery, among rolling hills and picturesque valleys. Founded by the Zebrzydowski family, the whole site is emblematic of the counter-reformation age. The church and monastery are works of an Italian architect, Giovanni Maria Bernardoni, and Flemish goldsmith and architect Pauwel Baudarth. The holy image of the Virgin in Zebrzydowski Chapel is said to have shed bloody tears in 1641. In front of the temple there is a plaza, called the Paradise Square. On either side it is lined with a 19th-century colonnaded gallery, and enclosed with an iron balustrade incorporating stone pillars and statues. Ascending to the church of Saint Mary of the Angels (Portiunculae) is a wide stairway built between 1927 and 1932. Inside, note the frescoes covering the vaults of the nave and the rainbow wall: work of Włodzimierz Tetmajer, a Polish art nouveau artist.

The famous paths of Christ's Passion (The Way of Condemnation, and the Stations of the Way of the Cross) were modeled upon those in Jerusalem, and constructed in the early 17th century. The paths of Virgin Mary (The Funerary Path and the Way of Triumph) were founded in 1632. On Palm Sunday, and then during the Easter Week, on Wednesday, Thursday, Good Friday, Easter Saturday and Sunday, full-fledged ceremonial Passion Plays are reenacted there, attracting thousands of pilgrims. Kalwaria is again flooded with pilgrims August 15–20 arriving for the Feast of Ascension of the Virgin Mary. At most other times, it is a peaceful retreat.

7 **Karol Wojtyła's Museum in Wadowice** (✉ Kościelna 7, Wadowice ☎ 033/823–26–62) is located in the very house where the Pope from Poland was born, "between five and six in the afternoon" on May 18, 1920. Among the memorabilia, you will find Karol Wojtyła's documents (including school certificates), photographs, as well as some modest personal objects. When in Wadowice, step into the church: in the chapel of St. Anne is the baptismal font where the future Pope was baptized. Admission to the museum is free, but donations are accepted. The museum is open Tuesday through Sunday; from May through September, 9–1 and 2–6, and from October through April, 9–1 and 2–5.

✉ *Train leaves from Kraków Główny, Kraków* ☎ *012/393–33–28, 012/393–33–29 in Kraków, 033/823–39–15 Ext. 340 in Wadowice* ⊕ *www.pociag-papieski.pl* ⧉ *zł 11.50 one-way, zł 18 round-trip* ☉ *Departures from Kraków daily at 8:55, 12:55, and 4:55; return from Wadowice daily at 10:30, 2:30, and 6:30.*

ALWERNIA

❽ *30 km (19 mi) west of Kraków.*

Enveloped in two landscape parks—Tenczyński and Rudniański—the quiet, small town of Alwernia most probably started as a settlement to serve the Franciscan Bernardine monastery and its arriving pilgrims. The first mention of Alwernia in written records dates back to 1778, when King Stanisław August granted it the privilege of holding 12 fairs per year. Alwernia did not receive its full town charter until 1903, and although it lost the charter 30 years later, it was officially reinstated as a city in 1993.

Alwernia's **Kościół i klasztor Bernardynów** (Bernardine Church & Monastery) is a large reason the town even exists. The pride of the church is a medieval painting of Jesus called Ecce Homo. Having hung in the church since 1686, the painting was probably brought from Constantinople and is believed to have miraculous powers. ☒ *Klasztorna 1* ☎ *012/283–12–13.*

Between the charming, oak-shaded square and the monastery, this little town is hiding a surprise, the **Małopolskie Muzeum Pożarnictwa** (Małopolska Firefighting Museum). Founded in 1953 by its future custodian, Zbigniew Gęsikowski, the museum has been run for the past half-century volunteer firefighters. Its collection includes nearly 25,000 items and over 300 technical exhibits dating back to the 19th century, all collected with the help of volunteer firefighters. The museum tells the story of more than a century of volunteer fire brigades mostly from the Małopolska and Podkarpacie regions. The collection is exhibited in a large, open hall and in several rooms of the fire station. Among the highlights are Austrian and Prussian horse-drawn carriages with fire hoses from the beginning of the 20th century, English motor pumps, and fire vehicles dating from 1940s and '50s; there's also a 1912 Mercedes and a 1936 Fiat. The Museum is open by appointment only, so you must call in advance (English is spoken). ☒ *Korycińskiego 10* ☎ *012/283–23–23 or 012/504–089–047* ⊕ *www.alwernia.pl.*

▌ NEED A BREAK?   If you need fortification before returning to Kraków, which has many (better) dining options, consider a short stop at **Kawiarnia Antidotum Alwernia** ☒ *ul. Skłodowskiej Curie 6* ☎ *012/888–640–712.*

NIEPOŁOMICE

❾ *12 km (7½ mi) east of Wieliczka, 25 km (15 mi) east of Kraków on the E40.*

The town of Niepołomice is on the western edge of the ancient Niepołomice Forest (Puszcza Niepołomicka). The name comes from Old Polish word *niepołomny,* which means "unbreakable"—and, indeed, the ancient oak trees seem that way. The town has a 14th-century castle and church built by Kazimierz the Great. From Kraków, you can reach Niepołomice by car by taking the E40 east and then turning north at

Wieliczka; the town is also accessible via PKS bus, train, or private minibus from plac Kolejowy.

Niepołomice Castle thrived during the reign of the Jagiellonian Dynasty— as the monarchs' retreat, as a site for political and diplomatic debates, and above all as a base for royal hunting escapades into the Puszcza Niepołomicka. The castle you see today dates to the reign of Zygmunt August and was built in Renaissance style between 1550 and 1571. In order to please the queen, Bona Sforza, a native of Bari in Itali, Italian gardens were planted next to the south wing. What followed is a long story of the vicissitudes of fortune, including Swedish raids in the mid-17th century and the partitions of Poland since 1772, when all of Niepołomice (the castle included) fell under the Austrian administration. Renovated in the 19th and then late 20th centuries, the castle is now an exhibition space and also hosts events. During the renovation of the Sukiennice in Kraków, which began in late 2006 and is not expected to finish until 2009, a portion of the collection of the Polish painting exhibition will be exhibited in the castle. ⊠ *Zamkowa 2* ☎ *012/389–20–44* 💰 *zł 6* ⊗ *Weekdays 10–5, weekends 10–4.*

The Gothic-style **Parish church in Niepołomice,** which is also known as the Church of Virgin Mary and the Ten Thousand Martyrs, was built by king Kazimierz Wielki (Kazimierz the Great) between 1350 and 1358. On the outside, the church is strangely irregular, with a somewhat haphazard appearance; indeed, the original Gothic structure received several later additions, notably the Renaissance and baroque chapels. Once you step inside, look up to see vaults with carved keystones in the presbytery and the sacristy, as well as the murals in the presbytery wall—these are the oldest surviving elements. The work of Italian artists, the murals in the blind windows of the presbytery depict Saint Michael Archangel and Saint George; in the old sacristy, you will find other paintings depicting the legend of Saint Cecilia. South of the main aisle, enter the domed Branicki Chapel, a typical Renaissance-Mannerist chapel following the pattern of Sigismund's chapel in the Wawel Castle in Kraków. The tombstone of Katarzyna and Grzegorz Branicki is situated opposite the chapel's entrance. The space in between their kneeling figures contains a relief depicting Christ and Doubting Thomas, as well as an epitaph of the couple's child; the tombstone of marble and sandstone is the work of a famous Italian artist Santi Gucci and was completed in 1596. ⊠ *Rynek, at ul. Piękna* 💰 *Free* ⊗ *Daily dawn–dusk.*

OFF THE BEATEN PATH

ZALIPIE – is the only village in Poland where houses are adorned with painted flowers—well, only about 20 of them. And the painting is the job of the local ladies. According to the tradition here, women-painters from Zalipie also adorn the interiors of the houses, as well as many other everyday objects. You will find beautifully painted roadside chapels, barns, covered wells, and even dog kennels. Traditionally, the women used simple and easily obtainable materials made from brown clay, soot, and lime. As a binder they used milk, sugar, egg whites, and water from their dumplings. The paint, which was prepared in a particular way, was then applied using a brush made of hay, horse hair, or a cow's tail. Some artists still use these traditional techniques today. A good opportunity to see the ladies at work comes on the weekend after Corpus Christi (a moveable feast, typically in June), when the "Painted House" competition is on. This village is definitely off the beaten path, 56 km (35 mi) northeast of Niepołomice and 65 km (40 mi) east/northeast of Kraków; you'll need a car to get to the village because public transport options are minimal.

Where to Eat

$–$$$ ✗ **Zamek Królewski.** In an elegant setting on the ground floor of the castle (in the summer there are also tables in the courtyard), this restaurant serves traditional, upmarket Polish food—poultry, venison, and the like—in rich, fragrant sauces. Because the restaurant is a popular setting for private functions, regular diners can be disadvantaged because the restaurant can be closed without any warning. ✉ *Niepołomice Castle, ul. Zamkowa 2* ☎ *012/28–13–260* ▭ *AE, MC, V.*

Sports & the Outdoors

There are several marked **walking trails** in the Niepołomice Forest. Get information—or arrange for a guided tour—at the Tourist Information Office that is located inside Niepołomice Castle (⇨ *above*). The forest trails are easily accessible if you are visiting the castle. Animals, including bison, still live in the forest, and you may be lucky enough to see some of them as you stroll under the ancient oak trees. There is a bison breeding center within the forest, but it is not open to visitors.

ZAKOPANE

★ *100 km (62 mi) south of Kraków on Hwy. E95.*

Nestled at the foot of the Tatra Mountains, at 3,281 feet above sea level, Zakopane is the highest town in Poland (it's the southernmost as well). Until the 19th-century Romantic movement started a fashion for mountain scenery, Zakopane was a poor and remote village. During the 1870s, when the Tatra Association was founded, people began coming to the mountains for their health and recreation, and Zakopane developed into Poland's leading mountain resort. At the turn of the 20th century, Zakopane was the place to be. Many artists, scientists, physicians, and politicians frequented this fashionable resort, and some called it home. Of these, the most famous are the composer Karol Szymanowski and the artist and playwright Stanisław Witkiewicz (Witkacy). The father of the latter, also named Stanisław Witkiewicz, was responsible for creating the so-called Zakopane style, inspired by traditional local wooden architecture.

The town is small, and the most important sights can easily be covered on foot. Ulica Krupówki, the main thoroughfare, runs downhill through the town from northwest to southeast. If you begin at the northwest end, you will pass many buildings in the Zakopane style. The street is lined with countless restaurants, bars, and souvenir shops. Ulica Kościuszki runs east to west across Krupówki and links the town with the railway and bus stations. At the bottom of the hill is ulica Kościeliska, another street with a wealth of traditional wooden architecture.

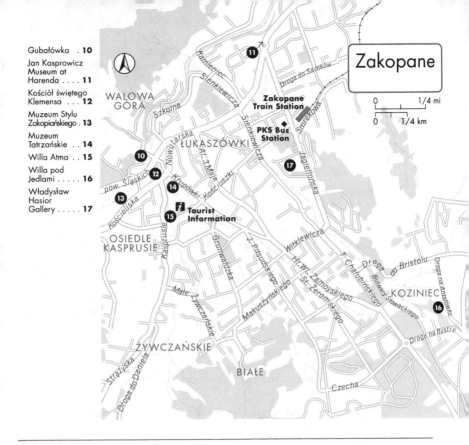

What to See

Numbers in the margins correspond to numbers on the Zakopane map.

10 Gubałówka. A cable railway can take you from the center of town up to this high ridge, where on a clear day you will have a fine view of the Tatras and of the town. An alternative to riding the cable car back into town is to walk: take the path along the ridge to Pałkówka and from there back down into town, about 9 km (5½ mi). Children can have their photograph taken on the Gubałówka **terrace** in a carriage drawn by four white mountain sheepdogs and driven by a man dressed in a white bearskin. ✉ *Down from corner of ul. Krupówki and ul. Kościeliska, at end of path lined with souvenir stalls* ☎ *018/201–48–30* ⊠ *zł8 one-way, zł 14 round-trip* ⊗ *8:30–6.*

11 Jan Kasprowicz Museum at Harenda. This lovely wooden villa, once the home of Kasprowicz, is now a museum dedicated to the Polish poet. Kasprowicz (1869–1926) is known mostly for his poetry (including some beautiful poems about the Tatras), but he was also a prolific translator from the English, French, and German, as well as a playwright and a theater critic. The house was originally intended as an inn, and built in 1920 by a local highlander, Jan Kluś Fudala. Soon afterward,

Fudala sold it to an English painter, Winifred Cooper, from whom Kasprowicz purchased it. He lived there with his wife Maria (née Bunin), a Russian whom he met in Italy. After he died, she herself organized the museum. The layout of the villa is based on a typical highlander cottage with the hall (or dining room) at the main axis opposite the entrance: the "black chamber" (or parlor) is on the left, and the "white chamber" (bedroom) is on the right. Next to the villa, among the trees, is a granite mausoleum where Maria and Jan Kasprowicz are buried. ⊠ *Harenda 12a* ☎ *018/206–84–26* 🖃 *zł 5* ⊙ *May–Sept., Wed.–Sun. 9–4; Oct.–Apr., Wed.–Sun. 10–3.*

⑫ **Kościół świętego Klemensa** (Church of St. Clement). At the foot of the hill in town is this wood church, which dates from the mid-19th century. The first church built in Zakopane, it has been decorated by the local artists. The pictures of the Stations of the Cross were painted on glass by Ewelina Pęksowa. At the adjoining **Cmentarz na Pęksowym Brzyzku** (Cemetery at Pęksów Bryzek), visitors are greeted with the following maxim: "A native country is the land and graves. / Nations may perish when they lose their memory. / Zakopane remembers." Here is the burial place of many famous artists, mountain guides, and other people of the Tatras: among them Stanisław Witkiewicz, writer Kornel Makuszyński, doctor Tytus Chałubiński, musician and storyteller Jan Krzeptowski Sabała, Alpine sport champions of the Marusarz family, and many others. This very atmospheric place is also a one-of-a-kind gallery that includes tombstones carved by Władysław Hasior, Antoni Rząsa, and other local artists who were masters at their art. ⊠ *Kościeliska, opposite Kasprusie.*

⑬ **Muzeum Stylu Zakopiańskiego im. Stanisława Witkiewicza** (Stanisław Witkiewicz Museum of the Zakopane Style). The "Swiss Alpine" style of architecture started to appear in Zakopane during the second half of the 19th century, provoking local architect Stanisław Witkiewicz to create a more appropriate "vernacular" style based on Podhale's folk traditions. His very first project in the so-called Zakopane style was the **Willa Koliba,** which is now this museum dedicated to the architect and his signature style. The beautiful wooden interior is filled with matching furniture and decorations and an ethnographical collection of Zygmunt Gnatowski, the original owner of the villa. ⊠ *Kościeliska 18* ☎ *018/201–36–02* 🖃 *zł 4* ⊙ *Wed.–Sun. 9–4.*

⑭ **Muzeum Tatrzańskie** (Tatra Museum). While this museum on Zakopane's main street is a little dusty and sleepy, if are patient, you will find a lot of information on the Tatra Mountains, both the geology and the culture of the region. The museum has two replicas of typical highland dwellings, examples of mountain crafts, and a collection of Zakopane's flora and fauna. The first room is a portrait gallery of local heroes and famous visitors to Zakopane, who have included writer Joseph Conrad and national hero Józef Piłsudski among many others. Ask for a audio tour in English. ⊠ *ul. Krupówki 10* ☎ *018/201–52–05* 🖃 *zł 4* ⊙ *Tues.–Thurs. and Sat. 9–5, Sun. 9–3.*

⑮ **Willa Atma.** A wooden structure in the Zakopane style, this villa was home to the great Polish composer Karol Szymanowski in the 1920s and

'30s. Szymanowski's best work—including *Harnasie* and *Pieśni kurpi-owskie*—was inspired by the local folk music, and he was the first Polish composer after Chopin to receive international recognition. Filled with Szymanowski's music played from the recordings—and sometimes during live recitals—the villa is now a museum dedicated to his life and work. ⊠ *Kasprusie 19* ☎ *018/201-34-93* 🖅 *zł 5* ⊘ *May–Sept., Tues.–Thurs. and weekends 10–4, Fri. 2–8; Oct.–Apr., Tues.–Sun. 10–4.*

🔟 **Willa pod Jedlami.** An elaborate villa and another of Stanisław Witkiewicz's Zakopane buildings, this villa is considered one of his most ambitious works. Since it's still a private home, it is not open to the public, but the outside is worth a look. ⊠ *Koziniec 1.*

🔟 **Władysław Hasior Gallery.** You can see the work of one of the most original and talented contemporary artists from Zakopane here. Hasior (1928–99) created idiosyncratic assemblages, including very original "banners" such as the "Star of the Watering Place." A wide range of examples of his work is on display. ⊠ *Jagiellońska 18b* ☎ *018/206-88-71* 🖅 *zł 4* ⊘ *Wed.–Sat 11–6, Sun. 9–3.*

Where to Eat

All restaurants in Zakopane follow pretty much the same pattern: regional wooden interior, live folk music, and traditional—tasty but heavy—food. Most are found on Krupówki Street or around it. For starters, try grilled *oscypek* (smoked sheep's cheese); for soup, try the famous *kwaśnica* (sour cabbage soup); and for the main course, look for local lamb or trout.

$–$$
Fodor'sChoice
★
✕ **Bąkowo Zohylina.** Friendly waiters in folk costumes serve hearty regional dishes while the band plays fiery folk music in the background—rather loudly. This kind of food is designed—and guaranteed—to keep you warm, be it potato pancakes, a "mountaineer's cauldron" (dense, goulashlike soup), or hot oscypek cheese with cranberries. On a chilly day, you can treat yourself to "tea, mountaineer style" (yes, it does include grog); the mirror and the alco-meter in the bathroom will tell you when you've had enough. ⊠ *ul. Piłsudskiego 5* ☎ *018/206-62-16* 🖃 *AE, DC, MC, V.*

★ **$–$$**
✕ **Obrochtówka.** This regional restaurant is run by two ladies, Irena Wieczorek and Małgorzata Zawadzka. Most of the time, they can be seen here cooking and supervising the preparation of food, which includes their own home recipes. Lamb dishes and potato pancakes are among the best choices, and if you like participating in the food-preparation process, you can grill your own shish-kebab or sausage in the open fireplace. Reputedly, this is a hangout of (harmless) "contemporary mountain robbers," one of whom made it to the finals of the Polish version of the "Big Brother" TV show. ⊠ *ul. Kraszewskiego 10a* ☎ *018/206–62–16* 🖃 *AE, DC, MC, V.*

$–$$
Fodor'sChoice
★
✕ **Sabała.** One of the most popular regional restaurants in Zakopane is nearly always full and lively. Given the number of restaurants in Zakopane and the size of this place, that's quite a recommendation indeed. The staff, in regional folk costumes, will bring you well-seasoned grilled meats on

wooden plates, and you can select your own fresh and pickled salads from a self-service salad bar. In summer, the elevated terrace, which overlooks the Krupówki promenade, offers perfect people-watching opportunities. You don't need to order food, either: it is fine if you just sip a drink. ✉ *ul. Krupówki 11* ☎ *018/201–50–92* ⊟ *AE, DC, MC, V.*

★ $–$$ ✕ **Zbójecka.** In one of the nicest traditional Zakopane-style restaurants is subterranean, reached via a stairs leading down to a cozy basement room bathed in light and warmth from a fireplace and an open grill. Diners sink back into wool-upholstered chairs and enjoy a selection of carnivorous delights, including fresh and expertly prepared lamb, beef, pork, and poultry. You'll easily feel you've gone a century back in time and will forget about the nearby bustle of ulica Krupówki. ✉ *ul. Krupówki 28* ☎ *018/201–38–54* ⊟ *AE, DC, MC, V.*

¢–$$ ✕ **Czarny Staw.** Hearty mountain fare in the traditional Zakopane "rustic" style is the trademark of the Black Pond. The restaurant serves good fish—especially mountain trout—as well as poultry, lamb, and beef dishes, plus a variety of pierogi. Traditionally dressed staff prepare meat on an open grill in the middle of the room. Nearly every night there is live folk music. ✉ *Krupówki 2* ☎ *018/201–38–56* ⊟ *AE, DC, MC, V.*

¢–$$ ✕ **Murowana Piwnica.** The dining room in the Giewont Orbis Hotel is high-ceilinged and galleried, decorated with crystal chandeliers and crisp, white tablecloths on well-spaced tables. Service is elegant and discreet, and while this restaurant aspires to be the best in Zakopane, the quality of the food can sometimes be a bit uneven. Wild game dishes are the best choices on the menu: try the roast pheasant when it's in season. Beef sirloin with boletus mushrooms is another house specialty. ✉ *Giewont Orbis Hotel, ul. Kościuszki 1* ☎ *018/201–20–11* ⊟ *AE, DC, MC, V.*

¢–$ ✕ **Gospoda Pod Niebem.** The name translates as "the Inn under the Sky," and indeed it is closer to the sky than most restaurants in Zakopane: 1,122 meters above sea level. The restaurant is just a small distance uphill from the upper station of the Gubałówka cable car, which is the only way to get here. The food is simple (regional), and the owners themselves say it is "quite tasty, but nothing too extravagant." Stick to such standbys as *pierogi* (filled dumplings) and *bigos* (a stew with meat and sauerkraut), and you won't be disappointed. What are wonderful are the views at this quiet, cozy spot—and if you don't feel like descending back to the valley after dinner, you can even rent one of the rooms (zł 50 per person for accommodation, without breakfast), which are popular with skiers. ✉ *Droga Stanisława Zubka 5* ☎ *018/206–29–09* ⊟ *No credit cards.*

Where to Stay

$$$ 🏨 **Belvedere Hotel.** Close to the center of Zakopane, in a quiet area adjoining the National Park, the Belvedere is probably the most upscale hotel in town. It's also the best. Comfortably furnished rooms come in two variations: "classic" and "wooden" (the latter have slanted ceilings). The hotel has a range of restaurants and bars, as well as great fitness and wellness facilities. At the "Thalgo" Marine Institute of Health and

Fodor's Choice
★

Beauty you can try thalassotherapy. On the whole, Belvedere is a great place to stay, especially if you want to slow down and relax for a few days in the fresh, mountain air. ⊠ *Droga do Białego 3, 34–500* ☎ *018/20–21–200* 🖷 *018/20–21–250* ⊕ *www.belvederehotel.pl* 🛏 *130 rooms, 30 suites* ⌂ *3 restaurants, café, minibars, in-room safes, in-room broadband, cable TV, pool, gym, hot tub, spa, bowling, squash, bowling, 2 bars, business services, meeting rooms, free parking* 🖃 *AE, DC, MC, V* 🍽 *BP.*

★ **$$$** 🏨 **Litwor.** This is one of the best hotels in Zakopane. Right on the town's main promenade, it adjoins a quiet, picturesque park. The rooms have all the amenities you might crave, including towel warmers, hair dryers, and heated floors in the plush bathrooms. Plus the hotel's own spa and fitness center has a great enclosed pool, a sauna, solarium, and a gym. Perhaps best of all, the friendly staff seem to enjoy perfecting their English. ⊠ *ul. Krupówki 40, 34–500* ☎ *018/201–71–89* 🖷 *018/201–71–90* ⊕ *www.litwor.pl* 🛏 *58 rooms, 5 suites* ⌂ *Restaurant, cable TV, indoor pool, in-room safes, gym, hot tub, sauna, steam room, bar, business services, convention center, some pets allowed; no a/c* 🖃 *AE, DC, MC, V* 🍽 *BP.*

★ **$$$** 🏨 **Villa Marilor Hotel.** This comfortable, upscale hotel, reminiscent of a luxurious alpine lodge, opened in 2001 in a tastefully restored 19th-century palace. In the very center of Zakopane, it is pleasantly hidden away in a private park. Some rooms have huge balconies with brilliant views of the Tatras. ⊠ *ul. Kościuszki 18, 34–500* ☎ *018/206–44–12* 🖷 *018/206–44–10* ⊕ *www.hotele-marilor.com.pl* 🛏 *20 rooms* ⌂ *Restaurant, minibars, in-room safes, in-room broadband, Wi-Fi, cable TV, tennis court, hot tub, massage, sauna, bar, meeting room, free parking; no a/c* 🖃 *AE, DC, MC, V* 🍽 *BP.*

$$ 🏨 **Sabała.** This large, historic hotel was built in 1897 in the then-emerging Zakopane style and named after a renowned 19th-century storyteller. The wood-panel rooms are also furnished in beeswax-treated, solid wood furnishings; many have the original fixtures. There's nothing outstanding about this hotel, but the reasonable prices are a draw, as is the excellent restaurant. ⊠ *ul. Krupówki 11, 34–500* ☎ *018/201–50–92* 🖷 *018/201–50–93* ⊕ *www.sabala.zakopane.pl* 🛏 *50 rooms* ⌂ *Restaurant, cable TV, in-room broadband, pool, sauna, some pets allowed; no a/c* 🖃 *AE, DC, MC, V* 🍽 *BP.*

$–$$ 🏨 **Giewont Orbis Hotel.** This late-19th-century hotel is right in the center of town. The rooms are furnished in traditional style but vary greatly in size, so it's a good idea to see the room before moving in. Try to get a room with a view of the peak after which the hotel is named. ⊠ *ul. Kościuszki 1, 34–500* ☎ *018/201–20–11* 🖷 *018/201–20–15* ⊕ *www.giewont.net.pl* 🛏 *44 rooms* ⌂ *Restaurant, cable TV, meeting room; no a/c* 🖃 *AE, DC, MC, V* 🍽 *BP.*

Shopping

Leather and sheepskin products are local specialties, along with hand-knitted socks, sweaters, and caps in white, gray, and black patterns made from rough, undyed wool. The best place to look for local handmade goods is at the **Zakopane market** (✉ ul. Krupówki), at the foot of the street on the way to the Gubałówka cable railway. Wednesday is the main market day, but some stalls are here all week. The whole of Krupówki Street is lined with shops and kiosks selling regional products.

Sports & the Outdoors

Biking

Mountain biking has become increasingly popular in the area. Expect to pay around zł 50 a day to rent a mountain bike. **Rent a Bike** (✉ Sienkiewicza 37 ☎ 018/201–42–66) has a small selection of mountain bikes available. You can hire a bike at **Sport & Fun Company Ltd.** (✉ Rondo 1 ☎ 018/201–56–03).

Hiking

The Gorczański, Pieniński, and Tatrzański (Tatra) national parks all have hiking territory. The routes are well marked, and there are maps at entrance points that give the distances, times, and degrees of difficulty of the trails. On the lower reaches of trails out of major tourist points (such as Zakopane, Szczawnica, and Krynica), walkers crowd the paths, but they thin out as you go higher up.

The Tatras are serious mountains: magnificent, but not to be trifled with. Unfortunately, every year, fatal accidents happen. Some trails—notably the so-(aptly)-called **Orla Perć** ("Eagles' Perch") and the last section of the ascent to **Rysy** (the "Rifts"), the Tatra's highest peak—have elements of *via ferrata*, routes where permanent chains are attached to the mountain wall for getting up the steeper slopes. Although you should be able to walk these trails without any specialized rock-climbing equipment, you need to be sure that you know what you are doing. You may have a close encounter with snow in May or even as late as June. Weather can turn rapidly, and you'll definitely find cooler temperatures at the higher elevations, so dress properly, and wear good walking boots or shoes. Even though the trails are well marked, never walk in the Tatras without a detailed map. Pack a bottle of water for proper hydration and a bar of chocolate for an energy boost. Be aware that the Tatra National Park is a natural habitat of other species than our own, including bears. You should never walk alone, and always let someone at your hotel know where you are going. Don't get too relaxed on your way down: even though descent may seem easier, this is when most accidents happen. And remember that it is okay to give up and turn back if you do not feel comfortable with your route.

EASY HIKES　The easiest and most accessible hike from Zakopane is to **Butorowy Wierch**. Begin by taking the cable-car to Gubałówka (⇨ *above*), a five-minute trip. You should certainly give yourself some time to admire the famous panorama of the Tatras, and then walk right in the direction of Butorowy (or Butorowski) Wierch. The perfectly flat trail should take about 40 minutes each way. Have a beer or *herbatka z prądem* (a "fortified" tea) to restore yourself before you take the cable car back down. Since this is a very easy trail, it's often quite busy.

Another easy walk is along the **Dolina Kościeliska** (aka Kościeliska Valley), an extremely picturesque place where you can feel the peace and grandeur of the Tatras despite the crowds that come here in the summer season. To get to the valley, take a minibus from outside the main bus station in Zakopane to Kiry; the journey takes about 20 minutes. The bus will let you off at the entrance to the valley. Walk along the flat, broad path—it takes about 90 minutes to reach the valley's end, where you'll find Hala Ornak, the meadow at the end of the valley, and the mountain hostel. You can always top for a snack of grilled oscypek, from one of the chalets on the way. If you don't want to do the entire route on foot, you can take a horse-drawn cart halfway into the valley, to Polana Pisana.

CHALLENGING HIKES These more challenging hikes should be attempted only from June through September, when the snow is gone and cold temperatures are much less likely. These walks are all longer and considerably more strenuous than the "easy" options. Although you must expend more energy, the chance to avoid some of the crowds makes these routes worth the trouble. Plan your travel carefully as some of these routes take an entire day. (For overnight stops, *see* Where to Stay & Eat *in* Dolina Kościeliska *or* Lake Morskie Oko).

The trip to **Dolina Pięciu Stawów** (Five Lakes Valley) offers such a breathtaking view that the trip is worth the considerable effort you'll expend reaching it (this walk is of medium difficulty). Start by taking a minibus from Zakopane's main bus station to **Palenica** (Łysa Polana); the trip takes about 30 minutes. You'll need to walk for about an hour along the paved road to the waterfall of **Wodogrzmoty Mickiewicza;** from there, find a green-marked trail to the right, which takes you into the cozy valley of **Dolina Roztoki.** You can reach another waterfall called **Siklawa** if you walk another 90 minutes along a steady but sharp ascent (the whole trail is 4 mi, with an increase of about 2,100 feet in elevation). The path, however, is well laid out in big stone "steps." And after the hard work comes your reward: a breathtaking view that was certainly worth it. It is another 30 minutes walk to the end of the valley. (The total time to get from Palenica to the end of the valley is about 4 hours; you'll need only 3½ hours for the trip back since it's downhill for much of the way.)

If you are looking for a somewhat shorter trip that's still medium-difficult, consider the trail to **Przełęcz Liliowe,** ("Purples" Pass). This trip begins in **Kuźnice,** which can be reached by frequent bus and minibus service from Zakopane (zł 2). In Kuźnice, you take the cable car up to **Kasprowy Wierch** (about 10 minutes). From here, choose the red trail; the ascent to Przełęcz Liliowe takes about 40 minutes. From the pass, take the green trail (via Beskid peak) down to **Hala Gąsienicowa,** where the so-called "Murowaniec" mountain hostel awaits you with tea and apple pie after about 90 minutes; this is a good place to rest a while. If you have time and strength left, you can walk up to **Czarny Staw Gąsienicowy,** a lake that is about 40 minutes further along. After spending some time enjoying the scenery, backtrack along the same trail—again, about 40 minutes—to Hala Gąsienicowa. From here, you can take the blue-marked trail down back to Kuźnice (about 90 minutes).

If you are looking for something more challenging, the difficult hike to the top of **Rysy** peak may be a worthy goal. As with the trip to Five Lakes

Valley, start by taking a minibus to **Palenica** (Łysa Polana), which takes approximately 30 minutes. Walk a longish way up the asphalt road—or take the horse-drawn cart, which carries about a dozen passengers at a time—to **Morskie Oko.** Many people stay long enough to see the lake and have a snack at the mountain hostel just above it, then go back down. Up to this point, the hike does not require any mountaineering experience or special preparation. It is quite a different story if you decide to set out toward the highest peak in the Tatras. Start out on the red trail down to the lake and around it; approximately 1 mi along (1 hour travel time) is another lake called the **Czarny Staw** (Black Lake). Stop here for a while to rest and enjoy the magnificent view. If you continue another 2 mi (about 3 hours) you'll reach **Rysy**, the highest point in the Tatras. Do note that the last part of the trail is in fact via ferrata, with chains attached to the rock to help your ascent. Along the 3-mi trail between Morskie Oko and Rysy, you gain 1,100 meters in height. The walk back down to the lake it will take about 3½ hours. You can do this hike in one day, but make sure to start early, and come well-prepared.

Skiing

Zakopane acquired snow-making machinery in 1990 and is still the region's major center for downhill skiing, although Krynica and Krościenko also have some slopes. You probably will not be traveling with your own skis, but plenty of places rent ski equipment, including these: **Sukces** (⊠ Sienkiewicza 39 ☎ 018/206–41–97 ⊕ www.ski-sukces.zakopane.pl); **Koziniec** (⊠ Na Antałówkę ☎ 018/206–64–39).

A two-person chairlift bring skiers to the peaks of **Butorowy Wierch** (⊠ Powstańców Śląskich ☎ 018/201–39–41), which has a relatively easy run, suitable even for beginners.

You'll find the most advanced runs at **Kasprowy Wierch** (⊠ Kuźnice ☎ 018/201–45–10 lower station, 018/201–44–05 upper station). The resort has a gondola cable car, which is very popular, so long lines should be expected (the good news is, you can book a timed ticket in advance through the Orbis office in Zakopane, and thus jump the line). Kuźnice, where the cable lift is found, can be reached by a minibus from outside Zakopane's PKS bus station.

Nosal (⊠ Balcera ☎ 018/201–31–81) has a chairlift and a number of T-bar lifts. You can buy tickets from the Orbis office in Zakopane, but you'll pay a surcharge of 30%.

Nightlife & the Arts

Zakopane's theatrical and musical performances are often connected with the artists and writers who have made the town their home, particularly Witkiewicz and Karol Szymanowski. Posters on kiosks announce performances. Tourist information will also provide schedules (or you can check them yourself at the tourist office's Web site). Traditional local folk orchestras also perform regularly—often in restaurants to accompany your meal. Every now and then there are jazz concerts and jam sessions. As for nightlife, Zakopane is not the all-night town that Kraków is, but there are some interesting options.

Bars

Ampstrong (✉ Jagiellońska 18   ☎ 018/20–12–904) used to be called "Pstrąg" (trout, pronounced p'*strong*) before it wisely changed its name. After all, it is not a fish restaurant, nor do they play Schubert's "Die Forelle." Instead, you can hear fashionable club music: new jazz, funk, reggae, and house. **Caffe Sanacja** (✉ ul. Krupówki 77   ☎ 018/20–13–140) is a dark, brick-vaulted and wooden enclave for the small but vibrant artistic community. It is an island of rock and jazz, while most restaurants and bars around play nothing but local folk music. **Paparazzi** (✉ Gen. Galicy 8   ☎ 018/20–63–251), the sibling of Kraków's own Paparazzi, is Zakopane's après-ski alternative to folksy traditionalism, offering well-shaken cocktails, a good wine menu, and fusion-style bar food. In summer, garden seating over a shimmering brook is very pleasant.

Music

Every August, Zakopane's International Festival of Highland Folklore takes place, with folk musicians arriving from all over the world. The United Europe Jazz Festival happens at the beginning of May. There is an organ music festival in the summer (June through August). A festival of Szymanowski's music, with concerts all over town, is held each July. The **Kulczycki Gallery** (✉ Koziniec 8   ☎ 018/201–29–36) occasionally hosts concerts and other events. Concerts are sometimes given at the **Willa Atma** (✉ Kasprusie 19   ☎ 018/206–31–50).

Theater

The **Teatr im. Stanisława Ignacego Witkiewicza** (✉ ul. Chramcówki 15   ☎ 018/206–82–97) has two stages and is considered one of the best theaters in Poland. Some performances are very visual and musical, so it is worth inquiring whether the theater is offering something for which understanding of Polish is not essential.

DOLINA KOŚCIELISKA

9 km (5 mi) southwest of Zakopane, on the road to Kiry and Witów.

⑲ The Kościeliska Valley falls within the confines of the **Tatrzański Park Narodowy** (Tatra National Park), which covers the entire mountain range in both Poland and Slovakia. The first part of the valley runs for roughly a mile through flat, open pasture, before the stream that gave the valley its name begins its descent through steep, rocky gorges. It ends at **Ornak,** 5½ km (3½ mi) from the road, where there are splendid views. Horse-drawn carriages (sleighs in winter) wait at the entrance to take visitors halfway up the valley (for about zł 50), but if you want to reach Ornak, you must cover the last stage on foot. **Harnaś** is a bar at the entrance to the valley, where locals come to drink beer, and where dishes such as *fasolka po bretońsku* (baked beans) or *bigos* (here made with sauerkraut, cabbage, sausage, apples, and bacon), *pstrąg* (trout) and oscypek cheese are available from 8 AM to 10 PM. Remember that you are not allowed to pick flowers here—a strong temptation in spring, when the lower valley is covered with crocuses. ✛ *Take a bus or a minibus to Kiry from Zakopane's PKS bus station on ul. Kościuszki, and catch a horse-drawn carriage there.*

Where to Stay & Eat

In addition to the mountain hostel at Lake Morskie Oko, there are two other recommendable hostels in the Tatras. These are, for the most part, fairly modest places that are meant for simple accommodations for skiers and hikers, so don't expect full hotel amenities.

$ ✕⊞ **Schronisko Murowaniec.** Built in 1920s, this mountain hostel (at an elevation of 4,938 feet) is approximately a 30- to 40-minute walk from the upper station of the Kasprowy Wierch cable car. It is a good starting point for an easy walk to Czarny Staw Gąsienicowy and for other hikes of varying difficulty (including the via ferrata at Orla Perć). It is also near the ski slopes of the Kasprowy. The bar-restaurant (¢–$) offers simple, nutritious food such as scrambled eggs, or bigos. The apple pie (*szarlotka*) is particularly famous. Book ahead if you're planning to stay overnight and want a bed rather than a mattress on the floor. ⊠ *Hala Gąsienicowa* ⌖ *Box 193, Zakopane, 34–500* ☎ *018/201–26–33* ⤳ *126 dormitory beds with shared bath, 2 rooms with private bath* ⚴ *Restaurant, bar; no a/c* ⊟ *No credit cards* ⓞ *EP.*

¢–$ ✕⊞ **Hotel Górski na Kalatówkach.** Of all mountain hostels, this one (at 3,930 feet) most resembles a hotel. It was built when the International Ski Championships were held in Kalatówki in 1938. There are rooms for two, three, and five persons (a total of 84 beds), a restaurant (¢–$$), a cozy café, a fireplace, fitness facilities (including a sauna), and even ski rentals (there are ski lifts and easy training grounds, suitable for beginners, in its immediate vicinity). The rooms are simply, yet comfortably, furnished with handmade wooden furniture; some have en suite baths. In September and October, the hotel hosts jazz concerts and jam sessions. It is always essential to book in advance. ⊠ *Kalatówki* ⌖ *Box 194, Zakopane, 34–500* ☎ *018/206–36–44* ✉ *hotel@kalatowki.pl* ⤳ *84 beds, most shared bath* ⚴ *Restaurant, café, gym, sauna; no a/c* ⊟ *No credit cards* ⓞ *BP.*

LAKE MORSKIE OKO

⓴ *30 km (20 mi) southeast of the center of Zakopane in the direction of Poronin or Cyrla.*

Morskie Oko is the largest and loveliest of the lakes in the High Tatras, at 4,570 feet above sea level. The name means "Eye of the Sea," and an old legend claims it has a secret underground passage connecting it to the ocean. The **Mięguszowiecki** and **Mnich** peaks appear to rise straight up from the water, and the depth of the lake permanently colors it an intense blue. In order to get there, you can take a PKS bus or a private minibus from the Zakopane bus station to Łysa Polana and follow the rather tedious marked trail along the asphalt road for 8 km (5 mi); for those who aren't into hiking, you can take a take a horse-drawn cart, which carries about a dozen passengers at a time right up to the lakeshore. There are no fixed hours for the operation of the carriages, which are individually owned and operated, but they operate year-round, usually from early morning to dusk, and if there are tourists to be carried, they'll generally find carriages to transport them. ⊠ *Morskie*

Oko 🚌 zł 45 round-trip for horse-drawn cart transportation.

Where to Stay & Eat

¢ ✕🏨 **Schronisko Morskie Oko.** This historical mountain hostel was built in 1908 as the "new" hostel (the "old" one at the time dated to the 1820s), and it was renovated in the 1990s. It is located right at the Morskie Oko Lake, and you can hike farther up to Czarny Staw—and even farther to the Rysy peak—from here. This establishment has a huge restaurant-cantine (¢–$) serving large portions of such basic but filling fare as *fasolka po bretońsku* (Breton-style baked beans, made with tomato sauce and bits of bacon) or pancakes with whipped cream. For a snack or a dessert, the homemade apple pie is excellent. You can obtain a bed in a spartan, clean three-, five-, or six-person room for very little; otherwise you'll be in a large dormitory. There is (usually) hot running water in basic, common bathrooms. During the summer season, ski season, and on holidays and weekends, it is a good idea to book in advance. ✉ *Morskie Oko* 🗋 *Box 201, Zakopane, 34–500* ☎ *018/207–76–09* 🖃 *No credit cards* 🛏 *77 beds with shared bath* ⚑ *Restaurant; no a/c* 🍽 *EP.*

NOWY TARG

㉑ *24 km (15 mi) north of Zakopane, 90 km (56 mi) south of Kraków.*

The unofficial capital of the Podhale region, Nowy Targ has been a chartered borough since the 14th century, when it stood at an intersection of international trade routes, and it remains an important market center for the entire mountain region. It is also an interchange point with routes to Kraków, Zakopane, Czorsztyn Lake, and Dunajec Gorge, and most tourists just pass through. If you want to make a brief pause in town, however, it is worth doing so on Thursday, market day, when farmers bring their livestock in for sale and when several stalls offer local products, including rough wool sweaters and sheepskin coats. The White Dunajec and Black Dunajec streams meet in Nowy Targ to form the Dunajec River, which then runs on through steep limestone gorges to Nowy Sącz. By car, take the main road from Zakopane to Kraków. Buses run from Zakopane every hour; there are also frequent minibuses. Nowy Targ is a place to pass through, not a place to stop (even for a meal).

OFF THE BEATEN PATH

On the road to Szczawnica, 12 km (8 mi) east of Nowy Targ, is **DĘBNO.** This village in the valley of the Dunajec River has a tiny wooden church dating from the 15th century (it's believed to be the oldest wooden building in the Podhale region); inside are medieval wall paintings and wooden sculptures. *Buses run from the marketplace in Nowy Targ.*

If you are exploring some of the smaller routes around Nowy Tag, another small town of interest is Chabówka, 17 km (11 mi) north of Nowy Targ, where you will find the **SKANSEN TABORU KOLEJOWEGO** (Rolling-Stock Heritage Park) – , which has a great collection of old steam locomotives and antique carriages, lovingly maintained by true fans. Note the elegant *salonka* (a drawing-room carriage) in which Władysław

Gomułka, the Polish communist leader in 1950s and '60s, used to travel; it's also bullet-proof. From May through September, on selected weekends, you can even ride in one of these beauties all the way to Zakopane for zł 10. Fans of old-time trains should not miss the Steam Show in July. ✉ *Chabówka* ☎ *018/267–62–00* ⊕ *www.parowozy.pl/steamtrains* 🎫 *zł 4; zł 15 for a guided tour* ⊙ *Weekdays 7–7.*

THE PIENINY & CZORSZTYN LAKE REGION

In the south of Poland, along the Slovakia border, the area that includes the Pieniny mountains and Czorsztyn Lake is among the most picturesque corners in Central Europe. The winding Dunajec River gorge cuts through Pieniny National Park, with its varied peaks—some sharp and rocky, others gentle and green—creating dramatic and unique scenery in this region. To the west of Pieniny lies the man-made Czorsztyn Lake, created from the dammed waters of the Dunajec River, primarily to remedy problems with frequent floods and to provide neighboring villages with fresh running water. The small village of Czorsztyn was sacrificed to this project, but much of the town's unique wooden architecture was saved as houses were dismantled and moved to higher ground. Overlooking the lake are two famous castles that once stood on the river's banks and guarded the border that lay between them, the Dunajec having once been the border between Poland and Hungary.

The origin of Pieniny range is replete with lore and legends, many of which are connected to the medieval-era local saint, Princess Kinga (Kundegund), the wife of Bolesław Wstydliwy (Boleslaus the Bashful). In the 13th century, their lands were plagued by Mongolian (Tartar) raids. During one of those raids, Saint Kinga—together with the Clare nuns of Stary Sącz—had to go into hiding. Legend has it that a ribbon, a rosary, and a comb that were cast behind by the runaways were to turn into protective obstacles, a river, a range of mountains, and a forest. That mountain range is the Pieninys, which we can still see today.

A farmer named Kras, whom Saint Kinga had taught always to tell the truth (as it was the only right thing to do) was asked by the Tartar invaders where the princess had fled. Replying truthfully, the farmer pointed them in the right direction. He was then working in the field, planting his wheat crop. Miraculously, the seeds sprouted, and the wheat grew high within seconds. The Tartars gave up the chase, as they were made to believe that too much time must have passed for them to ever catch up with the fugitive nuns.

Dunajec Gorge

㉒ Sromowce Wyżne-Kąty (starting point of the rafts) is 26 km (16 mi) southeast of Nowy Targ, 37 km (23 mi) southeast of Nowy Sącz. Szczawnica (landing point of the rafts) is 28 km (17 mi) east of Nowy Targ, 35 km (22 mi) southwest of Nowy Sącz.

A rafting trip down the Dunajec River through the picturesque limestone ravine known as the Dunajec Gorge (or Dunajec Canyon) is one of the longest-standing tourist activities not only in this region but in all of Poland. These boat trips have quite a history, having been in operation since the first half of the 19th century. In the 1840s, the town of Szczawnica—then the property of Szalay family—became a popular resort; it is then that the river trips started.

Where to Stay & Eat

$ ▣ **Osada Turystyczna "Czorsztyn."**

Fodor'sChoice ★ This is a unique place—an entire village rescued from a flood caused by the creation of a man-made lake. The lovely wooden buildings that were brought here from the old Czorsztyn village, now Czorsztyn Lake. Today three stylish, 19th-century villas have been turned into tastefully and comfortably furnished guest rooms and suites, meeting rooms, and a restaurant. If you stay here, you'll find serene rooms with natural, warm wood furnishings and crisp, white linens. The surroundings are marvelous, with the views of the lake, offering plenty of peace and quiet and a lot of fresh air. The restaurant serves delicious regional specialties, including sheep's cheese in the summer, baked mushrooms in the fall, and bigos in the winter. ☒ *Stylchyn 1, Kluszkowce 34-440* ☎ *018/265–03–02* 🖷 *018/265–03–55* ⊕ *www.osada.czorsztyn.pl* ⤵ *19 rooms, 5 suites* ⚅ *Restaurant, cable TV; no a/c* ☐ *AE, DC, MC, V* ⏸ *BP.*

Sports & the Outdoors

HIKING If you are looking to do a little hiking, the **Blue Tourist Trail** is a good option. This walk, which begins at the visitor center in Czorsztyn, will take approximately 5½ hours. It is of medium difficulty; and the path is well marked, so it's easy to do on your own. The path heads southeast from the ruins of the Dunajec Castle in Czorsztyn Tourist Village. Follow the blue markers, and you will pass the mountain hut on the Majerz Glade, then Macelak Summit (857 meters) and Trzy Kopce Pass (which has a junction with the Red Trail). Approximately 1½ hours from the starting point the hike, the trail reaches the Szopka Pass (and a junction with the Yellow Trail) and then climbs to the top of the Three Crowns (982 meters). When you climb to the observation point at the top of the peak, make sure that you keep to the left-hand path on the way back. After 2½ hours from the starting point, the path takes you down to Kosarzyska Glade (and a junction with the Green Trail) and to the Pieniny Castle ruins on the Castle Mountain (Góra Zamkowa). Another hour later (3½ hours from the start of the walk), the trail descends to Bajków Gronik (another junction with the Yellow Trail). From this point, the path starts to climb gently, passing the Burzana Glade (another junction with the Green Trail), and reaching the top of Czertezik Summit. The trail

---

HOW TO MAKE A MOUNTAIN GORGE

Geologists have different theories regarding the origin of the Dunajec Gorge, but local lore and legend provide even more interesting explanations. According to one legend, it was Polish king Bolesław Chrobry (Bolesłaus the Brave), who cut the way for Dunajec River with his sword. Another legend tells the story of a man named Ferkowicz, who was chasing the Serpent King. The latter on the run (or on the slide) knocked the mountains down and made way for the river.

7

then descends to the Sosnów Pass (yet another junction with the Green Trail), whence it climbs again, to the top of Sokolica Peak. At the end, the path descends to the Dunajec River, which you can cross by ferry (from mid-April to late October).

RIVER RAFTING Gentle rafting trips through the Przełom Dunajca is one of the region's most popular tourist activities, drawing tourists from throughout Poland and the world. (Incidentally, it is also one of the biggest attractions of Slovakia, with "mirror" tours starting on the other bank of Dunajec River, which marks the border between the two countries.) The route starts in Sromowce Wyżne–Kąty and continues in turns and twists for 18 km (11 mi) along the river to Szczawnica or a little farther to Krościenko. As the crow flies, you travel only about 6 km (4 mi) and make an elevation change of 36 meters. Each turn opens a new fantastic view of the rocks and peaks around you, and with all the twists, you never know on which side of the river the next peak will appear.

Depending on the water level, the trip takes from two to three hours. Rafting season usually runs from May through the end of October, weather permitting (it may start a little later or end a little earlier if there is snow, and rafting may be suspended temporarily if the water level is too high). It is a safe, leisurely trip, and you won't get wet. One raft seats a dozen passengers plus two raftsmen, called *flisacy* (one raftsman is a *flisak,* or "gondolier"). These guides are quite down-to-earth: they are usually local mountaineers and will be dressed in their folk costumes and tell stories in the local dialect while they steer the boat with a long pole.

Rafting trips are offered by the **Polskie Stowarzyszenie Flisaków Pienińskich** (⊠ Raft Wharf [Przystań Flisacka], Sromowce Wyżne–Kąty ☎ 018/ 262–97–21 ⊕ www.flisacy.com.pl). The cost for the trip is zł 39 for the shorter course, zł 48 for the longer course. Trips are offered from May through August, daily from 8:30 to 5; in September daily from 8:30 to 4; and in October daily from 9 to 2. You can get to the rafting wharf by PKS bus from Nowy Targ, Zakopane, Szczawnica, or Krościenko (from the latter two there is also seasonal minibus service). You'll find parking lots at both the embarkation and disembarkation points (Sromowce Wyżne–Kąty and Szczawnica, respectively) with a shuttle-bus service between the two for zł 5. It is not usually necessary to reserve a place on a rafting trip in advance.

Niedzica Castle

❷❸ *20 km (12 mi) southeast of Nowy Targ, 12 km (7 mi) west of Szczawnica*

Niedzica Castle is perched on a steep rock over the Dunajec River, which is dammed up in Zalew Czorsztyński. Once an important defensive stronghold at the Polish-Hungarian border, Niedzica was a part of Hungary at that time and ruled over the Spisz (Spiss). On the Polish side of the border, in Czorsztyn, was another large castle, which today is a ruin. Niedzica Castle was built in the 14th century in stone; later, it was rebuilt in the Renaissance style, and a lower castle was added at the turn

CLOSE UP

What Is Spiss?

"SPISS" IS BOTH THE GEOGRAPHICAL and historical denomination of the region that lies today mostly in Slovakia (where it is called *Spis*), though a small part of the region is within the boundaries of present-day southeastern Poland (where it is called *Spisz*.) It would be impossible to recount the Spiss's long and complex history in a few sentences. The border region has always been a melting pot of many nations, cultures, and religions. In addition to Slovaks, there were German colonists (who call the region Zips; awarded royal privileges to settle here, they started coming in the 12th century and went on to found many independent towns and villages.

Although the Spiss was part of the Kingdom of Hungary from the Middle Ages (the region is called *Szepes*), few ethnic Hungarians ever lived there. Some Hungarians did come to the southern part of the region in the 12th

century, while Polish *górale* (Spiss highlanders) settled close to the region's contemporary northern border. Russians and Ukrainians arrived in the 14th century, and they dwelt mostly in the mountains, bringing their own culture and language, but also Eastern Christianity. Beginning in the 15th century, many Jews and Roma settled in the region. This was one of the few parts of Europe where you might find Roman-Catholics, Greek-Orthodox, Protestants, and Jews working and living together. From the 15th century onward Poland governed the Spiss, but after Poland's partitions in the 18th century, it was seized by Austria. After World War II, the Spiss became part of the newly formed Czechoslovakia; since 1993, it has been largely a part of the Republic of Slovakia, though a small northwestern section remains within the borders of the Republic of Poland.

of the 17th century. From that moment on, the castle has remained nearly unchanged, even to this day. Shortly after World War II ended in 1945, the castle underwent renovation and conservation, and it was entrusted to the Polish Art Historians' Society. Today it houses a museum, a hotel, and a restaurant. The terrace of the upper castle affords magnificent views of the mountainous landscape of Spisz. ⊠ *Niedzica–zamek* ☎ *018/262-94-89* 🎟 *zł 6* 🕙 *May–Sept., Tues.–Sun. 9–5; Oct.–Apr., Tues.–Sun. 9–4.*

Where to Eat

$–$$ ✕ **Restauracja Dwór.** In an 18th-century wooden manor house, this
Fodor'sChoice restaurant serves the best Spiss cuisine—a mixture of Polish and Hun-
★ garian—in Poland. As is the tradition in the Spiss region, meat and fish dishes are prepared in original, old-fashioned stone ovens, fueled by beech wood. Highlights of the menu include broth with *kołduny* (little ravioli stuffed with meat), *halaszle* (a Hungarian fish soup), lamb cutlets, and goose with cranberries. ⊠ *Polana Sosny, Niedzica* ☎ *018/262-94-03* 🚫 *No credit cards.*

Lost Treasure of the Incas

SEBASTIAN BERZEVICY, a 17th-century owner of the Niedzica castle, traveled extensively in Peru with his family, who included his daughter Umina. During the trip, Umina met, fell in love with, and married a descendant of the last great Inca king Tupac Amaru, whose bloodline the Spanish had tried to wipe off the face of the earth. After their marriage, Umina became pregnant. When this became known to the Spanish rulers, she had to flee with her husband—who had adopted the name "Tupac Amaru," after his famed relation—escaping to Venice. Here, it is said, Spanish spies caught up with them and secretly murdered Tupac, prompting Sebastian Berzevicy to take his daughter and grandson back to Niedzica. In the castle, they hid a testament written by Tupac in the Quipu language of the Inca, while the treasures they had brought with them from Peru—including chests of gold—were buried somewhere in the surrounding mountains. The testament and the treasure have never been discovered.

Where to Stay

★ **$–$$** ⌂ **Niedzica Castle Hotel.** Under the expert management of the Polish Art Historians' Association, Niedzica Castle offers about a dozen rooms to rent (some in the actual castle, some in the lovely wooden outbuilding of Celnica). Most are stylishly furnished, but don't expect royal luxury. Only some rooms have private bathrooms. Still, it is definitely one of the most interesting and unique places to stay in the area and is filled far in advance. ✉ *Zamkowa 2, Niedzica 34-441* ☎ *018/262–94–89* 🖷 *018/262–94–80* 🛏 *14 rooms* ⚴ *Restaurant; no a/c* ▤ *AE, DC, MC, V* ❍| *BP.*

Krościenko

㉔ *25 km (15 mi) east of Nowy Targ, 35 km (22 mi) southwest of Nowy Sącz.*

Krościenko is one of the villages that became holiday resorts during the late 19th century, and it is still popular today as a center for walking vacations. It has many interesting Zakopane-style wooden structures but few actual tourist sights. It is a good base for mountain hiking, being located in a picturesque valley surrounded with three mountain ranges: the Pieniny, Gorce, and Beskid Sądecki. Since the 13th century, settlers of various nationalities have started to arrive here, creating a colorful multicultural landscape. Dunajec Gorge, which cuts through the Carpathians, marked the shortest and most convenient way to the south of Europe, and it has served as a busy trade route for many centuries. You will find more comfortable accommodations in Niedzica (⇨ *above*) or the Osada Turystyczna "Czorsztyn" (⇨ Dunajec Gorge, *above*), so few tourists actually stay here. There is, however, one very good restaurant.

Where to Eat

★ ¢–$$ ✕ **Restauracja U Walusia.** The most popular—and probably the best—restaurant in Krościenko is this cheerful, traditional wooden inn, serving regional dishes. It's been around since 1975. The specialties include an excellent *żurek* (sour soup), potato pancakes with meat and vegetables, and grilled trout. The restaurant has free Wi-Fi Internet access. ✉ *Jagiellońska, Krościenko* ☎ *018/262–30–95* ▭ *No credit cards.*

Szczawnica

㉕ *28 km (17½ mi) east of Nowy Targ, 35 km (22 mi) southwest of Nowy Sącz.*

The small spa of Szczawnica dates from the late 19th century, and you can still stroll around in the high-vaulted pump rooms and sip the foul-tasting mineral waters. The town also a landing point of the unforgettable smooth-water rafting trip from Sromowce Wyżne–Kąty through the Dunajec Gorge, a popular tourist attraction operated since the mid-19th century by the local mountaineer raftsmen. The best access to Szczawnica is by PKS bus from the marketplace in Nowy Targ or outside the train station in Nowy Sącz. From Szczawnica, there are frequent shuttle buses to the Kąty wharf, where you can buy a ticket for the river trip (⇨ Dunajec Gorge, *above*).

Muzyczna Owczarnia Szczawnica-Jaworki (Music Sheep-Fold ✉ Szczawnica-Jaworki 18a ☎ 018/2620–22–66 ⊕ www.muzycznaowczarnia.pl) an independent cultural center and music club run by "family and friends" and still one of the best-kept secrets of the region. Of course, it's existence is no secret, and it is immensely popular, hosting concerts by Polish and international stars that have included Nigel Kennedy, Bennie Maupin, and Jarosław Śmietana. The club books about 100 concerts every year in a wide range of musical styles, from jazz to blues to rock to folk. Also, the owners organize music workshops, live recordings, and art exhibitions.

Where to Eat

¢–$ ✕ **Karczma Pienińska.** Run by local chef Mariola Węglarz, this regional restaurant, which is on the main thoroughfare between Szczawnica and Krościenko, serves a variety of grilled meats, as well as excellent black sausage, accompanied by fried potatoes and fried cabbage. Granted, this is not the healthiest meal for everyday consumption, but once in a while these kinds of homey specialties are hard to resist. A bonus is folk music every weekend and a summer garden, weather permitting. ✉ *Główna 240, Szczawnica* ☎ *018/262–28–57* ▭ *No credit cards.*

NOWY SĄCZ

㉖ *70 Km (44 mi) northeast of Nowy Targ.*

Nowy Sącz has existed as a market town since the 13th century, and was founded in 1292 by Bohemian king Venceslaus (Václav) II. It was intended to replace Stary (or the Old) Sącz, whose inhabitants were designated to resettle. The layout of Nowy Sącz is one of the first implementations of an ideal city plan in Małopolska, drawing from both Silesian and Czech experiences. Its hub is a rectangular market square, from which the streets symmetrically feed out: three each to the east and the west, two each to the north and the south. Remnants from this early period include a ruined 14th-century castle, about 10 minutes from the market square on ulica Piotra Skargi, as well as the church on the northeast side of the market square and the 15th-century church and chapter house on the square's east side.

Sądecki Park Etnograficzny (Regional Ethnographic Park) encompasses the former village of Falkowa, today part of Nowy Sącz. Exhibits detail the folk art heritage of the key ethnic groups in the Sącz region (Sądecczyzna): the Sącz Lachs; the natives of Pogołrze; Sałddeczczyzna's highlanders; the Lemkos; and the Carpathian Roma. The pride of the collection, a wooden manor from Rodzawa, stands in the center of the park. The interiors of this 17th-century building are lined with religious polychromes. The manor originally belonged to Stanisław Baranowski, who gave it to canons regular of Trzciana. The monks adapted the house to suit their needs, and they left behind the aforementioned polychrome decorations. The architecture of Sałcz Lachs is exemplified by an 18th-century church from Łososina Dolna, while an Orthodox temple from Czarne reflects the religious architectural traditions of the Lemkos.

✉ *Wieniawy Długoszowskiego 83b* ☏ *018/441–44–12* ⊕ *www.muzeum. sacz.pl* ✑ *zł 10* ⊙ *May–Sept., Tues.–Sun. 10–5; Oct.–Apr., weekdays 10–2.*

▌OFF THE BEATEN PATH

About 2 km (1 mi) north of Stróże, which lies halfway between Gorlice and Nowy Sącz, is the **SĄDECKI BARTNIK APICULTURE MUSEUM** – Spread across rolling hills covered with woodland and orchards, Sądecki Bartnik, established in 1991, has an impressive collection of beehives as well as an active, honey-producing apiary. Its custodian, Janusz Kasztelewicz, has been keeping bees since 1973. The apiary consists of some 1,000 families of honey-producing bees. Since 2000, visitors have been able to admire a unique collection of more than 100 historical beehives, most of which were gathered by Mr. Bogdan Szymusik, a collector from Kraków. Some of the oldest beehives are actually parts of tree trunks, vertical or horizontal, housing one or more families of bees. There is also a group of extremely inventive beehives in the form of statues: including a monk from the Tyniec monastery, a devil, and Saint Ambrose. More simple and modern frame beehives astonish the beholder with a variety of forms and decorations: you may find architectural beehives fashioned like mountain chalets and churches, or thatched beehives adorned with funny scenes and sentences. ✉ *Stróże* ☏ *018/445–18–82* ⊕ *www.bartnik.pl* ✑ *zł 3* ⊙ *May–Sept., daily 9–5; Oct.–Apr., weekdays 9–4.*

Where to Eat

¢–$$ ✕ **Zajazd Sądecki.** This restaurant emphasizes regional cuisine, such as highland-style pancakes, which are stuffed with pork and onions. True, the place is not too attractive on the outside, but the dining room is cozy, with pine furniture and crisp white tablecloths. Zajazd Sądecki doubles as a small hotel with about a dozen rooms if you need a simple and cheap place to stay. ⊠ *Królowej Jadwigi 67, Nowy Sącz* ☎ *018/443–67–17* 🖃 *No credit cards.*

STARY SĄCZ

㉗ *5 km (3 mi) northeast of Nowy Sącz.*

The oldest town of the Sądecczyzna region is located on a hill between the Dunajec and Poprad rivers, at the crossroads of a former Hungarian thoroughfare and the Nowy Sącz–Nowy Targ route. Sącz was founded in the second half of the 13th century. In the beginning it developed rapidly, but soon it was overtaken by its rival Nowy Sącz. Yet the town survived and even received a new charter in 1358 from the hands of King Kazimierz Wielki. Since the beginning of its existence, Stary Sącz was closely related with a convent of Saint Clare nuns. The convent provided protection and nurtured the economical and cultural growth of the city. What makes Stary Sącz special is its historical layout as well as its traditional-scale architecture, which has remained virtually unchanged over the years, making it one of the best-preserved historical cities in this part of Poland. Key points of the medieval city included the market square, and three churches: St. Clare's convent, a Franciscan monastery, and the parish church. At the heart of the city is the square with eight streets starting in its corners.

Saint Kinga (Kunegund), daughter of the Hungarian king Bela IV, came to Poland in order to marry the Polish ruler Bolesław Wstydliwy (Boleslaus the Bashful). Upon their marriage, her husband endowed Kinga with the Sącz lands, and she decided to use her endowment to create the Convent of Saint Clare nuns in Stary Sącz. The construction of first buildings for the convent—as well as the church of Holy Trinity and Saint Clare—commenced around 1285, and the finished church was consecrated in 1332. The original buildings were made of wood, and in spite of numerous fires, the convent and the church endured. In 1605, Jan di Simoni, a Krakovian mason, was commissioned to erect new, brick buildings: this is when the cloister we see today was built, surrounded by four wings of the convent. Growing in the convent's courtyard is an ancient linden tree, which was planted by Saint Kinga herself, according to legend. The body of the Gothic-style church reveals a baroque interior, with paintings of scenes from the life of Saint Kinga, and marvelous black-marble altars by Baldasare Fontana.

When King Boleslaus died, the widowed queen entered the Franciscan convent. In the side chapel devoted to the church's foundress, you will see a Gothic figure of Saint Kinga standing on an inverted crown, which symbolizes her abandonment of royal power in order to follow the monastic life of contemplation. She died in Stary Sącz in 1292, was beatified in 1690, and was named a saint by Pope John Paul II in 1999. ⊠ *pl. Świętej Kingi 1* ☎ *018/446–04–99* ⊕ *www.klaryski.sacz.pl* 🖃 *Free* ☉ *Church daily, masses at 6:30* AM *and 6* PM.

7

Naive Epiphany

"MY PICTURES WILL REMAIN FOREVER as mementoes of me. They're different from other pictures because they are my own. Please take a closer look at them." These are the words of Nikifor of Krynica (1895–1968), a primitive Polish painter. One of the most fascinating personalities in 20th-century European art, the illiterate genius lived his life in loneliness and poverty. His real name was Epifaniusz Drowniak, and he signed his paintings *Nikifor, Netyfor,* or *Matejko* (the last name being that of a famous 19th-century Polish painter). Communist authorities insisted that the artist—like all Polish citizens of the era—carry an ID card that could be produced whenever the police demanded; because he was known far and wide by his *nom de plume,* they actually created one for "Nikifor Krynicki" so he would have a proper identification card.

He painted his landscapes and saints on scraps of paper and cardboard, notebook covers, chocolate wrappers, cigarette boxes—whatever he could find. He used mostly watercolors, but he branched out later into crayon and gouache. His workshop was the town of Krynica, where he would sit in the street and paint. He created countless views of his hometown and surroundings, including the interiors of wooden churches, spa-town villas, provincial train stations, and so on. He mostly sold his pictures to tourists who arrived in Krynica. Toward the end of his life, his genius became recognized in Poland and abroad, but fame didn't change his lifestyle. Just as before, he took his wooden box with paints and set off to paint what he modestly called his "little pictures."

KRYNICA

㉘ *32 km (20 mi) southeast of Nowy Sącz on Hwy. 99.*

Krynica is one of the oldest and better-known Polish spa towns in the Małopolska region, made famous by not only its medicinally valuable mineral waters but also by the Jan Kiepura European Festival, which brings opera, operetta, and ballet lovers to the resort every summer. Krynica is also a winter-sports center in a high valley. The salutary properties of Krynica's mineral waters were recognized during the 18th century, and the first bathhouse was built here in 1807. In the late 19th century, Krynica was developed in the classic spa style, gaining a tree-lined promenade, a pump room, and concert halls. The waters here may not be appetizing to the unaccustomed palate, but they are good for you. In fact, they are the most concentrated mineral waters in Europe.

The heart of Krynica is its **promenade** (called *Deptak* by the locals and tourists alike), adjoining the Spa Park, where you'll find the most important old and new spas. The promenade starts at the bridge that crosses the Kryniczanka Stream. On the right, note the wooden building of Old Baths, with their characteristic wooden turrets—and notice the clock that has been mounted in the middle turret. Farther up the promenade, you can sample the mineral waters in the Main Pump Room, the Old Spa House, or the Mieczysław and Jan pavilions.

Krynica's **Pijalnia Główna** (Main Pump Room) is a glass building filled with tropical plants, located at the mid-point of the Promenade. The pump room, which opened in 1971, offers nearly a full selection of Krynica's mineral waters, including those from the Jan, Słotwinka, Tadeusz, Zdrój Główny, and Zuber springs. ⊠ *ul. Nowotarskiego 9/3* ☎ *No phone* 🖃 *Free* ⊙ *Daily 6:30 AM–6 PM.*

The palatial, neo-Renaissance **Stary Dom Zdrojowy** (Old Spa House) was constructed in 1889 and is located on Promenade near the Main Pump Room. It has a grand ballroom and a small pump room with Mieczysław mineral water. ⊠ *ul. Nowotarskiego 2* ☎ *018/471–28–18* 🖃 *Free* ⊙ *Daily 6:30–9, 10–1, and 3:30–6.*

The **Mieczysław and Jan Pavilions** are located in the Spa Park at the foot of Góra Parkowa (Park Hill). They serve Jan and Józef waters. ⊠ *Aleja Nikifora Krynickiego, just below Góra Parkowa Hill* ☎ *No phone* 🖃 *Free* ⊙ *Daily 6:30–9, 10–1, and 3:30–6.*

Muzeum Nikifora, which is in the Romanówka villa, a beautiful wooden building painted in green, is dedicated to the work of one of the most interesting Polish artists: Krynica-born naive painter Nikifor, who is of Lemko origin. The museum exhibits a selection of his wonderful "primitive" paintings. 77 of his works, mostly from the period between the two world wars. His photographs and memorabilia are also displayed. ⊠ *Bulwary Dietla 19* ☎ *018/471–53–03* 🖃 *zł 6* ⊙ *Tues.–Sun. 10–1 and 2–5.*

Where to Eat

¢–$ ✕ **Pod Zieloną Górką.** Beyond the green facade of a picturesque, historic
Fodor's Choice 1850 villa, which is surrounded with green and covered by a red roof,
★ you'll find the idyllic restaurant "Under the Green Hill." The menu is filled with good and often creative interpretations of Polish cuisine, such as herring in honey, blood sausage with apples, or meat roulade baked inside a loaf of bread. You can also get excellent pizza, made from the restaurant's own recipe. The wine list is decent, and great beers are also on offer, including Czech Pilsner Urquell and Irish Guinness. ⊠ *ul. Nowotarskiego 5* ☎ *018/471–21–77* 🖃 No credit cards.

Where to Stay

$$–$$$ 🖭 **Hotel SPA Dr. Irena Eris.** The best spa hotel in Krynica is owned by the
Fodor's Choice most successful Polish entrepreneur in the cosmetics business, Dr. Irena
★ Eris. The rooms are comfortably accessorized and include deck chairs, bathrobes, slippers, hair dryers, tea/coffeemaker, and complimentary Internet access. You'll find an extensive menu of health and beauty treatments in the Dr. Irena Eris Cosmetic Institute (on premises). You can also buy a package; for instance, the hotel offers a 10-day slimming program with biological regeneration, a 5-day prenatal program, and even indulgent spa weekend packages. ⊠ *Czarny Potok 30, 33–380* ☎ *018/472–35–00* ⊕ *www.hotelspa.pl* ⇝ 49 *rooms* ⌂ *Restaurant, indoor*

7

pool, health club, hot tub, spa, minibars, in-room safes, cable TV, Wi-Fi, bar, business services, meeting rooms, parking (free); no a/c ⍾|⍾ *BP.*

¢–$ ⊞ **Pensjonat Czerwony Dwór.** Formerly called the "President Wilson," this family-run pension has been welcoming visitors since the 1920s. It is located in the oldest part of the Krynica spa town and adjoins a landscaped park. Thoroughly renovated in 1990s—and updated again in 2005—the hotel offers good standard rooms that are airy and light. The hotel's dining room is also stylish. ⊠ *ul. Jana Kiepury 3, Krynica 33–380* ☎ *018/471-23-04* ⇲ *45 rooms* ⚬ *Restaurant, cable TV; no a/c* ⊟ *No credit cards* ⍾|⍾ *BP.*

¢ ⊞ **Pensjonat Wisła.** This small, friendly pension has been serving guests since the 19th century. Famous for its old-fashioned hospitality and home cooking, Pensjonat Wisła is in the center of the Krynica spa area. If there are no available rooms here, the pension will provide information on vacancies elsewhere. Most rooms have a private bath. ⊠ *Bulwary Dietla 1, Krynica 33–380* ☎ *018/471-55-12* ⇲ *21 rooms, 18 with private bath* ⚬ *Restaurant, some microwaves, TV in some rooms; no a/c* ⊟ *No credit cards* ⍾|⍾ *BP.*

MAŁOPOLSKA & THE TATRAS ESSENTIALS

Transportation

BY AIR
The only airport in the Małopolska region is in Kraków(⇨ Chapter 6).

BY BUS
Zakopane is most easily accessible by bus from Kraków, a two-hour trip by express bus (via Nowy Targ), and seats can be reserved in advance. Nowy Targ is a transportation hub/interchange, and many buses head from here to the Pieniny as well as the Tatras. You can also get to the Pieniny and Krynica from Nowy Sącz. There are some limited-stop services from Warsaw to Zakopane (five hours). Almost all villages in the region, however isolated, can be reached by PKS bus or a private minibus. The buses themselves can be ancient and slow, so take an express bus if one operates to your destination. The best buses are privately operated and offer frequent service from just outside the PKS bus stations; the two biggest companies are Trans-Frej and Szwagropol, both offering regular connections from Kraków to Zakopane via Nowy Targ, and Kraków to Nowy Sącz via Bochnia-Brzesko; both routes take about two hours.

There is regular minibus service from Kraków to Wieliczka and Kraków to Niepołomice (all leaving from outside the main Kraków railway station), and Kraków to Ojców (leaving from the Nowy Kleparz bus stop in Kraków going in the direction of Olkusz). There are also buses to Oświęcim and Wadowice, but both these destinations can be reached faster and more easily by train.

🚍 Bus Stations **Zakopane PKS Bus Station** ⊠ Corner of ul. Kościuszki and ul. Chramcówki, Zakopane ☎ 018/201-44-53 ⊕ pks.zakopane.pl. **Nowy Targ PKS Bus Station** ⊠ al. Tysiąclecia, Nowy Targ ☎ 018/266-22-82 ⊕ www.ppks.nowy.targ.pl. **Nowy Sącz PKS Bus Station** ⊠ Wyspiańskiego 2, Nowy Sącz ☎ 018/443-82-02 ⊕ www.pks. pl.

🚌 Private Bus Companies **Szwagropol** ☎ 018/652–77–80 ⊕ www.szwagropol.pl. **Trans-Frej** ☎ 018/288-07-80 ⊕ www.trans-frej.com.pl.

BY CAR

It is not necessary to have a car to explore the southern region. Public transport will take you to even the most remote places—but it will take time and can be uncomfortably crowded. On the other hand, the narrow mountain roads can be trying and dangerous for drivers.

The 7 (E77) highway, which takes you roughly halfway from Kraków to Zakopane, is four-lane all the way. The road that runs the rest of the way, E95, was improved in summer 2006, but some stretches are still single-lane, and horse-drawn carts can cause major delays. Side roads in the region can be very narrow and badly surfaced. In Zakopane and other towns in the region, it is wise to leave your car at a guarded parking lot. If you wish to rent a car, it is most practical to do so in Kraków (⇨ Chapter 6).

BY TRAIN

From Kraków, the trip to Zakopane takes a full four to five hours because of the rugged nature of the terrain. Unless you take the overnight sleeper from Warsaw, which arrives in Zakopane at 6 AM, it's better to change to a bus in Kraków.

Trains move slowly in the hilly region south of Kraków, but most towns are accessible by train from Zakopane, and the routes can be very picturesque. The most scenic route is toward Krynica, and although it takes a long time (four or five hours, depending on the type of train), and the train cars are rather—well—vintage, to put it nicely; it is worth it if you like train journeys.

To visit the Auschwitz memorial, you can take a train to Oświęcim (about 90 minutes from Kraków). Basic regional trains (*przewozy regionalne*) will take you to Wieliczka. The brand-new and shiny "Pope's Express" from Kraków to Kalwaria Zebrzydowska and Wadowice remains in contrast to most Polish trains (save InterCity express routes), and is a tourist attraction in itself.

Train timetables can be found online at the Web site for Telekomunikacja Kolejowa. (In the English-language version of the site, look for a button on the left for the PKP Train Timetable.)
🚆 **Pociąg Papieski** (The Pope's Express) ⊕ www.pociag-papieski.pl. **Telekomunikacja Kolejowa** ⊕ www.tktelekom.pl. **Zakopane Train Station** ✉ ul. Chramcówki 23, Zakopane ☎ 018/201-50-31.

Contacts & Resources

EMERGENCIES

🚨 **Emergency Services Ambulance** ☎ 999. **Police Emergencies** ☎ 997. **TOPR Tatra Mountain Rescue** ☎ 048/601-100-300 has an emergency mobile phone number in the Tatra mountains.
🏥 **Hospitals Nowy Sącz Hospital** ✉ Młyńska 5, Nowy Sącz ☎ 018/443-88-77. **Krynica City Hospital** ✉ ul. Kraszewskiego 140,, Krynica ☎ 018/471-28-07. **Zakopane City Hospital** ✉ Kamieniec 10, Zakopane ☎ 018/201-20-21.

🔊 24-hour Pharmacies Apteka Pharbita Zakopane ☒ ul. Chramcówki 34, Zakopane ☎ 018/206-82-21. **Pharmacy Nowy Sącz** ☒ Rynek 27, Nowy Sącz ☎ 018/443-82-92. **Vita Pharmacy Krynica** ☒ ul. Kraszewskiego 61, Krynica ☎ 018/471-39-47.

INTERNET, MAIL & SHIPPING

🔊 Internet Cafés **Alfa Net** ☒ ul. Krupówki 2, Zakopane ☎ 018/206-42-31. **Internet Club** ☒ ul. Krupówki 54, Zakopane ☎ 018/201-33-10. **Alfa Net** ☒ ul. Krupówki 2, Zakopane ☎ 018/206-42-31.

🔊 Post Offices **Urząd Pocztowy Krynica** ☒ ul. Zdrojowa 28, Krynica ☎ 018/471-23-66. **Zakopane Post Office** ☒ ul. Krupówki 20, Zakopane ☎ 018/206-31-26.

SAFETY

If you are going into the mountains, make sure you are well prepared— in terms of fitness, proper clothing (remember it can be much cooler there, and the weather can change in an instant), and provisions (water and an energy snack). Bring a map and, ideally, a mobile phone (especially if you are going into high mountains). You should never hike alone, and always let somebody know where you are going and when you expect to be back.

TOUR OPTIONS

Although you will find it easy to travel around Małopolska on your own, for some destinations, you may wish to consider a guided tour. This is especially true of the Tatra mountains, particularly if you would like to go hiking but don't feel experienced enough to do it safely on your own. Klub Przewodników Tatrzańskich and Koło Przewodników Tatrzańskich are associations of experienced mountain guides who know the mountains as only natives can do, and you will definitely be safe in their company. Your visit to Auschwitz will be more valuable if you join one of the English-language guided tours of the camp, or you can book a private tour with a knowledgeable guide. In Wieliczka, you are not allowed to wander on your own, but there are English-language group tours.

🔊 **Auschwitz-Birkenau Memorial Museum** ☒ Więźniów Oświęcimia 20, Oświęcim ☎ 033/843-21-33 ⊕ www.auschwitz-muzeum.oswiecim.pl, tours by qualified museum guides. **Klub Przewodników Tatrzańskich PTTK-TPN** ☒ Chałubińskiego 42a, Zakopane ☎ 018/206-32-03 ⊕ www.klub-przew.home.pl. **Koło Przewodników Tatrzańskich** ☒ ul. Piłsudskiego 63a, Zakopane ⊕ kpt.zakopane.pl. **Raft Wharf** (Przystań Flisacka) ☒ 34-443 Sromowce Wyżne-Kąty ☎ 018/262-97-21 ⊕ www.flisacy.com.pl, for Pieniny Gorge. **Wieliczka Salt Mine Tourist Route** ☒ Daniłowicza 10, Wieliczka ☎ 012/278-73-02 ⊕ www.kopalnia.pl, guided tours of Wieliczka Salt Mine).

VISITOR INFORMATION

🔊 **Informacja Turystyczna Krościenko nad Dunajcem** ☒ ul. Rynek 32, Krościenko nad Dunajcem ☎ 018/262-33-04. **Informacja Turystyczna PTTK–Ojców** ☒ Ojców 15 ☎ 012/389-20-10 ⊕ ojcow.pttk.pl. **Informacja Turystyczna Szczawnica** ☒ ul. Zdrojowa 3, Szczawnica ☎ 018/262-23-70. **Krynica Tourist Information** ☒ ul. Piłsudskiego 8, Krynica ☎ 018/471-61-05 ⊕ www.kot.org.pl. **Nowy Sącz Tourist Information** ☒ Piotra Skargi 2, Nowy Sącz ☎ 018/443-55-97 ⊕ www.nowysacz.pl. **Orbis Zakopane** ☒ ul. Krupówki 22, Zakopane ☎ 018/201-22-38. **Zakopane Tourist Information (BIT)** ☒ ul. Kościuszki 17, Zakopane ☎ 018/201-22-11. **Wadowice Tourist Information (BIT)** ☒ Kościelna 4, Wadowice ☎ 033/873-23-65 ⊕ www.it.wadowice.pl.

UNDERSTANDING POLAND

A SHORT HISTORY OF POLAND

POLISH FOLK ART

DOING BUSINESS IN POLAND

RECOMMENDED BOOKS & FILMS

POLISH VOCABULARY

A SHORT HISTORY OF POLAND

THE STORMS OF HISTORY have swept back and forth across Poland, often using it as a battlefield. "Polonophile" British historian Norman Davies titled his book on Polish history *God's Playground* to convey just this image. As foreign armies marched through these lands, alliances were made and its territory divided—rarely with the consent of the Polish people—and more than once the country found itself wedged between overpowering neighbors who were at war. At one point, Poland even disappeared from the official map of the world. More recently, the country was under the yoke of half-a-century of communism.

And yet, the Poles are proud of this tumultuous history, and of the fact that the spirit of freedom never died, even through the worst times. Poland's history goes back 1,000 years, and her history is not all turmoil. Many periods of peaceful prosperity and development have left behind a rich culture in cities, villages, palaces, and castles, and it is for this culture that tourists mainly visit Poland. As the country has entered NATO (in 1999) and more recently the European Union (2004), its future once again looks bright.

Early History

The earliest traces of human habitation in the Polish lands—fossils of *Homo erectus* in the Trzebnica area—date back some 500,000 years. In prehistoric times, the territory that is now Poland was inhabited by a number of pre-Slavic, and then Slavic, tribes. One of these tribes, called the *Polanie,* gave Poland its name. The Polanie lived in the area around Poznań and were first united under Mieszko I, who is now acknowledged as the first historical ruler of Poland. He ruled over a large part of the area that is now Poland, though not quite as a king.

In order to protect the lands of Polanie, Mieszko accepted vassal status under Otto I, king of the Germans, but there was still a threat that the Polanie, who were pagans, would provoke military efforts aimed at their conversion and ultimate submission in this time of Christianization in Europe. Mieszko, therefore, decided to embrace Christianity voluntarily rather than have it thrust upon him and his people, and he made a significant decision regarding who he would allow to guide him in this conversion. Rather than turning to the Germans, Mieszko appealed to the Bohemians (now the Czechs), a kindred Slavic tribe. In AD 965, he married Dobrava, a Christian Czech Princess, and in 966 he accepted Christianity—on Easter Sunday no less—aligning himself with the Czech Catholic Church, which derived its ecclesiastical authority from the Pope in Rome.

This was a significant development, not only marking Poland's beginning as a modern state, but also placing it within the Latin sphere of influence, along with the rest of Western Europe. By contrast, in 988, Vladimir the Great of Kiev accepted Christianity but from the Patriarch of Constantinople, then a part of Byzantium, after the division of the Roman Empire. The schism continues to this day, and churches in Russia, Ukraine, and many parts of the former Soviet Union are Eastern Orthodox or a variation thereof, while the churches in Poland (not to mention the Czech Republic, Slovakia, and Croatia) adhere to the Roman Catholic faith. However, Poland was the easternmost country in Western Europe, and as such it was influenced by Eastern civilization and Byzantine culture.

Mieszko I was succeed by his son, Bolesław the Brave. In the year 1000, Otto III (King of the Germans and Holy Roman Emperor) came to Gniezno, recognizing Bolesław as the sovereign of an independent nation. Twenty-five years later, with the Pope's blessing, Bolesław was crowned the first King of Poland, founder of the Piast Dynasty, which continued to rule Poland for three centuries.

Early Medieval Poland

When the first capital and archbishopric was established in Gniezno, many of the country's other major cities had already been founded—including Kraków, Gdańsk, Poznań, Szczecin, and Wrocław. Other important settlements in early Poland, such as Kruszwica and, indeed, even Gniezno itself, are only small provincial towns today; though certainly of great historical interest, they no longer wield the political clout they did in the medieval period. Poland's center shifted away from Gniezno soon enough after its founding, and by the mid-11th century, Kraków was established as the royal seat and capital, an honor it held for almost 600 years.

Poland developed as a nation, but all was not smooth sailing. In his will, the 12th-century king Bolesław Krzywousty (Bolesław the Wry-mouthed) divided the state between his sons, and this weakened the unity of the country, which was divided into several feudal kingdoms. Despite the fragmentation, the common language, culture, and historical legacy of the people were able to survive the physical division of the country—as would be the case in centuries to come. And the Poles were even able to unite enough to repel invasions by the Mongols in the 13th century. Other forces were more difficult to repel. For example, the Teutonic Knights, who were invited to Pomerania in 1226 by Duke Konrad of Mazovia to help defend the region against the Baltic Prussians, evolved into a much more difficult strain on the union later on when they became a military force to be reckoned with and created their own fortified kingdoms within Polish territory. The feudal fragmentation ended in 1320, with the coronation of Władysław Łokietek (Ladislas the Short, or more specifically, the "Elbow-high"), who managed to unite the country once again.

The last ruler of Piast Dynasty was King Kazimierz Wielki (Casimir the Great), of whom it is said: "When he came to the throne, Poland was made of wood; at the close of his reign, it was made of brick." Kazimierz erected hundreds of castles, towns, and strongholds. Among his accomplishments was also the foundation—in 1364—of the Kraków Academy (which later, upon its endowment by Queen Jadwiga, became known as the Jagiellonian University), the second-oldest university in Central Europe after Prague's. Kazimierz was a progressive king. At that time, when Jews were being expelled and persecuted in many countries in Europe, he invited them to come and settle in Poland, where they would live under his protection. *So many came—then and later—that at one point three quarters of the Jews in the world were living peacefully in Poland.

Although Kazimierz had several (official and unofficial) wives, these unions produced only daughters, and by the laws of medieval succession, the throne passed first to a male heir, his nephew King Louis of Hungary (of the Anjou Dynasty), and only upon Louis's death to Louis's daughter Jadwiga (Hedvig) since there were no more male heirs and he wished to continue the family's dynasty. To avoid the problem of a woman ascending to the throne, Jadwiga was crowned as the Polish "king," since a "queen" could not rule over Poland. In the year 1386, Jadwiga (then aged 12) married Władysław Jagiełło, the Grand Duke of Lithuania, thus converting the grand duchy to Christianity and creating a union of the two independent states. It is from Jagiełło that the next powerful dynasty of Polish rulers takes its name.

Jadwiga's motivation to marry Jagiełło—and her willingness to combine her kingdom with that of Lithuania—was not unconnected to the extraterritorial domains belonging to the Teutonic Knights, known as Krzyżacy, who were flexing their legendary military muscles throughout the northern reaches of Polish territory. This military-religious order had originally been granted its domain by invitation from Prince Konrad of Mazovia back in 1226 to help defend Poland from the Baltic Prussians (and to convert the latter to Christianity). After the Teutonic Knights successfully reached those goals, they established their own state and sought to expand it at the cost of Poland and Lithuania, posing a constant threat to the borders of both countries. United, the two countries stood more of a chance to stop Krzyżacy. Indeed, in one of the biggest military confrontations of the Middle Ages, the Battle of Grunwald (1410), the Polish and Lithuanian armies, under the leadership of Jagiełło, crushed the Knights, though they continued to fight against Poland even in their diminished form until the mid-15th century.

The Jagiellons

The influence of the Jagiellonian Dynasty—and its influence on the rest of Europe—was immense. Kazimierz Jagiellończyk (Casimir Jagiellon), the son of Jagiełło and his fourth wife, came to be known as the "father of Europe." Of his nine children, four became kings, and three daughters were married off to produce heirs to various other dynasties throughout Europe. The Jagiellonian Dynasty was connected by marriage with many royal families of Europe, including the houses of Hapsburg, Hohenzollern, and Vasa. (A link can be traced back in the genealogical trees of most surviving monarchs in Europe today, including the House of Windsor.)

Because of these political marriages, the power of the kingdom and the commonwealth grew, and Poland's political position in Europe was strong. This was certainly one of Poland's greatest periods of prosperity, filled with political, cultural, and economic achievements. And gradually, the way the nation was governed became more democratic. A bicameral parliament (the *Sejm*) was first convened in 1493, and in 1505 it enacted a statute requiring the king to obtain prior approval of both chambers of the parliament before making any legal decree. Unfortunately, this law was both a blessing and a curse, as the wants and desires of the privileged nobility—who made up the parliament—did not always serve the country's best interests.

During the reign of the last two Jagiellons—Zygmunt I Stary (Sigismund the Old) and Zygmunt August (Sigismund Augustus)—Poland once again enjoyed a golden age. They brought the Renaissance to Poland, along with its art, architecture, and philosophy. Much of Poland's embrace of Renaissance values comes directly from Zygmunt I Stary's marriage to an Italian princess, Bona Sforza of Bari. After the marriage, many Italian artists and artisans came to Poland, leaving behind a rich architectural heritage—including the arcaded courtyard at the Royal Castle, the Wawel, and the entire town of Zamość. It was also during this period that Polish writers began to write in the Polish language rather than in Latin. Religious tolerance was enjoyed: one act, passed at the Confederation of Warsaw in 1573, recognized freedom for all to practice their faith without fear of persecution, a revolutionary idea at the time. Poland was quite an oasis of freedom in a time when religious wars consumed much of Europe and where burnings at the stake were not at all uncommon.

During the reign of Zygmunt August, the last of the Jagiellons, the Parliament convened in Lublin (1569), with two very important outcomes. The union between the Polish crown and Lithuania was renewed, proclaiming the "Republic of Two Nations" as a single, unified state. As there was no heir-apparent to the throne, a new system of royal succession was established, whereby the king was elected by the Parliament. Alas, the first king to be elected (in 1573) was Henri de Valois, who decided to return to France almost immediately after his coronation, ruling there as King Henry the III. The next king, Stefan Batory, was a much better choice: a great military strategist, he strengthened Poland's eastern frontier and won battles against the Tzars.

Despite the new law, in 1587, the throne passed to the grandson of Sigismund the Old, Zygmunt III Waza (Sigismund Vasa), who ruled until 1632. He had been raised a Catholic in Lutheran Sweden, and while his mother had taught him Polish, he aspired to be King of Sweden, as his father had been. He is perhaps best known in Poland as the king who moved the royal capital to Warsaw at the beginning of the 17th century (1609). He was one of the longest-ruling Polish kings, with interests in both alchemy and soccer (he organized soccer games in the Wawel castle). After his father's death (in 1592) Zygmunt III Waza inherited the throne of Sweden as well, but because he was a Catholic (and therefore in favor of the Counter-Reformation), he was unacceptable to the Swedes, and he was deposed in 1599. This entangled Poland in a series of disastrous wars with Sweden while other threats—the Ottoman Turks and Muscovites among them—were also lurking round the corner.

Sweden occupied Poland for five years, from 1655 to 1660, a period known in Poland as the "Swedish Deluge," when the country's population was reduced by as much as 40%. At one point, the whole of the country fell into Swedish hands, with one exception: the Jasna Góra monastery in Częstochowa. The Swedes lay siege to the monastery for over a hundred days, but the Poles did not surrender, a fact regarded as a miracle and attributed to the black Madonna icon in the monastery's shrine.

Poland in Pieces

After these dark times, Poland did have one brief period of glory, which began with the election of King Jan III Sobieski (in 1674), a brilliant military leader who came to be hailed as the "Liberator of Europe" and the "Savior of the Occident." After reuniting his own kingdom, which had fractured after a half-century of wars with Sweden, he led the battle of Vienna in 1683 and managed to expel the Ottoman

Turks who besieged the city. This was the last great victory of the Polish army, and after that the country became prey to the internal instability of the feudal republic, and external expansion.

Throughout the 17th century, the Polish gentry acquired numerous privileges and came to enjoy the so-called "golden freedom," a partial democracy that eventually evolved—or rather degenerated—into anarchy. Any deputy of the parliament, if he felt strongly enough about a matter, could exercise a personal veto (*liberum veto*) and bring the session to a close, which made effective governing of the country virtually impossible. Meanwhile, the fortunes of magnates grew, with individual nobles gaining absolute power over dozens of villages and cities. Also growing were the three power-hungry, mighty empires that surrounded Poland: Russia, Prussia, and Austria. As absolute monarchies, they considered Poland's traditions of freedom and tolerance politically dangerous. More than anything, however, they wanted to help themselves to a piece of the pie. The three formed a coalition to deal with Poland and circled for the kill.

Over the course of the 18th century, treaties were forced upon Poland limiting the size of its armed forces, stipulating the stationing of Russian troops on its soil, and generally aiming at subjugating the country. Until 1763, the rulers of Poland were mainly Dresden-based princes from Saxony, who cared little for the country's affairs. In 1764, Stanisław August from the Poniatowski family was elected king. A great patron of the arts and literature, full of good intentions, he endeavored reforms but ended up as a puppet in the hands of the Russian regime. Stanisław August Poniatowski bears a rather cheerless distinction of being the last king of Poland.

With a powerful coalition of neighbors allied against Poland, the situation was very serious; Poles came to realize that their country's freedom was at stake and that something had to be done. Some (though not King Stanisław August) favored a military solution. The patriotic Confederation of Bar, the last push to bring the disparate parts of the Polish Kingdom together, was created in 1768 to protect Polish interests, but it was eventually destroyed by the Russian army. Among the confederates was Kazimierz Pułaski, who for four years fought countless battles with the Russian troops stationed in Poland. A brilliant military tactician, he was forced into exile in 1772. He ended up lending his hand in the American Revolutionary War, organizing the U.S. Cavalry (and died at the siege of Savannah in 1779).

THE FIRST PARTITION OF POLAND (which peeled off roughly one-third of the Polish territory) was completed in 1772. One immediate result was the realization that the very existence of Poland was in danger. Internally, many saw the need for comprehensive reforms—social, educational, and administrative. An elite military academy, the Knights' School, was also founded. Although treaties Poland had been forced to sign allowed the country to have only a limited number of officers, the military felt these should be first-class. This was certainly true of one of the first graduates of the Academy, Tadeusz Kościuszko, who lived to personify Poland's struggle for freedom and who was another Pole destined to play a crucial role in the American Revolutionary War.

Perhaps the greatest legislative success of the reform period of 1788–92 was the proclamation on May 3, 1791, of a new democratic constitution, which the King signed into law. The first constitution in Europe—and second only to the American Constitution—it reorganized the government, abolished the liberum veto, assured religious freedom, and provided rights to the citizens.

It should come as no surprise that Poland's autocratic neighbors did not like this manifestation of the country's sovereignty. Soon, the Russian army invaded Poland. The Poles defended themselves bravely,

but in the end, the Constitution was suspended, and the second partition of Poland was effected. But Poland fought back.

On March 24, 1794, in Kraków's Market Square, Kościuszko proclaimed the national insurrection and vowed to serve the cause as the leader of the revolutionary government. Initially, the revolt was successful, but after a spectacular victory in the Battle of Racławice, the uprising was put down by Russian and Prussian forces. After only six months, the uprising was suppressed, and Kościuszko, badly wounded, was taken prisoner. King Stanisław August was forced to abdicate and was placed under house arrest (he died in Saint Petersburg in 1798). In 1795, Russia, Prussia, and Austria, annexed all the remaining Polish territory and divided it among themselves. Poland disappeared from the map of Europe for the next 123 years.

Although the kingdom of Poland had evaporated, Poland had never ceased to exist as a nation. Poles looked for ways and means to preserve their culture and fight for their independence. At one point, they put their hopes with Napoleón Bonaparte. A Polish Legion was organized in southern Italy in 1797, and the words written by one of the legionnaires, the poet Józef Wybicki, became Poland's current national anthem: "*Jeszcze Polska nie zginęła, póki my żyjemy! . . .*" ("As long as we live, Poland has not perished! . . ."). Later, when Napoleón became Emperor, he reestablished the small "Duchy of Warsaw." But when Napoleon was defeated, Polish hopes waned again.

In this period, Wielkopolska and Pomerania remained parts of Prussia; Kraków (since 1815) was a semi-independent minirepublic; Galicia (southern Małopolska and lands that are now part of Ukraine) was under Austrian (then Austro-Hungarian) rule; and the rest formed the so-called "Congress Kingdom of Poland," which was effectively a province of Russia. The situation in each occupied area was different, enhancing—or sometimes giving rise to—some of the regional differences we can still see in Poland today. To this day, it is common to drink tea from glass cups in the former Russian zone, but from porcelain cups in the Austrian-dominated Galicja.

Poles never gave up their fight for independence: patriotic associations and clandestine groups were formed and re-formed, and there were a series of national uprisings, including the November Rising in 1830, then the Kraków Rising of 1846, and the January Rising of 1863. Each of the uprisings was brutally suppressed, with the only positive outcome being more public sympathy for the Polish cause in Europe. More and more of Poland's bravest and brightest minds joined the Great Emigration, the first wave of forced exodus from Poland. However, the 123 years of foreign rule also produced some of the most famous expressions of Polish culture—especially in fine arts, music, and literature. Many artists took a political stand and were punished for their beliefs, or were forced to emigrate with no hope of returning to their homeland. Among these artists were Fryderyk Chopin and the Romantic poet Adam Mickiewicz. Other artists—notably the painter Jan Matejko and the novelist Henryk Sienkiewicz—sought to glorify the more golden moments of Polish history in order to preserve the nation's memory and inspire hope for the future.

The 20th Century

World War I, which changed the face of Europe, turned Poland's primary enemies—Russia to the east, Germany and Austria to the west—against each other and turned Poland into a battlefield. The front ran through the middle of Poland, and Poles were often forced to fight on opposite sides, depending on where they lived. But in November 1918, the Poles liberated themselves, and on November 11 they proclaimed their independence under the leadership of Marshal Józef Piłsudski. This day is now observed as Poland's Independence Day.

During the 21 years of independence that followed, Poland faced a ruined economy, social problems, and the necessity to rebuild every one of its state institutions, and the territorial struggle continued for a few years after the war itself ended. Polish borders were not officially redrawn until 1919–21. The Treaty of Versailles (1919) gave Poland access to the Baltic Sea, but Gdańsk was granted special status as the Free City of Danzig. In Silesia, after rebellions and plebiscites, a part of Upper Silesia was placed within the Polish borders. In the east, the Polish-Soviet war ended in Poland's victory over the Red Army. Interwar Poland was a multicultural state that adopted a new democratic constitution, based on the French model, in 1921. Not without internal controversies and problems, Poland grew in strength and stability, developed her economy (the construction of the Baltic port and city of Gdynia was an important event), and had a vibrant cultural life.

NEXT DOOR, IN 1930S GERMANY, the fanatical Nazi party with its leader Adolf Hitler rose to power. Preaching that the Germans were a superior race, the Nazis felt it was their destiny to secure *lebensraum* (living space) to the east, and this meant annexing territories occupied by the inferior Slavic race. On August 23, 1939, Germany and Soviet Union signed the so-called Ribbentrop-Molotov pact, which has a secret clause planning the fourth partition of Poland. Essentially, Stalin and Hitler planned to divide Poland between themselves. World War II started days later, when Germany invaded Poland in the early hours of September 1, 1939, at Westerplatte, the outpost of Gdańsk. Poland was left to her own devices, and her hopes for assistance from the rest of Europe were disappointed. Although Great Britain and France declared war on Germany on September 3, 1939, no help came for Poland, and Hitler completed his blitzkrieg of Poland unhindered.

If this were not bad enough, the Soviet Red Army also invaded Poland on September

17 from the east. The country was virtually ripped apart. From their zone of occupation, the Soviets started the systematic extermination of Polish elites—in the infamous massacre at Katyń, thousands of Polish officers were executed. Another 1.8 million Poles were deported to Siberia, where most of them perished. By October 1939, the westernmost part of Poland was considered part of the German Reich, and the remaining areas were turned into the so-called "General Government" under German rule, with governor Hans Frank residing at the Royal Castle in Kraków.

In the Nazi plan, Jews were doomed for extermination, while non-Jewish Poles were destined to become slaves, their nation eradicated. The Germans herded all the Poles who were Jewish into areas of the main cities, which were walled off in ghettos. Tens of thousands died from starvation and epidemics; hundreds of thousands more were shipped to death camps, where they were gassed. The Nazi concentration camps were built in both the annexed and occupied Polish lands—some in the "General Government" areas, and others in camps like Auschwitz–Birkenau that were in the German Reich proper. All told, some 3 million perished in the death camps, virtually all the Jews who had lived in Poland. Christian Poles perished in equal numbers. Executions, deportations, and imprisonment became a daily occurrence.

However, there was also a massive resistance to the German occupation. The Polish underground Home Army (AK) evolved; there were also clandestine educational, communications, and judicial systems in operation. A Polish government-in-exile was formed. And many Poles managed to find their way to the Allies and fought on many fronts: Britain, Norway, North Africa, Italy, the Netherlands, France, and on the Eastern Front. By the end of the war, the Polish forces were the fourth-largest in the Allied camp. Poland's contributions to the Allied victory antedated the war itself; in 1939, Polish cryptologists had managed to duplicate and provide the British with the Omega machine, which the Germans used to code messages they sent by radio. As a result, throughout the war, the Allies had access to many of Germany's secret messages.

Not all Poles stood by helplessly to watch the suffering of their fellow Jewish citizens. Assistance was organized in various forms and at great risk to individuals and their families—in German-occupied Poland, all members of a household were punished by death if a Jew was found hiding in their home. Of the 20,000-some people awarded the status of Righteous Among the Nations (*Hasidei Umot HaOlam,* an honor bestowed upon non-Jews who aided the Jews of Europe during the Holocaust), more than one fourth (about 6,000) were Poles.

Hitler's unexpected attack on his former ally, Soviet Russia, in June 1941 changed the course of the war. Stalin turned to Poland for help, and the official Polish army was formed under Soviet control, partly recruited from among the "pardoned" Poles who had been previously deported to Soviet camps. The leader of those forces, General Anders, led his people out of Russia and to the fronts in North Africa, where they played an important part in the Battle of Tobruk, and then to Italy, where they distinguished themselves in Monte Cassino.

POLAND PAID AN ESPECIALLY HEAVY PRICE in the war. Warsaw, the capital, was almost totally destroyed. It was heavily bombed during the German invasion in 1939, and again in 1943, following the Nazi deportation of most of the Jews confined in the Ghetto to death camps. The remaining Jews staged an uprising, preferring death with honor to being killed in gas chambers. Again, on August 1, 1944, with the Soviet army just across the river, the Polish Home Army staged an uprising in the rest of Warsaw and liberated most of it from German control. The Poles had expected to link up with the Soviet forces, sparing the city from any more major damage, and have a say in the formation of the forthcoming Polish state. The Soviets, however, halted their advance, failed to provide any assistance, and left the Poles to their fate. Without Soviet support, the Polish Home Army was unable to prevent the Germans from destroying what was left of Warsaw in their ensuing retreat.

After the Soviet massacres in Katyń were discovered in 1943, the Polish government-in-exile had refused to cooperate further with Stalinist Russia, fearing Poland's Sovietization. Upon the German retreat from much of Poland's territory in the summer of 1944, a Polish administration was introduced in (partly) liberated Poland, which was then already under Soviet control. The battle for the political supremacy in Poland continued between the legitimate Polish government and the Soviets. Already, those who had fought for Polish freedom on the wrong side were proclaimed traitors, and they were treated as criminals by the future Communist government. Many were prosecuted, sent to the worst prisons or to Siberia, or simply murdered, yet another great tragedy of 20th-century Poland.

Even before the war ended, the Allies sat down to work out a new political order. As a result of agreements reached by Churchill, Roosevelt, and Stalin at Yalta (in February 1945), Poland was consigned to the "Soviet sphere of influence" and thereby to Communist rule. As the result of the agreement, Poland's eastern border followed roughly the Soviet-German demarcation line of 1939 (thus, the Soviet Union retained a large portion of the pre-war eastern territory of Poland). In August 1945, the western border was settled, too, following the Nysa (Neisse) and Odra (Oder) rivers, assigning to Poland the lands that before the war had been German territory. Following these huge territorial changes were massive, organized repatriations. This became the lot of some 10 million people—most of them Poles from the east who were directed to western Poland, but also Germans, Ukrainians, and Belarusians.

Unfortunately for Poles, the end of the war did not signal a return of sovereignty and independence. Although officially the Yalta treaties included a guarantee for democratic elections in Poland after the war, Stalin had no intention of adhering to that part of the deal. A "People's Poland" with a government controlled from Moscow was created behind the Iron Curtain. In 1948, the Polish United Workers' Party (PZPR) was established; it was the one and only political party in Poland. Four years later, Poland received a new Soviet-style constitution, and the first secretary of the Party Central Committee received the power.

THE COMMUNIST YEARS were harsh for Poland. There would be no differences in opinions, no free expression. A planned, centralized economy led to much regimentation and a lack of consumer goods. Luckily for Poland, centralization and nationalization of agriculture was not wholly successful, so farmers did not suffer as much. During this time, any industrial development was mostly strategic heavy industry—steel, coal, iron, and armament—meant to benefit the Soviet empire. Nowa Huta, at the outskirts of Kraków, is a memento of those times. The people in the People's Poland were heavily controlled—Secret Police were everywhere. The Roman Catholic church was generally regarded as a reactionary relic of the old system—first prosecuted, then barely tolerated. After Stalin's death in March 1953, some controls were eased, and Poland came to be known as the "most fun of all the barracks in the eastern camp." In October 1956, Poland's new leader Władysław Gomułka, managed to negotiate some concessions, yet the situation was far from rosy, and central planning was destroying Poland's economy.

The Polish people had never lost their independent spirit and started to demand more civil rights. In June 1956, massive workers' protests in Poznań started with the slogan *chleba i wolności* (bread and freedom). Tanks were sent in immediately to crush the protesters, but dissent broke out again and again: in March 1968 in Warsaw, Gdańsk, and Kraków; in 1970 in Gdańsk and Szczecin (where 44 people died); in 1976 in Radom and Warsaw; and, finally, in the famous breakthrough year of 1980.

IN 1978, KAROL WOJTYŁA had been elected as the first Polish Pope, taking the name John Paul II. His elevation gave the nation real hope. After the Pope's significant first trip to his homeland in August 1980, the shipyard workers in Gdańsk started a strike under the leadership of Lech Wałęsa (an electrician by profession), which led to a nonviolent revolution. The protesters negotiated an agreement with the government, which accepted most of their demands. Perhaps the most significant, they were given the right to form an independent trade union, the first in a communist country and the whole Soviet bloc. That trade union, called *Solidarność* (Solidarity), soon grew into a huge national movement with 10 million members (60% of all working people in Poland). Many Communist party members tore up their membership cards and joined Solidarity. In a final attempt to preserve the communist system, General Wojciech Jaruzelski, Poland's communist ruler, declared a state of martial law on December 13, 1981. Solidarity was officially disbanded, many opposition members imprisoned (interned), and a wave of repression started. Despite that, underground work continued (it would have been impossible to arrest 60% of all citizens). All political prisoners were eventually released, but some languished until 1986.

IN 1983, LECH WAŁĘSA was awarded the Nobel Peace Prize, and the country became increasingly ungovernable for the Communists. The economy went from bad to worse. In 1989, after a wave of protests by workers, students, and youths, the government proposed holding talks with Solidarity, which came to be known as Round Table Talks. A compromise agreement was reached between the Communist regime and the leaders of Solidarity to hold semi-free elections, which produced an overwhelming victory for Solidarity, to which the Communists were forced to cede power. In 1990, the Communist Party dissolved itself, and the first free, parliamentary elections were held in October 1991, completing the peaceful revolution.

The happy ending was only the beginning of a long struggle to create democratic systems, a free-market economy, and a new way of life, but the changes continued. In 1997, a new democratic constitution was approved in a national referendum. In March 1999, Poland became a member of NATO. On May 1, 2004, after another referendum, Poland joined the European Union.

Today's Poland is a relatively prosperous and certainly an energetic European state. She has her own historical demons to face and tame—the problematic de-communization issue seems to return like hiccups every now and then. There are still essential (but not necessarily negative) tensions between liberal and conservative traditions. Poland's current prime minister and president are twin brothers, and political parties of the ruling coalition still bear names such as Law and Justice, Self Defence, and the League of Polish Families. However, as one of the most prosperous countries of the Eastern Bloc, Poland's transition back into full nationhood continues.

POLISH FOLK ART

SINCE LATE 19TH CENTURY, folk art, though variously defined, has been particularly important in creating a larger sense of Poland's culture, particularly when the country itself didn't survive on any map. The concept of folk art was being rediscovered in other European countries at the time, but for Poles, folk traditions held more significance, as the vestiges of a 1,000-year-old cultural tradition, manifested in the shape of cottages, in particular patterns and ornaments, eventually being turned into new styles of art and architecture that were distinctly Polish.

After Poland regained its independence in 1918, folk art became the basis on which an interesting national version of art deco emerged. After World War II, folk art and peasant traditions became an ideologically safe basis for artists in the communist regime. Many of the rediscovered village artists received exhaustive training in how to be untrained and were required to read long treatises on which folk tradition were genuine—and which were not. All of this led to amusing paradoxes, including a demand—in the regulations of various art competitions held in the 1950s—to deliver sculptures in raw wood only, so that they would look "original." Of course, the original 19th-century figures upon which these regulations were based only looked unpainted; because so much time had passed, they had a weather-beaten look, and the original paint had all flaked off. A surviving relict of those times of regulated spontaneity and skilful marketing is Cepelia, a state-owned chain that both employs and educates folk artists. Today, the stores are excellent sources for interesting pottery, wooden toys, embroidered table linens, and hand-woven gobelins.

More recently, folk art has experienced another renaissance, heightened by political changes and Poland's accession to the EU. As the country has looked to define itself and sharpen its own local color, folk art has left its dusty skansens and walked straight into music, architecture (particularly in the revival of timber as a building material), and interior design (in carpets designed by Moho).

Where to Find Folk Art

You may be delighted by the various ways was that Polish musical traditions have found their way into popular music. Some is historical folk, performed on reconstructed, long-forgotten instruments; at the other extreme, contemporary jazz, rock, or experimental artists are including folk influence in a more sophisticated way. Look for CDs by Orkiestra Św. Mikołaja, Trebunie Tutki, Kapela ze Wsi Warszawa, Kwartet Jorgi, Zakopower, and the Klezmer-influenced Kroke.

There are several excellent *skansens* (open-air museums) in Poland, with examples of the wooden architecture of various regions, complemented with local crafts and art. These can be found all over Poland. The paths of the Szlak Architektury Drewnianej (Wooden Architecture Route) in southern Poland winds through beautiful hilly and mountainous landscapes to real hidden gems—especially old wooden churches in unusual shapes, fragrant with a mixture of pine resin, incense, mold, and holiness. Many of these have breathtaking, minute polychromies in gold and rich colors. Several of these monuments, including the churches in Haczów, Blizne, Sękowa, Dębno, and Lipnica Murowana figure on the UNESCO heritage lists.

To see how traditional building methods have been transformed by artists, go to Zakopane and check on villas designed by Stanisław Witkiewicz, the creator of Zakopane Style at the turn of 20th century. Willa Koliba is now a museum and can be visited, but the best example of the Zakopane style is Willa pod Jedlami, though it must be admired from the outside as it is now private property.

Rich, delightful, moving, and sometimes kitschy folk paintings, graphics, and sculpture can be found nowadays in museums. The biggest and best of these is the Muzeum Etnograficzne in Kraków, the Muzeum Etnograficzne in Warsaw, or the excellent Muzeum Okręgowe in Nowym Sączu; the latter is famous for its collection of icons.

To get overwhelmed by the decorative power of floral ornament, travel well off the beaten path to Zalipie, a small village north of Nowy Targ, where the local women managed to cover every possible surface with drawings of flowers. In the *Gesamtkunstwerk* (total work of art) thus created, you can see blooming hut walls, stoves, dishes, fences, and even dog kennels. If you don't wish to travel so far off the beaten path, you can get a taste by visiting the famous Kawiarnia Zalipianki in Kraków, which was decorated by the village artists in 1960s.

–Sylwia Trzaska

DOING BUSINESS IN POLAND

OUTSIDERS MUST EARN THE TRUST of their Polish acquaintances before a close business relationship can form. For this reason, when conducting business in Poland, you may find that your Polish colleagues adopt a fairly formal approach in the beginning, and you may need to hold several meetings before any final decisions are made. There are a few things you can do to make the process work more smoothly.

Making Appointments

Generally speaking, official business hours are weekdays, from 8 to 4 with no official break for lunch. However, it is not uncommon for business lunches to take place around 4 PM in Poland and then continue well into the evening. The best times for scheduling nonlunch meetings are from 10 to 11 or from 2:30 to 4. When you make a business appointment, you should do it four to five days in advance and then confirm the meeting on the day before. Your Polish colleagues can still be flexible and are often prepared to change schedules if necessary. You can schedule appointments for any day but Sunday. Also, be aware that February, July, and August are popular vacation months, so consider this when setting up a meeting schedule.

It's important that you be punctual in Poland to establish your reliability, even though meetings often have no specific end time (and can often go longer than planned). If you cannot be on time, write an SMS text message or make a phone call to inform the other person about the circumstances that have delayed you. Refrain from calling your Polish partner after work hours. If it is important, write an SMS text message and ask for feedback. Remember that in Poland, as in most of Europe, the day comes first when writing dates (e.g., November 8, 2005 is written 8 November 2005 or 8.11.05). Most businesses in Poland follow the Continental system of writing dates.

Formality & Hierarchy

Generally speaking, organizations in Poland have a strong respect for hierarchy and authority, with structure and delegation coming from above. This hierarchical style is reflected in many Polish business formalities and settings, including the decision-making process and the use of professional titles. Titles are very important in Poland. Do not use first names unless asked to do so. You must use *pan* (Mr.) or *pani* (Mrs.) plus the family name to introduce someone to strangers. Follow the example of the associates as to how to address each other.

Age and educational background often form the basis for corporate hierarchy. For this reason, when negotiating, it is advised to send delegates of a similar status to those of your Polish colleagues, both in age and professional qualifications. Rules and regulations are an important part of the Polish business environment; therefore, your Polish counterparts will expect you to know and appreciate established protocol and business etiquette. Poles generally speak calmly and softly and resent raised voices. Loud, aggressive behavior is unacceptable, especially from women. Try to be restrained in your use of hand gestures. Poles will remain formal and reserved until they get to know you.

As for business dress, you should dress well, but modestly. The business culture in Poland dislikes ostentatious displays of wealth. Your Polish counterparts will take more notice if your clothing is clean, well-pressed, and in good condition. Smaller companies have accepted a more casual manner of dress in the workplace—certainly more than the larger companies—but avoid bright colors and busy patterns. The same goes for women, although a scarf in a color or pattern, along with a demure suit, is fine. Preferred colors are black, gray, brown, beige, and dark blue.

Use perfumes and aftershave sparingly. Men should wear subdued suits and ties to formal events. When wearing jewelry, keep it elegant but modest.

Business Meetings

Business meetings often contain long pauses in conversation, whereby your counterparts may simply want to consider everything. Do not attempt to fill in every lull in conversation. Your company will gain more respect if several people are present for negotiations—and particularly if there is at least one middle-aged representative. In many European countries, age is given much respect. In any situation you're expected to show respect to older persons and women. If you're in any crowded place, offer your seat to someone older than you. This will make a great impression.

In business discussions, Poles usually move fairly quickly to substantive issues. Presentations need not be fancy, as long as they are clear and easily understood. Presenting in English is fine, but back-up documentation should also be in Polish, if possible. Never be condescending or offer an ultimatum: bargaining is not the Polish style. Contracts are serious. They should be clear, concise, and translated into both Polish and English. The first meeting will usually be used as a time to get acquainted rather than to do serious business.

Presentations should be a blend of well-organized information backed with statistics and case studies plus a feel-good factor relating to you as a person and your experience and the proposed relationship. This is because Poles make decisions not only based on evidence but also on their own experience, beliefs, and sense of right and wrong. Concerning visual aids, a Powerpoint presentation is nowadays the standard. Do not forget to ask if the right equipment is available. The best solution would be, of course, to provide all presentation materials yourself.

Due to the hierarchical nature of business, it should be obvious if the meeting you are attending is for exploration or finalization. If the decision makers are present in a meeting, then decisions can be made; otherwise, the purpose of the meeting will be considered to be information sharing and discussion. Be patient. In Poland, the decision-making process is slower than in North America or Germany. So be prepared to have several meetings before clinching a business deal.

Many business meetings are conducted during lunch but rarely breakfast. Suppertime is usually reserved for family or romantic dining, though 4 PM business lunches are not uncommon. If dining, wait for the host to taste his food before you begin eating. It is common to make to toast before and/or after the meal. If your host stands, so should you. Do not sit down again until the host does. Keep wrists above the table during the meal. When finished eating, place utensils next to each other, on the right side of the plate (in Poland, crossing utensils on the plate means you're still eating). Pub meetings are common practice, particularly among the younger businesspeople.

Communication

Poland is a perfect example of a high-context country, where there is a strong preference for doing business face to face. In the United States, much business is done over the phone or via e-mail; this rarely happens in Poland. It is equally important to know that in Poland (as in many countries) building relationships is the key to successful cooperation. You'll need to build trust before any important decisions can be made, and sincere trust does not usually extend beyond the family circles. The family or the relationship will usually take precedence over work, rules, and decisions.

It is customary to start business meetings in Poland with some introductory small talk. This allows you to become more acquainted with your Polish counterparts and establish an initial business rapport. Conversational topics may cover a wide range of issues, including public life, the weather, your family, your trip to Poland, interesting facts about your homeland, your short-term plans, as well as your own work experience. However, the subjects of money and politics should be avoided. After initial contacts, Polish people like a fairly personal approach, certainly when business contacts will be conducted over a longer period of time. Meaningful conversation is appreciated after business is finished, as a way of becoming closer.

The exchange of business cards is an accepted part of Polish business etiquette and should be done at the start of any initial meeting. Be sure to hand over your card first. Business cards and other paperwork can be printed in English. Handshakes are the normal way of initial introductions; between men, they are more robust than between men and women. A man should wait until the woman extends her hand before shaking. Kissing is common between men and women, women and women, and sometimes men and men; three "air kisses" are the norm. Shake hands with everyone individually in a group before departing. It's not sufficient to give a nod and a wave. Maintain eye contact and smile when being introduced. When greeting and shaking hands on arrival, don't do it over a threshold; this is considered bad luck (according to a local superstition). Never sit with one ankle rested on the opposite knee and never stand with hands in pockets.

Business negotiations in Poland adopt a reserved and contemplative approach, so don't be surprised by extended periods of silence; these are not uncommon and are an essential part of negotiating. Do smile and maintain direct eye contact during conversation with your Polish counterparts, as it helps to develop a feeling of trust with the people you are meeting. The Polish are particularly perceptive to nonverbal cues. Don't be surprised if, after the first few business meetings, your business partner engages in more friendly conversation with physical gestures such as backslapping. A more personal approach is preferred once initial relationships have been established. Don't over-compliment your Polish business colleagues as it may create the impression that you are insincere in your business dealings. Don't try to disguise you feelings and emotions; openness and honesty are qualities that your Polish colleagues will appreciate, and they will help build trust for future business transactions. Do try to learn some basic Polish words and greeting phrases, for instance "hello," "good-bye," and "thank you." Your Polish business contacts will welcome your efforts and perceive them as gracious gestures.

Business Gifts & Socializing

In order to build relationships with your business partners, it is common to give a small gift at an initial business meeting or upon the signing of a contract. Avoid giving items that display your company logo (the idea here is to make a personal connection with your business partner). Books (particularly best sellers in English), CDs, DVDs, or pens are all appropriate; in terms of value, limit yourself to gifts worth €200 or less.

The business lunch or dinner is not the time to make business decisions. Wait for your Polish business associate to bring up business before speaking about it. If you are invited to a Polish home, expect that dinner will begin at 8:30 PM and end after midnight. Your hosts will be insulted if you leave early. You should bring a gift, such as flowers or candy, with you to the dinner, but not wine. Relationship-building may be done over food. Never talk business at such occasions unless it is brought up by the other party. This time should be used to get to know your counterpart better and vice versa. When invited to a restaurant, the host usually pays the bill; however, it is also polite for the guest to offer. If you plan on being the host, speak with the manager or headwaiter and explain that you, and *only* you, will be paying the bill.

—Marta Ślusarczyk–Snoch

RECOMMENDED BOOKS & FILMS

FOR AN INTRODUCTION TO POLISH HISTORY AND POLITICS, check out *Heart of Europe: A Short History of Poland,* or the more detailed *God's Playground: A History of Poland,* both by Norman Davies. *The Polish Way* by Adam Zamoyski is another outstanding history of Poland.

Polish Literature

Adam Mickiewicz (1798–1855) is considered the greatest Polish romantic poet; his *Pan Tadeusz,* one of the greatest epic novels ever, is all in verse (some 10,000 lines, each in 13 syllables (in English, the full title is *Sir Thaddeus, or the Last Foray in Lithuania: A History of the Nobility in the Years 1811 and 1812 in Twelve Books of Verse*). Most Polish scholars have declared *Pan Tadeusz* to be untranslatable, and indeed, to translate it is a tremendous challenge. There have been at least two attempts, both written in verse: one by Kenneth MacKenzie (written in iambic pentameter, typical of much English poetry) and one by Marcel Weyland (who attempted to reproduce the original rhythm). The original flows so seamlessly that it leaves you out of breath; although some of the charm is inevitably lost in translation, *Sir Thaddeus* is still a great read.

Polish classics include the works of Henryk Sienkiewicz (1846–1916); his trilogy—*With Fire and Sword, The Deluge,* and *Fire in the Steppe (Pan Wołodyjowski)*—which describes Poland's wars with the Tartars, the Swedes, and the Cossacks in the 17th century is one of the most important works of modern Polish literature. Sienkiewicz was the first Polish laureate of the Nobel Prize in Literature, granted to him in 1905. In addition to its historical interest, the trilogy is simply a great read: adventure novels spiced up with love, intrigue, and humor, filled with interesting and vivid characters.

Bruno Schulz (1892–1947), a Polish Jew from Drohobych (today's Ukraine) was an artist as well as a writer—and his stories have often been likened to canvases painted with words. *The Street of Crocodiles* (also known as *Cinnamon Shops*) is a fantastical mix of Kabala, Kafka, surrealism, expressionism, and magical realism (well before its time), to name but a few characteristics.

Snow White and Russian Red (Wojna polsko-ruska pod flagą biało-czerwoną; 2002) is the debut novel by Dorota Masłowska (1983–), enfant terrible of Polish literature. Innovative, fresh, and controversial, the book is, at turns, hilarious, irreverent, and overflowing with black humor.

Witold Gombrowicz (1904–62), a literary genius with a knack for the grotesque, is the author of the brilliant experimental novel *Ferdydurke* (1937) and many other novels and plays.

Brilliant Stanisław Ignacy Witkiewicz (1885–1939) was an artist and a philosopher, as well as the son of the creator of the Zakopane style. Most of his works are plays in the absurdist style, including *Mother/Matka* and *Cobblers/Szewcy.*

Tadeusz Borowski (1922–51) wryly explores the fate of the Jews in Nazi concentration camps in Germany-occupied Poland in *This Way for the Gas, Ladies and Gentleman.* Jerzy Andrzejewski (1909–83) vividly captures the small window in Polish history immediately after the war, when partisans were still hiding in the fields and before the Soviets and their regime had fully entered the scene in *Ashes and Diamonds.* The first of a trilogy and the basis for the Andrzej Wajda film of the same name, it's a poignant account of Poland in the mid-1940s.

Another excellent book is by Eva Hoffman (1945–). Her memoir *Lost in Translation* is an account of her Jewish-Polish childhood and subsequent sense of dislocation when she and her family moved to British Columbia.

The novelist, essayist, and poet Czesław Miłosz (1911–2004), winner of the Nobel Prize for Literature in 1980, was one of Poland's greatest writers. His major prose works include *Native Realm,* his moral and intellectual autobiography from childhood to the 1950s; and *The Captive Mind,* an exploration of the power of Communist ideology over Polish intellectuals.

Another Nobel Prize–winner (1996) is poet Wisława Szymborska (1923–); several volumes of her poems have been translated into English. Perhaps the best introduction to her work is *View with a Grain of Sand: Selected Poems.* The first-rate translation is by Stanisław Barańczak and Clare Cavanagh.

Recently departed Stanisław Lem (1921–2006) was a Polish science-fiction, philosophical, and satirical writer of international renown, author of *Solaris, The Cyberiad,* and many other excellent books.

Madame (1998), by Antoni Libera (1949–), is a late writing debut of the translator (of Beckett, among other authors) and theater director. It is a coming-of-age novel set in a realistically depicted Cold War Warsaw, about a high-school student obsessed with his French teacher. It is a beautifully written novel in classical tradition, with a well-designed, gripping plot.

Some newer, and very readable Polish novels include *Miss Nobody* (1994) by Tomek Tryzna, *White Raven* (1995) by Andrzej Stasiuk, and *Who Was David Weiser?* (1987) by Paweł Huelle.

Polish Cinema

Many movies by Polish directors are windows into Poland's 20th-century history. Roman Polański's *The Pianist,* and Andrzej Wajda's *Canal (Kanał)* are human dramas set in World War II Warsaw. *The Tin Drum,* German director Volker Schlöndorff's adaptation of the novel by Günter Grass, tells the story of a boy in wartime Gdańsk and is a metaphorical account of that region's history.

Andrzej Wajda, co-founder of the Polish Film school and winner of an Academy Award for his life's oeuvre, often addressed formative moments in modern Polish history: his *Ashes and Diamonds (Popiół i diament)* presents political and human dilemmas immediately after World War II; *Man of Marble (Człowiek z marmuru),* the dark years of Stalinism; and the sequel, *Man of Iron (Człowiek z żelaza),* the birth and first success of Solidarity. The director is now working on his new project on the Katyń massacre.

Another Polish classic is prematurely departed Krzysztof Kieślowski, writer and director of the *Dekalog (Decalogue),* 10 movies that constitute contemporary, philosophical commentaries to the Commandments, and *Trzy Kolory: Niebieski, Biały, Czerwony (Three Colors: Blue, White, and Red),* allegorical interpretations of liberty, equality, and fraternity (the three colors of the French flag denoting the ideals of the French Revolution).

Polish cinematography has its "cult" movies, typically grotesque comedies that may be difficult to comprehend for non-Polish audiences, but why not give it a try? Although cultural, political, and social context is crucial here, you can enjoy these comedies on many different levels, not least for their surreal elements. Some of these bizarre-but-brilliant cult movies include Marek Piwowski's *Rejs (A Trip Down the River;* 1970), about a cruise with no apparent purpose or sense; it's a hilarious comedy, but not without some depth. Andrzej Kondratiuk's *Hydrozagadka (Water Enigma;* 1970) is a fabulous and totally mad Polish version—or rather, a parody—of an American superhero, featuring a Maharaja and a Nile crocodile in the Mazurian lakes. Stanisław Bareja's *Miś (Teddy Bear;* 1980), one of the most famous and best loved Polish comedies, reveals the nonsensical and surreal quality to the Polish everyday life in the 1970s.

Juliusz Machulski's *Seksmisja* (*Sex-Mission*; 1984) is an entertaining sci-fi comedy, which turns out to be another satire on the Communist system.

Some of the most interesting recent works include *Jasminum* (2006), the latest movie by Jan Jakub Kolski, which has elements of the fantastic and the magical, in the setting of Polish provincial life and landscape. (This director specializes in warm and philosophical films with a message.)

Krzysztof Krauze and his partner Joanna Kos-Krauze, on the other hand, look more into the social domain, and to our behavior in contemporary reality, both at home and beyond, trying to understand what happens to the human soul in this context. Their film *Plac Zbawiciela* (*Saviour Square*; 2006) is a powerful and shaking session of social psychoanalysis.

If you are a serious movie fan, Poland has a lot of great film festivals. Two are particularly interesting: Era Nowe Horyzonty (Era New Horizons Film Festival) is held in Wrocw in late July; Camerimage is held in Łódź, usually in late November. Most films in Poland—at regular screenings and at festivals—are not dubbed; they are shown in the original version with Polish subtitles.

POLISH VOCABULARY

English	Polish	Pronunciation

Basics

English	Polish	Pronunciation
Yes/no	Tak/nie	tahk/nye
Please	Proszę	**pro**-sheh
Thank you	Dziękuję	dzhen-**koo**-yeh
Excuse me	Przepraszam	psheh-**prah**-shahm
Hello	Dzień dobry	**dzhehn dohb**-ry
Do you (m/f) speak English?	Czy pan (pani) mówi po angielsku?	chee **pahn** (**pahn**-ee) moovie poh ahn-**gyel**-skuu?
I don't speak Polish.	Nie mówię po Polsku.	nyeh **moohv**-yeh po-**pohl**-skoo
I don't understand.	Nie rozumiem.	nyeh rohz-**oo**-myehm
Please speak slowly.	Proszę mówić wolniej.	proh-sheh **moo**-veech **vohl**-nyah
Please write it down.	Proszę napisać.	proh-sheh nah-pee-sahtch
I am American (m/f)	Jestem Amerykaninem/Amerykanką	**yest**-em ah-mer-i-**kahn**-in-em/ ah-mer-i-**kahn**-ka
English (m/f)	Anglikiem/Angielką	ahn-**gleek**-em/ ahn-**geel**-ka
My name is . . .	Nazywam się . . .	nah-**ziv**-ahm sheh
On the right/left	Na prawo/lewo	nah-**prah**-vo/**lyeh**-vo
Arrivals/departures	Przyloty/odloty	pshee-**loh**-tee/ ohd-**loh**-tee
Where is . . . ?	Gdzie jest . . . ?	gdzhyeh yest
. . . the station?	. . . Dworzec kolejowy?	**dvoh**-zhets koh-lay-oh-vee
. . . the train?	. . . Pociąg?	**poh**-chohnk
. . . the bus?	. . . Autobus?	a'oo-**toh**-boos
. . . the airport?	. . . Lotnisko?	loht-**nees**-koh
. . . the post office?	. . . Poczta?	**poch**-tah
. . . the bank?	. . . Bank?	bahnk
Stop here, please.	Proszę się tu zatrzymać.	**proh**-sheh sheh too zah-**tchee**-mahch
I would like (m/f) . . .	Chciałbym . . . / Chciałabym . . .	**kh'chow**-beem/ kh'chow-**ah**-beem
How much?	Ile?	**ee**-leh
Letters/postcards	Listy/kartki	**lees**-tee/**kahrt**-kee
By airmail	Lotniczy	loht-**nee**-chee
Help!	Na pomoc!	na **po**-motz

Numbers

English	Polish	Pronunciation
One	Jeden	**yeh**-den
Two	Dwa	dvah

Three	Trzy	tchee
Four	Cztery	**chteh**-ree
Five	Pięć	pyehnch
Six	Sześć	shsyshch
Seven	Siedem	**shyeh**-dem
Eight	Osiem	**oh**-shyem
Nine	Dziewięć	**dzhyeh**-vyehnch
Ten	Dziesięć	**dzhyeh**-shehnch
One hundred	Sto	stoh
One thousand	Tysiąc	**tee**-shonts

Days of the Week

Sunday	Niedziela	nyeh-**dzhy'e**-la
Monday	Poniedziałek	poh-nyeh-**dzhya**-wek
Tuesday	Wtorek	**ftohr**-ek
Wednesday	Środa	**shroh**-da
Thursday	Czwartek	**chvahr**-tek
Friday	Piątek	**pyohn**-tek
Saturday	Sobota	soh-**boh**-ta

Where to Sleep

A room	Pokój	**poh**-kooy
The key	Klucz	klyuch
With bath/shower	Z łazienką/ prysznicem	zwah-**zhen**-koh/ spree-**shnee**-tsem

Food

The menu	Menu	**men**-yoo
The check, please.	Proszę rachunek	**proh**-sheh rah-**kh'oon**-ehk
Breakfast	Śniadanie	shnya-**dahn**-iyeh
Lunch	Obiad	**oh**-byat
Dinner	Kolacja	koh-**lah**-ts'yah
Beef	Wołowina	voh-woh-**veen**-a
Bread and butter	Chleb i masło	kh'lyep ee **mahs**-woh
Vegetables	Jarzyny	yah-**zhin**-ee
Salt/pepper	Sól/pieprz	sool/pyehpsh
Bottle of wine	Butelkę wina	boo-**tehl**-keh **vee**-na
Beer	Piwo	**pee**-voh
(Mineral) Water	Wodę (mineralną)	**voh**-deh (**mee-nehr**-ahl-nohn
Coffee with milk	Kawę z mliekiem	**kah**-veh **zmlehkyem**
Tea with lemon	Herbatę z cytryną	kh'ehr-**bah**-teh **ststrin**-ohn

Poland
Essentials

There are planners, and there are those who fly by the seat of their pants. We happily place ourselves among the planners. Our writers and editors try to anticipate all the issues you may face before and during any journey, and then they do their research. This section is the product of their efforts. Use it to get excited about your trip to Poland, to inform your travel planning, or to guide you on the road should the seat of your pants start to feel threadbare.

GETTING STARTED

We're very proud of our Web site: Fodors. com, a great place to begin any journey. Scan Travel Wire for suggested itineraries, travel deals, restaurant and hotel openings, and other up-to-the-minute info. Check out Booking to research prices and book plane tickets, hotel rooms, rental cars, and vacation packages. Head to Talk for on-the-ground pointers from travelers who frequent our message boards. You can also link to loads of other travel-related resources.

▌ RESOURCES

ONLINE TRAVEL TOOLS

The Polish National Tourist Office has a comprehensive Web site with information about every major and minor tourist destination in Poland, and it's a good place to start when you're planning a trip. When it comes time to book your hotels, you may wish to take a look at the Web site for Travel Poland, a booking engine for hotels in Poland that also has some general information about traveling in the country.

All About Poland Polish National Tourist Office ⊕ www.polandtour.org. **Travel Poland** ⊕ www.travelpoland.com.

Currency Conversion Google ⊕ www. google.com does currency conversion. Just type in the amount you want to convert and an explanation of how you want it converted (e.g., "14 Swiss francs in dollars"), and then *voilá.* **Oanda.com** ⊕ www.oanda.com also allows you to print out a handy table with the current day's conversion rates. **XE.com** ⊕ www.xe.com is a good currency conversion Web site.

Safety Transportation Security Administration (TSA) ⊕ www.tsa.gov

Time Zones Timeanddate.com ⊕ www. timeanddate.com/worldclock can help you figure out the correct time anywhere in the world.

Weather Accuweather.com ⊕ www. accuweather.com is an independent weather-forecasting service with especially good coverage of hurricanes. **Weather.com** ⊕ www. weather.com is the Web site for the Weather Channel.

Other Resources CIA World Factbook ⊕ www.cia.gov/cia/publications/factbook/index.html has profiles of every country in the world. It's a good source if you need some quick facts and figures.

VISITOR INFORMATION

Before you leave, you can get brochures about travel to Poland from the Polish National Tourist Office in the U.S. **Polish National Tourist Office** ☎ 201/420–9910 ⊕ www.polandtour.org.

▌ THINGS TO CONSIDER

GEAR

In general, you should pack comfortable and casual clothing that can be layered in case temperatures change throughout the day, as they often do in the spring and fall. There aren't many occasion where formal dress is required, so "dressy casual" will work in almost all circumstances. The only places where you might need smarter clothes would be at top-class restaurants, opera houses, and theaters—but even there, the degree of tolerance to more casual dress is high. Do bring comfortable walking shoes as cobblestones are not uncommon in historical parts of old towns. Summers can be hot, and winters bitterly cold, so dress appropriately for the season.

Except for top- to mid-range hotels, which supply towels, soap, and other toiletries, simpler accommodation (and particularly "rooms to rent" or "agrotourism" farms) may not have these, so come equipped. Although sanitation standards have improved over the recent years, some public toilets may not have toilet paper and it is wise to carry a packet of tissues.

Condoms are available from pharmacies, kiosks, supermarkets, and petrol stations, while contraceptive pills are prescription only. You cannot bring narcotics of any kind into Poland—unless you have a prescription (bring a copy).

GOVERNMENT ADVISORIES

As different countries have different world views, look at travel advisories from a range of governments to get more of a sense of what's going on out there. And be sure to parse the language carefully. For example, a warning to "avoid all travel" carries more weight than one urging you to "avoid nonessential travel," and both are much stronger than a plea to "exercise caution." A U.S. government travel warning is more permanent (though not necessarily more serious) than a so-called public announcement, which carries an expiration date.

The U.S. Department of State's Web site has more than just travel warnings and advisories. The consular information sheets issued for every country have general safety tips, entry requirements (though be sure to verify these with the country's embassy), and other useful details.

■ TIP→ If you're a U.S. citizen traveling abroad, consider registering online with the State Department (https://travelregistration. state.gov/ibrs/), so the government will know to look for you should a crisis occur in the country you're visiting.

There are no specific warnings against travel to Poland except the usual concerns about pick-pockets and street crime in major cities.

General Information & Warnings **Australian Department of Foreign Affairs & Trade** ⊕ www.smartraveller.gov.au. **Consular Affairs Bureau of Canada** ⊕ www.voyage.gc. ca. **U.K. Foreign & Commonwealth Office** ⊕ www.fco.gov.uk/travel. **US Department of State** ⊕ www.travel.state.gov.

SHIPPING LUGGAGE AHEAD

Imagine globetrotting with only a carry-on in tow. Shipping your luggage in advance via an air-freight service is an effective—albeit expensive—way to cut

WORD OF MOUTH

After your trip, be sure to rate the places you visited and share your experiences and travel tips with us and other Fodorites in Travel Ratings and Talk on www.fodors. com.

down on backaches, hassles, and stress—especially if your packing list includes strollers, car-seats, etc. There are some things to be aware of, though. First, research carry-on restrictions; if you absolutely need something that isn't practical to ship and isn't allowed in carry-ons, this strategy isn't for you. Second, plan to send your bags several days in advance to US destinations and as much as two weeks in advance to some international destinations. Third, plan to spend some money: it will cost least $100 to send a small piece of luggage, a golf bag, or a pair of skis to a domestic destination, much more to places overseas. Some people use Federal Express to ship their bags, but this can cost even more than air-freight services. All these services insure your bag (for most, the limit is $1,000, but you should verify that amount); you can, however, purchase additional insurance for about $1 per $100 of value.

Luggage Concierge ☎ 800/288-9818 ⊕ www.luggageconcierge.com. **Luggage Express** ☎ 866/744-7224 ⊕ www. usxpluggageexpress.com. **Luggage Free** ☎ 800/361-6871 ⊕ www.luggagefree.com. **Sports Express** ☎ 800/357-4174 ⊕ www. sportsexpress.com specializes in shipping golf clubs and other sports equipment. **Virtual Bellhop** ☎ 877/235-5467 ⊕ www. virtualbellhop.com.

PASSPORTS & VISAS

Americans traveling to Poland need to have a valid passport, but no visas are required for stays of up to 90 days. Your passport should be valid for at least three months after the time you enter the country. For the latest official policies regard-

PACKING 101

Why do some people travel with a convoy of huge suitcases yet never have a thing to wear? How do others pack a duffle with a week's worth of outfits *and* supplies for every contingency? We realize that packing is a matter of style, but there's a lot to be said for traveling light. These tips help fight the battle of the bulging bag.

Make a list. In a recent Fodor's survey, 29% of respondents said they make lists (and often pack) a week before a trip. You can use your list to pack and to repack at the end of your trip. It can also serve as a record of the contents of your suitcase—in case it disappears in transit.

Think it through. What's the weather like? Is this a business trip? A cruise? Going abroad? In some places dress may be more or less conservative than you're used to. As you create your itinerary, note outfits next to each activity (don't forget accessories).

Edit your wardrobe. Plan to wear everything twice (better yet, thrice) and to do laundry along the way. Stick to one basic look—urban chic, sporty casual, etc. Build around one or two neutrals and an accent (e.g., black, white, and olive green). Women can freshen looks by changing scarves or jewelry. For a week's trip, you can look smashing with three bottoms, four or five tops, a sweater, and a jacket.

Be practical. Put comfortable shoes atop your list. (Did we need to say this?) Pack lightweight, wrinkle-resistant, compact, washable items. (Or this?) Stack and roll clothes, so they'll wrinkle less. It's best to select luggage you can readily carry. Porters, like good butlers, are hard to find these days.

Check weight and size limitations. On many airlines, your checked bags may weigh no more than 50 pounds, and for some airlines, the limit is less. Always verify your airline's baggage size and weight limits since you'll be charged extra for every pound you go over.

Check carry-on restrictions. Research restrictions with the TSA. Rules vary abroad, so check them with your airline if you're traveling overseas on a foreign carrier. Consider packing all but essentials (travel documents, prescription meds, wallet) in checked luggage. This leads to a "pack only what you can afford to lose" approach that might help you streamline.

Rethink valuables. On U.S. flights, airlines are liable for only about $2,800 per person for bags. On international flights, the liability limit is around $635 per bag. But items like computers, cameras, and jewelry aren't covered, and as gadgetry regularly goes on and off the list of carry-on no-no's, you can't count on keeping things safe by keeping them close. Although comprehensive travel policies may cover luggage, the liability limit is often a pittance. Your home-owner's policy may cover you sufficiently when you travel—or not.

Lock it up. If you must pack valuables, consider using either plastic cable ties or twist-ties; while these can be easily broken, they may give luggage pilferers cause to look at more easily accessible bags. You can also use TSA-approved locks (about $10) that can be unlocked by all U.S. security personnel, but sometimes these are cut anyway if security wants to look inside your bag.

Tag it. Always tag your luggage; use your business address if you don't want people to know your home address. Put the same information (and a copy of your itinerary) inside your luggage, too.

Report problems immediately. If your bags—or things inside them—are damaged or go astray, file a written claim with your airline *before leaving the airport*. Most lost bags are found within 48 hours, so alert the airline to your whereabouts for two or three days. If your bag was opened for security reasons in the United States and something is missing, file a claim with the TSA.

ing travel to Poland, you can look at the Web site of the Embassy of Poland in Washington, DC. As a member of the European Union, Poland has immigration laws that are in line with other EU member countries.

Info Embassy of Poland ⊕ www.
polandembassy.org.

PASSPORTS

We're always surprised at how few Americans have passports—only 25% at this writing. This number is expected to grow in coming years, since you must now have a valid passport to fly into or out of the U.S. unless you are going to Puerto Rico or the U.S. Virgin Islands. Remember this: a passport verifies both your identity and nationality—a great reason to have one.

U.S. passports are valid for 10 years. You must apply in person if you're getting a passport for the first time; if your previous passport was lost, stolen, or damaged; or if your previous passport has expired and was issued more than 15 years ago or when you were under 16. All children under 18 must appear in person to apply for or renew a passport. Both parents must accompany any child under 14 (or send a notarized statement with their permission) and provide proof of their relationship to the child.

There are 13 regional passport offices, as well as 7,000 passport acceptance facilities in post offices, public libraries, and other governmental offices. If you're renewing a passport, you can do so by mail. Forms are available at passport acceptance facilities and online.

The cost to apply for a new passport is $97 for adults, $82 for children under 16; renewals are $67. Allow six weeks for processing, both for first-time passports and renewals. For an expediting fee of $60 you can reduce this time to about two weeks. If your trip is less than two weeks away, you can get a passport even more rapidly by going to a passport office with the necessary documentation. Private expediters can get things done in as little as

---

INSPIRATION

Adam Zamoyski's *The Polish Way: A Thousand Year History of the Poles and their Culture* is a comprehensive account of Polish history. *Mila 18,* by Leon Uris, tells the story of the Warsaw Ghetto Uprising during World War II in a novelistic form. Roman Polański's *The Pianist,* and Andrzej Wajda's *Canal (Kanał)* show human dramas set in World War II Warsaw. *The Tin Drum,* is an adaptation of the novel by Günter Grass, set in Gdańsk.

---

48 hours, but charge hefty fees for their services.

■ **TIP→** Before your trip, make two copies of your passport's data page (one for someone at home and another for you to carry separately). Or scan the page and e-mail it to someone at home and/or yourself.

VISAS

A visa is essentially formal permission to enter a country. Visas allow countries to keep track of you and other visitors—and generate revenue (from application fees). You *always* need a visa to enter a foreign country; however, many countries routinely issue tourist visas on arrival, particularly to U.S. or EU citizens. When your passport is stamped or scanned in the immigration line, you're actually being issued a visa. Sometimes you have to stand in a separate line and pay a small fee to get your stamp before going through immigration, but you can still do this at the airport on arrival. Getting a visa isn't always that easy. Some countries require that you arrange for one in advance of your trip. There's usually—but not always—a fee involved, and said fee may be nominal ($10 or less) or substantial ($100 or more).

If you must apply for a visa in advance, you can usually do it in person or by mail. When you apply by mail, you send your passport to a designated consulate, where your passport will be examined and the visa issued. Expediters—usually the same ones who handle expedited passport applications—can do all the work of obtaining your visa for you; however, there's always an additional cost (often more than $50 per visa).

Most visas limit you to a single trip—usually during the actual dates of your planned vacation. Other visas allow you to visit as many times as you wish for a specific period of time. Remember that requirements change, sometimes at the drop of a hat, and the burden is on you to make sure that you have the appropriate visas. Otherwise, you'll be turned away at the airport or, worse, deported after you arrive in the country. No company or travel insurer gives refunds if your travel plans are disrupted because you didn't have the correct visa.

U.S. Passport Information U.S. Department of State ☎ 877/487-2778 ⊕ http://travel. state.gov/passport.

U.S. Passport & Visa Expediters A. Briggs Passport & Visa Expeditors ☎ 800/806-0581 or 202/464-3000 ⊕ www.abriggs.com. **American Passport Express** ☎ 800/455-5166 or 603/559-9888 ⊕ www. americanpassport.com. **Passport Express** ☎ 800/362-8196 or 401/272-4612 ⊕ www. passportexpress.com. **Travel Document Systems** ☎ 800/874-5100 or 202/638-3800 ⊕ www.traveldocs.com. **Travel the World Visas** ☎ 866/886-8472 or 301/495-7700 ⊕ www.world-visa.com.

GENERAL REQUIREMENTS FOR POLAND	
Passport	Must be valid for 3 months after date of arrival.
Visa	Not required for Americans.
Vaccinations	No special vaccinations required.
Driving	No international driver's license required.
Departure Tax	There are no separate departure taxes in Poland.

SHOTS & MEDICATIONS

There are no special health concerns associated with travel to Poland. For more information *see* Health *in* On the Ground in Poland, *below.*

You might consider optional vaccinations. It is always a good idea to get a Hepatitis B vaccination (Hepatitis B is relatively common in Polish hospitals, making the vaccination important for a trip here). In flu season (autumn through spring) it is a good idea to get a flu vaccination; consult your physician. ■ TIP→ If you travel a lot internationally—particularly to developing nations (though Poland is not a developing nation)—refer to the CDC's *Health Information for International Travel* (aka Traveler's Health Yellow Book). Info from it is posted on the CDC Web site (www.cdc.gov/travel/yb), or you can buy a copy from your local bookstore for $24.95. **Health Warnings National Centers for Disease Control & Prevention** (CDC) ☎ 877/394-8747 international travelers' health line ⊕ www.cdc.gov/travel. **World Health Organization** (WHO) ⊕ www.who.int.

TRIP INSURANCE

What kind of coverage do you honestly need? Do you even need trip insurance at all? Take a deep breath and read on.

We believe that comprehensive trip insurance is especially valuable if you're booking a very expensive or complicated trip (particularly to an isolated region) or if you're booking far in advance. Who knows what could happen six months down the road? But whether or not you get insurance has more to do with how comfortable you are assuming all that risk yourself.

Comprehensive travel policies typically cover trip-cancellation and interruption, letting you cancel or cut your trip short because of a personal emergency, illness, or, in some cases, acts of terrorism in your destination. Such policies also cover evacuation and medical care. Some also cover you for trip delays because of bad weather or mechanical problems as well as for lost or delayed baggage. Another type of coverage to look for is financial default—that is, when your trip is disrupted because a tour operator, airline, or cruise line goes

Trip Insurance Resources

INSURANCE COMPARISON SITES		
Insure My Trip.com		www.insuremytrip.com
Square Mouth.com		www.quotetravelinsurance.com
COMPREHENSIVE TRAVEL INSURERS		
Access America	866/807-3982	www.accessamerica.com
CSA Travel Protection	800/873-9855	www.csatravelprotection.com
HTH Worldwide	610/254-8700 or 888/243-2358	www.hthworldwide.com
Travelex Insurance	888/457-4602	www.travelex-insurance.com
Travel Guard International	715/345-0505 or 800/826-4919	www.travelguard.com
Travel Insured International	800/243-3174	www.travelinsured.com
MEDICAL-ONLY INSURERS		
International Medical Group	800/628-4664	www.imglobal.com
International SOS	215/942-8000 or 713/521-7611	www.internationalsos.com
Wallach & Company	800/237-6615 or 504/687-3166	www.wallach.com

out of business. Generally you must buy this when you book your trip or shortly thereafter, and it's only available to you if your operator isn't on a list of excluded companies. Companies that are already in bankruptcy are always on these exclusion lists.

If you're going abroad, consider buying medical-only coverage at the very least. Neither Medicare nor some private insurers cover medical expenses anywhere outside of the United States, including Mexico and Canada (also including time aboard a cruise ship, even if it leaves from a U.S. port). Medical-only policies typically reimburse you for medical care (excluding that related to preexisting conditions) and hospitalization abroad, and provide for evacuation. You still have to pay the bills and await reimbursement from the insurer, though.

Expect comprehensive travel insurance policies to cost about 4% to 7% of the total price of your trip (it's more like 12% if you're over age 70). A medical-only policy may or may not be cheaper than a comprehensive policy. Always read the fine print of your policy to make sure that you are covered for the risks that are of most concern to you. Compare several policies to make sure you're getting the best price and range of coverage available.

BOOKING YOUR TRIP

Unless your cousin is a travel agent, you're probably among the millions of people who make most of their travel arrangements online. But have you ever wondered just what the differences are between an online travel agent (a Web site through which you make reservations instead of going directly to the airline, hotel, or car-rental company), a discounter (a firm that does a high volume of business with a hotel chain or airline and accordingly gets good prices), a wholesaler (one that makes cheap reservations in bulk and then resells them to people like you), and an aggregator (one that compares all the offerings so you don't have to)? Is it truly better to book directly on an airline or hotel Web site? And when does a real live travel agent come in handy?

ONLINE

You really have to shop around. A travel wholesaler such as Hotels.com or Hotel-Club.net can be a source of good rates, as can discounters such as Hotwire or Priceline, particularly if you can bid for your hotel room or airfare. Indeed, such sites sometimes have deals that are unavailable elsewhere. They do, however, tend to work only with hotel chains (which often makes them just plain useless for getting hotel reservations outside of major cities) or big airlines (so that often leaves out upstarts like jetBlue and some foreign carriers like Air India). Also, with discounters and wholesalers you must generally prepay, and everything is nonrefundable. And before you fork over the dough, be sure to check the terms and conditions, so you know what a given company will do for you if there's a problem and what you'll have to deal with on your own.

■ TIP➔ To be absolutely sure everything was processed correctly, confirm reservations made through online travel agents, discounters, and wholesalers directly with your hotel before leaving home.

Booking engines like Expedia, Travelocity, and Orbitz are actually travel agents, albeit high-volume, online ones. And airline travel packagers like American Airlines Vacations and Virgin Vacations—well, they're travel agents, too. But they may still not work with all the world's hotels.

An aggregator site will search many sites and pull the best prices for airfares, hotels, and rental cars from them. Most aggregators compare the major travel-booking sites such as Expedia, Travelocity, and Orbitz; some also look at airline Web sites, though rarely the sites of smaller budget airlines. Some aggregators also compare other travel products, including complex packages—a good thing, as you can sometimes get the best overall deal by booking an air-and-hotel package.

WITH A TRAVEL AGENT

If you use an agent—brick-and-mortar or virtual—you'll usually pay a fee for the service. And know that the service you get from some online agents isn't comprehensive. For example Expedia and Travelocity don't search for prices on budget airlines like jetBlue, Southwest, or small foreign carriers. That said, some agents (online or not) *do* have access to fares that are difficult to find otherwise, and the savings can more than make up for any surcharge.

A knowledgeable brick-and-mortar travel agent can be a godsend if you're booking a cruise, a package trip that's not available to you directly, an air pass, or a complicated itinerary including several overseas flights. What's more, travel agents who specialize in a destination may have exclusive access to certain deals and insider information on things such as charter flights. Agents who specialize in types of travelers (senior citizens, gays and lesbians, naturists) or types of trips (cruises, luxury travel, safaris) can also be invaluable.

Online Booking Resources

AGGREGATORS	
Kayak	www.kayak.com also looks at cruises and vacation packages.
Mobissimo	www.mobissimo.com.
Qixo	www.qixo.com also compares cruises, vacation packages, and even travel insurance.
Sidestep	www.sidestep.com also compares vacation packages and lists travel deals.
Travelgrove	www.travelgrove.com also compares cruises and packages.
BOOKING ENGINES	
Cheap Tickets	www.cheaptickets.com is a discounter.
Expedia	www.expedia.com is a large online agency that charges a booking fee for airline tickets.
Hotwire	www.hotwire.com is a discounter.
lastminute.com	www.lastminute.com specializes in last-minute travel; the main site is for the U.K., but it has a link to a U.S. site.
Luxury Link	www.luxurylink.com has auctions (surprisingly good deals) as well as offers on the high-end side of travel.
Onetravel.com	www.onetravel.com is a discounter for hotels, car rentals, airfares, and packages.
Orbitz	www.orbitz.com charges a booking fee for airline tickets, but gives a clear breakdown of fees and taxes before you book.
Priceline.com	www.priceline.com is a discounter that also allows bidding.
Travel.com	www.travel.com allows you to compare its rates with those of other booking engines.
Travelocity	www.travelocity.com charges a booking fee for airline tickets, but promises good problem resolution.
ONLINE ACCOMMODATIONS	
Hotelbook.com	www.hotelbook.com focuses on independent hotels worldwide.
Hotel Club	www.hotelclub.net is good for major cities worldwide.
Hotels.com	www.hotels.com is a big Expedia-owned wholesaler that offers rooms in hotels all over the world.
Quikbook	www.quikbook.com offers "pay when you stay" reservations that let you settle your bill at check out, not when you book.
Stay Poland	www.staypoland.com is a comprehensive booking engine.
Travel Poland	www.travelpoland.com is a booking engine for Poland, and sometimes offers good deals.
OTHER RESOURCES	
Bidding For Travel	www.biddingfortravel.com is a good place to figure out what you can get and for how much before bidding on, say, Priceline.

For example, a top-notch agent planning your trip to Russia will make sure you get the correct visa application and complete it on time; the one booking your cruise may get you a cabin upgrade or arrange to have bottle of champagne chilling in your cabin when you embark. And complain about the surcharges all you like, but when things don't work out the way you'd hoped, it's nice to have an agent to put things right.

■ **TIP→** Remember that Expedia, Travelocity, and Orbitz are travel agents, not just booking engines. To resolve any problems with a reservation made through these companies, contact them first.

You can sometimes get very good deals on travel to Poland if you book through the Polish tour operator at Orbis Travel, which was formerly the state-run tour company in the Communist days. You can arrange everything from a simple airfare and hotel package to a full-service, organized tour. The company's main office is in New York. But you shouldn't think that Orbis is your only option; it's just the biggest name. There are now a lot of other private companies, including Emmerson & Lumico, Visit.pl, and Mazurkas Travel, though these are all based in Poland rather than in the U.S.

Agent Resources American Society of Travel Agents ☎ 703/739-2782 ⊕ www.travelsense. org.

Poland Travel Specialists Emmerson & Lumico ⊕ www.lumico.pl. **Mazurkas Travel** ⊕ www.mazurkas.pl. **Orbis Travel** ☎ 212/867-5011 or 800/867-6526 ⊕ www. orbistravel.com. **Visit.pl** ⊕ www.visit.pl.

■ ACCOMMODATIONS

In general, the quantity, quality, and variety of accommodation choices in Poland has increased immensely over the last 15 years. Most Polish hotels are now on par with those in the rest of the EU, although you may still find places—usually at the lower end of the price scale—where both the facilities and the customer-service approach are more reminiscent of pre-liberation Poland.

With the development of better infrastructure, prices have also increased, although they are still lower than in much of Western Europe or the U.S. (this difference is more pronounced outside of the larger cities). High season is April through October, and prices go down slightly between November and March. Some hotels, especially those in major cities, offer lower weekend rates. Unlike in some Eastern European countries, prices for domestic and international tourists are the same.

The word for hotel in Polish is spelled the same as in English, but the pronunciation is slightly different—the stress falls on the first syllable, and the "o" sound is like in "hot." It is a broad term, usually encompassing also B&Bs and pensions (the latter are also sometimes called *pensjonat*).

It is worth noting that an increasing number of interesting hotels have been created in converted historical buildings, including some castles and palaces (the word for castle is *zamek,* and palace is *pałac*). You can also come across hotels with well-developed health and beauty facilities (mostly in holiday resorts), usually referred to as *hotel-spas.*

In seaside, lakeside, and mountain resorts, you can find also other types of accommodation: *pokoje* are private rooms to rent, usually pretty basic but also nice and neat. Rural tourism is popular, especially among domestic tourists—farms converted or partly converted into pensions are called *gospodarstwa agroturystyczne.* A *Dom wczasowy* or *ośrodek wczasowy* is a large hotel or resort, usually catering to long-term stays (a minimum of one week), with optional full board.

Despite an ever-expanding number of hotels in top tourist and business destinations—cities such as Kraków, Warsaw, Gdańsk, and Poznań—it is a good idea to book well in advance.

CATEGORY	COST
$$$$	Over zł 800
$$$	zł 500–zł 800
$$	zł 300–zł 500
$	zł 150–zł 300
¢	under zł 150

All prices are in Polish złoty for a standard double room in high season with a private bath and breakfast; in Poland, taxes are usually included in quote room rates.

Most hotels and other lodgings require you to give your credit-card details before they will confirm your reservation. If you don't feel comfortable e-mailing this information, ask if you can fax it (some places even prefer faxes). However you book, get confirmation in writing and have a copy of it handy when you check in.

Be sure you understand the hotel's cancellation policy. Some places allow you to cancel without any kind of penalty—even if you prepaid to secure a discounted rate—if you cancel at least 24 hours in advance. Others require you to cancel a week in advance or penalize you the cost of one night. Small inns and B&Bs are most likely to require you to cancel far in advance. Most hotels allow children under a certain age to stay in their parents' room at no extra charge, but others charge for them as extra adults; find out the cutoff age for discounts.

■ TIP→ Assume that hotels operate on the European Plan (**EP**, no meals) unless we specify that they use the Breakfast Plan (**BP**, with full breakfast), Continental Plan (**CP**, continental breakfast), Full American Plan (**FAP**, all meals), or Modified American Plan (**MAP**, breakfast and dinner).

APARTMENT & HOUSE RENTALS

Short-term apartment rentals are possible in Poland but are more prevalent in major cities such as Kraków or Warsaw. Local agencies are recommended in individual destination chapters. Some large interna-

10 WAYS TO SAVE

1. Join "frequent guest" programs. You may get preferential treatment in room choice and/or upgrades in your favorite chains.

2. Call direct. You can sometimes get a better price if you call a hotel's local toll-free number (if available) rather than a central reservations number.

3. Check online. Check hotel Web sites, as not all chains are represented on all travel sites.

4. Look for specials. Always inquire about packages and corporate rates.

5. Look for price guarantees. For overseas trips, look for guaranteed rates. With your rate locked in you won't pay more, even if the price goes up in the local currency (of course, you also won't pay less if the dollar goes up).

6. Look for weekend deals at business hotels. High-end chains catering to business travelers are often busy only on weekdays; to fill rooms they often drop rates dramatically on weekends.

7. Ask about taxes. Verify whether local hotel taxes are included in quoted rates. In some places taxes can add 20% or more to your bill.

8. Read the fine print. Watch for add-ons, including resort fees, energy surcharges, and "convenience" fees for such things as unlimited local phone service you won't use or a free newspaper in a language you can't read.

9. Know when to go. If your destination's high season is December through April and you're trying to book, say, in late April, you might save money by changing your dates by a week or two. Ask when rates go down, though: if your dates straddle peak and non-peak seasons, a property may still charge peak-season rates for the entire stay.

10. Weigh your options (we can't say this enough). Weigh transportation times and costs against the savings of staying in a hotel that's cheaper because it's out of the way.

tional rental companies represent properties in Poland.

Barclay International Group ☎ 516/364-0064 or 800/845-6636 ⊕ www.barclayweb.com. **Interhome** ☎ 954/791-8282 or 800/882-6864 ⊕ www.interhome.us.

HOME EXCHANGES

With a direct home exchange you stay in someone else's home while they stay in yours. Some outfits also deal with vacation homes, so you're not actually staying in someone's full-time residence, just their vacant weekend place.

Exchange Clubs Home Exchange.com ☎ 800/877-8723 ⊕ www.homeexchange.com; $59.95 for a 1-year online listing. **HomeLink International** ☎ 800/638-3841 ⊕ www.homelink.org; $80 yearly for Web-only membership; $125 includes Web access and two catalogs. **Intervac US** ☎ 800/756-4663 ⊕ www.intervacus.com; $78.88 for Web-only membership; $126 includes Web access and a catalog.

HOSTELS

Hostels offer bare-bones lodging at low, low prices—often in shared dorm rooms with shared baths—to people of all ages, though the primary market is young travelers, especially students. Most hostels serve breakfast; dinner and/or shared cooking facilities may also be available. In some hostels you aren't allowed to be in your room during the day, and there may be a curfew at night. Nevertheless, hostels provide a sense of community, with public rooms where travelers often gather to share stories. Many hostels are affiliated with Hostelling International (HI), an umbrella group of hostel associations with some 4,500 member properties in more than 70 countries. Other hostels are completely independent and may be nothing more than a really cheap hotel.

Membership in any HI association, open to travelers of all ages, allows you to stay in HI-affiliated hostels at member rates. One-year membership is about $28 for adults; hostels charge about $10–$30 per night. Members have priority if the hostel is full; they're also eligible for discounts around the world, even on rail and bus travel in some countries.

Hostelling International—USA ☎ 301/495-1240 ⊕ www.hiusa.org.

■ AIRLINE TICKETS

Most domestic airline tickets are electronic; international tickets may be either electronic or paper. With an e-ticket the only thing you receive is an e-mailed receipt citing your itinerary and reservation and ticket numbers. The greatest advantage of an e-ticket is that if you lose your receipt, you can simply print out another copy or ask the airline to do it for you at check-in. You usually pay a surcharge (up to $50) to get a paper ticket, if you can get one at all. The sole advantage of a paper ticket is that it may be easier to endorse over to another airline if your flight is canceled and the airline with which you booked can't accommodate you on another flight.

■ RENTAL CARS

When you reserve a car, ask about cancellation penalties, taxes, drop-off charges (if you're planning to pick up the car in one city and leave it in another), and surcharges (for being under or over a certain age, for additional drivers, or for driving across state or country borders or beyond a specific distance from your point of rental). All these things can add substantially to your costs. Request car seats and extras such as GPS when you book.

WORD OF MOUTH

Did the resort look as good in real life as it did in the photos? Did you sleep like a baby, or were the walls paper thin? Did you get your money's worth? Rate hotels and write your own reviews in Travel Ratings or start a discussion about your favorite places in Travel Talk on www.fodors.com. Your comments might even appear in our books. Yes, you, too, can be a correspondent!

In Poland, remember that children up to 12 years old or 150 cm (4 feet, 11 inches) have to be seated in the car seats. The requirement doesn't apply to children riding in taxis, however.

Rates are sometimes—but not always—better if you book in advance or reserve through a rental agency's Web site. There are other reasons to book ahead, though: for popular destinations, during busy times of the year, or to ensure that you get certain types of cars (vans, SUVs, exotic sports cars).

■ **TIP→** Make sure that a confirmed reservation guarantees you a car. Agencies sometimes overbook, particularly for busy weekends and holiday periods.

Car rentals in Poland are relatively expensive, particularly with large international companies. Prices vary within the range of zł 150 to zł 500 per day (24 hours), and some companies have a two-day minimum for rentals. Some companies require an additional credit-card deposit of between zł 1,500 and zł 3,000, depending on the class of the rented car. Many car-rental companies do not allow you to take the car across national borders (especially the eastern border of Poland).

CAR-RENTAL INSURANCE

Everyone who rents a car wonders whether the insurance that the rental companies offer is worth the expense. No one—including us—has a simple answer. It all depends on how much regular insurance you have, how comfortable you are with risk, and whether or not money is an issue.

If you own a car, your personal auto insurance may cover a rental to some degree, though not all policies protect you abroad; always read your policy's fine print. If you don't have auto insurance, then seriously consider buying the collision- or loss-damage waiver (CDW or LDW) from the car-rental company, which eliminates your liability for damage to the car. Some credit cards offer CDW coverage, but it's usually supplemental to your own insur-

10 WAYS TO SAVE

1. Nonrefundable is best. If saving money is more important than flexibility, then non-refundable tickets work. Just remember that you'll pay dearly (as much as $100) if you change your plans.

2. Comparison shop. Web sites and travel agents can have different arrangements with the airlines and offer different prices for exactly the same flights.

3. Beware those prices. Many airline Web sites—and most ads—show prices *without* taxes and surcharges. Don't buy until you know the full price.

4. Stay loyal. Stick with one or two frequent-flier programs. You'll rack up free trips faster and you'll accumulate more quickly the perks that make trips easier. On some airlines these include a special reservations number, early boarding, access to upgrades, and more roomy economy-class seating.

5. Watch those ticketing fees. Surcharges are usually added when you buy your ticket anywhere but on an airline Web site. (That includes by phone—even if you call the airline directly—and paper tickets regardless of how you book.)

6. Check early and often. Start looking for cheap fares up to a year in advance, and keep looking until you see something you can live with.

7. Don't work alone. Some Web sites have tracking features that will e-mail you immediately when good deals are posted.

8. Jump on the good deals. Waiting even a few minutes might mean paying more.

9. Fly mid-week. Look for departures on Tuesday, Wednesday, and Thursday, typically the cheapest days to travel.

10. Weigh your options. What you get can be as important as what you save. A cheaper flight might have a long layover rather than being nonstop, or it might land at a secondary airport, where your ground transportation costs might be higher.

Car Rental Resources

AUTOMOBILE ASSOCIATIONS		
U.S.: American Automobile Association (AAA)	315/797-5000	www.aaa.com; most contact with the organization is through state and regional members.
National Automobile Club for California residents only.	650/294-7000	www.thenac.com; membership
Polish Automobile & Motorcycle Federation	022/849-93-61, 9637	www.pzm.pl in Poland for emergency roadside assistance
LOCAL AGENCIES		
Express		www.express.pl
Sixt		www.sixt.pl
WHOLESALERS		
uto Europe	888/223-5555	www.autoeurope.com
Europe by Car	212/581-3040 in New York, 800/223-1516	www.europebycar.com
Eurovacations	877/471-3876	www.eurovacations.com
Kemwel	877/820-0668	www.kemwel.com

ance and rarely covers SUVs, minivans, luxury models, and the like. If your coverage is secondary, you may still be liable for loss-of-use costs from the car-rental company. But no credit-card insurance is valid unless you use that card for *all* transactions, from reserving to paying the final bill. All companies exclude car rental in some countries, so be sure to find out about the destination to which you are traveling.

■ TIP➔ Diners Club offers primary CDW coverage on all rentals reserved and paid for with the card. This means that Diners Club's company—not your own car insurance—pays in case of an accident. It *doesn't* mean your car-insurance company won't raise your rates once it discovers you had an accident.

Some countries require you to purchase CDW coverage or require car-rental companies to include it in quoted rates. Ask your rental company about issues like these in your destination. In most cases it's cheaper to add a supplemental CDW plan to your comprehensive travel-insurance policy (⇨ Trip Insurance *under* Things to Consider *in* Getting Started, *above*) than to purchase it from a rental com-

pany. That said, you don't want to pay for a supplement if you're required to buy insurance from the rental company.

In Poland, CDW coverage may or may not be included in the quoted price for car rentals, so be sure to read the contract and ask the car rental company. If your credit card doesn't give you coverage, it's usually a good idea to buy insurance because of the risk of car accidents and car theft throughout the country.

■ TIP➔ You can decline the insurance from the rental company and purchase it through a third-party provider such as Travel Guard (www.travelguard.com)—$9 per day for $35,000 of coverage. That's sometimes just under half the price of the CDW offered by some car-rental companies.

▌VACATION PACKAGES

Packages *are not* guided tours. Packages combine airfare, accommodations, and perhaps a rental car or other extras (theater tickets, guided excursions, boat trips, reserved entry to popular museums, transit passes), but they let you do your own thing. During busy periods packages may be your only option, as flights and rooms may be sold out otherwise. Packages will definitely save you time. They can also save you money, particularly in peak seasons, but—and this is a really big "but"—you should price each part of the package separately to be sure. And be aware that prices advertised on Web sites and in newspapers rarely include service charges or taxes, which can up your costs by hundreds of dollars.

■ TIP→ Some packages and cruises are sold only through travel agents. Don't always assume that you can get the best deal by booking everything yourself. Each year consumers are stranded or lose their money when packagers—even large ones with excellent reputations—go out of business. How can you protect yourself? First, always pay with a credit card; if you have a problem, your credit-card company may help you resolve it. Second, buy trip insurance that covers default. Third, choose a company that belongs to the United States Tour Operators Association, whose members must set aside funds to cover defaults. Finally, choose a company that also participates in the Tour Operator Program of the American Society of Travel Agents (ASTA), which will act as mediator in any disputes. You can also check on the tour operator's reputation among travelers by posting an inquiry on one of the Fodors.com forums.

Packages for travel to Poland may save you money, particularly in larger cities, but you are unlikely to be booked into unique places—and certainly never off the beaten path. If your preference is for a standard tourist- or business-class hotel, though, and you plan to stick to the proven destinations, then you can do well with a package.

Organizations American Society of Travel Agents (ASTA) ☎ 703/739-2782 or 800/965-2782 ⊕ www.astanet.com. **United States Tour Operators Association** (USTOA) ☎ 212/599-6599 ⊕ www.ustoa.com.

■ TIP→ Local tourism boards can provide information about lesser-known and small-niche operators that sell packages to only a few destinations.

10 WAYS TO SAVE

1. Beware of cheap rates. Those great rates aren't so great when you add in taxes, surcharges, and insurance. Such extras can double or triple the initial quote.

2. Rent weekly. Weekly rates are usually better than daily ones. Even if you only want to rent for five or six days, ask for the weekly rate; it may very well be cheaper than the daily rate for that period of time.

3. Don't forget the locals. Price local car-rental companies as well as the majors.

4. Airport rentals can cost more. Airports often add surcharges, which you can sometimes avoid by renting from an agency whose office is just off airport property.

5. Wholesalers can help. Investigate wholesalers, which don't own fleets but rent in bulk from firms that do, and which frequently offer better rates (note that you must usually pay for such rentals before leaving home).

6. Look for rate guarantees. With your rate locked in, you won't pay more, even if the price goes up in the local currency.

7. Fill up farther away. Avoid hefty refueling fees by filling the tank at a station well away from where you plan to turn in the car.

8. Pump it yourself. Don't buy the tank of gas that's in the car when you rent it unless you plan to do a lot of driving.

9. Get all your discounts. Find out whether a credit card you carry or organization or frequent-renter program to which you belong has a discount program. And confirm that such discounts really are a deal. You can often do better with special weekend or weekly rates offered by a rental agency.

10. Check out package rates. Adding a car rental onto your air/hotel vacation package may be cheaper than renting a car separately on your own.

▌ GUIDED TOURS

Guided tours are a good option when you don't want to do it all yourself. You travel along with a group (sometimes large, sometimes small), stay in prebooked hotels, eat with your fellow travelers (the cost of meals sometimes included in the price of your tour, sometimes not), and follow a schedule. But not all guided tours are an if-it's-Tuesday-this-must-be-Belgium experience. A knowledgeable guide can take you places that you might never discover on your own, and you may be pushed to see more than you would have otherwise. Tours aren't for everyone, but they can be just the thing for trips to places where making travel arrangements is difficult or time-consuming (particularly when you don't speak the language). Whenever you book a guided tour, find out what's included and what isn't. A "land-only" tour includes all your travel (by bus, in most cases) in the destination, but not necessarily your flights to and from or even within it. Also, in most cases prices in tour brochures don't include fees and taxes. And remember that you'll be expected to tip your guide (in cash) at the end of the tour.

Many large tour companies now offer some Poland options, if not entire tours in Poland. Lower-cost operators include Globus and Cosmos (with the same parent company). Mid-range operators like Collette and Gate 1 also offer good prices; Gate 1 is a particularly good value since its tours almost always include airfare. At the top end, Maupintour has some itineraries that include Poland. Abercrombie & Kent also offers some independent tours in Poland, always at the luxury end of the scale.

Recommended Companies Abercrombie & Kent ☎ 800/554-7016 ⊕ www.abercrombiekent.com. **Collette Vacations** ☎ 800/340-5158 ⊕ www.collettevacations.com. **Cosmos** ☎ 800/276-1241 ⊕ www.cosmos.com. **Gate 1 Travel** ☎ 800/682-3333 ⊕ www.gate1travel.com. **Globus** ☎ 866/755-8581 ⊕ www.globusjourneys.com. **Maupintour** ☎ 800/255-4266 ⊕ www.maupintour.com.

▌ CRUISES

Some northern European cruise itineraries include calls at Polish ports, primarily Gdańsk (the cruise-ship pier is in Gdynia), though the number of cruiseships that stop in Poland varies dramatically from year to year.

Cruise Lines Celebrity Cruises ☎ 305/539-6000 or 800/437-3111 ⊕ www.celebrity.com. **Costa Cruises** ☎ 954/266-5600 or 800/462-6782 ⊕ www.costacruise.com. **Crystal Cruises** ☎ 310/785-9300 or 800/446-6620 ⊕ www.crystalcruises.com. **Holland America Line** ☎ 206/281-3535 or 877/932-4259 ⊕ www.hollandamerica.com. **Oceania Cruises** ☎ 305/514-2300 or 800/531-5658 ⊕ www.oceaniacruises.com. **Princess Cruises** ☎ 661/753-0000 or 800/774-6237 ⊕ www.princess.com. **Regent Seven Seas Cruises** ☎ 954/776-6123 or 800/477-7500 ⊕ www.rssc.com. **Royal Caribbean International** ☎ 305/539-6000 or 800/327-6700 ⊕ www.royalcaribbean.com. **Seabourn Cruise Line** ☎ 305/463-3000 or 800/929-9391 ⊕ www.seabourn.com. **Silversea Cruises** ☎ 954/522-4477 or 800/722-9955 ⊕ www.silversea.com.

TRANSPORTATION

Warsaw is the primary entry point for international flights from the U.S., but it is also possible to fly into Kraków. Other cities with airports include Gdańsk, Katowice, Lublin, Poznań, Szczecin, and Wrocław. Europe-based budget airlines fly into a wide variety of these cities from hubs all over the continent.

TRAVEL TIMES FROM WARSAW			
To	By Air	By Car or Bus	By Train
Kraków	1 hour 45 minutes	5–6 hours	2 hours
Gdańsk	50 minutes	5–6 hours	4 ½ hours
Szczecin	1 hour 25 minutes	10–11 hours	5 ½ hours
Poznań	1 hour	4–5½ hours	3 hours
Wrocaw	1 hour	6–8 hours	5 hours
Łódź	40 minutes	5–6 hours	2 hours
Lublin	N/A	3 hours	2 ½ hours

When you are traveling between north and south by train, you are likely to have to pass through either Warsaw or Kraków. There are major highways connecting many parts of the country, but some travel (particularly if you are going to destinations that are farther off the beaten path) may be on smaller secondary roads, which are varying in quality. The eastern part of Poland is the least developed area of the country and has the worst connecting roads. If you are driving in the region to the southeast of Warsaw and east of Kraków, be prepared to spend extra time reaching your destination. Traffic can also be quite heavy and can also cause delays.

Most of the destinations of interest to tourists are reachable by public transportation of some kind, but it may not always be a train. Buses are also a vital link between certain destinations, and those who are trying to avoid renting a car are likely to need to use the bus system, which consists of both the national PKS line but also private local minibuses. For information on all the regions of Poland, see the Essentials sections in the destinations chapters.

■ TIP➔ Ask the local tourist board about hotel and local transportation packages that include tickets to major museum exhibits or other special events.

▮ BY AIR

■ TIP➔ If you travel frequently, look into the TSA's Registered Traveler program. The program, which is still being tested in several U.S. airports, is designed to cut down on gridlock at security checkpoints by allowing prescreened travelers to pass quickly through kiosks that scan an iris and/or a fingerprint. How sci-fi is that?

Airlines & Airports Airline and Airport Links.com ⊕ www.airlineandairportlinks.com has links to many of the world's airlines and airports.

Airline Security Issues Transportation Security Administration ⊕ www.tsa.gov has answers for almost every question that might come up.

AIRPORTS

The major international airport is in Warsaw, but Poland has many other airports for intra-Europe flights, which are detailed in the individual destination chapters.

FLIGHTS

There are relatively few domestic flights in Poland (distances within the country do not justify these). All domestic flights by LOT go via Warsaw (but a new airline, Directfly, may be worth checking of you need to travel across the country, for instance from Kraków to Gdańsk or Wrocław to Gdańsk).

Airline Contacts Aer Lingus ☎ 800/474-7424 ⊕ www.flyaerlingus.com. **Air Canada** ☎ 888/247-2262 ⊕ www.aircanada.com. **Air**

FLYING 101

Flying may not be as carefree as it once was, but there are some things you can do to make your trip smoother.

Minimize the time spent standing in line. Buy an e-ticket, check in at an electronic kiosk, or—even better—check in on your airline's Web site before leaving home. Pack light, and limit carry-on items to only the essentials.

Arrive when you need to. Research your airline's policy. It's usually at least an hour before domestic flights and two to three hours before international flights. But airlines at some busy airports have more stringent requirements. Check the TSA Web site for estimated security waiting times at major airports.

Get to the gate. If you aren't at the gate at least 10 minutes before your flight is scheduled to take off (sometimes earlier), you won't be allowed to board.

Double-check your flight times. Do this especially if you reserved far in advance. Schedules change, and alerts may not reach you.

Don't go hungry. Ask whether your airline offers anything to eat; even when it does, be prepared to pay.

Get the seat you want. Often you can pick a seat when you buy your ticket on an airline Web site. But it's not guaranteed so double-check. You can also select a seat if you check in electronically. Avoid seats on the aisle directly across from the lavatories. Frequent fliers say those are even worse than back-row seats that don't recline.

Got kids? Get info. Ask the airline about its children's menus, activities, and fares. Sometimes infants and toddlers fly free if they sit on a parent's lap, and older children fly for half price in their own seats. Also inquire about policies involving car seats; having one may limit seating options. Also ask about seat-belt extenders for car seats. And note that you can't count on a flight attendant to produce an extender; you may have to ask for one when you board.

Check your scheduling. Don't buy a ticket if there's less than an hour between connecting flights. Although schedules are padded, if anything goes wrong you might miss your connection. If you're traveling to an important function, depart a day early.

Bring paper. Even when using an e-ticket, always carry a hard copy of your receipt; you may need it to get your boarding pass, which most airports require to get past security.

Complain at the airport. If your baggage goes astray or your flight goes awry, complain before leaving the airport. Most carriers require that you file a claim immediately.

Beware of overbooked flights. If a flight is oversold, the gate agent will usually ask for volunteers and offer some sort of compensation for taking a different flight. If you're bumped from a flight *involuntarily*, the airline must give you some kind of compensation if an alternate flight can't be found within one hour.

Know your rights. If your flight is delayed because of something within the airline's control (bad weather doesn't count), the airline must get you to your destination on the same day, even if they have to book you on another airline and in an upgraded class. Read the Contract of Carriage, which is usually buried on the airline's Web site.

Be prepared. The Boy Scout motto is especially important if you're traveling during a stormy season. To quickly adjust your plans, program a few numbers into your cell: your airline, an airport hotel or two, your destination hotel, your car service, and/or your travel agent.

France ☎ 800/237-2747 ⊕ www.airfrance. com. **Alitalia** ☎ 800/223-5730 ⊕ www. alitaliausa.com in the U.S. **American Airlines** ☎ 800/433-7300 ⊕ www.aa.com. **Austrian Airlines** ☎ 800/843-0002 ⊕ www.aua.com. **British Airways** ☎ 800/247-9297 ⊕ www. britishairways.com. **Continental Airlines** ☎ 800/523-3273 for U.S. and Mexico reservations, 800/231-0856 for international reservations ⊕ www.continental.com. **Czech Airlines** (CSA) ☎ 212/223-2365 ⊕ www.csa. cz. **Delta Airlines** ☎ 800/221-1212 for U.S. reservations, 800/241-4141 for international reservations ⊕ www.delta.com. **Finnair** ☎ 800/950-5000 ⊕ www.finnair.com. **Iberia Airlines** ☎ 800/772-4642 ⊕ www.iberia. com. **LOT Polish Airline** ☎ 212/789-0970 ⊕ www.lot.com. **Lufthansa** ☎ 800/645-3880 ⊕ www.lufthansa.com. **Malév Hungarian Airlines** ☎ 212/566-9944 ⊕ www.malev.hu. **Northwest/KLM Airlines** ☎ 800/225-2525 ⊕ www.nwa.com. **SAS Scandinavian Airlines** ☎ 800/221-2350 ⊕ www.flysas.com. **Swiss** ☎ 877/359-7947 ⊕ www.swiss.com. **SN Brussels Airlines** ☎ 516/740-5200 ⊕ www.flysn.com. **United Airlines** ☎ 800/864-8331 for U.S. reservations, 800/538-2929 for international reservations ⊕ www.united. com. **USAirways** ☎ 800/428-4322 for U.S. and Canada reservations, 800/622-1015 for international reservations ⊕ www.usairways. com. **Virgin Atlantic** ☎ 800/821-5438 ⊕ www.virgin-atlantic.com.

Intra-European Airlines Aerosvit Airlines ⊕ www.aerosvit.com. **Airberlin** ⊕ www. airberlin.com. **Air Europa** ⊕ www.air-europa.com. **Belavia** ⊕ www.belavia.by. **Centralwings** ⊕ www.centralwings.com. **DirectFly** ⊕ www.directfly.pl. **Germanwings** ⊕ www.germanwings.com. **Norwegian** ⊕ www.norwegian.no. **Ryanair** ⊕ www. ryanair.com. **Sky Europe** ⊕ www.skyeurope. com. **Wizzair** ⊕ www.wizzair.com.

▌ BY BUS

Buses in Poland are operated mostly by PKS, the former national (state-managed) network that is now being decentralized into regional units. Buses are particularly useful if you need to get to smaller towns and resorts, and they tend to be more convenient for short-distance routes. In mountainous areas of southern Poland, the bus network is better developed than the railway network.

The most recent and reliable timetables can be found in bus stations, and they are usually posted on large boards—departures (*odjazdy*) are usually on a yellow background, and arrivals (*przyjazdy*) on white. Faster express buses (*pośpieszny*) are marked in red to distinguish them from regular, local buses, which are listed in black.

Although you can buy the ticket from the driver, it is better to buy it in advance from the *kasa* (ticket office) in the bus station (*dworzec autobusowy*, which may also be labeled *dworzec PKS* after the name of the national bus line. This guarantees that you have a seat.

▌ BY CAR

If your travel plans include only major cities such as Warsaw, Kraków, Wrocław, and Gdańsk, then you probably do not need to rent a car. You can reach many nearby places by public transit or organized tours. However, if you want to explore off the beaten path or at your own pace, then a car can be a very welcome luxury. Your valid driver's license, issued in any country, will allow you to rent a car in Poland. Be aware that if you are renting outside of Poland and planning to drive into the country, there may be restrictions on border crossings, special insurance requirements, or premiums you must pay. Manual transmissions are the norm, and you may not be able to get a car with an automatic transmission at all; when you can get one, it will often be a luxury car or a larger model. Roads in Poland can be very crowded, and accident rates are significantly higher in Poland than in other parts of Europe, so always drive with care.

It is possible for a group of more than four people to hire a car (or minibus) with a driver, and this can be arranged though a local travel agency. As a rule, you are expected to cover the expenses of the driver (accommodation plus meals); when making your arrangements, inquire if these are included in the quoted price. Travel agents are recommended in the individual destination chapters.

GASOLINE

Gas stations are plentiful along major roads, less so on smaller, secondary roads. It is recommended that you use only a major gasoline chain (i.e., BP, Shell, Jet, Orlen, or Statoil). They all will accept major credit cards.

Several useful words to know include the following: receipt (*rachunek*); unleaded (*bezołowiowa*); octane (*oktanowa*); diesel (*ropa*).

Gasoline prices are per liter and are significantly more expensive than in the United States; expect to pay a little more than $1 per liter, but prices can change. Most rental cars take either unleaded gas or diesel (be sure you know what kind of fuel your vehicle runs on before leaving the car-rental office). Most stations provide assistance in pumping your gas, but not all; if an attendant pumps your gasoline for you, a small tip is expected. Most chain stations are open 24 hours.

PARKING

Every bigger city has its own payment system for parking, including most street parking. For example, Warsaw is in the process of introducing parking meters, and Kraków uses the system of prepaid passes you can buy at kiosks or from the street sellers (dressed in bright yellow vests). All the tickets must be displayed in your window. If you are planning to drive and visit major cities, you should try to check the local tourist information site for the city; most major cities list a description of parking rules in English.

ROAD CONDITIONS

In general, the road conditions in Poland are rather bad, but the worst roads are the minor secondary and tertiary routes. Be particularly careful when driving on country roads, which tend to be narrow and winding, and where you can encounter much slow traffic (such as tractors or horse-drawn carriages). However, even along smaller routes, you can encounter cows and other animals when you are driving through the countryside. In larger cities such as Warsaw, Kraków, Łódź, Gdańsk, and Poznań, rush hour produces very large traffic backups from 7:30 to 10 and again from 3:30 to 6:30. In historical city centers, most streets are one-way, and the streets are often too narrow for the amount of traffic.

Speeding is a major problem in Poland, and a major factor in the high number of traffic accidents (one of the highest in Europe). Unfortunately, drivers are not only fast, but rather erratic and aggressive, and good manners on the roads are rare.

In 2007—and most probably for the next several years—it will be particularly difficult to drive in Poland because almost every town and city is experiencing a lot of construction work due to a major influx of funds from the EU for infrastructure improvements. While this work will no doubt help future generations, it is causing headaches for the current one.

Seasonal conditions can also make driving in Poland hazardous. High-country snow between fall and spring is not uncommon; in winter, roads can be very slippery, and you are more likely to come into contact with unlighted farm or other vehicles at night, not to mention many more pedestrians than you would encounter in the U.S. This can be a particularly dangerous condition outside of major cities and towns, so driving at night is not recommended.

It will be helpful if you know a few Polish signs in addition to the international traffic signs. A green arrow allows you to turn right even though the main signal is red. A blue circle with red border and a red slash means no parking on the road;

the words *dotyczy chodnika* mean that the rule applies to the pedestrian footpath and/or sidewalk as well. A yellow diamond with white border means that you have the right of way (if the diamond is crossed out in black, you no longer have right of way). A yellow triangle (pointing down) with a red border means stop.

ROAD DISTANCES FROM WARSAW (IN KM/MI)		
Warsaw	Kraków	300 km/186 mi
Warsaw	Gdańsk	387 km/240 mi
Warsaw	Szczecin	501 km/301 mi
Warsaw	Lublin	163 km/101 mi
Warsaw	Wrocaw	361 km/224 mi
Warsaw	Poznań	310 km/193 mi

ROADSIDE EMERGENCIES
The network to report roadside emergencies is not very well developed; in case of an accident or breakdown, you are better off calling the police number 112. Police will not always speak English, but they will make an effort to find someone who can. If your car is stolen, proceed directly to the nearest police station to file a report. If you are in an accident, call the police and do not sign any insurance documents produced by the other driver.
Emergency Services Police 📠 112.

RULES OF THE ROAD
The maximum speed limit is: 50 km/h in towns from 5 AM to 11 PM, and 60 km/h from 11 PM to 5 AM; 90 km/h outside urban areas; 110 km/h on dual carriageways; and 130 km/h on motorways. Speeds are monitored, but sometimes erratically. The fine for speeding can be up to zł 500.

Seatbelts must be worn by all passengers, both in the front and back seat. A right turn is permitted on a red light only if there is a green arrow. Children under 12 must sit in special child seats in the back passenger seat (a rule that is waived for taxis).

Rules regarding drunken driving are very severe, and the legally permissible level of alcohol in one's bloodstream is very low. If you are in an accident and there is any trace of alcohol at all, it is a criminal offense.

One unusual rule in Poland is that headlights must be used all day from November 1 to March 1.

Cars must be equipped with a fire extinguisher, a first-aid kit, and a hazard-warning reflexive triangle.

There are a lot of unguarded railway crossings, which require the driver's attention. Buses moving from a bus stop have the right of way, as do trams in cities. Large Polish cities are full of roundabouts, and the traffic is often coordinated by the police. There are some streets where only taxis and coaches are permitted to enter.
Driving Abroad ⊕ www.drivingabroad.co.uk.
Travel Island ⊕ www.travel-island.com.

▌ BY TRAIN

The Polish railway network is well developed. A full map of railway connections, covering Poland with a dense web, can be seen at the main Web site for PKP State Polish Railways. The State Polish Railways has struggled in the new post-Communist reality, but many improvements have been seen since the early 1990s. Particularly efficient are express trains operated by PKP Intercity, which connect the main cities in the country (including Gdańsk, Krak, Łódź, Poznań, Warsaw, and Wrocław, among others). These lines tend to have newer carriages and are cleaner and better serviced than some regional trains; they also tend to be very punctual. PKP Intercity has a bilingual Web site (in Polish and English), where you can check timetables and special offers and buy tickets online (but remember that you must print out and keep the confirmation). Regional connections and regular trains (*osobowy*) are more prone to delays, but schedules are fairly accurate. Delays are more likely in winter, when there is heavy snow.

The full train timetable (*rozkład jazdy pociągów*), including slow and fast, domestic and international trains, is available on the Web site of the PKP State Polish Railway company in Polish and English. Timetables for a given railway station are always posted in that station: traditionally on yellow boards or posters for departures (*odjazdy*) and white ones for arrivals (*przyjazdy*); of course, you will see more electronic than written boards today.

Although you can now purchase tickets for many trains online, most people buy their tickets at the train station or at travel agencies, including Orbis. Look for the *kasa* (ticket office) or *kasy* (ticket offices). You can also buy tickets on the train (there is a small surcharge), but be warned: old-fashioned regulations require you to notify the train attendant that you have no ticket and intend to buy one, **before** you actually board the train—otherwise, you may have to pay a substantial fine. Even though this regulation is clearly outdated and impractical, some inspectors tend to turn blind eye, but others won't, particularly on local trains. On Intercity trains, this is never a problem: you can buy your ticket onboard without any prior notification; you just need to pay a small surcharge of zł 8. On busy routes and peak times (e.g., morning express trains to Warsaw, and on holidays) all you risk is having to stand throughout the journey.

Although it is generally a good idea to buy your ticket in advance, if you can, in off-peak periods, it may be worth waiting until the last minute. From 30 minutes before departure, you can buy a cheap last-minute ticket for selected trains, but only from the *kasa* at the railway station.

When buying your ticket, specify whether you want first-class (*pierwsza klasa*) or second-class (*druga klasa*); in most trains this means six versus eight seats in a compartment. Specify also if you want a nonsmoking (*dla niepalących*) or a smoking (*dla palących*) seat. Most trains have separate compartments (and sometimes separate carriages) for smokers, and for many trains smoking is allowed in the corridors (unless the whole carriage is a nonsmoking carriage). This is slowly changing, and since 2006 smoking has been forbidden on all Intercity trains (but not express trains and Euro-city trains without the "Intercity" tag).

There are regional and commuter train networks, now managed by new units such as PKP Przewozy Regionalne (regional railways), PKP WKD (Warsaw commuter trains), PKP SKM (Tri-city commuter train). Some of these commuter trains can be very useful to tourists.

There are several convenient overnight connections, both domestic (Zakopane and Kraków to Gdańsk and Szczecin, for instance) and international (Warsaw and Kraków to Prague, Berlin, Budapest, or Vienna). These are worth considering: by spending the night on the train you can save time and money. It is worth paying the extra fee for a better cabin. (There are different options available: compartments with six berths, three berths, doubles, and singles—but the fewer beds in the compartment, the more expensive the fare.)

When traveling on overnight trains and moving through crowded railway stations, observe common-sense rules of safety, and keep your belongings and your wits about you. On the night train, you can lock your compartment and fasten the chain on the door (if it's an international train, expect to be woken up for the passport control). Busy railway terminals are favorite working spots for petty thieves and pickpockets, and although the stations are patrolled and monitored, it is better to be safe than sorry.

PKP Polish State Railways ⊕ www.pkp.pl.
PKP Intercity ⊕ www.intercity.pl. **PKP Polish State Railways Timetable** ⊕ www.rozklad. pkp.pl.

ON THE GROUND

■ COMMUNICATIONS

INTERNET
You should have no problems getting on-line in Poland. Internet service is common in three- to five-star hotels and at free-standing Internet cafés. In hotels, fast Internet connections may be either broadband and/or Wi-Fi—sometimes at an additional fee, but increasingly free of charge. In bigger cities, you will find Internet hotspots (their number is increasing every year). Internet cafés can now be found in some of the smallest villages. **Cybercafes** ⊕ www.cybercafes.com lists over 4,000 Internet cafés worldwide. **Free Hotspots** ⊕ www.free-hotspot.com lists free Wi-Fi service all over the world.

PHONES
The good news is that you can now make a direct-dial telephone call from virtually any point on earth. The bad news? You can't always do so cheaply. Calling from a hotel is almost always the most expensive option; hotels usually add huge surcharges to all calls, particularly international ones. In some countries you can phone from call centers or even the post office. Calling cards usually keep costs to a minimum, but only if you purchase them locally. And then there are mobile phones (⇨ *below*), which are sometimes more prevalent—particularly in the developing world—than land lines; as expensive as mobile phone calls can be, they are still usually a much cheaper option than calling from your hotel.

Telekomunikacja Polska is the main telecommunications provider, but the competition is gathering pace (with Netia as the main competitor). You will find card-operated phones around in spite of an increasing number of mobile phone users.

CALLING OUTSIDE POLAND
The country code for the United States is 1.

To call internationally, dial "00" followed by country code.

Access Codes AT&T ☎ 00-800/111-11-11. **Sprint** ☎ 00-800/111-31-77. **MCI** ☎ 00-800/111-21-22

CALLING CARDS
There are a number of international calling cards available, offering calls at competitive rates. Some of these can be purchased online as a "virtual" phone card. Or you can also buy them at newsstands and kiosks.

Phone Cards Foncard ⊕ www.foncard.pl. **Intrafon** ⊕ www.intrafon.pl. **Telerabat** ⊕ www.telerabat.pl.

CALLING WITHIN POLAND
All numbers in Poland have nine digits (the first two digits are the area code and must always be dialed). Mobile phone numbers are also nine digits, but they do not have an area code. You must also dial "0" before all numbers unless you are calling from a mobile phone.

If you make a call from your hotel, you will be charged a surcharge, which may be quite high—always check before dialing. You can also make a long-distance phone call from any post office.

To reach directory assistance, dial 118–811 to reach the English-language operator for Polish Telecom (Telekomunikacja Polska). This service is available 24 hours a day, 7 days a week. The cost of the connection is zł 2.44 per minute.

MOBILE PHONES
If you have a multiband phone (some countries use different frequencies than what's used in the United States) and your service provider uses the world-standard GSM network (as do T-Mobile, Cingular, and Verizon), you can probably use your phone abroad. Roaming fees can be steep, however: 99¢ a minute is considered reasonable. And overseas you normally pay the toll charges for incoming calls. It's almost al-

LOCAL DO'S & TABOOS

CUSTOMS OF THE COUNTRY

Strict punctuality in Poland is not common; except in business meetings, being late 5 to 10 minutes is completely accepted.

If you ask a Pole how he/she is, the person will probably give you a long answer expressing her/his troubles. Complaining (with a pinch of salt) is the Polish national sport.

Normal courtesies are observed when visiting private homes, and it is customary to bring flowers. Maintain direct eye contact when eye contact is made with you, especially when toasting. Hand gestures, in general, are limited. Flicking a few fingers against the neck is an invitation (usually between men) to join the person for a drink of vodka. Poles do not usually speak in loud voices. Avoid chewing gum when you are talking to someone.

Poles are not overly demonstrative, so avoid casual body contact, unless you're among close friends. Showing the single, middle finger upright is an offensive gesture. In general, Poles don't use hand gestures in conversation, or at least they are limited.

Poles usually treat women with a certain courtesy; that is, they will let a woman pass through a door first, holding it for her. One topic is off-limits in casual conversation: never ask a woman about her age.

GREETINGS

Poles are not very formal, and they do not often stand upon ceremony; they also tend to have high tolerance to possible faux-pas and blunders that foreign visitors might commit. The proper form of addressing strangers would be *pan* (when addressing men) and *pani* (when addressing women); while *ty* is used only when addressing children, family members, or close friends. The use of *ty* versus *pan/pani* is analogous to the difference between *du* and *Sie* in German, or *tu* and *vous* in French.

In small towns and villages, people tend to greet each other—and that includes strangers—with *dzień dobry* (good day). Incidentally, there is also a tradition of hikers greeting each other in the mountains—either with a *dzień dobry* or a more informal *cześć*. Of course, this practice isn't as common on very crowded trails, where the greetings might leave one out of breath.

Hand-shaking is quite common (especially between men), although it is polite to greet each other with merely a bow and a smile to accompany a greeting. Kissing is usually restricted to family and close friends, and is more popular in some circles than others—just observe and follow whatever seems to be the rule in a given context. But if you do kiss your friends on the cheek, remember: it is always three times!

Old-fashioned Polish men sometimes still kiss a lady's hand, but this is increasingly rare. If you're a man, a safe rule is: don't attempt to do it if you can't do it right; if you're a lady and want to avoid having your hand kissed, just shake hands firmly, and that should convey the message.

SIGHTSEEING

Tourists are expected to dress and behave appropriately when entering churches. Skimpy clothing (including shorts or tops that expose the shoulders) are considered disrespectful, as is loud talking. In most places (even churches), it is acceptable to take photographs without a flash; if photos are prohibited, there should be a sign. Swim attire should be limited to the beach, but in really hot weather, the rules of propriety in seaside resort areas can be stretched. One is generally expected to treat women and the elderly with some sense of chivalry; so it is considered proper and polite to give up your seat for a pregnant woman or an elderly person, to help someone with a baby stroller get into a bus, and so forth. In large cities,

Poles generally obey signals and cross the street with the lights only; in smaller towns (or on quiet streets), jaywalking is tolerated, but if you are seen by a policeman, you may be stopped.

OUT ON THE TOWN

In good restaurants, there will be no need to attract the waiter's attention, but if you need to do so, just raise your hand and look at him directly. Upmarket restaurants will probably have cloakrooms where you can check your coat, but some restaurants have hooks next to the table; at very casual places, you can put your coat on the back of your seat, but this is generally frowned on when there are alternatives.

In many pubs, you need to go to the bar to place your order, but most cafés have waiter service. The word for self-service is *samoobsługa*—and it will usually be clearly printed on a sign, in which case you can head straight to the counter. In very busy restaurants at the peak of tourist season it might be good policy to insist on paying immediately as your order is delivered, particularly when you're in a hurry. *Proszę rachunek* (proshe rahoonek) means "The bill, please."

If you are invited into someone's home, you're expected to bring a small gift. Flowers are particularly prized in Poland, but a bottle of wine will also do. Depending on how traditional the home is, you may be asked to change from your shoes into slippers (particularly when it is wet or muddy outside); it is generally considered polite to offer to do this.

DOING BUSINESS

Polish business culture has its own peculiarities and formalities, which are discussed in detail in the essay "Doing Business in Poland" in Understanding Poland section.

LANGUAGE

One of the best ways to avoid being an Ugly American is to learn a little of the local language. You need not strive for fluency; even just mastering a few basic words and terms is bound to make chatting with the locals more rewarding.

A phrase book and language-tape set can help get you started.

CON OR CONCIERGE?

Good hotel concierges are invaluable—for arranging transportation, getting reservations at the hottest restaurant, and scoring tickets for a sold-out show or entrée to an exclusive nightclub. They're in the know and well connected. That said, sometimes you have to take their advice with a grain of salt.

It's not uncommon for restaurants to ply concierges with free food and drink in exchange for steering diners their way. Indeed, European concierges often receive referral *fees*. Hotel chains usually have guidelines about what their concierges can accept. The best concierges, however, are above reproach. This is particularly true of those who belong to the prestigious international society of Les Clefs d'Or.

What can you expect of a concierge? At a typical tourist-class hotel you can expect him or her to give you the basics: to show you something on a map, make a standard restaurant reservation (particularly if you don't speak the language), or help you book a tour or airport transportation. In Asia concierges perform the vital service of writing out the name or address of your destination for you to give to a cab driver.

Savvy concierges at the finest hotels and resorts, can arrange for just about any good or service imaginable—and do so quickly. You should compensate them appropriately. A $10 tip is enough to show appreciation for a table at a hot restaurant. But the reward should really be much greater for tickets to that U2 concert that's been sold out for months or for those last-minute sixth-row-center seats for *The Lion King*.

ways cheaper to send a text message than to make a call, since text messages have a very low set fee (often less than 5¢).

If you just want to make local calls, consider buying a new SIM card (note that your provider may have to unlock your phone for you to use a different SIM card) and a prepaid service plan in the destination. You'll then have a local number and can make local calls at local rates. If your trip is extensive, you could also simply buy a new cell phone in your destination, as the initial cost will be offset over time.

■ TIP→ **If you travel internationally frequently, save one of your old mobile phones or buy a cheap one on the Internet; ask your cell phone company to unlock it for you, and take it with you as a travel phone, buying a new SIM card with pay-as-you-go service in each destination.**

Renting a mobile phone is uncommon in Poland, but it is easy to buy a Polish SIM card (and, if necessary, an inexpensive phone to go with it). Poland uses the GSM 900/1800 standard. While these frequencies are different than those used in North America, many tri- and quad-band phones from the U.S. will be usable in Poland; always check with your carrier to determine the frequencies of your phone. In Poland, the main mobile communications providers (at the time of this writing) are Era, Orange, and Plus.

Cellular Abroad ☎ 800/287-5072 ⊕ www.cellularabroad.com rents and sells GMS phones and sells SIM cards that work in many countries. **Mobal** ☎ 888/888-9162 ⊕ www.mobalrental.com rents mobiles and sells GSM phones (starting at $49) that will operate in 140 countries. Per-call rates vary throughout the world. **Planet Fone** ☎ 888/988-4777 ⊕ www.planetfone.com rents cell phones, but the per-minute rates are expensive.

Polish Mobile Companies Era ⊕ www.era.pl. **Orange** ⊕ www.orange.pl. **Plus** ⊕ www.plusgsm.pl.

▌CUSTOMS & DUTIES

You're always allowed to bring goods of a certain value back home without having to pay any duty or import tax. But there's a limit on the amount of tobacco and liquor you can bring back duty-free, and some countries have separate limits for perfumes; for exact figures, check with your customs department. The values of so-called "duty-free" goods are included in these amounts. When you shop abroad, save all your receipts, as customs inspectors may ask to see them as well as the items you purchased. If the total value of your goods is more than the duty-free limit, you'll have to pay a tax (most often a flat percentage) on the value of everything beyond that limit.

The official limit for duty-free items that can be exported from or imported to Poland is (per adult): 1 liter of spirits, 2 liters of wine, and 5 liters of beer. As far as tobacco products are concerned, 250 cigarettes or 50 cigars or 250 g of tobacco are allowed. There are strict regulations concerning the export of works of art. Any item created before 1945 needs special permission from the Regional Monument Conservation Authority. If it is considered to be an object of high cultural value, then permission to export may not be given. The same rule concerns works of art created by any artists who are no longer alive. If you purchase an older work of art, the gallery should be able to help you with the paperwork, but never make your final payment until the paperwork is finalized.

U.S. Information U.S. Customs and Border Protection ⊕ www.cbp.gov.

▌ EATING OUT

The Polish word for restaurant (*restauracja*) usually means a traditional sit-down restaurant, but sometimes also a fast-food cantine. Restaurants serving regional food are sometimes called *karczma, zajazd* (as in "roadside inn"), or *tawerna* (at the seaside). Eateries serving simple, cheap, and usually self-service food are called *bar* (sometimes also *bar szybkiej obsługi*). *Bar mleczny* (milk bars) are a particular style of self-service establishments, serving very

inexpensive, mostly flour and dairy based dishes. Sometimes you can also get a light meal at a *kawiarnia* (a café). For dessert, try *koktail bar, cukiernia,* or *lodziarnia.*

Polish food may look monotonous at a first glance. For some, the Polish culinary canon may seem little more than a tedious collation of pork, potatoes, and cabbage, and, indeed, traditional fare is often heavy and wholesome beyond reason. Breaking through these stereotypes, however, can be very rewarding. A lot of dishes are an acquired taste—this is true of *żurek* (soup made from the base of marinated rye flour) and red beet *barszcz* (borscht).

People of many different nationalities and traditions have left their marks in Poland's menus. Dishes now considered "typically Polish" are often a mixture of Russian, German, Ukrainian, Italian, Jewish, Lithuanian, Turkish, French, and other recipes, brought to Poland and happily assimilated and modified to suit the local palate.

A starter to be sampled by carnivores only is beef tartare (*befsztyk tatarski,* or simply *tatar*), consisting of scraped (rather than minced or chopped) raw beef sirloin, very fresh, with an addition of a raw egg yolk, chopped herbs, pickles, and spices, which you mix yourself depending on your preferences. A cold meat platter (*talerz wędlin*) should include tender cured ham, and *kiełbasa* (sausage). Grilled *oscypek* (sheep cheese), smoked eel (*węgorz wędzony*), and wild hare pâté (*pasztet z zająca*) are some savory staples to try.

Perhaps the most typical Polish soup is *barszcz czerwony* (red borscht), a beet broth that can be served clear (*barszcz czysty*), or with tiny meat-filled ravioli (*uszka z mięsem*) or, even better, forest mushrooms (*uszka z grzybami*). Red borscht with mushroom-filled ravioli is a part of traditional Christmas Eve dinner. Barszcz goes well also with a hot pastry filled with meat (*barszcz z pasztecikiem* or *barszcz z krokietem*) or cabbage (*barszcz z kapuśniaczkiem*). The stock for borscht is made either of meat or mushrooms; the soup base (leaven) made of beetroot, other vegetables, and herbs must be marinated for about a week. Proper barszcz is a very noble and elegant soup indeed.

Żurek is sometimes called *barszcz biały* (white borsch). The soup base is made from marinated rye flour, garlic, herbs, and whole-meal bread. Żurek is often served with boiled white sausage (*biała kiełbasa*) and/or hard-boiled egg and potatoes, although there are other variations as well (other vegetables, bacon). Żurek is a popular hangover remedy.

Very popular are *rosół* (chicken or beef bouillon), the eternal soup of the Polish Sunday dinner, most often served with noodles (*z makaronem*); *pomidorowa* (tomato soup), sometimes accompanied with rice (*z ryżem*) and often thickened with sour cream. Typical wholesome wintertime soups include *krupnik,* a thick barley soup with a variety of vegetables and chunks of meat, and *kapuśniak,* sauerkraut soup with potatoes. Mushroom soup served in bread (*zupa grzybowa w chlebie*) is popular year-round.

Chłodnik is a cold soup served in the summer. The most common variety is *chłodnik litewski* (Lithuanian style) made of beetroot, but some cold fruit soups, including raspberry (*chłodnik malinowy*) or strawberry (*chłodnik truskawkowy*) dash through the menus now and then like comets. *Zupa ogórkowa* (cucumber soup), though served warm in Poland, can also be quite refreshing.

Some starters that are frequently sufficient meals in themselves include *gołąbki, bigos,* and *pierogi.* Delicious gołąbki (literally "little pigeons") are cabbage leaves stuffed with rice and meat (not pigeon) filling, served with tomato or mushroom cream sauce. Bigos is a curious stew made of fresh cabbage and sauerkraut, apples, bacon, sausage, herbs, and spices. It is one of those rare and ancient dishes that get better day after day as you reheat them. Pierogi are boiled dumplings with different kinds

of fillings: the *pierogi ruskie* (the Russian pierogi) are made of potatoes, sour cottage cheese, onion, salt, and pepper; *pierogi z kapustą i grzybami* are composed of cabbage and mushrooms; *pierogi z kaszą gryczaną* are buckwheat; and *pierogi z mięsem* are meat dumplings. And there are sweet pierogis as well, both sweet cottage cheese and fruit: the unbeatable *pierogi z jagodami* (filled with fresh blueberries), *pierogi z truskawkami* (with strawberries), or *pierogi z wiśniami* (with cherries).

Of the most typical meat dishes, look for *schab ze śliwkami* (roast pork with prunes), *kaczka pieczona* (roast duck, often served with baked apples and potatoes), *zrazy zawijane z kaszą gryczaną* (a rolled slice of beef sirloin filled with smoked bacon and pickled cucumber, served with buckwheat), *pieczone prosię* (roast suckling pig), *żeberka* (spare-ribs), and *golonka* (pig's feet, which are surprisingly tasty). Polish *sznycel* is not the same as Wiener schnitzel—the latter is called *kotlet schabowy* (pork cutlet), while sznycel is the poorer version of the dish, made of ground meat.

To accompany your main course you can choose the unrivalled *buraczki* or *ćwikła z chrzanem* (boiled or lightly pickled beetroot), often with horseradish. Main courses are most commonly accompanied by potatoes (*ziemniaki*) in different styles, but keep your taste buds open for *kasza gryczana* (buckwheat).

Traditional sweets include *pączki* (doughnuts, full and round, often filled with wild rose confiture), *nugat* (two wafers with very sweet filling made from honey, nuts, and egg yolks), *piszinger* (many layers of wafer with chocolate filling), *szarlotka* (apple pie), *sernik* (cheese cake), or *cwibak* (baked cake with nuts and dried fruit).

International influence has entered the Polish culinary scene. The last 15 years have witnessed the arrival of French, Italian, Japanese, Chinese, Indian, Greek, Mexican and Ukrainian cuisines.

For information on food-related health issues, *see* Health *below.*

MEALS & MEALTIMES

Unless otherwise noted, the restaurants listed in this guide are open daily for lunch and dinner.

Traditionally, the Poles have their main meal at midday, between 1 and 3 PM, typically consisting of at least two courses: soup and the main course. For breakfast and light supper, many people once had (and still many of them have) just sandwiches. Traditions change, especially in cities, where it is becoming more common to have your main meal in late afternoon or evening.

Restaurants are usually open from noon (but some open earlier for breakfast). They usually close about 11 PM, but it may happen that the kitchen closes at 10. (In smaller towns, eateries tend to close even earlier.)

PAYING

For guidelines on tipping *see* Tipping *below.*

CATEGORY COST	
$$$$	over zł 70
$$$	zł 50–zł 70
$$	zł 30–zł 50
$	zł15–zł 30
¢	under zł15

All prices are per person for a main course at dinner.

RESERVATIONS & DRESS

Regardless of where you are, it's a good idea to make a reservation if you can. In some places, it's expected. We only mention them specifically when reservations are essential (there's no other way you'll ever get a table) or when they are not accepted. For popular restaurants, book as far ahead as you can (often 30 days), and reconfirm as soon as you arrive. (Large parties should always call ahead to check the reservations policy.) We mention dress

WORD OF MOUTH

Was the service stellar or not up to snuff? Did the food give you shivers of delight or leave you cold? Did the prices and portions make you happy or sad? Rate restaurants and write your own reviews in Travel Ratings or start a discussion about your favorite places in Travel Talk on www.fodors.com. Your comments might even appear in our books. Yes, you, too, can be a correspondent!

only when men are required to wear a jacket or a jacket and tie.

WINES, BEER & SPIRITS

All respectable restaurants these days have an at least adequate wine list, but in a typical café or a pub you are unlikely to find a really good wine. The selection of vodkas is impressive, however, and if you are not a connoisseur of clear vodka (consumed ice-cold), there is usually a selection of flavored vodkas and interesting cocktails.

In summer, cold beer will revive you. Polish beer, almost exclusively synonymous with lager, is quite good, although takeovers of local breweries by big multinationals have shaken the quality of production for some time. The brands of Żywiec, Okocim, or Leżajsk may be difficult to pronounce, but the word for beer—*piwo* (pronounced: pivo)—is refreshingly simple.

In large cities, bars (usually called pubs) are open until late.

▌ELECTRICITY

The electrical current in Poland is 220V, 50 Hz. The plugs/sockets are the same as in the rest of continental Europe (but different than U.K.), with two round prongs. Americans will need both an adaptor and a transformer for many electrical appliances. Consider making a small investment in a universal adapter, which has several types of plugs in one lightweight, compact unit. Most laptops and mobile phone chargers are dual voltage (i.e., they operate equally well on 110 and 220 volts), so require only an adapter. These days the same is true of small appliances such as hair dryers. Always check labels and manufacturer instructions to be sure. Don't use 110-volt outlets marked FOR SHAVERS ONLY for high-wattage appliances such as hair-dryers.

Steve Kropla's Help for World Traveler's ⊕ www.kropla.com has information on electrical and telephone plugs around the world. **Walkabout Travel Gear** ⊕ www. walkabouttravelgear.com has a good coverage of electricity under "adapters."

■ EMERGENCIES

From landline phones, there are different three-digit emergency numbers for ambulance, fire, police, roadside assistance, and municipal police. When calling from a mobile phone, you need to dial the local area code before the number, for instance 022–997 to call the police in Warsaw. Emergency calls from phone boxes are free of charge. If you do not know the local code, dial the general emergency number for mobile phones: 112. The operator will request the appropriate emergency unit. In some areas the general emergency number (112) may not work properly.

In larger cities, or in a given region, there is usually at least one 24-hour pharmacy in operation "on duty" (*apteka dyżurna*); usually pharmacies take turns for that duty. To check which pharmacy is open, consult daily paper. The list of on-duty pharmacies is usually also posted in the door/window of every pharmacy in town. **Foreign Embassies U.S. Embassy** ⊠ Al. Ujazdowskie 29–31, Warsaw ☎ 022/504–20–00 ⊕ www.usinfo.pl.

Australian Embassy ⊠ ul. Nowogrodzka 11, Warsaw ☎ 022/521–34–44 ⊕ www.australia.pl.

Canadian Embassy ⊠ ul. Jana Matejki 1/5, Warsaw ☎ 022/584–31–00 ⊕ www.canada.pl.

British Embassy ⊠ Al. Róż 1, Warsaw ☎ 022/311–00–00 ⊕ www.britishembassy.pl.

US Consulate ⊠ ul. Stolarska 9, Kraków ☎ 012/424–51–00 ⊕ http://krakow. usconsulate.gov ⊠ ul. Paderewskiego 8, Poznań ☎ 061/851–85–16.

General Emergency Contacts Ambulance ☎ 999. **Fire** ☎ 998. **General Emergencies** ☎ 112. **Municipal Police** ☎ 986. **Police** ☎ 997. **Roadside Assistance** ☎ 981.

■ HEALTH

The most common types of illnesses are caused by contaminated food and water, though these are not likely problems in Poland. If you have problems, mild cases of traveler's diarrhea may respond to Imodium (known generically as loperamide). In Poland this is a prescription drug, or Pepto-Bismol OTC. Be sure to drink plenty of fluids; if you can't keep fluids down, seek medical help immediately. Other OTC drugs to use in this case could be Smecta or Carbomedicinalis.

Infectious diseases can be airborne or passed via mosquitoes and ticks and through direct or indirect physical contact with animals or people. Some, including Norwalk-like viruses that affect your digestive tract, can be passed along through contaminated food. Condoms can help prevent most sexually transmitted diseases, but they aren't absolutely reliable and their quality varies from country to country. Speak with your physician and/or check the CDC or World Health Organization Web sites for health alerts, particularly if you're pregnant, traveling with children, or have a chronic illness.

For information on travel insurance, shots and medications, and medical-assistance companies *see* Shots & Medications *under* Things to Consider *in* Getting Started, *above.*

SPECIFIC ISSUES IN POLAND

Flu season in Poland starts in the autumn and continues until early spring. Some doctors would advocate flu vaccination, others advise against it. Traditional cold remedies used by the Poles include garlic or tea with lemon and/or raspberry juice.

In spring, particularly in Masuria and Pomerania, and in the woods, there is an increased risk of coming across a tick. If a tick bites you, remove it carefully (the best way is to turn it counter-clockwise). Observe the place of tick bite afterward, and look for signs of an *erythema migrans* (a traveling flush on the skin), which is a symptom of tick-borne encephalitis; if you see it, you should seek medical help immediately.

In summer, when it's hot with a lot of sunshine, try to avoid prolonged sun exposure, drink plenty of fluids, cover your head, and use sunscreen (plenty of international and local brands are available from pharmacies, cosmetics stores, supermarkets, and kiosks). In winter, when temperatures drop, dress adequately; you may also want to use protective face cream.

The *Żmija zygzakowata* (*vipera berus,* or European or crossed viper) is the only poisonous reptile native to Poland. It is venomous, but the venom's toxicity is relatively low. It is also a protected species.

Polish mosquitoes don't carry malaria, so the bites are merely unpleasant. Don't scratch them; it will only make it worse. You can use aerosol repellent, and skin tonic or cream to reduce skin irritation.

OVER-THE-COUNTER REMEDIES

Common over-the-counter remedies available both from pharmacy (*apteka*) and many supermarkets or even kiosks include aspirin, paracetamol (acetominophen), and ibuprofen.

■ HOURS OF OPERATION

Museums are often closed on Monday. Stores are open on most holidays, except for Christmas and Easter, and they do not close for lunch.

HOLIDAYS

In Poland, the major holidays include the following: New Year's Day (January 1); Easter Monday (the Monday after Easter, usually in late March to late April); Labor Day (May 1); Constitution Day (May 3); Corpus Christi (a Thursday, 60 days after Easter); Assumption Day (August 15); All Souls' Day (November 1); Independence Day (November 11); and Christmas (December 25 and 26).

■ MAIL

Poczta is Polish for post office. In larger cities, there are many post offices, the *poczta główna* being the main one. Most post offices are usually open 8 AM to 8 PM on weekdays (some smaller post offices close at 4 PM). Some post offices are open also on Saturday (usually until 2 PM). In larger cities there is usually one post office open 24 hours a day (often at or near the city's railways station).

A stamp (*znaczki pocztowe*) to mail a priority letter (up to 50 g) or postcard to the U.S. (*do Ameryki*) costs zł 3.20 at this writing. If your postcard or letter already has stamps, put it in a red mailbox; the transit time is about two weeks.

Parcels are best sent by courier mail (Fed Ex, UPS) or registered airmail; regular surface mail is very slow and may occasionally be unreliable. The Web site for the Polish Post has a list of all post offices in Poland (go to *Znajdź urząd pocztowy*) and the prices of postal services (go to *Cennik usług pocztowych*).

■ MONEY

Credit cards are widespread, but they are not accepted everywhere. Especially for small sums, you would usually be expected to pay in cash (you don't pay with a credit card for your coffee, a newspaper, or a taxi ride). Poland has a good network of ATMs, particularly in the larger cities, where they are numerous and common. Currency can be exchanged at either a *kantor* (exchange office) or a bank (usually the former offer better rates than the latter).

ITEM AVERAGE COST	
Cup of Coffee	zł 8
Glass of Wine	zł 15
Glass of Beer	zł 6
Sandwich	zł 10
One-Mile Taxi Ride in Capital City	Starting fee zł 7, then about zł 1.50–2 per km
Museum Admission	zł 5

Prices throughout this guide are given for adults. Substantially reduced fees are almost always available for children, students, and senior citizens.

■ **TIP→** Banks never have every foreign currency on hand, and it may take as long as a week to order. If you're planning to exchange funds before leaving home, don't wait until the last minute.

ATMS & BANKS

Your own bank will probably charge a fee for using ATMs abroad; the foreign bank you use may also charge a fee. Nevertheless, you'll usually get a better rate of exchange at an ATM than you will at a currency-exchange office or even when changing money in a bank. And extracting funds as you need them is a safer option than carrying around a large amount of cash.

■ **TIP→** PIN numbers with more than four digits are not recognized at ATMs in many countries. If yours has five or more, remember to change it before you leave.

Poland's ATM network is well developed, especially in cities, but you may have problems finding one in a village or a very small town. Visa, MasterCard, Cirrus, and Maestro are all common networks. Many ATMs limit you to zł 1,000 in withdrawals per day.

CREDIT CARDS

Throughout this guide, the following abbreviations are used: **AE**, American Express; **DC**, Diners Club; **MC**, MasterCard; and **V**, Visa.

It's a good idea to inform your credit-card company before you travel, especially if you're going abroad and don't travel internationally very often. Otherwise, the credit-card company might put a hold on your card owing to unusual activity—not a good thing halfway through your trip. Record all your credit-card numbers—as well as the phone numbers to call if your cards are lost or stolen—in a safe place, so you're prepared should something go wrong. Both MasterCard and Visa have general numbers you can call (collect if you're abroad) if your card is lost, but you're better off calling the number of your issuing bank, since MasterCard and Visa usually just transfer you to your bank; your bank's number is usually printed on your card.

If you plan to use your credit card for cash advances, you'll need to apply for a PIN at least two weeks before your trip. Although it's usually cheaper (and safer) to use a credit card abroad for large purchases (so you can cancel payments or be reimbursed if there's a problem), note that some credit-card companies *and* the banks that issue them add substantial percentages to all foreign transactions, whether they're in a foreign currency or not. Check on these fees before leaving home, so there won't be any surprises when you get the bill.

■ **TIP→** Before you charge something, ask the merchant whether he or she plans to do a dynamic currency conversion (DCC). In such a transaction the credit-card *processor* (shop, restaurant, or hotel, not Visa or MasterCard) converts the currency and charges you in dollars. In most cases you'll pay the merchant a 3% fee for this service in addition to any credit-card company and issuing-bank foreign-transaction surcharges.

Dynamic currency conversion programs are becoming increasingly widespread.

Merchants who participate in them are supposed to ask whether you want to be charged in dollars or the local currency, but they don't always do so. And even if they do offer you a choice, they may well avoid mentioning the additional surcharges. The good news is that you *do* have a choice. And if this practice really gets your goat, you can avoid it entirely thanks to American Express; with its cards, DCC simply isn't an option.

Most shops, restaurants, and hotels accept credit cards, but small kiosks, cheap self-service bars, and private rooms-to-rent won't. In most cafés and pubs, cash is king. Most taxis don't accept credit cards; and when you are buying your train or bus ticket onboard, you will have to pay in cash.

Reporting Lost Cards American Express
☎ 800/992-3404 in U.S., 336/393-1111 collect from abroad ⊕ www.americanexpress.com. **Diners Club** ☎ 800/234-6377 in the U.S., 303/799-1504 collect from abroad ⊕ dinersclub.com. **MasterCard** ☎ 800/622-7747 in U.S., 636/722-7111 collect from abroad ⊕ www.mastercard.com. **Visa** ☎ 800/847-2911 in the U.S., 410/581-9994 collect from abroad ⊕ www.visa.com.

CURRENCY & EXCHANGE

The *złoty* is the currency of Poland, subdivided into 100 *grosz*. At this writing, the exchange rate was approximately zł 3 to US$1, with fluctuations within 10% range (at the time of this writing, the dollar rate was at a low point of zł 2.8/ to US$1). Currency can be safely exchanged at any bank or *kantor* (currency exchange office); while traveler's checks are cashed at most (but not all) banks and few kantors.

The kantor's profit is the difference between the "buying" and the "selling" rate. These rates should be (and usually are) clearly posted. If you see that the gap is unreasonably wide, look for another kantor, where the exchange rate is healthier.

■ **TIP→** Unlike many destinations, you will usually get a better deal on your currency exchange at a kantor rather than a bank. If your

WORST-CASE SCENARIO

All your money and credit cards have just been stolen. In these days of real-time transactions, this isn't a predicament that should destroy your vacation. First, report the theft of the credit cards. Then get any traveler's checks you were carrying replaced. This can usually be done almost immediately, provided that you kept a record of the serial numbers separate from the checks themselves. If you bank at a large international bank like Citibank or HSBC, go to the closest branch; if you know your account number, chances are you can get a new ATM card and withdraw money right away. **Western Union** (☎ 800/325-6000 ⊕ www.westernunion. com) sends money almost anywhere. Have someone back home order a transfer online, over the phone, or at one of the company's offices, which is the cheapest option. The U.S. State Department's **Overseas Citizens Services** (☎ 202/647-5225) can wire money to any U.S. consulate or embassy abroad for a fee of $30. Just have someone back home wire money or send a money order or cashier's check to the state department, which will then disburse the funds as soon as the next working day after it receives them.

ATM doesn't charge a huge fee, you may do marginally better by taking your money directly from your account.

TRAVELER'S CHECKS & CARDS

Some consider this the currency of the cave man, and it's true that fewer establishments accept traveler's checks these days. Nevertheless, they're a cheap and secure way to carry extra money, particularly on trips to urban areas. Both Citibank (under the Visa brand) and American Express issue traveler's checks in the United States, but Amex is better known and more widely accepted; you can also avoid hefty surcharges by cashing Amex checks at Amex offices. Whatever you do, keep track of all the serial numbers in case the checks are lost or stolen.

Traveler's checks can be cashed in most—but not all—banks and at a very few kantors; moreover, there is a handling fee and a commission, which probably makes a traveler's check more expensive and definitely more awkward than exchanging or withdrawing cash.

American Express now offers a stored-value card called a Travelers Cheque Card, which you can use wherever American Express credit cards are accepted, including ATMs. The card can carry a minimum of $300 and a maximum of $2,700, and it's a very safe way to carry your funds. Although you can get replacement funds in 24 hours if your card is lost or stolen, it doesn't really strike us as a very good deal. In addition to a high initial cost ($14.95 to set up the card, plus $5 each time you "reload"), you still have to pay a 2% fee for each purchase in a foreign currency (similar to that of any credit card). Further, each time you use the card in an ATM you pay a transaction fee of $2.50 on top of the 2% transaction fee for the conversion—add it all up and it can be considerably more than you would pay when simply using your own ATM card. Regular traveler's checks are just as secure and cost less.

American Express ☎ 888/412-6945 in U.S., 801/945-9450 collect outside of U.S. to add value or speak to customer service ⊕ www. americanexpress.com.

▌ RESTROOMS

The general standard of restrooms in Poland has improved greatly over the last decade, but sometimes you may still come across unclean facilities, and especially in bars and cheaper establishments, toilet paper may be missing. Usually the more upscale establishment, the better the toilets. There are not very many public conveniences; it is better to use one in a café or a restaurant (it is easier if you at least buy a drink, but if you just walk in and ask for permission, it is unusual that you will be refused). You may be sometimes expected to pay a small fee (usually zł 1) to use the toilet (even if you are a customer), as well as in some public restrooms.

Gents' facilities are often marked with a triangle and ladies' with a circle.

Find a Loo The Bathroom Diaries ⊕ www. thebathroomdiaries.com is flush with unsanitized info on restrooms the world over—each one located, reviewed, and rated.

▌ SAFETY

▌ **TIP→ Distribute your cash, credit cards, IDs, and other valuables between a deep front pocket, an inside jacket or vest pocket, and a hidden money pouch. Don't reach for the money pouch once you're in public.**

Poland is a relatively safe country. Of course, some petty crime exists, but you should be fine as long as you exercise simple, common-sense safety protocols. The most risky places—where you might fall prey to pickpockets—would be the most crowded destinations: main streets, markets, pubs, and on public transportation. Don't leave your valuables in a jacket in an unprotected area, such as on a hanger in a pub or restaurant, or on the back of your chair.

▌ TAXES

Airport taxes are included in the price of your ticket, and there are no additional airport taxes to be paid when flying out of Poland. Hotel rates in Poland are quoted inclusive of V.A.T. In some destinations (mountains, seaside, spas, some historic cities) there is a small so-called "climate tax" (usually under zł 2 per person per day), which has to be paid separately.

When making a purchase, ask for a V.A.T. refund form and find out whether the merchant gives refunds—not all stores do, nor are they required to. Have the form stamped like any customs form by customs officials when you leave the country or, if you're visiting several European Union countries, when you leave the EU. After

EFFECTIVE COMPLAINING

Things don't always go right when you're traveling, and when you encounter a problem or service that isn't up to snuff, you should complain. But there are good and bad ways to do so.

Take a deep breath. This is always a good strategy, especially when you are aggravated about something. Just inhale, and exhale, and remember that you're on vacation. We know it's hard for Type A people to leave it all behind, but for your own peace of mind, it's worth a try.

Complain in person when it's serious. In a hotel, serious problems are usually better dealt with in person, at the front desk; if it's something quick, you can phone.

Complain early rather than late. Whenever you don't get what you paid for (the type of hotel room you booked or the airline seat you prereserved) or when it's something timely (the people next door are making too much noise), try to resolve the problem sooner rather than later. It's always going to be harder to deal with a problem or get something taken off your bill after the fact.

Be willing to escalate, but don't be hasty. Try to deal with the person at the front desk of your hotel or with your waiter in a restaurant before asking to speak to a supervisor or manager. Not only is this polite, but when the person directly serving you can fix the problem, you'll more likely get what you want quicker.

Say what you want, and be reasonable. When things fall apart, be clear about what kind of compensation you expect. Don't leave it to the hotel or restaurant or airline to suggest what they're willing to do for you. That said, the compensation you request must be in line with the problem. You're unlikely to get a free meal because your steak was undercooked or a free hotel stay if your bathroom was dirty.

Choose your battles. You're more likely to get what you want if you limit your complaints to one or two specific things that really matter rather than a litany of wrongs.

Don't be obnoxious. There's nothing that will stop your progress dead in its tracks as readily as an insistent "Don't you know who I am?" or "So what are you going to do about it?" Raising your voice will rarely get a better result.

Nice counts. This doesn't mean you shouldn't be clear that you are displeased. Passive isn't good, either. When it comes right down to it, though, you'll attract more flies with sugar than with vinegar.

Do it in writing. If you discover a billing error or some other problem after the fact, write a concise letter to the appropriate customer-service representative. Keep it to one page, and as with any complaint, state clearly and reasonably what you want them to do about the problem. Don't give a detailed trip report or list a litany of problems.

you're through passport control, take the form to a refund-service counter for an on-the-spot refund (which is usually the quickest and easiest option), or mail it to the address on the form (or the envelope with it) after you arrive home. You receive the total refund stated on the form, but the processing time can be long, especially if you request a credit-card adjustment.

Global Refund is a Europe-wide service with 225,000 affiliated stores and more than 700 refund counters at major airports and border crossings. Its refund form, called a Tax Free Check, is the most common across the European continent. The service issues refunds in the form of cash, check, or credit-card adjustment.

V.A.T. Refunds Global Refund ☎ 800/566-9828 ⊕ www.globalrefund.com.

∎ TIME

Poland is in a single time zone, which is GMT +1 (i.e., if it's noon in London, in Poland it is already 1 PM). Daylight Saving Time is observed: the clock is put forward one hour on the last Sunday in March. The time is put back one hour on the last Sunday in October.

∎ TIPPING

There are no strict rules when it comes to tipping in Poland; however, it is customary to show your appreciation if you have been served well. In restaurants, cafés, and pubs, you usually just round up the bill to the nearest whole figure. In cheaper places, often you don't leave a tip at all, and in upmarket restaurants, it is cus-

tomary to tip a bit more (up to 10%). In luxury hotels, tipping the staff (particularly the porters) is more expected than in moderate and inexpensive ones, but it is not mandatory. You don't usually tip taxi drivers in Poland (but again, you may want to round up to bill to the nearest whole złoty, just for convenience), but you might want to tip the driver if he helps with the luggage. It is customary to tip tour-guides (often by making a collection among the tour group).

TIPPING GUIDELINES FOR	
Bellhop	zł 2–zł 5 per bag, depending on the level of the hotel
Hotel Concierge	zł 10 if he or she performs a service for you
Hotel Doorman	zł 2–zł 5 if he helps you get a cab
Hotel Maid	zł 2–zł 5 a day (either daily or at the end of your stay, in cash)
Hotel Room-Service Waiter	zł 2–zł 5 per delivery, even if a service charge has been added
Taxi Driver	Round up the fare to the next złoty amount
Tour Guide	10% of the cost of the tour
Waiter	10% being the norm at high-end restaurants; or round up the bill to the next whole figure
Others	Toilet charge is zł 1–zł 2 (if there is a charge); coat-check fee is zł 1–zł 5 (if any)

INDEX

PHOTO CREDITS

Cover Photo *(Piwna Street in Warsaw's Old Town): Walter Bibikow/age fotostock.*
10, P. *Narayan/age fotostock.* 11 (left), *Jan Morek/PAI/Polish National Tourist Office.* 11 (right), *Atlantide S.N.C./age fotostock.* 12, *lookGaleria/Alamy.* 13, *Henryk T. Kaiser/age fotostock.* 14, *Jim West/Alamy.* 15, *Konrad Zelazowski/Alamy.* 16, *Walter Bibikow/age fotostock.* 17 (left), *Picture Contact/Alamy.* 17 (right), *Kevin Foy/Alamy.* 18, *Piotr Ciesla/age fotostock.* 19 (left), *Edward North/Alamy.* 19 (right), *Piotr Ciesla/ age fotostock.* 26, *Konrad Zelazowski/Alamy.* 27 (left), *Dallas & John Heaton/age fotostock.* 27 (right) *and* 28, *lookGaleria/Alamy.* 29 (left), *Maciej Wojtkowiak/Alamy.* 29 (right), *lookGaleria/Alamy.*

NOTES

NOTES

NOTES

NOTES

NOTES

NOTES

NOTES

NOTES

NOTES

ABOUT OUR WRITERS

Dorota Wąsik has been fond of museums and trips to the Polish seaside since her early years. No wonder she grew up to become a travel addict. But all the roads take her back to her native Kraków. With a degree in English Literature from Jagiellonian University, including a term at Oxford, she works as a writer and a translator, a part-time teacher, an accidental tour guide, and did a stint as an interpreter for members of the British Royal Family. Her published works include *Living in Kraków* and *Visible Cities Kraków*. She is the primary author of this guide.

Marcin Jasionowicz is an art historian by passion and education (with a degree from Jagiellonian University), and a court-certified expert on verifying the authenticity of artworks. This does not prevent him from being the owner of an IT company; and he has published in both art history and computers. Marcin is also a dedicated gourmet and, incidentally, an excellent cook who likes cats, classical music, beautiful paintings, and fine wines. In what little free time he has left, he enjoys horseback riding. For this book, he wrote the chapter "Wielkopolska."

Sylwia Trzaska, also art historian and writer, specializes in folk art, the history of design, and monument preservation. She is a keen explorer of artistic margins and a passionate researcher of towns and their histories. Although she lives her life in big cities—namely Berlin and Kraków—each year she scours the forests of northwestern Poland for mushrooms, berries, and other treasures. She has a fondness for luxury, camping, gardens, flea markets, and railway stations. Her favorite places include the Polish seaside and the lakes. She covered Szczecin, Wolin Island, and Pojezierze Drawskie—as well as writing an essay on folk art—for this book.

For many years the head of the International Department of the Małopolska Regional Government, **Marta Ślusarczyk-Snoch,** was responsible for organizing and receiving diplomatic visits and business missions from all over the world. She is now an independent consultant and trainer in diplomatic protocol and business etiquette. She often takes to the Polish road in her red Peugeot (and she happens to be an excellent driver). In addition to some general information and sound advice, she provided information about the Tri-City and about Polish business culture.

Dorota Leśniak–Rychlak has degrees in Art History and Architecture and for several years was the editor of the monthly *Architektura i biznes*. She loves mountain climbing and kayaking and contributed information on hiking trails in the Tatras, and the Krutynia River Trail for this book.

Acknowledgments

The authors wish to acknowledge the vital assistance of several individuals who helped in the preparation of this guide. Thanks to Anna Klaus and Iwona Pisiewicz, great travelers, for their help in travel research. Yoshiko Yoshino, Joanna and Kabir Mulji, and Olaf Mueller should be considered part-time honorary Poles for their honest impressions and useful tips. Dr. Piotr Rychlak contributed important health advice for "Poland Essentials." Wiesław Rychlik assisted the authors by offering advice based on his many years' experience in the hospitality industry. And finally, thanks to Aniela Deja-Wąsik and Michał Skiba for their contributions on music.